# The Law of
# Tax-Exempt Organizations
# Planning Guide

## Strategies and Commentaries

# The Law of Tax-Exempt Organizations Planning Guide

## Strategies and Commentaries

BRUCE R. HOPKINS

WILEY

John Wiley & Sons, Inc.

For general information on our other products and services, or
technical support, please contact our Customer Care Department
within the United States at 800-762-2974, outside the United
States at 317-572-3993 or fax 317-572-4002.

Wiley also publishes its books in a variety of electronic formats.
Some content that appears in print may not be available in
electronic books.

For more information about Wiley products, visit our web site
at *www.wiley.com*.

ISBN: 0-471-47122-4

10 9 8 7 6 5 4 3 2 1

*With this book, Hopkins has not merely given away the store, he has bared his soul.*

—Thomas K. Hyatt, Esq.

# Dedication

Few books are dedicated to an author's critics. This one is.

The most frequent criticism I have heard over the years (all 30-plus of them) of *The Law of Tax-Exempt Organizations* is that it is silent as to planning, guidance, and techniques. (You critics out there know who you are; I could name some names, but I desist.) With a few exceptions, this observation is true. Just *summarizing* the law in the eighth edition (2003) required more than 1,000 pages; the addition of planning material would balloon the book to a size beyond utility (and purchase).

As this criticism finally sunk in, it occurred to me that a planning component is in fact essential, given the increasing complexity of the law in this area, albeit in a separate volume. This is that book.

This book, then, is dedicated to these critics. Thank you, dear critics, for the idea. An extraordinary amount of pleasure has been derived from preparation of the book. It is my hope that it will help lawyers, accountants, managers, board members, and others more effectively grapple with and understand that marvelous body of evolving and expanding law known as the law of tax-exempt organizations.

# About the Author

Bruce R. Hopkins is a lawyer in Kansas City, Missouri, with the firm of Polsinelli Shalton Welte, P.C., having practiced law in Washington, D.C., for 26 years. He specializes in the representation of tax-exempt organizations. His practice ranges over the entirety of tax matters involving exempt organizations, with emphasis on the formation of nonprofit organizations, acquisition of recognition of tax-exempt status for them, the private inurement and private benefit doctrines, the intermediate sanctions rules, legislative and political campaign activities issues, public charity and private foundation rules, unrelated business planning, use of exempt and for-profit subsidiaries, joint venture planning, review of annual information returns, Internet communications developments, the law of charitable giving (including planned giving), and fundraising law issues.

Mr. Hopkins served as Chair of the Committee on Exempt Organizations, Tax Section, American Bar Association; Chair, Section of Taxation, National Association of College and University Attorneys; and President, Planned Giving Study Group of Greater Washington, D.C. He was accorded the Assistant Commissioner's (IRS) Award in 1984.

Mr. Hopkins is the series editor of Wiley's Nonprofit Law, Finance, and Management Series. In addition to *The Law of Tax-Exempt Organizations Planning Guide: Strategies and Commentaries,* he is the author of *The Law of Tax-Exempt Organizations, Eighth Edition; The Tax Law of Charitable Giving, Third Edition; The Law of Fundraising, Third Edition; The Nonprofits' Guide to Internet Communications Law; The Law of Intermediate Sanctions: A Guide for Nonprofits; The First Legal Answer Book for Fund-Raisers; The Second Legal Answer Book for Fund-Raisers; The Legal Answer Book for Nonprofit Organizations; The Second Legal Answer Book for Nonprofit Organizations; The Nonprofit Law Dictionary; Starting and Managing a Nonprofit Organization: A Legal Guide, Fourth Edition;* and is the co-author, with Jody Blazek, of *Private Foundations: Tax Law and Compliance, Second Edition;* also with Ms. Blazek, *The Legal Answer Book for Private Foundations;* with D. Benson Tesdahl, of *Intermediate Sanctions: Curbing Nonprofit Abuse;* and with Thomas K. Hyatt, of *The Law of Tax-Exempt Healthcare Organizations, Second Edition.* He also writes *Bruce R. Hopkins' Nonprofit Counsel,* a monthly newsletter, published by John Wiley & Sons.

Mr. Hopkins earned his J.D. and L.L.M. degrees at the George Washington University and his B.A. at the University of Michigan. He is a member of the bars of the District of Columbia and the state of Missouri.

# Preface

**B**ooks are born of many motives. One of my favorites is an attempt to capture, via the written word, all there is to know about a subject in my field of law practice. (I realize the attempt is futile but it remains challenging to try.) Hence the books on *The Law of Tax-Exempt Organizations, The Law of Fundraising,* and *The Tax Law of Charitable Giving.* These books are technical, with discussions of tax regulations, court opinions, and IRS rulings, replete with lots of citations and footnotes. It is all a grand exercise in translating.

Another of my motives is to share the experience with others in related fields—a mind expansion and learning effort. Thus, the co-authorship of books such as *Private Foundations: Tax Law and Compliance* and *The Law of Tax-Exempt Healthcare Organizations.*

A third motive is to attempt to explain all of this law to the citizenry at large. The result has been *Starting and Managing a Nonprofit Organization: A Legal Guide* and the several legal answer books.

Still another motive is the pleasure of delving deep into a discrete area of the law of tax-exempt organizations, thinking about the policy aspects and the issues, and writing an entire book about that area. Thus, *The Nonprofits' Guide to Internet Communications Law* and *The Law of Intermediate Sanctions: A Guide for Nonprofits.*

(I am in therapy at the present, attempting to ascertain the motive for undertaking the *Nonprofit Law Dictionary.*)

The motive for this book is different, and is noted in the dedication. Writing in response to criticism can prove dangerous, and often unwise if not unhealthy. With this project, however, once focused on it, I resolved to enjoy the process more than anything else. Despite Tom Hyatt's abjuration, I decided to take the perspective of 35 years of law practice and unburden myself of thoughts as to how to solve problems raised by the law of tax-exempt organizations.

I will not assert that herein lies the solution to all such problems. I have tried, nonetheless, to tackle most of them and I hope my exertions prove helpful. This book was well over a year in the writing and, as I practiced during those months, I tested what I was doing against the developing material. Obviously, then, much of what I do today and have done in my practice is reflected in these pages.

I thank my editor at John Wiley & Sons, Susan McDermott, for her support and encouragement in the development of this book and Petrina Kulek, senior production editor, for her skills in the production of it.

*July 2004*                                                                                   BRUCE R. HOPKINS

# How to Use This Book

This book—true to its name—is principally designed to be used, as a planning guide, in conjunction with the author's book titled *The Law of Tax-Exempt Organizations* (8th ed. 2003) and various IRS forms. Indeed, the first sentence of this book refers to the exempt organizations book as the "companion volume." For the most part, it is expected that the reader of this book, often referred to as the "planner," understands and frequently uses in a professional practice at least most of the material in the companion volume.

The *Planning Guide,* however, goes beyond the scope of the exempt organizations book. Other subjects are referenced, such as corporate law, details as to the private foundation rules, fundraising regulation, and charitable giving. When appropriate, reference is made to other books by your author for more information.

The *Planning Guide* is intended to be a medium of assistance for those who are engaged in planning in the context of the law of tax-exempt organizations. It is anticipated that the user of this book will likely be a lawyer, an accountant, or a sophisticated manager of an exempt organization. It serves as a *guide* to assist these *planners* in coping with the burgeoning law concerning exempt organizations and their legal problems. (The book is not a substitute for specific legal advice.)

This guide will probably be approached in one of two ways: the planner is trying to solve a particular problem involving the law of tax-exempt organizations or the planner is attempting to evaluate an organization's facts to determine if there is such a problem.

The *Planning Guide* can be accessed three ways. One, the table of contents points the planner in one or more general directions. Two, the same is true of the index. Three, the reader can turn to Chapter 12 and review the questions listed there.

The planner who is involved in the establishment of an organization should dwell in Chapter 1. If tax exemption for an organization has not yet been acquired, Chapter 2 should be consulted. Otherwise, the *Planning Guide* is subject matter oriented: it focuses on core subjects, such as public charity status, private benefit, private inurement, attempts to influence legislation, political campaign activities, unrelated business endeavors, use of subsidiaries, and involvement in joint ventures.

If the expectation as stated at the outset is correct, the planner knows something about the intertwining of these subjects. As examples:

- An issue as to the reasonableness of executive compensation can entail the intermediate sanctions rules, the doctrine of private inurement, and the developing concepts of private benefit.

- The calculation of public support for a charitable organization may be correct—or mistakes may have been made.

- What initially appears to be an attempt to influence legislation may be (or may also be) political campaign activity.

- What is assumed to be an exempt function may be an unrelated business.

- What is assumed to be taxable unrelated business income may be revenue that is protected by an exception.

- The many distinct uses of subsidiaries, both tax-exempt and for-profit (taxable).

- What is assumed to be a management contract or a fundraising agreement is instead a joint venture.

With whatever basics may initiate the inquiry, the planner can explore the appropriate portions of the *Planning Guide,* digging deeper into the aspects of the problem, eventually (this is certainly the intent) ferreting out a solution.

The subtitle of the *Planning Guide* is *Strategies and Commentaries.* Much of the book concerns the former. Thus, throughout, are tips, notes, and even graphics to help guide, stimulate, and find answers for the planner.

Commentary is also placed in the various chapters. In Chapter 11, however, the planner is taken into the realm of what is (often charitably) termed the *difficult cases.* There is little the planner can do *with* these opinions—they are what they are—but there is much the planner can do to *cope* with them. In this chapter, the planner is provided perspectives as to how to evaluate a court opinion and some examples of difficult opinions in the exempt organizations setting. Each of the summaries of the opinions is followed by a commentary and guidance.

For some, the most useful component of the book is Chapter 12. Titled "The Legal Audit," the chapter consists of a series of questions, correlated to the appropriate chapter in the *Planning Guide.* Armed with these 549 questions and fortified with the other material, the planner should be able, based on the planner's experience and the augmentations of the *Planning Guide,* to resolve legal issues raised by the law of tax-exempt organizations.

# Contents

## APPENDICES

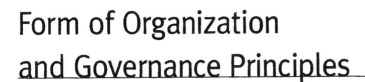

# Form of Organization and Governance Principles

The purpose of *The Law of Tax-Exempt Organizations* (hereinafter referred to as the companion volume)[1] is to summarize the federal tax law pertaining to tax-exempt organizations. The companion volume touches on, but certainly does not dwell on, the subjects of formation of nonprofit, tax-exempt organizations, and governance and liability issues, which are largely state corporate and other law matters. Nonetheless, those who advise in the realm of exempt organizations frequently face these issues.

Thus, unlike most of the other chapters in this book, the contents of this chapter go beyond the corresponding coverage in the companion volume and address the principal matters that arise when consideration is being given to formation of a tax-exempt organization. This chapter also focuses on matters with law implications that arise on an ongoing basis in connection with the management of exempt organizations.[2]

## Basic Decision: Nonprofit or For-Profit

The experience of planners in the realm of tax-exempt organizations (mostly lawyers and accountants) is that when they are approached by one or more individuals to establish a nonprofit, tax-exempt organization, the decision to do that usually has already been made by those parties. That is, it is rare for the planner to be approached by an individual who announces that he or she has an idea for an organization and then asks whether the entity should be nonprofit or for-profit. In most circumstances of this nature, the decision to form a nonprofit organization is the correct one. Still, in a given case, it may be appropriate to consider the two basic alternatives.

There are two thoughts to consider preliminarily. One is that establishing a nonprofit organization can be just as complex as creating a for-profit corporation. The other is that, in some instances, the same activity or activities being contemplated can be undertaken in either a nonprofit or a for-profit organization.

Many of the elements to consider are the same, irrespective of whether the entity is nonprofit or for-profit. These include the contents of the organizing document, the contents of bylaws, the composition of the board, officers, meetings, employees, furniture and equipment, and nature of the office space, finances, contracts, and insurance coverage(s).

The main distinction between the two types of entities concerns *control* versus *ownership*. The board of directors of a nonprofit organization does not own the organization's assets and income stream, although it controls them. Thus, the decision as to choice of entity at this level depends on the *motive* of those starting the entity. If the matter concerns money, the issue is not whether the organization can "make money" (as in earn a profit), inasmuch as both types of entities can do that; rather, the issue is what can be done with the money. If the individuals involved are satisfied with reasonable compensation, the nonprofit organization will suffice. If, however, the individuals involved want to personally receive the profits generated by the organization, the entity must be formed as a for-profit one, with the funds taken out as dividends.[3]

There is another consideration pertaining to this control/ownership dichotomy. If an organization is structured as a for-profit corporation and the enterprise is successful over the years, the result will be property of value, namely, stock. Thus, the creators of the company can create an asset that has value (so that it can be reflected on financial statements) and can be sold for a profit (capital gain). Even here, however, it is possible (though infrequent) to form a stock-based nonprofit organization, with the same ends achieved.

The ability to earn more money and build up a valuable asset needs to be compared to features of the nonprofit organization that the for-profit entity is not likely to have: tax-exempt status and the ability to attract tax-deductible contributions and grants.

The balance of this chapter is predicated on the assumption that the decision is made to create a nonprofit, tax-exempt entity. Yet many of the considerations reviewed next are equally applicable to for-profit entities.

## LOCATION

In almost all instances, the nonprofit entity is formed pursuant to the law of a state. (In a rare situation, the entity is created by federal or state statute, or perhaps a local ordinance.) The planner is likely to be often asked: which state?

The general rule is that the jurisdiction in which the organization is to be formed is the state in which the organization will be physically located. That is the state in which it will have its office, conduct its programs, and otherwise function. There may be, however, a feature of another state's law, not available under the law of the home state, that is desired, thereby compelling the organization to establish itself under the law of the other state. For example, a state's law may permit the nonprofit organization to be formed

### NOTE ✎

The stock in a stock-based corporation is used for ownership purposes only. It is not stock that pays dividends. Payment of dividends on such stock would violate the doctrine of private inurement or the doctrine of private benefit or both.[4]

as a stock-based corporation, a feature not available under the law where operations will be conducted. As another illustration, one state may require three or more directors; another state may tolerate one director.

For some, the decision regarding location will be affected (if not dictated) by appearances. A national organization, for example, may believe it is best formed pursuant to the law of the District of Columbia. A U.S.-based international organization may be of the view that formation should be in the state of New York. Some may opt for Delaware, the for-profit corporate mecca.

Consequently, in some circumstance, the dual-state approach is preferable. (Although it can operate in more than one jurisdiction, an organization can be formed under the law of only one jurisdiction (at a time).) The state in which the organization is organized is the *domestic* one; the state in which the organization is to operate (if different) is the *foreign* jurisdiction. As an illustration, assume the following decisions have been made: the nonprofit entity is to be formed as a corporation (see below), it is to be a corporation that can issue stock, and its only office is to be in Maryland (which does not allow stock-based corporations). This organization could be formed in Delaware (where stock-based corporations are permitted). Maryland, then, would be the foreign state, and Delaware would be the domestic state. The organization would incorporate in Delaware, then qualify to *do business* (operate its programs) as a foreign corporation in Maryland.

## CAUTION!

If this approach is to be used, the planner should determine in advance whether the foreign state will accept the application of the foreign corporation to do business within its borders as a stock-based nonprofit entity. Those states that do not permit the formation of stock-based nonprofit corporations in their jurisdiction will not allow them to operate there as foreign corporations.

The problem with the dual-state approach is that the organization must comply with the laws of both jurisdictions. If it is a corporation, for example, it must file articles of incorporation in the domestic state and an application to do business in the foreign state. (Both documents will look much alike.) The organization may have to maintain a registered agent in both jurisdictions. Both states may require an annual report and an annual filing fee. There are, thus, financial and efficiency issues associated with this approach.

## COMMENT >

As a related matter, a nonprofit organization can be formed under the law of a state and be principally located in the same state, yet *do business* in one or more other states. Generally, to do business in a state, as a foreign entity, means to have an office there, substantially conduct programs there, or own property there. The concept varies from state to state.[5] Indeed, in a few states, the mere act of fundraising in a state is deemed doing business there.

In conclusion, for some nonprofit organizations, the dual-state approach is necessary or desired. In the case of nearly all nonprofit entities, however, one state will do.

## FORM OF ORGANIZATION

Once the home state has been determined, the legal form of the nonprofit organization must be considered.[6] (For tax exemption to be available, there must be a separate legal entity.[7]) This is basically a matter of state law. (Again, this analysis assumes that the organization is not formed by statute.)

Tax-exempt, nonprofit organizations generally are of three types:

1. Corporation
2. Unincorporated association
3. Trust[8]

There are other ways to be tax-exempt, including qualification as a limited liability company[9] or perhaps a professional corporation.

### Documents

Generically, the document by which a tax-exempt organization is created is known, in the parlance of the tax law, as *articles of organization*.[10] There usually is a separate document containing rules by which the organization conducts its affairs; this document is most often termed *bylaws*. (The organization may also develop other documents governing its operations, such as various policies and procedures, an employee handbook, a conflict-of-interest policy (although that may be part of the bylaws), and/or a code of ethics.)

The types of articles of organization for each type of tax-exempt, nonprofit organization are:

- Corporation: articles of incorporation
- Unincorporated association: constitution
- Trust: declaration of trust or trust agreement

**NOTE**

Occasionally, a nonprofit organization will have both articles of incorporation and a constitution. This, technically, is incorrect.

The contents of a set of articles of organization should include:

- The name of the organization (see below)
- A general statement of its purposes
- The name(s) and address(es) of its initial directors or trustees
- The name and address of the registered agent (if a corporation)
- The name(s) and address(es) of its incorporator(s) (if a corporation)
- A statement as to whether the entity has members

- A statement as to whether the entity can issue stock (if a corporation)
- Provisions reflecting any other state law requirements
- A dissolution clause[11]
- Provisions reflecting any federal tax law requirements

The bylaws of a nonprofit organization (if any) will usually include provisions with respect to:

- The organization's purposes (it is a good idea to restate them in the bylaws)
- The origins (e.g., election) and duties of its directors
- The origins and duties of its officers
- The role of its members (if any)
- Meetings of members and directors, including dates, notice, quorum, and voting
- The role of executive and other committees
- The role of its chapters (if any)
- The organization's fiscal year
- A conflict-of-interest policy (if not separately stated)
- Reference to (any) affiliated entities
- Restatement of the federal tax law requirements

## Choice of Form

The planner, in deciding which form the nonprofit organization should select (assuming tax exemption is desired), should take into account:

- The exposure of members of the governing board to personal liability
- The answers to questions regarding operations that may be provided by state law
- Familiarity
- State law registration and reporting requirements
- Federal tax law requirements

**Personal Liability.**   The corporate form is the only form that provides the advantage of shielding board members from most types of personal liability. Liability, if any, is generally confined to the organization; that is, it does not normally extend to those who manage it. Thus, trustees and directors of trusts and unincorporated associations do not have this "corporate veil" to protect them.

**Answers to Questions.**   The law of a state usually provides answers to many of the questions that inevitably arise when forming and operating a nonprofit organization. These answers are most likely found in the state's nonprofit corporation act (which nearly every state has). Some examples are:

- How many directors must the organization have? What are their voting rights? How is a quorum ascertained? How is notice of meetings properly given? What are the length and number of their terms of office? Are there term limits?

- What officers must the organization have? What are their duties? What are the length and number of their terms of office? Are there term limits? Can an individual hold more than one office?

- How frequently must the governing board meet? Must the board members always meet in person, or can the meetings be by telephone conference call or video teleconferencing? Can the board members vote by mail or unanimous written consent?

- If there are members, what are their rights? When must they meet? What notice of the meetings must be given?

- What issues must be decided by members (if any)? Directors?

- May there be an executive committee of the governing board? If so, what are its duties? What limitations are there on its functions?

- What about other committees? What are their duties? Can the organization have an advisory committee?

- How are the organization's governing instruments amended?

- How must a merger involving the organization occur?

- What is the process for dissolving the organization? For distributing its assets and net income on dissolution?

If the organization is not a corporation, these and other questions are usually unanswered under state law. The organization must then add to its rules the answers to all the pertinent questions (assuming they can be anticipated) or live with the uncertainties.

**Familiarity.** People are more familiar with corporations than other entities. Thus, if the nonprofit organization is a corporation, more will know what the entity is. In general, the world in which the nonprofit organization will be functioning is comfortable with the concept of a corporation. Trusts are well known, too, particularly in the private foundations and other estate planning areas, although less known and used than corporations. Unincorporated associations are the least used of these three entities.

**Registration and Reporting.** Incorporation entails an affirmative act of a state government: it "charters" the entity (it issues a certificate of incorporation). In exchange for the grant of corporate status, the state usually expects certain forms of compliance by the organization, such as adherence to rules of operations, an initial filing fee, annual reports, annual fees, and public disclosure requirements. These costs are frequently nominal, however, and the reporting requirements are usually not extensive. There rarely are comparable filing requirements for trusts and unincorporated associations. Although articles of incorporation are public documents, trust documents and unincorporated association constitutions often are not.

**Federal Tax Law Requirements.** In most cases, federal tax law is silent as to the form of tax-exempt organizations; most of them can select from among the three types. In a few instances, however, a specific form of organization is required to qualify under federal law as a tax-exempt organization. For example, an instrumentality of the federal government[12] and a single-parent title-holding organization[13] must, under federal tax law, be formed as corporations, while entities such as supplemental unemployment benefit organizations,[14] Black Lung benefit organizations,[15] and multiemployer plan funds[16] must be formed as trusts. A multibeneficiary title-holding organization[17] can be formed as either a corporation or a trust. On occasion, a federal law other than the tax law will have a direct bearing on the form of a tax-exempt organization. For example, under the federal political campaign regulation laws, corporations cannot make political campaign contributions; a tax-exempt political organization[18] may, therefore, have to avoid the corporate form.

## More on Trusts

The trust form for a tax-exempt organization is rarely the appropriate choice except for certain charitable entities (most notably, private foundations), some labor organizations, and certain funds associated with employee plans. This form is also used when creating charitable giving vehicles in the planned giving setting, such as charitable remainder trusts[19] and charitable lead trusts.[20] By contrast, for example, membership organizations are ill-suited to the trust form.

The principal problem with structuring a nonprofit organization as a trust is that most state laws concerning trusts are written for the regulation of charitable trusts. These rules are rarely as flexible as contemporary nonprofit corporation acts, and the rules frequently impose fiduciary standards and practices that are more stringent than those for nonprofit corporations. The trust form may, however, provide more privacy to the founders of a trust (sometimes termed *grantors* or *settlors*) than the other forms.

It is unusual—although certainly permissible—for the trustee or trustees of a trust to adopt a set of bylaws.

## More on Unincorporated Associations

The term *unincorporated association* employs the word *association* for a reason: these entities are usually membership based. That is, societies and the like are often formed without the formalities of incorporation.

To the uninitiated, a nonprofit corporation and a nonprofit unincorporated association look alike. A membership association has many of the same characteristics, whether incorporated or not. The contents of a constitution are much the same as the contents

**COMMENT >**

As a general rule, the preferable form for a modern tax-exempt organization is the nonprofit corporation. This is because of the advantages referenced above, including the protection against personal liability (more on that below). The approach should be that the corporate form is the appropriate one, unless there are one or more specific reasons compelling another choice. Nonetheless, the facts and circumstances in each situation should be carefully examined to be certain that the most suitable form is selected.

of articles of incorporation. A set of bylaws for an unincorporated association looks much like those of a nonprofit corporation. One of the main distinctions between the two entities, however, is that the corporation is the organization that is "officially chartered" by a state (or the District of Columbia).

### NOTE

This choice is not necessarily immutable. A tax-exempt organization can change its form. (As a matter of state law, trusts are likely to be the most difficult of entities to change.) A common instance is conversion of an unincorporated association to a nonprofit corporation. (It is rare for a nonprofit corporation to unincorporate.) When this type of change is made, however, a new legal entity is created; this may require another filing with the IRS to procure a determination letter for the successor organization.[21]

## NAME

Planners, when involved in the establishment of a tax-exempt organization—particularly a charitable one—should assist the organization in giving serious consideration to the entity's *name*. Certainly, the organizational test[22] is silent on the point. The organization's eligibility for tax-exempt status is not going to pivot on its name.

Still, the organization's name sets a tone that overshadows the evaluation that is accorded the entity, whether it is by the IRS, a court, the media, or the general public. Thus, the name should do more than convey what the entity is about—it should be appropriate for a tax-exempt organization and, if applicable, an exempt charitable organization. Particularly in the case of a putative charitable entity, as a matter of sheer presentation and appearance, and of imbuing the exemption application process with a positive start (from the applicant's viewpoint), the planner should give more than passing consideration to the organization's name.

A case decided in 2000 nicely illustrates the point. A nonprofit organization was in court seeking a ruling that it was a tax-exempt charitable and educational entity. The organization audits structural steel fabricators in conjunction with a quality certification program conducted by a related trade association. The association (a business league[23]) was engaged primarily in the creation of standardized engineering codes and specifications for use in the fabrication and construction of steel-framed buildings and bridges. At the request of governmental agencies and others, the association developed a certification program for structural steel fabricators, which it placed in the related nonprofit entity. The essence of the program was to further structural integrity and quality within the steel fabrication industry. Ultimately, efforts of the association and its related organization were about safety—protection of members of the public in connection with their use of buildings and bridges constructed with steel. The organization failed in its effort to become tax-exempt, with the court rejecting the arguments that it was charitable (in part because of lessening of the burdens of government[24]) and educational, and finding unwarranted private benefit.[25]

The correctness of this opinion is arguable, particularly its application of the private benefit doctrine.[26] For purpose of the immediate topic, however, planners should consider the name given to this organization: Quality Auditing Company. While more or less descriptive of the organization's programs, that name does not sound plausibly charitable or educational. For one thing, the word *company* should be avoided; that terminology is best left to the realm of for-profit organizations. Second, the word *auditing* also has commercial overtones. The three words together simply do not sound like those associated with tax-exempt, charitable entities.

At the very least, the organization could have been the Quality Auditing *Foundation* or the Quality Auditing *Institute*. Given its overall objectives and programs, the organization could have been named the *Public Safety Institute*. A different name presumably would not have changed the outcome in this case, but it might be a factor in a closer one. Another illustration of a name that led the organization off to a poor (and ultimately unsuccessful) start is At Cost Services.[27]

A name can be clever and yet only provide a court with a basis for concluding that the undertaking was something less than serious, thereby tainting the entire cause; an example of this is Salvation Navy.[28] Likewise, if an organization is trying to qualify for exemption but probably is not entitled to it, it is not a good idea to select a name that conveys the individuals' true intentions (such as attempting to qualify an organization as a religious one because it conducts "worship services" on a yacht while floating around in a large bay): an example is The Southern Church of Universal Brotherhood Assembled (the acronym being SCUBA).[29]

By contrast, an argument can be made that one of the finest names ever assigned to a tax-exempt organization is this: the Vigilant Hose Company. In this context, the word *company* has a different meaning; the organization is a volunteer fire company.[30]

## GOVERNING BOARD

A tax-exempt organization—irrespective of form—must have one or more directors or trustees.[31] State law typically mandates at least three of these individuals, particularly in the case of nonprofit corporations. Some states require only one. Some nonprofit organizations have large governing boards, often to the point of being unwieldy. (State law does not set a maximum number of directors of nonprofit organizations.) The optimum size of a governing board of a nonprofit organization depends on many factors, including the type of organization involved, the nature and size of the organization's constituency, the way in which the directors are selected, and the role and effectiveness of an executive committee (if any).

### Nomenclature

State law generally refers to these individuals as *directors*. Some tax-exempt organizations use other terms, such as *trustees* or *governors*. Generally, organizations are free to use the terminology they want, although applicable state law should be checked on the point.

The choice of term is not usually a matter of law. Some organizations prefer to refer to their governing board as the *board of trustees* because it sounds more impressive. (Technically, only a director of a trust can be a trustee, but that formality has long disappeared.) This is particularly the case with charitable and educational institutions. Schools, colleges, and universities, for example, favor this approach.

Where organizations are related, this terminology can be used to reduce confusion. For example, in an instance of a tax-exempt membership association and its related foundation, the board of the former may be termed the *board of directors* and the board of the latter, the *board of trustees*.

## Scope of Authority

The directors are those who set policy for the organization and oversee its affairs; actual implementation of plans and programs, and day-to-day management, is to be left to officers and employees. In reality, however, it is difficult to mark precisely where the scope of authority of the board of directors stops and the authority of other managers begins. (In the parlance of the tax law, trustees, directors, officers, and key employees are *managers* of the organization.)

Frequently, authority of this nature (or "territory" or "turf") is resolved in the political arena, not the legal one. It may vary, from time to time, as the culture of the entity changes. In some organizations, the directors do not have the time or do not want to take the time to "micromanage"; others restrain themselves from doing so (and still others do not). Often, the matter comes down to the sheer force of personalities. In some organizations, the most dominant manager is the executive director rather than the president or chair of the board.

## Origins

The board of directors of a tax-exempt organization can be derived in several ways; indeed, there can be a blend of these ways. The basic choices are:

- Election by a membership
- Election by the other directors (such as a self-perpetuating board)
- Selection by the membership of another organization
- Selection by the board of another organization
- Ex officio positions
- A blend of two or more of the foregoing options

If there are bona fide members of the organization (such as an association), it is likely that these members will elect some or all of the members of the governing board of the entity. This election may be conducted by mail ballot or voting at the annual meeting. It is possible, however, for an exempt organization with a membership to have a governing board that is not elected by that membership.

In the absence of a membership or if the membership lacks a vote on the matter, the governing board of a tax-exempt organization may be a *self-perpetuating* board. With this model, the initial board continues with those it elects and those elected by subsequent boards.

Some boards have one or more *ex officio* positions. This means that individuals are board members by virtue of other positions they hold.[32] These other positions may be those of the organization itself or of another organization or a blend of the two.

In the case of many tax-exempt organizations, the source of the membership of the board is preordained. Examples include the typical membership organization that elects the board (such as a trade association, social club, or veterans' organization); a hospital, college, or museum that has a governing board generally reflective of the community; and a private foundation that has one or more trustees who represent a particular family or corporation.

## Control

With the rare exception of the stock-based nonprofit organization, no one "owns" a nonprofit entity. Control of a nonprofit organization, however, is another matter.[33] Certainly, the governing board of a nonprofit organization controls the organization.

There are, nonetheless, other manifestations of this matter of control that the planner is likely to confront. One is the situation where an individual or a close-knit group of individuals wants to control an organization. This can be of particular consequence in the case of a single-purpose organization that was founded by an individual or such a group. Those who launch a tax-exempt organization understandably do not want to put their blood, sweat, tears, and dollars into formation and growth of the organization, only to watch others assume control over it and freeze them out of the organization's affairs. The planner will be called on to create a system where this type of control exists, even while there is also a larger governing board in which those who want to retain control are in a minority.

The seven alternatives to achieve this end are:

1. **Trust.** Most individuals in this position assemble a board of friends and family members and hope that trust and loyalty will prevail. Usually, they do. Occasionally, however, there is internal conflict, a new majority emerges, and the founder or founders are ousted.

2. **Superterm.** Some individuals attempt to create for themselves a term longer than that of the others. Sometimes, an effort is made to have a term for life. This approach usually is untenable under state law.

3. **One director.** A founder of a nonprofit entity can form it in a state that requires only one director, then if necessary qualify it in the state in which it will operate.

4. **Membership classes.** One technique is to have two classes of board members: Class A and Class B. Class A consists of the founders; Class B is everyone else. The governing instrument is written in such a way that certain major decisions (such as

expenditures in excess of a set amount or dissolution of the organization) cannot be approved without a majority vote of those in Class A.

5. **Entity membership.** Another technique is to establish the organization as a membership entity and to have only the founders as members. The member/founders have the authority to elect the board members—and to remove them.

6. **Stock.** In a few states, a nonprofit organization can issue stock. Such an entity can be formed with the founders being the sole shareholders. The shareholders would have the authority to elect and remove board members.

7. **Advisory committee.** The governing board can be confined to a select few, coupled with an advisory committee. This is a group of individuals who are not on and do not substitute for the board of directors but provide policy and/or technical input in advancement of the organization's programs. Because members of an advisory committee lack voting rights, their number is governed only by what is practical. Committee members serve without the threat of personal liability that may accrue to the organization's directors and officers, and without incurring the larger set of responsibilities shouldered by the directors. Moreover, with an advisory committee, an organization can surround itself with some of the prominent names in the field.

Those involved with nonprofit organizations will discover, as most tax-exempt organizations planners already know, that techniques such as those described above in items 2 to 6 seem feasible in theory but rarely work in practice. This is because these approaches are divisive and are likely to cause more difficulties than they resolve. In the end, usually the first option is selected, perhaps augmented with the seventh.

## Other Considerations

The board of directors of a tax-exempt organization may decide to have a chair (chairperson, chairman, or chairwoman) of the board. This individual presides over board meetings. The chair position is not usually an officer position (although it can be made one). The position may (but need not) be authorized in the organization's bylaws.

Some organizations find it useful to stagger the terms of office so that only a portion of the board is up for election or reelection at any one time, thereby providing some continuity of service and expertise. A tidy model in this regard is the nine-person board, with three-year terms for members; one-third of the board is elected annually.

A board of directors of a tax-exempt organization usually acts by means of in-person meetings, where a quorum is present. Where state law allows, the members of the board can meet via conference call (a call where all participants can hear each other) or by unanimous written consent. These alternative procedures should be authorized in the organization's bylaws (indeed, that may be a requirement of state law).

Unless there is authorization in the law (and there is not likely to be), the directors of a tax-exempt organization may not vote by proxy, mail ballot, e-mail, or telephone call (other than by a qualified conference call).

Members of an organization have more flexibility as to voting than members of the board of the organization. For example, usually they can vote by mail ballot and by use of proxies.

**NOTE** ✎

The planner should consider creating the tax-exempt organization as a membership organization and making the board of directors the members of the entity if voting by means of proxy or mail ballot is of significance to the board. Indeed, in a few states, a nonprofit organization must have a membership; the board of directors can be that membership.

## Board Composition and the IRS

Generally, the federal tax law has nothing to say about the composition of the governing board of a tax-exempt organization; it is essentially a state law matter.[34] There are three prominent exceptions: (1) exempt healthcare organizations are required to satisfy a community benefit test, which includes a requirement of a community board;[35] (2) organizations that qualify as publicly supported entities by reason of a facts-and-circumstances test are likely to be required to have a governing board that is representative of the community;[36] and (3) the rules concerning supporting organizations often dictate the manner in which board members are selected.[37] Basically, then, those forming and operating a tax-exempt organization are free to structure and populate the organization's board in any manner they choose.[38]

Unfortunately, today, some in the IRS who process applications for recognition of tax exemption, or otherwise review the operations of tax-exempt organizations, are not well trained in the law of tax-exempt organizations. These individuals have a tendency to substitute their view as to what the law is (or should be) for the actual legal requirements, and demand that the organizations do something (or refrain from doing something) as a condition of exemption. In this regard, they usually are in error. Nowhere is this regrettable phenomenon more prevalent than in the case of the composition of the board of tax-exempt organizations.

Following are the positions of IRS reviewers that exempt organizations, most likely charitable ones, and their planners may encounter:

- **Public board.** The governing board of a tax-exempt organization must be reflective of the public. An IRS specialist asserted that "[u]nrelated individuals selected from the community you serve should control the non-profit." One applicant was directed to "expand your board at this time, so control no longer rests with related individuals." Another was told that the entity needs to enlarge its board "to remove the close control issue." Still another IRS specialist articulated the thought that the "structure [of the board] must be changed to allow members of the general public to control the non-profit organization."

- **Control by a for-profit organization.** An IRS specialist wrote: "No for-profit should have control of a non-profit organization."
- **Conflicts.** An IRS specialist asserted that a majority of an exempt organization's board may not be related to salaried personnel or to parties providing services to the organization.
- **One director.** An IRS law specialist was of the view that a tax-exempt organization could not have only one director, as state law permitted. This was seen by the specialist as a violation of the doctrine of private inurement. The specialist wrote that this individual "stands in a relationship" with the organization "which offers him the opportunity to make use of the organization's income or assets for personal gain."
- **Competence.** An IRS reviewer asked an organization for a statement as to the "qualifications" of the board members.
- **Experience.** An IRS reviewer asked an organization for a statement as to the board members' "experience" in serving on the board of a nonprofit organization.
- **Participation.** An IRS law specialist demanded that the applicant organization produce a statement, signed by each director, that they will "take an active part" in the operations of the organization.
- **Intermediate sanctions.** An IRS law specialist tried to force an applicant organization to provide a statement, signed by each director, that they were aware of and would abide by the intermediate sanctions rules[39] in their service to the organization.[40]

These assertions as to the state of the law, practices, and required statements have an element in common: they are nonsense. None of this is the law; none of this is required. The planner should stand up to these IRS representatives, explain to them (politely, of course) why they are flat wrong, make it abundantly clear that their demands are going to be disregarded, and state that if they persist with their position(s), the matter will be referred to the IRS National Office for resolution. They usually will back down, particularly in the face of an assertion that they are merely (and erroneously) inserting their personal views into the case. The problem is that an applicant organization is filing without the benefit of a tax-exempt organizations professional, or is using the services of a professional who is not sufficiently proficient in this area of the law and innocently believes that it must comply with the specialist's demand(s)—and does.

## OFFICERS

Nearly every tax-exempt organization has officers. A prominent exception is the trust, which usually has only one or more trustees.

## Scope of Authority

As with the board of directors, the scope (or levels) of authority of the officers of a tax-exempt organization is difficult to articulate. In the case of a nonprofit organization that has members, directors, officers, and employees (key or otherwise), setting a clear distinction as to who has the authority to do what is nearly impossible. General principles can be stated but will usually prove nearly useless in practice.

For example, it can be stated that the members of the organization (if any) set basic policy and the members of the board of directors set additional policy, albeit within the parameters established by the membership. The officers thereafter implement the policies, as do the employees, although this is more on a day-to-day basis. Yet, the reality is that, at all levels, policy is established and implemented.

In a typical tax-exempt organization, who decides what programs will be undertaken, who is hired and fired as employees, the nature of the retirement plan arrangements, who the lawyers and accountants for the organization will be, the type of fundraising program, the format of the journal, or the organization's physical location(s)? Depending on the circumstances, the answers may be the members, the board, the executive committee, the chair of the board, the president, the (or a) vice president, the executive director, and/or any number of others.

## Positions and Duties

As a general proposition, the officers of a tax-exempt organization, and their respective duties and responsibilities, are as follows.

**President.**  The president is the principal executive officer of the organization and in general supervises and controls all of the business and affairs of the entity. He or she presides at meetings of the governing board. The president signs, often with one other officer of the organization (usually the secretary), any contracts (including leases) or other documents required to be executed on behalf of the organization (such as mortgages, deeds, or bonds). The bylaws of the organization should provide that the president is to perform all duties "generally incident to" the office of president.

### NOTE

In some organizations, one or more of the roles of president (most notably, presiding over board meetings) are assumed by the chair of the board.

**Vice President.**  In the absence of the president, or in the event of the president's inability or refusal to act, the vice president performs the duties of the president.

**Treasurer.**  The treasurer has charge and custody of and is responsible for all funds, securities, and perhaps other property of the organization. He or she receives and gives receipts for money due and payable to the organization, and deposits such money in the name of the organization in the banks, trust companies, or other depositories selected by the organization. The treasurer may make investments, pursuant to an overall investment policy developed by the organization's board. The bylaws of the organization should provide that the treasurer is to perform all duties "generally incident to" the office of treasurer. If required by the board, the treasurer has to provide a bond (at the organization's expense) for the faithful discharge of the treasurer's duties in such sum and with such surety or sureties as the board determines.

**Secretary.** The secretary is responsible for the minutes of the meetings of the board of the organization. He or she has the responsibility to give all notices in accordance with the organization's bylaws or as required by law. The secretary is custodian of the records and of the seal (if any) of the organization. The secretary is to keep a register of the addresses of each member of the board of the organization (and perhaps each member of the organization). The bylaws of the organization should provide that the secretary is to perform all duties "generally incident to" the office of secretary.

## Origins

The officers of a tax-exempt organization are usually elected, either by a membership or by the board of directors. In some instances, the officers of an organization are ex officio with, or are selected by, another organization. The basic choices are:

- Election by a membership
- Election by the directors, who are elected by members
- Election by the directors, who are a self-perpetuating board
- Election (or appointment) by the board of another organization
- A blend of two or more of the foregoing options

## Governing Instruments

The governing instruments of the tax-exempt organization (usually the bylaws) should identify the officers of the organization and state the duties and responsibilities of each position (see above), provide for the manner of their election (or other selection), state the terms of the offices, and address the matter of reelections to office (including any term limits).

For the most part, the law allows a tax-exempt organization to use whatever governing structure it wants. In most states, a nonprofit corporations law contains rules (some mandatory, some optional) concerning officers, terms of office, and the like.

Particularly if the organization is a corporation, state law usually requires at least certain officers. In general, the same individual can hold more than one office; the positions of secretary and treasurer are commonly combined. The president and secretary, however, should not be the same individual. (The law in many states prohibits this duality.) Frequently, legal documents will require these two officers' separate signatures.

Officers are officers of the organization. They are not officers of the board of directors. An exception to this can be the chair of the board; this individual may be considered an "officer" of the board.

## KEY EMPLOYEES

The federal tax law recognizes that an individual can have significant duties and responsibilities with respect to a tax-exempt organization, and not be a trustee, director, or officer. The planner should assist the organization in identifying these persons, who are those who have responsibilities or powers "similar to" those of a trustee, director, or officer.[41] There often are, for example, special reporting requirements as to these individuals.[42] Also, they are usually disqualified persons for intermediate sanctions purposes[43] and insiders for private inurement purposes.[44] One likely candidate for key employee is the executive director of an exempt organization; other key employees are other chief management or financial individuals.

## MANAGEMENT COMPANIES

A tax-exempt organization may utilize the services of a management company. This type of company does not supplant the need for directors and officers of the exempt organization, although it may substitute for an organization's employees.

There is nothing inherently inappropriate about a tax-exempt organization's use of a management company. Nonetheless, the IRS tends to accord these arrangements particular scrutiny.[45] For example, if members of the board of the management company also serve as members of the board of the exempt organization (or there are other business and/or family ties between the two entities), the agency may be particularly sensitive to the potential for private inurement, private benefit, and/or excess benefit transactions.[46] In some instances, the IRS may be inclined to interpret a management company–exempt organization arrangement as a joint venture.[47]

## MINUTES

The proceedings of most tax-exempt organizations are (and should be) reflected in minutes. Essentially, there are two types of minutes: *organizational minutes* and ongoing *directors' meeting minutes*. There can, of course, be other sets of minutes, such as those of meetings of members and committees.

### Organizational Minutes

A document—in addition to articles of organization and bylaws—that is important when forming a tax-exempt organization is the organizational minutes. The organization's initial board of directors adopts these minutes.

At a minimum, this document, should reflect:

- Ratification of the articles of organization
- Adoption of the bylaws
- Election of any other directors

- Election of the officers (if appropriate)
- Passage of the requisite resolution(s) for establishment of a bank account (or accounts) or any other accounts at financial institutions[48]
- Passage of a resolution selecting legal counsel
- Passage of a resolution selecting an accountant
- Authorization (or ratification) of certain actions, such as preparation and filing with the IRS of an application for recognition of tax-exempt status
- Authorization of reimbursement of expenses incurred in establishing the entity

Other actions of the board can be reflected in these minutes, such as discussion of program activities, development of one or more components of a fundraising program, or selection of a management or fundraising consultant.

These minutes can reflect actions taken by means of an in-person meeting, a meeting by conference call, or a written unanimous consent document.

## Other Board Minutes

Each meeting of the board of directors of a tax-exempt organization should be the subject of a set of minutes. These documents should not be veritable transcripts of the proceedings but instead should memorialize material developments and decisions formally taken (as in resolutions). A current and complete minute book, reflecting explanation of important decisions and transactions, can go a long way in resolving disputes, shortening (or even forestalling) an IRS audit, and the like. They should be written with a certain amount of prescience, with the scrivener always thinking about how the document will look months and years to come.

> ### NOTE ✎
>
> A good practice is to have board meeting minutes drafted, then reviewed by a lawyer, before they are circulated to the full board for review and approval. In this way, inartful phraseologies can be eliminated and other potential problems minimized or eliminated. Some lawyers review and revise corporate minutes with the view that each document will someday be an exhibit in a trial.

Minutes should be kept in a minute book, along with other important documents, such as the articles of organization, bylaws, and IRS determination letter. Minute books can be purchased commercially, although a simple ring binder will suffice. The point is to initiate and maintain a substantive history of the board's decisions and the organization's progress toward the objective of achieving exempt purposes.

As with organizational minutes, these minutes can reflect actions taken by means of an in-person meeting, a meeting by conference call, or a written unanimous consent document.

COMMENT ➤

Each board member is well advised to maintain his or her personal board meeting book (see below). Copies of minutes of meetings long since held can be discarded from time to time, but the thoughtful board member should bring this book to each meeting, with copies of recent minutes readily available if needed.

## OTHER DOCUMENTS

A tax-exempt organization may have other documents, other than those discussed above, with legal import.

### Mission Statement

It is becoming increasingly popular for tax-exempt organizations to develop a full mission statement, explaining their purposes, programs, and objectives. This exercise often ties in with development of a business plan (see next item). There certainly is nothing wrong with this exercise. The only caution from the planner's standpoint is twofold:

1. Be certain that the mission statement is consistent with the organization's articles of organization and/or bylaws.
2. Be certain that the mission statement does not contain language that is inconsistent with the requirements for maintaining the organization's tax-exempt status.

### Business Plan

A tax-exempt organization may be operating in conformity with a business plan. Again, this is a commendable practice. The only caution from the planner's standpoint is expressed in the above two elements.

### Case Statement

A tax-exempt organization, most likely a charitable one,[49] may have a case statement used as part of its fundraising program. Again, the planner should test the contents of this document against the above two elements. Also, statements made in a case statement (or a fundraising solicitation letter) can be interpreted as the substance of a contract with contributors and grantors.

### Code of Ethics

Membership and some other tax-exempt organizations may have a code of ethics that they enforce and otherwise administer. This document will include criteria for membership and may be the basis for expulsion of an individual from membership. The organization may have an ethics committee that oversees and interprets application of the principles of this code. Because of the heightened potential for legal liability (such as for defamation) in cases of membership exclusion and expulsion, and other applications of a code of ethics, the planner should ensure that the code is reasonable and legal (tested, for example, against antitrust law principles), and enforced by means of a procedure that is fair (although the full panoply of due process rights need not be present).

## Conflict-of-Interest Policy

It has become increasingly popular (fueled in part by corporate governance developments, as discussed below) for a tax-exempt organization to have a conflict-of-interest policy. While this type of policy is not generally mandated by law,[50] it can be useful in protecting the interests of the exempt (particularly charitable) organization when it is contemplating entering into a transaction or other arrangement that might benefit the financial interest of the organization's directors, officers, and/or other interested persons (as that term may be defined).

Pursuant to these policies, interested persons are identified, then required to disclose to the board of directors, with regard to actual or possible conflicts of interest, the existence of their financial interest in connection with a transaction or arrangement. The policy should include a procedure by which the board determines if, in fact, a conflict of interest exists and, if so, whether to proceed with the transaction or arrangement. Compensation paid to all interested persons should be identified and periodically tested against the standard of reasonableness.

Directors and officers (and perhaps others, such as full-time employees) should sign a statement that affirms that they understand and agree to comply with the conflict-of-interest policy. Thereafter, the statement should be annually executed by these interested persons, disclosing any conflict of interest, relationships with other organizations and suppliers of goods and services to the exempt organization involved, and places of employment of family members.

# CORPORATE GOVERNANCE PRINCIPLES

In the wake of the collapse of and major public relations damage to large corporations and accounting firms in the early 2000s, there has been intense focus on matters pertaining to *corporate responsibility*. Massive statutory laws applicable to for-profit entities have been enacted, followed by sweeping rules and regulations. Litigation on the subject is ubiquitous.

This body of law does not apply to tax-exempt organizations (although comparable laws may be imminent). Nonetheless, there are some principles being developed in the realm of corporate responsibility that should at least be considered by the boards of exempt organizations:

- This is discussed elsewhere (see above) but can be noted here: should the board cause the organization to have a conflict-of-interest policy to which the directors, officers, key employees, and perhaps others must adhere?

- Should the board develop a code of ethics (see above) for its senior officers? This would go beyond a conflict-of-interest policy.
- Should the organization have an independent audit committee or comparable body?
- Should the organization require certification of the financial statements and/or information returns by its chief executive?
- Should the accounting firm retained by an exempt organization be a firm that is registered with the Public Company and Accounting Oversight Board?
- Should an exempt organization have a policy of prohibiting loans to its senior executives?
- Suppose there is a need for an accounting restatement by an exempt organization due to some form of misconduct. Should any bonuses and/or the like to executive personnel have to be reimbursed?
- Should an exempt organization follow the rules regarding audit partner rotation?
- Should an exempt organization have a rule requiring its lawyer (particularly outside counsel) to report to one or more board members where a legal matter is not being properly handled or resolved by the staff?

## BOARD MEMBER RESPONSIBILITIES AND DUTIES

In today's litigious society, avoidance of a lawsuit cannot be guaranteed. Even the rules prohibiting frivolous suits have gotten lax. There are, however, a number of steps that members of the board of a tax-exempt organization can take to minimize the likelihood of a lawsuit against the organization—and against themselves.

### Form

Every member of the board of a tax-exempt organization should understand the form of the organization.[51] The board member should also know what is required to maintain that form—and see to it that the necessary action (or actions) is taken. For example, an organization that is incorporated can lose its corporate status if it fails to timely file annual reports with the state in which it is incorporated.

Moreover, if the exempt organization is not incorporated, it is incumbent on the board member to understand why that is the case. If the entity is to remain unincorporated, the board member should be satisfied, by being provided (by a lawyer) at least one good reason for its status. An unincorporated organization almost always can become incorporated.

### Understand Organization's Purposes/Mission

The board member should understand, and be able to articulate, the tax-exempt organization's mission. This entails knowledge of the organization's *purposes*. For this, the individual should read the statement of purposes contained in the entity's articles of organization. If the purposes are not understood, a suitable explanation should be obtained. There may be a mission statement that, as noted, is in addition to, and perhaps more expansive than, the statement of purposes. The board member should be satisfied that the statement of purposes and the mission statement are consistent.

Statements of purpose and mission statements are not intractable. The board member should be satisfied with the language of both, particularly the statement of purposes. It may be that the statement should be updated (articles amended). The organization may have a statement of purposes that is not adequately reflective of its contemporary goals and objectives.

## Understand Its Activities and Why They Further Purposes/Mission

Just as the board member should understand the organization's purposes, the member should understand the organization's *activities*.

With regard to program activities, the board member should understand and remain informed as to each of them.[52] The member should be able to explain what they are and why they are conducted. The member should know the connection between the organization's operations and furtherance of its purposes.

The organization's activities may include lobbying. If so, the board member should be satisfied that the lobbying is appropriate for the organization and that such activity is not jeopardizing the organization's tax-exempt status.[53] The same is true with respect to any political campaign activities.[54]

If the organization engages in fundraising activities, the board member should understand what they are. The member should make some effort to be satisfied that the organization is using the types of fundraising that are suitable for it and its objectives. Fundraising is not program, however; rather, it is a means to advance program and should be kept in that perspective.

The organization may conduct one or more unrelated businesses.[55] There is nothing inherently wrong with unrelated activity, but the board member should know why the business is being conducted, be certain it does not detract from program undertakings, and be satisfied that the organization's tax-exempt status is not being endangered.

## Understand Its Articles of Organization

The board member should understand each article of the organization's articles of organization—what it means and why it is in the document. Of particular importance are the statement of purposes and the dissolution clause.

Other provisions to review and understand are those describing the organization's membership (if any) and provisions in the document that are reflective of federal tax law requirements and limitations.

## Understand Its Structure/Bylaws

The board member should understand the tax-exempt organization's bylaws. This document spells out (or should spell out) the entity's basic governance and operational structure.

Items to check are: (1) the origin, composition, and stated duties of the organization's directors; (2) the origins and duties of the organization's officers; (3) the qualification and functions of any members; (4) the rules as to conduct of meetings (such as notice, quorum, voting); (5) the organization's committee structure; (6) provisions as to any indemnification (although state law may require that the provisions be in the articles); and (7) provisions as to any immunity (again, the language may have to be in the articles).

## Understand Other Documents

The board member should understand the reason for, and the content of, other documents published by and/or prepared for the organization. These include annual reports, promotional materials (brochures, pamphlets), fundraising materials, newsletters, and journals. Of course, if a program activity of the organization is publishing, it is not necessary that the board member read every book or other publication of the organization.

There are other documents—those that have some import in the law—that the board member should understand. They include any documents that are required to be filed with a state, such as annual reports and reports filed pursuant to one or more charitable solicitation acts. The board member should understand the organization's conflict-of-interest policy (if any) and have at least a general familiarity with its insurance policies. Employment contracts should also be understood.

There are other documents of considerable importance that each board member should review in draft. These are the annual financial statement (if any), the annual information return filed with the IRS,[56] and any unrelated business income tax return[57] filed with that agency. If the board member does not understand material in these documents, questions should be asked. If the organization is not required to file an annual information return, the member should know why (such as the organization is small or is a church).[58]

## Related Entities

A tax-exempt organization often is not a solitary entity; it may be a part of a cluster of entities. For example, a membership association may have a related foundation, a political action committee, and/or a for-profit subsidiary. A charitable organization may have a separate organization that functions as a "lobbying arm," or an advocacy organization may have a related educational foundation. The board member should understand why these discrete entities exist, what their functions are, and how the relationships are structured.

Other entities that may be involved are partnerships, limited liability companies, and/or other forms of joint ventures.

In the case of multiple related entities, what has been said above may be true for all of them. For example, the board member may be well advised to review and understand the documents pertaining to each of these entities.

## Is the Organization Doing Business in One or More Other States?

The board member should know the jurisdiction(s) in which the tax-exempt organization "does business." (That term, while sounding as though it applies only to commercial enterprises, also applies to nonprofit organizations.) Certainly, the organization is "doing business" in the state in which its offices are located.

An exempt organization, however, may also be doing business in one or more other jurisdictions. An obvious illustration of this is an office or some other manifestation of a physical presence in another state. These precepts vary from state to state, however, and an organization can be deemed to be doing business in a state where there is less of a presence than a formal office.[59] If the organization is doing business in other jurisdictions, the board member should be advised of those locations and understand why the organization is deemed to be engaged in business.

## Public Charity Status

If the tax-exempt organization is a charitable one, the board member should know whether it is a public charity or a private foundation.[60] If it is a public charity, the board member should know the organization's classification for this purpose. The choices are: (1) one of the *institutions,* such as a school, college, university, hospital, other healthcare provider, medical research organization, church, or the like; (2) a *publicly supported organization,* with its support derived from gifts, grants, and/or exempt function (program service) revenue; or (3) a *supporting organization.*

Much of the law pertaining to private foundations focuses on transactions with, or in relation to, disqualified persons. In many instances, however, it is necessary that a public charity understand who the disqualified persons are with respect to it. The most obvious example in that regard is the intermediate sanctions rules.[61] Each board member should know who the organization's disqualified persons are.

## Perspective

The premise of the foregoing discussion is that the member of the board of directors of a tax-exempt organization who understands the legal aspects of the organization's structure and operations is far less likely to attract legal liability than the board member who acts (or fails to act) with lack of knowledge of these points.

# PROTECTIONS AGAINST PERSONAL LIABILITY

Actions by or on behalf of a tax-exempt organization can give rise to personal liability. The term *personal liability* means that one or more managers of an exempt organization (its trustees, directors, officers, and/or key employees) may be found personally liable for something done (commission) or not done (omission) while acting in the name of the organization.

Some of this exposure can be limited by:

- Incorporation
- Indemnification

- Insurance
- Immunity

**Incorporation.**   The matter of incorporation is discussed above, in the context of choice of form. To reiterate, a corporation is regarded in the law as a separate legal entity that can attract legal liability. This liability is generally confined to the organization and thus does not normally extend to those who set policy for or manage the organization. (This is one of the principal reasons a tax-exempt organization should be a nonprofit corporation.)

**Indemnification.**   *Indemnification* occurs (assuming it is legal under state law) when the organization agrees (usually by provision in its bylaws) to pay the judgments and related expenses (including legal fees) incurred by those who are covered by the indemnity, when those expenses are the result of a misdeed (commission or omission) by those persons while acting in the service of the organization. The indemnification cannot extend to criminal acts; it may not cover certain willful acts that violate civil law.

Because an indemnification involves the resources of the organization, the efficacy of it depends on the economic viability of the organization. In times of financial difficulties for a tax-exempt organization, with little in the way of assets and revenue flow, an indemnification of its directors and officers can be a classic "hollow promise."

**Insurance.**   *Insurance* (directors' and officers' (D&O) insurance) has features somewhat comparable to indemnification. Instead of shifting the risk of liability from the individuals involved to the nonprofit organization (indemnification), however, the risk of liability is shifted to an independent third party—an insurance company. Certain risks, such as criminal law liability, cannot be shifted by means of insurance (because it would be contrary to public policy). The insurance contract will likely exclude from coverage certain forms of civil law liability, such as defamation, employee discrimination, and/or antitrust matters.

Even where adequate insurance coverage is available, insurance can be costly. Premiums can easily be thousands of dollars annually, even with a sizable deductible.

A tax-exempt organization can purchase insurance to fund one or more indemnities it has made of its directors and officers.

**Immunity.**   *Immunity* is available when the law provides that a class of individuals, under certain circumstances, is not liable for a particular act or set of acts or for failure to undertake a particular act or set of acts. Several states have enacted immunity laws for directors and officers of nonprofit organizations, protecting them in case of asserted civil law violations, particularly where these individuals are functioning as volunteers.

## MINIMIZING BOARD MEMBER LIABILITY

The board member who is knowledgeable about the tax-exempt organization's programs and other operations is a board member who is not likely to do or not do, or say, something that will result in legal liability, for the organization or personally. Following are some practical steps the board members can take to enhance this knowledge and minimize the prospects of legal liability.

## Create Board Book

Each board member should have, and keep up to date, a board book. It need not be particularly formal or fancy; a simple three-ring binder will suffice. In the book should be, at a minimum: the board address list (see below), the organization's articles of organization, its bylaws, any other documents with legal overtones (such as a mission statement or conflict-of-interest policy), recent board meeting minutes, a copy of the ruling from the IRS recognizing the organization as a tax-exempt entity, the most recently filed state report, the most recent financial statement, and the most recent three annual information returns.

Other documents that may be included are recent committee reports, a copy of the organization's application for recognition of tax exemption, and the most recent unrelated business income tax return (if any).

## Board Address List

Each member of the board should have, and keep in the board book, a current list of the organization's board members. This list should contain each individual's mailing address, telephone numbers (office, home, cell, car, pager), fax number, and e-mail address.

## E-Mail Communications System

There should be a system by which the board members can communicate by e-mail. Each member should have a group listing of all of the board members. These individuals should communicate by e-mail to the extent practicable.

### CAUTION !

This does not mean that formal board meetings can be held via e-mail.[62] Also, board members should be careful what is said in e-mail messages; everything should be written from the perspective that it may someday become public. (Courts are ruling that e-mail messages can be used in civil cases as evidence.) Matters that have confidential aspects (such as the processing of ethics cases) should be discussed cautiously (if at all) by e-mail.

## Minutes

Careful consideration should be given to board meeting minutes.[63] There should be minutes of every board meeting. The minutes should be prepared with a heavy dose of common sense and perspective. These documents are not transcripts of the proceedings but are summaries of important actions, perhaps accompanied by resolutions.

It is difficult to generalize about the length and contents of board meeting minutes. Usually, whether something should have been in the minutes and is not, or whether something should not have been stated in the minutes and is, is determined in hindsight. The best practice is to be certain that all material decisions and actions are reflected, and be careful that nothing damaging to the organization is in the document.

### NOTE

A board member who opposes a majority board action on a matter, and is sufficiently concerned about the seriousness of the issue, should be certain that this opposition is reflected in the minutes, perhaps coupled with an explanation of the board member's position.

A good practice is for the secretary to provide a draft of the minutes to legal counsel for review, and if necessary revision, before they are circulated to the board members for their review and adoption.

In general, solid and current minutes are one of the most important of the "corporate" formalities to observe.

## Attend Meetings

It is critical that the board member attend each of the meetings of the board. Obviously, there will be occasional schedule conflicts; if the board member cannot attend a meeting, the minutes should reflect that fact and why. A board member cannot exercise the requisite degree of fiduciary responsibility without attending meetings and interacting with the other members.

The director should actively participate in the decision-making process. Silence is deemed to be concurrence. If a director is opposed to an action to be undertaken by the organization at the behest of the board, the director should speak up and, as noted, be certain to have his or her dissent noted in the minutes.

## Understand What Is Going On

Earlier, a summary of the aspects of an organization's structure and operations, involving legal matters, that a board member should know was provided. This understanding needs to be ongoing, as purposes are revised or expanded, programs change, and documents are amended. It is essential that the board member know these basics and then build on that base of knowledge as the organization evolves.

## Ask Questions

Probably one of the worst nonactions of a board member is failure to ask questions. The board member who merely pretends to understand what is taking place is only fooling himself or herself and is placed in a position to cause harm—to the organization or personally.

Questions may be asked of other board members, the organization's officers, and the staff. Questions may be posed during the course of a board meeting or on other occasions. Inquiries can be made by e-mail, although caution should be exercised as to how those messages are framed. Questions can be asked of lawyers and other professionals.

This is why some boards of tax-exempt organizations do not meet without the organization's lawyer present. Others make decisions conditioned on legal advice.

## Board Oversight of Staff

The board should oversee the activities of the organization's staff. Although board members should refrain from micromanaging, they should have sufficient knowledge of the role of each staff member and a general understanding as to their performance.

How this works in practice will vary considerably. If the organization has an executive director, most of this information should be provided by that individual. (Again, questions should be asked.) Some boards prefer to meet only when the organization's executive director is present. (Indeed, in some instances, the executive director is a member of the board, perhaps a nonvoting member.) Others do that but reserve some time to meet without that individual (or other staff) present.

## Conflict-of-Interest Policy

While for the most part it is not required as a matter of law, a nonprofit organization—particularly a charitable one—should give serious consideration to adoption of a conflict-of-interest policy (see above). For one thing, the IRS is pushing this as a condition of tax-exempt status. More importantly, this type of policy enables an organization to identify its disqualified persons and to know about any potential conflict at the time it is entering into transactions with such persons.

## Intermediate Sanctions Compliance

Board members of most tax-exempt organizations certainly want to be aware of the intermediate sanctions rules.[64] This is the case if only because the penalties for violation of these rules are imposed not on the organization but on the disqualified persons with respect to the organization. The disqualified persons with respect to the organization almost certainly will include members of the organization's board.

## Read Materials about Nonprofit Boards

An immense amount of literature concerns the role of members of the board of tax-exempt organizations, including material on the operations of exempt organizations as such.[65] Board members are well advised to read as much of this literature as possible.

## Attend Seminars

There are seminars that are of considerable utility to individuals in their capacity as board members of tax-exempt organizations.[66] Just as publications are recommended, so too are seminars of this nature—at least one annually.

## Retreats

The board of directors of a tax-exempt organization should consider having a periodic—perhaps even annual—board retreat. This is an opportunity for the board members to escape their employment and family responsibilities, and focus—if only for a few hours—on the contemporary mission and goals of the organization. This experience can help place the nonprofit organization's activities in perspective—and help the board member understand more fully the organization's structure and operations.

At this retreat, various outside consultants can make their appearance, share their expertise, give the board members the opportunity to ask questions, and provide the board a sense of the state of the organization. The board should consider use of a consultant for this purpose, to enhance the retreat with an outside perspective and a more directed focus.

## Overall Authority

The board should not exceed its authority. The members of the board serve as overseers. Their role is to make extraordinary, not ordinary, decisions. Day-to-day management of the organization should be left to the officers and the executive staff.

## Watchdog Agencies

Lawyers and other planners for tax-exempt organizations are principally concerned with seeing to it that the exempt organization involved is operating in conformity with the law or other rules of the profession involved (such as accounting principles). Indeed, the foregoing elements of this chapter and the other chapters in this book have been written to assist the planner in advising and assisting exempt organizations in connection with the requirements of the law.

There is, however, another consideration that, regrettably, planners cannot ignore: the role and influence of the so-called *watchdog agencies* that monitor and publicize the endeavors of tax-exempt organizations, principally those that solicit contributions from the public. These agencies have rules—euphemistically termed *voluntary standards*—which sometimes are inconsistent with or attempt to supersede law requirements. For example, one of the standards promulgated and enforced by the principal watchdog agency, the Better Business Bureau (BBB) Wise Giving Alliance, requires that a board of directors of a tax-exempt organization be comprised of at least five voting members—even though the law in most states requires only three directors and in some cases only one. As another example, these standards proclaim that only one meeting per year of the board of directors of an exempt organization can be by conference call—even though the law in the states does not place any limitation on the number of meetings that can be conducted using the telephone.

Even though these standards are by no means law, the planner may be forced to take them into account when advising a tax-exempt organization.

## Watchdog Agency Basics

This matter of standards enforcement by watchdog agencies is discussed elsewhere, including a summary of the various standards that are currently being applied.[67] Subsequent to publication of that material, however, the BBB Wise Giving Alliance promulgated its *Standards for Charitable Accountability* in final form. (These standards replaced the separate (and sometimes differing) standards utilized by the Philanthropic Advisory Service of the Council of Better Business Bureau's Foundation and the National Charities Information Bureau, which merged in 2001.) These standards are summarized under "Wise Giving Alliance Standards."

## COMMENT ►

**Y**our author is not enamored with the operations of these watchdog agencies. On balance, they are counterproductive—more trouble than they are worth. These agencies' collective portrayal of themselves is less than forthright; they loftily characterize themselves as *voluntary* organizations and their standards as *voluntary* ones. What they mean, of course, is that the agencies and standards are not *governmental* agencies and rules. Yet, there is nothing *voluntary* taking place in this context at all; a far more accurate term would be *extortionate*. Charitable organizations are coerced into compliance with these standards out of fear of the adverse publicity these agencies can quickly unleash in the form of a negative rating or report.

These agencies are, then, self-anointed. They are often staffed with individuals who are not adequately trained and experienced.[68] Some have a bias against the nonprofit sector; these agencies, as a justification for their existence, constantly portray the sector in the darkest of terms. When an issue arises, these agencies can be counted on to take the position most distant from that in the interest of the sector. It is maddening to watch the public, the media, government agencies, donors, and grantors—almost without exception—unquestioningly accept the pronouncements of these organizations. It is sad to see the charitable community capitulate to them. To exacerbate the situation, such agencies are proliferating.[69]

Most relevant, and most irksome to a lawyer, the standards meddle in areas where there is specific law on the point. These agencies can have a direct impact on the economics of a tax-exempt organization; they can adversely affect the flow of contributions and grants an organization receives. Yet they uniformly violate the most fundamental of procedural and substantive due process principles. Perhaps someday, a representative of the media or a court will expose the misleading rationale for the existence of these groups, and the often harmful and counterproductive outcomes they thrust on the charitable sector.[70] On the rare occasion when these agencies are publicly criticized, by the way, they do not respond in a forthright manner.[71] Rather, they retaliate with arrogance, misleading phraseology, misstatement of fact, innuendo, attention shifting to irrelevant points, and emphasis on insignificant detail to obscure and/or taint the larger picture.[72] In other words, they use the same techniques they often employ when writing reports about charitable organizations and publicly applying standards to them.

## Framework for Review of Agency Operations and Standards

A charity watchdog agency basically has three functions. One, it writes "standards" to which charitable organizations are expected to adhere. Two, it enforces the standards, in part by rating charitable organizations in relation to the standards and making the ratings public. Three, it prepares and circulates reports about charitable organizations to the public.

These agencies should be reasonable and truthful in respects to the content of their reports. They should be fair and reasonable when creating standards, and they should also do so when applying them. They may or may not, as a matter of law in a set of circumstances, follow due process and/or equal protection principles, but they should strive for basic fairness.

## Wise Giving Alliance Standards

The BBB Wise Giving Alliance issued the final version of its *Standards for Charitable Accountability* in 2003.[73] These standards replaced the separate (and sometimes differing) standards utilized by the Philanthropic Advisory Service of the Council of Better Business Bureau's Foundation and the National Charities Information Bureau, which merged in 2001.

These standards are replete with excellent suggestions/requirements for the operation of charitable (and, for that matter, many other nonprofit) organizations. Thus, there is a rule that the board of the organization should have a policy of assessing, at least every two years, the organization's "performance and effectiveness and of determining future actions required to achieve its mission."

Solicitation and other informational materials should be "accurate, truthful and not misleading." Although a nimiety of terminology, few can disagree with that requirement. There should be an "annual report," including a summary of the past year's program service accomplishments, basic financial information, and a roster of directors and officers. That is wholly redundant with the federal annual information return requirement but otherwise harmless.

The organization's board of directors should provide "adequate oversight" of its operations and staff. This includes regularly scheduled appraisals of the chief executive officer (CEO) and sufficient accounting procedures. There should be a board-approved budget. The charity's expenses should be "accurately" reported in its financial statements.

Audited financial statements should be obtained for organizations with annual gross income in excess of $250,000. For charities with less gross income, a review by a certified public accountant (CPA) is sufficient, although where annual income is less than $100,000, an internally produced financial statement is adequate. Financial statements should include a breakdown of expenses (such as salaries, travel, and postage) that also shows the portion of the expenses allocated to program, fundraising, and administration (again, as already required on annual information returns).

If the standards ended with only the foregoing, all would be well. But a charity is to "avoid accumulating funds that could be used for current program activities." In other words, it is impermissible to plan ahead and maintain reserves and endowment funds. Reading on, one learns that net assets available for program use should not be more than the greater of three times the size of the prior year's expenses or three times the size of the current year's budget. This is just one of many arbitrary rules. In some instances, that amount will be too low. The draft standards employed a two-year test; now two is low and three is acceptable.

Another questionable rule concerns the matter of conflicts of interest, which too many want to cast in the most derogatory of manner, equating them with illegal acts. Often, conflicts of interest are not a problem (indeed, they may be unavoidable or even beneficial to the charity), particularly if they are disclosed. Yet, the standards prohibit "material conflicting interests" involving the board or staff. This is overreaching. The emphasis should be on disclosure.

Matters worsen. The standards, like their predecessors, just cannot seem to get past the puerile insistence on application of fundraising percentages. Thus, there are the tiresome requirements that at least 65 percent of total expenses be for program and no more than 35 percent of contributions be expended for fundraising. (There are even blank ratios provided for those who have trouble computing percentages.) An organization that fails these capricious percentages is permitted to demonstrate that its use of funds is nonetheless reasonable. Were we in the 1970s, this approach might make sense. This mechanism, however, has been repeatedly struck down as unconstitutional when applied to charities and fundraisers as a matter of law, and it is irrational to have it embedded in "voluntary" standards.

It is hard to believe, but the standards require a board of directors of a charitable organization be comprised of at least five voting members. Not 4 or 7 or 23, but the magic number of 5. This goes beyond arbitrariness; it is silly. The standards should let the law take care of this (where usually three members are required) and stay out.

There is an arbitrary rule for board meetings. There must be three each year, "evenly spaced," with a majority in attendance. Only one of these meetings can be by conference call. This is the case even though the law does not require that many meetings, allows all of them to be by conference call, and allows boards to act by unanimous written consent. Here again, charities will be penalized for acting in ways that are quite lawful (not to mention, acting in ways that often make a lot of sense). These requirements also have cost implications (travel, lodging), siphoning off funds that could be devoted to programs.

No more than one individual on the board or 10 percent of the board, whichever is greater, can be compensated by the organization. The chair (president?) and treasurer cannot be compensated. These arbitrary and nonsensical rules were outmoded decades ago. The standards should stay away from aspects of operations like this that are already covered by the law.

Laughably, the last of the transgressions is failure to respond promptly to matters brought to the attention of the Alliance or local BBBs. This amply illustrates just how "voluntary" these standards are.

Had the essence of these standards be confined to the material summarized in the first five paragraphs of this analysis, they would have been a positive contribution to the operations of the nation's philanthropic organizations. As issued in final form, they are more trouble than they are worth. Charities should ignore these standards, but they will not (or, more accurately, they cannot).

These standards, by the way, place lawyers in a difficult position. The lawyer now has to say to a client charitable organization, "Yes, a board of three is perfectly legal and, yes, you can compensate the treasurer, and, yes, you can have a unanimous written consent document instead of a meeting, but if you do, you will be pilloried in public by the BBB Wise Giving Alliance." Charities today must function in a difficult regulatory environment; the BBB has made matters worse.

## NOTE ✎

The Society of Nonprofit Lawyers, a charitable and educational calendar-year organization that engages in considerable public fundraising, was wrapping up a board meeting in early March 2003. The Society's board, about to take up the final item on the agenda, which was approval of a new and ambitious fundraising program, learned of the BBB standards. In anger and in protest, the board decided to adjourn, and agreed to approve the fundraising program by means of written unanimous consent, in lieu of a meeting, within 30 days. The board also voted to conduct its next two board meetings, in July and in October (and thus "evenly spaced"), by conference call. The board was aware of the additional costs of using the unanimous written consent approach, instead of merely continuing the meeting, yet also knew that the immense cost savings to be realized by having its meetings by telephone would amply offset the expenses of the written consent process. The Society's board members departed by airplanes to their various home cities, satisfied that what they had just decided to do was perfectly legal, yet worried that, in the view of the Alliance, they had rendered the Society charitably unfit.[74]

## NOTES

1. Bruce R. Hopkins, *The Law of Tax-Exempt Organizations*, 8th ed. (Hoboken, NJ: John Wiley & Sons, 2003) (hereinafter *Tax-Exempt Organizations*).
2. Some of these matters have been addressed by the author in Bruce R. Hopkins, *Starting & Managing A Nonprofit Organization: A Legal Guide,* 4th ed. (Hoboken, NJ: John Wiley & Sons, 2004) (hereinafter *Starting & Managing*).
3. See Chapter 3; *Tax-Exempt Organizations,* chap. 19.
4. See Chapter 3; *Tax-Exempt Organizations,* chap. 19.

5. See Chapter 9, page 221.

6. See *Tax-Exempt Organizations,* §§ 4.1(a), 33.1(a).

7. Id., § 4.1(a), nn. 19, 20.

8. The application for recognition of exemption filed by charitable organizations (Form 1023; see Chapter 2), for example, contemplates that the applicant is one of these entities (Part I, line 10).

9. For example, a group of colleges and universities are members of an organization, structured as a limited liability company, that maintains a collective qualified tuition plan program (*Tax-Exempt Organizations,* § 18.16) for these institutions. (Internal Revenue Service (hereinafter IRS) Private Letter Ruling (hereinafter Priv. Ltr. Rul.) 200311033).

10. See *Tax-Exempt Organizations,* § 4.2.

11. Id., § 4.3.

12. Id., § 18.1.

13. Id., § 18.2(a).

14. Id., § 16.4.

15. Id., § 16.5.

16. Id., § 16.7.

17. Id., § 18.2(b).

18. Id., chap. 17.

19. See Bruce R. Hopkins, *The Tax Law of Charitable Giving,* 3rd ed. (Hoboken, NJ: John Wiley & Sons, 2004) (hereinafter *Charitable Giving*), chap. 12.

20. Id., chap. 16.

21. See *Tax-Exempt Organizations,* § 24.1.

22. Id., § 4.3.

23. Id., chap. 13.

24. Id., § 6.4.

25. Quality Auditing Co. v. Comm'r, 114 T.C. 498 (2000). See Chapter 11, pages 287–291.

26. See Chapter 3.

27. At Cost Servs., Inc. v. Comm'r, 80 T.C.M. 573 (2000).

28. Salvation Navy v. Comm'r, 84 T.C.M. 506 (2002). See Chapter 11, pages 291–292.

29. Southern Church of Universal Bhd. Assembled v. Comm'r, 74 T.C. 1223 (1980).

30. Vigilant Hose Co. of Emmitsburg v. United States, 2001-2 U.S.T.C. ¶ 50,458 (D. Md. 2001).

31. See *Tax-Exempt Organizations,* § 33.1(b).

32. Despite widespread belief to the contrary, this term has nothing to do with whether the individual in the position has the right to vote. Absent a provision in the document to the contrary, those holding office in this manner have the same voting rights as others on the board.

33. See *Tax-Exempt Organizations,* § 33.1(c).

34. Id., § 33.1(b).

35. See Thomas K. Hyatt and Bruce R. Hopkins, *The Law of Tax-Exempt Healthcare Organizations,* 2nd ed. (Hoboken, NJ: John Wiley & Sons, 2001) (hereinafter *Tax-Exempt Healthcare Organizations*), chap. 6.

36. See Bruce R. Hopkins and Jody Blazek, *Private Foundations: Tax Law and Compliance,* 2nd ed. (Hoboken, NJ: John Wiley & Sons, 2003) (hereinafter *Private Foundations*), § 15.4(c).

37. Id., § 15.7(h).

38. A small board, particularly one comprised of members of a single family, can (except in the private foundation setting) attract greater scrutiny from the IRS and/or a court. See *Tax-Exempt Organizations,* § 4.8.

39. See Chapter 3.
40. To compound this one, the applicant organization was a private operating foundation, so the intermediate sanctions rules did not apply to begin with.
41. See Chapter 9, pages 193, 200–201.
42. E.g., Form 990, Part V. See Chapter 9.
43. See Chapter 3.
44. Id.
45. E.g., Form 1023, Part II, question 10a. See Chapter 2.
46. See Chapter 3.
47. See Chapter 7.
48. The bank or other institution(s) will provide the form of the resolution that it wishes the organization to pass.
49. That is, an organization described in Internal Revenue Code section (hereinafter IRC §) 501(c)(3); thus, this term also includes educational, religious, scientific, and like entities.
50. The IRS is making every effort to force new charitable organizations, as a condition of recognition of tax exemption, to adopt a conflict-of-interest policy. The agency has been successful in this regard in the healthcare field, with such a policy now mandatory as part of the community benefit standard. See note 35 above. For all other tax-exempt organizations, however, the adoption of a conflict-of-interest policy remains voluntary.
51. See pages 4–8 above.
52. See, e.g., Form 990, Part III. See Chapter 9.
53. See Chapter 5.
54. Id.
55. See Chapter 8.
56. See Chapter 9.
57. See Chapter 8, page 180. Also see Appendix D.
58. See Chapter 9, pages 226–227.
59. See Chapter 9, page 221.
60. See Chapter 4.
61. See Chapter 3, pages 71–76.
62. See pages 32–33 below.
63. See pages 17–19 above.
64. See Chapter 3, pages 71–76.
65. E.g., Bruce R. Hopkins, *Legal Responsibilities of Nonprofit Boards* (BoardSource, 2003); *Starting & Managing.*
66. For example, several times each year, the Professional Education Systems Institute, LLC, sponsors one-day (and one annual two-day) seminars, held at locations throughout the United States, on The Law of Tax-Exempt Organizations, presented by your author.
67. See Bruce R. Hopkins, *The Law of Fundraising,* 3rd ed. (Hoboken, NJ: John Wiley & Sons, 2002) (hereinafter *Fundraising*), chap. 8.
68. A defender of a charitable organization, in response to criticism from the president of a watchdog agency, delicately characterized the critic thusly: he was "basically talking out of his hat." Ian Wilhelm, "Love Him or Hate Him, Charity Watchdog Garners Lots of Attention," *Chronicle of Philanthropy* 15, no. 4 (Nov. 28, 2002): 23. That was not a unique situation.
69. A survey of the watchdog agencies is in Ian Wilhelm, "Charity under Scrutiny," *Chronicle of Philanthropy* 15, no. 4 (Nov. 28, 2002): 22.

70. A fuller commentary in this regard appears in *Fundraising,* § 8.8.
71. See, e.g., id., § 8.9.
72. Id., § 8.10.
73. These standards took effect on March 3, 2003.
74. It is hoped that the reader understands that this paragraph is fiction (or is it?).

# CHAPTER 2

# Acquisition and Maintenance of Tax-Exempt Status

The focus of this book and the companion one is, of course, on the subject of the law of tax-exempt organizations. It is important, then, to dwell on the definition and ramifications of the phrase *tax-exempt organization*. Of greater importance are the matters of acquiring and maintaining exempt status.

## NONPROFIT ORGANIZATIONS

Nearly all tax-exempt organizations are nonprofit organizations. Essentially, a *nonprofit organization* is an entity that is not permitted to engage in acts of *private inurement,* that is, it may not allow its net earnings to flow to persons in their private capacity.[1] (By contrast, for-profit entities are expected to engage in forms of private inurement.)

For the most part, a tax-exempt organization is one of three types of entities:

1. Nonprofit corporation
2. Unincorporated association
3. Trust[2]

Occasionally, however, a tax-exempt organization will be another type of entity, such as a limited liability company or a for-profit corporation.

## CONCEPT OF *TAX EXEMPTION*

Usually, when an organization is referred to as a *tax-exempt organization,* the reference is to its status as an entity that does not have to pay federal income tax. This is somewhat of a misnomer, however, in that most of these organizations are subject to the unrelated business income tax.[3] Also, some exempt organizations must pay an income tax (or perhaps an excise tax) on their net investment income.[4] Moreover, these organizations may also be subject to other taxes, such as, in the case of public charities, excise taxes on excess lobbying expenditures and political campaign expenditures.[5] Indeed, private foundations are subject to a battery of excise taxes.[6]

There may be other federal taxes that a tax-exempt organization need not pay. Also, exemption from the federal income tax usually leads to exemption from state (and perhaps local) income tax. Depending on state law, an organization may be exempt from sales, use, tangible personal property, intangible personal property, real estate, and/or other taxes.

## ELIGIBILITY FOR TAX-EXEMPT STATUS

Eligibility for tax-exempt status is established by law, usually statutory law. With the emphasis on the federal income tax, nearly all organizations that are tax-exempt are expressly referenced in the Internal Revenue Code. IRC § 501(a) provides for tax-exempt status; the categories of exempt organizations are the subject of IRC §§ 501(c), and 526 to 529.[7] Tax exemption for governmental and quasi-governmental organizations is not provided by statutory law (although IRC § 115 provides for exclusion of gross income for certain political subdivisions).[8]

Thus, to be tax-exempt, it is not enough for the organization to be a nonprofit one. It must also meet the requirements stipulated in the law for exempt status.

## CATEGORIES OF TAX-EXEMPT ORGANIZATIONS

There is no uniform agreement as to the number of types of tax-exempt organizations; the number obtained depends on how the law is parsed. The number used in connection with the two books is 69.[9]

In order of Internal Revenue Code sections, the categories of tax-exempt organizations are:

- Instrumentalities of the United States — IRC § 501(c)(1) and (1)[10]
- Title-holding companies — IRC § 501(c)(2) and (25)[11]
- Charitable, educational, scientific, religious, and like organizations — IRC § 501(c)(3)[12]
- Social welfare organizations — IRC § 501(c)(4)[13]
- Local associations of employees — IRC § 501(c)(4)[14]
- Labor organizations — IRC § 501(c)(5)[15]
- Agricultural organizations — IRC § 501(c)(5)[16]
- Horticultural organizations — IRC § 501(c)(5)[17]
- Business leagues (associations) — IRC § 501(c)(6)[18]
- Social clubs — IRC § 501(c)(7)[19]
- Fraternal organizations — IRC § 501(c)(8) and (10)[20]
- Voluntary employees' beneficiary associations — IRC § 501(c)(9)[21]
- Teachers' retirement fund associations — IRC § 501(c)(11)[22]

- Benevolent or mutual organizations — IRC § 501(c)(12)[23]
- Cemetery companies — IRC § 501(c)(13)[24]
- Credit unions and mutual reserve funds — IRC § 501(c)(14)[25]
- Certain small insurance companies — IRC § 501(c)(15)[26]
- Crop operations finance corporations — IRC § 501(c)(16)[27]
- Supplemental unemployment benefit trusts — IRC § 501(c)(17)[28]
- Certain employee benefit trusts — IRC § 501(c)(18)[29]
- Veterans' organizations — IRC § 501(c)(19) and (23)[30]
- Black lung benefits trusts — IRC § 501(c)(21)[31]
- Multiemployer plan trusts — IRC § 501(c)(22)[32]
- Certain trusts described in the Employee Retirement Income Security Act — IRC § 501(c)(24)[33]
- High-risk individuals healthcare coverage organizations — IRC § 501(c)(26)[34]
- Workers' compensation reinsurance organizations — IRC § 501(c)(27)[35]
- National Railroad Retirement Investment Trust — IRC § 501(c)(28)
- Religious or apostolic organizations — IRC § 501(d)[36]
- Farmers' cooperatives — IRC § 521[37]
- Shipowners' protection and indemnity associations — IRC § 526[38]
- Political organizations — IRC § 527[39]
- Homeowners' associations — IRC § 528[40]
- Qualified tuition programs — IRC § 529[41]
- States, political subdivisions, instrumentalities, and integral parts[42]
- Native American tribes[43]

Some organizations are reflected in other provisions of the Internal Revenue Code yet must also meet the requirements of IRC § 501(c)(3):

- Cooperative hospital service organizations — IRC § 501(e)[44]
- Cooperative educational service organizations — IRC § 501(f)[45]
- Child care organizations — IRC § 501(k)[46]
- Charitable risk pools — IRC § 501(n)[47]

## DETERMINING APPROPRIATE CATEGORY OF TAX EXEMPTION

The appropriate category of tax exemption for an eligible organization is dictated by application of the *primary purpose test*.[48] Thus, the planner must work with the individuals who are creating the organization to first determine the primary purpose of the organization; that purpose will guide the planner and the others to the appropriate category of tax exemption, if any. (Not all nonprofit organizations are eligible for tax-exempt status.) Also, an entity's primary purpose can change; the change may cause the organization to evolve into a different type of exempt entity (or, in rare cases, to lose exempt status).

The nonprofessional, of course, is not likely to be able to correlate the organization's purpose or purposes with the pigeonholes of the law providing for categories of exemption. This task, then, is likely to fall to the planner. The usual choices are:

- Charitable
- Educational
- Religious
- Scientific
- Social welfare
- Labor
- Membership services
- Social and recreational services
- Advocacy (legislative or political)

It is common for an organization to have more than one of these (or other) purposes. Again, it is the primary purpose or purposes that must be ascertained in selecting the appropriate category of tax-exempt status. For example, an organization may have some charitable and educational purposes, yet its dominate ones are social and recreational; the entity will fail to qualify for exemption by reason of IRC § 501(c)(3) but satisfy the requirements of IRC § 501(c)(7).[49]

Moreover, in some circumstances, distinctions as to purposes will dictate more than one tax-exempt organization. Often, one entity will control the other (parent and subsidiary relationship).[50] One (or more) of these entities may be a supporting organization.[51] The planner should realize that these rules are not always understood by the IRS or the courts.[52]

The usual combinations are:

- Business league parent and charitable organization subsidiary
- Social welfare organization parent and charitable organization subsidiary
- Other noncharitable tax-exempt organization parent and charitable organization subsidiary
- Foreign charity parent and domestic charity subsidiary
- Charitable organization parent and charitable organization subsidiary
- Charitable organization parent and social welfare organization subsidiary
- Charitable organization parent and business league subsidiary

Other examples of bifurcations are the use of title-holding companies, political organizations, and employee benefit funds.

For that matter, this need for bifurcation (or trifurcation, and so on) may entail a for-profit corporation, a limited liability company, a taxable nonprofit organization, and/or some other entity.[53]

## CONCEPT OF *RECOGNITION* OF TAX EXEMPTION

As noted, eligibility for tax-exempt status is dictated by the provisions of (usually statutory) law. Thus, an organization either qualifies for a category of exemption or it does not (although the planner may have to exercise considerable judgment in this regard). Tax exemption is conferred by operation of law.

*Recognition* of tax-exempt status occurs when a governmental agency agrees with the organization that the organization is eligible for tax-exempt status. At the federal level, this is of course a function of the IRS. Thus, the IRS does not grant an organization tax-exempt status; the agency recognizes the exempt status that the organization already possesses as a matter of law.[54]

## APPLYING FOR RECOGNITION OF TAX EXEMPTION

The seeking of recognition of tax-exempt status by the IRS[55] is either mandatory or voluntary. For most types of exempt organizations, recognition of exempt status is not required. This is the case, for example, for social welfare organizations, labor organizations, business leagues, fraternal organizations, and veterans' groups.

Most charitable organizations, by contrast, are required—to be tax-exempt—to achieve recognition of exempt status.[56] There are exceptions to this requirement.[57] Certain employee benefit funds are likewise required to obtain recognition of exempt status.[58] (Political organizations, while not required to secure recognition of exempt status, must give notice of their formation to the IRS.[59])

Consequently, the planner may be called on to advise as to whether an organization should seek recognition of tax-exempt status. A controlling factor can be the expense of the process. Another may be aversion to interacting with the IRS if it is not absolutely necessary. Or the parties may be confident that the organization is eligible for exempt status, so that recognition of exemption is not necessary. The countervailing factor is, of course, the comfort of a ruling: knowing that the IRS agrees that the organization is a tax-exempt entity.

The body of law concerning the matter of seeking recognition of tax exemption is considerably different from the body of law concerning the matter of filing annual information returns. Despite the fact that many categories of exempt organizations need not, as a matter of law, pursue recognition of exempt status, nearly all exempt organizations are required to file annual information returns.[60] Thus, the IRS often receives annual returns from exempt organizations that do not have recognition of exempt status. The agency finds it difficult to process annual returns of this nature. Indeed, at one point, the IRS proclaimed that it would return annual returns filed by exempt organizations that did not have recognized exempt status unless they filed for that recognition or became taxable.[61] (This development placed the planner in a difficult position: since the filing of the returns is mandated by law, what should the organization do if its return is rejected by the IRS? Answer: send the return back to the IRS by registered mail or a similar approach that provides a formal record of the transmittal.) It is understood, however, that the IRS has quietly backed away from that heavy-handed (and contrary to law) approach.

For the most part, the process of seeking recognition of tax-exempt status from the IRS entails a filing of a formal application for that status. The IRS has promulgated application forms. They are:

- Form 1023, which is used to apply for IRS recognition of IRC § 501(c)(3) status[62]
- Form 1024, which is used to apply for IRS recognition of most other categories of exempt status[63]
- Form 1028

For some types of exempt organization, there is no formal application; recognition of exempt status is sought by the filing of a letter.

To state these requirements in another way, the filing of the Form 1023 usually is mandatory, while the filing of the Form 1024 or 1028 (or letter) is voluntary. The word *usually* in this context reflects the fact that some organizations that are not required to file a Form 1023 (yet can nonetheless be exempt by reason of IRC § 501(c)(3)) may elect to do so; an example of this type of organization is a church.[64]

## Legal Aspects of Form 1023

The Form 1023 is designed, of course, to reflect various aspects of the law that govern qualification of an organization for tax exemption by reason of IRC § 501(c)(3). (The planner may wish to make a photocopy of the application and have it at the ready to follow along in connection with this review of the form.) The principal considerations in this regard are:

- **Part I, line 1e.** The organization must provide its web site address if it has one. Thus, the planner should be certain that there is nothing posted on the organization's site that is inconsistent with tax-exempt status. (Indeed, the planner is well advised to monitor the site from time to time with this perspective.)
- **Part I, line 3.** A planner who is preparing and filing the application should see to it that his or her name and telephone number are provided. This will facilitate communication by the IRS with the planner, rather than directly with the client. (In this circumstance, the filing of a power of attorney (Form 2848) is required.)
- **Part I, line 5.** The planner should be certain that the date of formation of the organization is correct. (If the entity is a corporation, that date is the date on which the certificate of incorporation was issued. If the entity is a trust or an unincorporated association, there may be some uncertainty as to the date of formation.) When an organization files this application, it is seeking three rulings: recognition of tax-exempt status, recognition of public charity status (if applicable), and a determination that contributions to the organization are deductible. If the application is timely filed (see below), all three of these determinations will be effective as of the date the organization was formed. Thus, it is important that the date inserted on this line is the correct one.
- **Part II, question 1.** The applicant organization is required to provide a "detailed narrative" description of all its past, present, and planned activities. A mere recitation

of the organization's purposes should be avoided. Each activity should be listed separately in the order of importance; the percentage of time for each activity should be indicated.

Each of these descriptions should include (at a minimum):

- A detailed description of the activity, including its purpose and how the activity furthers the organization's tax-exempt purpose or purposes
- The date or time when the activity was or will be initiated
- The location of the activity
- The person or persons who will conduct the activity

The response to this question obviously is an important part of the application. This is not the place to be reserved. If anything, this narrative essay should be effusive, stating in some detail the various activities of the organization. The length of this statement will vary by organization, because of variations in size and complexity. A generalization as to the length of the essay thus is not possible; a suggested goal is a statement of at least five double-spaced pages. The IRS is scrutinizing applications for recognition of exemption with intensity; as many questions as possible should be anticipated and answered.

Usually, the facts contained in this statement will be provided by the individual or individuals involved in the organization of the entity. It may be derived from a business plan or draft of a brochure. The planner's role is to be certain that all of the relevant facts are in the statement and that the statement reads well and positively (within the bounds of veracity) tells the organization's story. Also, the planner needs to correlate the underlying law with the recitations of fact. A skill that the experienced planner brings to this exercise is an understanding of how the IRS views these documents; it is the planner's task to think the way an IRS reviewer does and see that the information is presented accordingly.

A court opinion that the planner should keep in mind in this context is a holding that an organization was ineligible for tax-exempt status as a charitable and educational entity because the organization's activities and those of its founder, sole director, and officer were essentially identical.[65] The court found private inurement because the affairs of the organization and of this individual were "irretrievably intertwined."[66] This case was wrongly decided. Often charitable organizations engage in activities that their founders would otherwise undertake personally (such as private foundations). Nonetheless, the planner should endeavor to be certain that the applicant organization is not perceived as a mere "alter ego" of one or more of its founders.

- **Part II, question 2.**  The applicant organization should list, in order of size (largest first), its sources of financial support. Typical entries are contributions from the general public, grants from private foundations, grants from governmental agencies, and various forms of exempt function revenue. Usually the list should include investment income (often as the last item). The planner should be certain that the information provided here correlates with the budget or other information that is provided in response to Part IV (see below).

- **Part II, question 3.** The organization is required to describe its fundraising program (if any), both actual and planned. Typical entries are descriptions of direct-mail letters, special events, capital campaigns, and planned giving programs. Also to be referenced (if applicable) are the formation of a fundraising committee and the use of a professional fundraiser and/or a professional solicitor. Representative copies of solicitations for financial support (if any) should be attached to the application. If the organization does not plan to have a fundraising program, a statement to that effect will suffice.

- **Part II, question 4a and b.** The organization must provide a list of its trustees, directors, and/or officers. This entry must include their addresses and annual compensation (if any). As to addresses, the planner may want to suggest that the individuals use their business address, rather than their personal residence address, because of privacy issues. As to compensation, the planner should keep in mind that *compensation* entails all economic benefits provided to the individual and that the totality of this compensation must be reasonable.[67]

- **Part II, question 4d.** In connection with this question, the planner should work with the organization in ascertaining its disqualified persons.[68] The applicant organization is required to identify the organization's board members who are disqualified persons (other than by reason of being organization managers). Also, the organization must disclose any business or family relationship between a board member and a disqualified person. (Members of the family of a disqualified person are themselves disqualified persons.[69])

- **Part II, question 5.** The organization must explain whether it controls one or more organizations or whether it is controlled by one or more organizations. This question can properly be answered yes or no, in that there is no "correct" answer. That is, it is not inconsistent with tax-exempt status for the applicant entity to be a controlling organization or a controlled organization.[70]

  This question has two other elements. One requires the organization to explain any "special relationship" with another organization (such as by means of interlocking directorates). Often the answer to the first part of this question is the answer to the second part of the question (in that the special relationship is one of parent and subsidiary).

  The third element of the question is whether the applicant organization is the "outgrowth" of or "successor" to another organization. This can occur, for example, when an unincorporated entity incorporates. This element of the question can also generate some difficulties for the planner. It is not uncommon for one or more individuals to, with considerable aspirations, form a nonprofit organization, only to thereafter lose interest in the project, to be followed by another group of individuals who wish to resurrect the project. Often, at this point, the group desires to start afresh, with a new entity, rather than utilize the first one. The documents of the first one may be defective and/or there may be fear of lurking legal liability. It is preferable to answer the "outgrowth" question no; the planner may have to struggle with the facts to determine whether that is the correct answer. If it is not, then the earlier efforts at forming the first organization must be disclosed, including, perhaps, the false start and imperfections in documents.

- **Part II, question 10.** The applicant organization is required to disclose any relationship with a management company or a lessor. Although there is nothing inherently inappropriate with either arrangement, the IRS may endeavor to ascertain the presence of any private inurement or private benefit,[71] an excess benefit transaction,[72] and/or a joint venture.[73]

- **Part II, question 12a.** The applicant organization may provide benefits, services, or products. If the recipients are required to pay for them, the organization is required to explain how the charges were determined. This is a sensitive and somewhat unfair inquiry; the planner may be required to give this answer careful consideration. In the background is the commerciality doctrine,[74] so factors such as profit or profit margin should be avoided, if possible.

- **Part II, question 13.** An applicant organization is not permitted to engage, as a substantial portion of its activities, in attempts to influence legislation.[75] Thus, the planner should see to it that this question is appropriately answered.

- **Part II, question 14.** This is one of the few questions on the application where the correct answer is clear, inasmuch as it is mandated by law. Charitable organizations are not permitted to intervene or participate in political campaign activities.[76] Therefore, if the answer to this question cannot be no, the planner's ability to help secure recognition of tax exemption for the organization will be severely compromised.

- **Part III, questions 1 to 6.** If the applicant organization files the application within the 15-month period (question 1) or the 27-month period (question 3), and the determination letter is favorable, the ruling will be retroactive to the date the organization was formed (see above). Most new organizations will not tolerate waiting that long to file, so the planner is not likely to be involved in a filing that occurs after the 27-month period. Even when the organization files the application after expiration of the 27-month period, there may be an opportunity to show reasonable cause and good faith (question 4). Otherwise, the ruling will be effective as of the date the IRS received the application (question 5).

  As noted, by filing the application, the organization is in fact pursuing three rulings:

  1. A determination that the organization can be recognized as a tax-exempt organization

  2. Classification as a public charity (assuming the applicant is not a private foundation)[77]

  3. A determination that contributions to the organization are deductible as charitable gifts[78]

  If the application process is successful from the standpoint of the organization, and if the application was filed within the 27-month period, all three of these determinations are retroactive to the date the organization was formed. If the filing is after that period, the matter of recognition of tax exemption can be remedied by treating the organization as an exempt social welfare organization[79] from the date the organization was formed until the date the determination letter becomes effective (question 6). The aspects of public charity and charitable donee status for this initial period cannot, however, be rectified.

> **NOTE**
>
> This matter of recognition of tax-exempt status as a social welfare organization is predicated on two elements of law: (1) an organization that qualifies as an exempt social welfare organization is not required to seek recognition of exempt status;[80] and (2) an organization that qualifies for exemption pursuant to IRC § 501(c)(3) usually simultaneously qualifies for exemption pursuant to IRC § 501(c)(4). The planner may have to ponder circumstances where the second element may not in fact be the case.

Certain organizations need not file this application to qualify for exemption pursuant to IRC § 501(c)(3) (question 2).[81]

- **Part III, questions 7 to 10.** The applicant organization must indicate whether it is a public charity or a private foundation (question 7).[82] If it is endeavoring to qualify as a public charity, it should select one of nine alternatives (question 9). (The planner should advise the organization as to the appropriate selection and as to the choices of publicly supported organization rather than expect the IRS to decide the proper classification (question 9j).) If the organization is to be a private foundation, it must indicate whether it is claiming to be a private operating foundation (question 8).[83]

- **Part III, questions 10, 12, and 13.** The applicant organization must decide whether to appropriately request an advance ruling or a definitive ruling, and respond accordingly.[84]

- **Part III, question 11.** The applicant organization may claim the receipt of one or more unusual grants.[85]

- **Part III, question 14.** Certain applicant organizations are required to provide additional information to the IRS, by means of a schedule. These schedules and entities are:
  - Schedule A—Churches[86]
  - Schedule B—Schools[87]
  - Schedule C—Hospitals[88]
  - Schedule C—Medical research organizations[89]
  - Schedule D—Supporting organizations[90]
  - Schedule E—Private operating foundations[91]
  - Schedule F—Homes for the aged or handicapped[92]
  - Schedule G—Child care organizations[93]

○ Schedule H—Organizations that provide or administer scholarship benefits, student aid, or the like[94]

○ Schedule I—Organizations that have taken over, or will take over, the facilities of a for-profit entity[95]

In some instances, the operation of only a component of an organization can trigger the requirement of filing one or more of these schedules. For example, only a part of an organization may be a school, hospital, medical research organization, home for the aged or handicapped, or a child care organization. Also, an organization may be required to file more than one of these schedules, such as a school with a student aid program. The planner should avoid filing blank schedules.

- **Part IV-A.** The applicant organization is required to submit information concerning its revenue and expenses. The five sets of circumstances in this regard are:

  1. The organization has been in existence for more than four full years. If that is the case, the information should be provided for the current year and the three immediate prior years.

  2. The organization has been in existence for more than three full years yet less than four full years. If that is the case, the information should be provided for the partial current year and the three immediate prior years.

  3. The organization has been in existence three full years. If that is the case, the information should be provided for the current year and the two immediate prior years.

  4. The organization has been in existence for less than three full years. If that is the case, the information should be provided for the partial current year and the two immediate prior years.

### NOTE

In the case of any of these instances, the planner should review the discussion above concerning the 15-month and 27-month periods.

  5. The organization has been in existence less than one year. In that case, it should provide the information for the partial current year and a proposed budget for the following two years.

### NOTE

This revenue information should be reviewed in relation to the requirements for qualifying as a publicly supported organization (assuming these rules are applicable). This consideration is particularly important if a budget is involved. In other words, the planner should be confident that the revenue information provided comports with the organization's claim to be or expectation that it is a publicly supported organization.

- **Part IV-B.** The applicant organization is required to provide a balance sheet show-ing assets, liabilities, and fund balance or net assets as of the financial period involved.

  If there have been any substantial changes in any aspect of the organization's financial activities since the end of the financial period involved, the organization is required to check the box at the bottom of page 9 of the application and attach a detailed explanation.

## BIZARRE POSITIONS TAKEN BY THE IRS

The IRS, in the aftermath of its reorganization, including the creation of the Tax Exempt and Governmental Entities Division, has been hiring and otherwise using some inexpe-rienced and not well-trained tax law specialists to review applications for recognition of exemption. On occasion these reviewers display ignorance of the law or invoke their personal judgment as to what the law should be. The planner must be ever cautious in identifying these situations.

### Examples of Positions

Some examples of these types of statements and questions, in connection with reviews of Forms 1023, are:

- An applicant organization was advised that, to obtain recognition of tax exemption, it must expand its board of directors, "so control no longer rests with related indi-viduals." With the exception of supporting organizations,[96] there is no such require-ment in the federal tax law. (Such a rule would void tax-exempt status for most private foundations.)
- In a variant of the foregoing, a tax law specialist advised that the organization's board structure "must be changed to allow members of the general public to con-trol the organization." There is no such requirement in the federal tax law.
- A tax law specialist advised that a tax-exempt organization is forbidden to allow its directors to vote on their compensation. That is not the case.
- A tax law specialist advised that a majority of an organization's board must not be salaried by the organization. That is not true.
- A tax law specialist advised that a majority of an organization's board may not be related to salaried personnel or to parties providing services. That is not the law.
- A specialist advised that, to be recognized as exempt, the organization must adopt a conflict-of-interest policy. Outside the healthcare context, that is not a requirement for tax-exempt status.
- A specialist stated that a tax-exempt organization may not be controlled by a for-profit corporation. That is not the law. (For example, for-profit corporations can have private foundations.)
- A specialist stated that, as a condition of exemption, the organization must provide a statement from each of its board members that "makes it clear" that they are aware of the intermediate sanctions rules. That is not a requirement of the law.[97]

- An applicant organization created a for-profit subsidiary. The tax law specialist demanded that it submit a completed Schedule I. This schedule, however, is to be filed by a tax-exempt organization that is taking over the activities of a for-profit corporation.

- An applicant organization was going to make grants to another exempt charitable entity to enable the grantee to make scholarships, including selecting the recipients. The tax law specialist demanded that the applicant organization submit a completed Schedule H. This schedule, however, is to be filed by an exempt organization that is itself maintaining a scholarship program.

- A tax law specialist insisted that dividends paid to an exempt organization from its for-profit subsidiary be reported as unrelated business income. Dividends of this nature are not taxable as unrelated income.[98]

## Résumés

Still another recent practice of these reviewers is to request the résumés of the organizations' trustees, directors, and officers. One IRS questioner noted that these résumés should "focus on their professional experience and training" in relation to these individuals' "oversight" of the organization.

It is certainly an optimum situation to have directors and officers of an organization who have experience and training in relation to the organization's purposes and activities. Or, to state the matter more directly, it is preferable to have officers and directors who know what they are doing.

The federal tax law (which, after all, the IRS is required to follow), however, is silent on this point. There is nothing—in a statute, regulation, ruling, form instruction, or court opinion—that requires, as a condition of recognition of tax exemption, an organization's officers and directors to have experience and training that comports with the organization's affairs. An exempt organization can, for example, add to its board one or more individuals who have absolutely no prior knowledge or understanding of what the organization does. Once state law standards are satisfied (such as the individual's being at least 18 years of age), the individual is eligible, as a matter of law, to serve. Ignorance, lack of schooling, apathy, or low IQ are not bars to such service. (Violations of principles of fiduciary responsibility are another matter; that can happen even though a director has experience and training.)

What this comes down to, then, is that the IRS is asking for information that is irrelevant to the task at hand. This subject provides the agency's specialists with fodder for asking follow-up questions but advances no other purpose.

## Perspective

Some organizations prepare and file an application for recognition of exemption without benefit of the services of a professional adviser. Often, they submit to demands such as the foregoing, not realizing that the IRS's position is not mandated by law. On occasion, a planner is retained once the application is under IRS review.

Certainly the planner is expected to differentiate between the demands of tax law specialists that are legitimate and those that are not. In the case of the latter, the planner may be told that the organization is going to adhere to the demand or demands so as not to tangle with the IRS and delay the issuance of a determination letter. Absent some potential harm to the organization, the planner may have to stand by while the organization capitulates. (A few of these demands may be followed without adverse consequences, such as the adoption of a conflict-of-interest policy.) Otherwise, the planner should resist the mistaken efforts of the tax law specialist. A technique that usually is successful is for the planner to advise the specialist that unless he or she revises the erroneous view, the planner will take the matter to the IRS National Office; that approach usually causes the specialist to reshape his or her views on the point.

## LEGAL ASPECTS OF FORM 1024

Form 1024 is designed, of course, to reflect various aspects of the law that govern qualification of a wide variety of organizations that qualify for tax exemption, such as entities that are exempt by reason of IRC § 501(c)(4) to (7). (Again, the planner should make a photocopy of the application and have it at the ready to follow along in connection with this review of the form.) The principal considerations in this regard are:

- **Part I, line 1e.** The comments about the web site address offered in connection with Form 1023 are also applicable in this context.

- **Part I, line 3.** The comments about the contact person offered in connection with Form 1023 are also applicable in this context.

- **Part I, line 5.** The planner should be certain that the date of formation of the organization is correct. The recognition of tax-exempt status usually will be effective as of the date the organization was formed.

- **Part II, question 1.** The comments made in connection with the comparable question on Form 1023, concerning the organization's activities, are also applicable in this context.

- **Part II, question 2.** The applicant organization should list, in order of size (largest first), its sources of financial support. Typical entries are membership dues, various forms of exempt function revenue, and investment income.

- **Part II, question 3.** The comments made in connection with the comparable question on Form 1023, concerning directors and officers, are also applicable in this context.

- **Part II, question 4.** The comments made in connection with the comparable question on Form 1023, concerning outgrowths and predecessors, are also applicable in this context.

- **Part II, question 5.** The comments made in connection with the comparable question on Form 1023, concerning relationships with one or more other organizations, are also applicable in this context.

- **Part II, question 7.** The planner for an applicant business league should be certain that the answer to this question, concerning membership qualifications, comports with the line-of-business requirement.[99]

- **Part II, question 8.** The law of tax-exempt organizations concerning the organizations that file this application is silent on dissolution requirements, as contrasted with the law concerning organizations that file Form 1023.[100] Nonetheless, the IRS inquires as to how the applicant organization's net income and assets (if any) will be distributed on dissolution.

- **Part II, question 10.** The comments made in connection with the comparable question on Form 1023, concerning payments for services provided, are also somewhat applicable in this context, although the commerciality doctrine does not apply to the applicant organizations.

- **Part II, question 14.** The comments made in connection with the comparable question on Form 1023, concerning leasing arrangements, are also applicable in this context, although the IRS is far more concerned with leases involving charitable organizations.

- **Part II, question 15.** The federal tax law is nearly silent as to political campaign activities by organizations that file Form 1024.[101] Often, these organizations engage in political activities by means of related political organizations.[102]

- **Part III-A.** The comments about the submission of information concerning revenue and expenses on this application are basically the same as those offered in connection with Form 1023.

- **Part IV.** The comments made about the 15-month period and the 27-month period in connection with Form 1023 are generally the same in this context.[103] (The considerations as to public charity and charitable donee status are inapplicable in this setting.)

- **Schedule A.** This portion of the application is to be completed by title-holding organizations.[104]

- **Schedule B.** This portion of the application is to be completed by social welfare organizations, local associations of employees, and certain veterans' organizations.[105]

- **Schedule C.** This portion of the application is to be completed by labor, agricultural, and horticultural organizations,[106] and business leagues, chambers of commerce, and the like.[107]

- **Schedule D.** This portion of the application is to be completed by social clubs.[108]

- **Schedule E.** This portion of the application is to be completed by fraternal organizations.[109]

- **Schedule F.** This portion of the application is to be filed by voluntary employees' beneficiary associations.[110]

- **Schedule G.** This portion of the application is to be filed by benevolent or mutual organizations.[111]

- **Schedule H.** This portion of the application is to be filed by cemetery (and comparable) organizations.[112]

- **Schedule I.** This portion of the application is to be filed by certain small insurance companies.[113]

- **Schedule J.** This portion of the application is to be filed by supplemental unemployment compensation organizations.[114]

- **Schedule K.** This portion of the application is to be filed by most veterans' organizations.[115]

## PREPARATION OF APPLICATIONS

An applicant organization is expected to fully describe the activities in which it intends to engage, including the standards, criteria, procedures, or other means adopted or planned for carrying out the activities, the anticipated sources of receipts, and the nature of contemplated expenditures. An organization filing an application for recognition of exemption has the burden of proving that it satisfies all of the requirements of the particular tax exemption category.

The planner involved in the preparation of an application must make a judgment as to the extent of the content of the document. Mere "vague generalizations" will not suffice,[116] in that "meaningful explanations" must be provided[117] along with "complete and candid" responses to any follow-up inquiries from the IRS.[118]

At the same time, an organization is considered to have made the requisite "threshold showing" where it describes its activities in "sufficient detail" to permit a conclusion that the entity will meet the pertinent requirements, particularly when it answered all of the questions propounded by the IRS.[119] A court observed that, although the law "requires that the organization establish reasonable standards and criteria for its operation as an exempt organization," this requirement does not necessitate "some sort of metaphysical proof of future events."[120]

It is within these boundaries, then, that the planner must work with the organization to present the most complete and favorable portrayal of the organization that is reasonably possible. Some organizations supply the planner with ample information to use to shape a full characterization of the entity; indeed, some provide overwhelming mounds of information. Other organizations grudgingly provide the planner with information, requiring the planner to return to the source again and again until sufficient information—again, a judgment call—is finally yielded.

The proper preparation of an application for recognition of exemption, therefore, involves far more than merely niggardly responding to questions on a government form. It is a process not unlike the preparation of a prospectus for a business in conformity with securities law requirements. Every statement made in the application should be carefully considered by the planner and tested against the applicable law. Indeed, some of the questions—on the application or in one or more follow-up letters from the IRS—may force the applicant organization to focus on matters that good management practices should cause it to consider, even in the absence of the application's requirements.

The prime objections must be completeness and accuracy; it is essential that all material facts be correctly and fully disclosed. Of course, the determination as to which facts are material and the marshaling of these facts requires judgment. Also, the manner in which the answers are phrased can be significant; in this regard, the exercise can be more one of art than science. The preparer or reviewer of the application should be able to anticipate the concerns the contents of the application may cause the IRS and to see that the application is properly prepared, while simultaneously minimizing the likelihood of conflict with the agency.

Organizations that are entitled to tax-exempt status have been denied recognition of exemption, or at least have caused the process of gaining the recognition to be more protracted (perhaps coming perilously close to failing to acquire recognition), because of inartful phraseologies in the application that motivated the IRS to muster a case that the organization did not qualify for exemption. Consequently, the application for recognition of tax exemption should be regarded as an important legal document and constructed accordingly. The fact that the application is available for public inspection and dissemination only underscores the need for the thoughtful preparation of it.[121]

The application for recognition of exemption seems to be a document that a tax-exempt organization misplaces more than any other. The organization should endeavor to maintain copies of it, as should the planner. An exempt organization is required to provide a copy of the application for inspection if it had a copy of it on or after July 15, 1987; the effective date for the document dissemination requirements is June 8, 1999.[122]

## RELIANCE ON DETERMINATION

In general, an organization can rely on a determination letter or ruling from the IRS recognizing its tax-exempt status. This is not the case, however, if there is a material change, inconsistent with exemption, in the character, purpose, or methods of operation of the organization.[123]

## MAINTENANCE OF EXEMPT STATUS

Once an organization achieves tax-exempt status—recognized or not—that qualification is maintained as long as the entity does not materially change its character, purposes, or methods of operation. A change in an organization's form is likely to have tax consequences. Of course, an organization's exempt status may be affected by a change in the law.

The planner thus will frequently be called on to make a judgment as to:

- Whether one or more material changes (see next item) have occurred, and if so,
- Whether the change or changes are inconsistent with the organization's tax-exempt status.

## MATERIAL CHANGES

An organization's tax-exempt status remains in effect as long as there are no substantial—*material*—changes in the organization's character, purposes, or methods of operation.[124]

(This language is from the tax regulations; the determination letter language adds sources of support to the list of changes involved.) The planner is likely to be called on from time to time to provide a judgment as to whether one or more of these changes is substantial (material).

This matter of substantiality can affect the *timing* of the communication of the change to the IRS. The IRS is supposed to be notified of every one of these changes. A material change should be communicated to the IRS as soon as possible after the change is made or becomes effective. In any event, each of these changes should be reflected in due course in the organization's annual information return.[125] Thus, from the standpoint of the planner, the issue will not be *whether* change should be communicated to the IRS but *when*.

A material change does not mean that the organization's tax-exempt status is imperiled. For example, a change in the facts may entail a substantial expansion or revision of exempt function activities. Or the change could involve a modification of the organization's purposes.

The foregoing considerations also apply to changes in the organization's governing instruments. Although all of these changes are to be reported as part of the filing of an annual information return, substantial changes should be communicated to the IRS contemporaneously. Again, the planner is likely to be called on to advise as to the materiality of changes.

Of course, the planner will be expected to monitor changes in the federal tax law, and to determine whether any of them affect—adversely or otherwise—the tax-exempt status of the organization involved.

## CHANGES IN FORM

A change in organizational form generally is treated as the creation of a new legal entity, which may require the filing of an application for recognition of exemption for the successor entity, even though the organization's purposes, methods of operation, sources of support, and accounting period remain the same as they were in its predecessor form.[126]

The planner should follow this principle of law in the event of:

- Conversion of a trust to a corporation
- Conversion of an unincorporated association to a corporation
- Reincorporation of an organization, incorporated under the laws of one state, pursuant to the laws of another state
- Reincorporation of an organization, incorporated under state law, pursuant to an act of Congress

Generally, the tax-exempt status of the predecessor entity will, in effect, be transmitted to the successor entity. If an application for recognition of status as a charitable entity is filed, a specific question about successor organizations must be answered.[127]

## GROUP EXEMPTION

In most instances, an organization is tax-exempt by operation of law, although in some instances, as discussed, recognition of that exemption by the IRS is required. Occasionally, however, tax exemption can be achieved by means of the group exemption procedure, summarized in the companion book.[128]

The principal advantage of the group exemption is that each of the organizations in the group is relieved from filing an application for recognition of exemption, irrespective of whether the filing is otherwise mandatory or voluntary. The planner, thus, should give consideration to the group exemption in circumstances where there are (or are expected to be) several chapters, locals, posts, units, or other affiliates of a tax-exempt organization. It is a useful procedure that can save the organizations (and the IRS) much time and effort.

There are difficulties with the group exemption procedure, however, and they start with the terminology involved. The organization that is the one with which the others are affiliated is termed the *central organization*. Worse, the affiliates are referenced as *subordinate organizations*. The human ego being what it usually is, many organizations do not like to consider themselves subordinated to and/or dominated (controlled) by another organization. Thus, the planner's first hurdle in this setting is likely to be getting the parties past the parlance. At a minimum, the group members should be referred to as *affiliates* rather than *subordinates*.

There are other disadvantages to the group exemption approach, including:

- There is a fear of "ascending liability"—the worry that an affiliate will incur legal liability for a commission or omission and that liability will reach to the central organization.

- The members of the group do not individually possess determination letters as to their tax exemption, perhaps posing difficulties for grantors and donors.

- State tax exemption(s) may be laborious to obtain, in that the state tax authorities usually expect submission of a federal determination letter as to tax-exempt status.

- In the case of charitable organizations, there is no separate assessment of their public charity status.

Nonetheless, the group exemption generally is a most favorable technique for clusters of nonprofit organizations that are affiliated in some manner. This approach to tax exemption obviates the need for each member entity in the group to file an application for recognition of tax exemption, and this can result in savings of time, effort, and expenses—for the organization and for the IRS. In the proper set of circumstances—something for the planner to determine—the group exemption arrangement is an effective, streamlined approach for the establishment of recognition of tax-exempt status.

## Notes

1. See Chapter 3.
2. See Chapter 1, pages 4–8.
3. See Chapter 8.
4. This is the case with social clubs, political organizations, and private foundations.
5. See Chapter 5.
6. See *Private Foundations,* chaps. 5–10.

7. See *Tax-Exempt Organizations,* pts. 2, 3.
8. Id., § 18.17.
9. Id., app. C.
10. Id., § 18.1.
11. Id., § 18.2.
12. Id., pt. 2.
13. Id., chap. 12.
14. Id., § 18.3.
15. Id., § 15.1.
16. Id., § 15.2.
17. Id., § 15.3.
18. Id., chap. 13.
19. Id., chap. 14.
20. Id., § 18.4.
21. Id., § 16.3.
22. Id., § 16.7.
23. Id., § 18.5.
24. Id., § 18.6.
25. Id., § 18.7.
26. Id., § 18.8.
27. Id., § 18.9.
28. Id., § 16.4.
29. Id., § 16.7.
30. Id., § 18.10.
31. Id., § 16.5.
32. Id., § 16.7.
33. Id.
34. Id., § 18.14.
35. Id., § 18.15.
36. Id., § 8.7.
37. Id., § 18.11.
38. Id., § 18.12.
39. Id., chap. 17.
40. Id., § 18.13.
41. Id., § 18.16.
42. Id., §§ 6.10, 18.17.
43. Id., § 18.18.
44. Id., § 10.4.
45. Id., § 10.5.
46. Id., § 7.7.
47. Id., § 10.6.
48. Id., § 4.4.
49. E.g., Wayne Baseball, Inc. v. Comm'r, 78 T.C.M. 437 (1999).
50. See Chapter 6.
51. See Chapter 4, pages 91–99.
52. As to the latter, see Quality Auditing Co. v. Comm'r, 114 T.C. 498 (2000). See Chapter 11, pages 287–291.

53. See Chapter 6.
54. *Tax-Exempt Organizations,* § 23.1.
55. Id., § 23.2.
56. Id., § 23.3(a).
57. Id., § 23.3(b).
58. Id., § 23.5.
59. Id., § 23.6.
60. *Tax-Exempt Organizations,* § 24.3.
61. IRS INFO [information letter] 2000-0260.
62. See Appendix A. The IRS is in the process of substantially revising Form 1023; the new version of the application for recognition of exemption is expected to be available in the fall of 2004.
63. See Appendix B.
64. A church that files a Form 1023 also must submit a Schedule A.
65. Salvation Navy v. Comm'r, 84 T.C.M. 506 (2002). See Chapter 11, pages 291–292.
66. Id., page 292.
67. See Chapter 3, pages 72–73.
68. Id., pages 71–72.
69. Id., page 71.
70. See, e.g., Chapter 6.
71. See Chapter 3, pages 65–71.
72. Id., pages 71–76.
73. See Chapter 7, pages 150, 158–164.
74. *Tax-Exempt Organizations,* chap. 25.
75. See Chapter 5, pages 110–112.
76. Id., pages 118–121.
77. See Chapter 4.
78. See *Charitable Giving,* § 3.6.
79. *Tax-Exempt Organizations,* chap. 12.
80. Id., § 23.1.
81. Id., § 23.3(b).
82. See Chapter 4.
83. See *Private Foundations,* § 3.1.
84. See Chapter 4, page 86.
85. See *Private Foundations,* § 15.5(c).
86. *Tax-Exempt Organizations,* § 8.3.
87. Id., § 7.3.
88. Id., § 6.3.
89. Id.
90. See Chapter 4, pages 91–99.
91. See note 83 above.
92. *Tax-Exempt Organizations,* § 6.2.
93. Id., § 7.7.
94. Id., § 6.6.
95. Id., § 33.4.
96. See Chapter 4, pages 91–99.
97. In this instance, as noted in Chapter 1, n. 40, the applicant organization was claiming status as a private operating foundation; thus, the intermediate sanctions rules were inapplicable in any event!

98. See Chapter 8, pages 178–179.

99. *Tax-Exempt Organizations,* § 13.1.

100. Id., § 4.3.

101. E.g., id., § 21.4.

102. Id., chap. 17.

103. See pages 45–46 above.

104. *Tax-Exempt Organizations,* § 18.2.

105. Id., chap. 12, §§ 18.3, 18.10, respectively.

106. Id., chap. 15.

107. Id., chap. 13.

108. Id., chap. 14.

109. Id., § 18.4.

110. Id., § 16.3.

111. Id., § 18.5.

112. Id., § 18.6.

113. Id., § 18.8.

114. Id., § 16.4.

115. Id., § 18.10.

116. Pius XII Acad., Inc. v. Comm'r, 43 T.C.M. 634, 636 (1982).

117. Public Indus., Inc. v. Comm'r, 61 T.C.M. 1626, 2629 (1991).

118. National Ass'n of Am. Churches v. Comm'r, 82 T.C. 18, 32 (1984).

119. E.g., The Church of the Visible Intelligence That Governs the Universe v. United States, 83-2 U.S.T.C. ¶ 9726 (Ct. Cl. 1983).

120. American Sci. Found. v. Comm'r, 52 T.C.M. 1049, 1051 (1986).

121. See Chapter 10, pages 236–237.

122. *Tax-Exempt Organizations,* § 24.4(b).

123. Id., § 23.2(c).

124. Id., § 24.1(a).

125. See Chapter 9, pages 202–203.

126. *Tax-Exempt Organizations,* § 24.1(b).

127. See pages 44–45 above.

128. *Tax-Exempt Organizations,* § 23.7.

# CHAPTER 3

# Private Benefit

Planners should be ever vigilant as to the presence of private benefit in the tax-exempt organizations context, particularly in instances involving charitable organizations. This is one of the most significant aspects of exempt organizations law and certainly one of the most controversial. For these purposes, the term *private benefit* is used to generically encompass four fundamental principles of the law of tax-exempt organizations:

1. Private inurement doctrine
2. Private benefit doctrine
3. Excess benefit transactions (intermediate sanctions) law
4. Self-dealing (private foundations) rules

Thus, there are four bodies of federal tax law that essentially address the same subject: inappropriate transactions involving types of tax-exempt organizations. From the planner's perspective, developments in all four of these areas should be constantly monitored, inasmuch as a development in one of these contexts is likely to influence development of the law in the other three settings. For example, a transaction that is found to be a self-dealing transaction is probably inherently a private inurement transaction, a private benefit transaction, and an excess benefit transaction, just as a finding that a person is a disqualified person is likely to mean that the person is an insider.

## OVERVIEW OF PRIVATE BENEFIT LAW

As noted, this area of the federal tax law embraces four discrete but overlapping bodies of jurisprudence, all directed to the same basic ends.

### Doctrine of Private Inurement[1]

Planners should approach the body of law consisting of the doctrine of *private inurement* on two levels. Being one of the most important sets of rules in the realm of the law of tax-exempt organizations, the doctrine is the fundamental defining principle distinguishing *nonprofit organizations* from *for-profit organizations*.[2] Thus, the planner may be called on to advise as to whether an entity should be one or the other.[3]

If the founder or founders of the organization are looking for ways to make a profit from the undertaking, in terms of net income and/or capital appreciation, the for-profit approach should be selected. This is because for-profit entities engage in forms of private inurement; that is their purpose.[4] By contrast, those involved with the operation of a tax-exempt organization can receive income in the form of reasonable compensation (see below) but cannot simply periodically take the organization's net profits. In some circumstances, this dichotomy is not so stark: two organizations are created, one tax-exempt and one for-profit.[5]

The planner is far more likely, however, to be concerned with the doctrine of private inurement as it is manifested at the other—more technical—level. Various types of transactions need to be planned or scrutinized with the private inurement doctrine in mind. These include the payment of compensation, rental arrangements, borrowing arrangements, sales transactions, and involvement in partnerships and other joint ventures. The underlying standard is that the terms and conditions of these transactions must be *reasonable*. The sanction for violation of the doctrine is denial or revocation of tax exemption.

A set of facts implicating the private inurement doctrine must have three components:

1. A tax-exempt organization that is subject to the doctrine[6]
2. One or more transactions[7]
3. Involvement of one or more insiders[8]

The private inurement doctrine is a statutory criterion for federal income tax exemption for the following types of exempt organizations:

- Charitable organizations[9]
- Social welfare organizations[10]
- Associations and other business leagues[11]
- Social clubs[12]
- Voluntary employees' beneficiary associations[13]
- Teachers' retirement fund associations[14]
- Cemetery companies[15]
- Veterans' organizations[16]
- State-sponsored organizations providing healthcare to high-risk individuals[17]

Despite the fact that this law is applicable to these many types of tax-exempt organizations, nearly all of the law concerning private inurement has been developed in the context of transactions with charitable (IRC § 501(c)(3)) organizations.

As to the second element, the planner should include in the list of transactions tested against the private inurement doctrine:

- Payment of compensation[18] to an employee
- Payment of compensation to a consultant (independent contractor)
- Borrowing of money or other property
- Lending of money or other property
- Rental of property, as landlord
- Rental of property, as tenant
- Availability of facilities or services
- Sales of property
- Purchase of property
- Involvement in a partnership (general or limited)
- Involvement in another form of joint venture

In addition to the involvement of a tax-exempt organization that is subject to the private inurement doctrine and the presence of one or more transactions, the doctrine requires that the transaction be with an *insider* with respect to the organization. An insider essentially is a person who is in a position to exercise a substantial degree of control over the organization. This definition is being significantly informed by the evolving definition of the term *disqualified person*.[19]

## Doctrine of Private Benefit[20]

The private benefit doctrine has, in recent years, been transformed from a relatively obscure area of tax-exempt organizations law to one of the most potent and controversial aspects of that law. The private benefit doctrine, applicable only with respect to charitable organizations, is broader than and subsumes the private inurement doctrine.

The private benefit doctrine differs from the private inurement doctrine in two significant respects. One is that the law recognizes the concept of *incidental* private benefit. (The IRS steadfastly maintains that there is no such thing as incidental private inurement, although that probably is not the case.) The other is that the private benefit doctrine can be applied in the absence of involvement of an insider. Like the private inurement doctrine, however, the underlying standard of the private benefit doctrine is that the terms and conditions of these transactions must be *reasonable,* and the sanction for violation of the doctrine likewise is denial or revocation of tax exemption.

## Excess Benefit Transactions[21]

The law concerning *excess benefit transactions* is found in the intermediate sanctions rules.[22] These rules, while utilizing much of the language of the self-dealing rules, are in many ways a restatement of the private inurement doctrine. The concept of the private inurement transaction and the excess benefit transaction is essentially the same, as is the concept of the insider and disqualified person.

Thus, like the private inurement doctrine, a set of facts implicating the excess benefit transactions rules must have three components:

1. A tax-exempt organization that is subject to this body of law
2. One or more transactions
3. Involvement of one or more disqualified persons

Unlike the private inurement doctrine, the excess benefit transactions rules apply only to two categories of tax-exempt organizations: all public charities[23] and all social welfare organizations.[24] Thus, there are no exceptions to these rules, such as for churches and small organizations.[25] Organizations caught up in this body of law are termed *applicable tax-exempt organizations.*[26]

The list of private inurement transactions (above) is equally applicable to the excess benefit transactions rules. The formal definition of an excess benefit transaction, however, is an overarching one: it is a transaction in which an economic benefit is provided by an applicable tax-exempt organization directly or indirectly to or for the use of a disqualified person, if the value of the economic benefit provided by the exempt organization exceeds the value of the consideration (including the performance of services) received for providing the benefit.[27] This type of benefit is known as an *excess benefit.*

In addition to the involvement of an applicable tax-exempt organization and the presence of one or more excess benefit transactions, the rules require that the transaction be with a disqualified person with respect to the organization. Basically, a *disqualified person* is a person who is in a position to exercise substantial influence over the affairs of the organization. The definition also includes family members and controlled entities.[28]

The sanctions for violation of these rules are excise taxes that are imposed on the disqualified person or persons involved. The sanctions do not fall on applicable tax-exempt organizations. The initial tax is 25 percent of the excess benefit. If that tax is not timely paid and the excess benefit transaction is not undone (corrected), there can be a tax of 200 percent of the excess benefit. In instances of reasonable cause, these taxes can be abated. If a member of the organization's board knowingly participates in (approves) an excess benefit transaction, he or she may be subject to a tax of 10 percent of the excess benefit.[29]

## Self-Dealing Rules[30]

In general, the federal tax law prohibits direct and indirect acts of self-dealing between a private foundation and a disqualified person. The types of transactions that constitute self-dealing are enumerated in the statute.[31] These transactions are essentially the same as those enumerated in the summary of the private inurement doctrine.

An initial tax is imposed on each act of self-dealing between a disqualified person and a private foundation; the tax is imposed on the self-dealer at the rate of 5 percent of the amount involved with respect to the act for each year. When this tax is imposed and the act of self-dealing is not timely corrected, an additional tax is imposed in an amount equal to 200 percent of the amount involved. A tax of $2\frac{1}{2}$ percent of the amount involved may be imposed on the participation of a foundation manager in the act of self-dealing where the manager knowingly participated in the act.

## ACTIONS BY EXEMPT ORGANIZATIONS

Tax-exempt organizations are, by application of many federal and state laws, commanded to act, and enjoined to not act, in a multitude of ways. Much of the law in this regard is found in the federal tax law. This is particularly the case with exempt charitable organizations and application of the laws proscribing unwarranted private benefit.

These (and other[32]) rules are written using language that assumes that tax-exempt organizations, as such, *act* or *refrain from acting* in various ways. For example, the rules as to exemption for charitable organizations include the requirement that the entities may not permit any of their net earnings to inure to the benefit of persons in their private capacity. This is, of course, a legal fiction. Tax-exempt organizations, like all other persons that are not natural persons, cannot alone *do* anything. They are animated only to the extent that one or more human beings cause them to function; this is as true with respect to omissions as it is with respect to commissions.

Until recently, little attention had been given to this point. Over the years, in the federal tax arena and elsewhere, regulations, rules, form instructions, and more have been written as if nonprofit organizations acted, or refrained from acting, or failed to act somehow independently of the human beings that control and serve them.

Generally, nonprofit organizations are controlled and have their policies set by boards of trustees or boards of directors. These organizations, of course, have officers and they often have employees. It is not uncommon for an individual to simultaneously serve in two or three of these capacities. Actions and nonactions of nonprofit organizations can also be manifested by persons acting as their agents.

Actions of one or more employees, officers, or board members can constitute actions of a public charity or other type of tax-exempt organization. Like all entities recognized in the law as persons, where the entities are not natural persons, exempt entities can *act* only as directed by one or more natural persons. The issue as to when a charity or other exempt organization *acts* arises in a variety of contexts in the law of tax-exempt organizations. One such area, which is forcing focus on just how an exempt organization acts or refrains from acting, is in determining whether a charity has undertaken an excess benefit transaction. This aspect of evolving law is shedding light on the point in general.

The general definition of the excess benefit transaction is provided above.[33] Not only does this statute require that an economic benefit be provided, but also it mandates that the economic benefit be provided *by* the applicable tax-exempt organization.

Clearly, a transaction approved by a majority of the board of trustees or directors of a tax-exempt organization with full awareness of the underlying facts, when undertaken, is an act of the organization. Likewise, a transaction undertaken by an officer or employee within the scope of his or her authority as delegated by such board or granted pursuant to the organizational documents is an act of the organization. An action taken by an employee or officer beyond the scope of his or her authority, however, without the knowledge of the directors and other officers of the organization, and in contravention of the organization's policy, may not be an act of the organization. The resolution of whether action of an employee, officer, or director of an exempt organization will be considered an act of the organization often lies in agency law.

In 1997, the IRS revealed that it developed attribution rules to fit a variety of exempt organizations situations, including lobbying, political campaign activities, and illegal activities of organizations.[34] The IRS stated that principles of agency law may apply to the determination of attribution. The application of agency law to exempt organization issues was further articulated when the IRS, in 2002, observed that "[w]here agency issues arise in federal tax cases, the courts typically look to federal case law and treatises on common law, particularly the Restatement (Second) of Agency (1958) . . . , rather than State law."[35]

The IRS described *agency* as a fiduciary relationship resulting from the manifestation of consent by one person (principal) to another person (agent), so that the agent will act on behalf of the principal subject to the principal's control and consent by the agent to so act. An agent may obtain authority to bind the principal through agreement with the principal (actual authority) or through actions of the principal (apparent authority or ratification).

In discussing possible illegal political activities of an exempt organization's officers or members, the IRS cautioned that actions of "members and officers do not always reflect on the organization."[36] On this occasion, the matter involved a determination as to whether the actions of certain officers and members of a tax-exempt charitable organization reflected actions of the organization itself in addressing whether to revoke the organization's tax exemption. Only certain acts, the agency wrote, "should be considered as activities 'of the organization.'" Those acts include: "(1) acts by [organization] officials under actual or purported authority to act for the organization; (2) acts by agents for the organization within their authority to act; or (3) acts ratified by the organization."

These agency standards are further supported by the IRS's stance in 2002 on political and lobbying activities. This article stated that the actions of employees within the context of their employment generally will be considered authorized by the organization. Furthermore:

> Acts of individuals that are not authorized by the IRC [§] 501(c)(3) organization may be attributed to the organization if it explicitly or implicitly ratifies the actions. A failure to disavow the actions of individuals under apparent authorization from the IRC [§] 501(c)(3) organization may be considered a ratification of the actions. To be effective, the disavowal must be made in a timely manner equal to the original actions. The organization must also take steps to ensure that such unauthorized actions do not recur.

Even criminal activity committed by an officer or director of a tax-exempt organization can be imputed to the organization for tax purposes, at least according to the IRS. In application of the private inurement doctrine, the U.S. Tax Court held that the doctrine did not apply when the exempt organization was the *victim* of the crime (in the case, embezzlement), writing that "we do not believe that the Congress intended that the charity must lose its exempt status merely because a president or treasurer or an executive director of a charity has skimmed or embezzled or otherwise stolen from the charity, at least where the charity has a real-world existence apart from the thieving official."[37] By contrast, the IRS, in considering whether embezzled amounts should be viewed as provided *by* a tax-exempt organization for intermediate sanctions purposes, stated that "any economic benefit received by a disqualified person from the assets of an [exempt] organization is considered to be provided by the organization even if the transfer was not authorized under the organization's regular procedures."[38] The agency concluded that "amounts embezzled by a disqualified person from an [exempt charitable] organization are considered an excess benefit transaction."[39]

The essence of the foregoing is that the law—at least the federal tax law interpretation of the law as to principal and agent—as to when and how a tax-exempt organization *acts* depends on whether the nonprofit actor is functioning in the role of a trustee or director, an officer, or an employee.

An action by an *employee* of a charitable organization generally is considered an action by the organization if it is undertaken within the scope of the employee's employment.

An action by an *officer* of a charitable organization generally is considered an action by the organization if it is undertaken pursuant to a delegation of authority by the governing board or is inherently within the scope of the duties and responsibilities of the office (and thus consistent with the organization's organizational and operating documents).

An action of a charitable organization, when precipitated by one or more *directors* or *trustees*, does not require a majority vote or a formal resolution or like conferral of authority. An individual in a position of leadership thus can single-handedly cause a nonprofit organization to act or refrain from acting. The federal law on the point—certainly the IRS's view of that law—is that an action (or nonaction) by a single director can be that of the charitable organization involved, particularly if one or more of the other directors or trustees knew (or should have known) of the action and/or if the board of directors or trustees by action or nonaction subsequently ratifies the action of the one director or trustee.

## ISSUES, STRATEGIES, AND COMMENTARIES

The planner faces a host of issues that must be resolved when applying the laws concerning private inurement, private benefit, excess benefit transactions, and self-dealing.

### Private Inurement

In analyzing a set of facts from the perspective of the private inurement doctrine, the planner should not have much difficulty in determining whether the tax-exempt organization involved is subject to the doctrine. Also, almost by definition, there are one or more transactions precipitating the inquiry. There can be an issue, however, as to whether a party to the transaction is an insider.

The task of the planner in identifying insiders has been made easier by reason of enactment of the bodies of law defining who is a disqualified person. Essentially, an insider is the same as a disqualified person—what may be termed a *control person* or a *person of influence.* There may be some difficulty, particularly in connection with large organizations, in determining which employees are *key employees.* The planner should remember, however—once control persons are identified—to include as insiders members of their family and entities controlled by them.

Under evolving law principles, consultants to a tax-exempt organization can be insiders. This includes lawyers, accountants, fundraisers, and management companies. The planner should disregard the appellate court opinion in the *United Cancer Council* case[40] when making judgments in this context.

If there is uncertainty when examining a set of facts in relation to the private inurement doctrine, the planner may wish to utilize, as a guide, the private foundation self-dealing rules.[41] This is because these rules amount to a codification of the private inurement doctrine. Thus, if a transaction would be a self-dealing transaction, it likely would be a private inurement transaction. It must be emphasized, however, that the self-dealing rules apply only with respect to private foundations.

Once the planner is satisfied that the three fundamental elements of the private inurement doctrine are present, the next step is to ascertain whether the terms and conditions of the transaction being evaluated are *reasonable.*[42] This is an issue of fact, rather than law, so that lawyers are not likely to be competent to render advice on the point, unless the facts are clear and obvious.

In the case of compensation arrangements (particularly in instances of employees), this issue of fact is to be resolved by application of the *multifactor test.* This determination can be aided by following the rules in the excess benefit transactions setting as to *appropriate data.*[43] The factors commonly applied in the private inurement (and intermediate sanctions) setting, to ascertain the reasonableness of compensation, are:

- The levels of compensation paid by similar organizations (tax-exempt and taxable) for functionally comparable positions, with emphasis on comparable entities in the same community or region
- The need of the organization for the services of the individual whose compensation is being evaluated[44]
- The individual's background, education, training, experience, and responsibilities
- Whether the compensation resulted from arm's-length bargaining, such as whether it was approved by an independent board of directors
- The size and complexity of the organization, taking into consideration elements such as assets, income, and number of employees
- The individual's prior compensation arrangement
- The individual's performance
- The relationship of the individual's compensation to that paid to other employees of the organization
- Dramatic increases (spikes) in the level of compensation, particularly when provided as a bonus
- The amount of time the individual devotes to the position

Many of these factors are derived from the case law arising in the for-profit setting. As discussed in the companion book, however, some federal courts of appeals are utilizing a dramatically different test: the *independent investor test*. In the exempt organization's context, nonetheless, planners should continue to apply the multifactor test. It may be noted that, in an intermediate sanctions case (which was settled before any law was developed), the IRS, in stating the factors the agency relied on in concluding that an individual's compensation, paid by a public charity, was excessive, invoked the independent investor test (writing, in the notice of deficiency, that "[i]t is not probable an outside investor would approve of such a compensation plan as reasonable").[45] Inasmuch as tax-exempt organizations do not have investors, however, it is improbable that the independent investor test is properly applicable in the exempt organizations context.

There are two factors that are largely unique to the law of tax-exempt organizations. One is the fact that an exempt organization may have a need for the services of a particular individual. Examples include the scientific research organization that has a need for a particular scientist, a college that has a need for a particular professor, or a university that has a need for a particular football coach. The exempt organization in this situation is entitled to pay a "premium" for acquisition of the individual's services, assuming the overall level of compensation is reasonable. As noted, the planner may utilize the tenets of the IRS's physician recruitment guidelines in making judgments in this area.

The other factor is the role of the board. The underlying assumption is that there *is* involvement of the board in this context. In many instances, however, the full board of directors or trustees of a tax-exempt organization does not know the details of the compensation arrangement the organization has with one or more of its executives. While there is no federal law on the point (although corporate governance principles are beginning to expect board involvement in these transactions), the IRS and state regulatory officials prefer to see situations where the entire board of an organization passes on these compensatory packages.

Conceptually, there are two types of governing boards: independent and captive. An independent board is one where none of its members are related by family or business ties to the executive whose compensation is being evaluated. A captive board is one where all of its members have one or more such relationships with the executive. Often, however, the board is a blend of these extremes.

In this setting, the distinction between the two types of boards goes to the credibility of their determination(s) as to compensation. A finder of fact (such as the IRS or a court) will grant the judgment and decision of an independent board more credence than those of a captive board. (There is nothing inherently inappropriate about a captive board—such as that of a private family foundation or small public charity—rather, the issue is the credibility of its decisions concerning the compensation of one or more of its members.) A solution in this regard, assuming it is valid under state law, is for the captive board to appoint an independent committee (perhaps consisting in whole or in part of non-board members) of the board to make judgments about a compensation arrangement with an insider.

If the board of an organization subject to the private inurement doctrine decides to compensate (or, for that matter, enter into any other business relationship with) an insider, it should have some objective information on which to base its decision. This may be derived from a study, one or more surveys, or an independent consultant's report. Again, the planner who is a lawyer probably is not trained to make these determinations. The lawyer, however, should be certain that all of the relevant factors in determining reasonableness are taken into account. For example, the IRS or a court may reject the conclusions of a consultant's report where the report fails to definitively address each of the relevant factors.

Another aspect of compensation arrangements that warrants considerable sensitivity and scrutiny on the part of the planner are those that are based, in whole or in part, on the revenue flow of the organization. These arrangements come with many names, such as commissions, incentive compensation, productivity compensation, revenue-sharing,[46] and gainsharing. In addition to the general requirement that the resulting compensation be reasonable, the planner should strive to build into the structure of the plan the elements of objective criteria and an independent assessment committee. Also, these plans function best when the compensation is dependent, in whole or in part, on the revenue flow of a discrete segment of the organization (such as a department of a hospital) rather than the entire organization. Overall, the difficulty with these forms of compensation arrangements is that their terms can come perilously close to entanglement with the proscription on inurement of *net earnings*.

The criteria the IRS will examine in the area of incentive compensation are:

- Was the compensation arrangement established by an independent board of directors or by an independent compensation committee (see above)?
- Does the compensation arrangement with the recipients result in total compensation that is reasonable?
- Is there an arm's-length relationship between the tax-exempt organization and the recipients of the compensation?
- Does the compensation arrangement include a "ceiling or reasonable maximum" on the amount an individual may receive to protect against "projection errors or substantial windfall benefits"?
- Does the compensation arrangement have the potential for reducing the charitable services or benefits that the organization would otherwise provide?
- Does the compensation arrangement "transform the principal activity" of the organization into a "joint venture" between it and the income recipients?
- Is the compensation arrangement "merely a device to distribute all or a portion" of the organization's profits to persons who control the organization?
- Does the compensation arrangement serve a "real and discernible business purpose of the exempt organization, such as to achieve maximum efficiency and economy in operations[,] that is independent of any purpose to operate the organization for the impermissible direct or indirect benefit" of the income recipients and/or insiders?
- Does the compensation arrangement result in "no abuse or unwarranted benefits because, for example, prices and operating costs compare favorably with those of other similar organizations"?

- Does the compensation arrangement "reward" an individual based on services actually performed, or is it based on performance in an area where the individual "performs no significant functions"?[47]

The IRS generally has been rather generous in this field. The agency has approved of many types of incentive compensation arrangements involving tax-exempt organizations, benevolently skirting potential private inurement concerns. As an illustration, the IRS approved of an incentive compensation arrangement whereby all of the scientists working at a medical research organization and responsible for producing certain intellectual property will receive all of the research organization's royalty interest resulting from commercialization of the property.[48]

There are other forms of private inurement. One is rental arrangements.[49] The factors to be considered in this context include the duration of the lease, and the amount and frequency of the rent payments. Lending arrangements also can entail private inurement.[50] The factors to be considered in this setting include the amount being borrowed, the rate of interest to be paid, the duration of the loan, the security underlying the loan, and the creditworthiness of the borrower. In either instance, the terms and conditions of the arrangement should be committed to writing (lease or note).

Another form of private inurement is the sale of an exempt organization's assets to one or more insiders.[51] There are many reasons as to why this occurs, such as the discontinuance of a program and the sale of the underlying assets to one or more board members who wish to perpetuate the function in another entity. As with other transactions of this nature, a principal role of the planner is to ensure that the terms and conditions of the sale are reasonable. For the most part, this entails a competent judgment that the property was properly valued at the time of the sale.

The three aspects of these sales transactions warranting emphasis are:

1. Just as the lawyer who is the planner is likely not competent to evaluate an executive's compensation package, he or she is not likely to be competent to value an item of property. This, of course, is the work of appraisers. Yet, like the lawyer who should be certain that the multifactor test in the realm of compensation is properly applied (see above), he or she should be certain that the appraiser took all relevant facts into account when valuing the property. In one instance involving a faulty appraisal, the court blamed the lawyer, not the appraiser.[52]

2. In the case of a dispute as to whether there was private inurement, by definition the matter is being evaluated (by the IRS or a court) in hindsight. There may be amply valid reasons as to why the property increased in value (if that is the case) following the sale of it by the tax-exempt organization to the insiders; this may enable the insiders to reap a profit unforeseen at the time of the sale by the exempt organization. These subsequent developments will color the judgment of the factfinder and increase the likelihood of a finding of private inurement. In these situations, a suitable appraisal and/or a favorable ruling from the IRS at the time of the sale may end up being disregarded.

3. This third aspect of the subject is related to the second one. In a case, a court held that, in evaluating the value of an item of property being sold by an exempt organization

to insiders, the parties were expected to take into account events that may occur as far as two years into the future.[53]

Other types of private inurement circumstances are discussed in the companion book. They are equity distributions,[54] certain assumptions of liability,[55] certain employee benefits,[56] various tax avoidance schemes,[57] the rendering of certain services,[58] the provision of goods or refreshments,[59] certain retained interests,[60] embezzlements,[61] and involvement by public charities in certain types of partnerships.[62]

## Private Benefit

The planner must be wary of the private benefit doctrine.[63] As noted, it has emerged as a powerful force in the law of tax-exempt organizations, despite the paucity of law on the point. It is a body of law that, today, knows no bounds and lurks as a trap for the unwary exempt charitable organization and its planner(s).

A charitable organization can engage in a private benefit transaction with anyone. If the transaction is with a board member, officer, and/or key employee, the private inurement doctrine may be employed instead of the private benefit doctrine. Otherwise, the transaction may be tested against the private benefit rules. In one case, for example, an appellate court concluded that the private inurement doctrine was inapplicable because the party to the transaction was not an insider, and the court remanded the case for consideration in light of the private benefit doctrine.[64]

One of the principal court opinions invoking the private benefit doctrine that the planner should always consider is that issued in the important *Redlands Surgical Services* case.[65] This case illustrates how a charitable organization can be involved in a private benefit transaction with a for-profit organization and how private benefit can arise in the joint venture context. Another aspect of *Redlands* that is significant is the selection of precedents on which the opinion rests. The principal case in this regard is the one concerning *est of Hawaii*.[66]

The planner must be extremely wary of the findings and import of the *est of Hawaii* case. The opinion is one of the most radical in the law of tax-exempt organizations—and the IRS follows its principles without hesitation. The essence of the case is that private benefit can occur even where (1) the tax-exempt charitable organization involved is exclusively engaged in exempt functions and (2) the terms and conditions of financial relationships with one or more for-profit entities is reasonable.

The extent to which the IRS follows this approach is illustrated by the manner in which it evaluates the tax consequences of a relationship between a charitable organization and a management company. Private benefit is deemed present even where the charitable entity is primarily engaged in exempt functions, the company is providing suitable services, and the compensation paid to the company by the exempt organization is reasonable, where one or more individuals serve simultaneously on the governing boards of the charitable organization and the management company.[67]

One of the most troubling aspects of the private benefit doctrine, however—one as to which the planner must be particularly attentive—is its application wholly in the tax-exempt organizations context. That is, there are situations emerging where an otherwise charitable organization is denied exempt status because of ostensible private benefit accorded another (noncharitable) exempt organization. Examples of this include situations where organizations have been denied tax exemption as charitable entities because of private benefit ostensibly thrown off on exempt social welfare organizations[68] and where an organization was denied exempt charitable status because of private benefit allegedly conveyed to an exempt business league.[69]

Aside from the unknown scope and reach of the private benefit doctrine, another trap lying in wait that this doctrine posits for the nondiligent planner is embedded in the facts that any transaction that constitutes private inurement also constitutes private benefit and that the private benefit doctrine does not require the involvement of an insider. Thus, the planner who is analyzing a set of facts from the perspective of the private inurement doctrine should not end the analysis if there is a finding that the transaction(s) did not entail the participation of an insider, so that the private inurement doctrine is inapplicable. The planner must press on and further examine the facts from the standpoint of the private benefit doctrine. Two examples of this point are an IRS private letter ruling holding that the private inurement doctrine would be applied (resulting in loss of exempt status) in a case involving a private foundation even though the self-dealing rules were inapplicable (because the self-dealer was not a disqualified person)[70] and a court opinion concluding that the self-dealing rules did not apply to an otherwise self-dealing transaction (because the self-dealer was not a disqualified person), even though the government could have (and should have) utilized the private inurement and private benefit doctrines as fallback arguments (to cause revocation of the exemption of the private foundation involved).[71]

## Excess Benefit Transactions

The rules concerning excess benefit transactions are far more a boon and blessing for planners than a problem or curse. This body of law is intellectually stimulating and—being relatively new—is pregnant with unresolved issues and planning opportunities. Indeed, this aspect of the law can be effectively used to navigate the other three bodies of private benefit law.

The least of the planner's worries in the intermediate sanctions context is likely to be determination as to whether the exempt organization involved is an applicable tax-exempt organization.[72] The planner should remember, however, that there is a lookback rule in this context, so that an organization is an applicable tax-exempt organization if it had that status at any time during the five-year period immediately preceding the transaction under examination.

The planner may have little difficulty identifying many of those who are disqualified persons with respect to an applicable tax-exempt organization.[73] This presumably is the case in connection with the organization's trustees, directors, and officers. Conversely, the planner may have considerable difficulty in this regard with issues such as:

- Identification of those employees of a large organization who are *key employees*
- Identification of *members of the family* of otherwise disqualified persons (taking into account births, adoptions, deaths, marriages, and divorces)

- Applying the facts-and-circumstances test to find control, such as analysis of those who may have managerial control over a discrete segment of the organization

- Identification of substantial contributors to the organization

- Identification of entities that are controlled by disqualified persons

- In general, identification of all who are in a position to exercise substantial influence over the affairs of the organization

- Identification of those who were in a control position during the lookback period.

The planner will likely be called on to ascertain whether a transaction has within it an *excess benefit*. This is the exercise, discussed above, that is employed to determine whether a transaction is *reasonable*.

The definition of the term *excess benefit transaction* is built on the contract law concept of *consideration*.[74] A contract, to be valid, must be supported by adequate consideration. This means that the parties to the arrangement must have roughly equal benefits arising out of it. For example, suppose an applicable tax-exempt organization is paying an individual $300,000 annually to be its chief executive officer. If that amount of compensation is reasonable, the organization is receiving services with a value of $300,000 (its consideration) and the individual is, of course, receiving the money (his or her consideration). (Any employment agreement would then be valid (enforceable).) Further suppose, however, that this individual's services are worth only $200,000 annually. This employment arrangement would then entail an excess benefit transaction, in that the economic benefit (consideration) provided by the exempt organization ($300,000) to the disqualified person is greater (by $100,000) than the value of the consideration it received for providing the benefit.

As also discussed above, the planner who is a lawyer is not likely to have the expertise to determine whether an excess benefit is lurking in a transaction involving an applicable tax-exempt organization. Nonetheless, the lawyer should be certain that all of the relevant factors are taken into consideration in ascertaining the possible presence of an excess benefit.

Nonetheless, the intermediate sanctions rules present a host of legal issues for the planner. The primary ones are:

- **Determining what is compensation.**[75] The term *compensation* is not confined to an individual's salary. Rather, at least for purposes of the intermediate sanctions rules (and undoubtedly also for the other rules), the term includes nearly all economic benefits provided by an applicable tax-exempt organization, to or for the use of a person, in exchange for the performance of services. Thus, compensation includes bonuses, commissions, most forms of deferred compensation, most insurance coverages, payments to welfare benefit plans, most fringe benefits, severance payments, and retirement arrangements.

- **Treating an economic benefit as consideration for the performance of services.**[76] For an economic benefit to be treated in this fashion, the applicable tax-exempt organization providing the benefit must clearly indicate its intent, at the time the benefit is paid, to treat the benefit as compensation. Generally, this is accomplished by the provision of written substantiation that is contemporaneous with the transfer of the economic benefit at issue. If an organization fails to provide this contemporaneous substantiation, any services provided by the disqualified person will not be treated as provided in consideration for the economic benefit for purposes of determining the reasonableness of the transaction.

• **Ascertaining the presence of any other direct provision of an excess benefit.**[77] Payment of excessive compensation is not the only way an applicable tax-exempt organization can be involved in an excess benefit transaction. Rental arrangements, borrowing transactions, sales transactions, and involvement in joint ventures are among the other ways an excess benefit transaction can occur.

• **Determining if there is or was an indirect provision of an excess benefit.**[78] An applicable tax-exempt organization may provide an excess benefit *indirectly* to a disqualified person by means of a controlled entity or through an intermediary.[79] *Control*, in this context, means more than 50 percent, and extends to all entities, including corporations, partnerships, and nonstock organizations. An *intermediary* is any person (an individual or a taxable or tax-exempt entity) who participates in a transaction with one or more disqualified persons of an applicable tax-exempt organization.

• **Determining if an excess benefit was provided for the use of a disqualified person.**[80] This is one of the biggest traps, in part because the concept of providing a benefit *for the use of* a disqualified person is not addressed in the tax regulations. The phrase is used in the self-dealing setting (see below), however, and thus some understanding of it can be derived from the little law there is in that context.

For example, in a matter involving a lawyer who was the sole trustee of a private foundation (and thus a disqualified person), the IRS ruled that the benefit to the lawyer from a loan by the foundation to an individual (not a disqualified person with respect to the foundation) who had substantial dealings with the lawyer and his firm was more than an insubstantial benefit, because the loan enhanced the lawyer's image in the view of his client and thus provided an economic benefit to him. The lawyer's procurement of the loan for this non-disqualified person was determined to be an act of self-dealing.[81]

Likewise, the IRS found that a bank, in extending credit to large for-profit corporations and tax-exempt organizations, where the notes were to be purchased by private foundations for which the bank acted as trustee (and thus was a disqualified person), was engaging in a substantial activity that enhanced the bank's reputation and significantly increased its goodwill, so that the transactions were acts of self-dealing.[82] On another occasion, the IRS suggested that marketing benefits provided by means of a transaction of this nature could amount to self-dealing.[83]

In another of these examples, the IRS found self-dealing where, in calculating the amount of collateral required to meet the margin requirements of personal trading accounts of disqualified persons, assets of the private foundation involved were taken into account.[84] The IRS saw this cross-collateral agreement as the means for allowing disqualified persons to improperly use the assets in the foundation accounts as collateral to meet the margin requirements of those persons on certain partnership trading accounts beneficially owned by those that were undermarginalized as the result of certain investments by one of the disqualified persons. Indeed, the IRS was so exercised about this arrangement that revocation of the foundation's tax exemption was proposed.

Yet, the IRS ruled that grants made by a charitable organization for purposes of community assistance, while characterized as "investments" for purposes of community reinvestment policy pursuant to the federal banking laws, were not excess benefit transactions, because undue benefits did not flow to disqualified persons, namely, the banks that were benefited by reason of credit for the charity's grants.[85] The IRS, however, did not subject these facts to analysis under the *for the use of* standard. This appears to be an error, with the IRS writing that banks' "main benefit" from a high rating from the Office of Thrift Supervision was "intangible public benefit," which presumably is akin to enhanced reputation and increased goodwill. Even if the banks were not disqualified persons, two individuals, who were disqualified persons with respect to the charitable organization, were benefited in their roles as chief executive officers and directors of the banks. The argument was there that these two disqualified persons were using the resources of the charitable organization to benefit the banks and their positions with the banks. This situation is scarcely different from the one referenced above concerning the taking of private foundation assets into account in calculating disqualified persons' trading accounts margin requirements. This ruling highlights the extent of the trap for the planner: if the IRS can miss this issue, so too can the unsedulous planner.

- **Assessing *revenue-sharing arrangements*.**[86] A revenue-sharing arrangement may, but need not always be, an excess benefit transaction. A *revenue-sharing arrangement* occurs when the amount of an economic benefit provided by an applicable tax-exempt organization to or for the use of a disqualified person is determined, in whole or in part, by the flow of the revenues of one or more activities of the organization. This type of transaction or other arrangement is, however, an excess benefit transaction only if the transaction results in private inurement (see above) and to the extent provided in tax regulations. There are no regulations on the point at this time, yet the IRS is interpreting these rules on the basis of the general definition of the term *excess benefit transaction*. As a matter of statutory construction, this approach is questionable.

- **Determining applicability of the *initial contract exception*.**[87] A huge exception is that the intermediate sanctions rules do not apply to a fixed payment made by an applicable tax-exempt organization to a disqualified person pursuant to an initial contract. Thus, application of these rules requires definition, with respect to the particular setting, of the terms *initial contract* and *fixed payment*. Also, a *material change* to a contract can cause it to become a *new contract*, thus voiding the exception.

- **Determining whether a benefit is incidental.** The formal law as to the intermediate sanctions rules is silent on the concept of the incidental transaction with a disqualified person. The IRS has, however, privately ruled that the "incidental and tenuous" standard, applicable in the self-dealing area (see below), also applies in the intermediate sanctions context.[88] Thus, the planner should, in appropriate instances, explore the likelihood of this defense.

- Utilizing the *rebuttable presumption of reasonableness*.[89] The presumption of reasonableness (a mechanism for shifting the burden of proof in an intermediate sanctions case to the IRS) presents the planner with a host of marvelous opportunities. Much of what this set of rules is about entails recommended management practices generally; an organization should strive to meet as many of the elements of these rules as it can, even if all of them cannot be satisfied. This presumption that the terms and conditions of a transaction or other arrangement are reasonable arises when the arrangement was approved by an *authorized body* of the exempt organization involved who lack a *conflict of interest,* the authorized body obtained and relied on *appropriate data,* and the body *adequately documented* the basis for its determination.

- **Calculating the penalty excise tax(es).**[90] For example, the initial tax imposed on a disqualified person is equal to 25 percent of the *excess benefit.* In some situations, such as an amount of excess compensation, a rental arrangement, or a borrowing arrangement, determining that benefit is relatively easy. In other instances, such as a *for the use of* transaction, the benefit may be sufficiently ethereal as to defy easy calculation of the benefit; guidance on this point is sparse.[91] Imposition of the 200 percent additional tax requires determination, not only of the excess benefit involved, but also the *taxable period* and the *correction amount* (see below). The 10 percent tax on organization managers requires calculation or determination of (in addition to identification of those who are managers in the first instance) the excess benefit involved, application of the words *participation* and *knowing,* and ascertainment as to whether the participation was *willful* and due to *reasonable cause.*

- **Preparing and filing Form 4720.** This Form is the IRS form by which a disqualified person reports involvement in an excess benefit transaction and calculates the tax or taxes involved. This is part of a self-reporting system; the parties are not to merely wait to see when and if the IRS discovers the transaction or other arrangement. Human beings can differ as to whether a transaction constituted an excess benefit transaction (see below); matters may evolve to the point where a disqualified person needs legal counsel, separate from that for the applicable tax-exempt organization.

- **Engaging in *correction* of an excess benefit transaction.**[92] An excess benefit transaction must be corrected; it is insufficient to merely pay one or more taxes. This type of *correction* is accomplished by a disqualified person by (1) undoing the excess benefit to the extent possible and (2) taking any additional measures necessary to place the applicable tax-exempt organization involved in the transaction in a financial position not worse than that in which it would be if the disqualified person had been dealing with the organization under the highest fiduciary standards. The law on this point is meager (although the phraseology is taken from the private foundation self-dealing rules). The *correction amount* is comprised of the sum of the excess benefit (see above) and suitable interest on that amount. The process can vary, depending on the type of applicable tax-exempt organization involved.

- **Seeking abatement of a tax.**[93] Unlike the self-dealing rules (see below), under certain circumstances, the IRS has the authority to abate the initial tax and must abate the additional tax.

- **Reimbursing an excess benefit tax.**[94] Under certain circumstances, an applicable tax-exempt organization may reimburse a disqualified person for an intermediate sanctions tax penalty. Planners should proceed carefully in this setting: not only should the reimbursement amount be treated as additional compensation to the disqualified person and tested against the standard of reasonableness, but also there is the matter of the propriety of this type of reimbursement in the first instance.

- **Using insurance.**[95] Under certain circumstances, an applicable tax-exempt organization may purchase insurance to cover the cost of intermediate sanctions penalty taxes imposed on disqualified persons. The above considerations and concerns as to reimbursement are equally applicable in the insurance context.

- **Reporting on the annual information return.**[96] It is often said that applicable tax-exempt organizations need not worry about the intermediate sanctions rules in that the penalties (excise taxes) fall only on disqualified persons. This dismissive attitude toward these rules should be rejected by the planner, however, because of a pointed question on the annual information return: "Did the [applicable tax-exempt] organization engage in any section 4958 excess benefit transaction during the year or did it become aware of an excess benefit transaction from a prior year? This sweeping and pointed question can generate considerable controversy; applicable tax-exempt organizations and their disqualified persons can, for example, passionately disagree as to whether a transaction embodied an excess benefit. Also, if the answer to the question is yes, the organization must gather the necessary information and prepare a statement to be attached to the return, which is a public document.

- **Ascertaining the interrelationship with the private inurement and private benefit doctrines.**[97] The planner should constantly monitor developments in the law pertaining to the private inurement and private benefit doctrines (and, for that matter, the self-dealing rules) to gain information, on an ongoing basis, as to the interpretation and amplification of the excess benefit transactions rules.

- **Valuing compensation or property.**[98] As referenced above, matters of valuation relate to issues of fact, not law. Nonetheless, it is the responsibility of the planner who is a lawyer to see to it that the valuation process is appropriate and complete. For example, if the issue is the valuation of a compensation arrangement, the planner should endeavor to be certain that all of the applicable elements of the multifactor test are taken into account.

## Self-Dealing

The planner who is advising a private foundation as to application of the self-dealing rules has the advantage of more than 30 years' accumulation of law in this area. While the regulations are sometimes sketchy and the court cases are few, an enormous wealth of private letter rulings (technically, of course, not law) has evolved since the inception of these rules in 1969.

The legal issues that are most likely to arise in the self-dealing context are:

- **Ascertaining the presence of an act of self-dealing.**[99] Once the planner has determined that an organization is a private foundation[100] and that one or more other parties to a transaction or other arrangement are disqualified persons,[101] the facts must be analyzed to ascertain whether the transaction or arrangement is or was an act of self-dealing.

- **Determining if there is or was an** *indirect* **act of self-dealing.**[102] The self-dealing rules differentiate between direct and indirect acts of self-dealing. These rules are somewhat different than those in the intermediate sanctions context, although developments in that context are likely to inform the self-dealing law.

- **Determining if an inappropriate benefit was provided for the use of a disqualified person.**[103] The concept of the *for the use of* transaction in the self-dealing context is the same as that in the intermediate sanctions context. Thus, again, a development in the law in one of these areas will have an impact on law development in the other area.

- **Applying the personal services exception.**[104] The planner may anguish over this one as much as any of the private foundation rules. Generally, the private foundation rules in effect prohibit self-dealing,[105] yet there is an exception in the case of payment of compensation to disqualified persons. That form of compensation is permissible, as long as the services that are the subject of the compensation are *personal services*—an undefined term. The services of lawyers, accountants, and investment advisors qualify and those of janitors do not, and the vast range of services in between must be evaluated by the planner, aided by a substantial number of private letter rulings on the point.

   There is one private letter ruling in particular that the planner may wish to review.[106] Although private letter rulings are not considered precedent, this particular ruling provides the fullest explication of this exception by the IRS. It lists both allowable and unallowable services.

- **Determining if an unwarranted benefit was incidental.**[107] The tax regulations in the self-dealing area expressly provide that the fact that a disqualified person receives an incidental or tenuous benefit from use by a private foundation of its income or assets will not, by itself, make the use an act of self-dealing. There are several IRS private letter rulings on the point; one in particular may stake out the outer reaches of the scope of this exception.[108]

- **Determining if a foundation manager** *knowingly participated* **in an act of self-dealing.**[109] These terms are defined in the same way as they are in the intermediate sanctions context. The definitions are adopted from the private foundation rules.

- **Calculating the penalty excise tax(es).**[110] The considerations in this regard are the same as those in the intermediate sanctions context (discussed above). The main difference is that, in the private foundation field, the term *amount involved* is used rather than *excess benefit*.

- **Preparing and filing Form 4720.** The considerations in this regard are the same as those in the intermediate sanctions context (see above).

- **Engaging in correction of an act of self-dealing.**[111] As noted, the concept of *correction,* used in the intermediate sanctions context, was taken from the private foundation rules. The law in the foundation setting, however, is even more sparse than is the case with the excess benefit transactions rules. Planners may use the elements of the correction rules in connection with intermediate sanctions to interpret and apply the private foundation correction requirements.

- **Ascertaining the interrelationship with the private inurement and private benefit doctrines, and the intermediate sanctions rules.** As observed, a development in one of these three aspects of the law is likely to directly shape the ongoing evolution of the self-dealing rules.

## CONCLUSIONS (REITERATIONS)

It is worth reiterating—one more time—that these four bodies of law are essentially targeted at the same problem: preventing or penalizing an instance of an excess benefit provided to an insider. Furthermore, a development in one of the four settings is likely to directly impact the unfolding of the law in the other three contexts. Indeed, as noted, much of the language used in the intermediate sanctions rules was taken directly from the self-dealing rules.

It thus is the responsibility (and obligation) of the planner to monitor the ongoing developments in each of these bodies of law and to apply these developments when considering particular fact situations. As an illustration, enforcement of the intermediate sanctions rules by the IRS is just getting under way; a substantial number of private letter rulings and technical advice memoranda, and amount of litigation are starting to materialize; and, in the interim, the planner must utilize precepts from these other fields.

The overall concept of private benefit will continue to be one of the most important and controversial aspects of the law of tax-exempt organizations in the months and years to come.

## NOTES

1. See *Tax-Exempt Organizations,* §§ 19.1–19.9.
2. Id., § 1.1.
3. In fact, since the law as to nonprofit organizations and the law of tax-exempt organizations do not precisely mesh, the choices are tax-exempt nonprofit organization, taxable nonprofit organization, or taxable for-profit organization.
4. See Chapter 2, page 37.
5. See Chapter 6.
6. *Tax-Exempt Organizations,* § 19.1.
7. Id., § 19.4.

8. Id., § 19.3.
9. Id., pt. 2.
10. Id., chap. 12.
11. Id., chap. 13.
12. Id., chap. 14.
13. Id., § 16.3.
14. Id., § 16.7.
15. Id., § 18.6.
16. Id., § 18.10.
17. Id., § 18.14.
18. The term *compensation* embraces a wide range of economic benefits paid by a tax-exempt organization to an employee or independent contractor, such as salary, bonus, commission, expense account, insurance, and retirement benefits.
19. *Tax-Exempt Organizations,* § 19.3.
20. Id., § 19.10.
21. Id., § 19.11.
22. In general, Bruce R. Hopkins, *The Law of Intermediate Sanctions: A Guide for Nonprofits* (Hoboken, NJ: John Wiley & Sons, 2003) (hereinafter *Intermediate Sanctions*).
23. That is, all IRC § 501(c)(3) organizations other than private foundations. See Chapter 4.
24. *Tax-Exempt Organizations,* chap. 12.
25. E.g., id., § 23.3(b).
26. *Intermediate Sanctions,* § 1.3.
27. Id., chap. 4.
28. Id., chap. 3.
29. Id., chap. 6.
30. *Tax-Exempt Organizations,* § 11.4(a). Also, *Private Foundations,* chap. 5.
31. IRC § 4941.
32. The observations made in this section are equally applicable in connection with the law pertaining to areas such as lobbying and political campaign activity (see Chapter 5) and unrelated business undertakings (see Chapter 8).
33. See text accompanied by note 27 above.
34. "Lobbying Issues," 1997 Continuing Professional Education (CPE) Text.
35. "Agency: A Critical Factor in Exempt Organizations and UBIT Issues," 2002 CPE Text.
36. IRS General Counsel Memorandum (hereinafter Gen. Couns. Mem.) 34631 (citing Gen. Couns. Mem. 34523, which was cited in the 1997 Lobbying Issues Article (see note 34 above), and in the 1994 CPE Text "Illegality and Public Policy Considerations" (hereinafter 1994 Illegality Article)).
37. Variety Club Tent No. 6 Charities, Inc. v. Comm'r, 74 T.C.M. 1485, 1494 (1997).
38. "Introduction to I.R.C. 4958 (Intermediate Sanctions)," 2002 CPE Text (hereinafter 2002 Intermediate Sanctions Article); T.D. 8920, 2001-8 I.R.B. 654 (Feb. 20, 2001) ("Explanation of Provisions" section of the preamble to the temporary regulations).
39. 2002 Intermediate Sanctions Article.
40. See Chapter 11, pages 266–270.
41. See pages 62–63 above.
42. *Tax-Exempt Organizations,* § 19.4(a).
43. *Intermediate Sanctions,* § 5.4.
44. In this regard, planners can extrapolate from the IRS's physician recruitment guidelines (Rev. Rul. 97-21, 1997-1 C.B. 121) to glean guidance when an exempt organization is inducing an

individual to become one of its employees. See *Tax-Exempt Organizations*, § 19.4(a), n. 120. For considerably more detail on this subject, see *Tax-Exempt Healthcare Organizations*, chap. 25.

45. *Tax-Exempt Organizations*, § 19.4(a), n. 104.
46. See *Intermediate Sanctions*, § 4.9.
47. These criteria are based on an IRS information letter (INFO 2002-0021).
48. Priv. Ltr. Rul. 200326035. As a reminder that other law may adversely apply, notwithstanding compliance with the exempt organizations rules, the IRS held that the commercialization arrangement satisfied the private business use test, thereby causing the interest on the bonds issued by the MRO to not be exempt from federal income tax. Priv. Ltr. Rul. 200347009.
49. *Tax-Exempt Organizations*, § 19.4(b).
50. Id., § 19.4(c).
51. Id., § 19.4(d).
52. Anclote Psychiatric Ctr., Inc. v. Comm'r, 76 T.C.M. 175 (1998). See Chapter 11, pages 297–300.
53. Id.
54. *Tax-Exempt Organizations*, § 19.4(e).
55. Id., § 19.4(f).
56. Id., § 19.4(g).
57. Id., § 19.4(h).
58. Id., § 19.4(i).
59. Id., § 19.4(j).
60. Id., § 19.4(k).
61. Id., § 19.4(*l*).
62. See Chapter 7.
63. *Tax-Exempt Organizations*, § 19.10.
64. United Cancer Council, Inc. v. Comm'r, 165 F.3d 1173 (7th Cir. 1999). See Chapter 11, pages 266–270.
65. See Chapter 7, pages 158–161.
66. est of Haw. v. Comm'r, 647 F.2d 170 (9th Cir. 1981). See Chapter 11, pages 280–282.
67. See *Tax-Exempt Organizations*, § 19.10(c), text accompanied by n. 333.
68. Id., text accompanied by n. 334.
69. Quality Auditing Co. v. Comm'r, 114 T.C. 498 (2000). See Chapter 11, pages 287–291.
70. Priv. Ltr. Rul. 200114040.
71. Graham v. Comm'r, 83 T.C.M. 1137 (2002).
72. *Tax-Exempt Organizations*, § 19.11(b); *Intermediate Sanctions*, § 1.3.
73. *Tax-Exempt Organizations*, § 19.11(c); *Intermediate Sanctions*, chap. 3.
74. *Intermediate Sanctions*, § 4.1.
75. Id., § 4.6(a).
76. Id., § 4.6(d).
77. *Tax-Exempt Organizations*, § 19.11(d); *Intermediate Sanctions*, § 4.7.
78. Id., § 4.1(c).
79. Id., §§ 4.2, 4.3.
80. Id., § 4.8.
81. IRS Technical Advice Memorandum (hereinafter Tech. Adv. Mem.) 8719004.
82. Gen. Couns. Mem. 39107.
83. Priv. Ltr. Rul. 9726006.
84. Tech. Adv. Mem. 9627001.
85. Priv. Ltr. Rul. 200335037.

86. *Intermediate Sanctions,* § 4.9.

87. Id., § 4.4.

88. Priv. Ltr. Rul. 200335037.

89. *Tax-Exempt Organizations,* § 19.11(e); *Intermediate Sanctions,* chap. 5.

90. *Tax-Exempt Organizations,* § 19.11(f); *Intermediate Sanctions,* chap. 6.

91. One of the few pronouncements on the point from the IRS is Tech. Adv. Mem. 9627001, where an analysis of calculation of the *amount involved* (the equivalent of the excess benefit) in the margin account collateralization case (see note 84 above) was provided.

92. *Intermediate Sanctions,* § 6.4.

93. Id., § 6.6.

94. *Tax-Exempt Organizations,* § 19.11(g); *Intermediate Sanctions,* § 6.11.

95. Id.

96. See Chapter 9, pages 206–207.

97. *Intermediate Sanctions,* § 1.4, chap. 2.

98. Id., § 4.5.

99. *Private Foundations,* chap. 5.

100. See Chapter 4.

101. Id., pages 85, 89–90.

102. *Tax-Exempt Organizations,* § 11.4(a); *Private Foundations,* § 5.11.

103. *Private Foundations,* § 5.8(c).

104. *Private Foundations,* § 5.6.

105. Technically, this is not accurate; the tax structure is so onerous, however, that the rules are regarded as amounting to this prohibition.

106. Priv. Ltr. Rul. 200315031.

107. *Private Foundations,* § 5.8(c).

108. Priv. Ltr. Rul. 199939049.

109. *Private Foundations,* § 5.14(d).

110. Id., § 5.14(b).

111. Id., § 5.14(a).

# CHAPTER 4

# Public Charity and Private Foundation Classification

Despite the fact that the federal tax rules differentiating public charities and private foundations have been in existence for nearly 35 years, there is still, on an ongoing basis, considerable confusion about these rules. Often it is clear whether a charitable organization is or is not a public charity. In some instances, however, much planning can go into determining whether an entity is a public charity, how to maintain that status, and what to do when the public charity status may be disappearing.

The public charity/private foundation rules were written by Congress (in 1969) when that legislative body was in an anti-private-foundation mood. Consequently, many of these rules are harsh, although some have been moderated. Nonetheless, the rules remain stringent, so that, from a law standpoint, there is no advantage to private foundation status.

## LAW BASICS

The companion book summarizes the categories of public charities,[1] the various ways in which persons can be a disqualified person,[2] the types of private foundations,[3] the private foundation rules,[4] and the consequences of private foundation status.[5]

Despite these summaries, it is appropriate to reiterate some of the basic principles:

- The world of tax-exempt charitable organizations is comprised solely of two types: public charities and private foundations. There are millions of the former; there are about 65,000 of the latter.

- A tax-exempt charitable organization is presumed to be a private foundation;[6] the entity may rebut that presumption by a showing that it qualifies as a public charity.[7]

- The federal tax law does not define the term *private foundation;* rather it enumerates the types of charitable organizations that are not private foundations (that is, are public charities).[8]

- There is a body of law, collectively known as the *private foundation rules,* that are often constrictive of private foundations' operations; these rules are applicable only to private foundations.[9]
- The charitable contribution deduction rules are generally tilted in favor of public charities rather than private foundations.[10]

## NOTE

It is often critical that those who represent and manage a charitable organization (that is not a private foundation) know its public charity status. In some instances, the status will be obvious, in that the entity is, for example, a university or a hospital. There are far too many individuals who are working, professionally, for charitable organizations who do not know the entity's public charity status or, if they know it, do not fully understand all of the nuances of that status. Outsiders, such as funders, usually are quite interested in that status; an inability to effectively explain that status to funders and others can work to the detriment of the organization.

## GLOSSARY

The rules pertaining to public charities and private foundations include some important terms of art. They are:

- **Private foundation.** The term *private foundation* is not affirmatively defined in the federal tax law. Nonetheless, a typical private foundation is a tax-exempt charitable organization;[11] it is funded from one source (such as an individual, family, or corporation); its ongoing funding is in the form of investment income (rather than from a flow of contributions and/or grants); and it makes grants for charitable purposes to other persons (rather than conducting its own programs). From a more technical perspective, a private foundation is a charitable organization that is not a public charity.
- **Public charity.** A *public charity* is an institution, an organization that has broad public financial support (a publicly supported charity), or a supporting organization.
- **Institution.** An *institution* is a church, certain organizations affiliated with a church, a school, a college, a university, a hospital, a medical research organization, or a governmental unit.
- **Publicly supported charity.** A *publicly supported charity* is a charitable organization that is principally financially supported by the public. Generally, this support must be at least one-third of total support (see below), with the amount of support measured over the organization's most recent four-year period (see below). There are basically two types of publicly supported charities: the donative publicly supported charity and the service provider publicly supported charity.
- **Donative publicly supported charity.** A charitable organization qualifies as a *donative* publicly supported charity if it normally receives a substantial part of its support (other than exempt function revenue) from a governmental unit or from direct or indirect contributions or grants from the general public.

- **Service provider publicly supported charity.** A charitable organization qualifies as a *service provider* publicly supported charity if (1) it normally receives more than one-third of its support from any combination of (a) contributions, grants, or membership fees, and/or (b) gross receipts from admissions, sales of merchandise, performance of services, or furnishing of facilities in activities related to its exempt purposes, as long as the support is from permitted sources, and if (2) it does not receive more than one-third of its support from gross investment income.

- **Exempt function revenue.** *Exempt function revenue* is what is referred to on the annual information return as *program service revenue;*[12] it is revenue (income) generated by a tax-exempt organization from the conduct of one or more related businesses (such as the performance of services and/or the sales of merchandise). Some or all of this type of revenue can count as public support for service provider publicly supported charities but is omitted from the support fraction in the case of donative publicly supported charities.

- **Normally.** Generally, an organization is considered as *normally* receiving its support, for its current year and immediately succeeding year, on the basis of its support over the four years immediately preceding its current year.

- **Permitted sources.** In the case of service provider publicly supported charities, *permitted sources* are public institutions (see above), donative publicly supported charitable organizations (see above), and persons other than disqualified persons (see below) with respect to the organization.

- **Disqualified persons.** A *disqualified person* is a person (such as an individual, corporation, partnership, trust, or estate) that has a particular, usually intimate, relationship with respect to a private foundation. These persons include trustees, directors, officers, key employees, substantial contributors, and members of their families.[13]

- **Support.** The term *support* means the two types of public support (see above), along with net income from unrelated business activities, gross investment income, tax revenues levied for the benefit of the organization and either paid to or expended on behalf of it, and the value of services or facilities (exclusive of services or facilities generally furnished to the public without charge) furnished by a governmental unit to the organization without charge. These are amounts that collectively comprise the denominator of the support fraction.

- **Support fraction.** Organizations that strive to be publicly supported charities must, on an ongoing basis, construct a support fraction so as to determine the percentage of their total support that is public support. As noted (see above), generally public support must be at least one-third of total support.

- **Supporting organization.** A supporting organization is a charitable organization that is sufficiently related to one or more qualified supported organizations. Usually, a supported organization is a public institution or a publicly supported charitable organization (see above). When the organization meets the service organization publicly supported entity support test (see above), a tax-exempt social welfare organization, labor organization, or business league can be a supported organization.

- **Advance ruling.** When a charitable organization seeks recognition of tax-exempt status from the IRS,[14] it simultaneously obtains (if it can) classification by the agency as a public charity. If the entity is new and if it is attempting to qualify as a publicly supported charity (see above), it must first show that, during the first five years of its existence, it meets one of the two public support tests. This, then, is a probationary period. The ruling issued by the IRS in this connection is an *advance ruling*.

- **Advance ruling period.** The probationary period referred to in the preceding definition is termed the *advance ruling period*.

- **Definitive ruling.** A charitable organization may receive a ruling from the IRS as to its public charity status, where that ruling is not dependent on passage of the advance ruling period; that ruling is known as a *definitive ruling*. A definitive ruling is issued to a charitable entity that is an institution, a supporting organization, or a publicly supported organization that has successfully completed its advance ruling period (see above).

## QUALIFYING FOR AND MAINTAINING PUBLIC CHARITY STATUS

As noted, nearly all tax-exempt charitable organizations in the United States are public charities. To reiterate, a *public charity* is an institution, a publicly supported charity, or a supporting organization.

### Institutions

Many public charities are *institutions*.[15] It is not likely that there will be much confusion as to whether an organization qualifies under one of these categories. Similarly, practitioners are not likely to frequently have the opportunity to create one of these institutions.

### Calculating Public Support

Mistakes are frequently made when calculating the public support ratios of donative publicly supported charities and service provider publicly supported charities. Sometimes these errors occur because of mathematical errors, but more often they take place because the individuals making the computations do not fully understand the rules. In some instances, these errors are of little consequence inasmuch as the public support percentage of the organization is so large. But, in close-call situations, knowledge of all of the problem areas and opportunities for securing relief can make the difference between ongoing status as a publicly supported charity and the conclusion that the organization must be a private foundation.

Suppose an organization has an advance ruling that it can reasonably be expected to qualify as a donative publicly supported charity[16] and its advance ruling period has just ended. The organization's accountants have concluded that the organization's public support is 25 percent of total support, so that the organization apparently has failed to garner the requisite minimum one-third public support and thus must be considered a private foundation. A lawyer has been asked to review the underlying facts and the calculations. Following is a checklist of what this lawyer should be double-checking:

1. The first step is to verify the accuracy of the numbers themselves. For example, did Donor A actually contribute $25,000, or was it $2,500? Likewise, was the grant from Private Foundation B really $500,000, or was it $50,000?

2. Once the reviewer is satisfied that the numerical data is correct, the calculations should be redone. Is the addition of items of support correct? Was the 2 percent threshold number properly determined? Was the public support ratio properly computed?

> ### TIP 1
>
> A common mistake occurs in connection with contributions or grants that are in excess of the 2 percent threshold. The individual who calculated the support may have excluded the entire amount from consideration as public support. The fact is that the amount of the gift or grant up to the 2 percent threshold qualifies an element of public support.

> ### TIP 2
>
> These calculations must be made on the cash basis method of accounting, even if the organization's annual information return is prepared on the accrual basis.

3. Once the reviewer is satisfied that the numbers on the face of the schedule are correct or have been corrected, the next step is to examine the underlying facts. For example, the contributions of two individuals may have been combined on the assumption that there was a particular relationship between them; this should be verified. As an illustration, H and W were divorced (not married) at the time of the gift, or X (a donor) no longer owned a controlling interest in Y business (also a donor) at the time of X's gift. The reviewer should examine the facts to determine if a payment was truly a *gift;* perhaps it (or a portion of it) was actually a *loan* or *exempt function revenue,* so that it can be excluded from the calculation. Conversely, perhaps all or a portion of what was thought to be exempt function revenue can be considered a gift or grant, and included, in whole or in part, as public support.

4. Support from a *governmental unit*[17] is included in full as public support, if it is in the form of a grant. Thus, the reviewer should ascertain whether any grantor is a governmental unit.

5. Support from other donative publicly supported organizations is included in full in computing public support; like support from governmental units, this type of support is *indirect* public support.[18] Thus, the reviewer should check to determine if any grant support was derived from one or more of such organizations and whether it has been included in full as public support. Failure to include grants of this nature as public support in their entirety is a common mistake.

6. This step is one that is often overlooked; it is an extension of the previous step. Not only is support from another donative publicly supported charity counted in full as public support, so too is support from a charitable organization that may be classified as another type of public charity but is *described in* the rules pertaining to donative publicly supported charities.

7. The reviewer should check the definition of the term *support* as it applies in the particular case. Perhaps one or more items can be added (so as to enlarge the 2 percent threshold amount) or one or more items can be deleted (so as to increase the numerator amount).

8. The reviewer should determine whether a gift or grant can be excluded from the public support calculation as an unusual grant (see below).

9. If the advance ruling period ends and the organization cannot meet the public support test, it becomes a private foundation beginning the next year. If, however, the organization is beyond the advance ruling period and fails to meet the public support test, the organization has a second (or grace) year in which to remain in compliance with the public support requirements.

10. If all of the above avenues of reexamination fail, so that the entity is a private foundation for the year following the advance ruling period, the planner should consider reconstituting the organization as a public charity as soon as possible, so as to minimize the period of time the organization is a private foundation. For example, the organization could launch a fundraising campaign and seek another advance ruling that it qualifies as a publicly supported charity or it could become a supporting organization (see below).

If the organization involved is attempting to qualify as a service provider publicly supported charity, the following checklist should be used:

1. The first, second, third, fourth, seventh, eighth, ninth, and tenth elements in the checklist for donative publicly supported charities apply in the case of service provider publicly supported charities.

2. The reviewer should be certain that the determination of those who are considered to be disqualified persons with respect to the organization is correct. As examples, the reviewer should determine whether (1) an individual is properly characterized as a *foundation manager* (he or she may not have duties or responsibilities similar to that of an officer);[19] (2) the calculation of a 20 percent or more interest in business enterprises[20] is correct; (3) an individual is properly characterized as a *member of a family;*[21] (4) the calculations as to ownership in corporations

and the like[22] is correct; and (5) a person is properly being characterized as a substantial contributor.[23] This exercise is required to be certain that the maximum amount of support from *permitted sources* is ascertained. The matter of substantial contributor status is sufficiently important as to warrant greater focus (see below).

3. In this context, certain amounts of exempt function income can count as public support. Thus, the reviewer should check on any calculations relating to the $5,000 or 1 percent thresholds.

4. This type of publicly supported organization has a limitation as to allowable gross investment income. The reviewer should check on the accuracy of this calculation as well.

## CAUTION !

If a service provider publicly supported charity receives support from a supporting organization, some or all of the support may retain its character as investment income for this purpose.[24] The reviewer should be careful in characterizing and tracing this income.

## Substantial Contributor Status

A *substantial contributor* to a private foundation is a person who contributed or bequeathed an aggregate amount to the organization of more than the higher of $5,000 or 2 percent of the total contributions and bequests received by the organization before the close of its tax year in which the contribution or bequest is received by the organization from that person. In making this $5,000/2 percent computation, all contributions and bequests to the foundation since its inception are taken into account.

The principal elements concerning the definition of the term *substantial contributor* that the planner should consider are:

- To be a substantial contributor, the person must be a *contributor*. Therefore, it is imperative that the payments taken into account in this regard are *contributions*.[25]

- All contributions from a donor are aggregated for this purpose.

- Contributions from spouses are aggregated for this purpose.

- When contributions are of property, the gift items must be valued for this purpose. The value assigned to an item of property can, by itself, determine whether a contributor is a substantial contributor.[26]

- The calculation as to substantial contributor status is, as noted, made as of the close of the organization's tax year. Thus, a person can "temporarily" be classified as a substantial contributor at a point in time during the year, yet contributions and bequests made subsequent to the gifts of the contributor in question, but within the same tax year, may ultimately operate to keep that person out of substantial contributor status.

- Another tax-exempt organization can be a substantial contributor to a private foundation.

- The law does not permit exclusion of unusual grants (see below) in calculating aggregate contributions for purposes of identifying substantial contributors.

- With one exception,[27] once a person becomes a substantial contributor to a private foundation, he, she, or it can never escape that status—even though the person might not be so classified if the determination were first made at a later date.

## Unusual Grants

A charitable organization attempting to qualify as a publicly supported charity—either type—can exclude from its support fraction (both the numerator and the denominator) an amount equal to one or more qualifying unusual grants.

> **NOTE**
>
> This term is somewhat of a misnomer. First, the rules apply with respect to contributions as well as grants. Second, as reflected below, the adjective should be *unexpected*, rather than *unusual*.

The concept of this exclusion applies with respect to "substantial contributions or bequests from disinterested parties,"[28] as well as grants from disinterested parties. A payment is an *unusual grant* if it (1) was attracted by reason of the publicly supported nature of the organization, (2) was unusual or unexpected with respect to its amount, and (3) would, by reason of its size, adversely affect the status of the organization as a publicly supported charity.[29]

In determining whether a grant or contribution may be excluded as being unusual, all pertinent facts and circumstances are taken into consideration; a single factor is not necessarily determinative.[30]

Some of the factors the IRS will consider are:

- Whether the grant or contribution was made by a person (or related persons) who created the organization, previously contributed a substantial part of its support or endowment, or stood in a position of authority (such as a foundation manager) with respect to the organization. A grant or contribution made by a person other than the foregoing will ordinarily be given more favorable consideration than a grant made by one of the foregoing persons.

- Whether the contribution was a bequest or an inter vivos (lifetime) transfer. A bequest is ordinarily accorded more favorable consideration than an inter vivos transfer.

- Whether the grant or contribution was in the form of cash, readily marketable securities, or assets that further the exempt purposes of the organization (such as the gift of a work of art to a museum).

- Except in the case of a new organization, whether, prior to the receipt of the grant or contribution, the organization (1) has carried on a program of public solicitation and exempt activities, and (2) has been able to attract a significant amount of public support.

- Whether the organization may reasonably be expected to attract a significant amount of public support subsequent to the particular contribution or grant. Continued reliance on unusual grants to fund an organization's current operating expenses (rather than new endowment funds) may be evidence that the organization cannot reasonably be expected to attract future support from the general public.

- Whether, prior to the year in which the particular grant or contribution was received, the organization met the general public support requirement without the benefit of exclusion of unusual grants.

- Whether the grantor or contributor (or related persons) continues directly or indirectly to exercise control over the organization.

- Whether the organization has a representative governing body.

- Whether material restrictions or conditions[31] have been imposed by the grantor or contributor on the charity in connection with the grant or contribution.[32]

As to the penultimate factor, the phrase *representative governing body* means a governing body that is comprised of: (1) public officials, or individuals chosen by public officials acting in their capacity as such; (2) persons having special knowledge in the particular field or discipline in which the organization is operating; (3) community leaders, such as elected officials, members of the clergy, and educators; or (4) in the case of a membership organization, individuals elected pursuant to the organization's governing instrument or bylaws by a broadly based membership. This characteristic does not exist if the membership of the organization's governing body is comprised of individuals in a way that indicates it represents the personal or private interests of disqualified persons rather than the interests of the community or the general public.[33]

## Facts-and-Circumstances Test

The facts-and-circumstances test, summarized in the companion volume,[34] is often overlooked or misunderstood. The test is available only for use by the donative publicly supported charitable organization. If all of the steps in the above checklist have been followed and the public support ratio is below the requisite one-third level, consideration should be given to the use of this test, because the organization can become or remain a donative publicly supported charity even where its public support ratio is as low as 10 percent.

A charitable organization may acquire a ruling from the IRS as to whether it qualifies under the facts-and-circumstances test, or it may hold itself out as qualifying under the test on its annual information returns.

## FOCUS ON SUPPORTING ORGANIZATIONS

One way to constitute a public charity is to qualify as a supporting organization.[35] The supporting organization is the most versatile planning tool in the realm of public charities. Indeed, this vehicle is one of the most useful of the planning vehicles available in the law of tax-exempt organizations generally.

As the companion volume explains, there are several varieties of supporting organizations; likewise, there are many ways to utilize them. What follows is an analysis of the most significant of these opportunities. More than one of these techniques may be used in a particular situation.

Part of the flexibility of supporting organizations is that they can be established by the organizations that are supported or by donors who want to use the supporting organization as a charitable donee.

The supported/supporting organization arrangement is another manifestation of the use of bifurcation in the tax-exempt organizations context.[36] The relationship, then, often looks like this:

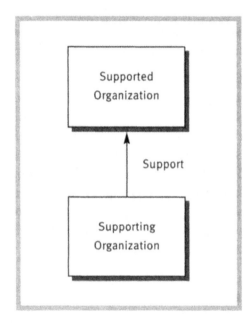

The planner should keep in mind that:

- There is no limitation in the law as to the number of organizations that can be supported by a supporting organization.
- There is no limitation in the law as to the number of supporting organizations a supported organization may have.

### Endowment Fund

It is common for a tax-exempt organization, particularly a charitable one, to have an endowment fund. Generally, an *endowment fund* is a collection of assets that are invested, with the resulting income used to generally support an organization or support one or more of its discrete programs. In many instances, the organization's policy (often reflected in a board resolution) is to use only the income for program; the principal (corpus) remains untouchable, usable only for investment purposes. Sometimes, a donor will make a gift restricted to an organization's endowment fund; when this occurs, once the donee accepts this type of gift, it is bound as a matter of contract to adhere to the restriction. Thus, there are two types of endowment funds: those that are *board directed* (in which case the restriction is not legally binding and can be changed) and *donor directed* (in which case the organization is legally obligated to follow the restriction, assuming it is legally permissible).

Many endowment funds are accounts within the tax-exempt organization. In other words, they are not separate legal entities. Sometimes, the assets and income are segregated by internal accounting record-keeping; in other instances, the fund is housed in a separate bank account.

The leadership of a tax-exempt organization, and/or those who represent it, may have two concerns. One, there may be some on the board of trustees who, either seeing dire economic times or wanting to expand program activity, wish to liquidate and spend some (or all) of the principal of the organization's endowment fund (assuming no donor restrictions). Two, there may be worry that the endowment fund can be reached by creditors in the event the supported organization is having economic difficulties. A solution to either or both of these concerns is to place the endowment fund in a separate organization, preferably a corporation.[37] The supporting organization is the ideal vehicle in this regard.

Maintenance of an endowment fund for a qualified tax-exempt organization is a suitable function for a supporting organization. Not only are the assets and income clearly segregated and held in a separate entity, but also it makes it more difficult for the parent organization to gain access to the assets. While it is true in most instances that the supported organization controls the supporting organization, and thus can gain access to the resources in the supporting entity, the interposition of the separate layer at a minimum makes that process more difficult. Whether assets in a separate, controlled organization can be protected from creditors is largely a matter of state law. Again, however, the process can be slowed; creditors would have to proceed separately against the supporting organization.

Some related points to consider are:

- The supported organization must reflect the existence of the supporting organization on its annual information return, as a related organization.[38] Likewise, the supporting organization must reflect the existence of the supported organization on its annual information return.

- The assets and income of the supporting organization are not reflected on the annual information return of the supported organization. If there are audited financial statements, however, the resources of both entities will almost always be shown on consolidated returns (inasmuch as the entities are regarded, pursuant to accounting principles, as related parties).

- If the supported organization is not a charitable one, the endowment fund can only be used to support and benefit programs that are charitable, educational, and the like.

- Where the supported organization is a donative publicly supported charitable organization, the grant support from the endowment fund in the supporting organization is subject to the 2 percent limitation in calculating the public support of the supported organization, unless the supporting organization is described in the rules defining the donative publicly supported charity.

- Where the supporting organization is a service provider publicly supported charitable organization, the grant support from the endowment fund in the supporting organization may be treated as a grant from a substantial contributor for purposes of calculating the public support of the supported organization.

- Where the supporting organization is a service provider publicly supported charitable organization, the grant support from the endowment fund in the supporting organization will retain its character for purposes of calculating the investment income of the supported organization.

- A supporting organization may not support or benefit another supporting organization.

## Fundraising

Many charitable organizations engage in fundraising. Often, this fundraising is undertaken directly by the organizations themselves. Some organizations, however, prefer to place the fundraising function in a separate organization. This, too, is an ideal use of a supporting organization.

There is rarely a federal income tax reason for this type of bifurcation, in that contributions to both organizations are deductible as charitable gifts.[39] Rather, this is done more for organizational and management reasons. Some organizations prefer to place the fundraising function in a separate organization so that the sole focus of that organization is on the generation of contributions and grants. That is, the fundraising program of the organization is not intermixed with the other governance aspects of the entity. This approach enables the use of a separate board of directors (albeit almost always controlled by the supported organization), the function and focus of which is on fundraising. (In many instances, members of the board of the supported organization are delighted at being relieved of the fundraising burden.) Thus, many universities, colleges, schools, healthcare institutions, churches, associations, and other tax-exempt organizations engage in fundraising through related organizations, often termed *foundations*. These entities are not (or certainly should not be) private foundations; they are public charities and in many instances are (or should be) supporting organizations.

The points made above in connection with the placement of endowment funds in supporting organizations are also applicable in this context.

## Programs

Just as the fundraising functions can be placed in a supporting organization, so too can one or more programs of a tax-exempt organization. These are either programs that are being conducted by an exempt organization and transferred to the supporting organization and/or programs that are commenced in the supporting organization. (These programs must, of course, be charitable, educational, or the like, and be operated for the benefit of a qualified supported organization.)

Where the supported organization also is a charitable organization, there rarely is a federal income tax reason for this form of bifurcation. Rather, it is done for structural or management reasons. An illustration of this type of bifurcation is the use, by a tax-exempt hospital, of a supporting organization to purchase a motel and convert it into a temporary residential facility for patients facing major surgery, and their family members and friends.[40]

This is illustrative of the point that a supporting organization can support and benefit a supported organization in ways other than the transfer of funds. That is, the support and benefit provided by a supporting organization can be the operation of one or more programs (related businesses). A supporting organization may conduct unrelated business[41] for the support of a supported organization.

Matters become even more dramatic where the supported organization is a qualified tax-exempt organization other than a charitable one.[42] Here, the supported organization can transfer one or more programs that inherently qualify as charitable, educational, scientific, or the like to the supporting organization. Programs of this nature include seminars, speakers' series, publications (such as books and papers), research, maintenance of a library, scholarships, fellowships, and awards. The great virtue of this approach is that these programs can be funded with gifts and grants, rather than with the conventional revenues of the parent organization. This model is as follows:

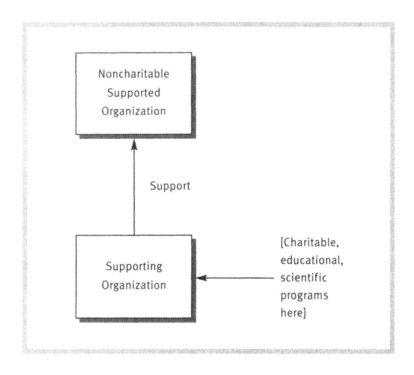

By contrast, the noncharitable organization can maintain or grow programs within it, with the supporting organization making restricted grants in support of those programs. This approach is depicted as follows:

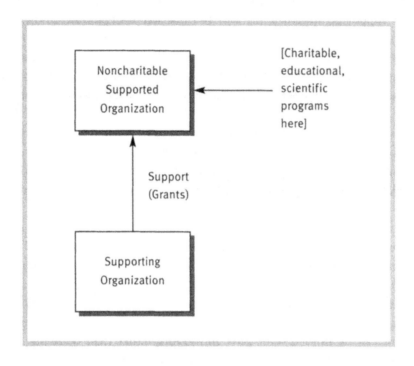

A supporting organization can be utilized for both program and fundraising purposes. As an illustration, the IRS glowingly approved of a structure where a tax-exempt medical research organization established a supporting organization to manage the intellectual property developed by the research organization (including transfer of the technology for commercialization) and to engage in fundraising for the benefit of the supported organization.[43]

## Property

A qualified supported organization can use a supporting organization to hold title to property. This approach is much like the use of a supporting organization to hold an endowment fund (see above). That is, this use of a supporting organization is usually undertaken for management reasons, where the leadership of the parent organization determines that the property would be better placed in the supporting organization. For example, the property may carry with it a potential for legal liability, and it is determined that the property should be held in a separate corporation.

An alternative to this approach is a title-holding company[44] or a single-member limited liability company.[45] Generally, a supporting organization provides more flexibility than the other two approaches, particularly the title-holding company. Also, gifts and grants are far more likely to flow to a supporting organization than to the other organizations. Conversely, one of the disadvantages of a supporting organization is that its tax-exempt status must be secured by filing an application for recognition of tax exemption with the IRS.

## Large Contributions

An organization that is publicly supported may find itself in a position where it is presented with a large gift of money or property, such that the acceptance of it would cause the organization to lose or at least jeopardize its publicly supported charity status. If other planning techniques are not available—such as the use of the unusual grant rules (see above) or the facts-and-circumstances test (see above)—consideration should be given to the use of a supporting organization.

With this approach, the property is contributed to the supporting organization. If the transfer is by contribution, the donor would receive the same tax deduction as if the property had been contributed to the supported organization. If the transfer is by grant, the considerations to the grantor should be the same as if the property had been contributed to the supported organization. If the gift or grant is one of property, the property may be sold by the supporting organization. The money in the supporting organization can thereafter be granted to the supported organization in increments, so as not to disturb its publicly supported charity status, or the money can be distributed to one or more third parties in conformance with the supporting organization rules.

## Advance Ruling Period

A charitable organization that was regarded by the IRS as a publicly supported charity on an advance ruling basis (see above) may find, as the months of that period unfold, that it will not be able to meet either public support test by the close of the period. If nothing is done, the organization will lapse into private foundation status.[46]

One way to prevent loss of the organization's public charity status is to convert it to a supporting organization *before* expiration of the advance ruling period. This is accomplished by affiliating the organization with one or more qualified supported organizations.

### CAUTION!

If the conversion is accomplished *after* expiration of the advance ruling period, the organization will be a private foundation for the year or years of the gap. Even if the conversion took place one day after the close of the advance ruling period, the organization would be a private foundation for the entity's ensuing year.

## Other Conversions

A publicly supported charity may be converted to a supporting organization at any time. For example, a charitable organization that has been in existence for 50 years, and has maintained publicly supported status, can convert to a supporting organization. This can be done because public support is waning or because the organization no longer wishes to keep the records and make the ongoing calculations of public support.

This seems to happen quite often with "foundations" that are related to trade and business associations. It may become more difficult, as the years go by, to continue to satisfy the public support requirements. This can be remedied by converting the organization to a supporting organization with respect to the association. (Indeed, the appropriate planning approach usually is to make the organization a supporting organization in the first instance.)

## NOTE

The process for achieving these conversions is relatively simple. There is no need to file another application for recognition of exemption. First, the organization should amend its articles of organization[47] to satisfy the organizational test that is mandated of supporting organizations.[48] Second, the Schedule D that accompanies the application should be prepared and sent to the IRS with a cover letter, explaining that the organization desires to be reclassified as a supporting organization. If this documentation is properly prepared, a favorable determination by the IRS should be forthcoming in a few months.

## Private Foundation Conversions

If a private foundation desires to convert to a public charity, the most likely candidate for its public charity status will be a supporting organization (see below). Indeed, in some instances, a private foundation is functioning as a supporting organization. Again, amendment of the articles of organization and preparation and filing of the above schedule is all that is required to cause the conversion.

## Joint Ventures

Two or more tax-exempt organizations may decide to engage in a joint venture.[49] This does not always necessitate use of a separate organization. When a new entity is needed, however, the supporting organization can be the ideal vehicle, particularly if gifts and grants are desired for the joint venture entity. (An alternative, which does not require the filing of an application for recognition of exemption, is use of a multimember limited liability company.)

## Holding Companies

Much like use of a supporting organization as a joint venture vehicle, a supporting organization may be used to coordinate the operations of one or more other tax-exempt organizations. Utilization of a supporting organization in this manner often causes the entity to be given the ungainly (and decidedly noncharitable) name of *holding company*. This approach has become quite common, for example, in the healthcare field.

With this model, the supporting organization can be the coordinating mechanism with respect to any number of charitable (and perhaps some noncharitable) organizations. On an organization chart, the entity may be at the top, with lines of authority running up to it from the organizations below. Or the supporting organization can be pictured as in the center of a cluster of eligible entities.

Often, in this case, the supporting organization is seen as just the opposite of a supporting organization, in that all of the support is flowing *to* it. Nonetheless, over the years, the IRS has come to accept this type of supporting organization.

## Donor-Created Supporting Organizations

The foregoing examples of the use of supporting organizations have one element in common: the supporting organization was created (by establishing a new entity or by conversion) by one or more tax-exempt organizations. A supporting organization may, however, be created by one or more donors.

As noted, a supporting organization functions much like a private foundation. It can be seen as a foundation dedicated to one or more eligible supported organizations. Therefore, when an individual (or a married couple, family, other group of individuals, or a corporation) is contemplating establishment of a private foundation, the prospective donor should give some consideration to creation of a supporting organization instead.

The advantages to this approach are that the organization does not have to comply with the private foundation rules (including payment of the tax on net investment income), the organization does not have to prepare and file the more complex annual information returns required of private foundations (Form 990-PF), and the donor is likely to receive a larger and/or otherwise more preferable charitable contribution deduction.

The chief disadvantage to this approach is that those who would otherwise be the managers of the private foundation must give up formal legal control to those who manage the supported organization or organizations involved. (Disqualified persons cannot control a supporting organization.) This is the principal reason for selection of the private foundation option over the supporting organization option.

## TERMINATIONS

A private foundation may decide to terminate its private foundation status. There are several ways to accomplish this—all known as *voluntary terminations*.[50] Until recently, private letter rulings were sought from the IRS; they have been issued by the agency over the years by the dozens.

The IRS issued guidance in 2002 and 2003, in part to discourage the filing of what are now unnecessary ruling requests. The first of these rulings pertains to transfers of assets among related private foundations.[51] The second of these rulings concerns transfers by private foundations to public charities.[52] The planner is likely to find that the second of these rulings[53] is of greater applicability.

The second of these rulings takes into account the four basic fact situations in which this type of transfer may occur.

## Assumptions

The four situations discussed in the ruling are predicated on the following assumptions:

- The private foundation has not committed either willful repeated acts (or failures to act) or a willful and flagrant act (or failure to act) giving rise to tax liability under the private foundation rules.
- The foundation is not a private operating foundation.
- The transferee organization or organizations are not controlled, directly or indirectly, by the foundation or by one or more disqualified persons with respect to it.
- The foundation has not previously terminated (or had terminated) its private foundation status.
- The transferee organization(s) is a public charity that retains its public charity classification for at least three years following the date of the distribution.
- The foundation does not impose any material restrictions on the transferred assets.
- The foundation retains sufficient income or assets to pay any private foundation taxes, such as the tax on investment income for the portion of the tax year prior to the distribution, and pays these taxes when due.

## Other Facts

As noted, the ruling addresses the four types of situations in which this type of transfer may occur.

**Situation 1.**    A private foundation (PF) distributes, pursuant to a plan of dissolution, all of its net assets to a public charity (PC). PC is a public charity by reason of classification as an institution or a donative publicly supported organization. PC has been in existence and a public charity for a continuous period of at least 60 calendar months immediately preceding the distribution. After PF completes the transfer, it files articles of dissolution with the appropriate state authority.

**Situation 2.**    The facts are the same as in the first situation, except that PC has been in existence for fewer than 60 calendar months immediately preceding the distribution. Moreover, it was not formed as a result of a consolidation of other public charities of the same classification that would have been in existence for a continuous period of 60 calendar months prior to the distribution had they continued in existence.

**Situation 3.**    The facts are the same as in the first situation, except that PC is a public charity by reason of classification as a service provider publicly supported charitable organization.

**Situation 4.**    The facts are the same as in the first situation, except that PC is a public charity by reason of classification as a supporting organization.

## Summary of This Law

The private foundation status of an organization, as to which there have not been either willful repeated acts (or failures to act) or a willful and flagrant act (or failure to act) giving rise to a liability for a private foundation tax, shall be terminated if the foundation distributes all of its net assets to one or more public charities (institutions or donative publicly supported charities), each of which has been in existence and so classified for a continuous period of at least 60 calendar months immediately preceding the distribution.

The law imposes a tax on each organization the private foundation status of which is voluntarily or involuntarily terminated. This tax is the lower of the aggregate tax benefits resulting from tax-exempt status or the value of the net assets of the foundation. (The tax can, in other words, amount to a confiscation of the net income and assets of the foundation.)

In order to voluntarily terminate private foundation status, an organization must submit a statement to the IRS of its intent to terminate foundation status. This statement must set forth in detail the computation and amount of the termination tax. Unless abatement is requested, full payment of the tax must be made at the time the statement is filed. An organization may request abatement of all of the tax, or pay a portion of the tax and seek abatement of the balance. If abatement is requested and denied, the organization must pay the tax in full on notification by the IRS that the tax will not be abated.

A transfer of all of the assets of a private foundation does not result in a termination of the transferor foundation unless the entity voluntarily terminates or there is an involuntary termination.

A private foundation may, as noted, terminate its private foundation status by distributing all of its net assets to one or more public charities, each of which has been in existence and so described for a continuous period of at least 60 calendar months immediately preceding the distribution. These public charities, however, must be institutions or donative publicly supported charities. The general rules do not apply to this type of termination, which can be thought of as the *favored termination;* thus, notification to the IRS is not required. A private foundation that engages in a favored termination does not incur the tax; therefore, there is no need for any abatement.

An organization that terminates in the favored manner remains subject to the private foundation rules until it distributes all of its net assets to qualified distributee organizations. A foundation meets the requirement that it distribute all of its net assets only if it transfers all of its right, title, and interest in and to its net assets to one or more qualified distributee organizations. To accomplish this, the foundation may not impose any material restriction or condition that prevents the transferee organization from freely and effectively employing the transferred assets, or the income derived from them, in furtherance of its exempt purposes.

If a private foundation transfers all or part of its assets to one or more public charities and, within a period of three years from the date of the transfers, one or more of the transferee organizations loses their public charity status (thus becoming a private foundation), the transfer will be treated as one involving a transfer to one or more other private foundations.

The value of net assets for these purposes is determined at whichever time the value is higher: the first day action is taken by the organization that culminates in its ceasing to be a private foundation or the date it ceases to be a private foundation.

## Analysis

In Situation 1, the distribution was made in accordance with the rules concerning favored terminations. This means that PF's status as a private foundation is terminated at the time of the distribution to PC. PF is not subject to the termination tax. PF is not required to give notice to the IRS to terminate its foundation status.

The distributions in Situations 2, 3, and 4 were not made in accordance with the favored termination rules. Thus, the status of PF as a private foundation is not terminated until it gives notice to the IRS. If PF does provide the notice (and thus terminates), it becomes subject to the termination tax. If, however, PF does not have any net assets on the day it provides the notice (such as because it gives the notice the day after it distributed all of its net assets), the tax is zero.

In all four situations, the distributions do not constitute an investment by PF for purposes of the investment income tax. (This and the other private foundation rules are discussed below.) Therefore, the distributions do not give rise to net investment income.

In these four situations, the distributions are to tax-exempt charitable organizations, which are not disqualified persons. Thus, the self-dealing rules are not implicated. In these instances, the payments are made in accomplishment of charitable purposes and are not to organizations controlled by PF. Thus, the transfers are qualifying distributions. These distributions do not cause PF to have excess business holdings, nor are they jeopardizing investments. Further, the distributions are to public charities and thus are not taxable expenditures (and, therefore, expenditure responsibility is not required).

## PRIVATE FOUNDATION RULES

The *private foundation rules*[54] stand as most of the reasons, in law, why private foundation status is disadvantageous to a charitable organization. These rules are summarized in the companion volume.[55] No other category of tax-exempt organization is subject to the degree of regulation and constriction as to operations as are private foundations.

The basic rules are:

- Prohibitions[56] on self-dealing between a private foundation and disqualified persons with respect to it (see above)
- Minimum distribution requirements
- Limitations on holdings in business enterprises (excess business holdings rules)
- Restrictions as to speculative investments (jeopardizing investments rules)
- Limitations as to lobbying activities (taxable expenditures)
- Limitations as to political campaign activities (taxable expenditures)
- Rules pertaining to grants to noncharitable organizations (taxable expenditures)
- Rules pertaining to grants to individuals (taxable expenditures)
- Rules pertaining to noncharitable expenditures (taxable expenditures)
- Tax on net investment income
- Taxes in the case of willful violations of these rules (involuntary terminations)

Thus, among the various reasons why it is disadvantageous to be a private foundation are the foregoing elements. Which will be of greatest concern in a particular case will depend on the facts and circumstances of each situation. For some, the self-dealing rules will be the largest problem, while for others concern with the payout rules, the excess business holdings rules, or the various elements of the taxable expenditures rules will predominate. Some organizations will be distressed about the tax on net investment income. Also, the annual information return that must be filed by private foundations[57] is more complex than the return filed by other types of tax-exempt organizations.

Still other aspects of the law that are unfavorable to private foundations are found in the charitable giving rules.

## CHARITABLE GIVING RULES

One of the features of the federal tax law directly relevant to charitable organizations is the charitable contribution deduction. While outside the scope of the companion volume,[58] these rules[59] are certainly relevant when private foundation status is being considered or faced.

One of the factors governing the deductibility of gifts is whether the charitable donee is a public charity or a private foundation. This distinction is manifested in several ways, including the percentage limitations that govern the extent of the deductibility of gifts by individuals.[60] These limitations are more restrictive with respect to gifts to private foundations than is the case with gifts to public charities. Here is the basic distinction:

- A deductible contribution of money to a private foundation by an individual who itemizes deductions is limited in any year to an amount equal to 30 percent of the donor's adjusted gross income. By contrast, the percentage is 50 percent in the case of these gifts to public charities and private operating foundations.

- A deductible contribution of property to a private foundation by an individual who itemizes deductions is limited in any year to an amount equal to 20 percent of the donor's adjusted gross income. By contrast, the percentage is 30 percent in the case of these gifts to public charities and private operating foundations.[61]

Another aspect of this public charity/private foundation dichotomy pertains to the calculation of the charitable deduction in the case of contributions of property, particularly where the property has appreciated in value. As a general rule, the charitable deduction can be based on the full fair market value of the property (enabling the donor to avoid recognition of the capital gain element inherent in the property, if any) only where the charitable donee is a public charity or private operating foundation.[62] In the case of a gift to a private foundation, however, there is a deduction reduction rule: When a charitable gift of capital gain property is made to a private foundation, the amount of the charitable deduction that would otherwise be determined must be reduced by the amount of gain that would have been long-term capital gain if the property contributed had been sold by the donor at its fair market value, determined at the time of the contribution. In other words, property gifts to private foundations generally result in a charitable deduction confined to the donor's basis in the property—which can be a considerable disincentive for giving in the case of highly appreciated property.[63]

There is, however, a significant exception to this rule concerning gifts of property to private foundations that planners readily embrace. This rule pertains to *qualified appreciated stock*. Thus, where this exception is available, the charitable deduction for a contribution of stock to a private foundation is based on the fair market value of the stock at the time of the gift. (This, then, is the same rule that applies in situations involving contributions to public charities.)

The term *qualified appreciated stock* basically is stock that is capital gain property and for which (as of the date of the contribution) market quotations are readily available on an established securities market.[64]

The planner involved in the establishment of a private foundation—if that is what the charitable organization must be—will undoubtedly find that this exception for qualified appreciated securities is indispensable.

## DONOR-ADVISED FUNDS

The planner considering establishment of a private foundation or a supporting organization should give some consideration to an alternative: use of the donor-advised fund. Although this option will be of service in only a few circumstances, the planner's client should know that this choice is available.

A donor-advised fund, unlike a supporting organization or a private foundation, is not a separate legal entity. Rather, it is a fund—a component of or an account within—a public charity, such as a community foundation or other publicly supported charity, including a charitable gift fund affiliated with an investment firm. This type of fund is established by a contribution to the charitable organization, where the gift involved is placed in a fund, which is named after the donor (or donor's family or comparable name). The donor (or donor's designee) is provided the opportunity to make subsequent recommendations as to use of the resources of the fund, such as grants to other charitable organizations.[65]

Consequently, the donor-advised fund is a legitimate alternative to the standard grant-making private foundation. With a foundation, the donor retains control over the gift amount(s) and other resources (including investment income); with the donor-advised fund, the recipient charitable donee controls the gifts and their subsequent uses. Otherwise, the similarities are notable: the recipient of the grant receives a check from the fund that looks like it is from a private foundation.

The advantages of the use of a donor-advised fund are:

- There is no need to establish a separate organization.
- There is no need for a board of directors or officers.
- There is no need to seek recognition of tax-exempt status (the host charity has done that).
- There is no need to worry about maintaining publicly supported charity status (the host charity does that).

- There is no need to file annual information returns (the host charity does that).
- The donor(s) have what appears to be a foundation and thus can be a philanthropist from that perspective.

The disadvantages of the use of a donor-advised fund are:

- The host charity controls the funds.
- Donor-advised funds usually cannot be used to make grants to individuals.
- There is no opportunity for creation of employment for the donor and/or family members.
- The IRS is not particularly fond of donor-advised fund programs.

Nonetheless, just as an individual or company should consider a supporting organization as an alternative to a private foundation, so too should contemplation be given (however briefly) to the use of a donor-advised fund.

## NOTES

1. *Tax-Exempt Organizations,* § 11.3; also *Private Foundations,* chap. 15.
2. *Tax-Exempt Organizations,* § 11.2; *Private Foundations,* chap. 4.
3. *Tax-Exempt Organizations,* § 11.1; *Private Foundations,* chap. 3.
4. *Tax-Exempt Organizations,* § 11.4; *Private Foundations,* chaps. 5–10.
5. Id., § 11.5. Also, in general, Bruce R. Hopkins and Jody Blazek, *The Legal Answer Book for Private Foundations* (Hoboken, NJ: John Wiley & Sons, 2002).
6. IRC § 508(b).
7. IRC § 509(a).
8. Id.
9. See pages 102–103 below. As noted (Chapter 3), however, the private foundation self-dealing rules are the basis for the intermediate sanctions rules that are applicable to public charities.
10. See pages 103–104 below.
11. That is, an organization that is tax-exempt by reason of IRC § 501(a) because it is described in IRC § 501(c)(3).
12. See Chapter 9, pages 191, 196–197.
13. See Chapter 3, pages 71–72.
14. See Chapter 2, pages 41–42.
15. *Tax-Exempt Organizations,* § 11.3(a); *Private Foundations,* § 15.3.
16. *Tax-Exempt Organizations,* § 11.3(b)(i).
17. Id., §§ 6.10, 18.17.
18. See Chapter 9, page 196.
19. *Tax-Exempt Organizations,* § 11.2(b); *Private Foundations,* § 4.2.
20. *Tax-Exempt Organizations,* § 11.2(c); *Private Foundations,* § 4.3.
21. *Tax-Exempt Organizations,* § 11.2(d); *Private Foundations,* § 4.4.
22. *Tax-Exempt Organizations,* § 11.2(e)–(g); *Private Foundations,* §§ 4.5, 4.6.
23. *Tax-Exempt Organizations,* § 11.2(a); *Private Foundations,* § 4.1.
24. *Private Foundations,* § 15.5.
25. For an analysis of the concept of a contribution, see *Charitable Giving,* § 3.1.

26. See the discussion of Graham v. Comm'r in Chapter 11, pages 311–314.

27. IRC § 507(d)(2)(C). See *Private Foundations,* § 4.1, text accompanied by nn. 15–17.

28. Reg. §§ 1.170A-9(e)(6)(ii), 1.509(a)-3(c)(3).

29. Id.

30. Reg. §§ 1.170A-9(e)(6)(iii), 1.509(a)-3(c)(4).

31. These are enumerated in Reg. § 1.507-2(a)(8). See *Private Foundations,* § 15.5(c).

32. Reg. § 1.509(a)-3(c)(4).

33. Reg. § 1.509(a)-3(d)(3)(i).

34. *Tax-Exempt Organizations,* § 11.3(ii). Also *Private Foundations,* § 15.4(c).

35. *Tax-Exempt Organizations,* § 11.3(c); *Private Foundations,* § 15.7.

36. See Chapter 6, pages 134–136.

37. See Chapter 1, pages 4–8.

38. See Chapter 9, page 202.

39. There can be some subtleties in this regard; for example, only public charities described in IRC § 170(b)(1)(A)(i) to (vi) can maintain pooled income funds (IRC § 642(c)(5)(A)). See *Charitable Giving,* § 13.2(a).

40. Tech. Adv. Mem. 9847002.

41. See Chapter 8.

42. That is, an organization described in IRC § 501(c)(4), (5), or (6).

43. Priv. Ltr. Rul. 200326035.

44. *Tax-Exempt Organizations,* § 18.2.

45. See Chapter 7, pages 156–158.

46. This is because of the presumption that all charitable organizations are private foundations (see text accompanied by note 6 above).

47. See Chapter 1, pages 4–5.

48. See *Private Foundations,* § 15.7(a).

49. See Chapter 7.

50. *Private Foundations,* § 13.1.

51. Id., § 13.5.

52. Id., § 13.4.

53. Rev. Rul. 2003-13, 2003-4 I.R.B. 305.

54. IRC Subchapter 42 (§§ 4940–4948).

55. *Tax-Exempt Organizations,* § 11.4; *Private Foundations,* chaps. 5–10.

56. See Chapter 3, note 106.

57. See *Private Foundations,* chap. 12.

58. *Tax-Exempt Organizations,* § 2.5.

59. In general, see *Charitable Contributions.*

60. Id., chap. 7.

61. *Private Foundations,* § 14.3.

62. *Charitable Contributions,* § 4.2.

63. *Private Foundations,* § 14.4(a).

64. Id., § 14.4(b).

65. *Tax-Exempt Organizations,* § 11.6; *Private Foundations,* chap. 16.

# CHAPTER 5

# Advocacy Activities

A singular component of the law of tax-exempt organizations focuses on advocacy efforts by these organizations, consisting primarily of attempts to influence legislation and involvement in political campaigns for public office. There are, of course, other forms of advocacy, such as demonstrations, boycotts, and litigation. Some educational undertakings can amount to advocacy activities.

A considerable portion of this area of the law is devoted to placement of limitations on advocacy efforts by tax-exempt charitable organizations. Other exempt organizations, however, are caught up in these rules, such as social welfare entities and business leagues.

## CONCEPT OF ADVOCACY

The term *advocacy* generally refers to the action of recommending, arguing for (pleading), supporting, and/or defending a cause. Individuals and organizations can engage in advocacy in many ways, using many forms of communication. As to the latter, the forms include publishing, correspondence, personal visits, tapes, facsimiles, telephone calls, radio, television, and the Internet.

The federal tax law concerning advocacy is, as noted, largely devoted to two aspects of the practice: attempts to influence legislation (lobbying) and participation in political campaign activities (electioneering).

## ATTEMPTS TO INFLUENCE LEGISLATION[1]

A tax-exempt organization often is required to ascertain whether it is engaging (or planning to engage or has engaged) in an attempt to influence a *legislative* process. This is of particular concern to charitable organizations, which are constrained by the federal tax law as to the extent of permissible lobbying. No other type of exempt organization is limited by the federal tax law as to the amount of lobbying in which it can engage, although there are special rules for membership organizations. (There may be state law on the point.)

## Introduction

There is considerable law, at the federal level, as to the matter of attempting to influence legislation. The task of the planner may be to ascertain those bodies of law (one or more) that are applicable in a particular case. In the tax context, there are four bodies of applicable law: two sets of rules applicable to public charities, rules applicable to private foundations, and rules pertaining to membership associations. There are three other nontax bodies of law in this setting as well.[2] The planner may find it useful, perhaps necessary, to extrapolate from one of these bodies of law in interpreting another of them.

As a general rule, therefore, these rules do not apply to attempts to influence the executive branch or independent regulatory agencies of a government. Thus, this body of law is generally inapplicable to attempts to influence the development of regulations, rules, form instructions, and the like. Also, the rules generally do not apply to attempts to influence the judicial branch of a government. This type of advocacy usually constitutes the preparation and filing of amicus curiae briefs or other participation in litigation.

In some instances, of course, it is obvious that the organization is engaged in lobbying, as evidenced by the activities of one or more staff members (sometimes comprising a "government relations" department) or the use of an outside lobbyist. In other instances, the matter is not so clear, often with the organization of the view that its involvement with a legislative body (members of the body or their personal or committee staff) is an *educational* undertaking.

There is no question that a tax-exempt organization can meet with members of a legislative body or staff members without the interaction consisting of lobbying. Many exempt organizations make it a practice to maintain regular contact with these individuals, who function with respect to the areas of interest to the organization. The provision of general information, technical advice, and the like is not lobbying. Likewise, the monitoring of legislation is not lobbying.

The planner is likely to encounter situations where the tax-exempt organization involved is of the view that its activities with respect to an item of legislation are educational in nature, while the facts indicate or at least strongly intimate that the activity, or one or more components of it, amount to attempts to influence legislation. This will require the planner to make a judgment about the situation, with the most critical factors being the imminence of particular legislation, and the timing (in relation to the status of the legislation) and the purpose of the communication(s).

## Necessity of Legislation

Usually, attempts to influence legislation concern efforts to pass, defeat, and/or amend legislation that is working its way through a legislature. Thus, one of the critical factors the planner must evaluate in this context is whether an item of *legislation* is involved.[3]

Although these rules are found in the federal tax law, the applicability of them is not confined to actions by Congress. The term *legislation* also embraces actions by state legislatures, local councils, and other legislative bodies. Thus, the planner may have to ascertain whether a governmental body is a *legislative* or other type of entity, the latter usually an *administrative* body. Action by a legislative body is manifested in bills, resolutions, and the like.

Consideration of a treaty is action by a legislative body. Also, action by the general public in a referendum, initiative, constitutional amendment, or similar procedure is treated by the law as legislating—with the public constituting the legislative body.

One of the traps in this area for charitable organizations, and the planner, is that a charitable organization can be considered to be engaging in an attempt to influence legislation even though particular legislation is not involved. This is because, if the organization's primary objective can be attained only by legislative action, the organization is treated for federal tax purposes as if it is substantially involved in a legislative process.

This aspect of the law is nicely illustrated by a case involving a fund associated with a commission formed to study alternatives to the federal income tax system and to present its findings to Congress. The commission could have discussed various options to the federal income tax (such as a flat tax, a value-added tax, or a national sales tax) and offered the pros and cons of each choice to Congress; had it done so, its activities would have been considered educational and the commission and its related fund would have achieved tax-exempt status. This was not, however, the approach selected by the commission, which instead recommended only one alternative (a flat tax) and advocated adoption of it to Congress. The commission (and the fund) were considered to be substantially involved in an attempt to influence legislation and the fund was denied tax-exempt status by the IRS, with that action upheld in the courts.[4]

The planner should study these opinions to divine the distinction between activities that amount to *propaganda* (advocacy) and *education*. At the same time, however, the planner should ponder the meaning of a curious and oblique footnote that is part of the appellate court opinion, which the court characterized as being "quite narrow."[5]

- The court wrote that it was "not holding that any organization which studies an issue touching on legislation, reaches a conclusion with respect to that issue, and then argues the merits of that conclusion must necessarily be characterized" as an action organization (see below).

- The court also wrote: "We are simply holding that an organization which assumes a conclusion with respect to a highly public and controversial legislative issue and then goes into the business of selling that conclusion may properly be designated" an action organization.

These distinctions make little sense. Advocacy is advocacy, whether it is characterized as "arguing the merits" of a conclusion or being "in the business of selling" that conclusion. Also, it makes no difference as to whether the conclusion being advocated by a charitable organization was preceded by "study" or based on an "assumption." Further, it is irrelevant whether the legislative issue involved is "highly public and controversial"; the rules as to lobbying by charities do not differentiate between legislation that is eristic or mundane.

## Lobbying by Public Charities

Lobbying basically is of two types: direct and indirect. Although this dichotomy is applicable with respect to all types of tax-exempt organizations, it is expressly reflected in the law concerning public charities.

*Direct* lobbying includes meetings with legislators and their staff (personal and/or committee), presentation of testimony at public hearings, publication of documents, and communications by electronic means. The underlying concept is that this type of lobbying involves interaction directly with those who are responsible for framing legislation.

There is another fundamental way by which the development of legislation may be influenced, and that is by aiming the appeal at the general public. This is the *indirect* form of lobbying, often referred to as *grassroots* lobbying. Thus, grassroots lobbying consists of appeals to the general public or segments of the general public to contact legislators or take other specific action as regards legislative matters.

The planner may have to determine whether there is direct or indirect lobbying. Whether this distinction is required depends on which body of law is applicable. That is, the substantial part test and the private foundation rules do not differentiate between these two types of lobbying, while the expenditure test does.

For a public charity, the core issue is likely to be whether the lobbying is substantial (as discussed below), rather than whether any lobbying is taking place. If a substantial part of a charitable organization's activities is attempting to influence legislation, the organization is denominated an *action organization* and hence cannot qualify as a tax-exempt charitable entity.

Thus, the role of the planner in these regards includes monitoring these circumstances to determine (1) if the charitable organization is engaging in lobbying activities, and (2) if so, if the activities are approaching, or are exceeding, the limits as to substantiality. These determinations should be made at the outset of the organization's existence and periodically during the course of its existence:

- The application for recognition of exemption filed by entities seeking IRS recognition as tax-exempt charitable organizations pointedly poses this question: "Does or will the organization attempt to influence legislation?"[6] (The planner will note that the element of substantiality or insubstantiality is not built into the question.)

- The annual information return requires charitable organizations to report the extent of their lobbying activities[7] and the amount of tax (if any) imposed on the organization during the reporting year because of excessive lobbying activities.[8]

## Public Charities and Substantial Part Test

One of the criteria for qualification as a tax-exempt charitable organization is that "no substantial part of the activities" of the organization may constitute "carrying on propaganda, or otherwise attempting, to influence legislation."[9] This is known as the *substantial part test*.[10]

The planner will be among the hordes of others who have long ruminated over the meaning of the word *substantial* in this setting. The term is undefined. Usually, substantiality is measured in terms of time or money expended. The IRS and the courts, however, view this as a facts-and-circumstances inquiry, and are not to be held to a particular standard, formula, or percentage.[11] Indeed, this dilemma is compounded in the context of lobbying efforts by means of the Internet.[12]

Nonetheless, the task will likely fall to the planner to determine and advise the charitable organization as to whether its lobbying activities are substantial. Although it can only be used as a rule of thumb, the planner may consider, when expenditures of money or time are being regarded, outlays of less than 15 percent to be insubstantial and thus outlays in excess of that percentage to be substantial. If it appears that the amount of lobbying conducted by a charitable organization is or will be substantial, the planner should consider the use of another organization to conduct the lobbying activity.[13]

## Public Charities and Expenditure Test

The *expenditure test*[14] was created because of the vagaries of the substantial part test. This test, which must be elected by the charity,[15] employs a mechanical standard for measuring permissible and impermissible ranges of lobbying expenditures by organizations that are eligible to make the election, and does so in terms of the expenditure of funds and sliding scales of percentages.

The details of the expenditure test are provided in the companion volume.[16] This test, which generally permits lobbying expenditures up to 20 percent of total expenditures, is a "safe harbor" body of law. A charitable organization is subject to the substantial part test until the expenditure test is elected.

## Exceptions for Public Charities

There are no exceptions to the rules for charitable organizations that are subject to the substantial part test. A charitable organization that merely responds to an invitation from a legislative committee to testify and provides technical expertise is not considered to be engaged in unwarranted lobbying. An organization may engage in nonpartisan analysis, study, and research, and publish its results.[17] These are, however, charitable and educational undertakings and not really exceptions to the substantial part test.

By contrast, five categories of activities are excluded by statute from the term *influencing legislation* for purposes of the expenditure test. Three of these "exceptions" are not really exceptions and mirror the rules of the substantial part test: lobbying does not include (1) making available the results of nonpartisan analysis, study, or research; (2) providing technical advice or assistance to a governmental body or legislative committee in response to a written request by that body or committee; and (3) routine communications with government officials or employees.

There is an exception for communications between a charitable organization and its members with respect to legislation or proposed legislation of direct interest to it and them, unless the communications directly encourage the members to influence legislation or directly encourage the members to urge nonmembers to influence legislation.

The most interesting, and potentially effective, of these five exceptions, however, is the one that is informally known as the *self-defense exception*. This exception shelters appearances before or communications to any legislative body with respect to a possible decision of that body that might affect the existence of the organization, its powers and duties, its tax-exempt status, or the deduction of contributions to it. Thus, once the fact of an appearance or communication of this nature is established, the charitable organization may attempt to influence the legislation without limitation. The planner should be alert to the use of this exception.[18]

A sixth exception is in the tax regulations. This rule excuses examinations and discussions of broad social, economic, and similar problems from the ambit of direct lobbying communications and grassroots lobbying communications, even if the problems are of the type with which government would be ultimately expected to deal.[19]

## Expenditure Test Election

The planner is certain to be called on from time to time to advise as to whether a charitable organization should elect the expenditure test. This election is made by filing Form 5768 with the IRS.[20]

The first of two steps in this analysis is to determine whether the particular charitable organization involved is *eligible* to make this election. All public charities[21] are permitted to elect the expenditure test except:

- Churches
- Conventions or associations of churches
- Integrated auxiliaries of churches
- Supporting organizations to noncharitable tax-exempt organizations
- Private foundations

The second step for the planner is to consider the variables that swirl about the contemplation as to the making of the election.[22] The positive variables are:

- The principal virtue of the expenditure test is that it provides relative certainty as to determination of the amount of lobbying that is allowable for a charitable organization. Of course, this is because of the mechanical manner in which permissible lobbying is calculated.
- Another helpful feature of the expenditure test is that the calculation as to allowable lobbying is made using a four-year average. A charitable organization thus may engage in considerable lobbying in one year and refrain from much lobbying in surrounding years, and not transgress the rules. By contrast, lobbying is evaluated annually pursuant to the substantial part test.
- In most instances, the expenditure test allows a greater degree of lobbying than does the substantial part test. There are three reasons for this:
  - Presumably, a 20 percent lobbying expenditure, allowed by the expenditure test, is greater than what would be allowed under the substantial part test.

- ○ As noted, the four-year averaging mechanism can accommodate even greater amounts of lobbying in a year.
  - ○ As noted, the availability of certain exceptions can increase the amount of allowable lobbying.
- The time expended by volunteers for lobbying is disregarded for purposes of the expenditure test. This time is taken into account when applying the substantial part test.
- There are certain exceptions to these rules that may be availed of only by charitable organizations that have elected the expenditure test (see above).
- The IRS may enforce the substantial part test using one or more standards other than the volume of legislative activity measured in terms of expenditures, so that a charitable organization covered by the expenditure test would be immunized by that development.
- An organization under the expenditure test is not subject to the taxes that may be imposed in instances of substantial lobbying, which include the potential of taxes on the organization's managers (see below).
- A public charity that has elected the expenditure test may satisfy its requirement to report lobbying activities to Congress[23] using the definition of lobbying under the test.
- A public charity that has elected the expenditure test may satisfy its requirement to report lobbying expenses to Congress by filing a copy of the schedule that is part of the entity's annual information return.
- A charitable organization, remaining under the substantial part test, desiring to engage in a substantial amount of lobbying, can convert to a social welfare organization[24] to pursue those activities.

There are negative variables as well:

- More extensive record-keeping and reporting responsibilities are imposed on organizations under the expenditure test.[25]
- A charitable organization that seeks to engage primarily or entirely in grassroots lobbying is undoubtedly best advised to not make the election, because the limitation on that type of lobbying is probably more stringent under the expenditure test than under the substantial part test.
- The affiliation rules have a greater impact under the expenditure test.[26]
- A charitable organization that has elected the expenditure test cannot, having made excessive lobbying expenditures, convert to a social welfare organization.
- A charitable organization that has made the expenditure test election should be concerned about revoking the election, inasmuch as the IRS believes the test is a more generous interpretation of the rules limiting lobbying by public charities. Such a revocation may be interpreted by the IRS to mean that the organization cannot meet the substantial part test either, causing the organization to be examined by the IRS.

Overall, the best policy for a charitable organization is to remain under the substantial part test unless it is quite clear that it is advantageous for it to elect the expenditure test. In fact, a tiny percentage of organizations that are eligible to make this election have done so.

If the decision is made to elect the expenditure test, the planner may want to consider the timing of the filing of the election form. The election may be made anytime during a charitable organization's year and be effective for that year. Once the election is made, it remains in effect until it is revoked.

## Public Charities—Expenditure Test Issues

In applying the expenditure test, the planner is likely to confront one or more issues. The principal issues are:

**Direct Lobbying.**    A communication with a legislator or other relevant person is a *direct lobbying communication* only where the communication refers to specific legislation and reflects a view on that legislation. The term *specific legislation* means either (1) legislation that has been introduced in a legislative body or (2) a specific legislative proposal that the charitable organization supports or opposes.[27] Thus, the planner may have to determine whether there is a legislative proposal being advocated by the organization or whether the organization is reflecting (or has reflected) a view on specific legislation.

**Grassroots Lobbying.**    A communication is regarded as a *grassroots lobbying communication* only where the communication refers to specific legislation (see above), reflects a view on the legislation, and encourages the recipient of the communication to take action with respect to the legislation. Thus, the planner may, in this context, have to make a judgment as to whether the facts entail specific legislation, a view on the legislation expressed by the organization involved, and an encouragement by the organization to take action. This latter element—also known as a *call to action*—is the subject of a detailed four-point definition.[28]

**Mixed-Purpose Expenditures.**    The planner may have to struggle with cost allocation issues. A communication's costs may entail direct lobbying expenditures, grassroots lobbying expenditures, and/or nonlobbying expenditures. For example, in the case of a lobbying communication that is not to an organization's members and that also has a bona fide nonlobbying purpose, an organization must include as lobbying expenditures all costs attributable to the parts of the communication that are on the same specific subject as the lobbying message. The planner may also be required to apply the phrase *same specific subject,* the definition of which is largely dependent on the pertinent facts and circumstances.

As another example, in the case of lobbying expenditures for a communication that also has a bona fide nonlobbying purpose and that is sent only or primarily to members, the charitable organization involved must make a reasonable allocation between the amounts expended for the two purposes.[29]

**Mass Media Advertisements.**    There is a rebuttable presumption that a paid mass media advertisement is grassroots lobbying. The planner, therefore, may be called on to ascertain whether (1) a communication constitutes a *paid mass media advertisement,* (2) the facts give rise to the presumption, and/or (3) there are facts that support rebuttal of the presumption.[30]

**Fundraising Units.**    The expenditure test utilizes, as noted, a mechanical standard for measuring permissible and impermissible ranges of lobbying expenditures by eligible charitable organizations. The percentages that are a component of that standard are applied to total *exempt purpose expenditures,* which include eight elements.[31] One of the types of expenditures that are excluded from that base, however, is amounts paid to or incurred for a separate fundraising unit of the charitable organization or an affiliated entity.

The planner, then, may have to ascertain whether the charitable organization involved is engaged in *fundraising,* as that term is (expansively) defined for this purpose,[32] and, if so, whether the organization has a *separate fundraising unit.*[33]

**Communications with Members.**    There is, as noted, an exception in the context of the expenditure test concerning certain communications between the charitable organization and its members. This exception presents a plethora of potential issues for the planner, including whether (1) the members are *bona fide* ones, (2) there is specific legislation, (3) the organization has reflected a view on the legislation, (4) the *direct interest* element is present, (5) the *direct encouragement* element is present, and/or (6) if the one or more elements of the exception are not available, the communication is direct or indirect lobbying.[34]

**Affiliated Organizations.**    One of the more complex aspects of the expenditure test for the planner can be the matter of lobbying by affiliated organizations. For purposes of this test, the expenditures of related organizations are required to be aggregated so as to forestall the creation of numerous organizations in an effort to avoid the limitations of the test.

Where two or more charitable organizations are members of an affiliated group and at least one of the members has elected coverage under the expenditure test, the calculation of lobbying and exempt purpose expenditures must be made by taking into account the expenditures of the group. If these expenditures exceed the permitted limits, each of the electing member organizations must pay a proportionate share of any penalty excise tax (see below), with any nonelecting members treated under the substantial part test.

Thus, among other issues, the planner may have to determine whether there is an affiliated group. Generally, under these rules, two organizations are considered *affiliated* where:

- One organization is bound by decisions of the other on legislative issues, pursuant to its governing instrument.
- The governing board of one organization includes enough representatives of the other to cause or prevent action on legislative issues by the first organization.

If a group of autonomous organizations controls an organization but no single organization in the controlling group can control that organization by itself, the organizations are not considered an affiliated group by reason of the second of these two definitions.[35]

## Sanctions—Public Charities

The general sanction imposed on a charitable organization for engaging in excessive lobbying activities is revocation or denial of the tax-exempt status of the organization. In the case of a charitable organization that is under the substantial part test, the IRS has the discretion to impose an excise tax on the excessive lobbying expenditures. A tax may also be imposed on the charity's managers.[36] Indeed, the IRS has the discretion to (1) revoke tax exemption on these grounds, (2) impose the tax instead, or (3) utilize both sanctions.

A charitable organization that has elected the expenditure test and that exceeds either the limitation on direct lobbying expenditures or the one on grassroots lobbying expenditures becomes subject to an excise tax. If an electing organization's lobbying expenditures normally exceed 150 percent of either limitation, it will lose its tax-exempt status as a charitable entity.[37]

Again, the role of the planner in this context is to monitor the affairs of the charitable organization (1) to ascertain whether any lobbying activities are occurring and (2), if they are, to advise and assist the organization in avoiding taxation under either body of law (if possible) and avoiding loss of exempt status (again, if possible).

## Public Charities' Use of Social Welfare Organizations

There are no federal tax law limitations on attempts to influence legislation by tax-exempt social welfare organizations other than the general requirement that the organization must primarily engage in efforts to promote social welfare.[38]

Consequently, it is common for a public charity, which has or intends lobbying activities that are more extensive than permitted for exempt charitable organizations, to conduct the activities in a related social welfare organization. Thus, this relationship is depicted as follows:

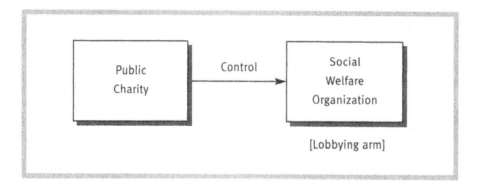

The planner should take into account that:

- This structure is one of the many manifestations of *bifurcation* of functions.[39] Thus, it is essential that both organizations have appropriate exempt functions.

- This is often a parent-subsidiary relationship. The requisite element of control can be established and maintained by a variety of mechanisms, most likely interlocking directorates or the membership feature (where the parent is the sole member of the subsidiary).[40]

- The charity should not be involved in the day-to-day management of the subsidiary. Where that is the case, the subsidiary will be considered the mere instrumentality of the parent or the arrangement will be regarded as a sham. Either outcome can lead to a collapsing of the arrangement for tax purposes, so that the lobbying activities are attributed to the charitable parent, with the attendant adverse tax consequences.

- The funding of the lobbying subsidiary needs, of course, to be considered. Funding by the charitable parent is not a likely solution, in that such a grant or grants would usually be considered lobbying expenditures by the parent. The lobbying subsidiary can be funded by nondeductible contributions, grants, dues, exempt function revenue, and/or unrelated business income.

- As discussed below in connection with Internet communications, there is a possibility that a web site link between the charitable organization and the social welfare organization could cause lobbying by the social welfare organization to be attributable to the charitable organization.

## Business Leagues

Just as is the case with social welfare organizations, there is no restriction, from the standpoint of the tax exemption for membership associations and other business leagues, on the amount of legislative activity these organizations may conduct. Nonetheless, there is an interaction between the rules restricting the deductibility of business expenses for legislative activities and this type of tax-exempt organization. That is, there generally is no business expense deduction available for amounts paid or incurred in connection with the influencing of legislation.

The business expense deduction denial rule is applicable to dues paid to associations, which generally are deductible. Thus, if an association engages in lobbying, a ratio of these expenses to total expenses must be created, with the portion of the dues that is considered allocable to the lobbying effort rendered nondeductible.[41]

## Private Foundations

Generally, private foundations may not engage in attempts to influence legislation. That is, they are not accorded the standard of insubstantiality granted to public charities.[42]

Nonetheless, private foundations are permitted to make available the results of nonpartisan analysis, study, or research.[43] Also, they can provide technical advice or assistance to a legislative body in response to a written request for the advice or assistance.[44]

Further, private foundations can, without limitation, engage in self-defense lobbying.[45] That is, a foundation can appear before or otherwise communicate with a legislative body with respect to a possible decision of that body that might affect the existence of the foundation, its powers and duties, its tax-exempt status, or the deductibility of contributions to the foundation.[46]

If a private foundation violates the legislative activities constraint, it is possible that its tax-exempt status would be revoked. More likely, however, inasmuch as an attempt to influence legislation by a private foundation generally is a taxable expenditure, lobbying by a foundation may well subject it to an excise tax on the expenditure and perhaps trigger a companion tax on those managing the foundation.[47]

## Research

One of the areas where the planner must be cautious in the lobbying setting is in connection with exempt organization research. Generally, conducting research is an exempt function—it can be a charitable, educational, and/or scientific endeavor. In some instances, however, the research activity can be considered a component part of an attempt to influence legislation, in which case it may be considered, for tax purposes, a lobbying activity rather than exempt program activity.

The substantial part test does not entail any specific rules on this point. Thus, the planner must evaluate the possibility that a research effort will be considered lobbying on a case-by-case basis (remembering that the analysis likely will be done in hindsight).

As for the expenditure test, an expense incurred for a nonlobbying communication can subsequently be characterized as a grassroots lobbying expenditure where the materials or other communications are later used in a lobbying effort. For this result to occur, the materials must constitute *advocacy communications* or *research materials,* where the primary purpose of the organization in undertaking or preparing the communications or materials was for use in lobbying. In the case of subsequent distribution of the materials by another organization, there must be "clear and convincing" evidence of collusion between the two organizations to establish that the primary purpose for preparing the communication was for use in lobbying. In any event, this subsequent-use rule applies only to expenditures paid less than six months before the first use of the nonlobbying material in the lobbying campaign.[48]

The rules for membership associations are more stringent. An amount paid or incurred for research for, or preparation, planning, or coordination of, any lobbying activity subject to these rules is treated as paid or incurred in connection with the lobbying activity. The intent of this rule is to convert what might otherwise be a function constituting nonpartisan analysis, study, or research into a lobbying undertaking where the research is subsequently used in an attempt to influence legislation.[49]

The planner may expect that, in a particular situation, the association rule may be applied even though the research was undertaken by a charitable organization.

## PARTICIPATION IN POLITICAL CAMPAIGN ACTIVITIES[50]

A tax-exempt organization may be required to ascertain whether it is participating or intervening (or is planning to do so or has done so) in a political campaign. This is of considerable concern to charitable organizations, which are prohibited, by the federal tax law, from engaging in political campaign activities. No other type of exempt organization is restricted in this manner, although the federal and state laws regulating the conduct and financing of political campaigns operate to impose limitations on some exempt organizations in this area.

## Introduction

There is little law, in the federal tax arena, as to the matter of participating or intervening in political campaigns. One of the tasks of the planner is to ascertain the nontax federal and state laws that may apply in a particular fact situation, inasmuch as these laws may trump a federal tax limitation. For example, federal law prohibits political contributions by corporations, and this rule applies to nonprofit, tax-exempt corporations;[51] thus a charitable organization formed as a corporation is barred from making political campaign contributions—the tax law prohibition on participation in political campaigns notwithstanding.

The planner may also be required to differentiate between *political campaign activities* and *political activities*. The latter phrase is a term of art used in the political organizations context.[52] A political activity is one of three undertakings:

1. Influencing, or attempting to influence, the selection, nomination, election, or appointment of an individual to a federal, state, or local public office.
2. Influencing, or attempting to influence, the selection, nomination, election, or appointment of an individual to an office in a political organization.
3. Influencing, or attempting to influence, the election of presidential or vice presidential electors.

Thus, the concept of the *political activity* is broader than, and subsumes, the concept of the *political campaign activity*. (The first type of political activity includes the usual political campaign activities.) For example, a political activity includes attempts to influence the nomination of an individual to be a justice of the Supreme Court or be a member of a president's cabinet.

This distinction is of particular importance to tax-exempt charitable organizations. An exempt charitable organization is permitted to engage in a political activity that is not a political campaign activity (although a tax may be incurred[53]).

## Political Campaign Activities by Public Charities

The planner must be cautious when advising on matters pertaining to public charities and political campaign activities, inasmuch as the prohibition is sweeping and (in the view of the IRS) absolute.[54] The statutory language of the prohibition makes the point: a tax-exempt charitable organization may "not participate in, or intervene in (including the publishing or distributing of statements), any political campaign on behalf of (or in opposition to) any candidate for public office."[55]

There are several words in that rule of law that require definition, although the IRS has a tendency to not be deterred by niceties of language in this context. The planner may be placed in the position of contending that this prohibition has a de minimis exception—an argument that has yet to be successfully made.

Also, the IRS has the discretion, in the event of political campaign activity by a charity, to (1) revoke tax-exempt status, (2) impose an excise tax,[56] or (3) do both. Recent action by the IRS indicates that it is not reticent to revoke an organization's exempt status for violating this rule and not bother with the tax.[57]

## Glossary

As noted, there are terms in this rule of law that, technically at any rate, require definition. The four principal ones are discussed next.

**Candidate.**    It is, of course, essential that, for the prohibition on political campaign activity by charitable organizations to be triggered, the facts include the presence of a candidate.[58] This term has not been given much attention in the federal tax setting.

Certainly, an individual who has formally declared that he or she is running for a particular office is a *candidate*. That formality is not always required, however; the IRS and the courts may consider an individual a candidate based solely on prominence and/or media speculation about a candidacy.

This matter can be compounded when the holder of a particular office is running for reelection. A charitable organization may interrelate with an individual believing the individual is acting in the capacity of a public official, only to be subsequently regarded as having provided some form of assistance to that individual in his or her capacity as a candidate.

Because of an absence of clear standards in this area, the planner should be careful when resting a defense on the proposition that, at the time when the charity's participation or intervention occurred, the beneficiary of the assistance was not a candidate. This aspect of the analysis is exacerbated when the determination on the point is made on the basis of hindsight.

**Campaign.**    The statute admonishes charitable organizations to not participate or intervene in a political *campaign*. There is almost no guidance on this point.[59] Therefore, here too, the planner must be careful. Often, it is next to impossible to identify a discrete undertaking that can be labeled a campaign; for the holder of a seat in the House of Representatives, from a closely divided district, for example, the boundaries of two-year terms are artificial, in that the *campaign* is an ongoing exercise.

**Public Office.**    The statute requires that the candidate be seeking a *public office*. This term is not defined in the federal tax law in this context, although the phrase *elective public office* is defined in the settings of the private foundation and political organizations rules.[60]

It is with respect to this point that the tendency of the IRS to be less than fastidious about the exactness of the language of the political campaign prohibition is well illustrated. Thus, the agency has, for example, extended the reach of the rule to encompass those who are seeking election to a precinct committee — an intraparty post. The view of the IRS is that, if the position is the subject of a ballot entry, it is a public office.[61]

**Participation or Intervention.**    The planner will likely find that, if there is an issue as to this aspect of the law, it will concern whether the charitable organization *participated* or *intervened* in a political campaign.[62] (Apparently, the two terms have the same meaning.) Although the definition of these words has not been accorded much attention in this setting, it is clear that they embrace nearly every way to be involved in political campaign activity. As noted, most of the obvious ways for an organization to involve itself in a political campaign—contributions, endorsements, provision of facilities, lending of employees, and the like—are forbidden by federal and/or state campaign financing laws.

Therefore, the scope of this prohibition is broader than that of the laws regulating political campaign financing and activity. This aspect of the law is detailed in the companion volume; illustrations of the point are private letter rulings concerning direct-mail fundraising letters sent by charitable organizations.[63]

The planner should monitor the possibility of political campaign activity by charitable organizations. Of note in this regard are:

- The application for recognition of exemption filed by organizations seeking recognition of tax-exempt status as charitable entities includes this question: "Does or will the organization intervene in any way in political campaigns, including the publication or distribution of statements?"[64] If the answer is yes, an explanation is to be attached.

- The annual information return requests identification of direct or indirect political expenditures[65] and requires charitable organizations to report any tax paid for engaging in political campaign activity.[66]

Two aspects of this area of the law that the planner should contemplate and perhaps utilize are:

1. Individuals retain their civil rights to engage in political campaign activities (within limitations). An argument may be made that an individual was acting in this context in his or her personal capacity and not as a representative of an organization.[67]

2. Charitable organizations often do not function in a vacuum in this regard. As an illustration, a charitable entity may be related to a business league[68] that maintains a political action committee.[69] The objective, of course, is to preclude the activities of the PAC from tainting the tax-exempt status of the charitable entity. An IRS private letter ruling provides an excellent example as to how this can be accomplished.[70] Also, the planner should monitor web sites and link arrangements to avoid circumstances where political content on the site of one of the other organizations is attributed, for tax purposes, to the charitable organization.[71]

## Voter Education Activities

A charitable organization (and perhaps other categories of exempt organizations) may engage in educational activities, albeit in a political milieu. The law in this regard is detailed in the companion volume.[72]

For this approach to be successful, a core requirement is that the (nonpolitical) activity be nonpartisan. Underlying intent can be a factor in this analysis, as can the timing of a particular initiative.

## Sanctions—Public Charities

The general sanction imposed on a charitable organization for engaging in political campaign activity is revocation or denial of the tax-exempt status of the organization. Also, a tax may be imposed on the organization; there may also be a tax on the organization's managers.[73] As noted, the IRS possesses the discretion as to which sanction to impose, or to impose both.

The IRS has two other tools at its disposal:

1. The agency is empowered to commence an action in federal district court to enjoin a tax-exempt charitable organization from the further making of political expenditures and for other relief to ensure that the assets of the organization are preserved for exempt purposes.[74]
2. If the IRS finds that a charitable organization has flagrantly violated the prohibition against the making of political expenditures, the agency is required to determine and assess any income and/or excise tax(es) due immediately, by terminating the organization's tax year.[75]

## Political Campaign Activities of Other Exempt Organizations

The federal tax law provides little guidance as to the consequences of political campaign activity by types of tax-exempt organizations other than charitable ones. What law there is concerning social welfare organizations, for example, is summarized in the companion volume.[76]

Other types of tax-exempt organizations tend to engage in political campaign activities, if they do so at all, by means of related political organizations. There are two reasons for this: (1) the federal campaign regulation laws encourage and sometimes mandate this form of bifurcation (using what that body of law refers to as the *separate segregated fund*); and (2) in this fashion, the tax on political expenditures[77] can be avoided.

The business expense deduction denial rule is also triggered in instances of political campaign activity, particularly by business leagues.[78]

## Private Foundations

Private foundations, being tax-exempt charitable organizations, are subject to the same proscription on political campaign activities that apply to these organizations generally.[79] Under certain circumstances, a private foundation may fund a voter registration drive.[80]

Political campaign activity by a private foundation could cause it to have its tax-exempt status revoked. It may be more likely, however, that the IRS would treat the matter as the making of a taxable expenditure and levy one or more taxes.

# POLITICAL ORGANIZATIONS

Among the various categories of tax-exempt organizations is the political organization.[81] The planner should, in the context of political campaign activities by the types of exempt organizations reviewed above, utilize the law pertaining to political organizations in two basic ways:

1. A tax-exempt organization can (and, in most instances, should), rather than engage in political campaign activities directly, conduct them indirectly by means of a related political organization (another illustration of the concept of bifurcation).

2. A tax-exempt organization can use the services of a related political organization to avoid payment of the political organizations tax.

## Political Organization in General

A *political organization* is an entity that is organized and operated primarily for the purpose of directly or indirectly accepting contributions or making expenditures for an exempt function. The two principal *exempt functions* in this setting are:

1. Influencing or attempting to influence nomination or election of an individual to a federal, state, or local public office.

2. Influencing or attempting to influence the selection or appointment of an individual to a federal, state, or local public office (such as within the judicial branch).

Thus, the exempt function of a political organization can include attempts to cause an individual to be elected to a public office or to prevent election of an individual to a public office. This function can also include efforts to secure the successful nomination of an individual to a public office, such as (at the federal level) appointment to a judgeship (including a member of the Supreme Court) or to the President's Cabinet.[82]

Particularly when serving a tax-exempt charitable organization, the planner needs to differentiate between political campaign activities and political activities. The latter subsumes the former. Charitable organizations can, without endangering tax-exempt status, engage in political activities that are not political campaign activities.

An exempt charitable organization generally may not utilize a related political organization, such as a political action committee, because the activities of the political entity are attributed, for tax purposes, to the charitable organization. An exempt charitable organization may, however, use a related political organization to engage in political activities that are not political campaign activities (such as influencing nominations to judgeships).

To be exempt, a political organization does not have to engage exclusively in exempt function activities; rather, it is subject to a primary purpose test.[83] Thus, a tax-exempt political organization may sponsor nonpartisan educational workshops, carry on social activities that are unrelated to an exempt function, or pay an incumbent's office expenses, as long as these are not the organization's primary activities. Caution needs to be exercised in this context, however, because of the different forms of advocacy: for example, an organization that engages entirely in legislative activities cannot qualify as a political organization.[84]

## Political Organizations Tax

Although political organizations are generally tax-exempt, they are subject to tax on their *political organization taxable income,* which basically is gross income less exempt function income. One of the principal examples of this type of taxable income is investment income.

An aspect of this area of the law is that the political organizations tax can be levied on other types of tax-exempt organizations. Particularly vulnerable in this regard are tax-exempt social welfare organizations and business leagues.

Stated more technically, although a political organization is exempt from taxation on amounts expended for an exempt function, if another type of tax-exempt organization expends an amount during a year, directly or indirectly (that is, through another organization), for what would be a political organization exempt function, it must include in its gross income for the year an amount equal to the lesser of:

- Its net investment income for the year, or
- The aggregate amount expended during the year for the exempt function

This rule does not apply, however, in instances of nonpartisan activities such as voter registration efforts and "get-out-the-vote" campaigns, where these undertakings are not specifically identified with any candidate or political party.[85]

Thus, tax-exempt organizations can avoid the tax on political organization exempt functions by utilizing a related political organization. The planner must be cautious here in distinguishing between the types of expenditures an exempt organization can permissibly make in support of (establishment and maintenance of) a related political organization and the types of expenditures that are subject to this tax. As to the former, an exempt organization may pay for the legal expenses associated with creation of the political organization, as well as its annual accounting costs. Much of the law in this area is informed by the federal election law rules.[86]

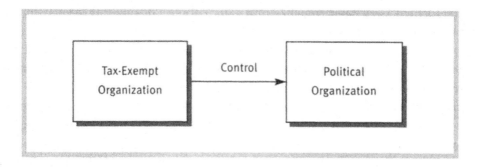

## INTERNET ACTIVITIES

Advocacy activities by tax-exempt organizations by means of the Internet include attempts to influence legislation and political campaign activity.[87]

## Attempts to Influence Legislation

The planner's review of attempts to influence legislation, particularly by charitable organizations, should include communications made by means of the Internet. The lobbying communication may be a publication on an organization's web site or it may be by means of e-mail. The difficulty for the planner in this regard is that there is no law directly on this point; considerable extrapolation from existing law principles is required.

The principal issues concerning lobbying by means of the Internet (particularly for charitable organizations) for the planner to contemplate are:

- For purposes of the substantial part test, how is substantiality determined in instances of Internet lobbying communications? The traditional elements of money or time do not fit well in this context.

- The expenditure test may accommodate a tremendous amount of Internet lobbying, in that this form of lobbying is so cost-effective.

- When determining whether a charitable organization that has elected the expenditure test is engaged in grassroots lobbying on the Internet, what facts and circumstances are relevant as to whether the organization made a *call to action?* These facts and circumstances are summarized above.

- Does publication of a web page on the Internet by a charitable organization that has elected the expenditure test constitute an appearance in the mass media? One would think so, yet the phraseology used in the definition of the term *mass media* does not encompass Internet communications (see above).

- A lobbying communication posted on a web page, even one that takes a position with respect to specific legislation, is a grassroots communication rather than a direct lobbying communication.

- What facts and circumstances are relevant in determining whether an Internet communication is a communication directly to or primarily with members of the organization for a charitable organization that is under the expenditure test? These facts and circumstances are no different than those presently in the law (see above).

- Is an Internet lobbying communication by an exempt organization a single publication or communication? It may be a single publication, but it is not likely to be a single communication. The law is silent as to the methodology to use when allocating expenses for different communications on a web site. The planner should remain alert to developments in the law on this point, inasmuch as allocations of this type are likely to be necessary in ferreting out legislative activities.

- Should an organization maintain the information from prior versions of its web site? There is no legal requirement that this be done, although the IRS has suggested that the policy may be necessary.

- To what extent are lobbying statements made by subscribers to a forum, such as a listserv or newsgroup, attributable to an exempt organization that maintains the forum? Existing law indicates that the general answer to this question must be that this type of attribution is not appropriate (or fair).

- A difficult question concerns the provision by an exempt organization of a link to the web site of another organization that engages in lobbying activity. As a general rule, the lobbying of the latter organization is not attributable to the former organization simply because of the link. Conversely, if the lobbying organization's site contains lobbying information posted by or endorsed by the first organization, that is likely to be considered lobbying by the first organization.[88] The planner should be careful in situations where a public charity is closely related to a social welfare organization or a business league, where the latter organization engages in lobbying and there is a link between the two.

- Can a communication become a grassroots lobbying communication because a call to action is on the organization's web site? That is, a communication may reference specific legislation and a view with respect to that legislation and not include a call to action in the communication but make reference to a web site where such a call appears.

## Political Campaign Activities

The planner's review of the conduct of political campaign activities, particularly by charitable organizations, should include communications made by means of the Internet. The difficulty for the planner in this regard is that there is no law directly on this point; considerable extrapolation from existing law principles is required.

The principal issues for the planner to contemplate are:

- The posting by a tax-exempt organization of a political campaign message on its web site would be a political campaign activity.

- An e-mail message from an exempt organization, urging the election or opposing the election of an individual to a public office, would constitute political campaign activity.

- Should an organization maintain the information from prior versions of its web site? There is no legal requirement that this be done, although the IRS has suggested that the policy may be necessary.

- To what extent are political campaign statements made by subscribers to a forum, such as a listserv or newsgroup, attributable to an exempt organization that maintains the forum? Existing law indicates that the general answer to this question must be that this type of attribution is not appropriate (or fair).[89]

- A difficult question concerns the provision by an exempt organization of a link to the web site of another organization that engages in political campaign activity. As a general rule, the political activity of the latter organization is not attributable to the former organization simply because of the link. Conversely, if the political campaign activity organization's site contains political campaign information posted by or endorsed by the first organization, that is likely to be considered political campaign activity by the first organization.[90] The planner should be careful in situations such as where a public charity is closely related to a social welfare organization or a business league, where the latter organization, either directly or by means of a related political organization, engages in political campaign activity and there is a link between the two.

## OTHER FORMS OF ADVOCACY

Aside from the types of activity traditionally considered by the federal tax law to be *action* efforts—substantial legislative and political campaign activities—there is a broad range of advocacy undertakings that may be described as *activist* in nature. These activities often can be regarded as *educational* efforts and/or communications sheltered by free speech principles. These advocacy efforts may be manifested in a variety of ways, such as writings, demonstrations, boycotts, strikes, picketing, and litigation.

Aspects of this matter that the planner should consider are:

- Some of these activities can qualify, as noted, as being inherently educational.[91]

- Some of these activities, such as litigation and boycotts, are not inherently exempt functions but can be rationalized as a means to achieve exempt ends.[92]

- An activity that is illegal or otherwise contrary to public policy[93] (such as promotion of violence, trespassing, or forms of vandalism) cannot be protected by these principles.[94]

## NOTES

1. In general, *Tax-Exempt Organizations*, chap. 20.
2. See id., nn. 4–9.
3. The concept of *legislation* is the subject of *Tax-Exempt Organizations*, § 20.1.
4. Fund for the Study of Econ. Growth & Tax Reform v. Internal Revenue Serv., 997 F. Supp. 15 (D.D.C. 1998), *aff'd*, 161 F.3d 755 (D.C. Cir. 1999). See Chapter 11, pages 309–311.
5. Id., 161 F.3d at 760 n. 9.
6. Form 1023, Part II, question 13. If the answer to this question is yes, an explanation is to be attached to the application, including an "estimate of the percentage of the organization's time and funds that it devotes or plans to devote to this activity." See Chapter 2, page 45.
7. Form 990, Schedule A. See Chapter 9, pages 212–213.
8. Form 990, Part VI, question 89a. See Chapter 9, page 206.
9. IRC § 501(c)(3).
10. *Tax-Exempt Organizations*, § 20.2(b).
11. Id., § 20.3 (a).
12. See Bruce R. Hopkins, *The Nonprofits' Guide to Internet Communications Law* (Hoboken, NJ: John Wiley & Sons, 2003) (hereinafter *Internet Communications*), § 5.5.
13. See Chapter 6, pages 136–137.
14. *Tax-Exempt Organizations*, § 20.2(c).
15. Id., § 20.5(a).
16. Id., § 20.3(b).
17. Id., § 20.4(a).

18. This exception was taken from the private foundation rules. See *Private Foundations*, § 9.1(e). As an illustration of effective use of this exception, the private foundation community was able to lobby against a proposal, considered in the fall of 2003, to revise the private foundation payout rules without causing any of the charitable organizations involved (public charities and private foundations) to transgress the limitations on lobbying activities.

19. *Tax-Exempt Organizations*, § 20.4(b).

20. Id., § 20.5(a).

21. See Chapter 4, pages 86–89.

22. *Tax-Exempt Organizations*, § 20.5(e).

23. See id., chap. 20, n. 7.

24. Id., chap. 12.

25. Id., § 20.5(b), (d).

26. Id., § 20.5(c).

27. Id., § 20.2(c)(i).

28. Id.

29. Id., § 20.2(c)(ii).

30. Id., text accompanied by nn. 50–51.

31. Id., § 20.3(b).

32. Id., § 20.3(b), text accompanied by n. 87.

33. Id., § 20.3(b), text accompanied by n. 88.

34. Id., § 20.4(b), text accompanied by nn. 120–124.

35. Id., § 20.5(c).

36. Id., § 20.6.

37. Id., § 20.3(b).

38. Id., § 20.7.

39. See Chapter 6, pages 134–136.

40. Id., pages 131–134.

41. Id., § 20.8.

42. *Private Foundations*, § 9.1(a), (b).

43. Id., § 9.1(d).

44. Id.

45. Id., § 9.1(e).

46. See note 18 above.

47. *Private Foundations*, § 9.1(b).

48. *Tax-Exempt Organizations*, § 20.2(c)(i), text accompanied by n. 52.

49. Id., § 20.8(a), text accompanied by nn. 181–183.

50. In general, id., chap. 21.

51. Federal Election Comm'n v. Beaumont, 539 U.S. 146 (2003).

52. See *Tax-Exempt Organizations*, chap. 17.

53. Id., § 21.3.

54. Id., § 21.1(b).

55. IRC § 501(c)(3).

56. *Tax-Exempt Organizations*, § 21.2.

57. Branch Ministries, Inc. v. Rossotti, 40 F. Supp. 2d 15 (D.D.C. 1999), *aff'd*, 211 F.3d 137 (D.C. Cir. 2000). See *Tax-Exempt Organizations*, § 21.1(d), text accompanied by n. 40. See Chapter 11, pages 300–304.

58. *Tax-Exempt Organizations*, § 21.1(f).

59. Id., § 21.1(g).
60. Id., § 21.1(h).
61. Id., text accompanied by nn. 70–75.
62. Id., § 21.1(d).
63. Id., text accompanied by nn. 29–30.
64. Form 1023, Part II, question 14. See Chapter 2, page 45.
65. Form 990, Part VI, question 81a. See Chapter 9, page 205.
66. Form 990, Part VI, question 89a. See Chapter 9, page 206.
67. *Tax-Exempt Organizations,* § 21.1(d), text accompanied by nn. 32–33.
68. Id., chap. 13.
69. Id., chap. 17.
70. Priv. Ltr. Rul. 200103084.
71. See *Internet Communications,* §§ 1.8(b), 6.5(b)(ii); id., 258–262.
72. *Tax-Exempt Organizations,* § 21.1(e).
73. Id., § 21.2.
74. Id., text accompanied by n. 112.
75. Id., text accompanied by n. 113.
76. Id., § 21.4.
77. Id., § 21.3.
78. See text accompanied by note 41 above.
79. *Private Foundations,* § 9.2(a), (b).
80. Id., § 9.2(c).
81. In general, *Tax-Exempt Organizations,* chap. 17.
82. Id., § 17.1(a).
83. Id., § 4.4.
84. Id., § 17.2.
85. Id., § 17.3.
86. Id., § 17.4.
87. In general, see *Internet Communications,* chaps. 5, 6.
88. See text accompanied by note 71 above.
89. *Tax-Exempt Organizations,* § 21.1(d), text accompanied by notes 19–20.
90. See text accompanied by note 71 above.
91. E.g., *Tax-Exempt Organizations,* § 7.2.
92. Id., § 5.5(e), (f).
93. Id., § 5.3.
94. Id., § 21.1(i).

# CHAPTER 6

# Subsidiaries

One of the most significant—and often vital—techniques available to the planner in the tax-exempt organizations context is the use of subsidiaries. It is frequently appropriate or even necessary to structure the operations of an exempt organization so that they are housed in two or more organizations. The many forms of bifurcation of this nature are dictated by law and/or management considerations.

In nearly all of these instances, the tax-exempt organization desires separation of functions (by placement in separate entities), yet also wishes to retain control over them (and their underlying assets and income). The resolution of these potentially contradictory objectives is the utilization of one or more subsidiaries.

## DEFINITION OF *SUBSIDIARY*

A *subsidiary organization* is an entity that is controlled by another organization, with that other entity often termed the *parent organization*. Thus, the element of *control* is built into the definition of the term—the subsidiary organization is subordinate or supplementary to the parent entity. By contrast, organizations can be *related* or *affiliated* without the presence of a control relationship.

The parent-subsidiary relationship, therefore, is as follows:

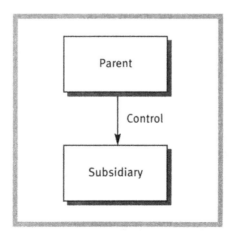

The planner will likely be called on to advise as to (1) whether a subsidiary is desirable or mandatory, (2) what the legal form of the subsidiary should be, and (3) how the control relationship is to be manifested.

As to the third aspect of this matter,[1] the planner essentially has one of three choices:

1. **Interlocking directorate.** One way for an organization to control another one is by means of the origin and composition of the subsidiary's governing board. That is, an organization can be the parent of another organization by having the power to determine who constitutes at least a majority of the other organization's board of directors or trustees. There are many mechanisms for achieving this; the common ones are:

   o The board of the parent organization appoints at least a majority of the board of the subsidiary organization.

   o Individuals holding certain positions within the parent organization (such as officers) are members of the board of the subsidiary organization by virtue of those positions (termed *ex officio* positions[2]), with those positions representing at least a majority of the subsidiary's board.

   o There may be a blend of the foregoing options.

   o The members of the board of the parent organization are also members of the board of the subsidiary organization.

2. **Membership.** The subsidiary organization can be organized as a membership organization, with the parent entity serving as the sole member of the subsidiary. The member is responsible for selecting the board of the subsidiary.

3. **Stock.** The subsidiary organization can be organized as a stock-based corporation, with the parent organization owning a majority or all of the stock of the subsidiary entity. The stockholder is responsible for selecting the board of the subsidiary.

The federal tax law generally is silent on this subject. Tax-exempt organizations are generally free to structure parent-subsidiary relationships as they wish, subject to the particulars of state law. For example, it is rare for a state to allow the formation of a non-profit organization as a stock-based corporation.[3] At the federal level, one of the few pronouncements of the law on this point is that supporting organizations may not be controlled by disqualified persons.[4]

## DETERMINING NEED FOR SUBSIDIARY

Conceptually, the principal reasons a tax-exempt organization may desire to utilize one or more subsidiaries is that a facet of the law and/or a management consideration suggests or requires it.

A nontax law reason for using a subsidiary is to avoid or minimize legal liability on the part of the parent organization. That is, the parent-subsidiary relationship will (or is intended to) insulate assets in the two entities from liability that may be incurred by the parent.

The chief tax law reason for a subsidiary is to house an activity, in which the parent organization may not or should not engage, in the subsidiary organization. Thus, deployment of a subsidiary is used to preserve the exempt status of the parent. The common types of activities that are preferably spun off to or incubated in a subsidiary are unrelated business, attempts to influence legislation, and political campaign efforts.

Another tax law use for a subsidiary is its function as a partner in a limited partnership or limited liability company. A for-profit entity may be used to attract capital and/or create assets (stock).

Management considerations (other than law ones) often lead to a decision to place the fundraising function of a tax-exempt organization and/or one or more program activities of an exempt organization in a subsidiary organization.

Bifurcation involving fundraising, where both entities are tax-exempt charitable organizations, is a classic example of the use of a subsidiary primarily for nonlaw reasons. (Where the two organizations are charitable, contributions to either of them are deductible.) This type of bifurcation is predicated on two factors: fundraising usually is not program, and the fundraising function often is best separated from the overall governance function. With a related fundraising foundation, there can be a board of directors (or trustees) that has fundraising as the sole function. Board members of the parent organization may be averse to fundraising; others relish the opportunity. By means of bifurcation, the fundraising function is placed in an entity where those who direct it know that fundraising (not governance) is their responsibility.[5]

Where the parent tax-exempt organization is not a charitable entity, placement of the fundraising function in a separate foundation is nearly essential. In this fashion, contributions and grants can be attracted, to support the charitable programs within the entity; without the separate charitable organization, this type of gift support would not be available because of the absence of the charitable contribution deduction.[6] Once the two entities are operational, one of two models (or, perhaps, a blend of the two) can be selected. Under one approach, all of the charitable activities are placed in the charitable organization and the fundraising supports these activities.[7]

Pursuant to the other approach, the charitable activities remain in the parent organization and the fundraising entity makes restricted grants to the parent organization in support of these programs.[8]

Allocation of programs between two exempt charitable organizations may be appropriate, depending on the facts and circumstances of the particular case. Generalizations as to which of these types of bifurcation is suitable are not possible; much depends on the personalities and politics involved.

An example of placement of a program in a separate entity was provided in the facts of a ruling where the IRS held that the operation of a motel by a supporting organization was a related business; the organization supports a hospital and the motel was used as a temporary living facility for patients awaiting surgery (and their family members and friends).[9]

A subsidiary may be essential to maximizing an income flow or creating a more favorable (from a tax standpoint) type of income. Thus, for example, a tax-exempt educational organization was ruled to be able to, without adversely affecting its exempt status, create and wholly own (and receive tax-free licensing income from) a for-profit subsidiary formed to maximize for membership and business purposes what would otherwise be the organization's web site.[10] Likewise, a medical research organization formed a supporting organization that in turn created a for-profit subsidiary to facilitate the transfer of technology incubated in the research organization; following commercialization of the technology, the for-profit subsidiary will provide tax-free royalty income to the research organization.[11]

The planner should give thought to the spin-off approach as opposed to the incubation approach. In some instances, this election is not available, such as in the case of an association (business league) that must utilize a political action committee to avoid tax.[12] In other situations, an activity can begin as a function of the exempt organization and be transferred to a subsidiary when and if the activity expands to the point where the spin-off is desirable or necessary. For example, the lobbying activity of a public charity may be appropriately transferred to a controlled social welfare organization if that activity increases beyond the bounds of insubstantiality.[13] Similarly, an unrelated business of a tax-exempt organization may have to be moved to a subsidiary if it becomes too extensive to be conducted within the exempt organization.[14] It may well become the planner's task to determine the point in time the spin-off must occur—a judgment that will turn on the facts and circumstances of each case.

## Legal Form of Subsidiary

Once the decision is made to create and use a subsidiary, the question as to its form may arise. If the subsidiary entity is to be a tax-exempt organization, the choices as to form are nonprofit corporation, trust, or unincorporated association (or, perhaps, limited liability company). If the subsidiary organization is to be a taxable entity, the choices as to form are regular (C) corporation, small business (S) corporation, limited liability company, or, perhaps, a nonprofit, nonexempt corporation.

The factors that dictate the nature of the subsidiary include:

- The value of or need for tax exemption for the subsidiary
- The motives of those involved in the enterprise (such as a profit motive)
- The desirability of creating an asset (such as stock that may appreciate in value and/or serve as the means for transfer of ownership) for equity owners of the enterprise
- The compensatory arrangements contemplated for employees

## Bifurcation Basics

The creation and maintenance of a fruitful parent-subsidiary relationship require a variety of elements. One, for example, is that the organizations must have real and substantial business functions. Success of the venture, however, fundamentally necessitates a certain degree of separation of the entities. That is, it is essential that, as a matter of tax law, the substance and independence of the entities are respected.

If the extent of control is inordinate, so that the parent organization's control of the affairs of the subsidiary is so pervasive that the latter is merely an extension of the former, the subsidiary may not be respected as a separate entity. In extreme situations, the parent-subsidiary relationship is regarded as a sham and thus ignored for tax purposes—with this outcome, the (undesirable) tax consequences are the same as if the two "entities" are one.

All of this pivots on the element of *day-to-day management:* if the parent organization is involved in the day-to-day management of the subsidiary organization, the two are likely to be regarded as one. The factors to evaluate in this regard are the identity (and overlap) of the officers and employees, location(s), office-sharing, and co-investing. Also important is record-keeping (as to expenses and time allocations) and contracts between the organizations (such as for cost reimbursement and/or rental arrangements). The history and the substance of the law on this point are summarized in the companion volume.[15] There are recent IRS private letter rulings, however, that the planner should peruse; these rulings illustrate how close and intertwined operations do not necessarily defeat a parent-subsidiary structure.

In one instance, a tax-exempt organization established a for-profit subsidiary to serve as the sole general partner in a limited partnership, to limit legal liability for legal claims to the assets of the two organizations, and to isolate exempt functions from unrelated business activities. The exempt organization elected all of the directors of the subsidiary; no more than three of the seven members of the subsidiary's board of directors were also members of the board of the exempt organization. The subsidiary rented office space and purchased professional services from the parent; the two organizations shared employees. The two entities shared investment leads and made joint investments, and the subsidiary generally, in the words of the IRS, had a "close working relationship" with the parent organization. Both organizations maintained separate accounting and corporate records. The IRS ruled that this subsidiary had a "separate corporate existence and business purpose" and that the tax-exempt parent did not "actively participate" in the day-to-day management of the subsidiary, so that the subsidiary was not a mere instrumentality of its parent and the "corporate existence" of the subsidiary would not be disregarded for federal tax purposes.[16]

This is a significant ruling on this point for planners. To reiterate: (1) the two organizations will be sharing office space (albeit pursuant to a lease), (2) the subsidiary will be purchasing administrative and professional services from the parent, (3) the subsidiary will reimburse the parent for the services of some of the parent's employees, (4) the two organizations will co-invest in companies, (5) the two entities will be "sharing investment leads," and (6) the parent and the subsidiary will "maintain a close working relationship." This is not to say that these six facts are the equivalent of day-to-day involvement by the exempt organization in the affairs of its subsidiary. Nonetheless, this ruling reflects a most munificent view of the facts by the IRS and illustrates how closely a tax-exempt organization and its subsidiary (in this instance, a for-profit one) can operate in tandem without crossing the line into attribution and causing the exempt entity to become entangled in what the IRS termed the "daily operations" of the subsidiary.

The planner should consider the tax consequences of a finding that a parent-subsidiary relationship will not be respected for tax purposes. A large unrelated business in the subsidiary could cause the parent to lose its tax-exempt status if the subsidiary is treated as a mere instrumentality of the parent (that is, the relationship is regarded as a sham). The same adverse outcome could result if the parent is a charitable entity and lobbying activities in the subsidiary are attributed to it. By contrast, if both the parent and the subsidiary are charitable organizations, the collapsing of operations presumably would not have any adverse tax consequences—and thus there is little likelihood that attribution would be imposed.

## TAX-EXEMPT SUBSIDIARIES

It is common, in a parent-subsidiary relationship, for the parent entity and the subsidiary entity to both be tax-exempt organizations. An illustration of this type of in-tandem arrangement is the supporting organization.[17]

### Choice of Form

The form selected for the tax-exempt subsidiary is essentially the same as for its parent: nonprofit corporation, trust, unincorporated association, or limited liability company.[18] The planner is likely to be called on to make the determination (or at least recommendation) as to form of entity. For the most part, the form selected will be the nonprofit corporation.[19]

### Bifurcation Revisited

The elements discussed above as to successful bifurcation usually apply when both organizations are tax-exempt. For example, the exempt charitable organization does not want the activities of its exempt lobbying subsidiary to be attributed to it, nor does the exempt business league want the functions of its exempt political action committee attributed to it. Where both organizations are exempt charitable entities,[20] the adverse tax consequences of attribution are minimized, although in most instances attribution should be avoided.

### Common Relationships

Following are the most common forms of these relationships when an exempt charitable organization is the parent:

- A charitable organization with an exempt social welfare organization[21] as its subsidiary. The function of the subsidiary may be lobbying.[22]
- A charitable organization with an exempt business league[23] as its subsidiary. The function of the subsidiary may be a certification program.[24]

Following are the most common forms of these relationships when an exempt charitable organization is the subsidiary:

- An exempt business league with a charitable foundation. This subsidiary is likely to be a supporting organization.

- An exempt social welfare organization with a charitable foundation. This subsidiary is likely to be a supporting organization.

- Another type of noncharitable tax-exempt organization with a charitable foundation. These exempt parent organizations include labor organizations,[25] agricultural organizations,[26] social clubs,[27] fraternal organizations,[28] and veterans' organizations.[29] The subsidiary is likely to be, in cases involving labor and agricultural organizations, a supporting organization.

- A foreign charitable organization with an exempt U.S.-based charitable entity.[30] This subsidiary (usually a fundraising entity) is likely to be a supporting organization.

- An exempt charitable organization (parent) with an exempt charitable organization (subsidiary).[31] The function of this type of charitable organization subsidiary will probably be fundraising, holding one or more endowment funds, or operating one or more programs. This subsidiary is likely to be a supporting organization.

As to supporting organizations, it is important to reiterate that there are different types of them.[32] Only one of these types is the parent-subsidiary model. The so-called "brother-sister" model can look much like the parent-subsidiary structure. With the *operated in connection with* approach (disfavored by the IRS[33]), however, a supporting organization can function without being formally controlled by one or more supported organizations.

The following tax-exempt organizations are subsidiary organizations, with the parent exempt organization potentially one of a wide variety of tax-exempt organizations:

- Political organizations[34]
- Title-holding companies[35]
- Employee benefit funds[36]

## TAXABLE SUBSIDIARIES

Nearly all tax-exempt organizations may utilize a taxable subsidiary. This is less common than the use of a tax-exempt subsidiary, with the issues in play nonetheless often more serious, given the fact of the taxable nature of the subsidiary.

### Choice of Form

The taxable subsidiary of a tax-exempt organization is likely to be a corporation. Here, the interests of the exempt organization and those of the subsidiary may diverge. The exempt organization presumably would want the subsidiary to be a regular (C) corporation, so that resulting income would be tax-free dividends. Those involved with the subsidiary may want it to be a small business (S) corporation or a limited liability company so as to avoid double taxation. The exempt organization, however, should avoid use of an S corporation, if only because all resulting income and gain are automatically considered unrelated business income,[37] and be cautious when contemplating use of a limited liability company, because the exempt organization's share of income (whatever its nature) is automatically passed along to it (either in actuality or for tax purposes).[38]

Another choice is the taxable nonprofit corporation. These entities are taxed the same as the for-profit corporation, yet it may prove advantageous for the parent entity to have its subsidiary cast as a nonprofit organization.

## Capitalization

Although there is no law on the point, consideration should be given to the amount of capital contributed to a taxable subsidiary by a tax-exempt organization, particularly where the parent is a charitable organization. The best guiding standard in this regard is that of the prudent investor.[39]

## Bifurcation Revisited

The elements discussed above as to successful bifurcation certainly apply when the parent organization is tax-exempt and the subsidiary is a taxable entity. Almost always, the planner will want to ensure that the activities of the subsidiary are not attributed to the parent. Even in the best of circumstances, treatment of this type of subsidiary as an instrumentality of the parent is almost certain to result in unrelated business income to the parent.

Thus, a tax-exempt organization needs to be cautious when using a taxable subsidiary, so as not to be placed in a position where it is cast (or perceived) as being involved in the day-to-day management of the subsidiary, so that the subsidiary is disregarded for tax purposes. Following are the elements the planner should take into account in assessing these situations:

- Overlap of board directors (although this element is of lesser concern because control is assumed; at the same time, control is manifested by means of stock, so there is no need to have a complete or majority overlap of directors)
- Overlap of officers
- Overlap of employees
- Sharing of office space, furniture, and/or equipment
- Co-investment arrangements
- Other circumstances that indicate undue involvement by the parent in the daily operations of the subsidiary

## Liquidations

If a taxable subsidiary liquidates and distributes its assets to its tax-exempt parent, the general rule is that the distribution is treated for tax purposes as though the assets are being sold to the parent organization. This means that, to the extent these assets are capital assets, there is a potential for payment of the tax on capital gains.[40]

The planner may wish to consider:

- If a capital asset transferred in this fashion is used by the parent in an unrelated business, capital gains taxation is not triggered (as long as the asset is used in that manner).[41]

- The rules as to liquidation are basically the same, irrespective of whether the liquidating entity is a subsidiary of the transferee or not.[42]

- These rules generally apply when a taxable entity converts (assuming that is permissible under state law) to a tax-exempt organization.

- In a situation where the transferee is *not* the parent of the liquidating entity, there are exceptions that should be considered.[43]

- Where these exceptions are applicable, the IRS is requiring the organization to file an application for recognition of tax-exempt status, even though the regulations expressly provide that the application does not have to be filed if it is not otherwise required.[44]

## SUBSIDIARIES IN PARTNERSHIPS

As noted, one use of a subsidiary is its participation as a partner in a partnership, in lieu of participation by the parent tax-exempt organization.[45] One reason to do this is to avoid endangering the exempt status of the parent entity.

This can be an effective stratagem as long as all of the requirements of the law as to the bona fides of the subsidiary are satisfied, including the requirement that the subsidiary organization be an authentic business entity. As discussed, however, if the tax-exempt organization parent is intimately involved in the day-to-day management of the subsidiary, the IRS or a court may impute the activities of the subsidiary to the parent, thereby (in this context) endangering the exempt status of the parent by treating it as if it were directly involved as a partner in the partnership. In one instance, for example, the IRS (without explanation) expressly ignored a tax-exempt organization's use of a for-profit subsidiary as the general partner in a partnership, reviewing the facts as though the exempt organization was directly involved in the partnership.[46]

## TAX TREATMENT OF REVENUE FROM SUBSIDIARY

While not always the case, most tax-exempt organizations develop an unrelated business with the anticipation that it will serve as a source of revenue. If the unrelated business is housed in a subsidiary, presumably a revenue flow to the parent organization is nonetheless desired.

Generally, passive income received by tax-exempt organizations is not taxable as unrelated business income.[47] An exception to this rule pertains to the receipt of certain income by a tax-exempt parent organization from a subsidiary. That is, interest, rent, annuity, or royalty payments made by a controlled entity to an exempt organization are includable in the exempt organization's unrelated business income and are subject to the unrelated business income tax to the extent the payment reduces the net unrelated income (or increases any net unrelated loss) of the controlled entity (determined as if the entity were tax-exempt).[48]

A *controlled entity* is a taxable or tax-exempt subsidiary that is at least 50 percent controlled by the parent tax-exempt organization. In the case of a stock-based subsidiary, *control* means ownership by vote or value of 50 percent or more of the stock. In the case of a partnership or other entity, *control* means ownership of 50 percent or more of the profits, capital, or beneficial interests. Moreover, there are constructive ownership rules[49] by which a parent exempt organization is deemed to control any subsidiary in which it holds more than 50 percent of the voting power or value, directly (as in the case of a first-tier subsidiary) or indirectly (as in the case of a second-tier subsidiary).[50]

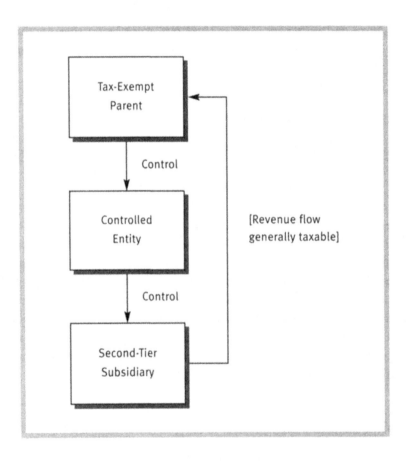

These rules do not apply to the payment of dividends by a taxable subsidiary to a tax-exempt parent organization.[51]

# FOR-PROFIT SUBSIDIARIES AND PUBLIC CHARITY STATUS

Just as it is possible for the operations of a for-profit subsidiary to have an adverse impact on the tax-exempt status of a parent organization (by an attribution of the activities for tax purposes), so too is there potential that the functions of a for-profit subsidiary will have a pernicious effect on the public charity status of the exempt charitable parent organization.

## Publicly Supported Organizations

Any impact of a for-profit subsidiary on the status of a tax-exempt charitable organization that is its parent, where the parent is classified as a publicly supported organization, is derived from funding of the parent by the subsidiary.

Where a parent charitable organization has its non-private-foundation status based on classification as a donative type of publicly supported charity,[52] a transfer of money or property to it by the subsidiary will, if treated as a dividend, not qualify as public support. Where the item or items transferred to the publicly supported donative parent are considered gifts, they are not forms of public support to the extent the amount exceeded the 2 percent limitation threshold. The planner should note that, particularly if the subsidiary is wholly owned, funding cast as a charitable contribution may be regarded for tax purposes as a dividend.

If the parent organization is not a private foundation by reason of categorization as a service provider type of publicly supported charity,[53] any amount paid to it by a subsidiary would not be public support if the amount was regarded as a dividend. Moreover, a payment of this nature that is accorded dividend treatment would be investment income, as to which there is a one-third limitation with respect to receipt of this type of revenue. If the item or items transferred to the publicly supported service provider parent are considered gifts, they would not constitute public support if the subsidiary is a disqualified person with respect to the parent organization.

A charitable organization that has a large endowment, such as one housed in a supporting organization, may find that it is difficult to sustain the requisite level of public support because of extensive investment income. Also, prospective donors and grantors may decline to provide support to a charitable organization with a sizable endowment—in the belief that the organization does not really need that financial support (often a mistaken notion). The charitable organization in this position may have to become a supporting organization, some other type of public charity, or a private operating foundation.

## Supporting Organizations

Some tax-exempt charitable organizations are classified as public charities by virtue of the rules concerning supporting organizations.[54]

Because the public charity status of a supporting organization is not derived from the nature of its funding, the considerations pertaining to publicly supported organizations summarized above are inapplicable (although a transfer from a for-profit subsidiary to a supporting organization may nonetheless be considered a dividend).

Although there initially was doubt on the point, the IRS ruled that a supporting organization can have a for-profit subsidiary and not disturb its status as a supporting entity.[55]

## SOCIAL ENTERPRISE

One of the principal contemporary forces with the potential for meaningfully shaping the law of tax-exempt organizations is emergence of what is known as *entrepreneurialism*: the open and accepted conduct of businesses by exempt organizations, on a for-profit basis, to the end of supplementing or even supplanting charitable contributions and grants. The unabashed aim of organizations undertaking entrepreneurial activities is to make money for the mission, upgrade the quality of staff and other resources, and become self-sufficient (that is, not dependent on external funders).

The nomenclature surrounding this phenomenon is illuminating: *social enterprises, business ventures, corporate partnerships, strategic partnerships,* and *cause-related marketing.* This parlance is decorated with verbs such as *leverage, develop* (the mission), *license, capitalize,* and *invest.*

There is, of course, nothing new in the fact that tax-exempt organizations undertake related and unrelated businesses.[56] What is different is the underlying spirit or philosophy of entrepreneurialism. Its proponents see heavy reliance on contributors and grantors as arcane and confining. They disregard concern about traditional federal tax law constraints; rarely in the literature of entrepreneurialism is much written about the impact of these business ventures on organizations' tax-exempt status or susceptibility to unrelated business income taxation. Instead, the emphasis is on business opportunities, asset expansion, productivity incentives, employee training and advancement, and public relations. Terms heretofore uttered only in the setting of the for-profit sector now dominate the social enterprise lexicon: *profit margin, return on investment, accountability, risk tolerance, capacity building, self-sufficiency, diversified revenue strategy,* and the irrepressible *new paradigm.* The vocabulary of entrepreneurialism is a blend of New Age platitudes, business-school-speak, and advocacy of a revolution in vision and accomplishments.

The thinking and actions of today's entrepreneurialism dramatically clash with the commerciality doctrine.[57] That doctrine holds that a charitable organization's tax-exempt status is endangered when elements such as focusing on the wants and needs of the general public, profits, and marketing are taken into account by it, not to mention trained employees and decreased reliance on gifts and grants.

Social entrepreneurialism tends to eschew the use of for-profit subsidiaries (and formal joint venture vehicles such as limited liability companies[58]). Rather, the attraction is to *partnerships*—not in the sense of discrete legal entities but rather direct interrelationships with for-profit businesses, where the entities function in-tandem ("partner" or form a "strategic alliance") to advance charitable causes ("missions"), rely on in-kind gifts, engage in unique fundraising promotions, utilize technical assistance, and operate using other forms of "mission alignment."

A survey conducted in 2002 of 72 tax-exempt organizations, entailing 105 ventures,[59] resulted in these findings:

- Tax-exempt organizations that engage in business ventures tend to offer some type of social service to at-risk populations in their communities (such as employment training programs), as contrasted with educational, arts, and religious organizations.

- Eighty percent of the organizations had been in existence at least nine years, suggesting that business ventures are not normally part of organizations' initial plans.

- Business ventures are not confined to large exempt organizations; one-third of the organizations have an annual operating budget under $1 million and another third has a budget of $1 million to $5 million.

- Nearly one-half (46 percent) of these organizations are community-based, 38 percent operate on a regional basis, and 14 percent operate on a national basis.

- Nearly one-half (46 percent) of these organizations operate multiple ventures; 25 percent of them manage at least three ventures.

- Eighty-nine percent of these organizations indicated that their ventures were related (or nearly so) to their exempt purpose.

- Most of these business ventures generate modest revenue; about one-third of these organizations generate annual gross revenue in the range of $100,000 to $500,000.

- Sixty-nine percent of these organizations reported that their ventures either made a profit or broke even; of the 42 percent that were profitable, 16 percent netted less than $25,000 and 13 percent generated more than $50,000.[60]

- It took organizations with profitable ventures an average of 2.5 years to break even.

- Initial capitalization for these ventures averaged $200,000 (with a mean of $90,000).

- Eighty-nine percent of these exempt organizations operated their ventures as a department or division of the entity; only 10 percent established the venture using a for-profit corporation, partnership, limited liability company, other joint venture, or other structure.

- Tax-exempt organizations that are interested in social enterprise tend to believe that planning and research are important.

- The greatest impact of operating a social enterprise was the creation of a "more entrepreneurial culture," although many organizations were of the view that it helped to attract and retain staff and contributors, and it enabled the organization to achieve greater self-sufficiency.

Public charities contemplating involvement in social enterprises may give consideration to do so other than by directly "partnering" with a for-profit business. Alternatives include the use of a supporting organization,[61] a for-profit subsidiary, a limited liability company, or a partnership or other form of joint venture vehicle. Entrepreneurialism can have an adverse impact on tax-exempt and/or public charity status, cause application of the unrelated business rules, and/or attract forms of legal liability. Also, as noted, there may be management or other reasons for the placement of functions in separate vehicles.

To date, the federal tax law has done little (if anything) to dampen the enthusiasm or curb the innovativeness of the structures of this social enterprise movement. This is somewhat surprising, given robust expansion of the private inurement and private benefit doctrines,[62] the potency of the intermediate sanctions rules,[63] and the relentless attention and application of the unrelated business rules.[64]

Perhaps coming developments in the law of tax-exempt organizations will compromise or even frustrate the trend toward more social enterprising. But, at the present, entrepreneurialism appears healthy and expansive, and no regulatory impulse has materialized to circumscribe the flowering of the movement.[65]

Nonetheless, the planner should be cautious, and envision possible developments and outcomes in the law in this area. Prognostications can be risky or even wrong, yet it does not seem possible that evolution of the law of commerciality and the techniques of the social enterprise movement can coexist along parallel planes forever. The planner advising the social enterprising charity should monitor the ongoing evolution of the commerciality doctrine, and be ready to advise the charity accordingly. The planner also may want to advise this type of client to make more ready use of for-profit subsidiaries (and/or one or more of the other vehicles available in this context).

## PRACTICAL OPERATIONAL CONSIDERATIONS

In general, as the foregoing indicates, there should be the requisite separation between the parent and subsidiary organizations to avoid attribution of functions of the subsidiary to the parent. This matter may be of little concern where both organizations are tax-exempt and both have the same exempt status (such as a public charity with a fundraising foundation), although even in that context, for management reasons, the entities may want to evidence an appreciable degree of separation.

The features the planner can attempt to work into the facts to build elements of independence (if necessary) between a tax-exempt parent organization and its subsidiary are:

- To the extent feasible, there should be a minimum of overlap of directors and officers of the two organizations.

- The parent and subsidiary may have separate leases with a third party, rather than have the parent lease property to the subsidiary or the subsidiary lease property to the parent.

- The parent and subsidiary may have separate locations or at least separate, discrete offices within one location.

- The parent and subsidiary may have separate telephone (including facsimile) lines.

- The parent and subsidiary may have separate equipment and furniture; if there must be sharing, there should be a written agreement on the point, including the basis of allocation of expenses.

- If there is employee-sharing, there should be a written agreement on the point, including the basis of allocation of (and reimbursement of) compensation, with the employees involved keeping records as to their expenditures of time.

- The parent and subsidiary should have separate bank accounts.
- The parent and subsidiary should have separate books of account and report separately to the IRS (although consolidated financial statements may be unavoidable).

## Notes

1. See *Tax-Exempt Organizations*, § 31.1(c).
2. There is confusion about the meaning of this term. The Latin words mean "by reason of the office." Thus, an individual can have a position on the board of directors of an organization and/or be an officer of it solely by reason of having a position with another organization. An *ex officio* position has all of the powers and responsibilities of any other board or officer position (such as elected positions), including voting (unless the organization's governing documents provide otherwise). The control relationship, however, cannot be established by means of individuals who are unable to vote.
3. Should this option be one of serious consideration and the law of the state where the subsidiary is to operate does not permit stock-based nonprofit corporations, the planner may consider formation of the subsidiary organization in a state where nonprofit organizations may be created as stock-based corporations, then qualifying that corporation (as a *foreign corporation*) in the state of operation. The law of the state of operation should be reviewed, nonetheless, to be certain that qualification of the foreign corporation is permissible.
4. *Tax-Exempt Organizations*, § 11.3(c); *Private Foundations*, § 15.7(h).
5. See Chapter 4, page 94.
6. Occasionally, a noncharitable organization will attempt to raise funds by inducing sponsors to utilize the business expense deduction (IRC § 162) for their payments. This approach rarely is successful. Also, if a payment is in fact a gift, it cannot lawfully be deducted as a business expense. Reg. § 1.162-15(a). See *Charitable Giving*, § 3.1(a).
7. See Chapter 4, page 95.
8. Id., page 96.
9. Tech. Adv. Mem. 9847002.
10. Priv. Ltr. Rul. 200225046.
11. Priv. Ltr. Rul. 200326035.
12. *Tax-Exempt Organizations*, § 17.4.
13. See Chapter 5, pages 116–117.
14. See Chapter 8, page 181.
15. *Tax-Exempt Organizations*, § 31.1(d). In a recent private letter ruling, the IRS captured the state of the law on the point as follows: "The activities of a separately incorporated subsidiary cannot ordinarily be attributed to its parent organization unless the facts provide clear and convincing evidence that the subsidiary is in reality an arm, agent or integral part of the parent." Priv. Ltr. Rul. 200132040.
16. Priv. Ltr. Rul. 200132040. Other recent private letter rulings where the activities of a (for-profit) subsidiary were not attributed to a tax-exempt parent include Priv. Ltr. Ruls. 200149043, 200152048, and 200225046.
17. See Chapter 4, pages 91–99.
18. See Chapter 1, pages 4–8.
19. Id., page 7.
20. That is, both organizations are tax-exempt by reason of the description in IRC § 501(c)(3).

21. *Tax-Exempt Organizations,* chap. 12.
22. See Chapter 5, pages 116–117.
23. *Tax-Exempt Organizations,* chap. 13.
24. Id., § 13.3.
25. Id., § 15.1.
26. Id., § 15.2.
27. Id., chap. 14.
28. Id., § 18.4.
29. Id., § 18.10.
30. Id., § 30.2(d).
31. Id., § 30.2(c).
32. See Chapter 4, page 92.
33. E.g., Lapham Found., Inc. v. Comm'r, 84 T.C.M. 586 (2003); Christie E. Cuddeback and Lucille M. Cuddeback Mem'l Fund v. Comm'r, 84 T.C.M. 623 (2003).
34. *Tax-Exempt Organizations,* chap. 17.
35. Id., § 18.2.
36. Id., chap. 16.
37. Id., § 27.2(m).
38. See Chapter 7, pages 150–151.
39. *Tax-Exempt Organizations,* § 31.2(a).
40. IRC § 337(b). In general, *Tax-Exempt Organizations,* § 31.2(d).
41. IRC § 337(b)(2)(B)(ii).
42. IRC § 337(d). In general, *Tax-Exempt Organizations,* §§ 33.4(b), (c), 33.5.
43. Reg. § 1.337(d)-4(a)(3)(i).
44. Reg. § 1.337(d)-4(a)(3)(ii). E.g., Priv. Ltr. Ruls. 200217044, 200333008.
45. In general, *Tax-Exempt Organizations,* § 31.4.
46. Tech. Adv. Mem. 8939002.
47. See Chapter 8, pages 178–179.
48. IRC § 512(b)(13).
49. IRC § 318.
50. In general, *Tax-Exempt Organizations,* §§ 27.1(n), 31.3.
51. Id. § 31.3, text accompanied by n. 69.
52. See Chapter 4, pages 86–88.
53. Id., pages 88–89.
54. Id., pages 91–99.
55. E.g., Priv. Ltr. Rul. 9637051. In general, *Tax-Exempt Organizations,* § 31.5.
56. See Chapter 8.
57. See *Tax-Exempt Organizations,* chap. 25.
58. See Chapter 7, pages 154–158.
59. *Powering Social Change: Lessons on Community Wealth Generation for Nonprofit Sustainability* (Washington, DC: Community Wealth Ventures, Inc., 2003), www.communitywealth.com; the survey results are at 52–62.
60. On this point, the survey summary noted that the "more successful ventures may be underrepresented in this survey since there is a greater likelihood that busy managers of larger operations will opt out of this sort of interview" and "ventures that are not profitable may be less forthcoming with financial results." Id. at 58.
61. See Chapter 4, pages 91–99.

62. See Chapter 3, pages 65–71.

63. Id., pages 71–76.

64. See Chapter 8.

65. In general, J. Gregory Dees, Jed Emerson and Peter Economy, eds., *Strategic Tools for Social Entrepreneurs: Enhancing the Performance of Your Enterprising Nonprofit* (Hoboken, NJ: John Wiley & Sons, 2002); J. Gregory Dees, Jed Emerson and Peter Economy, eds., *Enterprising Nonprofits: A Toolkit for Social Entrepreneurs* (Hoboken, NJ: John Wiley & Sons, 2001). An extensive bibliography on this subject is available in "Powering Social Change," note 59 above, pages 106–111.

# CHAPTER 7

# Partnerships and Other Joint Ventures

The use of joint venture vehicles is one of the most predominant forms of planning and operations in the law of tax-exempt organizations today. Over past years, this law has focused on the involvement of exempt organizations in partnerships. Recently, however, the emphasis has shifted to the use of other types of joint ventures, most notably those structured using limited liability companies. Almost all of the developments in this regard to date concern public charities. The principal issues are the ongoing exempt status of the nonprofit organization or organizations involved and the potential generation of unrelated business income. The law doctrines underlying the exemption issue tend to be private inurement or private benefit.[1] The intermediate sanctions rules[2] may also be implicated in this setting.

## PARTNERSHIPS AND JOINT VENTURE BASICS

A *partnership* is a form of business entity, recognized in the law as a separate legal entity, as is a corporation or trust. It is usually evidenced by a document (partnership agreement). The term *joint venture* is broader than, and subsumes, the concept of a partnership. There can be a joint venture without establishment of an entity and without a document signifying it; in fact, the joint venture form can be imposed on parties in particular factual circumstances, even contrary to their intent and wish.[3] A joint venture can, however, be a formal legal entity other than a partnership; the best example of this is the *limited liability company*.

The parties to a partnership are *partners*. Parties to a joint venture arrangement, including a limited liability company, are *members*.

### Partnerships

Partnerships basically are of two types. This delineation largely turns on the nature of the partners, who can be *general* or *limited*. Generally, liability for the consequences of a partnership's operations rests with the general partner or partners, while the exposure to liability for the functions of the partnership for the limited partners is confined to the amount of the limited partner's or partners' contribution(s) to the partnership.

The partnership that has only general partners is the *general partnership*. In this type of partnership, the interests of the general partners may or may not be equal. These partners are generally equally liable for satisfaction of the obligations of the partnership and can be called on to make additional capital contributions to the entity.

Capital in a partnership can come from investors, that is, limited partners. A limited partner is in the venture not to control and administer the underlying business but rather to obtain a return on the investment and perhaps to procure some tax advantages. A partnership with both general and limited partners is the *limited partnership*.[4]

## Joint Ventures in General

A *joint venture* conceptually is an association of two or more persons with intent to carry out a business enterprise for joint profit, for which purpose they combine their efforts, property, money, skill, and knowledge. Often, as noted, this arrangement is something less than a formal legal entity such as a partnership.[5]

The three types of joint ventures are:

1. One or more of the venturers places itself, in its entirety, in the venture.
2. One or more of the venturers places a primary portion of its operations in the venture.
3. One or more of the venturers places a small portion of its operations in the venture.

The first type of these joint ventures is the *whole entity joint venture*, started in the healthcare context (and thus known in that setting as the *whole hospital joint venture*[6]). The third of these joint ventures is the *ancillary joint venture*.[7]

## Limited Liability Companies

A limited liability company is a legal entity that has some of the attributes of a corporation (e.g., limitations as to legal liability for persons other than the entity) and (by means of an election) some of the characteristics of a partnership (principally, taxation as a partnership). A limited liability company is evidenced by a document forming the entity.[8]

## FLOW-THROUGH ENTITIES

Partnerships and these other joint venture entities are, for federal tax purposes, *flow-through entities*. This means that these entities are not taxpaying organizations—rather, they are conduits of net revenue (and other items) to the partners, who bear the responsibility for the payment of tax on their net income.

For tax-exempt organizations, the receipt of income from a joint venture vehicle raises issues as to unrelated business income taxation (and, in some instances, ongoing eligibility for tax-exempt status). In resolving these issues, a *look-through rule* is used. Pursuant to that rule, if a business regularly carried on by a partnership or other joint venture, of which an exempt organization is a member, is an unrelated business with respect to the organization, in computing its unrelated business income the organization must include its share of the gross income of the venture. Likewise, if the business in the venture is a related one as to the organization, the resulting income is treated as exempt function revenue. Thus, in application of the look-through rule, the business conducted by the joint venture is evaluated to determine what the outcome would be if the exempt organization directly conducted the business.[9]

## PARTNERSHIPS—DETAILS

The law regarding the involvement by public charities as general partners in limited partnerships—once one of the most controversial aspects of the law of tax-exempt organizations—has stabilized. The concern of the IRS in this regard has always been and continues to be that the resources of a charitable organization are being used to provide substantial benefits to for-profit participants in the partnership (usually the limited partners) where the exempt organization is a general partner in the partnership. It remains the view of the IRS that there is an inherent tension between the ability of a charitable organization to function exclusively in furtherance of its exempt functions and the obligation of a general partner to operate the partnership for the economic benefit of the limited partners. Indeed, the original position of the IRS was that a public charity would lose its tax-exempt status if it became a general partner in a limited partnership; that stance was predicated on application of the private inurement or private benefit doctrine.[10]

The posture of the IRS changed over the years as it lost all of the court cases on the point but one. The evolution of the law in this regard is discussed in the companion volume.[11] The aberrant court opinion is discussed there[12] and elsewhere in this book.[13]

The prevailing models in the partnership area, involving tax-exempt organizations, thus are partnerships entailing only general partners and partnerships consisting of general and limited partners.

Today, the criteria to be applied are far more refined; a three-step analysis is used:

1. Does the partnership further a charitable purpose?

2. If so, does the partnership agreement reflect an arrangement that permits the exempt organization to act primarily in furtherance of its exempt (charitable) purposes? That is, does the organization's role as general partner preclude or deter it from advancing its charitable ends?

3. If the primary purpose of the organization is not being thwarted, does the arrangement cause the exempt organization to provide an impermissible private benefit to the limited partners?

The planner should not have undue difficulty in assessing the first and third of these criteria. Indeed, as the examples below indicate, involvement in a limited partnership by a public charity as a general partner is almost always in furtherance of charitable ends. The principal rationales the planner may use in applying the first criteria are:

- The raising of needed capital[14]
- The creation of new programs

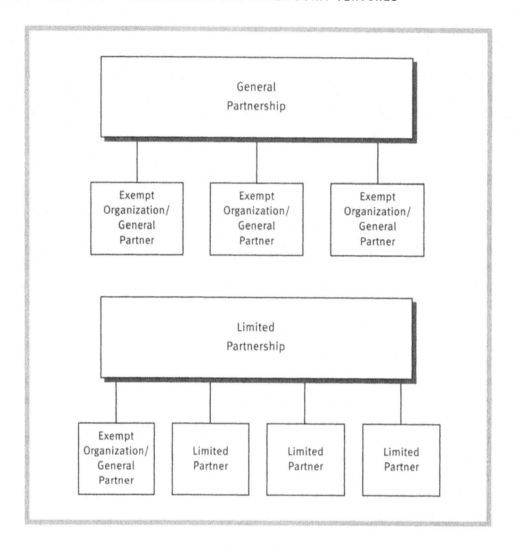

- The sharing of a risk inherent in a new exempt activity
- The pooling of diverse areas of expertise

The second criterion is troublesome; here, the IRS looks to means by which the organization may, under the particular facts and circumstances, be insulated from the day-to-day responsibilities as general partner. This element of the equation is conceptually difficult: once an entity is a general partner in a partnership, it cannot escape the responsibility and potential liability of that position.

The favorable factors that the IRS takes into consideration in evaluating a tax-exempt charitable organization's involvement as a general partner in a limited partnership are:

- Limited contractual liability of the exempt partner
- Limited (that is, reasonable) rate of return on the capital invested by the limited partners
- An exempt organization's right of first refusal on the sale of partnership assets

- The presence of additional general partners obligated to protect the interest of the limited partners
- Lack of control over the venture or the exempt organization by the for-profit limited partners
- Absence of any obligation to return the limited partners' capital from the exempt organization's funds
- Absence of profit as a primary motivating factor for the exempt organization's involvement in the partnership
- Arm's-length transactions with partners
- Management contract terminable for cause by the venture, with a limited term, renewal subject to approval of the venture, and preferably with an independent entity
- Effective control in the exempt organization over major decisions as to the venture
- Written commitment in the joint venture governing document to the fulfillment of charitable purposes in the event of a conflict with a duty to maximize profit

Not all of these criteria need be met and not all are of equal weight. For example, as to the fifth element, the IRS has approved of the arrangement where all of the limited partners in a limited partnership are members of the board of the charitable organization that is the general partner.[15] As another illustration, the last of these elements has taken on enormous importance; in one instance, the case largely turned (in favor of the exempt organization) on this point.[16]

The IRS looks at certain unfavorable factors as well:

- Disproportionate allocation of profits and/or losses in favor of the limited partners
- Commercially unreasonable loans by the exempt organization to the partnership
- Inadequate compensation received by the exempt organization for services it provides or excessive compensation paid by the exempt organization in exchange for services it receives
- Control of the exempt organization by the limited partners (see above) or lack of sufficient control by the exempt organization to ensure that it is able to carry out its charitable activities
- Abnormal or insufficient capital contributions by the limited partners
- Profit motivation on the part of the exempt partner
- Guarantee of the limited partner's projected tax credits or return on investment to the detriment of the exempt general partner

The state of the law in this regard is illuminated by IRS private letter rulings, almost all of them in the healthcare context:

- The IRS ruled that the tax-exempt status of a charitable organization should not be revoked; the issue was its participation as a general partner in seven limited partnerships.[17]
- The IRS ruled that a charitable organization, created by 10 unrelated hospitals, could remain exempt, even though it, as its only function, became a sole general partner in

a limited partnership, including individuals as limited partners, because the purpose of the partnership was furtherance of exempt purposes (operation of a lithotripsy center) and because the benefit to nonexempt limited partners (including physicians) was incidental.[18]

Two other relevant aspects of the law that the planner should consider are:

1. **Aggregate approach rule.** The IRS and the courts apply an *aggregate approach rule* in this setting.[19] This means that, when the eligibility for tax-exempt status of the nonprofit organization is being evaluated (anew or on an ongoing basis), the activities of the organization *and* the activities of a joint venture in which the organization is a member are taken into consideration.

2. **Involvement of subsidiary.** Some tax-exempt organizations, rather than becoming directly involved in a joint venture, will indirectly participate. This is accomplished by causing a subsidiary (controlled entity) to be a member in the parent's stead. Depending on the circumstances, the subsidiary may be a for-profit organization or a tax-exempt organization (the latter often a supporting organization).[20]

## LIMITED LIABILITY COMPANIES—DETAILS

Just as law developments concerning the involvement of public charities in partnerships have subsided, developments in the law concerning the use of limited liability companies by charitable and other tax-exempt organizations are on the increase. It appears today that the limited liability company is the joint venture vehicle of choice in the exempt organizations context.

Limited liability companies are of two varieties: the multimember limited liability company and the single-member limited liability company.[21]

### Multimember LLC

A limited liability company can have two or more members. One or more of the members may be tax-exempt organizations; there may be for-profit co-venturers as well. All of the members of the limited liability company may be exempt organizations.

In assessing whether the participation by a charitable organization as a member of a multimember limited liability company, consisting of one or more nonexempt persons, will have an adverse impact on the charitable organization's tax-exempt status, the planner should extrapolate from the criteria used by the IRS in making the same determination when the vehicle involved is a partnership (see above).

Again, private letter rulings illustrate this use of the multimember limited liability company (and, again, many of these rulings are in the healthcare context):

• An institution of higher education operates two neonatal intensive care units as part of being a component of an academic medical center. A hospital also operates a neonatal intensive care unit. The two organizations formed a limited liability company for the purpose of administering the hospital's existing facility and a new and expanded neonatal intensive care unit.[22]

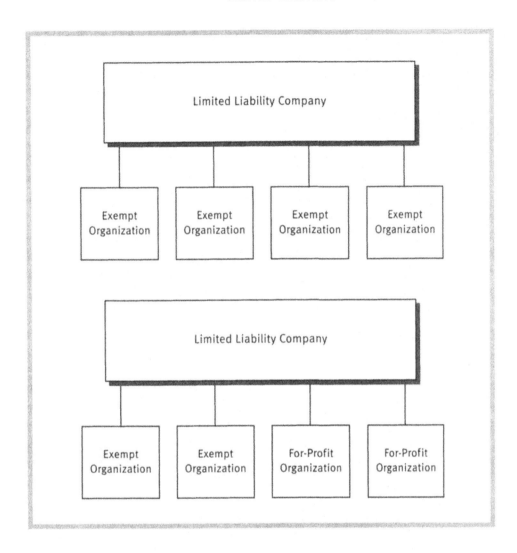

- A tax-exempt organization that provides supportive services to a healthcare provider and an exempt long-term healthcare facility formed a limited liability company for the purpose of providing rehabilitation services in a community.[23]

- A tax-exempt healthcare system and a group of physicians formed a limited liability company for the purpose of owning and operating an ambulatory surgery center.[24]

- A tax-exempt hospital owned and operated six cardiac catheterization laboratories; these facilities are in the hospital building. The hospital wanted to develop a seventh cardiac catheterization laboratory as an outpatient facility and wanted to involve the physicians who have staff privileges at the institution. The hospital created a limited liability company consisting of its supporting organization and the physicians.[25]

- Private colleges and universities can maintain their own qualified prepaid tuition plans.[26] A single plan has been established, structured for use by private colleges and universities throughout the nation; this program is stitched together by means of a "consortium agreement." The vehicle for this plan is a limited liability company, with the colleges and universities its members.[27]

- Three trade associations (business leagues) having comparable (but not similar) exempt purposes and members with congruent interests for years operated their own trade shows. To reduce the administrative costs of the shows, the associations created a limited liability company for the purpose of conducting a single trade show.[28]

The principal problem facing the planner in this context may be the ongoing tax-exempt status of the charitable organization that is a member of a limited liability company. This issue will likely arise if the charitable organization has lost control (or is perceived to have lost control) of its resources to one or more of the for-profit members. The extreme in this regard is the *whole entity joint venture,* detailed in the companion volume.[29]

Again, as the fourth of these examples illustrates, a charitable organization may cause a related entity to be the member of the limited liability company in lieu of itself. In that example, the form of the related entity was a tax-exempt supporting organization. The aggregate approach rule (see above) is applicable in this context as well.

## Single-Member LLC[30]

A limited liability company may be formed with only one member. This type of entity is disregarded for federal tax purposes.[31] This means that, while the company has the feature as to limitation on liability afforded pursuant to state law, the federal tax law regards the economic activity in the tax-exempt organization and in the limited liability company as conducted in one entity (the exempt organization). Consequently, the exempt organization in this situation must report on its annual information return the economic activity, assets, and/or liabilities of the limited liability company.

A disregarded limited liability company is regarded as a branch or division of its member owner. Thus, although the single-member limited liability company is a separate legal entity for nontax purposes, it is treated as a component of its owner for federal income tax purposes; thus, in that sense, it is not a subsidiary of the member. The IRS observed that, when the sole member of a limited liability company is a tax-exempt organization, the function of the company is treated as an "activity" of the exempt organization.[32]

Usually, the single-member limited liability company is created, with the tax feature of being disregarded deliberate. It is possible, however, for a multimember limited liability company to be treated for tax purposes as a single-member limited liability company. For example, the IRS ruled that a limited liability company with two members is nonetheless a disregarded entity because one of the members did not have any economic interest in the company and thus failed to qualify as a *member* for tax purposes.[33]

Tax-exempt organizations are making creative use of the single-member limited liability company. Some examples are:

- A public charity was working with a city government to transform the older, downtown sections of the city into a center of industry, commerce, housing, transportation, government services, and cultural and educational opportunities. These sections lack adequate parking due to the completion of several major development projects. The charity organized a single-member limited liability company to address the need

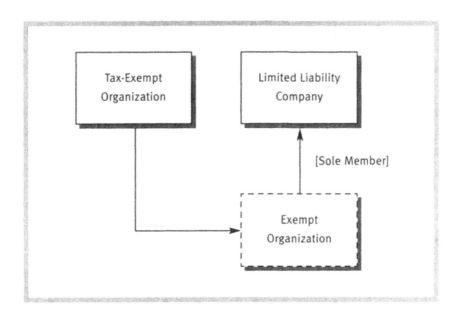

for affordable downtown parking; it will acquire a parking garage and two parking lots by means of a bond issue. The IRS ruled that the company is a disregarded entity and that its operations will not jeopardize the charity's tax-exempt status because it, by means of the company, is lessening the burdens of government[34] (the city).[35]

- A charitable organization may accept a gift of property that carries with it exposure of the donee to legal liability (such as environmental or premises tort liability). Before the advent of the single-member limited liability company, a charitable organization could attempt to shield its other assets from liability by placing the gift property in a separate exempt entity, such as a supporting organization[36] or a title-holding company.[37] Among the difficulties with this approach is the need or desire to file an application for recognition of tax exemption for the new entity and/or file annual information returns on its behalf. As an alternative, however, a charitable organization can utilize a single-member limited liability company as the vehicle to receive and hold a contribution of this nature. Each of these contributed properties can be placed in a separate single-member limited liability company, thereby offering protection in relation to each of the other properties and providing the charity overall liability protection.[38]

- A tax-exempt museum, organized as a private operating foundation,[39] owned and operated a racetrack and a campground, with these activities in a single-member limited liability company. The IRS ruled[40] that these activities were functionally related businesses.[41]

- A public charity, with the objective of constructing, owning, and leasing student housing for the benefit of a tax-exempt college, developed and operated the project through a single-member limited liability company. In this fashion it issued taxable and tax-exempt bonds, and provided temporary construction jobs and permanent employment opportunities in the community.[42]

- A charitable organization that provided educational opportunities, including housing, to low-income and other students provided facilities for various colleges, with the ownership and operation of each facility in a separate limited liability company.[43]

In the unrelated business setting, a supporting organization[44] affiliated with an operating educational institution[45] was the sole member of a limited liability company. The IRS ruled that when the single-member limited liability company receives real property encumbered by debt, it and the supporting organization will be afforded an exemption from the rules concerning acquisition indebtedness[46] for purposes of determining debt-financed income.[47]

## OTHER JOINT VENTURES

Tax-exempt organizations may be involved in relationships or arrangements with other entities (exempt or nonexempt) that constitute joint ventures, although there is no formal joint venture vehicle (namely, a partnership or limited liability company). Often, however, these arrangements are not viewed by the parties as joint ventures at all— although the law may see things differently (see below).

One of the issues the planner may have to face in this context is the filing of a partnership return.[48] The law is unclear as to when an arrangement becomes sufficiently "formal" as to trigger this reporting.

## WHOLE ENTITY JOINT VENTURES—COMMENTARY

The U.S. Tax Court's sole decision, in 1999, in the whole entity joint venture setting, which was affirmed,[49] is reflected in a momentous opinion; it is having a major impact on the operation of healthcare entities. From a larger perspective, however, it is fascinating to speculate on what this case means for public charities in general.

The case is one in a series of cases (more assuredly will follow) where a variety of major law doctrines in the exempt organizations field swirl about: private inurement, private benefit, intermediate sanctions, involvement in partnerships and other joint ventures, and the commerciality doctrine.

From a health law perspective, the case is seen as an example of the whole hospital joint venture, which it obviously is. The case provides judicial underpinning for the IRS's position as to these ventures.[50] The fundamental principle is this: when a public charity (in the case, a surgical center) cedes authority over its operations to a related for-profit organization, it will quite likely lose its tax-exempt status.

From the larger perspective, however, this case is a *private benefit* case; indeed, it is a significant private benefit case. In the past, some advisers would evaluate a set of facts involving a transaction between a public charity and a for-profit person and determine if that person was an *insider* (for private benefit purposes) or a *disqualified person* (for excess benefit transaction purposes). If the answer to both questions was no, the analysis ended. Clearly, this can no longer be the practice because of the sudden emergence of the private benefit doctrine as a major force. This is because private benefit can occur even where the person being benefited is not an insider or disqualified person. In the case, the Tax Court wrote that impermissible private benefit can be conferred on "unrelated or disinterested" persons.[51]

Another reason the private benefit doctrine has not received much attention until recent years is that it is somewhat hidden. It is not in the Code nor is it in the regulations. There have been, until recently, few court opinions on the subject. As the Tax Court nicely stated in this case, the private benefit proscription "inheres in the requirement that an organization operate exclusively [primarily] for exempt purposes."[52]

Until recently, most of the private benefit cases concerned public charities' relationships with individuals. The prime case had been the one involving a school, which failed to gain exemption because it conferred private benefit (other than insubstantially) on individuals in their private capacity.[53] The whole entity joint venture case, however, should be forcing public charities to face another application of the private benefit doctrine: their relationships with for-profit organizations.

This joint venture case teaches that a fundamental concept in this context is *control*. The opinion stands as a warning to all public charities to examine their relationships with for-profit entities to see if they have lost control of their resources to a for-profit entity. Examples are relationships as reflected in management agreements, leases, fundraising contracts, and, of course, partnership or other joint venture agreements. The scary aspect of all of this is that it is irrelevant if the public charity is in fact engaging in exempt activities and if the fees paid by the exempt organization to the for-profit one are reasonable (traditional private inurement analysis). There still can be private benefit.

That rule of law is the essence of a case decided by the Tax Court in 1979.[54] The point has been made subsequently, however. In a case decided by the U.S. Court of Appeals for the Ninth Circuit in 1985, the court wrote: "The critical inquiry is not whether particular contractual payments to a related for-profit organization are reasonable or excessive, but instead whether the entire enterprise is carried on in such a manner that the for-profit organization benefits substantially from the operation of" the nonprofit organization.[55]

The case in this area that has been regarded as being on the outer reaches of all this is the Tax Court's 1979 decision. That case—20 years of age at the time of the whole entity joint venture decision—had almost been forgotten—until now. One of the underdiscussed aspects of the whole hospital joint venture case is its resurrection of the law embodied in the 1979 case. The problem is that the 1979 case involved extreme facts, and the Tax Court took a hard line.

In the 1979 case, several for-profit organizations that did not have any formal structural control over the nonprofit entity in question nevertheless exerted "considerable control" over its activities.[56] The for-profit entities set fees that the nonprofit organization charged the public for training sessions, required the nonprofit organization to carry on certain types of educational activities, and provided management personnel paid for by and responsible to one of the for-profit organizations. Under a licensing agreement with the for-profit organizations, the nonprofit entity was allowed to use certain intellectual property for 10 years; at the end of the licensing period, all copyrighted material, including new material developed by the nonprofit organization, was required to be turned over to the for-profit organizations. The nonprofit organization was required to use its excess funds for the development of related research. The for-profit organizations also required that trainers and local organizations sign an agreement not to compete with the nonprofit entity for two years after terminating their relationship with comparable organizations.

The Tax Court concluded in 1979 that the nonprofit organization was "part of a franchise system which is operated for private benefit and . . . its affiliation with this system taints it with a substantial commercial purpose."[57] The "ultimate beneficiaries" of the nonprofit organization's activities were found to be the for-profit corporations; the nonprofit organization was "simply the instrument to subsidize the for-profit corporations and not vice versa."[58] The nonprofit organization was held to not be operating exclusively for charitable purposes.

This 1979 case, then, has framed the borders (to date, anyway) of this analysis. Even without formal control over the ostensible tax-exempt organization by one or more for-profit entities, the ostensible exempt organization can be seen as merely the instrument to subsidize a for-profit organization. The nonprofit organization's "affiliation" with a for-profit entity or a "system" involving one or more for-profit entities can taint the nonprofit organization with a substantial commercial purpose. The result: private benefit that causes the nonprofit organization to lose or be denied tax-exempt status.

Matters worsen within these boundaries when there is actual control. This is the message sent by the whole hospital joint venture decision. In that case, the public charity became a co-general partner with a for-profit organization in a partnership that owns and operates the surgery center. The arrangement was managed by a for-profit management company that was affiliated with the for-profit co-general partner. The participation in the partnership was the public charity's sole activity. (Hence the name *whole hospital joint venture.*) The court termed this "passive participation in a for-profit health-service enterprise."[59]

The Tax Court concluded that it is "patently clear" that the partnership was not being operated in an exclusively charitable manner.[60] The income-producing activity of the partnership was characterized as "indivisible."[61] No "discrete part" of these activities was "severable from those activities that produce income to be applied to the other partners' profit."[62]

The heart of the whole hospital joint venture case is this: to the extent that a public charity "cedes control over its sole activity to for-profit parties [by, in this case, entering into the joint venture] having an independent economic interest in the same activity and having no obligation to put charitable purposes ahead of profit-making objectives," the charity cannot be assured that the partnership will in fact be operated in furtherance of charitable purposes.[63] The consequence is the conferring on the for-profit parties "significant private benefits."[64]

This matter of control is not always so stark as was the situation in the whole hospital joint venture case. For example, the litigation involving the United Cancer Council[65] shows how courts can differ over whether a nonprofit organization is controlled by a for-profit one. This matter is also reflected in the definitions of *disqualified person* in the intermediate sanctions context.[66]

Further, it would be a mistake for a public charity to disregard the whole hospital joint venture case on the basis that the charity is not involved in a partnership. As discussed below, there does not have to be a formal partnership agreement for the rules to apply. The law can characterize the relationship between two organizations as a *joint venture* even though neither organization has an intent or desire to be in a joint venture. In some of the cases that the IRS lost on the issue of whether revenue constitutes a royalty, the IRS asserted that the exempt organizations involved were effectively participating in a joint venture.[67]

The IRS exempt organization continuing professional education technical instruction program textbook for fiscal year 2001 contains an article discussing the private benefit doctrine. There, the IRS conceded that "in reality it is difficult to apply the private benefit analysis." The doctrine is applied in this discussion to charter schools and organizations providing low-income housing.

What can a public charity do to protect itself against allegations of this type of private benefit? Obviously, the main factor is to not lose control over program activities. Another element is one of documentation; the agreements and other documents involved should stress the powers and functions of the nonprofit organization. Contracts should be negotiated at arm's length. Contracts for services should not have long terms. (The management agreement in the whole hospital joint venture case had the partnership, and thus the charity, locked in for at least 15 years.) If a partnership is involved, the public charity should try to have assets and other resources apart from those invested in the partnership. The public charity should try to receive gifts and grants on an ongoing basis, and not rely solely on exempt function revenue. (This factor is prompted by the commerciality doctrine.) Overall, the exempt organization should not be operated so as to provide to a for-profit entity a nonincidental "advantage; profit; fruit; privilege; gain; [or] interest."[68]

## ANCILLARY JOINT VENTURES

A pending issue is the extent to which the principles of law being developed in the whole entity joint venture setting are applicable in connection with the operations of ancillary joint ventures. An *ancillary joint venture* is a joint venture involving a public charity where less than the entirety of the charity's resources are placed in the venture (see above). The ancillary joint venture is sometimes termed the *programmatic joint venture*.

The law on this point is just evolving. In one instance, the IRS approved a proposed joint venture to operate an ambulatory surgery center.[69] This joint venture, which involved a public charity and nonexempt entities (physicians), serves as an illustration of the type of these ventures.

### Facts

The charitable organization involved was a supporting organization (SO) that operated a community-based healthcare system. SO and its affiliates provided hospital, physician, home health, hospice, nursing home, and other healthcare services. Other functions constituted the primary activities of SO.

In order to better serve community needs, SO and a group of local physicians formed a limited liability company (LLC) to own and operate an ambulatory surgery center. The ruling stated that SO formerly owned and operated the center, but somehow the center became owned by a for-profit subsidiary of SO (FP). Inasmuch as involvement in the center was not the primary activity of SO, this was an *ancillary joint venture*.

SO acquired a 70 percent ownership interest in LLC. The physicians acquired the remaining 30 percent interest. SO was to reduce its percentage interest in LLC by selling membership interests to board-approved purchasers until its percentage interest was 51 percent. Profits and losses were to be allocated to the members based on membership percentage.

LLC leased the center from FP. It also leased the equipment used in the center pursuant to a separate lease agreement. SO represented to the IRS that both of the lease agreements were negotiated at arm's length and that they reflected the fair market rental value of the facilities and the fair market purchase value of the equipment.

The operations of LLC were conducted pursuant to the terms of an operating agreement. That agreement provided that the purpose of LLC was to lease and/or own and operate an ambulatory surgery center in furtherance of charitable purposes by promoting health for a broad cross section of the community. It further provided that LLC and its board of directors would at all times cause LLC to be operated for these purposes and that this duty overrode any duty to operate LLC for the benefit of its members. SO represented that this override was enforceable under state law.

LLC was managed on a day-to-day basis by a board of directors; the total number of directors was six. SO appointed two of the directors; the physician members elected four of the directors. Each director appointed by SO had three votes on all matters coming before the board. Each of the other directors had one vote. Board decisions were by majority vote. The directors appointed by SO were community leaders experienced in healthcare matters, were not on the medical staff of the hospital or on the medical staff of the center, and were not otherwise engaged in business transactions with SO, LLC, or the center.

LLC had a charity care policy that was consistent with SO's charity care policy. This policy was made known to potential patients. Charity care was not included in bad debt. The percentages of patients that were expected to be served by LLC, as to indigents, Medicare and Medicaid patients, self-pay patients, and the like, were approximately equivalent to the percentages of patients served at the center when it was owned by SO.

Physician privileges at LLC's facility were not dependent on ownership of a membership interest in LLC. Medical staff members applied for and were granted privileges at the facility based on credentialing criteria. LLC did not have nor plan for any employees; SO provided support services to LLC. SO leased nursing, clinical, administrative, clerical, and other personnel to LLC. Medical staff members were independent practitioners. Professional services were billed separately by the independent practicing medical staff members providing the service.

## Law and Analysis

The IRS began the analysis of these facts by emphasizing three fundamental points of law: the promotion of health is a charitable purpose,[70] whether a healthcare organization promotes health in a charitable manner is determined under the community benefit standard,[71] and the activities of a partnership are attributed to a tax-exempt member for purposes of application of the *operational test*.[72] As discussed, this third element of the law is known as the *aggregate principle;* it was articulated in the IRS revenue ruling concerning whole hospital joint ventures.[73] In the ruling in this case, the IRS wrote that "[a]ggregate treatment is also consistent with the treatment of partnerships for purposes of the unrelated business income tax."

The IRS observed that a charitable organization may form and participate in a partnership, as well as a limited liability company, and meet the operational test if (1) participation in the partnership furthers a charitable purpose and (2) the partnership arrangement permits the exempt organization to act exclusively in furtherance of its exempt purposes and only incidentally for the benefit of for-profit partners. The agency also said that, based on its revenue ruling, whether a nonprofit organization, the principal activity of which is the ownership of a membership interest in a limited liability company that is engaged in healthcare activities, satisfies the community benefit standard depends on all of the facts and circumstances.

In this case, the IRS ruled that, following the formation and operation of LLC, SO would continue to be primarily involved in furthering the needs of the exempt hospital system and its tax-exempt entities. Also, its participation in this venture was ruled to further its exempt purposes. SO's participation in LLC and operation of the ambulatory surgery center was said to promote health for the community. The structure of LLC and operation of the center was portrayed by the IRS as allowing SO to act exclusively in furtherance of charitable purposes with no undue private benefit to the physician members.

As is the case with other joint ventures, the IRS focused on *control*. As noted, SO owned at least 51 percent of LLC. It had six of the 10 votes on LLC's board of directors. Because a majority of votes was needed to approve decisions, SO exercised effective control over the major decisions of LLC and over the operations of the center. This control ensured that the assets SO owned through LLC and the activities it conducted through LLC at the center would be used primarily to further tax-exempt purposes. Also, the IRS reiterated that the operating agreement of LLC provided that the duty of its members and board was to operate LLC in a manner that furthered charitable purposes and that this duty overrode any duty to operate LLC for the financial benefit of its members.

## Commentary

This ruling is the first effort by the IRS to extend the principles of law in the realm of whole hospital joint ventures to other types of joint ventures. But the ruling is confusing as to the facts and legal principles.

Thus, the ruling stated that SO "formerly owned" the ambulatory surgery center before it became LLC's operation, yet it also stated that LLC leased the center from a for-profit subsidiary of SO. The "primary business" of SO was said to be a set of unidentified activities, so the involvement of SO in LLC presumably was less than primary. Yet, the law analysis speaks of a "nonprofit organization whose principal activity is the ownership of a membership interest in a limited liability company."

As discussed above, there are essentially three types of these ventures. In one, the entirety of the exempt organization is in the venture (e.g., whole hospital joint venture). In the second, the primary operations of the exempt organization are in the venture. In the third, something less than primary operations of the exempt organization are in the venture.

It makes sense to apply the aggregate principle and the control test in determining eligibility for tax-exempt status in connection with the first two types of these ventures. More specifically in the healthcare setting, the community benefit standard is involved in both instances.

In the ancillary joint venture setting, however, the milieu is different. The IRS said in this ruling that the aggregate principle applies in the unrelated activity context. Fair enough. But where the involvement in a venture is a small portion of its overall activities, the operational test is not involved (assuming that the exempt organization continues to be primarily operated for exempt purposes).

Then there is this matter of control. Assuming the public charity must retain control of its assets in connection with entire and primary involvement in joint ventures, it does not necessarily follow that control is needed in the ancillary venture setting. Suppose a public charity is involved in such a venture and does not retain control of the assets it transferred. Does that automatically mean that the venture is an unrelated business? Does that automatically mean that undue private benefit is conferred? There are some unexplained leaps and gaps in reasoning here.

The test should be the facts and circumstances of whether charitable ends are being furthered. In the healthcare arena, the test should be whether the community benefit standard is being met. There are extrapolations here from the law of whole entity joint ventures to the law of ancillary joint ventures that require more exploration and analysis.

## LAW-IMPOSED JOINT VENTURES

In some instances, the law will treat an arrangement as a general partnership (or other joint venture) for tax purposes, even though the parties involved intended (or insist they intended) that their relationship is something else. The ostensible true relationship may be that of landlord and tenant, parties pursuant to a management agreement, or payor and payee of royalties. As discussed in the companion volume, the law is unclear as to the criteria used in making these assessments.[74]

Case law on this point, concerning landlord-tenant relationships, is summarized in the companion volume.[75] As another illustration, the IRS asserted there was a joint venture relationship involving a volunteer fire company and taverns in a county in which the organization placed "tip jars." This was a fundraising program conducted by the fire company; the court declined to find the presence of a joint venture.[76]

## LOOK-THROUGH RULE—DETAILS

As noted, when a tax-exempt organization is a member of a joint venture, the look-through principle applies in determining whether any resulting income is or is not unrelated business income. The planner is required to evaluate the nature of the business in the venture in relation to the purposes of the exempt organization and assess what the tax outcome would be if the exempt organization conducted the business directly. That evaluation will lead to the conclusion as to whether the revenue from the venture is taxable or not.

The same unrelated business rules apply in this setting as apply generally. This includes the modification rules for passive and other income.

Following are some examples of this point:

- A tax-exempt group trust arrangement has as its principal purpose serving as a medium for the collective investment of the funds of pension, profit-sharing, and other qualified benefit trusts in real estate and real estate interests. This entity has interests in partnerships and limited liability companies; the properties owned therein are held for leasing purposes. The IRS ruled that to the extent the organization receives income from a partnership or limited liability company, the character of the income as rent from real property[77] is retained and its flow through the partnerships and limited liability companies does not preclude the income from being received by the organization tax-free.[78]

- Three trade associations (business leagues) having comparable (but not similar) exempt purposes and members with congruent interests for years operated their own trade shows. To reduce the administrative costs of the shows, the associations created a limited liability company for the purpose of conducting a single trade show. The IRS ruled that the trade show income is protected by the special trade show rules in the unrelated business setting[79] and thus that the income is received by each of these associations free of tax.[80]

## NOTES

1. See Chapter 3.
2. Id., pages 71–76.
3. See pages 164–165 below.
4. In general, see *Tax-Exempt Organizations,* § 32.1.
5. Id., § 32.3.
6. Id., § 32.4.
7. Id., § 32.5.
8. Id., §§ 4.1(b), 30.7, 32.4.
9. Id., § 28.4.
10. Id., § 32.2(a).
11. Id.
12. Id., § 32.2, text accompanied by nn. 27–31.
13. See Chapter 11, pages 282–287.

14. Involvement of a charitable organization in a partnership is often a means to an end: raising of capital for one or more projects that advance the organization's exempt purposes. A partnership is, for the most part, a fundraising vehicle. The major problem in the federal tax setting is that, in its zeal to raise needed capital, the charitable organization transgresses the private inurement or private benefit doctrine. E.g., Redlands Surgical Servs. v. Comm'r, 113 T.C. 47 (1999), *aff'd*, 242 F.3d 904 (9th Cir. 2001); Rev. Rul. 98-15, 1998-1 C.B. 718. In general, *Tax-Exempt Organizations*, § 32.4.

15. E.g., Tech. Adv. Mem. 200151045; Priv. Ltr. Rul. 8541108.

16. St. David's Health Care Sys., Inc. v. United States, 2002-1 U.S.T.C. ¶ 50,452 (W.D. Tex. 2002), *vacated and remanded*, 349 F.3d 232 (5th Cir. 2003). Following a trial ordered on the remand, a jury, on March 4, 2004, found that the healthcare system should retain its tax-exempt status.

17. Priv. Ltr. Rul. 8938001.

18. Priv. Ltr. Rul. 200151045.

19. Rev. Rul. 98-15, note 14 above. One of the principal decisions on the aggregate approach rule is Butler v. Comm'r, 36 T.C. 1097 (1961).

20. See Chapter 6, pages 131–134.

21. State law needs to be checked on this point, inasmuch as the law may not permit single-member limited liability companies.

22. Priv. Ltr. Rul. 200044040. Likewise, Priv. Ltr. Ruls. 200325003, 200325004.

23. Priv. Ltr. Ruls. 200102052, 200102053.

24. Priv. Ltr. Rul. 200118054. Likewise, Priv. Ltr. Rul. 200117043.

25. Priv. Ltr. Ruls. 200304041, 200304042.

26. See *Tax-Exempt Organizations*, § 18.16.

27. Priv. Ltr. Rul. 200311034.

28. Priv. Ltr. Ruls. 200333031–200333033.

29. *Tax-Exempt Organizations*, § 32.4.

30. In general, see *Tax-Exempt Organizations*, § 30.7.

31. Id., § 4.1(b).

32. Priv. Ltr. Rul. 200134025.

33. Priv. Ltr. Rul. 200201024.

34. For a discussion of lessening the burdens of government as a charitable purpose, see *Tax-Exempt Organizations*, § 6.4.

35. Priv. Ltr. Rul. 200124022.

36. See Chapter 4, pages 91–99.

37. *Tax-Exempt Organizations*, § 18.2.

38. Priv. Ltr. Rul. 200134025.

39. *Tax-Exempt Organizations*, § 11.1(b).

40. Priv. Ltr. Rul. 200202077.

41. *Tax-Exempt Organizations*, § 11.3(c).

42. Priv. Ltr. Rul. 200249014.

43. Priv. Ltr. Rul. 200304036.

44. *Tax-Exempt Organizations*, § 11.3(c).

45. Id., § 11.3(a).

46. *Tax-Exempt Organizations*, § 29.3.

47. Priv. Ltr. Rul. 200134025.

48. See *Tax-Exempt Organizations*, § 32.6.

49. See note 14 above.

50. Id.

51. Redlands Surgical Servs. v. Comm'r, note 14 above, 113 T.C. at 74.

52. Id.

53. American Campaign Acad. v. Comm'r, 92 T.C. 1053 (1989). See Chapter 11, pages 276–280.

54. est of Haw. v. Comm'r, 71 T.C. 1067 (1979), *aff'd,* 647 F.2d 170 (9th Cir. 1981).

55. Church by Mail v. Comm'r, 48 T.C.M. 471 (1984), *aff'd,* 765 F.2d 1387 (9th Cir. 1985).

56. est of Haw. v. Comm'r, note 54 above, 71 T.C. at 1080.

57. Id.

58. Id. at 1082.

59. Redlands Surgical Servs. v. Comm'r, note 14 above, 113 T.C. at 77.

60. Id.

61. Id.

62. Id.

63. Id. at 78.

64. Id.

65. United Cancer Council, Inc. v. Comm'r, 109 T.C. 326 (1997), *rev'd,* 165 F.3d 1173 (7th Cir. 1999). See Chapter 11, pages 266–270.

66. See Chapter 3, pages 71–72.

67. *Tax-Exempt Organizations,* § 27.1(g).

68. American Campaign Acad. v. Comm'r, note 53 above, 92 T.C. at 1065–1066.

69. Priv. Ltr. Rul. 200118054.

70. *Tax-Exempt Organizations,* § 6.3.

71. *Tax-Exempt Healthcare Organizations,* chap. 6.

72. See text accompanied by note 19 above.

73. Rev. Rul. 98-15, note 14 above.

74. *Tax-Exempt Organizations,* § 32.1, text accompanied by nn. 9–16.

75. Id., text accompanied by nn. 17–18.

76. Vigilant Hose Co. of Emmitsburg v. United States, 2001-2 U.S.T.C. ¶ 50,458 (D. Md. 2001). See Chapter 11, pages 318–320.

77. *Tax-Exempt Organizations,* § 27.1(h).

78. Priv. Ltr. Rul. 200147058.

79. *Tax-Exempt Organizations,* § 27.2(f).

80. Priv. Ltr. Ruls. 200333031–200333033.

# CHAPTER 8

# Unrelated Business Rules

Nearly every organization that is exempt from federal income taxation is subject to the rules concerning unrelated business activities.[1] This body of law is one of the oldest components of the law of tax-exempt organizations (having originated in 1950) and one of the most extensive elements of it. The statutory law, regulations, case law, and IRS rulings (public and private) on the subject are plentiful. Yet, this area of the law of tax-exempt organizations remains complex and thus fertile ground, augmented by traps and exceptions, for planning opportunities.

## LAW BASICS

The companion book describes this law in considerable detail.[2] Topics include:

- Rationales underlying these rules[3]
- Definition of the term *business*[4]
- Determination of when a business is *regularly carried on*[5]
- Ascertaining whether a business is or is not *substantially related* to the furtherance of an organization's exempt purposes[6]
- Modifications[7]
- Exceptions[8]

The companion book also explores the contemporary applications of these rules,[9] the feeder organization rules,[10] the unrelated debt-financed income rules,[11] the tax-exempt entity leasing rules,[12] the application of these rules to business conducted in partnerships,[13] and the tax computations.[14]

## PERSPECTIVES

Lawyers and accountants are comfortable with the following notion, although most others in the nonprofit sector are not: tax-exempt organizations engage, exclusively or at least primarily, in *business*. The term is, in many ways, unfortunate, and certainly confusing. Those in management of nonprofit organizations prefer terms such as *activities* or (even better) *program*.

The difficulty here, of course, is that *business* is commonly perceived as what happens in the for-profit sector. (The nonprofit sector generally regards itself as above such conduct.) While a visit to the dictionary yields a wide range of applications of the word, the overwhelming emphasis in defining the word *business* is commercial and industrial enterprises, engaged in for profit. The term is often contrasted with undertakings such as hobbies, professions, sports, and (most relevant) the arts.

In the law of tax-exempt organizations, however, the term *business* is a neutral one. Basically, the term is synonymous with *function*. Just about everything a tax-exempt organization does amounts to the conduct of a business. This perspective is repeatedly reflected in the construct of the annual information return, for example, where the filing organization is required to report its expenses on a functional basis, its program service accomplishments, and its income-producing activities.[15]

**CAUTION!**

⌐his element of neutrality of the term *business* is not always fully recognized by courts. For example, a federal court of appeals wrote: "The fact that an organization's primary activity may constitute a trade or business does not, of itself, disqualify it from classification under § 501(c)(3), provided the trade or business furthers or accomplishes an exempt purpose."[16] First, an organization's "primary activity" *must be* (not *may be*) the conduct of one or more businesses. Second, obviously the conduct of a business per se by an organization does not (or cannot or will not) disqualify it for tax-exempt status. Third, the court too closely blended the notions of *business* and *related business*.

Thus, when the managers of a tax-exempt organization, and their professional advisers, confront, and plan in connection with, the law of unrelated business, it is essential that they do so with this mindset. From this tax law perspective, the organization is a cluster or bundle of businesses. That sometimes indigestible fact is mirrored in the *fragmentation rule*.[17] This rule requires an exempt organization to be conceptually fragmented into its various discrete parts—whether by the IRS, a court, or the organization's lawyer—for purposes of independent evaluation in light of the unrelated business law (and, as noted, elsewhere).

The fragmentation rule was written from a negative standpoint. The rule states, in essence, that a tax-exempt organization cannot hide a business (such as an unrelated business) for tax purposes merely by nestling it in among a number of related activities. Here is the rule, clunkily stated as it is: "An activity does not lose identity as trade or business merely because it is carried on within a larger aggregate of similar activities or within a larger complex of other endeavors which may, or may not, be related to the exempt purpose of the organization."[18]

Consequently, when evaluating the undertakings of an existing tax-exempt organization, or planning new endeavors for an exempt organization, the concept of *fragmentation* is critical. Just like the word *business* is neutral, however, so is the idea of *fragmentation*. An exempt organization can employ the concept for its benefit; the rule is not merely a device to facilitate and enhance unrelated business income taxation.[19]

## Unrelated Business Evaluation—Steps

In evaluating the status of a tax-exempt organization in relation to the unrelated business rules—which is to say, deciding whether the conduct of an activity will expose the organization to tax and, if so, how much—planning may have to entail as many as 12 steps. They are:

1. Determining whether the tax-exempt organization involved is subject to the unrelated business rules

2. Determining whether the activity involved or being contemplated is a *business*

3. Determining whether the business is or will be *regularly carried on*

4. Determining whether the business is or will be *related* to the exempt purposes of the exempt organization

5. Determining whether the business is or will be *substantially related* to the exempt purposes of the exempt organization

6. Ascertaining whether some or all of the exempt organization's unrelated business *income* is sheltered from taxation by an exception

7. Ascertaining whether some or all of the exempt organization's income from unrelated business *activity* is sheltered from taxation by an exception

8. Computing unrelated business *taxable* income, by marshaling an appropriate amount of expenses (if any) that can be used to minimize or even eliminate tax

9. Determining if there are one or more unrelated businesses conducted by the exempt organization that generate a loss, so that that loss can be offset against the gain generated by another unrelated business

10. Ascertaining how much unrelated business activity the exempt organization can engage in without endangering its tax-exempt status

11. Deciding whether one or more unrelated businesses should be transferred to or initially placed in another organization

12. In connection with the previous step, deciding what the form and tax status of that other organization should be

### Step 1:  Ascertain Whether the Rules Apply

This first step is likely to be one of the easiest. It is also quite common that the outcome of the determination will be favorable to the government. This is because the unrelated business rules are applicable to nearly all categories of tax-exempt organization.[20]

The organizations that are *not* subject to the unrelated business rules are:

- State and local governmental units[21]

- Instrumentalities of the federal government[22]
- Certain religious and apostolic organizations[23]
- Farmer's cooperatives[24]
- Shipowners' protection and indemnity associations[25]

Notwithstanding the first of these categories, however, there is an exception to the exception: the unrelated business rules are applicable to colleges and universities that are agencies or instrumentalities of a government or political subdivision of a government, or that are owned or operated by a government or such political subdivision or by any agency or instrumentality of one or more governments or political subdivisions of them; the rules also apply to any corporation wholly owned by one or more of these colleges or universities.[26]

## COMMENT ➤

A planning element in this setting, then, is to determine whether it may be appropriate to form an organization as, or convert the tax-exempt organization that is in nongovernmental form (other than an institution of higher education) to, a governmental entity.[27] There are other benefits to this approach; this type of organization is not subject to the intermediate sanctions rules[28] nor is it required to file an annual information return with the IRS.[29]

## NOTE ✎

This type of *conversion* may not be easy to effectuate. The IRS has pointed out that there is no procedure by which a tax-exempt organization can jettison its exempt status.[30] One way out of exempt status, however, is to violate an element of the applicable organizational test[31] or operational test.[32] For example, an exempt charitable organization could repeal its dissolution clause[33] and report itself to the IRS. Another approach would be for the tax-exempt (most likely, charitable) organization to assert that the IRS ruling (determination letter) recognizing its exempt status was issued in error and that it is the type of governmental entity that does not qualify as an exempt organization, so that the ruling is void.[34]

## Step 2: Ascertain Whether the Activity Is or Will Be a *Business*

From an unrelated business law planning standpoint, the logical place to begin (assuming the tax-exempt organization is subject to the rules) is to determine whether the activity in question (existing or planned) amounts to a *business*.[35] Certainly, an activity cannot be an *unrelated business* if it is not a *business*. As noted, however, nearly every activity of a tax-exempt organization constitutes a *business*.[36] Thus, if this is raised as an issue, the exempt organization will likely lose the argument. This nearly predetermined outcome is based in large part on the sweeping and encompassing statutory definition of the term, which is that it includes "any activity which is carried on for the production of income from the sale of goods or the performance of services."[37]

Courts, however, occasionally supply their own definition of the term *business*. This fact basically is the planner's only hope in this setting. Three court opinions illustrate the point.

In one case, the tax-exempt organization involved, a volunteer fire department, raised funds to support its firefighting activities by receiving the proceeds from the operation of "tip jars" placed in taverns. This is a legal gambling activity by which patrons purchase pieces of paper (tickets) that may entitle them to cash or other prizes. The IRS asserted that the net tip jar proceeds received by this exempt organization constituted unrelated business taxable income. The court disagreed.[38] Clearly, this activity of the volunteer fire department was carried on for the production of income from the sale of goods. Yet this court looked at other law informing the concept of *business* and noted that, at least for tax purposes, an activity, to rise to the level of a business, must be engaged in extensively over a substantial period of time. The court concluded that the exempt organization's role in this endeavor was confined to joint (with the taverns) application to the county for a gaming permit and purchasing the tip jar tickets. The court held that the organization was not engaged in a business because the activity was not sufficiently extensive.[39]

In another case, the tax-exempt organization was a labor organization funded by means of the collection of per capita "taxes" from affiliated labor unions. The IRS contended that the net dues payments were forms of unrelated business income. The court disagreed.[40] It could not find any activity performed by the labor organization that was in competition with for-profit entities.[41] The court wrote that an exempt labor organization levying this type of tax on other labor organizations, so that the taxing organization may perform its exempt functions, "simply is not conducting a trade or business."[42]

In the third case, the receipt of payments by a tax-exempt association pursuant to its involvement in insurance plans was ruled to not constitute a business because the activity did not possess the general characteristics of a business.[43] An unrelated for-profit corporation handled all of the promotion, marketing, and administration of the insurance programs; another unrelated company processed the insurance applications and made decisions about coverage. The organization was perceived by the court as the passive recipient of income generated by an asset owned by the association (an interest in insurance reserves).

These three court opinions illustrate the fact that a court may refuse to confine its analysis of the law on this point to the statutory definition of the term *business*—or simply ignore that definition—but instead turn its attention to, and apply to the advantage of the tax-exempt organization involved, other elements of the law, tax or otherwise.[44] Planners should surely take this conflicted aspect of the law into account when structuring an exempt organization's operations. The facts of each case will determine, however, if this approach is suitable as an affirmative planning technique or is to be mustered only as the last desperate act.

## NOTE

There is still another element that the courts have engrafted onto the statutory definition of the term *business*: the matter of a *profit motive*.[45] This aspect of the definition is discussed as part of the fifth and ninth steps in the analysis.

## Step 3: Determine Whether the Business Is or Will Be *Regularly Carried On*

Assuming that (1) the tax-exempt organization involved is subject to the unrelated business rules and (2) the activity involved is a business, the planner should determine whether the business is regularly carried on.[46] This is where the factor of competition is most pertinent—the underlying purpose of the unrelated business rules is to prevent tax-exempt organizations from unfairly competing with for-profit organizations.[47]

There are three considerations—some would say traps—that planners should take into account when considering this element.

One consideration is that this element always matches what is occurring in the for-profit sector. Usually, the business being evaluated is regularly carried on in both sectors. If, however, the activity is normally undertaken commercially only on a *seasonal* basis, then regularity for a tax-exempt organization is measured over that period. Because, generally, regularity is determined by an assessment of activity during a full year, the use of a season as the measuring period will almost always mean that it will be easier to conclude that the activity is regularly carried on.[48]

Another consideration stems from the contemporary proclivity of tax-exempt organizations to sidestep unrelated business income taxation by outsourcing activities that would or may be unrelated businesses if undertaken directly by the exempt organization. While transferring the activity to another tax-exempt organization may accomplish this objective (albeit usually also transferring the problem), most likely the transferee will be a for-profit entity. Also, it is likely that the transferee will be unrelated to the transferor exempt organization.

There is, however, a nontax law aspect of all this that may trump the tax law considerations and thus defeat the tax reasons for the maneuver: the law pertaining to principals and agents. When a person (the principal) authorizes another person to act in the stead of the first person (making the second person the agent of the first person), the acts of the second person are, for law purposes, deemed to be acts of the first person. In other words, the act of the agent is regarded as the act of the principal; differentiation between the parties is disregarded.

Tax-exempt organizations have a tendency to "want it both ways" in this context. For example, an exempt entity, planning to outsource a function to an unrelated party, may wish to retain a form of quality control over the product or service involved. To that end, the exempt organization includes in the contract between the parties a provision stating that the other party is functioning as an agent of the exempt organization. From a tax-exempt status viewpoint, however, this is a mistake—for the obvious reason that the acts of the other party will be attributed by the IRS to the exempt organization for tax purposes, thus placing the exempt organization in the same position (or perhaps a worse one) it would be in had it engaged in the activity involved directly.[49] Thus, planners should work with their exempt organizations clients to avoid this approach.

The third of these considerations can, in the appropriate set of circumstances (such as in the fundraising setting), be the most serious. This is the matter of *preparatory time*.[50] Traditionally, when evaluating whether a business is regularly carried on, the fact-finder looks only at the amount of time consumed by the activity itself (such as a weekend per year). The IRS, however, in recent years, has also been taking into consideration the amount of time the exempt organization expended in preparing for the event. An activity by itself may not be considered regularly carried on, but when coupled with preparatory time it may be deemed to be regularly carried on.

The best illustration of the IRS's approach in this area was provided in a technical advice memorandum issued in 1997.[51] The matter concerned a tax-exempt labor organization that sponsored concerts, for fundraising purposes, two weekends on a semiannual basis; the concerts were, of course, a business (Step 2) and were not related to exempt (labor) purposes (Step 4). The conduct of a business four days per year is not the regularly carrying on of a business. Because of the preparatory time element, however, the IRS concluded that the concert activity was regularly carried on. In its most recent private letter ruling on the point, however, the IRS ruled that two fundraising special events, conducted by an exempt charitable organization, were not regularly carried on; there was no mention of the preparatory time component.[52] Also, the preparatory time argument has been rejected in the courts.[53] Nonetheless, planners should not disregard the preparatory time factor in advising tax-exempt organizations on this point.

## Step 4: Determine Whether the Business Is or Will Be *Related* to Exempt Purposes

It is rare for a court to separately analyze whether a business is *related* to an organization's exempt purposes (this step) and then whether the business is *substantially related* to exempt purposes (Step 5). Indeed, it is infrequent for the IRS to split these steps.[54] Yet, the tax regulations separate the two elements.[55] In most instances, however, the two factors are blended, with the fact-finder focusing on whether a business is substantially related to exempt purposes.

A business is *related* to exempt purposes where the conduct of the business activities has a "causal relationship" to the achievement of exempt purposes. As is discussed in connection with the next step, a business is *substantially related* to exempt purposes where the causal relationship between the conduct of the activity and the achievement of exempt purposes is substantial.

The IRS provided an excellent illustration of this two-step process.[56] A tax-exempt organization had as its purpose the establishment and maintenance of a "place for the reception, exhibition and sale of articles, [that are] the product and manufacture of industrious and meritorious women." To enable "needy and deserving" women to earn an "honest livelihood by their own industry," the organization operated three contiguous shops, all of equal size: a consignment shop, a gift shop, and a small restaurant (tearoom). The purpose of the organization then was to enable deserving women to earn their living by means of their own handiwork, by providing a place where they can sell foodstuffs and other articles prepared by them.

Goods made by the needy women were sold and displayed in the consignment shop. The organization purchased decorative items from for-profit vendors and sold them to the public in the gift shop. The tearoom was a luncheon facility, consisting of a dining area and a kitchen, that sold to the general public. Each of these three operations was operated by volunteers[57] and employees.

The organization was of the view that the consignment activity would not, by itself, bring many prospective customers into the shop inasmuch as the operation would be perceived as a "craft fair." If that were the case, the consignment shop would not attract "top dollar" for the handmade items and would not generate confidence in the quality of the items for sale. The organization's marketing strategy, based on the view that it must attract and serve "quality clientele" who will support the consignors, was to have a reason for customers to come to the premises (which exposed them to the consigned items), to have a showroom with ambiance that repeatedly attracts "high end clientele," and to "showcase merchandizing that implies quality." Thus, the items in the gift shop were "sophisticated, tasteful, and fashionable"; because they were in the same showroom with the consignment items, the gift shop items "enhanced" the consignment items.

Adjacent to the consignment and gift shops was the tearoom, which served light lunches; the organization advised the IRS that the menu selections, décor, room arrangement, and tableware were designed to be "sophisticated and tasteful." This facility enabled individuals to "socialize and shop simultaneously," and was seen by the organization as (like the gift shop) attracting customers for the consignment shop. Also, the gift shop and tearoom provided funds to support the consignment function.

The operation of the consignment shop was not at issue in this case; that was considered by the IRS to be a business, regularly carried on, that was related to the organization's exempt purposes and was substantially related to exempt purposes. The gift shop, however, was found to be an unrelated business. The IRS appeared to accept the argument that the operation of the gift shop imbued the consignment items with an "aura of sophistication and tastefulness"; that was sufficient to make the enterprise related to exempt purposes. Nonetheless, the agency then proceeded to rule that the "gift shop items have no substantial causal relationship to the sale of handicraft items produced by needy and deserving women in a contiguous shop." (The tearoom was found to not be related, let alone substantially related, to exempt purposes.)

## Step 5: Determine Whether the Business Is or Will Be *Substantially Related* to Exempt Purposes

As noted, a business is *substantially related* to exempt purposes where the causal relationship between the conduct of the activity and the achievement of exempt purposes is substantial. Thus, for the conduct of a business from which an amount of gross income is derived to be substantially related to purposes for which tax exemption was granted, the production or distribution of the goods or the performance of the services from which the gross income was derived must contribute importantly to the accomplishment of those purposes. Where the production or distribution of the goods or the performance of the services does not contribute importantly to the accomplishment of the exempt purposes of the exempt organization, the income from the sale of the goods or the performance of the services is not derived from the conduct of related business.

Whether activities productive of gross income contribute importantly to the accomplishment of any purpose for which an organization is granted tax exemption depends, in each case, on the facts and circumstances involved.

Thus, it often falls to the exempt organizations planner to make—or at least help make—judgments of this nature. Because each case is fact specific, it is difficult to generalize on the point. As examples of this, the companion volume contains summaries of the law in this area directly pertinent to organizations such as healthcare institutions, colleges, universities, museums, and associations.[58]

There are a number of considerations in this regard. One is that this aspect of the law can involve fine distinctions and even inconsistencies. An example of this is provided in the discussion in connection with Step 4, where the IRS ruled that the operation, by an organization assisting needy women, of the tearoom was an unrelated business. Yet, the IRS allows museums to operate dining rooms, cafeterias, and snack bars, for their staff and members of the public visiting the museum, without adversely affecting tax-exempt status.[59] One of the distinctions the IRS makes in this context is that these facilities, while accessible from the museum's galleries, are not directly accessible from the street. A recent private ruling from the IRS, however, did not make that distinction.[60] The point is understandable—the exempt organizations' restaurants should not be directly competing with commercial establishments—yet the underlying purpose for these facilities is the same: to facilitate lengthy visitation and purchases in the gift shops.

There can be a conflict between the IRS and the courts in this setting. For example, the sale of standard legal forms by a local bar association to its member lawyers, which purchased the forms from the state bar association, was ruled by the IRS to be an unrelated business because the activity did not contribute importantly to the accomplishment of the association's exempt purposes.[61] A court held, however, that the sale of standard real estate legal forms to lawyers and law students by an exempt bar association was an exempt function inasmuch as it promoted the common business interests of the legal profession and improved the relationship among the bench, bar, and public.[62]

Another aspect of this that can prove frustrating for the planner is that the law is not always applied consistently as it relates to the size of the entities. Sophisticated transactions that are permissible when undertaken by colleges, universities, healthcare entities, museums, and the like—complex leasing arrangements, joint ventures, use of for-profit subsidiaries, and the like—often are barriers to exempt status when attempted by smaller entities.

Still another aspect, more suitable for analyzing the operations of organizations on an ongoing basis (as contrasted with new ones), is the tendency of the courts to infer non-exempt purposes from the presence of certain facts concerning activities.[63] The courts also hold that a single activity may be carried on for more than one purpose; thus, if one of the activity's purposes is substantial and nonexempt (perhaps because it is commercial), the organization will be denied (or lose) exempt status, even if the activity also furthers an exempt purpose. Factors regarded by the courts as indicative of nonexempt purposes include generation of profits, competition with for-profit entities, and commerciality.

The planner may be called on to be rather creative in this regard. Obviously, how the facts are stated has a bearing on whether the business is regarded as substantially related or not—with the planner, of course, always wanting to stay within the bounds of veracity. Lawyers strive for precedent, so the place to begin in all instances is a search for a case or ruling that directly buttresses the organization's position concerning characterization of the business. Failing that, the planner must *extrapolate* from existing law in an attempt to arrive at the correct (and desired) conclusion.

The IRS, in a private letter ruling, provided a perfect example of this process. The issue presented to the agency was whether distributions to a tax-exempt private university from the redemption of tuition certificates pursuant to a qualified prepaid tuition program[64] constitute unrelated business income to the university. In concluding that the distributions would not be taxable,[65] the IRS observed, based on long-standing law, that "[t]uition and required fees paid by a student to attend a college or university for purposes of obtaining higher education do not constitute income from the conduct of unrelated trade or business." With that the agency went on to conclude that, likewise, tuition and fees paid under a qualified tuition program are forms of gross income from charges by the educational institution for the performance of an exempt function. Thus, the process of collecting distributions pursuant to these plans is not an unrelated business—it is a substantially related business.

### Step 6:  Ascertain Whether Some or All of the Exempt Organization's Unrelated Business *Income* Is Sheltered from Taxation by an Exception

Even if a tax-exempt organization is conducting a business, the business is regularly carried on, and the business is not substantially related to the organization's exempt purposes, all is not necessarily lost. There are a variety of exceptions from unrelated business income taxation in the law for forms of *income*.[66]

Many of these exceptions are for forms of *passive income*. This includes most dividends, annuities, most forms of interest, most forms of rent from real property, capital gain, and the like. There are, however, some exceptions to these exceptions. The principal ones are:

- The unrelated debt-financed income rules[67] override these exceptions.
- Revenue from a controlled entity may be taxable.[68]
- Income generated from the conduct of an active business of renting property usually is taxable.[69]
- If the tax-exempt organization is too involved in development and/or disposition of property, what may initially appear to be (nontaxable) capital gain may in fact be (taxable) ordinary income.[70]

From a planning perspective, the most useful of these exceptions from income taxation is the one concerning *royalties*.[71] These rules are discussed in the companion volume.[72] In general, however, the royalty exception offers a great opportunity to convert what otherwise would be unrelated business taxable income into tax-free income. The principal element of the law in this regard to be concerned with is the extent of the services provided by the tax-exempt organization in conjunction with the revenue-producing activity;

the greater the extent of the services, the greater the likelihood that the payment cannot be considered a royalty.

Other exceptions in this context concern the rental of mailing lists,[73] the tax treatment of certain dues paid by associate members,[74] payments in connection with the lending of securities,[75] and even the rental of certain types of poles.[76]

The newest and one of the most interesting exceptions for forms of income is the rule concerning corporate sponsorships.[77] Unlike most of these exceptions, however, the one for corporate sponsorships is a "safe haven." If the terms of the exclusion are not met, there is nonetheless an opportunity to use one or more others.

Tax-exempt organizations that file annual information returns are required to identify each of their income-producing activities, and then characterize the income as from a related business, from an unrelated business and thus taxable, or sheltered from taxation by reason of an exception.[78]

## Step 7: Ascertain Whether Some or All of the Exempt Organization's Income from Unrelated Business *Activity* Is Sheltered from Taxation by an Exception

There are a number of exceptions in the tax law that protect from unrelated business taxation the conduct of certain activities that may otherwise be characterized as unrelated businesses. The usefulness of a particular exception usually depends on the type of tax-exempt organization involved.

### NOTE

The principle of law that offers the most extensive "exception" in the unrelated business setting is not really an "exception" at all. This is the rule that an activity must be regularly carried on to be a taxable business (Step 3). For example, in the fundraising context, this is the rule that most often shields fundraising activities (such as special events) from taxation as unrelated businesses.[79]

For colleges, universities, and hospitals, the most useful of these exceptions is the convenience doctrine.[80] This can be a mammoth exclusion, in that it shields from taxation businesses conducted for the convenience of the institution's students or patients.

For some organizations, utility is found in the rule that an activity conducted substantially by volunteers is not taxable.[81] Other organizations can make effective use of the exception for a business consisting of the sale of donated items.[82] For example, although this exception was installed for the benefit of nonprofit thrift stores, charities that engage in donated vehicle fundraising programs can rely on this rule to avoid taxation on the basis that they are involved in the unrelated business of selling the vehicles.[83] Still other entities rely on one or more of the various exceptions for the conduct of research,[84] entertainment activities,[85] trade show activities,[86] distribution of low-cost articles,[87] and even the rental of certain poles.[88]

## Step 8:  Compute Unrelated Business *Taxable* Income, by Marshaling an Appropriate Amount of Expenses (If Any) That Can Be Used to Minimize or Even Eliminate Tax

These rules are discussed in the companion volume.[89] The principal difficulty in this context is that the law requires that the deductions be *directly connected* with the carrying on of the business. In practice, however, exempt organizations often make reasonable allocations in differentiating between expenses that relate to related activities and those that relate to unrelated activities. These computations are made on Form 990-T (see Appendix D).

The planner may find that the tolerance of the leadership and management of the exempt organization involved for the amount of unrelated business being undertaken (see below) is dependent, at least in part, on the amount of tax (if any) being paid on the unrelated business taxable income.

## Step 9:  Determine If There Are One or More Unrelated Businesses Conducted by the Exempt Organization That Generate a Loss, So That the Loss Can Be Offset against the Gain Generated by Another Unrelated Business

This approach, which is, of course, predicated on an aggressive (perhaps exuberant) application of the fragmentation rule, works only where there is a relatively complex set of facts. Most tax-exempt organizations do not have unrelated business activities, let alone several.

There can be difficulties in this area, however. As discussed in the companion volume, the courts have engrafted onto this aspect of the law the requirement that, for an activity of a tax-exempt organization to be a business (really, an unrelated business), it must be conducted with a *profit motive*.[90] If the loss activity consistently (year-in and year-out) produces losses, the IRS may take the position that the activity is not a business, because of absence of the requisite profit motive, and disallow the loss deduction. Occasional losses, however, should not lead to this result.

## Step 10:  Ascertain How Much Unrelated Activity the Exempt Organization Can Engage in without Endangering Its Tax-Exempt Status

The exercise of ascertaining how much unrelated business activity a particular tax-exempt organization can engage in, without endangering its tax exemption, can be a difficult one. This is largely because, with one minor exception,[91] there is no law on the point. That is, there is no percentage, formula, or other rule by which the outer limits of tolerated unrelated business can be measured.

The underlying principles are found in the *primary purpose rule*.[92] To be tax-exempt, an organization must engage in activities that are sufficient to advance its exempt purpose. These activities must be *primary* or *substantial*. Once that standard is achieved, what is left over can be unrelated business activity.

Thus, in many ways, this is a facts-and-circumstances test. The planner may struggle (even agonize) over the analysis. It is impossible to generalize on the point, other than to offer a simple rule of thumb: if the unrelated business is close to or more than 20 percent of the organization's undertakings (whether measured in terms of revenue or time), the planner should begin to worry. The options at this point are few:

- Reevaluate the analysis, to be certain that all activities are properly classified as related and unrelated in nature.
- Discontinue or decrease one or more unrelated activities.
- Increase or create one or more related activities.
- Transfer one or more unrelated businesses to another entity (Step 11).
- Do nothing and hope that nothing adverse comes of the situation (essentially an unacceptable outcome for the planner).

This 20 percent figure, by the way, is not entirely arbitrary. There are instances in the law of tax-exempt organizations where the term *substantial* is defined to be in the 80 percent range. Also, the phrase *substantially all* is defined to represent the 85 percent range.

## Step 11:  Decide Whether One or More Unrelated Businesses Should Be Transferred to or Initially Placed in Another Organization

This step is previewed in the previous step. The planner in this situation should decide whether the tax-exempt organization is conducting unrelated business that is sufficiently extensive to jeopardize the organization's exempt status. As noted, this is a facts-and-circumstances test. (Nonetheless, the 20 percent rule of thumb may be applied.) Aside from the substance of the activity or activities, the planner is likely to find that much of the decision will turn on the tolerance of the exempt organization's leadership and management for the risk of loss of exempt status.

## Step 12:  Decide What the Form and Tax Status of That Other Organization Should Be

The essence of this subject is discussed elsewhere.[93] Presumably, the other organization is a subsidiary and a for-profit entity. Most likely that for-profit entity will be a regular (C) corporation, so that the revenue flow to the tax-exempt parent can be structured as a dividend. Most other forms of revenue from a subsidiary are taxable as unrelated business income.[94] A flow-through entity usually will not be appropriate because of the automatic flow-through of the unrelated business income.[95] Certainly the one entity that will not suffice is the single-member limited liability company.[96]

## COMMERCIALITY DOCTRINE

A body of law that, until recently, has been developing and applied parallel to the unrelated business rules is the commerciality doctrine. This doctrine is discussed in the companion volume.[97] The doctrine, utilized by the courts as a basis for denying or revoking tax-exempt status as a charitable organization, is evolving as a component of the operational test.[98] The focus in this setting is on whether or to what extent the organization is conducting its activities in a commercial manner, that is, in ways in which for-profit companies conduct comparable activities.

Courts look to several factors in assessing the extent of commerciality by charitable organizations. These factors tend to be:

- Competition with for-profit entities
- Pricing policies, including fee amounts and profit margins
- Audience(s) selected
- Extent and degree of low-cost services provided
- Advertising and other promotional methods (including catchphrases and jingles)
- Extent of financial reserves
- Utilization of employees and volunteers
- Extent to which the organization receives charitable contributions

When applying or even considering applying the commerciality doctrine, the planner should keep in mind:

- The doctrine has not been well articulated.
- The doctrine is unevenly applied.
- Hundreds or perhaps thousands of organizations (particularly institutions such as colleges, universities, and healthcare providers) would lose their tax-exempt status if the doctrine were applied to them.[99]
- Many elements of the doctrine do not make much sense in the modern era, particularly factors such as reliance on fee revenue (as opposed to contributions), the extent of advertising, the use of employees (as opposed to volunteers), and the practice of maintaining financial reserves.

There are two court opinions of which the planner should take particular cognizance.[100] As these opinions reflect, the IRS and the courts are looking to determine if the operations of charitable organizations reflect a *commercial hue*. There is an important appellate court opinion with analysis that runs counter to this application of the commerciality doctrine.[101]

An organization may engage (or be perceived to be engaging) in conduct that is partially exempt activity and partially commercial undertakings. The extent to which the commerciality doctrine will preclude or cause revocation of tax-exempt status will then depend on application of the primary purpose test.[102]

The IRS has begun utilizing the commerciality doctrine in determining whether an activity of a tax-exempt organization is a related or unrelated business.[103] Consequently, planners should evaluate various activities that are undertaken by exempt organizations to ascertain whether the IRS or a court might consider them to be operated in a commercial manner and thus unrelated businesses. Because application of the doctrine is so inconsistent, however, this attempt at analysis is likely to prove difficult. For example, colleges, universities, and healthcare institutions often operate fitness centers; although these operations are frequently competitive with for-profit health clubs, the IRS has consistently held that these centers are charitable and educational (related) functions.[104] As another illustration, the IRS finds that restaurants, snack bars, and the like are related businesses when conducted by museums[105] but are unrelated businesses when conducted by other types of charitable entities—by application of the commerciality doctrine.[106]

## Notes

1. IRC §§ 511–514.
2. *Tax-Exempt Organizations,* chaps. 26–29, with reference to the subject in several instances elsewhere throughout the book.
3. Id., § 26.1.
4. Id., § 26.2.
5. Id., § 26.3.
6. Id., § 26.4.
7. Id., § 27.1.
8. Id., § 27.2.
9. Id., § 26.5.
10. Id., § 28.6.
11. Id., §§ 29.1–29.4.
12. Id., § 29.5.
13. Id., § 28.4.
14. Id., §§ 28.1, 28.2.
15. See Chapter 9, pages 199–200, 207–210.
16. Living Faith, Inc. v. Comm'r, 950 F.2d 365, 370 (7th Cir. 1991). See Chapter 11, pages 314–318.
17. *Tax-Exempt Organizations,* § 26.2(f).
18. IRC § 513(c).
19. That is, a seemingly single activity can be fragmented into more than one activity, enabling at least one of the resulting activities to avoid unrelated business income taxation, such as by application of an exception. For example, an association that sold commercial advertising in its publications sidestepped unrelated business income taxation of the enterprise because the work involved was provided solely by volunteers. Priv. Ltr. Rul. 9302023.
20. IRC § 511(a)(2)(A).
21. *Tax-Exempt Organizations,* § 18.17.
22. Id., § 18.1.
23. Id., § 8.7.
24. Id., § 18.11.
25. Id., § 18.12.
26. IRC § 511(a)(2)(B).
27. *Tax-Exempt Organizations,* §§ 6.10, 18.17.
28. See Chapter 3, pages 71–76.
29. *Tax-Exempt Organizations,* § 24.3(b)(iii).
30. Priv. Ltr. Rul. 9141050.
31. *Tax-Exempt Organizations,* § 4.3.

32. Id., § 4.5.

33. Id., § 4.3(b).

34. This outcome was recognized by the IRS in Tech. Adv. Mem. 200126032.

35. Technically, the term is *trade or business*; nonetheless, the term *business* is used throughout.

36. In general, see *Tax-Exempt Organizations*, § 26.2.

37. IRC § 513(c).

38. Vigilant Hose Co. of Emmitsburg v. United States, 2001-2 U.S.T.C. ¶ 50,458 (D. Md. 2001).

39. The element as to whether an activity is engaged in over a substantial period of time is more relevant, for federal tax purposes, in ascertaining whether the activity is regularly carried on than whether it is a business to begin with.

40. Laborer's Int'l Union of N. Am. v. Comm'r, 82 T.C.M. 158 (2001).

41. See *Tax-Exempt Organizations*, § 26.2(c).

42. Laborer's Int'l Union of N. Am. v. Comm'r, note 40 above, 82 T.C.M. at 160.

43. American Acad. of Family Physicians v. United States, 91 F.3d 1155 (8th Cir. 1996).

44. In general, see *Tax-Exempt Organizations*, § 26.2(g).

45. Id., § 26.2(b).

46. Id., § 26.3.

47. Id., § 26.1.

48. Id., § 26.3(b).

49. Id., § 26.3(b), text accompanied by n. 144.

50. Id., § 26.3(d).

51. Tech. Adv. Mem. 9712001.

52. Priv. Ltr. Rul. 200128059.

53. *Tax-Exempt Organizations*, § 26.3(d), text accompanied by nn. 153–155.

54. Worse, the infrequency of application of this dichotomy occasionally leads the IRS to misstate the law. For example, the agency wrote: "To be related, in the statutory sense, the relationship must be a causal and substantial relationship." Tech. Adv. Mem. 200021056. The IRS, in that sentence, defined what is required to be *substantially* related.

55. Reg. § 1.513-1(d)(2).

56. Tech. Adv. Mem. 200021056.

57. *Tax-Exempt Organizations*, § 27.2(a).

58. Id., § 26.5.

59. Rev. Rul. 74-399, 1974-2 C.B. 172.

60. Priv. Ltr. Rul. 200222030.

61. Rev. Rul. 78-51, 1978-1 C.B. 165.

62. San Antonio Bar Ass'n v. United States, 80-2 U.S.T.C. ¶ 9594 (W.D. Tex. 1980).

63. E.g., the "purposes for which an organization is operated are discerned not from the organization's activities but from the end for which those activities are undertaken." Junaluska Assembly Hous., Inc. v. Comm'r, 86 T.C. 1114, 1121 (1986).

64. That is, a plan that qualifies under IRC § 529. See *Tax-Exempt Organizations*, § 18.16.

65. Priv. Ltr. Rul. 200313024.

66. *Tax-Exempt Organizations*, § 27.1.

67. Id., §§ 29.1–29.4.

68. Id., §§ 27.1(n), 31.3.

69. Id., § 27.1(h).

70. Id., § 27.1(j).

71. IRC § 512(b)(2).

72. *Tax-Exempt Organizations,* § 27.1(g).

73. Id., § 27.2(k).

74. Id., § 27.2(*l*)

75. Id., § 27.1(d).

76. Id., § 27.2(i).

77. Id., § 27.2(n).

78. See Chapter 9, pages 207–210.

79. E.g., Priv. Ltr. Rul. 200128059.

80. *Tax-Exempt Organizations,* § 27.2(b).

81. Id., § 27.2(a).

82. Id., § 27.2(c).

83. Priv. Ltr. Ruls. 200230005, 200230007.

84. *Tax-Exempt Organizations,* § 27.1(*l*).

85. Id., § 27.2(e).

86. Id., § 27.2(f).

87. Id., § 27.2(j).

88. Id., § 27.2(i).

89. Id., § 28.2.

90. Id., § 26.2(b).

91. Id., § 28.3, text accompanied by nn. 38–39.

92. Id., § 4.4.

93. See Chapter 6, pages 134, 136–139.

94. See text accompanied by note 68 above.

95. See Chapter 7, pages 150–151.

96. Id., pages 156–158.

97. *Tax-Exempt Organizations,* chap. 25.

98. Id., § 4.5.

99. See Chapter 6, pages 142–144 (discussion of *social enterprise*).

100. Living Faith, Inc. v. Comm'r, 950 F.2d 365 (7th Cir. 1991) (see Chapter 11, pages 314–318), and Airlie Found. v. United States, 283 F. Supp. 2d 58 (D.D.C. 2003) (see Chapter 11, pages 295– 297).

101. Presbyterian & Reformed Publ'g Co. v. Comm'r, 743 F.2d 148 (3d Cir. 1984) (see Chapter 11, pages 263–265).

102. *Tax-Exempt Organizations,* § 4.4.

103. E.g., Tech. Adv. Mem. 200021056.

104. E.g., Priv. Ltr. Rul. 200101036.

105. E.g., Priv. Ltr. Rul. 200222030.

106. E.g., Tech. Adv. Mem. 200021056.

# CHAPTER 9

# Annual Information Returns

Nearly every organization that is exempt from federal income taxation must, as required by statute,[1] file an annual information return with the IRS. This return, consisting of six pages plus two schedules amounting to another 14 pages, calls for considerable information, some of it financial and some of it in prose form. The document, being an information return rather than a tax return, is available for public inspection.[2] (By contrast, the Form 990-T, used to report unrelated business income,[3] is a tax return and is not publicly available.) For most tax-exempt organizations, this information return that must be annually filed is Form 990.

> **NOTE**
>
> The version of the Form 990 referenced in this chapter is that for 2003, a copy of which is in Appendix C.

## LAW BASICS

The companion book summarizes the contents of the annual information return, the due dates for filing the return, the exceptions from the reporting requirements, and the penalties that may be imposed for insufficient, late, or no filings of the return.[4]

> **NOTE**
>
> The IRS attempts to summarize this body of law in 43 pages of instructions for the Form 990 and 15 pages of instructions for two schedules. The instructions to the Form 990 consist of 15 pages of General Instructions and 28 pages of Specific Instructions.[5]

There is another body of law that relates to the filing of annual information returns: the various state charitable solicitation acts that regulate fundraising for charitable purposes.[6]

Some states accept the federal annual information return in place of their own form. As the instructions to the Form 990 state, however (in more than a mild understatement), some states that accept the form "require additional information." Other states, of course, insist on their own forms. The interrelationship of the Form 990 and state filing requirements is discussed more fully below.

## FORMS

As noted, most tax-exempt organizations are required to annually file Form 990. Some exempt organizations, however, file other returns. These are:

- **Form 990-EZ.** This return, consisting of two pages, may be filed by small organizations, that is, organizations that have gross receipts that are less than $100,000 and total assets that are less than $250,000 in value at the end of the reporting year.

- **Form 990-PF.** This return is filed by private foundations.[7]

- **Form 990-BL.** This return is filed by black lung benefit trusts.

- **Form 1120-POL.** This return, which is a tax return, is filed by political organizations.[8] These organizations also, however, file a Form 990 or Form 990-EZ.[9]

- **Schedule A.** This schedule must be filed by all tax-exempt charitable organizations other than private foundations.[10]

- **Schedule B.** This schedule of contributors must be filed by every filing organization that has received contributions and grants.

- **Form 990-W.** This is the form by which any estimated tax on unrelated business taxable income of tax-exempt organization, payable in installments, is calculated.

**COMMENT ➤**

The most typical set of circumstances in this regard is the filing of a Form 990. Where the filing organization is a charitable one, the most likely outcome is the filing of Form 990, plus Schedules A and B.

**NOTE ✎**

The federal tax law differentiates between exempt organization's income, revenue, and receipts. The Form 990, in Part I, requires an organization to report its *revenue*. Yet, in determining whether an organization does not have to file an annual information return because it is small, the measurement is on the basis of *receipts*.[11] Certain revenue items are netted in Part I in calculating total revenue. This netting process is not allowed in computing total receipts. Thus, the amount of a tax-exempt organization's gross receipts can be greater than the amount of its total revenue.

There are, therefore, two ways to compute gross receipts in Part I of the Form 990:

1. Gross receipts are the sum of lines 1d, 2, 3, 4, 5, 6a, 7, 8a (both columns), 9a, 10a, and 11.

2. Gross receipts are the sum of total revenue reported on line 12 plus the amounts on lines 6b, 8b, 9b, and 10b.[12]

## GLOSSARY

The rules pertaining to the annual information return filing requirement include some terms of art (in addition to *annual information return* and *gross receipts*). They are:

- **Contribution.** In the instructions to the Form 990, the IRS employs the term *voluntary contributions,* which is redundant. The term *contribution,* as defined in the instructions, is a payment, or the part of any payment,[13] for which the payor (donor) does not receive full retail value (fair market value) from the recipient (donee) organization.[14] The usual sources of contributions are individuals, corporations, partnerships, limited liability companies, estates, and perhaps trusts.[15]

- **Grant.** A grant has the attributes of a contribution. The Form 990 instructions state that *grants* are payments (made by a grantor) that encourage the organization receiving the grant (grantee) to carry on programs that further its tax-exempt purposes.[16] The usual sources of grants are public charities, private foundations, other tax-exempt organizations, government agencies, and perhaps trusts.

- **Contract revenue.** A payment made to a tax-exempt organization is not a grant if, in the language of the Form 990 instructions, the arrangement requires the recipient to provide the payor with a specific service, facility, or product (as opposed to providing a direct benefit to the general public or a segment of the public).[17] This, instead, is contract-for-service revenue.

## COMMENT ➤

There can be considerable confusion on this point. A document can have the title *grant* even though the funding arrangement generates contract-for-service revenue. A document can have the title *contract,* yet the arrangement constitutes a grant. Indeed, a grant agreement is a contract, although the funding is still considered a grant. The Form 990 instructions intensify the confusion by unnecessarily mixing the concepts of *contributions* and *grants.* Thus, the instructions advise the reporting organization to "not report as contributions any payments for a service, facility, or product that primarily give some economic or physical benefit to the payor (grantor)."[18] That is good advice, indeed, but payments of this nature should not be reported as grants, either. Moreover, in that quotation, the payor is not a *grantor.*

## NOTE ✎

The Form 990 itself perpetuates the confusion by making reference on line 1 of Part I to "contributions, gifts, grants, and similar amounts." For this purpose, the words *contribution* and *gift* mean the same; the latter term should be dropped. The Form 990 instructions do not mention *similar amounts;* there is no such thing, and that phrase

*(continues)*

**NOTE** *(Continued)*

should also be deleted. Thus, all would be well (or better, anyway) if that line referred solely to "contributions and grants." Further, instead of the phrase in line 1c "government contributions (grants)," the term should simply be "government grants." (Governments do not make contributions, just as individuals do not make grants.)

- **Direct public support.** The term *direct public support* means the gross amount of contributions and grants the organization received from members of the public.[19] Presumably all gifts are direct public support. A grant may be direct or indirect (see below) public support, depending on the source. Contract revenue is never direct public support.

- **Indirect public support.** There are many forms of *indirect public support*. Generically, this type of support is provided in the form of a *grant,* with the donors who contributed directly to the grantor considered as having indirectly contributed to the grantee. The Form 990 instructions identify two types of indirect public support: (1) funding from "federated fundraising agencies and similar fundraising organizations (such as a United Way organization and certain sectarian federations)," and (2) "other organizations closely associated with the reporting organization," such as funding from a parent organization, a subordinate organization, or another organization with the same parent.[20] Funding from a supporting organization[21] may be public support. The third type of public support (ignored in the instructions) is funding in the form of a grant from one donative publicly supported organization[22] to another such organization, or from an organization that meets the definition of a donative publicly supported organization to a donative publicly supported organization, regardless of whether the organizations are "closely associated."

- **Exempt function income.** The phrase *exempt function income* means income derived from the conduct of a related business.[23] Essentially, a *business* is an activity carried on to produce revenue from the sale of goods or services. For this purpose, the terms *related business, exempt function,* and *program* are identical. Thus, the Form 990 instructions state that "[p]rogram services are primarily those that form the basis of an organization's exemption from tax."[24] (It is not clear why the reference to "primarily" is there.) Exemption function income, program service revenue (see below), and (usually) contract revenue (see above) mean the same. Thus, as to the third of these items, the instructions provide that "[p]rogram service revenue includes income earned by the organization for providing a government agency with a service, facility, or product that benefited that government agency directly rather than benefiting the public as a whole."[25]

- **Dues.** The term *dues* (and this includes other member assessments and fees) means payments by the organization's members (and perhaps affiliates[26]) in exchange for a package of membership benefits and other services. The concept is that the value of the dues paid is roughly equivalent to the value of services received. This is the case even if a benefit provided is not used. Thus, dues are merely one form of exempt function income, program service revenue, contract revenue, and related business income (see above).

## COMMENT ►

This is another area of confusion. A payment may be termed *dues*, yet not be dues. As the Form 990 instructions note, if a "member pays dues mainly to support the organization's activities and not to obtain benefits of more than nominal monetary value," the payment is a *contribution* (see above) and should be reported as such.[27] (The quotation, then, should not use the word "dues," and often payments of this nature come from persons who are not really "members.") Moreover, if amounts that are paid are denominated as dues, but the monetary value of the membership benefits available to the payor are less, the difference is a contribution that should be reported as such.

- **Special events.** A *special event* is an event, usually conducted by a charitable organization, for fundraising purposes. The revenue raised is not always in the form of contributions, however; often there are fees paid for the acquisition of goods and/or services. The amount paid may be part charitable gift and part payment for a good or service. From the charity's viewpoint, the purpose of the event may go beyond revenue-raising and extend to community relations and outreach and increase in public awareness of the organization and its programs (what some in the fundraising profession term *friend-raising*). The Form 990 instructions observe that the "sole or primary purpose" of a special event "is to raise funds that are other than contributions to finance the organization's exempt activities"; special events "only incidentally accomplish an exempt purpose."[28] (As to the latter observation, the fact is that a special event rarely partakes of an organization's program.) Examples of special events are dinners, dances, theater outings, sports tournaments, carnivals, auctions, raffles, and bingo games and other forms of gambling.

- **Functional accounting.** The Form 990 instructions define *functional accounting* by stating that an organization's expenses, having been "designated by object classification (e.g., salaries, legal fees, supplies, etc.)," must then be "allocated into" three functions: program services, management and general, and fundraising.[29]

- **Program services.** The Form 990 instructions state that *program services* are "mainly those activities that the reporting organization was created to conduct and which, along with any activities commenced subsequently, form the basis of the organization's current exemption from tax." Also, these activities "may be self-funded or funded out of contributions, accumulated income, investment income, or any other source."[30] In other words, program activities are exempt functions, related businesses, and sources of contract revenue (see above).

- **Management and general.** The Form 990 instructions loosely define the term *management and general* by referring to the organization's "overall function and management." Thus, the distinction is between expenses for that type of management activity and expenses for the "direct conduct" of program services or fundraising activities. The instructions state that *overall management* "usually includes the salaries and expenses of the chief officer of the organization and that officer's staff." Other expenses of this category include those for meetings of the governing board; committee and staff meetings; general legal services; accounting services; general liability insurance; office management; auditing, personnel, and other centralized services; preparation, publication, and distribution of annual reports; and investment expenses.[31]

- **Fundraising.** The Form 990 instructions state that *fundraising expenses* are the expenses "incurred in soliciting contributions, gifts, grants, etc." The instructions detail these items: publicizing and conducting fundraising campaigns; soliciting bequests and grants from foundations and other organizations, including governments; participating in federated fundraising campaigns; preparing and distributing fundraising manuals, instructions, and other materials; and conducting special events (see above) that generate contributions This includes allocable overhead costs.[32]

- **Primary purpose.** A tax-exempt organization, to be and to remain exempt, must operate primarily in furtherance of its exempt purposes; this is the *primary purpose test*, which is most developed in conjunction with charitable organizations.[33] The activities of a tax-exempt organization are to be evaluated in light of its primary purpose or purposes.

- **Program service accomplishments.** The Form 990 requires a reporting organization to provide information about its *program service accomplishments*. These are the accomplishments achieved by the organization resulting from the conduct of program services (see above), also known as exempt functions, related businesses, and activities generating contract revenue (see above). Oddly, however, the Form 990 instructions state, in this context, that a "program service is a major (usually ongoing) objective of an organization."[34] This is a confusion of *purposes* (objectives) and *activities* (services). Examples given of program services are adoptions, recreation for the elderly, rehabilitation, and publication of journals or newsletters.

- **Trustee.** A trustee is a person (usually an individual) who is a member of the organization's governing body (when it is termed a board of trustees).

- **Director.** An organization most likely terms its governing body the board of directors; a director then is a person (most frequently an individual) who is a member of that governing body.

- **Officer.** An officer (who may also serve as a trustee or director) is the organization's president, vice president, secretary, treasurer, and/or the like.

- **Creator.** The creator of an organization is the organization's founder (or one of the founders).

- **Substantial contributor.** A substantial contributor is a person who contributed or bequeathed an aggregate amount of more than the higher of 2 percent of the total contributions and bequests received by the organization (private foundation) before the close of its tax year in which the contribution or bequest is received by the organization from that person, or $5,000 to the private foundation.[35]

- **Key employee.** The Form 990 instructions provide that a *key employee* is "any person having responsibilities or powers similar to those of officers, directors, or trustees." The term includes the chief management and administrative officials of an organization (such as an executive director or chancellor) but does not include the heads of separate departments or smaller units within an organization. A chief financial officer and the officer in charge of administration or program operations are key employees if they have the authority to control the organization's activities, its finances, or both. The phrase *heads of separate departments* means persons such as the head of the radiology department or coronary care unit of a hospital or the head of the chemistry, history, or English department at a college. These persons are managers within their specific areas but not for the organization as a whole and, therefore, are not key employees.[36]

- **Member of the family.** An individual is a *member of the family* if he or she is related to a disqualified person, such as by being a parent, child, grandchild, or great-grandchild.

- **Program service revenue.** The phrase *program service revenue* means revenue (income) derived from the conduct of a program, exempt function, or related business (see above). Program service revenue and contract-for-service revenue (see above) are thus essentially the same.

- **Disregarded entity.** A *disregarded entity* is a limited liability company that has only one member. For federal tax purposes, the income and activity of the company is treated as if it was received and conducted by the member.[37] That is, the company is disregarded for tax purposes. When the sole member of a limited liability company, then, is a tax-exempt organization, the activities, income, and assets of the company are reflected on the exempt organization's annual information return, just as if these elements were conducted, received, and held by the exempt organization. The Form 990 instructions do not define the term *disregarded entity*.

- **Personal benefit contract.** The term *personal benefit contract* generally means any life insurance, annuity, or endowment contract that benefits, directly or indirectly, a transferor of money or property to a charitable organization, a member of the transferor's family,[38] or any other person designated by the transferor, other than a charitable organization.[39]

- **Unrelated business income.** Income is from an *unrelated business* when it is from a business that is regularly carried on and is not substantially related to the exempt purposes of the reporting organization.[40] Thus, it is income that is not from a related business (see above) or from an activity or income type that is sheltered by statute from taxation. Part I of Form 990, where revenue items are listed, does not include a line for unrelated business income. Rather, any income of that nature is determined on line 103, Part VII, and then carried back to line 11, Part I.

## REVIEW OF FORM 990—A LAW PERSPECTIVE

The Form 990 is a remarkable document. There are those who criticize it as not containing sufficient information about tax-exempt organizations and not being user-friendly. Yet, if the return is properly prepared, it can be a source of a wealth of information about the organization that filed it.

The IRS states the point this way: "Some members of the public rely on Form 990, or Form 990-EZ, as the primary or sole source of information about a particular organization. How the public perceives an organization in such cases may be determined by the information presented on its return. Therefore, please make sure the return is complete and accurate and fully describes the organization's programs and accomplishments."[41]

## NOTE

The reader may find it convenient to have a copy of this return at hand to refer to in connection with the following discussion of the document. As noted, a copy is in Appendix C.

The primary purpose rule requires, as noted, that an organization's initial and ongoing eligibility for tax-exempt status be evaluated in light of its purposes. Again, a particular activity can be an exempt activity or not an exempt activity, depending on the context in which it is conducted; the scope of the organization's purpose or purposes provides that evaluative framework.

Therefore, when reviewing a Form 990 (and after reading the organization's name and address), the first step is to go to page 2, Part III. The first question there is: "What is the organization's primary exempt purpose?" (This question should, given the primary purpose rule, be on page 1 of the form, preceding Part I.) Unfortunately, some organizations do not answer this question. Others insert something nearly useless, such as "charitable" or "educational." Admittedly, the form does not provide much space for a suitable answer. Often the best answer, then, is "see attached." The organization would attach a carefully constructed statement of its exempt purposes.

Once the primary exempt purpose is understood, the reviewer should return to the beginning of the form. At the very top, the reviewer will find such information as the accounting method used in preparing the return; the category of tax exemption involved; whether the return is the initial, amended, or final one; whether the organization's application for recognition of exemption (if any) is pending; the organization's web site address (if any); and whether the return is being filed by a central organization as a group return for affiliates or the return of an organization covered by a group ruling.[42]

The balance of page 1, consisting of Part I, looks like a conventional tax return. This is also the case with respect to Part IV, comprising page 3, which is a balance sheet. Unlike a tax return, however, an exempt organization must also, in Part II on page 2, report its expenses on a functional basis. Certain joint costs must also be reported.

Part III of Form 990 is one place where the reviewer should linger. This is where the organization describes its program service accomplishments. This obviously is one of the most important elements of the form.

Part V on page 4 of the form is where some reviewers first turn. This is because it (if properly prepared) reflects the compensation paid (if any) to the organization's trustees, directors, officers, and key employees.

Part VI of Form 990, occupying page 5, contains a list of questions, some mundane, others of considerable significance. Part VII, on page 6, is another place where the reviewer should dwell. Here is where the organization is forced to report all of its income, and classify it as (1) related business income, (2) unrelated business income, or (3) income that is not inherently related but that is shielded from taxation by statute. Part VIII on page 6 is where the organization explains why it believes the income it has reported as exempt function income qualifies as such.

Part IX on page 6 is where the organization reports as to its taxable subsidiaries and/or disregarded entities (if any). Part X on page 6 is where the organization provides information concerning any transfers associated with personal benefit contracts.

Thus, as observed at the outset, a properly prepared Form 990 can yield an enormous amount of useful information about the filing organization. What follows is a legal perspective on preparation of the form and some thoughts on the appropriate perspective to have when preparing the return.

# PREPARATION OF FORM 990—A LAW PERSPECTIVE

Lawyers are not usually involved in the preparation of a Form 990. That function is most often undertaken by one or more representatives of the organization or by one or more independent accountants. The lawyer's role with respect to annual information returns most likely will be, as noted, to review them. It is not normally the lawyer's job to determine if the numbers are accurate (in and of themselves and in conjunction with any related financial statement) or whether the mathematics are correct. Nonetheless, there are a number of aspects of preparation of the return that should be viewed from a legal perspective, including proper characterization of the numbers, making certain they are correctly inserted on the appropriate line, and careful attention to the answers that are comprised of words and sentences.

## Preliminary Section of the Form

It needs to be reiterated that the Form 990 is open to public inspection.[43]

The organization is required to indicate whether it is required to file a Schedule B, which is used to report contributions and grants. This schedule is not open to public inspection.

The Form 990 requires a filing organization to state whether the organization's name or address has changed; whether the return is an initial, amended, or final one; or whether its exemption for recognition of exemption is pending (item B). As to a change of name, the appropriate document evidencing the change must be attached to the return. In the case of a corporation, this document is articles of amendment (coupled with proof of filing with the state of incorporation).[44] If the organization is a trust, the document is an amendment to a trust agreement or declaration of trust (coupled with the signature of the trustee). When the organization is an unincorporated association, the document is an amendment to articles of association, constitution, or other organizing document (coupled with the signatures of at least two officers or members of the entity).[45]

The Form 990 requests that the tax-exempt organization provide its web site address (item G). The IRS surfs the Internet, looking at exempt organizations' sites. The agency has been known to send letters to exempt organizations, asking them if they would like to comment on material posted on the site (without revealing what it is about the site content that prompted the inquiry). Therefore, an exempt organization should design and maintain its web site with the assumption that the IRS will periodically pay a visit. This may be true of other government agencies as well. Also, members of the staff of congressional committees or individual members of Congress may visit exempt organizations' sites.

## Part I

**Gifts, Grants, and Exempt Function Revenue.** In Part I of Form 990, the filing tax-exempt organization is required to report, on line 1, its total amount of revenue (if any) received in the form of *contributions* and *grants*. (These terms are defined above.) The organization is also required to report, on line 2, its *program service revenue* (also defined above). It is necessary, therefore, for the organization to differentiate between (1) contributions and grants and (2) program service revenue. For this purpose, although the form employs both terms on line 1, *contributions* and *gifts* mean the same.

A *contribution* can arise in connection with the operation of a special event, as discussed below.

The Form 990 uses the term *program service revenue* in this context to mean the same as *exempt function income* or *related business income* (see the discussion of Part VII).

This distinction between grants and program service revenue is not always an easy one. For example, the funding of an exempt organization by means of a contract may be program service revenue, rather than a grant, even though the document uses the term *grant*.

This is why line 2 makes reference to "government fees and contracts." The exempt organization is expected to differentiate between funding pursuant to a *government grant* (see line 1c) and funding pursuant to a *government contract*.

Form 990, line 3, requires an organization to report any membership dues and assessments. This type of funding is a form of program service revenue but nonetheless is separately broken out for reporting purposes.

As to contributions and grants, the organization is also required to distinguish between *direct public support* (line 1a) and *indirect public support* (line 1b). This differentiation is made in the context of *donative type publicly supported charities*.[46]

**NOTE**

These distinctions are not required just for Part I reporting purposes. They also need to be made when computing the public support ratio of publicly supported charities.[47]

The reporting exempt organization is expected, when reporting any contributions and/ or grants, to differentiate, on line 1d, between such funding in the form of money (cash) or property (noncash). For purposes of the latter, the organization must value the property received.[48]

> ## NOTE
>
> Contributions and grants of other items should not be reported as revenue. (Likewise, they cannot be considered when computing public support.) These other items are contributions of services and gifts of the use of property. (See the discussion of Part VI.)

**Other Revenue.**    All revenue other than contributions, grants, and program service revenue must be reported. Much of this will be nontaxable investment income, such as interest (lines 4 and 5), dividends (line 5), rent (line 6), and capital gain (line 8).[49]

> ## NOTE
>
> Some of this revenue may be unrelated business income. This can arise, for example, if the organization is in the business of renting property,[50] selling property when functioning as a dealer in the property,[51] receiving interest income from a controlled entity,[52] or receiving investment income from debt-financed property.[53]

**Special Events.**    The reporting of revenue from a special event can be a particularly aggravating exercise. This is one of the few instances on the annual information return where allocations and netting of revenue is permitted in the revenue portion of the return. Thus, in computing "gross revenue" from a special event, the organization must strip out the portion of the revenue (if any) that is considered *contributions*. This amount is then reported twice: as contributions on line 1a (direct public support) and on line 9a (within the parentheses) as an amount to be excluded from special event gross revenue.[54]

If a patron at a special event sponsored by a charitable organization pays more for goods or services than their fair market value, the difference is a *contribution*. The instructions to the Form 990, however, add to the confusion by blending special events and quid pro quo contribution activities. (The IRS's definition of a *special event* does not include the solicitation of quid pro quo contributions; this is rightly so, since such a fundraising undertaking is not an *event*.) The solicitation of quid pro quo contributions is a fundraising activity that primarily solicits gifts but has within it the sale of a good or service.[55]

Following are examples showing the difference between the two:

- **Quid pro quo contribution.** Charity A announces that anyone who contributes $50 or more to the organization will receive, in exchange for the gift, a book having a retail value of $20. This gives rise to a contribution of $30 and a sale of an item worth $20. The $30 is reported on line 1a and on line 9a within the parentheses, and the $20 is reported in the right-hand column on line 9a.

- **Special event # 1.** Charity B conducts a golf tournament. The tickets for the event have a face value of $200. The value of participation in the tournament is $150.

The patron purchasing the ticket has made a gift of $50. The $50 is reported on line 1a and on line 9a within the parentheses, and the $150 is reported in the right-hand column on line 9a.

- **Special event # 2.** Charity C conducts an auction. A patron purchases a painting for $1,500, although its retail value (as reflected in the auction catalog[56]) is $1,000. The patron purchasing the painting has made a gift of $500.[57] The $500 is reported on line 1a and on line 9a within the parentheses, and the $1,000 is reported in the right-hand column on line 9a.

The Form 990 instructions further the confusion in still another respect, this time by misstating the law (as correctly articulated by the IRS elsewhere). This error occurs in connection with factual situations reflected in the first example above. The IRS states that a person who contributes $50 and "who chooses the book" has actually made a gift of $30 and a purchase of $20. This is certainly true, but the outcome is the same if the person does not "choose" the book. The element of *choice* is irrelevant in the quid pro quo contribution setting. The IRS has made it clear that in these contexts, the *opportunity to receive* the item offered has the same value as the item itself; a donor in this context has the charitable deduction reduced even if the participant declines the item.[58] If, in a situation like the first example, the donor wants a deduction for the full amount, the gift should be made *outside the context of* the quid pro quo contribution solicitation activity.[59]

Once the reporting organization has computed its gross revenue from one or more fundraising events (line 9a, right-hand column), it is required to determine its expenses that are *directly related* to the conduct of the event or activity and report them (line 9b). The difference between the two is net income (or loss) from special events (line 9c). Notwithstanding this exercise, however, the charity must break out the expenses attributable to *fundraising* (namely, the raising of contributions that are shown both on line 1a and on line 9a (within the parentheses)), and report those expenses in Part II, column (D), and on Part I, line 15.

Another refinement: If an organization offers, by means of a special event or distribution of low-cost articles,[60] goods or services having only a nominal value,[61] the *entire amount* received is reported as contributions (Part I, line 1a) and the related expenses are reported as fundraising expenses (Part II, column (D), and Part I, line 15).

**NOTE** ✎

These various forms of contributions will count, most likely in full, as public support for those charitable organization that are endeavoring to qualify or remain qualified as publicly supported charities.

**COMMENT** ➤

The cost of these machinations (internal and/or outside bookkeeping and accounting expenses) may well exceed any otherwise-ascertained net income from special event fundraising!

Form 990, line 9, requires attachment of a schedule concerning special events and activities. The instructions state that the schedule should list the three largest special events conducted, as measured by gross receipts. These events must be described; the following must be included: gross receipts, the amount of contributions included in gross receipts, the gross revenue (gross receipts minus contributions), direct expenses, and the net income (or loss) (gross revenue less direct expenses). The same information is to be included, in total figures, for all other special events.[62]

## Part II

In addition to conventional reporting of a tax-exempt organization's expenses (in Part I), the organization must report these expenses on a functional basis. Donors, grantors, the IRS, other governmental agencies, and representatives of the media are quick to turn to the bottom lines of fundraising expenses (column (D)) and management expenses (column (C)).

The IRS and other readers of the Form 990 are sensitive to the matter of the reporting of fundraising expenses. Many large charitable organizations that clearly engage in fundraising activities report little or no fundraising expenses. Thus, organizations should be accurate in calculating and reporting fundraising costs on the Form 990.

Another subject of some sensitivity is the matter of joint costs. The Form 990 includes a question as to whether any joint costs from a combined educational campaign and fundraising solicitation are reported in the amount of program services. If the answer to this question is yes, the following must be reported: the aggregate amount of these joint costs, the amount allocated to program services, the amount allocated to management and general, and the amount allocated to fundraising.

The instructions state that an organization conducts a *combined educational campaign and fundraising solicitation* when it solicits contributions (by mail, telephone, broadcast media, or other means) and includes, with the solicitation, educational material or other information that furthers a bona fide nonfundraising exempt purpose of the organization.[63] Any method of allocating joint costs to program service expenses must be reasonable under the facts and circumstances of each case.

**NOTE**

The instructions state that expenses attributable to the provision of information about the organization, its use of past contributions, or its planned use of contributions received are not program service expenses.[64] This injunction is frequently not followed in the preparation of annual information returns.

## Part III

The Form 990 requires the filing organization to inventory its *program service accomplishments* (defined above). This should be the most delectable portion of the annual information return for the exempt organization, because it offers a marvelous opportunity for it to showcase its programs. "See attached" can often be the answer here, as this is the place for the organization to discuss *in detail* the various ways in which it is furthering its exempt purposes. This is the place to "tell the story," for the benefit of funders, the IRS, the media, and others. The only true limitation here is veracity.

From time to time, these programs should be compared to the organization's formal statement of purposes (such as the one in its articles of incorporation) to be certain the organization has not wandered beyond the bounds of those purposes. If that is the case, in most instances the statement of purposes can be amended (perhaps expanded).

NOTE

If the statement of purposes is amended, the organization should be certain to reflect that fact in line 77 of the appropriate annual information return (see below).

The organization should also be certain that these programs have been reflected on its application for recognition of exemption (if any) or on line 76 of one or more appropriate annual information returns (see below).

## Part IV

Part IV of the form, which basically is a standard balance sheet, is not usually the province of lawyers. It may be noted, however, that there are lines (50 and 63) requesting information about receivables from and loans to trustees, directors, officers, and key employees.

## Parts IV-A and IV-B

These portions of the form likewise rarely pertain to legal issues, because they concern any necessary reconciliation of revenue and expenses reported on the return with the comparable items reflected in audited financial statements. It may be noted, nonetheless, that completion of these parts is not required if the organization's financial statements (if any) are not *audited*.

## Part V

This portion of the form can be the most difficult for the tax-exempt organization filing it, in that it concerns the sensitive matter of compensation. The factor is, of course, exacerbated by the fact that the annual information return is a public document.

The exempt organization is required to list each of its trustees, directors, and officers (column (A)). Presumably, these individuals will be easy to identify. The organization is also required to list its *key employees* (column (A)); determining who these individuals are is often difficult—the exercise may involve politics as much as law. All of these individuals must be listed irrespective of whether they are compensated.

The form calls for insertion of the address of these individuals (Column (A)). Their residential addresses should not be used. Rather, their business address or the address of the filing organization should be inserted.[65]

The form requires not only recitation of the individual's title or titles (such as President and Director) but also the average number of hours devoted, on a weekly basis, to the position (column (B)). A number is required here. It is insufficient to use phrases such as "an needed."

The form calls for reporting the *compensation* paid to these individuals (column (C)). This term means more than simply a salary or wage. It includes all benefits paid (unless reported elsewhere), including nontaxable benefits. Separate reporting is required of contributions to employee benefit plans and deferred compensation (column (D)) and expense accounts and similar allowances (column (E)).

**NOTE**

The amount (if any) that is the total of column (C) should equal the amount (if any) shown on line 25, column (A) of Part II. (By picking up little discrepancies like this, the lawyer can at least evidence the fact that he or she carefully reviewed the return.)

Most tax-exempt organizations need to be concerned about the *reasonableness* of the compensation they pay, particularly where it is paid to *insiders* and/or *disqualified persons*.[66] Thus, when the amounts in these three columns are totaled up, the organization should be confident that the total number comports with the requirement that the compensation be reasonable. If the compensation is excessive, the organization's tax-exempt status may be endangered, either because of private inurement[67] or any other form of private benefit.[68] There may also be a problem in terms of the intermediate sanctions rules.[69]

If a trustee, director, officer, or key employee of a tax-exempt organization received compensation of more than $100,000 from the exempt organization and one or more related organizations, an explanatory statement must be attached where the compensation provided by one or more related organizations was more than $10,000 (line 75). For this purpose, the term *compensation* includes any amount that would be reportable as compensation (columns (C), (D), or (E)) if provided by the filing organization.

If an organization is in this position, it must attach a schedule listing, for each trustee, director, officer, or key employee receiving the compensation, the name and tax identification number of each related organization that provided the compensation, and the amount each provided.

A *related organization* is any entity (whether tax-exempt or taxable) that the filing organization directly or indirectly owns or controls, or that directly or indirectly owns or controls the filing organization. The word *owns* means holding, directly or indirectly, 50 percent or more of the voting membership rights, voting stock, profits interest, or beneficial interest.

## EXAMPLE ▼

Organization A owns 90 percent of Organization B. B owns 80 percent of Organization C. A, of course, directly owns B. Also, A indirectly owns 72 percent (90 percent of 80 percent) of C.

The term *control* means that (1) 50 percent or more of the filing organization's trustees, directors, officers, or key employees are also trustees, directors, officers, or key employees of the second organization being tested for control; (2) the filing organization appoints 50 percent or more of the trustees, directors, officers, or key employees of the second organization; or (3) 50 percent or more of the filing organization's trustees, directors, officers, or key employees are appointed by the second organization. Control exists if the 50 percent test is met by any single group of persons even if collectively the 50 percent test is not met.

Irrespective of whether any elements of ownership or control are present, a related organization includes (1) a supporting organization operated in connection with the filing organization[70] where one of the purposes of the supporting organization is to benefit or further the purposes of the filing organization, and (2) a supported organization operated in connection with the filing organization where one of the purposes of the filing organization is to benefit or further the purposes of the supported organization.

## EXAMPLE ▼

Hospital auxiliary A raises funds for Hospital H. A is a supporting organization of H and thus an organization related to H, even if H does not own or control A. H, in turn, is a supported organization of A. In any case where the $10,000 and $100,000 thresholds are met, H must report (on an attachment to its return) the compensation paid by A to the trustee, director, officer, or key employee of H. This reporting requirement also applies to compensation paid by H to a trustee, director, officer, or key employee of Y.

One of the more controversial statements in the instructions is this: "If you [the filing organization] pay any other person, such as a management services company, for the services provided by any of your officers, directors, trustees, or key employees, report the compensation and other items in Part V as if you had paid the officers, etc., directly." In most instances involving the use of a management company, this rule will not apply because the services provided are not provided by the organization's officers, directors, trustees, or key employees. Even in situations where this rule may be applicable, it is not clear how the filing organization is to obtain that information from the management company, where it is being paid a fee for its services.

### Part VI

There is a host of problems, traps, and other interesting aspects lurking in Part VI of the Form 990. The first of the questions is whether the organization engaged, during the reporting year, in any activity not previously reported to the IRS (line 76). Although the Form 990 refers to *any* activity, the rule is tempered in the instructions to pertain to any *significant* activity. The instructions also state that the filing organization is to include new or modified activities (1) not listed as current or planned in the organization's application for recognition of exemption, (2) not reported to the IRS by letter, or (3) not reported to the IRS by an attachment to a prior annual information return filed by the organization. Further, the organization should report any major program activities that are being discontinued.

All too often, year in and year out, this question is answered by checking the no box, when the correct answer is yes. It simply is not realistic to assume that a tax-exempt organization will remain so static over a multiyear period. The proper approach is to report the significant changes incrementally. This is done by attaching a statement explaining the changes. It is to be hoped that the changes will be related to the organization's tax-exempt purposes. If there is uncertainty about whether a newly undertaken activity is related or unrelated, a lawyer should be consulted.

The concept, then, is that each significant activity of the tax-exempt organization should be reflected in its application for recognition of exemption or in an annual information return.

## CAUTION!

If a change is *material* in nature, it should be reported to the IRS at the time of the change, rather than waiting to file the Form 990.[71] The material change should also be reported on the Form 990 in response to this question. The organization thus needs to make a judgment as to whether an activity it conducts or is discontinuing is *significant, major,* or *material.*

## NOTE

Generally, a material change need only be *reported* to the IRS. It is unlikely that the agency will respond to the filing, but it may. In rare instances, a tax-exempt organization may be best advised to request a ruling from the IRS that one or more activities are exempt functions.

A comparable question pertains to any changes made in the organizing or governing documents of the organization (line 77). This question literally relates to *any* change in these documents, which usually are articles of incorporation, constitution, trust agreement, declaration of trust, or bylaws. A *conformed copy* must be attached to the return; this is a copy that, in the language of the instructions, "agrees with the original document and all amendments to it."[72] If the copies are not signed, they must be accompanied by a written declaration signed by an officer authorized to sign for the organization, certifying that they are complete and accurate copies of the original documents. Photocopies of articles of incorporation showing the certification of an appropriate state official, however, do not have to be accompanied by a declaration. In an instance of a number of changes, the IRS prefers to see a copy of the entire revised organizing instrument or governing document.

This question also is often wrongly answered no; there seems to be a propensity here for miscommunication (or no communication) between those who prepare the return and those who are involved in the amendment of these documents. There also is a tendency, as is the case with the previous question, to answer this question no for no other reason than the fact that it was answered no in the past.

---

**NOTE** ✎

If a tax-exempt organization changes its legal form, such as from a trust to a corporation, an application for recognition must be filed for the new organization. This is because a new legal entity has been formed.

---

The return asks whether the organization had gross unrelated business income of $1,000 or more in the reporting year (line 78a). The question is framed in this fashion because there is a $1,000 standard deduction in this context.[73] If the question is answered yes, the IRS expects the filing of the unrelated business income tax return.[74]

An explanatory statement must be attached to the Form 990 if, as to the organization, there was a liquidation, dissolution, termination, or substantial contraction during the year (line 79). The statement must show whether the assets of the organization have been distributed and the date of distribution. The IRS also wants (1) a certified copy of any resolution, or plan of liquidation or termination, with all amendments or supplements not already filed and (2) a schedule listing the names and addresses of all persons who received the assets distributed in liquidation or termination, the kinds of assets distributed to each one, and each asset's fair market value.

A *substantial contraction* is a partial liquidation or other major disposition of assets, other than transfers for full consideration (usually, sales) or distributions from current income (such as grants). A *major disposition of assets* means any disposition for the tax year that is (1) at least 25 percent of the fair market value of the organization's net assets at the beginning of the tax year, or (2) one of a series of related dispositions commenced in prior years that add up to at least 25 percent of the net assets the organization had at the beginning of the tax year when the first disposition in the series was made. Whether a major disposition of assets took place through a series of related dispositions depends on the facts in each case.

---

**NOTE** ✎

In the case of a complete liquidation of a corporation or unincorporated association, or termination of a trust, the organization should check the "Final return" box in the heading of the annual information return.

The organization is required to report whether it is related to one or more other organizations (line 80a). These other organizations (if any) are to be identified by name, and the reporting organization is required to indicate whether the other organizations are tax-exempt or not (line 80b). This definition of *relatedness* is broad, including arrangements such as common membership, common governing boards, and/or common officers. The instructions state, however, that there has to be more than a 50 percent overlap for relatedness to exist.[75]

These rules do not pertain to situations where there is what the regulations term a "coincidental overlap" of membership with another organization, which occurs when membership in one organization is not a condition of membership in another organization.[76]

## EXAMPLE ▼

A majority of the members of a tax-exempt civic organization also belong to a tax-exempt local chamber of commerce. The civic organization should answer the question no if it does not require its members to belong to the chamber of commerce.

Also disregarded are mere affiliations with any statewide or nationwide organizations.

## EXAMPLES ▼

A tax-exempt local civic organization is a member of a state federation of similar organizations. The answer of the local civic organization to the question would be no. A tax-exempt local labor union's members are also members of a national labor organization. The answer of the local labor union to the question would be no.

The Form 990 inquires as to whether the organization made, during the year, any direct or indirect political expenditures and requires insertion of any such amount (line 81a). This question pertains to *political expenditures*[77] and not just *political campaign expenditures*.[78] The form also reflects the fact that the organization may have to file a tax return (Form 1120-POL) to report these expenditures (and calculate any tax) (line 81b).

The Form 990 inquires as to whether the organization received contributions of services or the use of materials, equipment, or facilities, either at no charge or at substantially less than fair market value (line 82a). Although these items cannot be treated as revenue (Part I) (or taken into account by charitable organizations in computing public support), they can be valued and reflected on the return (line 82b). The IRS, however, wants the organization to maintain records that either show the amount and value of the items or provide a "clearly objective basis" for an estimate of that value.[79]

The Form 990 asks the organization to indicate whether it complied with the public inspection requirements that apply with respect to applications for recognition of exemption and annual information returns (line 83a).[80] The appropriate answer to this question is yes, inasmuch as the law *mandates* such compliance. (The organization should consult a lawyer if the answer must be no.) Nonetheless, in a surprising number of instances, this question is answered no—because the organization was never asked for a copy of the documents and thus literally was unable to comply. That is not the suitable way to read the question. An organization can be in compliance with these requirements by being *ready* to provide the documents (or by posting them online). The question should be answered as if it read: "If asked to provide one or more copies of its application for recognition of exemption or an annual information return, did the organization comply with the public inspection requirements?"

A similar question is asked about compliance with the disclosure requirements pertaining to quid pro quo contributions (line 83b).[81] The comments above pertaining to the public inspection requirements apply in this context as well. Thus, the question should be answered (it is hoped, yes) as if it read: "If the organization received any quid pro quo contributions, did it comply with the disclosure requirements concerning these gifts?"

A somewhat similar question concerns the solicitation of contributions by organizations in situations where the gifts are not deductible (line 84a).[82] This question pertains, then, to tax-exempt organizations other than charitable ones. It applies, for example, to contributions solicited by exempt social welfare organizations.[83] As the form indicates, there is a requirement that a statement be made in connection with the solicitation of these types of contributions that they are not tax deductible (line 84b). Thus, it is to be hoped that the question can be answered yes. (If the answer must be no, the organization should consult a lawyer.)

A somewhat redundant question asks whether the organization, at any time during the year, owned 50 percent or more of the stock of a taxable corporation or owned 50 percent or more of an interest in a partnership or disregarded entity (line 88).[84] This is somewhat redundant because of the question asked above (line 80a) and below (Part IX).

Tax-exempt charitable organizations are required to enter the amount of tax (if any) imposed on them for engaging in excessive legislative activity or any political campaign activity (line 89a).[85] Any amount of these taxes imposed on organization managers or disqualified persons during the year must be disclosed (line 89c), along with any amount of the tax that the exempt organization reimbursed (line 89d).

Tax-exempt charitable and social welfare organizations are asked whether they (1) *engaged in* an excess benefit transaction during the year or (2) *became aware of* an excess benefit transaction that took place in a prior year (line 89b).[86] If the answer to either question is yes, an explanatory statement must be attached.

This question can place organizations of this type—termed *applicable tax-exempt organizations*—in a difficult position. The taxes imposed for engaging in excess benefit transactions fall on the disqualified persons who engaged in the transaction—not the applicable tax-exempt organization—yet the exempt organization has this annual reporting responsibility. These disqualified persons are likely to be board members, officers, or key employees. There may be a dispute as to whether a transaction constituted an excess benefit transaction—the exempt organization may be of the view that the transaction did so qualify and the board member may be of the opposite view. To say the least, the filing of a statement (on Form 4720) by the exempt organization identifying a board member as a participant in such a transaction can be problematic. (This is exacerbated by the fact that the document is open to public inspection.) There is a story circulating—it may only be apocryphal—about a disqualified person/board member who, because of such a statement filed with a Form 990, sued an applicable tax-exempt organization for defamation.

The Form 990 also asks the organization to report the amount of tax imposed on the organization managers or disqualified persons during the year because of one or more excess benefit transactions (line 89c). It is not clear as to how the exempt organization learns of this information. Also, any amount of the tax that the exempt organization reimbursed must be disclosed (line 89d).

There are special questions applicable only to tax-exempt social welfare organizations, labor organizations, and business leagues, concerning the extent of the deductibility of dues to them (line 85a to h);[87] social clubs (line 86a and b);[88] and mutual organizations (line 87a and b).[89]

## Part VII

From a federal tax law perspective, Part VII of the Form 990 is the most important portion of the document. It forces the tax-exempt organization filing the form to tally each of its sources of *income* and list them in the far left column. Contributions and grants, not being income, are not reflected here.

The form enables the exempt organization to list up to five items of program service revenue (line 93a to e). A statement can be attached if the organization wishes to identify additional items of this type of revenue. These income items will almost always be from related business activity. The differentiation as to these activities is based on application of the *fragmentation rule*.[90]

The form also lists three forms of program service revenue: payments from the Medicare and Medicaid programs (line 93f), funding from government agencies pursuant to a fee-for-service arrangement (contract, not grant) (line 93g), and membership dues and assessments (line 94).

The form then lists forms of what is usually investment income: interest (lines 95 and 96), dividends (line 96), rental income (lines 97 and 98), and other investment income (line 99). As discussed above, items such as interest and rent usually are not taxable, although there are circumstances where they can be unrelated business income. Indeed, this portion of the form requires a reporting of income from the holding of real property, when it is debt-financed (line 97a) and when it is not (line 97b).[91]

There is a line for income from the sale of property that is not inventory (this will often be capital gain) (line 100) and a line for the sale of property that is inventory (line 102).

There is a line for net income or loss from special events (line 101). These events are discussed above. The amount on this line should be the same amount as is being reported on line 9c.

This listing of income items concludes with a catchall series of lines by which the organization reports any other forms of revenue (line 103).

Once all of these income-producing activities have been identified and the associated amounts determined, the reporting of each item requires further classification of it into one of three categories.

> ## NOTE
>
> The amount entered as total income on line 105, plus the amount of gifts and grants stated in Part I, line 1a, should be the same as that provided on line 12 of Part I.

If the organization is of the view that the income item is derived from a related business,[92] the income item is reflected on the appropriate line in column (E). This then requires an explanation, in Part VIII, as to how the activity contributes importantly to the accomplishment of the organization's exempt purposes. These explanations should be crafted with care, not to mention a clear understanding of the law on the point.

If the income item is considered to be from an unrelated business,[93] the amount is reported on the appropriate line in column (B). The organization is expected to identify the type of business involved, associate it with a business code (found in the instructions that accompany the unrelated business income tax return (Form 990-T)), and insert that code on the appropriate line in column (A).

> ## NOTE
>
> As observed above, if an organization has gross unrelated business income of at least $1,000 in the reporting year, it should report that income (and calculate any tax) on a tax return (Form 990-T). The numbers reported in this part should, obviously, be reconciled with those reported on the unrelated business income tax return.

If the income item is not from a related business but is believed to be sheltered from federal income taxation by statute, the amount is entered on the appropriate line in column (D). The organization is expected to identify the statutory provision by correlating it with the corresponding exclusion code (found in the instructions[94]). Completion of this portion of the Form 990, then, requires an understanding of the various exclusions.

An exclusion code must also be assigned to items of nontaxable investment income. The most common of these are:

- Dividends, interest, payments with respect to securities, loans, annuities, income from notional principal contracts, loan commitment fees, and other such income derived from ordinary and routine investments (exclusion code 14)[95]
- Royalty income (exclusion code 15)[96]
- Rental income from real property that is not dependent on the income or profits derived by the person leasing the property (exclusion code 16)[97]
- Rent from personal property leased with real property and incidental in relation to the combined income from both types of property (exclusion code 17)[98]
- Gain or loss from the sale of investment property and other noninventory property (exclusion code 18)[99]

If more than one exclusion code applies to a particular revenue item, the IRS requests that the lowest numbered exclusion code be used. If nontaxable revenues from several sources are reportable on the same line in column (D), the exclusion code to use is the one that applies to the largest revenue source.

The most common of these exclusions are:

- Income from an activity that is not regularly carried on (exclusion code 01)[100]

- A business that is conducted substantially by volunteers (exclusion code 02)[101]

- A business conducted for the convenience of the charitable organization's students, patients, or members (exclusion code 03)[102]

- A business consisting of the sale of items that were donated to the organization (exclusion code 05)[103]

Some other codes, more suited to specific types of tax-exempt organizations, are:

- Income from the distribution of low-cost articles in connection with the solicitation of charitable contributions (exclusion code 12)[104]

- The conduct of an agricultural or educational fair or exposition (exclusion code 06)[105]

- The conduct of a qualified convention and trade show activity (exclusion code 07)[106]

- Income from the provision of certain hospital services (exclusion code 08)[107]

- Income from the conduct of certain bingo games (exclusion code 09)[108]

- Income from research for the United States, its agencies or instrumentalities, or a state or political subdivision of a state (exclusion code 20)[109]

- Income from research conducted by a college, university, or hospital (exclusion code 21)[110]

- Income from research conducted by an organization the primary activity of which is the conduct of fundamental research, the results of which are freely available to the general public (exclusion code 22)[111]

- Non-exempt function income set aside by a tax-exempt social club for charitable purposes (exclusion code 25)[112]

- Income exempt from the debt-financed income rules because substantially all of the use of the property is for the organization's exempt purposes (exclusion code 30)[113]

- Income from property received in return for the obligation to pay a charitable gift annuity (exclusion code 36)[114]

## NOTE ✎

There may be an argument that the income-producing activity is not a *business* to begin with and thus not an unrelated business.[115] The only definition that the IRS follows in this context, however, is the one that an activity is not a business if it is not conducted with the requisite profit motive (that is, there are "continuous losses sustained over a number of tax periods"). The IRS has provided an exclusion code for this purpose (41).

Once this exercise is completed, the total of the amounts in columns B, D, and E should reflect the total amount of income-producing activity of the organization.

## NOTE ✎

In doing the math, the total of these income items plus the amount of gifts and grants (line 1d) must equal the total amount of revenue being reported (line 12). Again, this portion of the Form 990 forces the organization to display and otherwise account for each discrete revenue item—assuming, as always, that the return is properly prepared.

## Part VIII

As noted, Part VIII is devoted to recitations as to why the activity underlying each income item contributes importantly to the furtherance of the organization's exempt purpose. Each of these items is to be identified by the corresponding line in Part VII. There is not much space afforded for this purpose; often Part VIII is best complied with by attachment of a statement. It goes without saying that this statement should be carefully crafted.

## TIPS

- The organization should endeavor to be certain that it clearly and concisely describes its exempt programs.
- The organization should make certain that this description meshes nicely with and is not inconsistent with its statement of program service accomplishments (Part III).
- The organization should make certain that more than 50 percent of the total revenue (including contributions and grants) is derived from exempt function revenue. This is in reflection of the *primary purpose rule*.[116]
- The organization should not attempt to justify the activity as a related one on the ground that it generates net income for exempt purposes.[117]
- Once this list of activities is completed, the return preparer should compare it to comparable lists filed in previous years to determine if one or more activities are newly added; if that is the case, that fact should be reflected in the answer as to whether the organization engaged in an activity not previously reported to the IRS (line 76) (see above).

## Part IX

The tax-exempt organization is required to identify any corporation, partnership, or disregarded entity in which it has an ownership interest. The name, address, and employer identification number of the entity must be provided (column (A)), as must the percentage of ownership interest (column (B)), the nature of the entity's activities (column

(C)), the total income of the organization (column (D)), and the organization's assets as of the end of the reporting year.

## Part X

Form 990 asks the filing organization whether, during the year involved, it received any funds, directly or indirectly, to pay premiums on a personal benefit contract (defined above) (question (a)). This question is simply to be answered yes or no.

What is being sought here is information about arrangements whereby a payor makes what the parties treat as a *contribution* to a charitable organization, with respect to which there is an expectation or other understanding that some or all of the funds will be used to pay premiums on a life insurance, annuity, or like contract through which there will be benefits flowing to the payor, the payor's family, and/or designee of the payor.[118] This is because a charitable deduction is disallowed for a transfer to or for the use of a charitable organization if, in connection with the transfer, (1) the organization directly or indirectly pays, or has previously paid, any premium on a personal benefit contract with respect to the transferor, or (2) there is an understanding or expectation that any person will directly or indirectly pay any premium on a personal benefit contract with respect to the transferor.[119] This rule applies with respect to transfers of this nature to charitable remainder trusts.[120]

There are two exceptions to this charitable deduction disallowance rule:

1. If in connection with a transfer to or for the use of a charitable organization the organization incurs an obligation to pay a charitable gift annuity[121] and the organization purchases an annuity contract to fund the obligation (termed *reinsurance*), persons receiving payments pursuant to the charitable gift annuity contract are not treated as *indirect beneficiaries* under the contract if (a) the charitable organization possesses all of the incidents of ownership under the contract, (b) the organization is entitled to all of the payments under the contract, and (c) the timing and amount of payments made under the contract are substantially the same as the timing and amount of payments to each such person under the obligation (as the obligation is in effect at the time of the transfer).[122]

2. A person is not treated as an *indirect beneficiary* under a life insurance, annuity, or endowment contract held by a charitable remainder trust solely by reason of being entitled to an income interest payment if (a) the trust possesses all of the incidents of ownership under the contract and (b) the trust is entitled to all of the payments under the contract.[123]

An excise tax is imposed on a charitable organization equal to the premiums paid by the organization on a life insurance, annuity, or endowment contract if the payment of premiums on the contract is in connection with a transfer for which a deduction is disallowed under these rules, determined without regard to when the transfer is made.[124] For this purpose, payments made by any other person pursuant to this type of an understanding or expectation are treated as made by the charitable organization.[125]

An organization on which this tax is imposed is required to file an annual return, which includes the amount of the premiums paid during the year and the name and identification number of each beneficiary under the contract to which the premium relates.[126] The penalties applicable with respect to annual information returns apply in connection with this return.[127]

The form also asks whether the organization, during the year, paid premiums directly or indirectly on a personal benefit contract (question (b)). Again, this question is to be answered yes or no. If, however, this question is answered yes, the organization becomes required to file two forms. It must report the premiums it paid, and any premiums paid by others but treated as paid by the organization, on Form 8870. The organization must report and pay the excise tax on Form 4720.[128]

## Schedule A

Schedule A is a supplemental form, accompanying Form 990 or Form 990-EZ, that must be filed by every tax-exempt charitable organization that is required to file an annual information return.[129] This schedule is used to report compensation arrangements, any transactions with insiders and/or noncharitable exempt organizations, public charity status, policies and activities of private schools, and lobbying activities.[130] The schedule should cover the same period of time as that for the Form 990 or Form 990-EZ it accompanies. The schedule is part of the annual return and, therefore, the penalties applicable with respect to the annual information return also are applicable with respect to this schedule.

Part I of Schedule A is used to report information about compensation, in excess of $50,000, of the five highest-paid employees of the filing organization (if any), other than what the return refers to as trustees, directors, and officers. The instructions, however, expand this to encompass key employees. Thus, the filing organization should not include in Part I of Schedule A information about employees listed in Part V of Form 990 (or Part IV of Form 990-EZ).

The information requested includes the name and address of the employee, his or her title, and the average number of hours devoted to the position each week (columns (a) and (b)). Also required is the amount of compensation paid (such as salary, fees, bonuses, and severance payments) (column (c)), contributions to employee benefit plans (plans providing benefits such as medical, dental, life insurance, severance pay, or disability) (column (d)), all forms of deferred compensation and future severance payments (whether funded, whether vested, and whether the deferred compensation plan is a qualified plan) (column (d)), and taxable and nontaxable fringe benefits (column (e)).

The organization also reports the total number of other employees (but not any additional information) with annual compensation of more than $50,000.

**NOTE**

The Schedule A instructions include this intriguing invitation: The organization can provide an attachment explaining the "entire year . . . compensation package" for any individual listed in Part I.[131] This attachment (which an organization could attach in the absence of the instruction), of course, would offer information rationalizing the compensation package as *reasonable*.[132]

In Part II, the filing organization is required to report on compensation, in excess of $50,000, of the five highest-paid independent contractors (individuals or firms) who performed personal services[133] of a professional nature for the organization. Independent contractors are persons (not employees) such as lawyers, accountants, and fundraisers. Expense reimbursements are not reported here.

As with Part I, the filing organization must also show the number of other independent contractors who received more than $50,000 for the year and may attach an explanatory statement concerning one or more compensation packages. For example, if the filing organization was embroiled in extensive litigation during the year and incurred substantial legal fees, it may wish to explain the extraordinary circumstances to the IRS.

Part III of Schedule A essentially delves into four aspects of an organization's operations: lobbying, transactions with insiders, certain grants, and maintenance of a section 403(b) annuity plan.

The total amount of expenses paid or incurred in connection with any lobbying activities[134] must be entered on line 1. If the answer on line 1 is yes, the organization must complete either Part VI-A or VI-B (see below).

The question on line 2 inquires as to certain transactions the organization may have engaged in, directly or indirectly, with one or more insiders[135] during the reporting year. These insiders are the following persons (defined above): trustees, directors, officers, creators (founders), substantial contributors, key employees, and members of their families.

The question on line 2 also inquires as to certain transactions engaged in, directly or indirectly, with a taxable organization with which any of the foregoing persons is affiliated as a trustee, director, officer, majority owner, or principal beneficiary.

The transactions involved are those reflected in the concept of self-dealing applicable in the private foundation setting. Thus, even though the tax-exempt organization is not a private foundation, it (or at least the return preparer) must respond to the question on line 2 with knowledge of the private foundation self-dealing rules. These transactions are:

- Sale, lease, or exchange of property[136]
- Lending of money or other extension of credit[137]
- Furnishing of goods, services, or facilities[138]
- Payment of compensation (or payment or reimbursement of expenses (if more than $1,000))[139]
- Transfer of any part of the organization's income or assets[140]

If the organization engaged in one or more of these transactions with one or more insiders, a "detailed statement" must be attached to the return, explaining the transactions. In the language of the instructions, these requirements apply with respect to "both sides" of a transaction. Reporting is required, for example, whether the reporting organization is a payer or payee, buyer or seller, or lender or borrower.[141]

In this part, the filing organization must respond to the question as to whether it makes grants for scholarships and/or fellowships, student loans, and the like. If the answer to this question is yes, the organization must attach a statement explaining how it determines that individuals or organizations receiving grants or loans from it in furtherance of its exempt programs qualify to receive the payments. Individuals or organizations *qualify* for the assistance if (1) they use the funds for purposes that are inherently charitable, educational, and the like[142] or (2) the individual recipients belong to a charitable class[143] and the payments are to aid them. As to the latter, the instructions provide these examples: providing assistance to the "aged poor,"[144] training teachers and social workers from underdeveloped countries, and awarding scholarships to individuals.[145]

Question 4 in Part III inquires as to whether the organization has a section 403(b) annuity plan[146] for its employees. The question is to be answered yes or no. A statement is not required, irrespective of the answer.

Part IV of Schedule A requires the organization to check one of 11 boxes, indicating its public charity (non-private foundation) status.[147]

Part V of Schedule A is to be prepared only by private schools.

Part VI of Schedule A concerns lobbying activities by public charities.[148]

Part VII of Schedule A is used to report direct and indirect transfers to, direct and indirect transactions with, and relationships the filing tax-exempt charitable organization may have with any noncharitable exempt organization.[149] A *noncharitable exempt organization* is (1) an organization that is tax-exempt by reason of being one of the entities listed in the conventional grouping of exempt organizations[150] (other than an exempt charitable one) or (2) a tax-exempt political organization.[151] A noncharitable exempt organization is, in this context, likely to be:

- A social welfare organization[152]
- A labor organization[153]
- A business league (association)[154]
- A social club[155]
- A fraternal organization[156]
- A veterans' organization[157]

The filing organization is required to differentiate between circumstances where it is related to a noncharitable exempt organization and where it is unrelated to such an organization. A noncharitable exempt organization is *related* to (or *affiliated* with) the reporting organization if the two organizations share an element of common control or a historic and continuing relationship exists between the two organizations. A noncharitable exempt organization is *unrelated* to the reporting organization if the two organizations do not share any element of common control and a historic and continuing relationship does not exist between the two organizations.[158]

An *element of common control* is present when (1) one or more of the trustees, directors, or officers of one organization are elected or appointed by the trustees, directors, officers, or members of the other organization, or (2) more than 25 percent of the trustees, directors, or officers of one organization serve as trustees, directors, or officers of the other organization. A *historic and continuing relationship* exists when (1) two organizations participate in a "joint effort to work in concert toward the attainment of one or more common purposes on a continuous or recurring basis rather than on the basis of one or several isolated transactions or activities," or (2) two organizations share facilities, equipment, or paid personnel during the year, regardless of the length of time the arrangement is in effect.[159]

## EXAMPLE 1 ▼

ABC Association is a noncharitable exempt organization. Some members of the Association formed the ABC Foundation, as a tax-exempt charitable entity, 20 years ago, as a nonmembership corporation. There is no overlap of directors and/or officers between the two organizations; all of these individuals are members of the association. The offices of the two organizations are in separate locations. There have been only two financial transactions between the two organizations; one was 10 years ago (a loan to the Association from the Foundation) and one was in the reporting year (a cash grant from the Association to the Foundation). While each has a somewhat common objective (furthering ABC), the organization always functions separately. Under these facts (which, in real life, are highly unlikely), ABC Foundation would answer question 51a(i) no. (The amount of the grant would still be reflected as public support in Part I, Form 990, and perhaps be reflected on Schedule B.)

## EXAMPLE 2 ▼

The facts are the same as in Example 1, except that instead of the grant, the Foundation sold an item of property, having a fair market value of $400, to the Association. The Association paid the Foundation $400 for the property. The Foundation would answer question 51b(i) no.

## EXAMPLE 3 ▼

The facts are the same as in Example 2, except that the fair market value of the property and the price paid for it was $600. The Foundation would answer question 51b(i) yes.

The filing organization is required to report on line 51 any transfer to or transaction with a noncharitable exempt organization even if the transfer or transaction constituted the only connection between the two entities. If the noncharitable exempt organization is related to or affiliated with the reporting organization, the reporting organization is required to report all direct and indirect transfers and transactions, except for contributions and grants received by the reporting organization. All transfers from the reporting organization to an unrelated noncharitable exempt organization must be reported on line 51a. All transactions between the reporting organization and an unrelated noncharitable exempt organization must be shown on line 51b (unless an exception, referenced below, is applicable).

The reporting organization must answer yes to line 51a(i) if it made any direct or indirect transfers of money (cash) to a noncharitable exempt organization. Likewise, it must answer yes to line 51a(ii) if it made any direct or indirect transfers of other property of any value to a noncharitable exempt organization. A *transfer* is any transaction or arrangement by which one organization transfers something of value (such as money, other property, services, or use of property) to another organization without receiving something of more than nominal value in return.[160] Although contributions and grants obviously constitute transfers, if the only transfers between the two organizations were contributions and/or grants made by the noncharitable exempt organization to the reporting organization, the reporting organization should answer the appropriate question(s) on line 51a no.

The reporting organization must answer yes for any transaction described in lines 51b(i) to (vi), irrespective of the amount, if the transaction was with a related or affiliated organization. The organization must answer yes for any transaction between it and an unrelated noncharitable exempt organization, irrespective of the amount, if the reporting organization received less than adequate consideration. There is *adequate consideration* where the fair market value of the goods, other assets, or services furnished by the reporting organization is not more than the fair market value of the goods, other assets, or services received from the unrelated noncharitable exempt organization. The exception described next does not apply to transactions for less than adequate consideration.

The reporting organization must answer yes for any transaction, including transfers for adequate consideration, between it and an unrelated noncharitable exempt organization if the amount involved is more than $500. The *amount involved* is the fair market value of the goods, services, or other assets furnished by the reporting organization. As an "exception," if a transaction with an unrelated noncharitable exempt organization was for adequate consideration and the amount involved was no more than $500, it is not necessary for the reporting organization to answer yes for that transaction.

The transactions that must be reported in response to the question involving line 51b are:

- Sales or exchanges of assets with a noncharitable exempt organization (line 51b(i))
- Purchases of assets from a noncharitable exempt organization (line 51b(ii))
- Rental of facilities, equipment, or other assets; the reporting organization must answer yes for any transactions in which it was the lessor or the lessee (line 51b(iii))
- Reimbursement arrangements; the reporting organization must answer the question yes if either organization reimbursed expenses incurred by the other (line 51b(iv))
- Loans or loan guarantees; the reporting organization must answer yes if either organization made loans to the other or if the reporting organization guaranteed the noncharitable organization's loans (line 51b(v))
- Performance of services or membership or fundraising solicitations; the reporting organization must answer yes if either organization performed services or membership or fundraising solicitations for the other (line 51b(vi))

---

**NOTE** ✎

This last item is troublesome, going far beyond the intricacies of coping with Part VII of Schedule A. It is somewhat common, for example, for an exempt charitable organization to be engaged in the raising of contributions for a noncharitable exempt organization, such as in the case of a supporting organization for a business league (although the support must be restricted for the charitable, educational, and/or scientific programs of the supported organization). By contrast, it is highly unlikely that a charitable organization would be providing services to enable a noncharitable exempt organization to enhance its membership. If a noncharitable exempt organization is raising contributions for a charitable organization, the former would be expected to comply with one or more states' charitable solicitation acts because it would be functioning as a professional fundraiser or professional solicitor.[161] The services described in this item are, in the unrelated business setting, known as *corporate services;* the provision of these services, however, does not give rise to unrelated business income taxation inasmuch as the exempt organizations are related.[162]

Line 51c inquires as to whether there was a sharing of facilities, equipment, mailing lists, other assets, or paid employees. For this purpose, the term *facilities* includes office space and any other land, building, or structure whether owned or leased by, or provided free of charge to, the reporting organization or the noncharitable exempt organization.

**EXAMPLE 4 ▼**

The facts are the same as in Example 1, except that the Association and the Foundation share office space. Under these facts, the two organizations are *affiliated.* The answer in Example 1 would remain no, while the answer in Example 2 would become yes. These facts would also entail a response to line 51c.

**EXAMPLE 5 ▼**

The leadership of the two organizations decides to make the ABC Foundation a supporting organization.[163] Consequently, the two organizations become *related,* with the corresponding consequences in the preparation of Part VII.

If the answer to one or more of the questions on lines 51a through 51c is yes, the reporting organization must prepare the schedule that follows line 51d. Each of the transfers or transactions must be separately described, although the organization may combine all of the cash transfers (line 51a(i)) to each organization into a single entry.

In column (a) of this schedule, the appropriate line number must be entered. In column (b), the amount involved must be inserted. In column (c), the reporting organization must enter the name of the noncharitable exempt organization involved. Column (d) is used to describe the transfer(s), transaction(s), and/or sharing arrangement(s); attachments, when more space is needed, are permissible.

The reporting organization must enter in column (a) of line 52b the name of each noncharitable exempt organization to or with which the reporting organization is related or affiliated. If the control factor or the historic and continuing relationship factor (or both) was present at any time during the year, the reporting organization must identify the noncharitable exempt organization even if neither factor was present at the close of the year. The category of tax exemption is entered in column (b) and the nature of the relationship is described in column (c). As to the latter, attachments, when more space is needed, are permissible.

If the reporting organization reported a transfer or transaction with an unrelated non-charitable exempt organization on line 51, it should not list the organization on line 52.

## Schedule B

**General Rules.**   Schedule B is a schedule to accompany Form 990 (as well as Form 990-EZ and Form 990-PF). The purpose of this schedule is to collect certain information about contributions the organization received during the filing period.[164]

Generally, this schedule must be filed by six categories of organizations (some tax-exempt, some not). If the organization is filing Form 990 or Form 990-EZ, it is a conventional tax-exempt organization,[165] a nonexempt charitable trust[166] that is not treated as a private foundation, or a political organization.[167] If the organization is filing Form 990-PF, it is a tax-exempt private foundation, a nonexempt charitable trust that is treated as a private foundation, or a taxable private foundation. An organization that believes it is not required to file this schedule must certify to that effect by checking the box in the heading of the appropriate annual information return that indicates it is not required to file it.

The general purpose of Schedule B—stated in the schedule to be the *general rule*—is to collect information about persons who contributed to the filing organization, during the year, $5,000 or more in the form of money or other property. This information must be provided in Part I of the schedule. If the contribution is not of money (a noncash contribution (Part I, column (d)), additional information about the gift must be provided in Part II. If more of these contributions were received than can be accommodated on the two pages of Part I and/or the two pages of Part II, copies of these pages should be used.

Part I of Schedule B has four columns. In column (a), the organization lists contributors to the organization by consecutive numbering. The information to be shown is the contributor's name, address, aggregate contributions for the year, and the type of contribution. If a contribution came directly from a contributor, the organization should check the "Person" box. The "Payroll" box is to be checked in the case of employees' contributions forwarded by an employer. The instructions state that if an employer withholds contributions from employees' pay and periodically gives them to the reporting organization, the organization should report only the employer's name and address, and the total amount given—unless the organization knows that a particular employee gave enough to be listed separately.[168]

In the case of political organizations that file a notice of tax-exempt status,[169] the names and addresses of contributors that are not reported on the organization's report of contributions and expenditures[170] do not need to be reported in Schedule B, Part I, if the organization paid the penalty for failure to adequately disclose information.[171] In this situation, the organization enters "Pd. 527(j)(1)" in column (b) instead of a name, address, and zip code, but it must enter the amount of contributions in column (c).

In Part II, the filing organization reports on property with readily ascertainable market value (such as quotations for securities) by listing its fair market value. In the case of marketable securities registered and listed on a recognized securities exchange, the market value is measured by the average of the highest and lowest quoted selling prices (or the average between the bona fide bid and asked prices) on the contribution date.[172] The instructions state that if the reporting organization cannot readily determine the fair market value of a property, the organization may use an appraised or estimated value.[173] The amount of a noncash contribution of property subject to a debt is the amount of the property's fair market value less the amount of the debt.

A *special rule* applies to tax-exempt charitable organizations (other than private foundations) that meet the rules concerning donative publicly supported entities.[174] An organization must follow this special rule even if its public charity status is predicated on another classification.[175] Thus, entities such as schools, colleges, universities, and hospitals may have to adhere to this special rule. Organizations that do not meet the donative publicly supported entity rule but are nonetheless public charities—such as organizations that are service provider publicly supported charitable organizations[176] or are supporting organizations[177]—always prepare Schedule B in conformity with the general rule.

Pursuant to this special rule, the organization lists in Part I (and, if applicable, Part II) only those contributors whose contribution(s) of $5,000 or more was greater than 2 percent of the total amount of the organization's gifts and grants for the reporting period (namely, the amount reflected on line 1d, Part I, of Form 990 (or line 1 of Form 990-EZ)). This special rule supersedes the general rule for these organizations. In this instance, the organization checks the first of the special rule boxes on the front of Schedule B.

## EXAMPLE ▼

Charity X qualifies for this special rule. During the reporting period, it received a total of $700,000 in gifts and grants. X must list in Part I of Schedule B (and, if applicable, Part II) each person who contributed more than the greater of $5,000 or 2 percent of $700,000 (which is $14,000). Thus, a contributor to X who gave a total of $10,000 in the form of money during the period would not be reported in Part I. This is because the contribution, although it exceeded $5,000, did not exceed $14,000.

There are two other special rules, both of which may apply to tax-exempt social clubs[178] and exempt fraternal organizations.[179] The general rule may also apply—or the general rule and a special rule may apply. The rules are:

1. In the case of contributions to one of these organizations that were *not* for an *exclusively* religious, charitable, or similar purpose, the organization lists in Part I (and, if necessary, Part II) each contributor who, during the year, contributed $5,000 or more.

2. In the case of contributions or bequests to one of these organizations that *were* for use *exclusively* for charitable and like purposes, the organization lists in Part I (and, if necessary, Part II) each contributor whose aggregate contributions for charitable purposes were more than $1,000 during the year. In this case, the organization checks the box relating to the second of the special rules reflected on the front of Schedule B.

3. If one of these organizations listed an exclusively charitable contribution on Part I (and perhaps on Part II), it must also complete Part III to:

   a. Provide further information on such contributions of more than $1,000 during the year; and

   b. Show the total amount received in the form of such contributions that were for $1,000 or less during the year.

4. If one of these organizations *did not* receive a contribution of more than $1,000 during the year for exclusively charitable purposes and consequently was not required to complete Parts I to III, it need only check the third of the special rule boxes on the front of Schedule B and enter, in the space provided, the total contributions it received during the year for charitable purposes.

If an amount is set aside for an exclusively charitable purpose, the organization must report in column (d) how the amount is held (for example, whether it is commingled with amounts held for other purposes). If the organization transferred the gift to another organization, the reporting organization is to show the name and address of the transferee organization in Part III, column (e), and explain the relationship between the organizations.

## Public Inspection Considerations

Schedule B *is* open to public inspection in the case of the filing of it (in conjunction with Form 990-PF) by a private foundation or in the case of the filing of it (in conjunction with Form 990 or Form 990-EZ) by a political organization.

For other tax-exempt organizations, the names and addresses of contributors are not open to public inspection. All other information, including the amount of contributions and the description of noncash contributions, is open to public inspection, unless it clearly identifies the contributor.

If an organization files a copy of Form 990 or Form 990-EZ, and attachments, with a state, it should not include its Schedule B in the attachments for the state, unless a schedule of contributors is specifically required by the state. The problem in this regard is that a state that does not require this information might inadvertently make the schedule available for public inspection along with the rest of the Form 990 or Form 990-PF.

## STATE LAW FILING REQUIREMENTS

The Form 990 is primarily an information return filed in adherence to federal tax law requirements. It has, however, roles to play in connection with filings required under state law.

## Fundraising

As noted at the outset, some states utilize the Form 990 as part of compliance with their charitable solicitation act, which is the body of law by which states regulate fundraising for charitable and sometimes other purposes. Often, localities have similar requirements. These bodies of law entail initial registration and usually annual reporting thereafter. Sometimes, the Form 990 can be used to submit financial information in this context.

## Doing Business

The concept of *doing business* in a state or locality is vague and is dependent on the law of the jurisdiction. The Form 990 instructions, however, undertake to explain the concept.[180] The instructions state that *doing business* in a jurisdiction *may* include: (1) soliciting contributions or grants by mail or otherwise from individuals, corporations, charitable organizations, or others; (2) conducting programs in the jurisdiction; (3) having employees in the jurisdiction; (4) maintaining a checking account in the jurisdiction; or (5) owning or renting property in the jurisdiction.[181]

### NOTE

This is a most expansive definition of the term *doing business*, and thus planners should be cautious in relying on it too literally. For example, the definition asserts that charitable fundraising by mail constitutes doing business in a jurisdiction. Were that the case in every state, for example, charities soliciting gifts by mail nationwide would have to register under and otherwise comply with 47 state charitable solicitation acts and 51 statutes regulating doing business in the jurisdictions! This would be compounded by similar registration and the like with thousands of counties, townships, cities, towns, villages, and more. Likewise, owning property in a jurisdiction, such as for investment purposes, is not doing business in that jurisdiction.

## Role of Form 990 in Both Settings

As the instructions to Form 990 observe, some states and local governments accept a copy of the annual information return (Form 990 or 990-EZ) and the accompanying schedules (A and B) "in place of all or part of their own financial report forms."[182] This may be the case if the filing is pursuant to a charitable solicitation law or a doing business requirement.

Some or all of the dollar limitations applicable in connection with the annual information return filing requirements may not apply in the state or local law context. For example, the $25,000 gross receipts threshold for filing the return with the IRS[183] may not apply under a state's law. Another example is the $50,000 minimum for listing professional fees.[184]

State or local filing rules may require the organization to attach to the annual information return one or more elements of information, including: (1) additional financial statements, such as a complete analysis of functional expenses or a statement of changes in net assets; (2) notes to financial statements; (3) additional financial schedules; (4) a report on the financial statements by an independent accountant; and/or (5) answers to additional questions. Moreover, as the IRS instructions note, "[e]ach jurisdiction may require the additional material to be presented on forms they provide."[185]

## INTERNET RESOURCES

The annual information returns of tax-exempt organizations are posted on the Internet by Guidestar (*www.guidestar.org*).

The Urban Institute has a web site, intended to improve the quality of annual information returns (*www.qual990.org*).

## PENALTIES

A penalty of $25 per day, not to exceed the smaller of $10,000 or 5 percent of the gross receipts of the organization for the year, may be charged when an annual information return is not filed on a timely basis, unless the organization can show that the late filing was due to reasonable cause.[186] Organizations with annual gross receipts exceeding $1 million are subject to a penalty of $100 for each day the failure continues (with a maximum penalty of $50,000 with respect to any one return).[187] This penalty begins on the due date for filing the annual information return. This penalty may also be charged if the organization files an incomplete return or furnishes incorrect information.

If the organization does not file a complete return or does not furnish correct information, the IRS may send the organization a letter that includes a fixed time to fulfill these requirements.[188] After that period expires, the person failing to comply may be charged a penalty of $10 a day. The maximum penalty on all persons for failures with respect to any one return may not exceed $5,000.[189]

Moreover, there are penalties—fines and imprisonment—for willfully not filing returns, and for filing fraudulent returns and statements with the IRS.[190]

A person who does not comply with the public inspection requirements pertaining to annual information returns[191] may be assessed a penalty of $20 for each day inspection was not permitted, up to a maximum of $10,000 for each return.[192] These penalties are the same as those referenced above for annual information returns, except that the $10,000 limitation does not apply. Any person who willfully fails to comply with the public inspection requirements for annual information returns may be subject to an additional penalty of $5,000.[193]

## COMMENTARIES

### Annual Information Return Preparation Perspective

The annual information return that tax-exempt organizations must file is not merely a government form to be mindlessly filled out. It is an important document for an exempt organization, often—since it is a public document—the principal basis used by government officials, prospective contributors, representatives of the media, and others to assess the merits of the organization. This return should accordingly be prepared with care.

This is not the place to be frugal with information. An organization should regard the Form 990 as its annual report to the world. It is not inappropriate to regard the document as akin to a prospectus prepared by a for-profit entity.

The form should be prepared robustly. The preparer is not confined to the spaces on the pages (often far too skimpy). An appropriate answer often is "see attached." Programs and purposes should be explained in some detail. There is nothing wrong with laudatory language and a positive spin on what the organization is doing (as long as the preparer stays within the bounds of veracity and does not breach a duty of confidentiality to a director, officer, and/or funder).

As noted, the Form 990 is not a tax return, it is an information return. This means that many questions are answered using sentences rather than numbers. The writing of these sentences and paragraphs should, as also noted, be done with both care and vigor, even advocacy.

## Interrelationship of Return with Exemption Application

Some, but not all, tax-exempt organizations are required to file an application for recognition of exemption with the IRS to become exempt.[194] Some of the principal organizations that are not required to file the application are social welfare organizations, labor organizations, associations and other forms of business leagues, social clubs, fraternal organizations, veterans' organizations, and title-holding companies.

The exemption application filing requirements and the annual return filing requirements are discrete bodies of law. The requirements and exceptions of one have no bearing on the requirements and exceptions of the other. Thus, for example, nearly all of the seven categories of exempt organizations just referenced are required to file annual information returns.

The IRS, nonetheless, despite these formalities, lacks an adequate procedure for correlating the filings of these applications and returns. That is, the agency finds it difficult to process an annual information return filed by a tax-exempt organization that has not filed—because it is not required to file—an application for recognition of exemption.

The IRS has decided to resolve this dilemma by rejecting annual information returns filed by organizations that have not filed an application for recognition of tax exemption, including situations where the return is not required.[195] The agency literally mails the return back to the exempt organization. Moreover, the agency takes the position that if the organization does not file an application, it must begin filing tax returns as a taxable entity.

The IRS has no authority to do this. The statutes are clear as to the organizations that are required to file an application for recognition of exemption[196] and those that are required to file an annual information return.[197] The agency simply cannot override this statutory structure. The audacity of the agency in this regard was reflected in this comment of an IRS representative at a nonprofit organizations law conference: "The statute requires tax-exempt organizations to file annual information returns but it does not require the IRS to accept them."

## RECOMMENDATION ✔

If the IRS sends an annual information return back to a tax-exempt organization for this reason, the organization should refile the return, sending it back to the IRS by registered mail. (Indeed, it may be a good idea to originally file this way.) If the IRS sends it back again, send it to the agency again in this fashion. If necessary, the matter should be brought to the attention of the Commissioner of Internal Revenue or a member of Congress, inasmuch as the IRS is flat wrong in engaging in this practice.

## Personal Benefit Contracts

The rules as to personal benefit contracts and the attention accorded them on the Form 990 could be troublesome for charitable organizations and their planners. These rules were hastily written, thrown together in nearly panic conditions by members of Congress and committee staff personnel in rapid response to some inflammatory articles that stressed some of the most abusive of these plans. There were no committee hearings; the legislation was whipped through Congress so quickly that there was no time to allow reason to prevail. There is a role for life insurance in underlying charitable organizations' endowment and other fundraising programs; the bugaboo of private benefit was invoked, deceptively, to wipe out nearly all of the charitable split-dollar life insurance program alternatives.

Decades ago, some in the charitable sector were lamenting the advent of various fundraising vehicles that are today encompassed by the most respectable term *planned giving,* such as charitable remainder trusts and charitable gift annuity contracts. These critics and fretters were alarmed at the prospects of undue private benefit being generated by these arrangements. The plans were also seen as too sophisticated, too slick, too beneficial to the wealthy. The critics then said that there was insufficient donative intent, that these arrangements were entered into primarily to provide personal benefits and only secondarily (at best) to further charitable purposes. The integrity of the charitable sector was said to be at stake. Today, of course, planned giving programs are a staple for charitable institutions; the use of planned gift vehicles continues to grow.

There were many variations of these arrangements, reflected today in charitable remainder trusts, pooled income funds, charitable gift annuity contracts, charitable lead trusts, and the like. There were abuses in these areas. In response, Congress enacted various provisions as part of the Tax Reform Act of 1969 and subsequent legislation. Congress did not eliminate planned gift arrangements; instead, it legislated criteria by which the charitable deductions would be available with respect to appropriate charitable giving techniques.[198] This practice persists today, with Congress not only continuing to refine the criteria for planned gift arrangements but also, in other fundraising contexts, carving out rules under which the gift solicitation practices are suitably permitted.[199] These plans and programs, then, have not been legislated away in the face of fear of private benefit; rather, those with appropriate features are allowed.

This process was not followed by Congress when it briefly considered charitable split-dollar life insurance plans. There were several variations of these plans; some involved abuses (perhaps constituting abusive tax shelters). There were forms of private benefit flowing from these plans (just as there is in the now-conventional planned giving setting).

At the same time, some of these plans could create, in a relatively short period of time, sizable endowments for charitable organizations. Now, charities are, because of the law concerning personal benefit contracts, severely penalized if they invest in any of these insurance plans. This is the first time, by the way, that the federal tax law places restrictions on the investment opportunities available for tax-exempt charitable organizations (other than certain limitations placed on investments by private foundations[200]).

This legislation places higher standards in this area compared with other giving plans in the tax law of charitable giving. It should go without saying that there are many charitable gift arrangements where donors and their family members receive "personal" or "private" benefits. (In one of the many ludicrous incidents surrounding these unfortunate developments, the first bill introduced in an effort to eradicate charitable split-dollar insurance plans provided for forfeiture of any charitable contribution deduction for any transaction "which provides a personal benefit directly or indirectly to the donor or any designee of the donor."[201] A rule like this would torpedo the charitable deduction for just about every major charitable gift.)

The fact that charitable giving and private benefit can co-exist in a lawful way is reflected in the statute. When an individual makes a gift to a charitable organization by means of a charitable remainder trust, for example, private benefit is created in many ways, including the creation of the income interest.[202] This seemingly discrepant dilemma is resolved, in part, by confining the charitable deduction to the value of the remainder interest. The same is true, as another illustration, in the case of a charitable gift annuity arrangement. This statute barring personal benefit contracts had to be revised and refined several times to take account of this fact; thus, there are exceptions in the context of charitable remainder trusts,[203] charitable gift annuities,[204] and gift annuity reinsurance arrangements.[205]

As far as this matter of *understandings* and *expectations* are concerned, critics of these arrangements were particularly hypocritical. In and out of the realm of planned giving, there are understandings and expectations involving donors and charitable donees. For example, a donor contributes to a donor-advised fund at a community foundation with the understanding and expectation that the advice tendered will be followed. An individual contributes to a charitable remainder trust, with certain understandings and expectations with the trustee as to whether gift property will be sold or whether the trust's investment philosophy will nicely change once the income beneficiary reaches retirement age. Parents make substantial contributions to a college with the expectation (and perhaps the understanding) that their child will be admitted.

The better approach in this area would have been to develop a statute that permits charitable deductions with respect to appropriate split-dollar life insurance plans. Just as in the various charitable giving techniques noted above, the charitable deduction could be confined to the value passing to charity. (If there can be qualified appreciated stock,[206] a qualified conservation contribution,[207] qualified convention and trade show activity,[208] qualified public entertainment activity,[209] a qualified sponsorship payment,[210] qualified tuition programs,[211] and qualified terminable interest property,[212] not to mention qualifying split-interest trusts,[213] surely there could be the qualified charitable split-insurance life insurance plan.) In this way, there would be a "carve-out" for the qualified arrangements, rather than an outright prohibition.[214] But, in 1999, when this legislation was hastily cobbled together, Congress had no interest in the virtue of this approach. It was only concerned with responding to a public outcry generated by a few newspaper and magazine articles. The process was a classic illustration as to how legislation should not be developed. This subject warrants revisit and reform.

Planners need to be careful in this area, however, for another reason. Split-dollar life insurance arrangements still lawfully exist in the charitable setting. This type of insurance can be part of a compensation package, with the employee, family members of the employee, and the tax-exempt employer sharing in the insurance benefits. Compensatory arrangements of this nature should not, however, involve personal benefit contracts.[215]

### Exceptions from Filing

The exceptions to the filing requirements are, for the most part, straightforward.[216] That is, the organization is a church, small entity, or governmental unit—or it is not. There is one exception, however, that can be made available to a tax-exempt organization with some planning. This is the exception for an entity that is an affiliate of a governmental unit.[217] Entities that are *governmental units* include (1) a state or local governmental unit as defined in the rules providing an exclusion from gross income for interest earned on bonds issued by those units[218] and (2) an entity that is entitled to receive deductible charitable contributions as a unit of government.[219]

An *affiliate of a governmental unit* is a tax-exempt organization[220] that meets one of two sets of requirements:

1. It has a ruling or determination letter from the IRS that (a) its income, derived from activities constituting the basis for its exemption, is excluded from gross income under the rules for political subdivisions and the like;[221] (b) it is entitled to receive deductible contributions on the basis that contributions to it are for the use of governmental units;[222] or (c) it is a wholly owned instrumentality of a state or political subdivision of a state for employment tax purposes.[223]

2. It does not have such a ruling or determination letter from the IRS but (a) it is either operated, supervised, or controlled by one or more governmental units, or by one or more organizations that are affiliates of governmental units, or the members of the organization's governing body are elected by the public at large, pursuant to local statute or ordinance; (b) it possesses two or more of certain affiliation factors;[224] and (3) its filing of an annual information return is not otherwise necessary to the efficient administration of the internal revenue laws.[225]

It is not as difficult as might be supposed to qualify as an affiliate of a governmental unit. An IRS private letter ruling proves the point.[226] In that case, there were eight tax-exempt, public charities, including a hospital, a home health services agency, a hospice care facility, a health maintenance organization, and a skilled nursing facility. Each of these organizations filed annual information returns. As part of a reorganization, a governmental unit, created to operate a hospital, transferred substantially all of its assets to the tax-exempt hospital entity. The governmental unit became the sole member of that corporation; both entities had identical board members. The governmental unit became the sole member of the other exempt organizations as well. The IRS concluded that each of these entities became affiliates of the governmental unit, thereby relieving them of the responsibility of filing annual information returns. Thus, most supporting organizations[227] of governmental units would seem to be exempt from the requirement of filing annual information returns.

## Notes

1. IRC § 6033(a)(1).
2. See Chapter 10, pages 236−237.
3. See Chapter 8.
4. *Tax-Exempt Organizations,* § 24.3.
5. The General Instructions, which also apply to Form 990-EZ, are assigned a letter and are referenced in this book by both the letter and the page or pages on which they appear. The Specific Instructions are correlated to the line of Form 990 involved and are referenced in this book by the page or pages on which they appear.
6. See *Fundraising,* particularly chap. 3.
7. See Chapter 4.
8. IRC § 6012(a)(6).
9. Rev. Rul. 2000-49, 2000-2 C.B. 430.
10. This document must also be filed by nonexempt charitable trusts (IRC § 4947(a)(1) entities).
11. An organization (other than a private foundation) that normally has gross receipts that are not less than $25,000 is not required to file an annual information return. *Tax-Exempt Organizations,* § 24.3(b)(ii).
12. General Instruction B, p. 2.
13. See *Charitable Giving,* §§ 3.1(b), 23.2.
14. Specific Instructions, p. 17.
15. In general, *Charitable Giving,* § 3.1.
16. Id., p. 18.
17. Id.
18. Id.
19. Id.
20. Id.
21. See Chapter 4, pages 91−99.
22. Id., pages 86−88.
23. See Chapter 8, pages 175−178.
24. Specific Instructions, p. 18.

25. Id.
26. See, e.g., Laborer's Int'l Union of N. Am. v. Comm'r, 82 T.C.M. 158 (2001).
27. Specific Instructions, p. 19.
28. Id., p. 20.
29. Id., p. 21.
30. Id.
31. Id.
32. Id.
33. *Tax-Exempt Organizations,* § 4.4.
34. Specific Instructions, p. 24.
35. *Private Foundations,* § 4.1.
36. Specific Instructions, p. 26.
37. See Chapter 7, pages 156–158.
38. See IRC § 170(f)(10)(H).
39. IRC § 170(f)(10)(B). Also General Instruction V, p. 14.
40. See Chapter 8.
41. Introduction to the Instructions, p. 1.
42. *Tax-Exempt Organizations,* § 23.7.
43. See Chapter 10, pages 236–237.
44. If the organization is doing business in one or more other states (see below), this change of name should be properly communicated to the other jurisdiction(s) as well.
45. The Form 990 specific instructions for item B state, as to this last point, that an amendment to bylaws may be submitted. A set of bylaws, however, is not an *organizing document*.
46. See Chapter 4, pages 86–88.
47. Id., pages 86–89.
48. See, e.g., Chapter 10, pages 246–250.
49. See *Tax-Exempt Organizations,* § 27.1.
50. Id., § 27.1(h).
51. Id., § 27.1(j).
52. Id., §§ 27.1(n), 31.3.
53. Id., §§ 29.1–29.4.
54. The phraseology of the return and the instructions is not helpful in this regard. The return states that the gross revenue from special events is to be reported, "not including" contributions reported on line 1a (line 9a), yet the specific instructions state that the contribution element is to be reported "both" on line 1a and line 9a (within the parentheses) (p. 17). Also see the specific instructions that accompany Part I, lines 9a–9c.
55. See Chapter 10, pages 239–240.
56. Id., page 240.
57. Problems can arise, however, in connection with the substantiation of a gift of this nature. See Chapter 10, page 240.
58. *Charitable Giving,* § 3.1(b).
59. Likewise, in the third example, the patron/donor would be well advised to write two checks: One for $1,000 in purchase of the painting and one (perhaps on another day) for $500 as a contribution (which the charity could more comfortably substantiate).
60. *Tax-Exempt Organizations,* § 27.2(j).
61. *Charitable Giving,* § 3.1(c).
62. The specific instructions accompanying Part I, lines 9a to 9c, include an example of this schedule (p. 20).

63. Specific Instructions for Part II, p. 23.
64. Id.
65. The instructions state that the organization should provide the "preferred address" at which these individuals "want the Internal Revenue Service to contact them." Specific Instructions, p. 26. In some quarters, there is no such address.
66. See Chapter 3, pages 60, 65–66, and 71–72.
67. Id., pages 65–70.
68. Id., pages 70–71.
69. Id., pages 71–76.
70. See Chapter 4, pages 91–99.
71. *Tax-Exempt Organizations,* § 24.1.
72. Specific Instructions for line 77, p. 27.
73. *Tax-Exempt Organizations,* § 28.2.
74. Id., § 24.3(a)(v).
75. Specific Instructions for line 80, p. 27.
76. Id.
77. See Chapter 5, pages 123–124.
78. Id., pages 118–122.
79. Specific Instructions for line 82, p. 28.
80. See Chapter 10, pages 235–237.
81. Id., pages 239–240.
82. Id., pages 240–243.
83. *Tax-Exempt Organizations,* chap. 12.
84. See Chapters 6, 7.
85. See Chapter 5.
86. See Chapter 3, pages 71–76.
87. *Tax-Exempt Organizations,* chap. 12, § 15.1, and chap. 13, respectively.
88. Id., chap. 14.
89. Id., § 18.5.
90. See Chapter 8, pages 170–171.
91. *Tax-Exempt Organizations,* §§ 29.1–29.4.
92. See Chapter 8, pages 175–178.
93. Id., page 171.
94. These codes are listed on the last page of the Specific Instructions for Form 990, p. 33.
95. *Tax-Exempt Organizations,* § 27.1.
96. Id., § 27.1(g).
97. Id., § 27.1(h).
98. Id.
99. Id., § 27.1(j).
100. See Chapter 8, pages 174–175.
101. Id., page 179.
102. Id.
103. Id.
104. Id.
105. *Tax-Exempt Organizations,* § 27.2(e).
106. Id., § 27.2(f).
107. Id., § 27.2(g).

108. Id., § 27.2(h).
109. Id., § 27.1(*l*).
110. Id.
111. Id.
112. Id., 28.3.
113. Id., §§ 29.1–29.4.
114. Id., § 29.3, text accompanied by n. 44.
115. Id., § 26.2.
116. Id., § 4.4.
117. Id., § 26.4, text accompanied by n. 159.
118. An illustration of this type of an arrangement is in Addis v. Comm'r, 118 T.C. 528 (2002). See Chapter 11, pages 271–274. A variant of it also appears in Notice 99-36, 1999-26 I.R.B. 3.
119. IRC § 170(f)(10)(A).
120. IRC § 170(f)(10)(C). In general, *Charitable Giving*, chap. 12.
121. *Charitable Giving*, chap. 14.
122. IRC § 170(f)(10)(D). There is a special rule for certain charitable gift annuity arrangements where state law requires that charitable gift annuitants be named as beneficiaries under the annuity contract, as a condition of exemption from insurance regulation by the state. IRC § 170(f)(10)(G).
123. IRC § 170(f)(10)(E).
124. IRC § 170(f)(10)(F)(i).
125. IRC § 170(f)(10)(F)(ii).
126. IRC § 170(f)(10)(F)(iii).
127. Id. See *Tax-Exempt Organizations*, § 24.3(a)(vii).
128. These rules are briefly summarized in Form 990, General Instruction V. Filers of Form 990-EZ are required to make a declaration, which is the equivalent of Part X, on a statement attached to the return. Additional information as to these filing requirements is available in Notice 2000-24, 2000-17 I.R.B. 952, and Ann. 2000-82, 2000-42 I.R.B. 385.
129. That is, an organization described in IRC § 501(c)(3), including organizations the tax-exempt status of which is based on IRC § 501(e), (f), (k), or (n). This filing requirement is also applicable to nonexempt charitable trusts (IRC § 4947(a)(1) entities).
130. IRC § 6033(b). Also Rev. Proc. 75-50, 1975-2 C.B. 587.
131. Specific Instruction for Part I, p. 2.
132. See Chapter 3, pages 66–68.
133. *Private Foundations*, § 5.6(a).
134. See Chapter 5, pages 107–118.
135. See Chapter 3, pages 65–66.
136. *Private Foundations*, § 5.4.
137. Id., § 5.5.
138. Id., § 5.4(d).
139. Id., § 5.6. If the only compensation, payment, or reimbursement amount involves amounts the organization reported in Form 990, Part V (or Form 990-EZ, Part IV), the question should be answered yes, with a cross-reference entered to the appropriate part.
140. Id., § 5.8.
141. Specific Instructions for Part III, p. 2.
142. See *Tax-Exempt Organizations*, chaps. 6, 7.
143. Id., § 5.5(a).
144. In fact, the categories of "poor" and "aged" are discrete classes. Id., §§ 6.1, 6.2.

145. Specific Instructions for Part III, pp. 2–3).
146. See *Tax-Exempt Organizations,* § 16.1.
147. See Chapter 4.
148. See Chapter 5, pages 107–118.
149. IRC § 6033(b)(9).
150. IRC § 501(c).
151. That is, an organization described in IRC § 527. See *Tax-Exempt Organizations,* chap. 17.
152. See *Tax-Exempt Organizations,* chap. 12.
153. Id., § 15.1.
154. Id., chap. 13.
155. Id., chap. 14.
156. Id., § 18.4.
157. Id., § 18.10.
158. Specific Instructions for Part VII, p. 12.
159. Id.
160. Special Instructions to accompany Part VII, line 51a, p. 12.
161. See *Fundraising,* §§ 3.6, 3.7.
162. *Tax-Exempt Organizations,* § 26.5(i).
163. See Chapter 4, pages 91–99.
164. A *contributor* includes an individual, fiduciary, corporation, association, trust, partnership, and other tax-exempt organization (grantor).
165. That is, an entity described in IRC § 501(c).
166. That is, an entity described in IRC § 4947(a)(1).
167. That is, an entity described in IRC § 527.
168. Specific Instructions to Schedule B, p. 9.
169. Form 8871; *Tax-Exempt Organizations,* § 23.6.
170. Form 8872; *Tax-Exempt Organizations,* § 24.3(d).
171. IRC § 527(j)(1).
172. See Reg. § 20.2031-2.
173. Specific Instructions to Schedule B, p. 10.
174. That is, organizations meeting the tests of IRC §§ 170(b)(1)(A)(vi) and 509(a)(1). See Chapter 4, pages 86–88.
175. That is, the organization is otherwise described in IRC § 170(b)(1)(A).
176. That is, an organization described in IRC § 509(a)(2). See Chapter 4, pages 88–89.
177. That is, an organization described in IRC § 509(a)(3). See Chapter 4, pages 91–99.
178. That is, entities described in IRC § 501(c)(7). See *Tax-Exempt Organizations,* chap. 14.
179. That is, entities described in IRC § 501(c)(8) or (10). See *Tax-Exempt Organizations,* § 18.4.
180. It may be wondered why this concept is seemingly gratuitously addressed in the instructions to a federal government form. It is an illustration of the cooperation between the IRS and the states when tax-exempt organizations are concerned, and the extent to which the IRS is willing to tailor the Form 990 and its instructions in this regard.
181. General Instruction E.
182. Id.
183. *Tax-Exempt Organizations,* § 24.3(b)(ii).
184. Schedule A, Part II.
185. General Instructions E.
186. An organization can obtain one or more extensions of time in which to file an annual information return. An automatic three-month extension of time to file may be obtained by filing

Form 8868. This form may also be used to apply for an additional three-month extension of time to file; reasonable cause for this extension must be shown.

187. IRC § 6652(c)(1)(A).

188. The IRS instructions to Form 990 (General Instruction K), in articulating this warning, use the word "will" rather than "may," but in fact the sending of this letter is a rare occasion, due to lack of IRS resources. Also, in many instances, an omission or misstatement of information cannot be detected by merely reviewing the return.

189. IRC § 6652(c)(1)(B)(ii).

190. IRC §§ 7203, 7206, 7207.

191. See Chapter 10, pages 236–237.

192. IRC § 6652(c)(1)(C).

193. IRC § 6685.

194. *Tax-Exempt Organizations,* §§ 23.3, 23.5.

195. IRS INFO [information letter] 2000-0260.

196. IRC §§ 505, 508(b).

197. IRC § 6033.

198. E.g., IRC §§ 642(c)(5), 664. See *Charitable Giving,* chaps. 13, 12, respectively.

199. E.g., the rules pertaining to qualified corporate sponsorship contributions. IRC § 513(i); *Tax-Exempt Organizations,* § 27.2(n).

200. IRC §§ 4943, 4944. See *Private Foundations,* chaps. 7, 8.

201. H.R. 572, 106th Cong., 1st sess. (1999), grandly titled the Charitable Integrity Restoration Act.

202. Other private benefits may include the ability to avoid capital gains tax by transferring appreciated property to the trust, the creation of an ability to generate more income to the donor and/or more favorably taxed income as the result of the gift, and professional money and property management of the resources of the trust, paid for by the trust. There are also, of course, the charitable contribution deduction and the public recognition resulting from establishing and naming the trust.

203. IRC § 170(f)(10)(D).

204. IRC § 170(f)(10)(E).

205. IRC § 170(f)(10)(G).

206. *Private Foundations,* § 14.4(b).

207. *Charitable Giving,* § 9.6.

208. *Tax-Exempt Organizations,* § 27.2(f).

209. Id., § 27.2(e).

210. Id., § 27.2(n).

211. Id., § 18.16.

212. *Charitable Giving,* § 8.3.

213. Id., § 9.20. If the law can tolerate a split-interest trust, it should be able to cope with a split-interest life insurance arrangement.

214. When the IRS weighed in on this subject, trying to regulate in this area administratively, it was careful to note that it was proceeding against only "certain" charitable split-dollar insurance arrangements. Notice 99-36, note 118 above.

215. In one instance, for example, the IRS considered, from the standpoint of private inurement, a compensation package involving a private foundation and its chief executive officer. The compensation arrangement included a split-dollar life insurance agreement among the parties. The IRS not only ruled that the compensation package was reasonable (thus precluding private inurement or self-dealing) but also concluded that the insurance contract in this case was not

among the type of split-dollar life insurance arrangements that are subject to this punitive rule. Priv. Ltr. Rul. 200020060.

216. *Tax-Exempt Organizations,* § 24.3(b)(i), (ii).

217. Id., § 24.3(b)(iii).

218. IRC § 103.

219. IRC § 170(c)(1). The definition of the term *governmental unit* is in Rev. Proc. 95-48, 1995-2 C.B. 418, § 4.01.

220. That is, it is described in IRC § 501(c).

221. IRC § 115.

222. IRC § 170(c)(1).

223. IRC §§ 3121(b)(7), 3306(c)(7). This definition is provided by Rev. Proc. 95-48, note 219 above, § 4.02(a).

224. Rev. Proc. 95-48, note 219 above, § 4.03.

225. Id., § 4.02(b). Relevant facts and circumstances as to whether an annual return is necessary include those provided at id., § 4.04.

226. Priv. Ltr. Rul. 9825030.

227. See Chapter 4, pages 91–99.

# CHAPTER 10

# Disclosure Requirements

Ⓞne of the major trends affecting development of the law of tax-exempt organizations is the dramatic expansion of the disclosure requirements imposed on these organizations. Two principal reasons account for this phenomenon are:

1. **Abuse.** There have been some abuses in various exempt organization fields, prompting enactment of disclosure rules. This has been largely the case in the context of charitable giving. Thus, the federal tax law contains rules imposing gift substantiation requirements, quid pro quo contribution disclosures, property appraisal requirements, and rules concerning personal benefit contracts.

2. **Transparency.** There is a view, particularly in government circles, that intense disclosure of exempt organizations' operations is required simply because they are tax-exempt. (Tax exemption is accorded nonprofit organizations because of their contributions to a democratic state and a pluralistic society, and not so governmental officials and others can take away rights of privacy and confidentiality that other entities in society have.) Many calls ensue these days for greater "transparency" of the affairs of exempt organizations. Examples of this type of disclosure include public availability of the application for recognition of exemption[1] and annual information returns.[2]

It is thus incumbent on planners to not only be aware of these laws but also constantly evaluate the impact that disclosure has on the conduct of exempt organizations' programs and other activities.

## APPLICATIONS FOR RECOGNITION OF TAX EXEMPTION

Generally, a tax-exempt organization is required to make a copy of its application for recognition of exemption[3] available to those who request it.

## Summary of Rules

Tax-exempt organizations that have a determination letter from the IRS recognizing their tax-exempt status[4] are required to provide a copy of their application for recognition of exemption to requesting members of the public. These rules, and the exceptions to them, are summarized in the companion volume.[5] The principal exception in this regard is available when the document is posted on the Internet,[6] which obviously vastly increases the number of individuals who have access to and review it.

Some of the elements of these rules that the planner may be required to consider are:

- Whether the organization has principal, regional, and/or district offices.[7]
- Whether the organization has copies of the document ready to respond to in-person requests.[8]
- Whether the organization is able (if necessary) to avail itself of the *unusual circumstances* exception.[9]
- Whether the organization will charge a fee for providing copies of the document.[10]
- Whether the organization is able (if necessary) to avail itself of the *harassment campaign* exception.[11]

## Form 990 Question

Tax-exempt organizations that file annual information returns are required to respond to a question as to whether they have complied with the law requiring disclosure of applications for recognition of exemption.[12]

## Penalties

There is a penalty for failure to comply with this disclosure requirement, amounting to $20 per day.[13]

## ANNUAL INFORMATION RETURNS

Generally, a tax-exempt organization is required to make copies of its annual information returns[14] available to those who request them.

## Summary of Rules

Tax-exempt organizations are required to provide copies of their annual information returns (if any) to members of the requesting public. This requirement pertains to the most recent three annual information returns. These rules, and the exceptions to them, are summarized in the companion volume.[15]

The same rules, as summarized above with respect to disclosure and dissemination of applications for recognition of exemption, apply in this setting, including the exception for returns that are posted on the Internet. Likewise, the same four elements for the planner to consider apply in this context.

## Form 990 Question

Tax-exempt organizations that file annual information returns are required to respond to a question as to whether they have complied with the law requiring disclosure of these returns.[16]

## Penalties

There is a penalty for failure to comply with this disclosure requirement, amounting to $20 per day ($10,000 per return).[17]

# GIFT SUBSTANTIATION REQUIREMENTS

The federal tax law imposes rules requiring written substantiation of certain contributions, which must be adhered to by charitable donees if the donor is to receive a charitable contribution deduction for the gift (assuming the deduction is otherwise available).

## Summary of Rules

A contribution of $250 or more must be substantiated by means of a contemporaneous written acknowledgment of the contribution by the charitable donee.[18] This substantiation must be in the form of a *contemporaneous written acknowledgment.*
An acknowledgment meets this requirement if it includes:

- The amount of money and a description (but not value) of any property (other than money) that was contributed
- Whether the donee organization provided any *goods or services*[19] in consideration, in whole or in part, for the contribution
- A description and good faith estimate[20] of the value of any goods or services provided[21]

A donee organization provides goods or services *in consideration for* a person's payment if, at the time the donor makes the payment to the donee, the payor receives or expects to receive goods or services in exchange for that payment.[22] The planner should note that goods or services a donee charity provides in consideration for a payment by a person include any goods or services provided in a year other than the year in which the payment is made.

This can be a difficult area for the planner—and the charity. For these rules to be triggered, it is not enough that the donor is provided goods or services; the goods or services must be provided *in consideration for* the gift. This is particularly problematic in the fundraising context. For example, it is common for a charitable organization to decide, months after contributions have been made, to honor a class of donors by providing them with a tangible benefit, such as a thank-you dinner. The event or other benefit may be provided in a year subsequent to some or all of the gifts. The fair market value of this benefit does not have to be subtracted from the amount of the gift for deduction purposes because it was not provided at the time the payment was made. That is, in this example, the donors did not receive or expect to receive a dinner at the time of their gifts. By contrast, if a charitable organization develops a regular pattern of providing these benefits after the fact, at some point it may be reasonable to take the position that donors are receiving that tangible benefit at the time of the gift and thus in consideration for it.

The written acknowledgment of a gift is not required to take any particular form. These acknowledgments may be made by letter, postcard, or computer-generated form; they may be made by e-mail.[23] A donee charitable organization may prepare a separate acknowledgment for each contribution or may provide donors with periodic (such as annual) acknowledgments that set forth the required information for each contribution of $250 or more made by the donor during the period.[24]

For the substantiation to be *contemporaneous,* it must be obtained no later than the date the donor filed a tax return for the year in which the contribution was made. If the return is filed after the due date or extended due date, the substantiation must have been obtained by the due date or extended due date.

It is the responsibility of a donor to obtain the substantiation and maintain it in his, her, or its records. (Again, the charitable contribution deduction is dependent on compliance with these rules.) Nonetheless, the charitable donee—if for no other reason than donor relations—has ample incentive to see to it that the proper substantiation of gifts to it is timely made.

The planner should remember that the substantiation rules do not apply to a transfer of property to a charitable remainder trust[25] or a charitable lead trust.[26] These rules apply, however, with respect to transfers by means of pooled income funds.[27] The reason for this distinction is grounded in the fact that the grantor of a charitable remainder trust or charitable lead trust is not required to designate a specific organization as the charitable beneficiary at the time property is transferred to the trust, so in these instances there is no designated charity available to provide a contemporaneous written acknowledgment to a donor. Moreover, even when a specific beneficiary is designated, the identification of the charity is revocable. By contrast, a pooled income fund must be created and maintained by the charitable organization to which the remainder interests are contributed.

The U.S. Supreme Court has written that the "sine qua non of a charitable contribution is a transfer of money or property without adequate consideration."[28] Other such pronouncements from the Court include the statement that a "payment of money [or transfer of property] generally cannot constitute a charitable contribution if the contributor expects a substantial benefit in return"[29] and that a gift is a transfer motivated by "detached or disinterested generosity."[30] Likewise, the IRS stated that a *contribution* is a "voluntary transfer of money or property that is made with no expectation of procuring financial benefit commensurate with the amount of the transfer."[31]

### The *Addis* Case

The U.S. Tax Court ruled that payments made to a charitable organization were not deductible as charitable gifts, because the substantiation requirements were not met, in that there was an undisclosed return benefit.[32] This benefit was reflected in an "understanding" or "expectation" between the donors and the donee organization. Planners for charitable organizations and donors have been placed in a most difficult position because of the holding in this case.[33]

### Penalty

The charitable contribution deduction is not available to a donor who does not timely receive the required substantiation document.[34]

## Quid Pro Quo Contributions

The federal tax law imposes certain disclosure requirements on charitable organizations that receive quid pro quo contributions.[35]

### Summary of Rules

A *quid pro quo contribution* is a payment that has two components: partially a contribution and partially a purchase of goods and services. The term is formally defined as a payment "made partly as a contribution and partly in consideration for goods or services provided to the payor by the donee organization."[36]

If a charitable organization receives a quid pro quo contribution that is in excess of $75, the organization is required, in connection with the solicitation or receipt of the contribution, to provide a written statement that:

- Informs the donor that the amount of the contribution that is deductible for federal income tax purposes is limited to the excess of the amount of any money or the value of any property (other than money) contributed by the donor over the value of the goods and services provided by the organization, and
- Provides the donor with a good faith estimate of the value of the goods or services.[37]

Thus, in the case of a contribution of this nature, the donor must be provided an estimate of the value of the goods or services received and notice that only the difference (the charitable contribution element of the payment) is deductible.

The planner may face some difficulties in this setting. For example, a charitable organization is able to use "any reasonable methodology in making a good faith estimate, provided it applies the methodology in good faith."[38] A good faith estimate of the value of goods or services that are not generally available in a commercial transaction may be determined by reference to the fair market value of similar or comparable goods or services. Goods or services may be *similar or comparable* "even though they do not have the unique qualities of the goods or services that are being valued."[39]

Another problem concerns the matter of the involvement of celebrities in a charity event. The performance by such an individual, engaging in an activity for which he or she is known, for the benefit of a charitable organization clearly constitutes the provision of a service (as noted, the value of it is a separate matter), and the good faith estimate of the value of that service would be determined, at least in part, by the fees and expenses paid to that individual when performing in a commercial setting. If, however, the celebrity provides some other service, that effort may have no value at all.[40]

The ultimate difficulty for the planner may well lie in the element of this law, by which no part of this type of payment can be considered a deductible charitable contribution unless two factors exist:

1. The patron makes a payment in an amount that is in fact in excess of the fair market value of the goods or services received, and

2. The patron intends to make a payment in an amount that is in excess of fair market value (*donative intent*).[41]

Proving the first of these two elements may be relatively easy. Often, for example, the charity sponsoring the event has made its good-faith estimate amount known in advance, such as by distribution of a catalog in the instance of an auction. Nonetheless, as to the second element, demonstrating *intent* can be problematic. Divining the thought process of an individual in any context is always an exercise in uncertainty; a payment made to a charitable organization in excess of an item's fair market value is not necessarily the consequence of donative intent. (In the case of an auction, for example, the patron who was the successful bidder may simply have intensely wanted the item, may have been motivated by peer pressure, or may have been animated by extensive access to an open bar; charity may have been the farthest thing from the patron's mind.)

The planner is likely to find that this development in the law is unfortunate, inasmuch as the law has been evolving in the direction of a more mechanical (and thus less reliant on subjective proof) test: any payment to a charitable organization in excess of fair market value of goods or services received is regarded as a charitable gift.[42]

## Form 990 Question

Tax-exempt organizations that file annual information returns are required to respond to a question as to whether they have complied with the law requiring adherence to these rules.[43]

## Penalties

There is a penalty for violation of these requirements.[44]

## DISCLOSURE BY NONCHARITABLE ORGANIZATIONS

A set of disclosure rules is applicable to all types of tax-exempt organizations—other than charitable ones.[45] These rules are targeted at social welfare organizations.[46] The rules

are intended to prevent noncharitable exempt organizations from engaging in gift-solic-
itation activities under circumstances in which donors will assume, or be led to assume,
that the contributions are tax-deductible as charitable gifts, when in fact they are not.

## Summary of Rules

An organization that has annual gross receipts that are normally not more than $100,000
is not subject to these rules. Where all of the parties being solicited are tax-exempt organizations, the solicitation does not have to include the disclosure statement (inasmuch as
these grantors have no need for a charitable contribution deduction).

This law applies in general to any organization to which contributions are not deductible as charitable gifts and that:

- Is tax-exempt[47]
- Is a political organization[48]
- Was either type of organization at any time during the five-year period ending on
  the date of the solicitation, or
- Is a successor to one of these organizations at any time during this five-year period.

The IRS has the authority to treat any group of two or more organizations as one entity
for these purposes where necessary to prevent the avoidance of these rules by means of
the use of multiple organizations.

Under these rules, each fundraising solicitation by or on behalf of a tax-exempt noncharitable organization must contain an express statement, in a "conspicuous and easily
recognizable format," that gifts to it are not deductible as charitable contributions for
federal income tax purposes. The term *fundraising solicitation* is defined as any solicitation of gifts made in written or printed form, and/or by television, radio, or telephone
(although there is an exclusion for letters or calls that are not part of a coordinated fundraising campaign soliciting more than 10 persons during a calendar year). Despite the
clear reference in the statute to "contributions and gifts," the IRS interprets this rule
to mandate the disclosure when any tax-exempt organization (other than a charitable one)
seeks funds, such as dues from members.

The IRS promulgated rules in amplification of this law, particularly the requirement
of a disclosure statement.[49] These rules, which include guidance in the form of "safe-
harbor" provisions, address the format of the disclosure statement in instances of the use
of print media, telephone, television, and radio. They provide examples of acceptable disclosure language and methods, and of included and excluded solicitations. They also contain guidelines for establishing the $100,000 threshold.

The safe-harbor guideline for print media (including solicitations by mail and in newspapers) is fourfold:

1. The solicitation should include language such as the following: "Contributions or
   gifts to [name of organization] are not deductible as charitable contributions for
   federal income tax purposes."

2. The statement should be in at least the same type size as the primary message stated in the body of the letter, leaflet, or advertisement.

3. The statement should be included on the message side of any card or tear-off section that the contributor returns with the contribution.

4. The statement should be either the first sentence in a paragraph or itself constitute a paragraph.

The safe-harbor guidelines for telephone solicitations are:

- The solicitation includes language such as the following: "Contributions or gifts to [name of organization] are not deductible as charitable contributions for federal tax purposes."

- The statement must be made in close proximity to the request for contributions, during the same telephone call, by the same solicitor.

- Any written confirmation or billing sent to a person pledging to contribute during the telephone solicitation must be in compliance with the requirements for print media solicitation.

To conform to the guideline, solicitation by television must include a solicitation statement that complies with the first of the print medium requirements. Also, if the statement is spoken, it must be in close proximity to the request for contributions. If the statement appears on the television screen, it must be in large, easily readable type appearing on the screen for at least five seconds.

In the case of a solicitation by radio, the statement must, to meet the safe-harbor test, comply with the first of the print medium requirements. Also, the statement must be made in close proximity to the request for contributions during the same radio solicitation announcement.

When the soliciting organization is a membership entity, classified as a trade or business association or other form of business league,[50] or a labor or agricultural organization,[51] the following statement is in conformance with the safe-harbor guideline: "Contributions or gifts to [name of organization] are not tax-deductible as charitable contributions. They may, however, be deductible as ordinary and necessary business expenses."

If an organization makes a solicitation to which these rules apply and the solicitation does not comply with the guidelines, the IRS will evaluate all of the facts and circumstances to determine whether the solicitation meets the disclosure rule. A "good faith effort" to comply with these requirements is an important factor in the evaluation of the facts and circumstances. Nonetheless, planners should note that disclosure statements made in "fine print" do not conform to the statutory requirement.

This disclosure requirement applies to solicitations for voluntary contributions as well as solicitations for attendance at testimonials and like fundraising events. The disclosure must be made in the case of solicitations for contributions to political action committees.

Exempt from the disclosure rules are the billing of those who advertise in an organization's publications, billing by social clubs[52] for food and beverages, billing of attendees of an exempt organization's conference, billing for insurance premiums of an insurance program operated or sponsored by an exempt organization, billing of members of a community association for mandatory payments for police and fire (and similar) protection, and billing for payments to a voluntary employees' beneficiary association,[53] as well as similar payments to a trust for pension and/or health benefits.

Material generally discussing the benefits of membership in a tax-exempt organization, such as an association or labor organization, does not have to include the disclosure statement. The statement is required, however, where the material requests payments and specifies the amount requested as membership dues. If a person responds to the general material discussing the benefits of membership, the follow-up material requesting the payment of a specific amount of membership dues (such as an association billing statement for a new member or a union check-off card) must include the disclosure statement.

Material discussing a candidate for public office and requesting individuals to vote for the candidate or support the candidate does not need to include the disclosure statement, unless the material specifically requests either a financial contribution or a contribution of volunteer services in support of the candidate.

## Form 990 Question

Tax-exempt organizations that file annual information returns are required to respond to a question as to whether they have complied with the law requiring adherence to these rules.[54]

## Penalties

Failure to satisfy this disclosure requirement can result in imposition of a penalty.[55] This penalty is $1,000 per day (maximum of $10,000 per year), albeit with a reasonable cause exception. In an instance of intentional disregard of these rules, however, the penalty for the day on which the offense occurred is the greater of $1,000 or 50 percent of the aggregate cost of the solicitations that took place on that day; the $10,000 limitation is inapplicable. For these purposes, the days involved are those on which the solicitation was telecast, broadcast, mailed, otherwise distributed, or telephoned.

## DISCLOSURE OF GIFTS OF PROPERTY

A donor to a charitable organization is required to disclose to the IRS, by means of the appropriate federal income tax return, certain information in the case of a claimed deduction for noncash contributions in excess of $500. This filing requirement is applicable in the case of contributions by individuals, partnerships, personal service corporations, closely held corporations, and other corporations. C corporations (that are not personal service corporations or closely held corporations) are required to make this disclosure only if the amount claimed as a deduction is more than $5,000.

The IRS form by which this disclosure is made is Form 8283. This form consists of Section A and Section B. A donor may need to complete one of these sections or the other, or both, depending on the type of property donated and the amount claimed as a deduction.

## Appropriate Income Tax Returns

A donor who is an individual must file the Form 8283 (when required) with his or her federal income tax return (Form 1040) for the year in which the property was contributed and in which the deduction was first claimed.

A partnership or S corporation that claims a charitable deduction for noncash gifts of more than $500 must file Form 8283 with Form 1065, Form 1065-B, or Form 1120S. If the total deduction for any item or group of similar items exceeds $5,000, the partnership or S corporation must complete Section B of Form 8283 even if the amount allocated to each partner or shareholder does not exceed $5,000.

The partnership or S corporation must provide a completed copy of Form 8283 to each partner or shareholder receiving an allocation of the contribution deduction reflected in Section B of the Form 8283 prepared by the partnership or S corporation. The partnership or S corporation is expected to provide information about an individual donor's share of the contribution on the Schedule K-1 associated with either Form 1065 or Form 1120S. If the donor received a copy of Form 8283 from the partnership or S corporation, the donor should attach a copy of the form to his or her appropriate income tax return. (The amount to be deducted is that shown on Schedule K-1.)

If the partnership or S corporation is not required to give the donor a copy of its Form 8283, the donor should combine the amount of noncash contributions shown on Schedule K-1 with his or her other noncash contributions to determine if the donor is required to file Form 8283. If the donor needs to file the form, the donor does not have to complete all of the information requested in Schedule A for his or her share of the partnership's or S corporation's contributions. The IRS's instructions that accompany Form 8283 state that the donor is only required to complete Part I, line 1, column (g), with his or her share of the contribution and enter "From Schedule K-1 (Form 1065 or 1120S)" across columns (c) to (f).

## Section A

The donor includes in Section A only references to items (or groups of similar items (see below)) for which the donor claimed a deduction of $5,000 or less per item (or group of similar items). The following information is required in Part I (except as noted above):

- Name and address of the donee organization
- Description of the donated property in sufficient detail, with more detail the greater the value of the property[56]
- Date of the contribution
- Date the donated property was acquired by the donor[57]
- How the property was acquired by the donor (such as purchase, gift, inheritance, or exchange)
- Donor's cost or adjusted basis in the property
- Fair market value of the property

- Method used to determine this fair market value (such as appraisal, comparable sales, or catalog price)

Also, the donor is required to list the following publicly traded securities even if the claimed deduction is more than $5,000:

- Securities listed on an exchange in which quotations are published daily

- Securities regularly traded in national or regional over-the-counter markets for which published quotations are available

- Securities that are shares of a mutual fund for which quotations are published on a daily basis in a newspaper of general circulation throughout the United States

The donor must respond to question 2 in Part II if the donor contributed less than the entire interest in the property. A response to question 3 in Part II is required if the donor placed conditions on one or more items of donated property listed in Part I.

If Part II applies to more than one property, a separate statement must be attached to the return, providing the required information for each property. The donor should identify the property listed in Part I to which the information relates.

### Section B

The donor includes in Section B (appraisal summary (see below)) only items (or groups of similar items) for which the donor claimed a deduction of more than $5,000 per item or group. (This rule does not apply with respect to publicly traded securities that are reportable in Section A.) Generally, the donor must have a written appraisal from a qualified appraiser that supports the information in Part I of Section B (see below). If the total deduction for art is $20,000 or more, the donor must attach a complete copy of the signed appraisal; a photograph must be provided to the IRS on request.

A separate qualified appraisal and a separate Form 8283 are required for each item of property, except for an item that is part of a group of similar items. If the donor gave similar items to more than one charitable donee for which the donor claimed a total deduction of more than $5,000, the donor must attach a separate form for each donee.

The donor should complete Part II of Section B for each item included in Part I of the section that has an appraised value of $500 or less. Because the donor does not have to show the value of these items in Part I of the donee's copy of the Form 8283, these items should be identified for the donee in Part II. Then, the donee does not have to file with the IRS if the property is sold within two years of the date of the gift.

If the donor was required to obtain an appraisal, the appraiser must complete Part III of Section B to be qualified (see below). The charitable donee that received the property is required to complete Part IV of the section. The donor must provide a copy of Section B of Form 8283 to the donee.

## DISPOSITIONS OF CONTRIBUTED PROPERTY

Charitable organizations that dispose of certain charitable deduction property within two years of the gift must disclose the transaction to the IRS. This is done by filing Form 8282.

There are two situations in which this form does not have to be filed:

1. This form does not have to be filed if, at the time the original donee signed the appraisal summary, the donor signed a statement on Form 8283 that the appraised value of the specific item was not more than $500. If the Form 8283 contains more than one similar item, this rule applies only to those items that are clearly identified as having a value of $500 or less.

2. The charitable donee is not required to file this form if an item is consumed or distributed, without consideration, in fulfillment of its exempt purpose or function.

The charitable donee, where neither exception is available, is required to file Form 8282 within 125 days after the date of disposition.

If the gift property is transferred by the donee charitable organization (the *original donee*) to another charitable organization (the *successor donee*) within the two-year period, the original donee must provide the successor donee with:

- The name, address, and tax identification number of the organization
- A copy of the appraisal summary
- A copy of the Form 8282 involved, within 15 days of filing by the original donee

The first two of these items must be furnished to the successor donee within 15 days after the latest of the date the original donee transferred the property, the original donee signed the appraisal summary, or the original donee received a copy of the appraisal summary from the preceding donee if the charity is also a successor donee.

A successor donee must provide the original donee with the successor organization's name, address, and tax identification number within 15 days after the later of the date the property was transferred by the original organization or the date the successor organization received a copy of the appraisal summary.

A charitable organization must provide a copy of the completed Form 8282 to the original donor of the property.[58]

## Penalty

A charitable organization may be subject to a penalty if it fails to timely file Form 8282, fails to include all of the information required to be shown on the form, or fails to include correct information on the form. Generally, this penalty is $50.[59]

## APPRAISAL REQUIREMENTS

There are disclosure requirements in connection with the substantiation of deductions claimed by an individual, a closely held corporation, a personal service corporation, a partnership, or an S corporation for charitable contributions of certain property.[60]

### Summary of Rules

Property to which these rules apply is termed *charitable deduction property*. If the contributed property is a partial interest in an item of property,[61] the appraisal must be of the partial interest. These requirements apply to contributions of property (other than money and publicly traded securities) if the aggregate claimed or reported value of the property—and all similar items of property for which deductions for charitable contributions are claimed or reported by the same donor for the same tax year whether or not donated to the same charitable donee—is in excess of $5,000.

The phrase *similar items of property* means "property of the same generic category or type," including stamp collections, coin collections, lithographs, paintings, photographs, books, non-publicly traded stock, other non-publicly traded securities, parcels of land, buildings, clothing, jewelry, furniture, electronic equipment, household appliances, toys, everyday kitchenware, china, crystal, or silver.

For this type of gift, the donor must obtain a qualified appraisal and attach an appraisal summary to the federal income tax return on which the deduction is claimed. In the case of non-publicly traded stock, however, the claimed value of which does not exceed $10,000 but is greater than $5,000, the donor does not have to obtain a qualified appraisal but must attach a partially completed appraisal summary form to the federal income tax or information return on which the deduction is claimed.

A *qualified appraisal* is an appraisal document that:

- Relates to an appraisal that is made not earlier than 60 days prior to the date of contribution of the appraisal property
- Is prepared, signed, and dated by a qualified appraiser (or appraisers)
- Contains the requisite information
- Does not involve a prohibited type of appraisal fee

The qualified appraisal must include:

- A description of the property in sufficient detail, for a person who is not generally familiar with the type of property, to ascertain that the property that was appraised is the property contributed
- The physical condition of the property (in the case of tangible property)
- The date of contribution of the property
- The terms of any agreement between the parties relating to any subsequent disposition of the property, including restrictions on the charitable organization's use of the gift property
- The name, address, and tax identification number of the appraiser
- The qualifications of the qualified appraiser (or appraisers)
- A statement that the appraisal was prepared for income tax purposes
- The date or dates on which the property was appraised
- The appraised fair market value of the property on the date of contribution
- The method of valuation used to determine the fair market value of the property
- The specific basis for the valuation

The qualified appraisal must be received by the donor before the due date (including extensions) of the return on which the deduction for the contributed property is first claimed or, in the case of a deduction first claimed on an amended return, the date on which the amended return is filed.

A separate qualified appraisal is required for each item of property that is not included in a group of similar items of property. One qualified appraisal is required for a group of similar items of property contributed in the same tax year, as long as the appraisal includes all of the required information for each item. The appraiser may select any items the aggregate value of which is appraised at $100 or less, for which a group description (rather than a specific description of each item) is adequate.

The appraisal must be retained by the donor "for so long as it may be relevant in the administration of any internal revenue laws."

The *appraisal summary* must be made on Section B of Form 8283, signed and dated on behalf of the charitable donee and by the qualified appraiser (or appraisers), and attached to the donor's federal income tax return on which a deduction with respect to the appraised property is first claimed or reported. The signature by the representative of the charitable donee does not represent concurrence by the donee in the appraised value of the contributed property.

The appraisal summary must include:

- The name and taxpayer identification number of the donor (such as the social security number of an individual)
- A description of the donated property in requisite detail
- A brief summary of the condition of the property at the time of the gift (in the case of tangible property)
- The manner and date of acquisition of the property by the donor
- The cost basis of the property
- The name, address, and taxpayer identification number of the charitable donee
- The date the donee received the property
- A statement explaining whether the charitable contribution was made by means of a bargain sale[62] and amount of any consideration received from the donee for the contribution
- The name, address, and taxpayer identification number of the qualified appraiser (or appraisers)
- The appraised fair market value of the property on the date of contribution
- A declaration by the appraiser (see below)

The rules pertaining to separate appraisals, summarized above, also apply with respect to appraisal summaries. A donor who contributed similar items of property to more than one charitable donee must, however, attach a separate appraisal summary for each donee.

Every donor who presents an appraisal summary to a charitable organization for signature must furnish a copy of the appraisal summary to the charitable organization. If the donor is a partnership or S corporation, the donor must provide a copy of the appraisal summary to every partner or shareholder who receives an allocation of a deduction for a charitable contribution of property described in the appraisal summary. The partner or shareholder must attach the appraisal summary to the partner's or shareholder's federal income tax return. If a donor (or partner or shareholder of a donor) fails to attach the appraisal summary to the return, the charitable deduction will not be disallowed if the donor (or partner or shareholder of a donor) submits an appraisal summary within 90 days of being requested to do so by the IRS, as long as the failure to attach the appraisal summary was a good faith omission and certain other requirements are met (including timely completion of the appraisal).

An appraisal summary on Section B of Form 8283 must be filed by contributors where the total value of all noncash contributions exceeds $500 and is less than $5,000. This portion of the form must also be used to report contributions of publicly traded securities, even where the value of them is in excess of $5,000.

The term *qualified appraiser* means an individual who includes on the appraisal summary a declaration that:

- He or she holds himself or herself out to the public as an appraiser to perform appraisals on a regular basis.
- Because of the appraiser's qualifications as described in the appraisal, he or she is qualified to make appraisals of the type of property being valued.
- The appraiser is not one of the persons excluded by these rules from being a qualified appraiser.
- The appraiser understands that an intentionally false or fraudulent overstatement of the value of the property described in the qualified appraisal or appraisal summary may subject the appraiser to a civil penalty for aiding and abetting an understatement of tax liability,[63] and consequently the appraiser may have appraisals disregarded.

Notwithstanding these requirements, an individual is not a qualified appraiser if the donor had knowledge of facts that would cause a reasonable person to expect the appraiser to falsely overstate the value of the donated property. Also, the donor, donee, or certain other related persons cannot be a qualified appraiser of the property involved in the gift transaction.

More than one appraiser may appraise the donated property, as long as each appraiser complies with these requirements, including signing the qualified appraisal and appraisal summary. If more than one appraiser appraises the property, the donor does not have to use each appraiser's appraisal for purposes of substantiating the charitable deduction.

Generally, no part of the fee arrangement for a qualified appraisal can be based on a percentage of the appraised value of the property. If a fee arrangement is based, in whole or in part, on the amount of the appraised value of the property (if any) that is allowed as a charitable deduction, after IRS examination or otherwise, it is treated as a fee based on a percentage of the appraised value of the property. (This rule does not apply in certain circumstances to appraisal fees paid to a generally recognized association that regulates appraisers.)

In any situation involving a gift of property, the charitable organization that is the recipient of the gift must value the property for its own record-keeping, reporting, and (if applicable) financial statement purposes. The charitable donee, however, is not required to share that valuation amount with the donor.

Many of these requirements apply to the donor. Therefore, technically, compliance with them is the responsibility of the donor and not the charitable donee. Nonetheless, if only as a matter of donor relations (inasmuch as availability of the charitable deduction may be dependent on adherence to these rules), the planner for the charitable organization should endeavor to be certain that a procedure is in place to make donors aware of these rules, and perhaps assist them in assembling the necessary records and in otherwise complying with the requirements.

## Substantial Compliance Doctrine

These rules are subject to the *doctrine of substantial compliance*. Pursuant to this doctrine, where the rules involved are procedural or directory in nature, strict adherence to them is not required; substantial compliance is sufficient. It has been held that in this context, the requirement that certain documentation be attached to the donor's federal income tax return is directory rather than mandatory.[64]

## C Corporation Rules

A separate set of rules applies appraisal requirements to regular corporations (that is, corporations other than those referenced above, termed *C corporations*). These rules, in general, require these corporations to obtain a qualified independent appraisal to validly claim a charitable contribution deduction for gifts of most items of property, other than money, having a value in excess of $5,000.[65]

There are special rules concerning contributions of inventory. These corporations are required to include summary information in their annual federal income tax return, such as a description of the inventory contributed and the valuation method used (for example, retail pricing). This information is to be embodied in a *partially completed appraisal summary*.[66]

## Penalty

These substantiation requirements must be complied with if the charitable contribution deduction is to be allowed.[67]

# OFFERING OF INFORMATION OR SERVICES

A tax-exempt organization[68] is required to adequately disclose that information or services it is offering to the public are available without charge from the federal government, assuming that is in fact the case.[69]

## Summary of Rules

This disclosure requirement is violated where:

- A tax-exempt organization offers to sell (or solicits money for) specific information or a routine service for an individual that could be readily obtained by that individual without charge (or for a nominal charge[70]) from an agency of the federal government,

- The exempt organization, when making the offer or solicitation, fails to make an "express statement (in a conspicuous and easily recognizable format)" that the information or service can be so obtained, and

- The failure is due to intentional disregard of these requirements.

This requirement applies only if the information to be provided involves the specific individual solicited. Thus, for example, the requirement applies with respect to obtaining the social security earnings record or the social security identification number of an individual solicited, while the requirement is inapplicable with respect to the furnishing of copies of newsletters issued by federal agencies or providing copies of or descriptive material concerning pending legislation.

This requirement is also inapplicable to the provision of professional services (such as tax return preparation, assistance with respect to the submission of an application for a grant, or medical services), as opposed to routine information retrieval services, to an individual even if they may be available from the federal government without charge or at a nominal charge.

### Penalty

There is a penalty for failure to comply with this rule, which is applicable for each day on which the failure occurred. It is the greater of $1,000 or 50 percent of the aggregate cost of the offers and solicitations that occurred on any day on which the failure occurred and with respect to which there was this type of failure.[71]

## PERSONAL BENEFIT CONTRACTS

Congress has essentially legislated the use of personal benefit contracts, in the charitable giving context, out of existence.[72] This was accomplished by the enactment of rules denying an income tax charitable contribution deduction for transfers, and imposing excise tax penalties, associated with the use of charitable split-dollar insurance plans.[73]

A *personal benefit contract* is a life insurance, annuity, or endowment contract where any direct or indirect beneficiary pursuant to the contract is the transferor, a member of the family of the transferor, or any other person (other than a charitable organization) designated by the transferor. There is no charitable contribution deduction for any transfer to or for the use of a charitable organization if, in connection with the transfer:

- The charitable organization directly or indirectly pays, or has previously paid, a premium on a personal benefit contract with respect to the transferor, or

- There is or was an understanding or expectation that any person will directly or indirectly pay any premium on any personal benefit contract with respect to the transferor.[74]

A charitable organization must disclose, on its appropriate annual information return, whether, during the year involved, it:

- Received any funds, directly or indirectly, to pay premiums on a personal benefit contract
- Paid premiums, directly or indirectly, on a personal benefit contract[75]

## Form 990 Questions

Tax-exempt organizations that file annual information returns are required to respond to a question as to whether they have complied with the law concerning personal benefit contracts.[76]

## Penalty

The federal tax law imposes an excise tax on a charitable organization in an amount equal to the premiums paid by the organization on any life insurance, annuity, or endowment contract if the payment of the premiums on the contract is in connection with a transfer involving a personal benefit contract.[77]

# Tax Shelters

There is considerable interest in tax shelters, by promoters and users of them, by the media, and by federal and state regulators. Much attention is being given to inversions, conversions, improper use of trusts, inflated business expense deductions, off-sheet financing schemes, unfounded legal or constitutional law arguments, frivolous refund claims, and the like. This matter of tax shelters is not confined to for-profit businesses and the for-profit sector in general; tax shelter activity is also taking place in the non-profit sector.

## General Concept of *Tax Shelter*

There is no single, and certainly no simple, definition of the term *tax shelter*. Some aspects of a comprehensive definition may be gleaned from three provisions in the Internal Revenue Code.

In the statute requiring registration of tax shelters,[78] the term *tax shelter* is defined as an "investment" (1) with respect to which any person could reasonably infer from the representations made, or to be made, in connection with the offering for sale of interests in the investment that the tax shelter ratio for any investor as of the close of any of the first five years ending after the date on which such investment is offered for sale may be greater than two to one, and (2) that is (a) required to be registered under a federal or state law regulating securities, (b) sold pursuant to an exemption from registration of the offering, or (c) a substantial investment.[79] Thus, this definition of a tax shelter focuses on an offering of an investment vehicle to a number of potential investors.

This statute also provides that the term includes any "entity, plan, arrangement, or transaction" (1) a "significant purpose" of the structure of which is the "avoidance or evasion" of federal income tax for a direct or indirect participant which is a corporation, (2) that is offered to any potential participant under conditions of confidentiality, and (3) for which the tax shelter promoters may receive fees in excess of $100,000 in the aggregate.[80] Thus, this type of confidential tax shelter is limited to certain corporate tax shelters. Still, the first of the three factors offers important elements of the types of tax shelters opposed by the IRS.

The federal tax law includes a penalty imposed on those who promote abusive tax shelters.[81] That section references a partnership or other entity, an investment plan or agreement, or any other plan or agreement.

Consequently, a unitary definition of the term *tax shelter* can be constructed from these definitions. Basically a tax shelter has two elements. One, it can be an entity (such as a partnership) or a plan, transaction, or other arrangement (investment or otherwise). Two, the sole or principal purpose of the entity or arrangement is avoidance or evasion of taxes.

Thus, there are *tax shelters* and *abusive tax shelters*. The latter may be defined as schemes created and used to obtain, or to try to obtain, tax benefits that are not allowable by law.[82]

### Judicial Doctrines Used to Combat Tax Shelters

The doctrines developed by the courts to deny certain tax-motivated transactions their intended tax benefits consist of the law concerning sham transactions,[83] economic substance, business purpose, substance over form, and step transactions.[84]

### Reportable Transactions

Tax regulations[85] established disclosure obligations of taxpayers that participate in *reportable transactions*. There are six types of these transactions, including *listed transactions*. These are transactions that the IRS has identified as having a tax avoidance purpose and whose tax benefits are subject to disallowance under existing law. The IRS, from time to time, identifies these transactions, some of which are in the tax-exempt organizations context.

### Tax Shelters in Exempt Organizations Context

Examples of tax shelters in the tax-exempt organizations context include the accelerated charitable remainder trust,[86] overvaluation of property (such as used vehicles) contributed to charity,[87] certain trust arrangements that purport to qualify as multiple-employer welfare benefit funds in order to deduct what would otherwise be nondeductible life insurance premiums,[88] and misuse of the tax exemption afforded small insurance companies.[89] Other abuses have occurred in the employee benefits and exempt bond contexts.

Indeed, depending on the definition of the term that is applied, tax shelters may embrace certain supporting organizations,[90] certain donor-advised fund arrangements, charitable split-dollar insurance plans (now outlawed (see above)), and charitable family limited partnerships.[91] This is because, in late 1999, the IRS observed that it was being "confronted" with a number of "aggressive tax avoidance schemes," referencing these four subjects as examples.[92]

## IRS Initiatives

The IRS has deployed various initiatives to attack promotions of abusive tax shelters. One is the establishment, within the Large and Mid-Size Business Division of the IRS, of the Office of Tax Shelter Analysis. Also, within the Small Business and Self-Employed Division is the Office of Flow-Through Entities and Abusive Tax Schemes.

Other compliance and enforcement efforts undertaken by the IRS include the National Fraud Program, criminal law investigations, and information about tax schemes on the IRS web site and in the agency's publications.

## Tax Shelter Tax Penalties and Other Sanctions

There are various statutory provisions limiting tax benefits in certain transactions.[93] Also, there are various penalties and sanctions applicable to tax shelters: the accuracy-related penalty,[94] a fraud penalty,[95] a penalty for understatement of a taxpayer's liability by an income tax return preparer,[96] penalties with respect to the preparation of income tax returns for others,[97] the penalty for promoting abusive tax shelters,[98] a penalty for aiding and abetting an understatement of tax liability,[99] a penalty for failure to register tax shelters,[100] and a penalty for failure to maintain lists of investors in potentially abusive tax shelters.[101]

The IRS also has the authority to pursue litigation to enjoin income tax return preparers from engaging in inappropriate conduct[102] and to enjoin promoters of abusive tax shelters.[103]

There are other laws used by the IRS to combat unwarranted tax practices in the tax-exempt area, such as the property appraisal requirements[104] and various anti-abuse rules in the tax regulations.

## Planner's Obligations

The obligations of the planner in this context are just emerging. Presumably the planner has no interest in having a tax-exempt organization with which he or she is associated be classified as an abusive tax shelter.[105] The planner's obligations in this regard include monitoring developments in the law, including changes in exempt organizations statutes and pronouncements from the IRS as to new forms of listed transactions.

# PROSPECTIVE (POSSIBLE) DISCLOSURE REQUIREMENTS

The tax-exempt organizations disclosure requirement movement has by no means abated. New disclosure requirements beget more of these proposals. More disclosure generates demand for still more. Advocates of fuller disclosure want to see some or all of the following documents made publicly available:

- All closing agreements involving tax-exempt organizations
- The results of IRS audits of exempt organizations
- Applications for recognition of tax exemption, as of the time they are filed
- The unrelated business tax return (Form 990-T)
- All returns filed by organizations that are affiliated with exempt organizations
- All written determinations from the IRS, including background file documents, involving exempt organizations
- Greater disclosure of lobbying activities, including self-defense lobbying[106]

Also, some are pressing for rules giving the IRS authority to disclose more information, including the results of examinations, about tax-exempt organizations to state officials. Another effort under way is enactment of law requiring the IRS to notify members of the public, by means of form instructions and publications, that the applications for recognition of exemption and annual information returns are publicly available.[107]

## Commentary

This litany of recommendations is overkill, far beyond anything that can be considered reasonable. It sounds of the "kitchen sink" approach: just throw in whatever can be thought of. It does not appear that there is any form of disclosure that is not on this list. Perhaps all employees of and independent contractors with tax-exempt organizations should be required to disclose their personal income tax returns.

Just because an organization is tax-exempt does not mean that it should be automatically set up for burdensome government regulation, almost in the nature of punishment, that far exceeds what its taxpaying counterparts must endure. This appears as a bias against organizations simply as a result of their tax exemption, which should not be manifested in this extreme fashion. These recommendations are unbalanced and unfair, bred of a complete loss of perspective as to why this country has the concept of tax-exempt organizations.

Tax exemption is not accorded nonprofit organizations just so governments can pummel them with regulatory requirements that impede their ability to carry out their charitable and other exempt functions. As noted at the outset of this chapter, nonprofit organizations exist as essential components of a free society; they are necessary for the pluralism of institutions. These organizations serve as an alternative to government. The fundamental theoretical framework underlying the concept of tax-exempt, nonprofit organizations is not found in the tax law; it is a political, philosophical law that reflects the unique nature of our democratic state. The tax law mirrors the way U.S. society is structured.

It is not surprising that some in government want to minimize the scope and meaningfulness of the services of nonprofit organizations. Increasingly, there is talk from legislators and other representatives of government that there are too many nonprofit organizations. Heavy-handed regulation, as reflected by the above proposals, is one way to reduce the effectiveness of tax-exempt organizations—simply strangle them with paperwork.

The public interest is, undoubtedly, served by disclosure of the activities and finances of tax-exempt organizations. Yet, there should be a limit; even exempt organizations surely have some privacy rights. Existing law provides considerable disclosure of financial and program activities of exempt organizations. Policymakers should think carefully before imposing more regulatory burdens on the sector; its contributions to society are too important.

## Notes

1. See Chapter 2.
2. See Chapter 9.
3. In general, see Chapter 2, page 42.
4. Id., page 41.
5. *Tax-Exempt Organizations,* § 24.4(b).
6. Id., § 24.4(b)(v).
7. Id., § 24.4(b)(ii).
8. Id., § 24.4(b)(iii).
9. Id.
10. Id.
11. Id., § 24.4(b)(vi).
12. See Chapter 9, pages 205–206.
13. IRC § 6652(c)(1)(D).
14. In general, Chapter 9.
15. *Tax-Exempt Organizations,* § 24.4(b).
16. See Chapter 9, pages 205–206.
17. IRC § 6652(c)(1)(C).
18. IRC § 170(f)(8). In general, *Charitable Giving,* § 21.1(b).
19. The term *goods or services* means tangible items—money, property, services, benefits, and privileges (Reg. § 1.170A-13(f)(5))—and not intangible, ephemeral things such as understandings and expectations (see text accompanied by notes 32–33 below).
20. The planner may wish to ponder the fact that a *good faith estimate* means the donee charitable organization's estimate of the fair market value of any goods or services "without regard to the manner in which the organization in fact made that estimate." Reg. § 1.170A-13(f)(7).
21. Special rules apply in the case of *intangible religious benefits.*
22. Reg. § 1.170A-13(f)(6).
23. *Internet Communications,* § 7.8(b).
24. A charitable organization that knowingly provides a false written substantiation to a donor may be subject to the penalty for aiding and abetting an understatement of tax liability. IRC § 6701.
25. *Charitable Giving,* chap. 12.
26. Id., chap. 16.
27. Id., chap. 13.
28. United States v. American Bar Endowment, 477 U.S. 105, 118 (1986).
29. Id. at 116–117.

30. Comm'r v. Duberstein, 363 U.S. 278, 285 (1960).

31. Reg. § 1.170A-1(c)(5). In general, *Charitable Giving*, § 3.1(a).

32. Addis v. Comm'r, 118 T.C. 528 (2002).

33. See Chapter 11, pages 271–274.

34. IRC § 178(f)(8)(A).

35. IRC § 6115. In general, *Charitable Giving*, § 22.2.

36. IRC § 6115(b). These rules are inapplicable with respect to *intangible religious benefits*.

37. IRC § 6115(a).

38. Reg. § 1.6115-1(a)(1).

39. Reg. § 1.6115-1(a)(2).

40. *Charitable Giving*, § 22.2, text accompanied by nn. 38–40.

41. Reg. § 1.170A-1(h)(1).

42. *Charitable Giving*, § 3.1(b).

43. See Chapter 9, page 206.

44. IRC § 6714.

45. IRC § 6113. See *Tax-Exempt Organizations*, § 22.2; *Charitable Giving*, § 23.3.

46. *Tax-Exempt Organizations*, chap. 12.

47. That is, is described in IRC §§ 501(a) and 501(c) (other than, as noted, charitable organizations described in IRC § 501(c)(3)).

48. That is, is described in IRC § 527. See *Tax-Exempt Organizations*, chap. 17.

49. Notice 88-120, 1988-2 C.B. 459.

50. *Tax-Exempt Organizations*, chap. 13.

51. Id., chap. 15.

52. Id., chap. 14.

53. Id., § 16.3.

54. See Chapter 9, page 206.

55. IRC § 6710.

56. As the IRS's instructions describe this distinction, a "car should be described in more detail than pots and pans."

57. If the property was created, produced, or manufactured by or for the donor, the date to be used is the date the property was substantially completed.

58. See *Charitable Giving*, § 21.3.

59. IRC § 6721.

60. Reg. § 1.170A-13(c). See *Charitable Giving*, § 21.2.

61. See *Charitable Giving*, § 9.22.

62. See *Charitable Giving*, § 9.18.

63. IRC § 6701.

64. A full discussion of the application of the doctrine of substantial compliance to these appraisal requirements is in § 21.2(v) of *Charitable Giving*.

65. Reg. § 1.170A-13(c)(2)(ii).

66. Additional details about this set of rules are in *Charitable Giving*, § 21.2(vi).

67. Reg. § 1.170A-13(c)(2).

68. That is, an entity described in IRC § 501(c) or (d) and exempt from federal income tax pursuant to IRC § 501(a) (*Tax-Exempt Organizations*, Part 2), or a political organization as defined in IRC § 527(e) (id., chap. 17).

69. IRC § 6711(a). *Tax-Exempt Organizations*, § 24.5.

70. If materials and/or services are available from the federal government for less than $2.50 (including postage and handling costs), the materials are considered by the IRS as being available from the federal government at a nominal charge. Notice 88-120, note 49 above).

71. IRC § 6711(b).

72. IRC § 170(f)(10).

73. See *Charitable Giving,* § 17.6.

74. A personal benefit contract was involved in the facts of Addis v. Comm'r, note 32 above.

75. Form 990, Part X.

76. See Chapter 9, pages 211–212.

77. IRC § 170(f)(10)(F).

78. IRC § 6111.

79. IRC § 6111(c)(1).

80. IRC § 6111(d)(1).

81. IRC § 6700.

82. Rather incredibly, a report presented to the IRS's Advisory Committee on Tax-Exempt and Government Entities (*Report of the TE/GE Abusive Tax Shelters Involving Tax-Exempt and Government Entities Project Group* (May 20, 2003)) offered the thought that tax-exempt organizations (like tax-qualified retirement plans and tax-exempt bond offerings) are "legitimate tax shelters." Abusive tax shelters were cast as "schemes consisting of abusive transactions that are aggressively sold by promoters in reckless disregard of Code provisions and that, under any reasonable interpretation, provide no basis for the tax advantages purportedly offered by these transactions."

83. E.g., *Tax-Exempt Organizations,* § 31.1(d).

84. See *Charitable Giving,* § 4.8.

85. These rules are promulgated under IRC § 6011.

86. See *Charitable Giving,* §§ 12.2(c), 12.3(c).

87. Id. § 9.23. In the first of the technical advice memoranda concerning the intermediate sanctions rules (Tech. Adv. Mem. 200243057), the IRS assessed penalties for aiding and abetting understatements of tax liabilities (IRC § 6701; see note 63 above) in the case of an individual's practice of providing donors with the full fair market value of contributed vehicles even where many of the vehicles could only be sold for salvage or scrap.

88. E.g., Neonatology Assocs., P.A. v. Comm'r, 299 F.3d 221 (3d Cir. 2002) (see *Charitable Giving,* § 16.3).

89. The law concerning tax-exempt small insurance companies (see *Tax-Exempt Organizations,* § 18.8) was revised, on enactment of the Pension Funding Equity Act of 2004, to place tighter restrictions on eligibility for the exemption, to prevent these companies from being used to shelter millions of dollars in investment income while providing little insurance coverage.

90. See Chapter 4, pages 91–99.

91. See *Charitable Giving,* § 9.23.

92. IRS CPE text for FY 2000.

93. IRC §§ 269, 446, 469, 482, 7701(l), 7805.

94. IRC § 6662.

95. IRC § 6663.

96. IRC § 6694.

97. IRC § 6695.

98. IRC § 6700.

99. IRC § 6701.

100. IRC § 6707.

101. IRC § 6708.
102. IRC § 7407.
103. IRC § 7408.
104. See *Charitable Giving,* § 22.2.
105. It is most unfortunate that some have chosen to portray tax-exempt organizations as tax shelters (legitimate or not) in the first instance. See note 82 above.
106. See Chapter 5, page 112.
107. All of these proposals are contained in a study published by the Joint Committee on Taxation in early 2000. Some of these proposals are part of legislation passed by the Senate in early 2003. Charity Aid, Recovery, and Empowerment (CARE) Act of 2003, S. 476, 108th Cong., 1st sess. (2003). Counterpart legislation subsequently passed by the House of Representatives in 2003 (Charitable Giving Act of 2003, H.R. 7, 108th Cong., 1st sess. (2003)) does not contain any of these disclosure proposals.

# CHAPTER 11

# Planning in the Face of Difficult Court Opinions

The complexity of the legal system and the fantastical development of the law in the United States being what it is, most fields of the law are amply informed by a multitude of court opinions. There is, of course, usually a base, established by one or more statutes; that core body of law is often leavened by regulations promulgated by one or more administrative agencies. Frequently, the law field is also expanded by rules, forms, form instructions, and the like. Yet, almost always, it is court opinions that give a body of law its energy and essence.

Every court opinion in a field contributes to the body of law involved. Some opinions obviously contribute more than others; some may "contribute" in a negative fashion. Some opinions are major forces from the moment they are written.[1] The significance of others may emerge with the passage of time.[2] Yet, as law ebbs and flows, an opinion that seems important at a point in time can lose luster, just as one that at a point in time seemed trivial (or an aberration or an anachronism) can later balloon into a court opinion of major significance.[3] Some court opinions are stellar (both in terms of accuracy on the point involved and as literature);[4] others can be humorous (either intentionally[5] or unintentionally[6]) and/or are nothing short of terrible.[7]

These judgments about court opinions, it need hardly be said, are highly subjective. These evaluations do not amount, by any means, to a scientific process. A court opinion deemed major by one observer may be deemed to be of little significance by another. An opinion considered "wrong" by one reader can appear quite reasonable if not "correct" to another reader. The importance of these writings turns on the commentators' views as to what the law should be, philosophies, political leanings, and other such nonobjective factors.

## INTRODUCTION: EVALUATION OF COURT OPINIONS

By any reckoning, there is in the United States the finest judicial system at the federal level that humankind has ever fashioned. The components of this element of the tripartite system of government—the judiciary, as framed by Article III of the Constitution—are the Supreme Court, the courts of appeal, and the district courts, as well as several other courts, including the U.S. Tax Court and the U.S. Court of Federal Claims. This system, then, is populated and served by hundreds of judges.

This is all very impressive and to many a mind-boggling array of judicial mind power. Yet, as impressive as this system is, it is—being fueled by the thinking of human beings— not perfect. Some court opinions are more "correct" than others. A few are just plain wrong.

A distinction needs to be drawn between a court's decision and a court's opinion. The *decision* of a court is its conclusion as to which party in the litigation prevailed. Almost always, one of the parties to a tax-exempt organizations case is the federal government. The decision, then, often is whether or not the United States won the case.

The *opinion* of a court, of course, embodies its decision. The opinion, however, also summarizes the facts of the case and the law involved, and (usually) explains how the court reached its decision. Here is to be found the court's reasoning and selection of precedents. Here, too, can occasionally be found wonderful literature and dazzling humor, or fuzzy thinking and other forms of humor, albeit unintended.

Sandwiched between these two concepts is *the law of the case*. This consists of the court's decision plus a summary of what it held.

A court may, in writing an opinion, meander a bit, pausing along the way to make observations that are not directly germane to its findings. These wanderings are known as *dicta*.

As noted, judging the correctness—or lack thereof—of a court opinion is an exercise of considerable subjectivity. The principal criterion, nonetheless, should be: was the decision by the court *correct*—that is, did the court properly state and apply the law? Is the opinion *accurate*? This entails an understanding of the statutory and regulatory structure of the body of law involved, as well as court-made precedents. With all that in mind, it comes down to this: did the court get the thing right?

There are other factors, again subjective ones. Does the opinion make sense, from a real-world perspective? That is, is the opinion too theoretical or impractical, or did the writing of it advance the law by providing some useful understanding and guidance as to how the rules are supposed to work? Some judges (or their clerks), in the process of deciding a case on its unique facts, lose perspective as to how the opinion would be applied in similar fact situations. Did the court interpret the law or did it make up some law? These can be fine and controversial distinctions.

Other factors that a reviewer of an opinion may want to consider are the reasoning in the opinion, the tone of the opinion, and the handling of precedents (assuming any are cited). An opinion can be evaluated as literature: its structure and the style in which it was written.

The analysis in this book, as to the difficult court opinions, is confined to one body of jurisprudence: the federal law of tax-exempt organizations. It is the take of one lawyer—albeit one with more than 30 years' experience (practicing, writing, teaching, lecturing) in the field—as to the most difficult court opinions in the exempt organizations area, and the major impact they are having on the development of exempt organizations jurisprudence. These opinions are intended to be of assistance to the exempt organizations planner who is trying to cope in their aftermath.

Since the federal constitutional income tax system commenced in 1913, there have been a multitude of court opinions on tax-exempt organizations issues, including charitable giving and fundraising matters. What follows is an inventory of the most difficult court opinions on tax-exempt organizations matters ever authored by a U.S. federal court, coupled with analyses as to why they were selected and the mammoth impact—for better or for worse—they are having on the ongoing development of the law of tax-exempt organizations.

For purposes of this analysis, there are two categories of court opinions that are *difficult* from a planning perspective. One is the set of opinions that were wrongly decided. The other is the collection of court opinions as to which one cannot say are wrong so much as they are difficult to apply in a real-world context. (Of course, the erroneous decisions can be difficult, if not impossible, to apply as well.)

## POSITIVE COURT OPINION

Before proceeding with the erroneous and otherwise difficult court opinions, some objectivity can be achieved by a brief focus on what may be termed a positive court opinion. Here is one of the finest.

### PRESBYTERIAN & REFORMED PUBLISHING CO. v. COMM'R[8]

CASE STUDY

#### INTRODUCTION TO THE CASE

In a case involving alleged commerciality by a religious publishing company, a federal court of appeals held that the standards to apply are the purposes for which the organization is operated and the extent of any private inurement, rather than factors such as profits, audience reached, influence, and affiliation with other religious entities.

#### SUMMARY OF THE FACTS

The Presbyterian and Reformed Publishing Company (hereinafter Company) was formed in 1931 to disseminate, largely by means of publishing, the system of belief and practice taught in the Bible, as that system is now set forth in the Confession of Faith and Catechisms of the U.S. Presbyterian Church. The essential exempt function of the Company, recognized by the IRS in 1939, was publication of *Christianity Today,* a Presbyterian journal.

From the beginning, the Company was closely linked—albeit not formally affiliated—with a Presbyterian group (OPC) dedicated to its view of reformed Presbyterian theology and, in particular, to the doctrine of Biblical Christianity set forth in the Westminster Confession of Faith.

One of the Company's incorporators and original directors founded the OPC in 1932. Seven of its nine directors were either officials at Westminster Theological

Seminary or are pastors of OPC or OPC-affiliated denominations. The Seminary was named in the Company's dissolution clause. Since 1931, the publishing house was operated by three successive generations of the Craig family. The individuals, all ministers, worked without compensation at what amounted to a "family concern whose business was conducted at the Craig's kitchen table."[9] The record was "devoid of evidence indicating any lessening or attenuation of ties between [the Company] and the OPC."[10]

Until 1969, the Company did not have any net income. The Craigs often contributed money to keep the operation afloat. Until 1973, the Company relied exclusively on volunteers to help the Craigs with editing, packing, shipping, and clerical work.

Beginning in 1969, however, the Company experienced a "considerable increase in economic activity."[11] This was because of the "sudden and unexpected" popularity of books written by a faculty member of the Seminary.[12] Gross profits began to materialize. The organization developed the need for seven employees; indeed, the Craig family member involved began receiving a salary.

The Company notified the IRS that it was accumulating funds as a "building fund."[13] Thereafter, the Company purchased $5\frac{1}{2}$ acres of land close to an OPC community and the press involved. After that, an office building/warehouse was constructed, and equipment was purchased.

The IRS revoked the tax-exempt status of the Company, on the grounds that it was not operating exclusively for exempt purposes and was engaged in a "commercial enterprise."[14] The Tax Court agreed that the Company had "acquired a truly commercial hue" and came to be "animated" by a substantial commercial purpose.[15] The court relied on the fact that the Company had "soaring" net and gross profits, set prices so as to return profits, and sold publications that "overlapped in subject matter" with commercial publishers.[16] In a separate opinion, the court concluded that the Company's new building, development of a professional staff, and accumulation of capital furthered commercial purposes.

## Summary of the Opinion

The appellate court wrote that the principal issue before it in this case was "at what point the successful operation of a tax-exempt organization should be deemed to have transformed that organization into a commercial enterprise and thereby to have forfeited tax exemption."[17] It reviewed the criteria relied on by the Tax Court and found them "relevant," yet the court was "troubled by the inflexibility of the Tax Court's approach."[18] Under the lower court's analysis, it was "doubtful that any small-scale exempt operation could ever increase its economic activity without forfeiting its tax-exempt status under such a definition of nonexempt commercial character."[19]

The court said that the correct approach is a two-prong one: what is the purpose of the organization claiming tax-exempt status, and to whose benefit does its activity inure? The "hallmarks of non-taxable activity" were said to be the purpose of the entity and the absence of personal profit, rather than the "volume of business."[20]

The court first addressed the matter of private inurement. It found "no basis" in the facts for a conclusion that the Company's activity caused inurement to anyone.[21] The salaries involved were held to be "modest," and thus reasonable.[22]

Then, the court returned to the first prong—that of purpose. The court struggled, not with "surface manifestation" of an action, but on the "undisclosed motivation of the actor."[23] It focused on the finding of the Tax Court that the Company was not affiliated or controlled by a particular church and that this contributed to its commercial and competitive character. The appellate court dismissed this factor, because of the "close connection" between the Company and the OPC.[24]

The court concluded that the principal concern of the Tax Court was the presence of "substantial profits."[25] The element of profits does not go to the question of purpose. The appellate court observed that "unexplained accumulations of cash may properly be considered as evidence of commercial purpose."[26] Yet, in this case, that fact did not prove an inappropriate purpose.

The court then turned to other evidence in the record. It noted that "success in terms of audience reached and influence exerted, in and of itself, should not jeopardize the tax-exempt status of organizations which remain true to their stated goals."[27] The court did not want organizations to have to choose between expanding influence and audience and remaining exempt. It observed that if "this were a stagnant society in which various ideas and creeds preserve a hold on a fixed proportion of the population, this concern would evaporate."[28]

A large religious institution, such as an established church, could be the "springboard for large-scale publishing houses dedicated to advancing its doctrines and be assured" of qualifying for tax exemption.[29] A small denomination "could then have within its penumbra only a small-scale operation run off a kitchen table."[30] That view, wrote the court, "does not reflect" the "dynamic quality of our society."[31] Such a standard "would lead to an inequitable disparity in treatment for publishers affiliated with mainstream churches as opposed to small off-shoots."[32]

The court of appeals reversed the Tax Court and allowed the Company to retain its tax-exempt status.

## COMMENTARY

This court opinion is one of the few to attempt to ward off coming encroachments by bodies of jurisprudence such as the commerciality doctrine.[33] It is, in many ways, the sole antidote to the principal commerciality doctrine opinion.[34]

## GUIDE FOR PLANNERS

If a charitable organization is facing a charge of commerciality, this is the court opinion to which the planner should initially turn for guidance (and, if needed, comfort). The Tax Court opinion in this case, however, is all too typical of these cases.

The planner should constantly remember, particularly when reviewing some of the opinions summarized below, what this court of appeals wrote about the lower court's opinion: it was "troubled by the inflexibility of the Tax Court's approach."[35]

# ERRONEOUS COURT OPINIONS

Inasmuch as a ranking of wrongly decided court cases is even more subjective than concluding they are wrong to begin with, these opinions are discussed in alphabetical order —with one exception: the worst court opinion of them all is discussed first.

## UNITED CANCER COUNCIL, INC. v. COMM'R[36]

### INTRODUCTION TO THE CASE

The U.S. Court of Appeals for the Seventh Circuit reversed the U.S. Tax Court, concluding that the fundraising company by the name of Watson & Hughey (W&H) was not an insider, for private inurement purposes, with respect to the public charity known as the United Cancer Council (UCC). This decision preserved the tax-exempt status of UCC, which the IRS proposed to revoke and the Tax Court held should be revoked. The case was remanded to the Tax Court for a determination as to whether UCC was operated for the private benefit of W&H and was settled before the lower court could consider the case from the perspective of the private benefit doctrine.

### SUMMARY OF THE FACTS

UCC was (it became bankrupt) a public charity, so recognized by the IRS in 1969. In 1984, UCC entered into a five-year direct-mail fundraising contract with W&H. This contract embraced a five-year period (1984–1989). While UCC received about $2.25 million as the result of the fundraising, W&H received more than $4 million in fees. The parties had co-ownership rights in UCC's mailing list; W&H was able to exploit those rights to derive substantial income for itself.

The Tax Court evaluated the position that W&H occupied in relation to UCC during the years at issue. It was observed that UCC was "heavily financed and kept in existence" by W&H by reason of the fundraising arrangement they had.[37] This relationship, wrote the court, "was in many ways analogous to that of a founder and major contributor to a new organization."[38]

In general, the Tax Court concluded that W&H exercised "substantial control" over UCC's finances and direct-mail fundraising campaigns over a period of several years.[39] Thus, the court concluded that because of W&H's "extensive control" over UCC, W&H should be considered an insider with respect to UCC.[40]

Having found the presence of an insider, the court proceeded to conclude that private inurement had occurred, in the form of excessive compensation to and manipulation of charitable assets for the direct benefit of W&H. The court conceded that the contract between the parties was bargained for but then found that that factor alone did not "by itself conclusively protect an arrangement from a determination that the compensation was unreasonable."[41] The private inurement was said to have taken place in the form of the fees paid by UCC to W&H and W&H's use (exploitation) of the UCC list for its private gain. The court upheld the IRS's retroactive revocation of UCC's exempt status in 1990, to the date in 1984 when the contract began.

### SUMMARY OF THE OPINION

The court of appeals grounded its findings on the premise that the "Tax Court's classification of W&H as an insider of UCC was based on the fundraising contract."[42] That is, the focus was on the contract's terms. The Tax Court and the IRS were characterized as contending that the "contract was so advantageous to W&H and so disadvantageous to UCC that the charity must be deemed to have surrendered the control of its operations and earnings to the noncharitable enterprise that it had hired to raise money for it."[43]

The appellate court wrote that "[f]undraising has become a specialized professional activity and many charities hire specialists in it."[44] It continued: "If the charity's contract with the fundraiser makes the latter an insider, triggering the inurement clause of section 501(c)(3) and so destroying the charity's tax exemption, the charitable sector of the economy is in trouble."[45]

UCC's "sound judgment" in entering into the contract with W&H was questioned by the appellate court.[46] It wrote that UCC "drove (so far as the record shows) the best bargain that it could, but it was not a good bargain."[47] Nonetheless, the court continued, the private inurement proscription "is designed to prevent the siphoning of charitable receipts to insiders of the charity, not to empower the IRS to monitor the terms of arm's-length contracts made by charitable organizations with the firms that supply them with essential inputs, whether premises, paper, computers, legal advice, or fundraising services."[48] The Tax Court's and IRS's position "threatens to unsettle the charitable sector by empowering the IRS to yank a charity's tax exemption simply because the Service thinks the charity's contract with its major fundraiser too one-sided in favor of the fundraiser, even though the charity has not been found to have violated any duty of faithful and careful management that the law of nonprofit corporations may have laid upon it."[49]

The court said it could not find anything in the facts to support the "theory" that "W&H seized control of UCC and by doing so became an insider."[50] Said the court: "There is nothing that corporate or agency law would recognize as control."[51] It wrote that the Tax Court used the word control "in a special sense not used elsewhere, so far as we can determine, in the law, including the federal tax law."[52] (The Tax Court defined an insider as a person who has "significant control over the [charitable] organization's activities."[53])

The appellate court concluded that "[t]here was no diversion of charitable revenues to an insider here, nothing that smacks of self-dealing, disloyalty, breach of fiduciary obligation or other misconduct of the type aimed at by a provision of law that forbids a charity to divert its earnings to members of the board or other insiders."[54]

As to the remand, the court wrote that the "board of a charity has a duty of care . . . and a violation of that duty which involved the dissipation of the charity's assets might (we need not decide whether it would—we leave that issue to the Tax Court in the first instance) support a finding that the charity was conferring a private benefit, even if the contracting party did not control, or exercise undue influence over, the charity. This, for all we know, may be such a case."[55]

## COMMENTARY

This opinion, as these things go, is quite extraordinary, in the most negative sense. It is wrong in so many ways, both procedurally and substantively. It is one of the worst court opinions ever. It is the most atrocious and embarrassing federal appellate court opinion in the law of tax-exempt organizations.

## Procedure

Regarding procedure, it is common for a federal appellate court opinion to begin by discussing the appropriate standard for the court's review. It is noteworthy that the Seventh Circuit skipped this step in its *UCC* opinion.

Yet, here is what this same court had to say on the subject in 1984: "The Tax Court's holding . . . [that an organization was not entitled to exemption] must be sustained on appeal unless clearly erroneous."[56] The *UCC* case should have also been reviewed under the *clearly erroneous* standard.

The Seventh Circuit is not alone in adhering (except in the *UCC* case) to this standard. Here is the Fifth Circuit: "A finding [by a lower court] that a corporation is not operated exclusively for charitable purposes cannot be disturbed unless clearly erroneous."[57] Second Circuit: "We review the Tax Court decision [finding an organization to not be entitled to exemption] for clear error."[58] Ninth Circuit: The "factual finding [that an organization is operated for a substantial nonexempt purpose] [is] reviewable under the clearly erroneous standard."[59] District of Columbia Circuit: "[O]ur review [of a denial of tax exemption] is on a clearly erroneous basis."[60]

It thus obviously was outside the province of the Seventh Circuit to decide whether the Tax Court was right or wrong. The most it should have done is determine if the Tax Court was clearly erroneous in its *UCC* decision. Certainly, right or wrong, the Tax Court's judgment in the case was not clearly erroneous. Again, it is telling that the Seventh Circuit simply left this part of the analysis out of its opinion.

## Substance

As to substance, many in the nonprofit sector were cheered by this finding that a fundraising company was not functioning as an insider with respect to a charitable organization, for purposes of the private inurement proscription. Those who supported this outcome did so because, quite simply, they like what the appellate court said. But the court lacked the authority to say what it said and what it said did not have much to do with the facts of the case.

Everyone likes to win; no one likes to lose. This is certainly true in litigation. Here, the nonprofit sector won and the government lost. Yet, there are wins and there are wins. Some wins rest on reason; they are correct outcomes. Indeed, most wins are of this category. Other wins, however, are flukes, oddball results that are not deserved. This opinion from the Seventh Circuit—this sad excuse for an appellate opinion, this rambling, nearly incoherent, nonsensical string of paragraphs[61]—is of the oddball category. The court, in trying to help the nonprofit sector, distorted or strayed widely from the facts of the case and the applicable law.

The court, as is painfully manifest, was abjectly fearful of the IRS. It saw that agency poised to run amok in this area, out to revoke the tax-exempt status of every charity that gets entangled in what in hindsight is a bad business deal. The IRS was viewed as "yanking"—inelegant phraseology for a court—charitable exemptions for those who enter into "one-sided" contracts.[62] The court mused, in one of its sillier moments, that, if the "charity's contract with the fundraiser makes the latter an insider, . . . the charitable sector of the economy is in trouble."[63]

An argument cannot get any more disingenuous than that. The Tax Court never made any such statement. In fact, the Tax Court went out of its way to write: "We are not holding that an arm's-length arrangement that produces a poor result for an organization necessarily would cause the organization to lose its tax-exempt status."[64]

The fact is that the Seventh Circuit's position is rested on a false premise. It was simply wrong for it to state that the "Tax Court's classification of W&H as an insider of UCC was based on the fundraising contract."[65] Rather, the conclusion as to insider status was based on the actual relationship between the parties that arose as the consequence of the contract. The facts are crystal clear that W&H had UCC in its clutches and exploited the charity for its private ends. It is nothing short of unbelievable for the appellate court to sweepingly assert that this contract was an arm's-length one and regard it as typical of a fundraising contract.

In its anti-IRS diatribe, the Seventh Circuit faulted the IRS for being "ignorant" of contract law.[66] The reverse is true: the court was ignorant of the law of tax-exempt organizations. How else to explain the astoundingly erroneous statement that the Tax Court's use of the word *control* is "not used elsewhere, so far as we can determine, in the law, including federal tax law"?[67] To what extent did the court make a determination? It could have looked in the Internal Revenue Code, where the term *disqualified person,* as applied with respect to public charities, is defined as any person who was "in a position to exercise substantial influence over the affairs of the organization."[68] That statutory definition is, by the way, almost identical to the definition crafted by the Tax Court.[69]

How about the assertion that "nothing [here] smacks of self-dealing"?[70] Again, a glance at the Code would have been enlightening to the court. Although the self-dealing rules[71] do not apply in this case, it was the appellate court that brought them up. Self-dealing includes furnishing of services between a charity and a disqualified person, payment of compensation by a charity to a disqualified person, and use of the assets of a charity by or for the benefit of a disqualified person.[72] Contrary to the Seventh Circuit's belief, the facts in this case reflect rampant self-dealing (in the generic sense).

This case, following the Seventh Circuit's disposition of the private inurement approach, was to have been resolved by application of the private benefit doctrine. What a mess. The Seventh Circuit never really addressed the question as to whether there was private inurement; it essentially focused on the question as to whether W&H was an insider in relation to UCC. If there was private inurement (and there was) and that inurement was not insubstantial (and it was not), how could there not be private benefit? (The Tax Court had already held that all forms of private inurement are also forms of private benefit.[73] Apparently, the appellate court did not know that.)

There was, at the time, little law on the private benefit doctrine (a byproduct of the operational test). The then principal court opinion[74] also was wrongly decided.[75] It appeared that the *UCC* case would bring some illumination of the reaches of the private benefit doctrine—because of the Seventh Circuit's opinion, itself being a strange and wrong decision. But with the settlement even that aspect of this opinion was lost. (The Tax Court assuredly would have reached the same conclusion in this case that it did beforehand, resting its conclusion on the private benefit doctrine rather than the private inurement doctrine.)

In short, the Seventh Circuit had the opportunity to nicely solidify the law in this area and interlace the private inurement doctrine with the excess benefit transaction rules. But the court, straying from the proper form of appellate court opinions and writing out of trepidation of perceived IRS expansionist tendencies rather than objective application of the law, blew it.

### Intermediate Sanctions

Incredibly, matters are worse. As it happened, this decision was handed down between the time of issuance of the proposed intermediate sanctions regulations and issuance of the temporary regulations. The IRS used this opinion as the basis for formulating what is the *initial contract exception.*

Thus, in the preamble to the final intermediate sanctions regulations, the IRS wrote that the Seventh Circuit held that private inurement "cannot result from a contractual relationship negotiated at arm's length with a party having no prior relationship with the organization, regardless of the relative bargaining strength of the parties or resultant control over the tax-exempt organization created by the terms of the contract."[76]

In fact, that was not the holding of this court of appeals. The opinion is silent on the implications of an entity having a form of "prior relationship" with a tax-exempt organization. The court found that the "party" did not control the exempt organization in the first instance. It is not clear what really motivated the IRS to create the initial contract exception, but it is a stretch of some elongation to assert that the court reached the *conclusions* formulated by the IRS. The most that can be said in this regard is that some elements of the initial contract exception can be gleaned or inferred from the facts of the case.

In this case, then, the court of appeals misconstrued the holding of the trial court and the IRS misconstrued the holding of the appellate court. This is not a stable foundation on which to rest a major tax regulation.

### GUIDE FOR PLANNERS

A lawyer almost always disregards a court opinion, just because of dislike of it, at his or her peril. The fact that a lawyer is of the view that the facts of a case are misstated or misconstrued, and/or that the court's decision was incorrect, is a risky rationale for ignoring a court's holding. Other lawyers, and judges, may easily disagree.

In this case, however, the lawyer or other planner has no choice: this opinion must be overlooked (or, if that cannot be mustered, substantially discounted). (The only principle this opinion stands for, for planners, is that, occasionally, the IRS animosity card can be played to successfully fake out a court.[77]) The facts of this case are so clear and compelling, the Tax Court's decision is so obviously correct, and the Tax Court's definition of an insider having been explicitly ratified by Congress when defining the term *disqualified person* in the intermediate sanctions setting, there can be no doubt that, today, an insider is just what the Tax Court said: a person who is in a position to exercise substantial control over the activities of the tax-exempt organization involved.

Thus, in the appropriate circumstances, the concept of an *insider* can, for private inurement doctrine purposes, include a fundraising company, a management company, a law firm (or individual lawyer), an accounting firm, and the like—despite what the Seventh Circuit said.

## Addis v. Comm'r[78]

### Introduction to the Case

The U.S. Tax Court ruled that payments made to a charitable organization were not deductible as charitable gifts, because the substantiation requirements were not met, in that there was an undisclosed return benefit. The amounts received by the charity were used to acquire a charitable split-dollar life insurance policy. The court held that there was a reasonable expectation that the charity would purchase the policy, which included a death benefit to one of the donors.

### Summary of the Facts

A married couple (H and W) claimed charitable contribution deductions for their payments (in 1997 and 1998) to the National Heritage Foundation (NHF) of money, which NHF used to pay premiums on a life insurance policy for the life of W. The policy was a charitable split-dollar life insurance contract. Under this contract, NHF was entitled to receive 56 percent of the death benefit, and the couple's family trust was entitled to receive 44 percent of the benefit.

Eleven years before the first of these payments, the couple formed a family trust. They are the trustors, first designee trustees, and initial beneficiaries of this trust. Their children and W's parents or siblings become beneficiaries of the trust on the death of the couple.

In October 1997, H and W established a "foundation" (a donor-advised fund) within NHF. On the same day, H wrote to NHF stating that the family trust intended to purchase an insurance policy on the life of W and would grant NHF an option to acquire an interest in that policy. The policy was issued. The couple owned the policy through the trust.

H, as trustee of the trust, and NHF entered into a death benefit option agreement, relating to the policy. H agreed to pay $4,000 of the $40,000 annual premium on the life insurance policy. H and NHF agreed that if NHF paid $36,000 of the annual premium, NHF would be entitled to its share of the death benefit. The agreement provided that the family trust and NHF each own a separate interest in this life insurance policy.

Later in 1997, H & W sent money ($36,000) to NHF for deposit into their foundation. An accompanying letter from H stated that NHF was not required to use the payment to pay the premium on the life insurance policy but that H "expected" NHF to use the payment to pay the premium. The next day, the couple paid the $4,000 of the premium.

NHF credited $36,000 to the foundation account. It simultaneously debited the foundation account $36,000 to pay NHF's portion of the life insurance policy premium. Also on the same day, NHF paid its $36,000 portion of the premium to the insurance company. The same series of transactions occurred the next year. As to both years, NHF provided the couple with a document that stated that it did not provide any goods or services to the donors in return for the contribution.

The couple stopped making payments to NHF after 1998. The statute that was designed to shut down these programs[79] took effect for transfers after February 8, 1999.

The IRS disallowed the charitable contribution deductions claimed by the couple for the transfers in 1997 and 1998 to NHF.

## SUMMARY OF THE LAW

A person may not deduct a contribution of $250 or more unless the person substantiates the contribution with a contemporaneous written acknowledgment of the contribution by the charitable donee.[80] This acknowledgment must include a statement as to whether the donee organization provided any goods or services in consideration for the contribution, and must provide a good faith estimate of the value of any goods or services provided.

A donee organization provides goods or services in consideration for a person's payment if, at the time the donor makes the payment to the donee, the payor receives or expects to receive goods or services in exchange for that payment.[81]

The U.S. Supreme Court wrote that a charitable contribution is one for which the donor has "no expectation of any quid pro quo."[82] The Court also wrote that the "sine qua non of a charitable contribution is a transfer of money or property without adequate consideration."[83]

## ANALYSIS

The couple argued (as the planner would expect) that NHF was not required, and did not promise, to use the contributions to pay the premiums on the insurance policy on the life of W. The court held, however, that NHF "provided consideration" for the payments because, at the time the payments were made to NHF, the couple "expected" to receive a share of the death benefit under the policy. Also, they "expected" NHF to use the funds they provided to pay NHF's portion of the premiums on the policy in 1997 and 1998.[84]

This "expectation" on the part of the couple was deemed "reasonable" by the court because it was in NHF's financial interest to pay premiums on the couple's life insurance policy in return for a guaranteed death benefit.[85]

NHF did not state in its substantiation documents that it paid premiums for the insurance policy on the life of W under which the couple would receive a portion of the death benefit. Also, NHF failed to make a good faith estimate of the value of these benefits. This arrangement was characterized by the court as a "scheme," including a "pot sweetened by charitable contribution deductions."[86]

The court held that the charitable contribution deduction was not available to this couple because the substantiation provided by the charitable donee was deficient.

## COMMENTARY

This is a classic example of a court decision that is not just incorrect but is simply unrealistic. Beating up on charitable split-dollar life insurance programs is easy, in the aftermath of the frenzied and unprincipled reaction in Congress that resulted in the statute that essentially outlawed these programs,[87] but the court should have given some thought to the real-world consequences of its holding.

The substantiation rules are designed to cause disclosure of, and reduction of a charitable contribution deduction by the amount of, the provision of a *good* or a *service* by the recipient charitable organization. The personal benefit contract rules reference *understandings* and *expectations*. If Congress meant these two sets of law to be identical, it would have used identical phraseology. The Tax

Court, in this case, blithely slid around, equating the provision of *goods and services* with *consideration* with *understandings* and *expectations*. This was a careless reading of the law.

Individuals and other persons make charitable contributions with expectations all the time. A person donates a parcel of land to a charity, expecting that the charity will improve the property, thereby enhancing the value of a neighboring piece of property that the person owns. An individual makes a charitable contribution to a donor-advised fund, with the expectation that the charity will always follow the advice of the donor. A parent makes charitable contributions to a university, with the expectation that the institution will admit the donor's child. These expectations are not goods or services; it has not been thought that these types of situations trigger a good faith estimate by the charity of the "value" of these expectations.

It would have been perfectly acceptable for the court to rule that NHF was not under any legally binding mandate to pay the premiums and that NHF elected to *invest* the money, in an opportunity provided by the couple, in a manner to generate a reasonable rate of return.

Now, instead, if the court is correct, an *expectation* is consideration defeating the concept of a charitable gift. Search in vain for authority for this conclusion in the opinion—it is not there. As noted, donors make (deductible) charitable gifts with expectations all the time.

This is one of the court opinions where the court simply lost its perspective. It was not sufficiently careful in its writing; the least it could have done was narrowly tailor its conclusions to the facts of the case. For example, the court sloppily wrote that the "NHF receipts [more correctly, substantiation documents] do not comply with the substantiation requirements . . . because NHF incorrectly stated in the receipts that [H & W] received no consideration for their payments."[88] The substantiation requirements, however, do not call for disclosure of *consideration;* they call for an estimate of *goods or services* provided.

It may well be that, as the court wrote, H & W "received substantial benefits from NHF under the life insurance policy."[89] But that is just how matters turned out. In any event, it is not these benefits that the substantiation requirements are, according to the court, intended to disclose. Rather, the ostensible good or service provided was the expectation of receiving these benefits.

If this court opinion was correct, a charitable organization, in preparing substantiation documents, would not only have to value what it *provided* in exchange for a gift, it would have to peer into the misty reaches of donor motivation and intent to discern what donors *expect to be provided*—and value that.

This is the great fault with this opinion. If literally followed, donors and donees —and their planners—are being placed in a precarious position. Mere expectations can—according to this decision—defeat, in whole or in part, charitable contributions. The lack of substantiation alone can preclude a charitable deduction. And just how does one value an *expectation?*

Unnecessarily, this court opinion has injected great confusion and anguish into the realm of substantiation that, obviously, was not needed. Had the insurance benefit been provided in exchange for the transfer of the money, that clearly would have to be valued and made the subject of a good faith estimate. But the expectation that the investment would be made in the insurance should not have to be valued and made part of the substantiation documentation. This is a most unfortunate decision—one that is greatly lacking in common sense and applicability in the real world.

## GUIDE FOR PLANNERS

This is another court opinion that the planner must disregard—at least until courts address the point further. Charities should stick to disclosure of goods and services provided (if any), and the provision of good faith estimates thereof. They should not try to struggle with disclosure and valuation of expectations.

## AIRLIE FOUNDATION, INC. v. UNITED STATES[90]

CASE STUDY

## INTRODUCTION TO THE CASE

A federal district court upheld the decision of the IRS to revoke the tax-exempt status of an organization on the ground that it was significantly operated for the private benefit of its founder and his family.

## SUMMARY OF THE FACTS

The IRS examined the appropriateness of tax exemption for this organization (AFI) after obtaining information at a tax fraud trial involving its founder, Dr. Murdoch Head. AFI had been tax-exempt as a charitable and educational organization since 1963. The court wrote that the IRS revoked this exemption because of Dr. Head's "control over a network of organizations, including AFI, that were involved in numerous transactions and exchanges of money, marketable assets and land."[91]

The court found that Dr. Head controlled AFI. He and his wife were partners in a partnership, succeeded by a corporation, that leased land to AFI. Their children were directors of the corporation. Dr. Head also controlled another entity that provided services to AFI. These two organizations had some common directors and officers. Dr. Head controlled a trust that provided some life income to him.

The facts included use of a fishing trawler and a condominium where Dr. Head's reimbursements for personal use were not backed up by records, sales of property from Dr. Head to AFI, a purchase of property by AFI from a trust controlled by Dr. Head, and leasing arrangements between a Dr. Head–controlled organization and AFI.

## SUMMARY OF THE OPINION

The court wrote that, by controlling the various organizations, Dr. Head was "able to manipulate the funds and assets of AFI, as well as to use AFI's exempt status, to benefit the non-exempt entities and himself."[92] The court concluded that all of this amounted to private inurement.

The findings of private inurement were based on inadequate recordkeeping, misinformation as reported on tax returns, and "profitable" business opportunities for Dr. Head–controlled organizations that provided services to AFI.[93]

## COMMENTARY

This opinion is a bit of a contretemps, with the court not really understanding all of the factors comprising the private inurement doctrine. The court saw a complex web of transactions and relationships between a public charity and its founder and entities he controlled, and just assumed that all was amiss. Revocation of the tax exemption of the charitable entity struck the court as an appropriate remedy.

There can be no doubt that Dr. Head was an insider with respect to AFI, so that the private inurement doctrine was properly invoked as the body of law containing the framework for analysis. The standard to be used, however, was whether the various transactions involved amounts that were excessive or otherwise unreasonable. The standard is not whether the transactions occurred, as is the case with the private foundation self-dealing rules (a distinction not even hinted at by the court). The word "reasonable" cannot be found in the opinion.

One basis of finding private inurement was personal use by Dr. Head of a condominium owned by AFI as the result of a gift of the property to it from Dr. Head. The record is clear that AFI used that facility for exempt purposes and that Dr. Head reimbursed the organization for the personal use. There was no finding that the reimbursements were inadequate or that the personal use was too extensive—the usual bases for finding private inurement under these circumstances. Instead, the court found private inurement because AFI failed to show the condominium on its books as an asset after Dr. Head transferred the property to it. There is no authority for a conclusion that this type of failure in the realm of recordkeeping amounts to private inurement.

Another basis for a finding of private inurement in this case was the alleged transfer of AFI property to a trust controlled by Dr. Head. While the opinion did not explain why these transfers were made, it also did not cite any authority for its findings of private inurement. The transfers appear to be legitimate; the court seemed to be concerned that the trust might purchase property from Dr. Head, yet absent a showing of unreasonable sales prices, that practice is lawful. The court also found that the trust served Dr. Head's "personal interests" because it provided him with some "life income."[94] The court thus evidenced its unfamiliarity with charitable remainder trusts, pooled income funds, and similar permissible planned giving arrangements.

Private inurement was also found in the business dealings between a Dr. Head–controlled entity and AFI. Yet the court did not find that the fees paid were unreasonable. Instead, it mused about some (admittedly sleazy) practices about backdating leases and untimely payments of rent.

The court, obviously impressed by (and overwhelmed by) the administrative record in this case (which included considerable information plucked from evidence obtained in Dr. Head's trial for personal tax fraud), wrote glowingly of the fact that the "government has marshalled an impressive array of undisputed facts showing how the network of organizations controlled by Dr. Head operated to his benefit."[95] AFI was faulted for not meeting its burden of proof to show an absence of private inurement.

The following quotation from this opinion is worth pondering: "Given Dr. Head's control of AFI, . . . [and the other entities], the various transfers of money and land among the organizations and to others, the trust, the cash fund, the condominium, and the lack of any evidence presented by AFI that Dr. Head or his family did not benefit, the Court finds that AFI was not operated exclusively for an exempt purpose but for the private benefit of Dr. Head and his family."[96] That is not the state of the law.

This opinion is devoid of any recognition that the word *exclusively* means, in this context, *primarily* rather than *solely*, that mere *benefit* to insiders is not sufficient to cause private inurement, and that the standard of *reasonableness* applies in this setting. The court was bamboozled by an IRS sound and light show, and got trapped in its facile research, overzealous application of burden of proof requirements, and lack of understanding of the applicable federal tax law.

Following is a quick review of points of law that this court ignored:

- A public charity can be established and controlled by those who are insiders with respect to it—mere *control* is no basis for an assumption of private inurement.

- An insider with respect to a public charity can engage in business dealings with it, including transactions that would constitute self-dealing if a private foundation were involved.

- A public charity can weave a complex web of affiliated entities, including one or more for-profit subsidiaries.

- Receipt by a donor of income for life from a charitable trust is quite lawful, and certainly not a form of private inurement.

- An insider can properly use the facilities of a public charity for his, her, or its personal or private use, as long as reasonable reimbursement for that use is timely made and the use does not inhibit the advancement of exempt functions.

## Guide for Planners

This opinion stands as a warning to those who apply the law of tax-exempt organizations in a sophisticated manner, particularly where an activity has an "appearance" of being "inappropriate." The planner needs to beware interlocking directorates or a multiplicity of intertwining organizations that may stump the fact-finder. This is a twist on this old adage: where there is smoke, there is fire. Courts are supposed to sift through facts such as these, correctly applying the law in all its niceties and subtleties. This opinion illustrates the unfortunate fact that sometimes they fail.

---

## American Campaign Academy v. Comm'r[97]                    CASE STUDY

### Introduction to the Case

The U.S. Tax Court held that an organization cannot be classified as a tax-exempt educational entity where it operated a school to train individuals for careers as political campaign professionals, because of the private benefit accruing to those who employ them after graduation.

## Summary of the Facts

This school was established to train individuals for careers as campaign managers, communications directors, finance directors, and other political campaign professionals. It clearly qualified as a school, in that it had a regularly scheduled curriculum, a regular faculty, training materials, and a full-time enrolled student body at the facilities it occupied. The school was an outgrowth of a program of instruction at the National Republican Congressional Committee (NRCC), an association comprised of Republican members of the U.S. House of Representatives.

It was agreed that the organization did not intervene in political campaigns nor did it engage in any legislative activities. The IRS conceded that the school's net earnings did not inure to the benefit of any individuals in their private capacity. The school did not assume any formal placement responsibilities.

The school admitted students on the basis of competitive admissions criteria. Applicants were not required to formally declare their political affiliation to attend the school. The court concluded, however, that the candidates and students were affiliated with the Republican Party. Following graduation, students were expected to apply their knowledge and skills in political campaigns.

The school also published a newsletter, reports, and books, and engaged in research. It was funded exclusively by the National Republican Congressional Trust.

## Summary of the Opinion

The court, agreeing with the IRS, concluded that this school was not primarily engaging in activities that accomplish educational purposes because it benefited private interests to more than an insubstantial extent. The court found that the school was operated in a way that substantially benefited the private interests of Republican Party entities and candidates.

Thus, this case involved the private benefit doctrine rather than the private inurement doctrine. The first issue considered by the court was whether the prohibition against private benefit was limited to situations where the benefits accrue to an organization's insiders with respect to it (as is the case with the private inurement rule). The court held that this prohibition is not so limited (that is, not limited to persons having a personal and private interest in the activities of the organization) and embraced benefits to what the court labeled "disinterested persons."[98]

Having thus defined the bounds (or lack thereof) of the private benefit doctrine, the court ruled that the doctrine was transgressed in this case. The court wrote that the school "conducted its educational activities with the partisan objective of benefiting Republican candidates and entities."[99] Elsewhere in the opinion, the court wrote that the school operated to "advance Republican interests."[100]

The court found that a substantial number of the members of the school's admission panel were affiliated with the Republican Party. Also, some of its directors were found to be involved with Republican organizations. Some of its curriculum items and studies were found to unduly focus on the Republican Party.

The court noted that 85 of the school's graduates were placed in the campaigns of 98 Republican Senatorial and House campaigns. The court twice noted that the lawyer for the NRCC was the one who had incorporated the school. Because of all this and other facts noted above, the school was deemed to be "partisan."[101]

The heart of this opinion is the analysis of the concept of *primary* private benefit and *secondary* private benefit. In this setting, the beneficiaries of primary private benefit were the students; the beneficiaries of secondary private benefit were the employers of the students. In the case, it was the secondary private benefit that caused to school to fail to acquire tax exemption.

The court accepted the IRS's argument that "where the training of individuals is focused on furthering a particular targeted private interest, the conferred secondary benefit ceases to be incidental to the providing organization's exempt purposes."[102] The beneficiaries, at the secondary level, were found to be a "select group."[103] The "particular targeted private interest" and the "select group" were, in the court's view, the Republican entities and candidates served by the school's graduates.

The school unsuccessfully used as precedent several IRS revenue rulings holding tax-exempt (under IRC § 501(c)(3)) organizations that provide training to individuals in a particular industry or profession. The court accepted the IRS's characterization of these rulings, which was that the "secondary benefit provided in each ruling was broadly spread among members of an industry . . . , as opposed to being earmarked for a particular organization or person."[104] The court said that the secondary benefit in each of these rulings was, because of the spread, "therefore incidental to the providing organization's exempt purpose."[105]

The school argued in part that the concept of secondary private benefit was inapplicable to it because the secondary beneficiaries were representatives of a charitable class. The school asserted that there was such a class under these facts because the Republican Party is comprised of millions of individuals. The court held, however, that size alone does not transform a benefited class into a charitable class. Thus, the argument that the ultimate beneficiaries of the school were members of the Republican Party, which constitutes a charitable class, failed. Moreover, the court held that, even if political entities and candidates can comprise a charitable class, the school did not prove that its activities benefited the members of the class in a nonselect manner.

## COMMENTARY

This is an unfortunate opinion, with the rationales for its conclusion obviously contrived to justify preconceived ends. The school satisfied all of the exemption criteria in the statute; the private benefit doctrine was all that remained for the court's use. The opinion is suffused with the view that a school for Republican campaign staffers and consultants should not be tax-exempt, on the ground of fear of exemption-sponsored partisanship.

The court, in this opinion, invented the distinction between primary and secondary private benefit—a principle of law that had not been previously invoked and has not been conjured up since. The court also misapplied the concept of a charitable class and distorted the long-standing body of law concerning educational activities.

Throughout this opinion, the school is reproved for not citing authority in support of its positions. Yet the court created the concept of primary and secondary private benefits; there was no authority cited in support of that concoction either (because there is not any).

The school was correct in relying on IRS rulings concerning other training organizations, such as an organization providing training to bank employees in a geographic area[106] and an organization maintaining a law library for members of a bar association.[107] There is far more "private benefit" in those situations than is in the facts of this case.

Private benefit, within the appropriate meaning of that term, was not present in this case. (The doctrine was invoked because that was the only body of law the court could grasp in justification for its conclusions.) Every tax-exempt school confers private benefit—first, on its students, and, second, on those for whom the students subsequently work as employees or consultants. As an illustration, were the court correct, every nonprofit college and university in the nation with a law school would not be entitled to tax exemption because of the private benefit generated by their graduates who become associates in law firms and have their 2,000-plus annual billable hours billed at rates that cause considerable private benefit to flow to the firms' partners. Staying with the legal profession, a college or university law school confers private benefit when it provides courses to lawyers who are motivated to undertake the instruction solely for the purpose of obtaining continuing legal education credits.

The court's finding that the school's training was "focused on furthering a particular targeted private interest" is incompatible with the law as developed (principally by the IRS) to date. There are many tax-exempt schools that have a far smaller base of primary and secondary beneficiaries. Some have a relationship with a specific business entity, where their graduates become employed. Beyond schools, there are other exempt organizations that serve a constituency that is "targeted," including publishing and counseling organizations. In any event, the school in this case has no control over the employment of its graduates.

The introduction of the precept of a *charitable class* in this setting also is wrong, in the sense of being contrary to previous IRS positions. First, the concept of a charitable class is applicable when analyzing the tax status of a putative charitable organization; it is not applicable in cases of educational entities.

Second, the IRS has long held that the training activity is the exempt function of a school, without regard to why the students are taking the training or what they are going to do with their education following graduation. The school in this case was a bona fide school that met all of the criteria for tax exemption (until this case); schools are not required to serve a charitable class.

To properly withhold tax exemption from this school, the court should have expanded on its finding that the school was operated in a partisan manner. The court could have found that the school was intervening in political campaigns and thus that its tax exemption should be denied on that basis. This would have been an incorrect conclusion, but use of the partisanship/political campaign approach would have made more sense than minting the doctrine of secondary private benefit—and the decision would have had less far-reaching consequences.

## GUIDE FOR PLANNERS

The private benefit doctrine is one of the aspects of the law of tax-exempt organizations that torments planners. Certainly, it is an expansive body of law, one that the IRS and the courts continue to push to its unknown boundaries.

Planners may look to other court opinions to ascertain the substance and scope of the private benefit doctrine. This opinion, once the most oft-cited of the private benefit cases, has lost its luster. Inasmuch as the primary private benefit/secondary private benefit dichotomy would nullify the tax-exempt status of every school, college, university, and other types of educational institutions in the United States, planners can safely conclude that it is not, in fact, a contemporary component of exempt organizations law.

## EST OF HAWAII V. COMM'R[108]

CASE STUDY

## INTRODUCTION TO THE CASE

The U.S. Tax Court held that a nonprofit organization could not qualify for tax-exempt status because it was part of a franchise system, controlled by for-profit corporations, and thus was operated for private and commercial purposes.

## SUMMARY OF THE FACTS

"est" is the acronym for Erhard Seminars Training which encompasses the general theory, body of knowledge, and method and techniques used in "est" programs as developed by Werner Erhard. These programs concern the areas of intrapersonal awareness and communication. By the mid-1970s, est was rapidly growing throughout the United States and in other parts of the world.

Activities related to est were conducted by several corporations. Three for-profit corporations entered into an agreement with the sole objective of establishing a system for the presentation of est to the public through the organization of tax-exempt corporations covering different geographical areas throughout the United States.

One of the for-profit corporations had the responsibility of training individuals to present est to the public. It also was charged with providing materials and management services to local exempt organizations and to assume responsibility for the quality of the operations of these organizations. The for-profit corporation employed the trainers.

Another for-profit corporation engaged in the ownership and promotion of literary, artistic, and educational publications, patents, and licenses. It did business throughout the world, except in the United States. It owned and controlled all rights outside the United States to the body of knowledge, publications, processes, methods, and the like pertaining to est. It licensed all of its rights to the third for-profit corporation.

The third corporation engaged in the development, promotion, sale, and licensing of artistic and educational materials and works. It licensed its rights to est to tax-exempt organizations established in all of the states. These organizations made royalty payments to this corporation, which compensated the second corporation, which compensated the first corporation.

This third corporation set the tuition for the training provided by the nonprofit organization involved in this case and required a minimum number of such trainings. It required the organization to conduct regular seminars and to host special events. It provided trainers who were salaried by and responsible to one of the other for-profit corporations.

The nonprofit organization was formed as the first step in the implementation of these agreements. Its objective was to develop and expand the principles and concepts of est. It planned to provide est training and seminars, to promote and sell est publications, engage in est educational work, and generally engage in related educational efforts in Hawaii. Its rights in relation to the for-profit corporations were dependent on the existence of its tax-exempt status.

The organization intended to derive all of its funds from student fees, lecture admissions, and occasional contributions. It did not contemplate a fundraising program. It satisfied the organizational test.

## Summary of the Opinion

The court observed that the IRS claimed that this nonprofit organization was "part of a franchise system which is operated for private benefit and that its affiliation with this system taints it with a substantial commercial purpose."[109] The court agreed with this view.

The third for-profit corporation was said to exert "considerable control" over the nonprofit organization's activities by virtue of the contractual relationship.[110] The organization's "only function" was portrayed as "present[ing] to the public for a fee ideas that are owned by [the third for-profit corporation] with materials and trainers that are supplied and controlled by" another of the for-profit corporations.[111] The court referenced the "possibility, if not likelihood" that the for-profit corporations were "trading on" the organization's prospective tax-exempt status.[112]

The court rejected the proposal that the "critical inquiry" is whether the payments made by the nonprofit entity to the for-profit entity were reasonable.[113] Irrespective of that fact, two of the for-profit corporations were said to have "benefited substantially" from the operation of the nonprofit entity.[114] The third for-profit corporation could license the nonprofit organization for up to 10 years. Copyrighted material had to be transferred to two of the for-profit corporations if the agreement was terminated. The nonprofit entity was required to use its excess funds for the development of est or related educational and scientific research. The court wrote that, to the extent that the nonprofit organization's activities increase interest and participation in est, the "ultimate beneficiaries" were the three for-profit corporations.[115]

Other factors were said to show that the nonprofit organization was operated for a "commercial purpose."[116] Trainers and local organizations were required to sign an agreement not to compete with est for two years after terminating their relationship with est organizations. The nonprofit entity, the court observed, "does not expect to derive funds from donations, as is typical of section 501(c)(3) organizations, but rather will depend upon tuition and lecture fees."[117] Tuition for the training was set by a for-profit corporation. The fees for lectures were set "with regard to the eminence of the speaker."[118]

The court noted that it did not "question the sincerity or dedication" of the non-profit organization's members.[119] But it was the organization's activities that determine its eligibility for tax exemption. "This is not a case where an organization engaged in an admittedly exempt activity and also engages in a non-exempt activity closely associated with, and incidental to, its exempt purposes," the court wrote.[120] Rather, the nonprofit organization's income-producing activities "are not incidental to its educational activities but are the very justification for its existence."[121]

In conclusion, as the court viewed this case, the nonprofit entity "was simply the instrument to subsidize the for-profit corporations and not vice versa and had no life independent of those corporations."[122] Thus, the nonprofit organization was ruled to not be entitled to tax exemption.

## COMMENTARY

This opinion may be viewed as one of the most radical of tax-exempt organization opinions. It certainly is the most actinoid of private benefit cases.

The opinion is placed in the erroneous category because, without more substantial explanation (or a confining of the reach of the opinion to its unique facts), it is not reasonable to hold that an exempt charitable organization that is exclusively engaged in exempt functions and that is paying only fair value fees to a vendor of services is nonetheless engaged in private benefit.

## GUIDE FOR PLANNERS

Despite the above protest, this is exactly the position of the IRS in these fact circumstances.[123] Thus, the planner must be uneasy when facing a situation such as this, inasmuch as showing ample program activities and reasonable terms and circumstances in a transaction with a for-profit organization may not be sufficient.

## HOUSING PIONEERS, INC. V. COMM'R[124]

CASE STUDY

## INTRODUCTION TO THE CASE

A federal court of appeals held that the involvement of a public charity in a limited partnership furthered substantial nonexempt purposes and caused private inurement, thereby precluding the organization from qualifying as a tax-exempt organization.

## SUMMARY OF THE FACTS

This organization was formed to provide affordable housing to low-income and handicapped individuals. It was organized as a charitable entity under federal and state law. Its plan of operation was correlated with a state's property tax exemption.

Where a managing general partner of a partnership holding property used for low-income rental housing is a qualified nonprofit entity, the property is entitled to state tax exemption. Among the qualifications are the requirements that at least 20 percent of the tenants meet certain low-income requirements and that the owner of the property be eligible for and receive low-income housing tax credits pursuant to federal law.[125]

This charitable organization executed an agreement with a property management company, formed as a partnership, to—as the appellate court put it—"participate in a project by which . . . [the company's] property would be exempt from property tax."[126] The company lent the charity $5,000 to purchase a 1 percent interest in the partnership as a general partner. An investment firm was the other general partner, holding a 9 percent interest.

The limited partners consisted of A, the founder of the charity (with 30 percent), B (40 percent), C (5 percent), D (5 percent), and E (10 percent). C and D are brothers of A. B is A's father. E is A's grandfather. The investment company/general partner is owned by A and B. A and B are on the board of directors of the charitable organization, which also consisted of nine individuals who were unrelated to this family and selected for their interest in housing and social services.

The charity's plan was to form low-income housing partnerships, with part of the property tax savings retained by the partnership and used to keep the rents low, with part paid to the charity to be used for other charitable purposes. In the partnership, the first year of savings was to be divided as follows: 40 percent to the investment firm for arranging the transaction and 60 percent to the partnership. In subsequent years, the partnership would retain 50 percent of the savings and the charity would receive cash from the partnership equal to the other 50 percent.

The charity's partnership duties were restricted by the agreement to ensure that the savings were applied in reduction of the rents charged by the partnership and that the properties owned by the partnership complied with the federal low-income housing credit and state tax law requirements.

Subsequently, the charity entered into another partnership agreement similar to the above one, except that these partners did not include anyone from the family of A.

## SUMMARY OF COURT OPINION # I

The case was first decided by the U.S. Tax Court, which concluded that this organization was disqualified from charitable status because its proposed activities included a substantial nonexempt purpose. This nonexempt purpose was said to be the provision of the benefits of the state property tax exemption and the federal low-income housing tax credit to partnerships that are not themselves charitable. The Tax Court also found private inurement. The beneficiaries of this inurement were the family members of A in the first partnership and the limited partners in the second partnership.

The Tax Court wrote that the state "property tax reductions, even though they are to be used exclusively for the purpose of reducing the rents or otherwise maintaining the affordability of the residential units, inure indirectly at least to the benefit of the non-exempt partners in that the partnerships are thereby relieved of the necessity of maintaining rents at a level sufficient to cover operating expenses which would otherwise have to be paid out of partnership capital."[127]

The U.S. Court of Appeals for the Ninth Circuit wrote that the charitable organization "present[ed] an argument that is ultimately unpersuasive but is nonetheless attractive enough to deserve elaboration and powerful enough to require refutation."[128]

The organization's argument was as follows. Federal and state law intend that in the production of low-income housing, there will be collaboration between an exempt entity and for-profit partners. This federal tax policy is reflected in the statutory law.[129] Congress has sought to encourage the development of low-income housing by encouraging nonprofit organizations to join with for-profit entities in providing it. The IRS's interpretation of the requirements for tax exemption[130] would make the tax credit inoperable.

This argument continued by observing that participation by a qualified nonprofit organization will inescapably bestow benefit from the tax credit on the for-profit partners. Once a partnership is formed involving nonprofit and for-profit entities, one purpose—necessarily a substantial one—will be for the nonprofit entity to endeavor to have the partnership succeed. This purposeful endeavor will inescapably generate some private benefit to the private investors.

This argument concluded with the injunction that it is the function of the court to harmonize these two Internal Revenue Code provisions.

While acknowledging that the charitable organization's argument "might well be a successful" one,[131] the appellate court sidestepped a finding directly on the point by concluding that the organization failed to show that it was a *qualified nonprofit organization.*[132] This type of organization must, in addition to owning an interest in the project (including by means of a partnership), "materially participate" in the development and operation of the project." A participation of this nature must be "regular," "continuous," and "substantial."[133] The appellate court found that none of these three criteria were met.

The appellate court also held that despite the requirement of the tax credit rules, there was nothing in the record establishing that the organization was "determined by the State housing credit agency not to be affiliated with or controlled by a for-profit organization."[134]

Thus, because the organization did not prove that it is a qualified nonprofit organization, the appellate court concluded that it had "no reason" to decide the relationship between the two Code provisions.[135] The court then found that the Tax Court's fact-findings in the case were not "clearly erroneous" and upheld that court's judgment.[136]

## COMMENTARY # I

At the outset, the nonprofit organization in this case is to be faulted for launching this litigation without proof in the record that it is a qualified nonprofit organization for purposes of the tax credit. That omission gave the court of appeals an out it seemed to be looking for. This organization probably would have lost on appeal even if this escape passage had not been provided to the court. This is because the lower court and appellate court opinions reflect a complete lack of understanding of the basic law in this area.

This fundamental failure in the analysis can be observed in the very tenor in which the appellate court wrote the fact summary—a portion of a court opinion that is supposed to be objective. The court of appeals wrote that the organization's "plan of operation was keyed to the property tax exemption."[137] It also stated that the organization's "plan was to form partnerships in which the other partners would benefit from the property tax exemption obtained by" the participation of the organization in the partnership.[138] With "objective" statements of "fact" like that, the organization was on its way to defeat before the intricacies of the low-income housing tax credit were parsed.

The Ninth Circuit's opinion is materially defective on two grounds. First, its bias belies the fact that an organization is entitled to structure its governance and operations to achieve tax-exempt status. So what if its "plan of operation was keyed to the [state's] property tax exemption"? There are thousands of nonprofit organizations that are tax-exempt because they deliberately structured themselves to satisfy tax law requirements. The organizational and operational tests dictate as much. This is a fact that should not have been mentioned this way in the opinion; the law is crystal clear that the motive of the founder in setting up a tax-exempt, nonprofit organization is irrelevant (absent fraud or like abuse). The issue of law is whether the organization qualifies for the desired status.

Second—and this is far more egregious—the appellate court opinion is devoid of any analysis of the substantial body of law concerning public charities as partners in limited partnerships. Had this jurisprudence been even superficially explored, the court would have discovered that other federal courts have approved the participation of public charities in partnerships (indeed, this case is the only one to the contrary) and that the IRS has extensive criteria on the point. If this body of law had been properly applied in this case, the outcome would have been substantially different.

Under prevailing court and IRS criteria, the tax exemption of a public charity will not be disturbed merely because it is a general partner in a limited partnership. The first inquiry is whether the organization's exempt purpose is furthered by its participation in the partnership. Here, that test was easily met: the nonprofit organization used a partnership—expressly approved under federal and state law—to further its purposes of providing low-income housing.

Also, the criteria look to see if the public charity is engaged in the day-to-day management of the partnership; if it is, it cannot qualify for tax-exempt status. The appellate court opinion does not address the point, which is understandable in that the opinion failed to review the law in this area in general. The court, however, noted in passing that the charity's partnership duties were curtailed in some respects. This it took to be a factor mitigating against the organization—apparently not realizing that provisions in the partnership agreement limiting charities' involvement in this regard are an IRS requirement. (The litigators for the government elected to not apprise the court of the point.)

Third, the law requires an analysis as to whether the economic return of the limited partners is *undue*—if it is, tax exemption is not available. This is where the Ninth Circuit's approach is the most abominable. Without any discussion, it blandly accepted the Tax Court's finding of private inurement. This occurred without any fact-finding as to whether all of the limited partners in the first partnership were insiders and whether their economic return was reasonable. Even more astonishing, the appellate court found private inurement in relation to the second partnership without any exploration whatsoever as to whether insiders were involved.

What is here is an opinion written by one or more individuals who made no effort to understand the most fundamental points of the law in this area. What happened is all too clear: a judge saw a sophisticated partnership arrangement involving a charitable organization and a bunch of related individuals, and just assumed wrongdoing and private benefit. The nonprofit organization in this case made a fundamental error in resting its argument on the low-income housing rules alone. The larger picture concerning public charities in partnerships should have been presented to the court.

Aside from the part concerning the tax credit, this opinion is a juvenile analysis of this type of fact situation, and the absence of any discussion of the applicable law is telling. Despite the government's arguments, this was not really a private inurement case. If the court was correct on the factual issue as to the requirements for the tax credit, then fine. Otherwise, this facile opinion is one of the worst as to law analysis of a tax-exempt organizations case.

The "law" formulated in this opinion would undo the law on public charities in partnerships that has been built up so assiduously over the years. There is private benefit in every one of these partnerships—it is literally unavoidable—but the courts and the IRS now have finely crafted rules that amply guard against nearly all abuses. It is a shame that these two opinions were written without taking the appropriate law into account.

## SUMMARY OF COURT OPINION # 2

The appellate court amended its opinion, although the additions did not change the basic finding. The court wrote that the case was "governed by a single statute,"[139] namely, the one providing the basis for tax exemption.[140] It also acknowledged, for the first time, the fact that there is case law on the point, citing the seminal decision (which it wrote).[141] The facts underlying this decision, however, were held to be distinguishable, because in the earlier case the "investors were not shareholders nor officers nor directors of the theatre group."[142] In the immediate case, two of the partners in the partnership were also directors of the nonprofit organization that sought recognition of tax exemption.

## COMMENTARY # 2

By amending its opinion without changing the outcome, the Ninth Circuit managed only to dig itself even deeper into its hole of unenlightenment. The second time around, the appellate court wrote that the exemption statute was the operative law. But, in the first version of its opinion, the court ruled entirely on the basis of another provision—the tax credit rules for low-income housing projects. Not only was the second position contrary to the first position, the court ignored two other federal tax provisions that are very much involved because they expressly contemplate public charities in partnerships.[143]

It is good that the Ninth Circuit ultimately recognized the existence and relationship of its earlier court opinion. (It is unfortunate that the court continued to ignore the many IRS rulings on the subject.) The court's attempt, however, to distinguish the case was formulated on a classic distinction without a difference. The IRS policies in this area clearly entail situations in which those who are directors and officers of the public charity are investors in the partnership (namely, limited partners). There are tens of IRS private letter rulings approving this structure.

Both efforts by the Ninth Circuit are devoid of any analysis of the substantial body of law concerning public charities as partners in a limited partnership. A belated, passing reference to an earlier court opinion—albeit one of its own—did not remedy the many deficiencies in this set of opinions from the Ninth Circuit.

## Guide for Planners

Were it not for this case, it could be said that the IRS lost every one of the cases it litigated involving public charities serving as a general partner in a limited partnership. The opinion is deficient, as noted, because it does not reflect the substantial amount of law that has accreted in this area.

The planner cannot disregard this opinion, however, if only because it was recently cited in a pronouncement from the IRS.[144] All the planner can do is be aware and wary of this case, and focus on the other court opinions and IRS rulings in this area.

## Quality Auditing Co. v. Comm'r [145]

CASE STUDY

### Introduction to the Case

The U.S. Tax Court held that a nonprofit organization that audits structural steel fabricators in conjunction with a quality certification program conducted by a related trade association does not constitute a charitable organization that lessens the burdens of government, and yields private benefit to the association and to the fabricators who are inspected. This is the first case in which the private benefit doctrine was applied with respect to a benefit conferred on a tax-exempt, noncharitable organization.

### Summary of the Facts

Developments and concerns within the structural steel fabrication industry, and particularly the response to them by the American Institute of Steel Construction, Inc. (AISC), led to the formation of Quality Auditing Company (QAC). QAC was organized as a nonprofit charitable and educational entity. AISC, a tax-exempt business league, has been engaged primarily in the creation of standardized engineering codes and specifications for use in the fabrication and construction of steel-framed buildings and bridges.

During the 1960s, a number of governmental agencies and private industrial owners and developers approached AISC and requested that it develop a certification program for structural steel fabricators. Technological advances had increased both the predominance and the complexity of steel's role in commercial and residential structures; a growing concern over potential differences in quality had arisen among entities attempting to select contractors for this component of a building project. Yet few owners and developers had sufficient expertise, time, or funds to adequately investigate the fabricators submitting project bids. AISC undertook to create a program that would afford the requested quality assurances.

Working in collaboration with engineers, architects, contractors, and other industry participants (including government agencies), AISC developed and trademarked the AISC Quality Certification Program. The Program incorporates codes, standards, and specifications for particular aspects of the fabricating process. It is designed to verify that fabricators have in place a quality control system that will ensure compliance with construction standards and contract requirements. Ongoing revision and upgrading of the Program track changes and advancements within the industry.

Fabricators desiring certification, often because the owner or developer of a project conditioned bid awards on that requirement, submit an application and appropriate fee to AISC. The fees are determined in accordance with a schedule set by AISC and are based on the fabricator's status as a member or nonmember of AISC, the type of certification being sought, and the number of employees at the facility. The Program is open to all fabricators, regardless of AISC membership.

AISC then contracts with and pays for an independent entity to perform the actual audit investigation of the fabricator's facility. The auditor evaluates the fabricator's quality control procedures to determine whether the procedures adequately test for and ensure compliance with the industry specifications incorporated in the Program. No particular structure, project, or product is certified; the construction process itself is examined.

Following the audit, the auditor communicates the findings to the fabricator and recommends to AISC whether certification should be awarded. Upon receipt of a positive recommendation from the auditor, AISC forwards to the fabricator documentation reflecting AISC-certified status. If the auditor does not believe certification is warranted, the fabricator may choose to be reevaluated after corrective actions have been implemented. The specific report pertaining to a particular audit is not disseminated to the public, although AISC publishes the names of the certified companies.

In administering the Program, AISC initially contracted with a for-profit company to conduct the facility audits. This approach was not successful, however, in that (in the words of the court) a "profit-driven enterprise was unwilling to reinvest a sufficient portion of the fees charged to achieve the level of auditor training and audit consistency necessary for a uniform, reliable certification program."[146]

Consequently, AISC provided the start-up capital to establish QAC as a nonprofit corporation. QAC's purpose is to conduct quality certification and inspection programs that meet the requirements of private and public standards-setting bodies and governmental agencies. No other organization presently provides this service. The boards of directors of AISC and QAC are overlapping.

QAC hires and trains independent contractors to inspect and audit the facilities of fabricators applying to AISC for certification. It pays royalties to AISC for use of its trademarked certification program. QAC's income is derived solely from the fees charged AISC for conducting the quality audits. Fees are set at a level that approximates actual costs.

The AISC certification program is increasingly becoming recognized as furthering structural integrity and quality within the steel fabrication industry. Numerous private and public owners, developers, and contractors (including the Army Corps of Engineers and as many as 40 state highway departments) require AISC certification for bridges and other metal work. To promote the Program, AISC solicits owners and developers to require certification of fabricators submitting bids.

The IRS ruled that AISC was not entitled to recognition of tax-exempt status as a charitable entity.

## Summary of the Opinion

QAC asserted that its purpose and activities are charitable in that quality auditing of steel fabrication firms lessens the burdens of government and encourages the safe construction of buildings and bridges for the benefit of the general public. The IRS's view was that QAC's inspection activity does not lessen the burdens of any government and does not confer upon the public any benefit that is not merely incidental to QAC's furthering of the private interests of AISC and firms within the steel industry.

*Lessening the burdens of government* is one way for a nonprofit organization to be charitable for federal income tax exemption purposes. Generally, however, two criteria must be satisfied. One is that the activities engaged in by the organization must be those that a governmental unit considers to be its burden. The other is that the organization's performance of the activities must actually lessen the burdens of a government.

QAC failed the first of these tests. The court observed that there is no indication in the record that governmental units consider it their burden to inspect or certify the quality control procedures in place in the facilities of private fabricators. It was noted that governmental agencies were among those who initially requested that AISC develop a certification program and who have since made use of the Program in awarding bids. But, wrote the court, these facts "fall short of demonstrating that governmental units view a program for auditing steel fabricators as a Government responsibility and recognize [QAC] as acting on their behalf."[147]

The court added that to the extent QAC facilitates government in selecting qualified fabricators, an equivalent benefit is conferred on private owners and developers. Private entities joined with public ones in requesting the AISC program and likewise utilize the Program in awarding bids. The court concluded that if QAC is operated to lessen the burdens of government, it also operates to lessen the burdens on private parties.

The court wrote that "furthering public safety is indeed a charitable objective."[148] It agreed that the certification program and QAC's audit activities promote increased structural integrity and safety in steel buildings and bridges. Nonetheless, it concluded that QAC's activities also further private interests to a degree that is more than insubstantial.

The court reiterated that QAC performs quality audits at the request of AISC, which in turn acts at the request of steel fabricators applying for certification. The association and the fabricators are not, however, *public* entities.

It was written that the "development and administration of a quality certification program, at the request of and for the structural steel industry, would appear to be consistent with AISC's mission" as a business league.[149] The court added that the "focus thus seems to be on aiding industry participants, with any benefit to the general public being merely secondary."[150]

The court thus saw more than insubstantial private benefit in two contexts. One was the extent to which QAC serves AISC's interests in carrying out its role of industry betterment. QAC's efforts prevent problems in the industry that could flow from hiring fabricators with inadequate quality control, such as increased nonconformities, delays, project cost overruns, reduced structure longevity, and frequent repair expenditures. The court noted that safety is never mentioned in the solicitations of owners and developers.

The other type of private benefit is that accruing to the steel fabricators who request audits and whose facilities are inspected by QAC. These are commercial entities, and the court was "constrained to assume" that they largely apply for certification when to do so furthers their primary objective of making a profit.[151] The fabricators "likely wish to pursue revenues from a contract requiring certification, or they see the certification process as a vehicle to increased work through an improved control process and reputation for quality."[152]

Both types of private benefit were found to be *substantial,* notwithstanding some "benefit reaped by the general public."[153]

### COMMENTARY

This is a case amplifying and illuminating a body of law that is emerging as a major component of the law of tax-exempt organizations: the *private benefit doctrine.* This opinion illustrates the basic points that, unlike the *private inurement rule* (or the *intermediate sanctions rules*), there is no requirement that a party who privately benefits be an *insider,* and the law tolerates an *insubstantial* amount of private benefit.

This case also illustrates the perils of placing certification programs in charitable (IRC § 501(c)(3)) organizations. (This is true irrespective of whether the certification is of individuals or programs. Certification of organizations is termed *accreditation*; that usually is an exempt function.) The law is that although there is some public benefit to be gained from certification, the primary beneficiaries are those who are certified.[154]

From a larger perspective, the case further serves as a reminder that charitable organizations (often termed *foundations*) affiliated with associations (IRC § 501(c)(6) ones) need to be careful. The association and its members usually are *private* parties. Unwarranted programmatic relationships between the two entities can lead to denial or revocation of tax exemption for the related charitable foundation. (The association alone is likely to be an *insider* and/or *disqualified person* as well.)

Then there is this matter of definition of the term *charitable* for federal tax purposes. This is a concept that the courts are free to embellish. The Internal Revenue Code provides that *testing for public safety* is a charitable purpose—in the tax exemption setting (but not the charitable deduction setting). The Tax Court expanded the scope of the exemption somewhat by proclaiming that *furthering public safety* is a charitable objective.

### GUIDE FOR PLANNERS

Planners should be deeply concerned with (indeed, troubled by) this opinion. Like the Tax Court's opinion in the charitable gift substantiation case,[155] this one fails the test of real-world application. Once again, the inflexibility of the court is troublesome.[156]

Association-related foundations are commonplace. They reflect the dynamics of a marvelous technique known as *bifurcation:* the housing of functions in two entities rather than one, usually for tax-planning reasons. With these foundations, the charitable, educational, scientific, and like programs of associations can be funded with charitable contributions and grants.

Congress has expressly endorsed this type of in-tandem operating relationship involving tax-exempt organizations. The supporting organization rules permit an exempt business league (like AISC) to utilize a related charitable organization (like QAC).[157] (The court opinion failed to acknowledge even the existence, let alone applicability, of this law.)

The planner must be ever cautious in this setting, always fearful that the related charitable organization (supporting organization or not) will be seen as—because of its program and/or fundraising activities—throwing off private benefit to its parent exempt organization. Most of these activities do not amount to private benefit at all or, if the benefit exists, it is incidental.

It is unfortunate, for the tax-exempt organizations community in general and planners in particular, that this opinion has raised the specter of one exempt organization's conferring private benefit on another exempt organization. The situation worsens when the fact that the IRS agrees with this extension of the law[158] is taken into consideration.[159]

## SALVATION NAVY, INC. v. COMM'R[160]

CASE STUDY

### INTRODUCTION TO THE CASE

The U.S. Tax Court ruled that an organization cannot qualify for tax-exempt status as a charitable or educational entity because of violation of the *operational test*, in that the organization's activities and those of its founder, sole director, and officer were essentially identical.

### SUMMARY OF THE FACTS

The organization was created by an individual who previously engaged in charitable activities as a volunteer. The application for recognition of tax exemption stated that the purpose of the organization was to do "good deeds." The application contained documents referencing the founder's charitable activities; it was clear that the organization would be engaging in the same activities. The application also stated that the organization wanted a determination letter from the IRS so it could obtain a grant to procure a computer, printer, and software. The founder was the only funder of the entity; it did not have a fundraising program.

### SUMMARY OF THE OPINION

The court concluded that the organization was being operated for the benefit of a private individual—the founder. According to the court, the affairs of the organization and of this individual were "irretrievably intertwined," so that the "benefits" of tax exemption would "inure" to him.[161] The court concluded that exemption was not available for an "individual engaged in various activities, charitable or otherwise."[162]

## COMMENTARY

This is still another one of the Tax Court's opinions that were written without regard to their applicability and repercussions in the real world. Many charitable organizations engage in activities that their founders would otherwise or did undertake personally.[163] The structure and operation of the organization in this case is much like that of a private foundation.

It is clear that the organizational documents and application for recognition of exemption were inartful. Still, the court should have done more to distinguish this "alter ego" case from other similar situations. This is indeed a strange interpretation of the organizational test. The shortness and anticipated obscurity of this opinion does not belie its large, albeit incorrect, present import.

## GUIDE FOR PLANNERS

In a sense, planners need not worry too much about this opinion; the case is an anomaly and is destined to not likely be cited often (if at all).

Yet, this case teaches planners a lesson: in the application for recognition of exemption's statement of activities, the wording should be "institutionalized." That is, reference to "my" or "our" programs is to be avoided; the appropriate phraseology is the "programs of the organization." Even if the applicant entity will be engaging in programs that one or more founders have or otherwise would have undertaken, there is no need to get into that; the question is concerned with the "organization's activities" and not those of others or those that might be engaged in by some other person if the organization did not exist. Indeed, this caseneed not have come into being. Slightly more artful wording of the answer would have prevented it.

The Tax Court must have known this. Nonetheless, while courts generally are supposed to confine their attention to the facts of the cases before them, on occasion it would help if courts would make an effort to explain what they are *not* holding.

## STANBURY LAW FIRM, P.A. v. INTERNAL REVENUE SERVICE[164]

CASE STUDY

### INTRODUCTION TO THE CASE

The U.S. Court of Appeals for the Eighth Circuit held that a district court properly dismissed a lawsuit seeking disclosure of the annual information return of a public charity containing donor information, undertaken to ferret out potential conflicts of interest, but in doing so misconstrued the federal tax law as to the classification of charities as public and private.

## SUMMARY OF THE FACTS

A lawyer established a public charity, with the goal of promoting opportunities for minority education. Although he made some initial contributions to it, the charity was primarily funded by contributions from many of the largest, most prominent businesses and law firms in a particular state. Subsequent to creation of the charity, its founder was elected to the state's supreme court.

During its first eight years, the charity voluntarily filed a copy of its annual information return (Form 990) with the state's attorney general's office. By so doing, the charity made the information in the returns available for public inspection. This disclosure included the identities of the contributors and the amounts given. Thereafter, the charity ceased this practice, so as to keep the names of its supporters from public view.

A law firm was concerned that frequent appearances by many contributors to this charity before the state supreme court could result in conflicts of interest and violations of legal ethics. The law firm asked the charity to voluntarily disclose its list of donors, but the charity failed to respond to that request.

The firm then filed a Freedom of Information Act request with the IRS, seeking the information return that the charity refused to divulge. The IRS did not respond; the law firm filed a lawsuit. A district court dismissed the suit, noting that the tax law[165] precludes the IRS from releasing the information being sought.

The firm, on appeal, however, countered with the assertion that another body of tax law[166] applied, which enabled the disclosure of contributors to private foundations. The language of the IRC provision, the firm asserted, permits disclosure of the documents requested.

## SUMMARY OF THE OPINION

The Eighth Circuit found its way to the correct conclusion, although in doing so misstated the law. The appellate court wrote that a "tax-exempt organization is not automatically classified as a private foundation."[167] The court added: "Indeed, if a § 501(c)(3) organization does not meet the distinct requirements provided by § 509(a), the organization is treated as a public charity."[168]

In fact, the process works just the opposite. The law provides the ways for a charity to be a public charity, that is, a charity that is not a private foundation.[169] A charity is "automatically classified" as a private foundation, in the sense that it is presumed to be one.[170] That presumption can be rebutted by a showing that the entity qualifies as a form of public charity. Thus, the law is that to be a public charity, the organization must meet the "distinct requirements" for public charity status. Thus, the default is to private foundation status, not public charity status.

The appellate court wrote that from the charity's inception, the IRS determined that it "failed to meet the criteria established for private foundations and therefore classified it as a public charity."[171] This casting of the law makes it sound like private foundation status is preferable to public charity status, which rarely is the case, and that public charity status is the default classification. Instead, what happened was that the charity was able to rebut the presumption as to private foundation status, enabling the IRS to categorize it as a public charity.

Nonetheless, the Eighth Circuit was correct in concluding that the charity is a public one, so that the names of its donors and amounts of the contributions need not be disclosed.

Then, however, the law firm made a remarkable argument: the district court should have reclassified the charity as a private foundation! Once again, the appellate court found its way to the correct result, while distorting the law. The Eighth Circuit ruled that the district court lacked the jurisdiction to reclassify the charity. This is true, in that the charity met the criteria for a public charity, thus precluding a court from characterizing it as a private foundation.

The rationale used by the Eighth Circuit, however, was that "reclassification would require the [district] court to effectively issue a declaratory judgment."[172] The appellate court noted that charitable organizations can pursue a declaratory judgment "with respect to their own tax-exempt status."[173] The court then wrote that "all other actions seeking declaratory judgments with respect to federal taxes appear to be barred by the Declaratory Judgment Act."[174] This is incorrect; the exempt organizations declaratory judgment procedure also allows charities to litigate as to their public charity status.[175]

In any event, the charity was a public charity and thus did not have to disclose its donors. The district court appropriately dismissed the case; this dismissal was affirmed by the court of appeals.

## Commentary

Although this opinion is amusing to read, it is sad to see a federal court of appeals so thoroughly botch an understanding and application of the law about which it is writing.

## Guide for Planners

There is not much that planners can do to help bring about a correct and well-written court opinion—other than to make cogent arguments and write crisp, accurate briefs.

There are several aspects of the law of tax-exempt organizations that are, to some, enigmatic, perhaps counterintuitive. The law as to public charities and private foundations may constitute one of those arcane areas. The planner should not assume that the court is, in advance of the unfolding of a particular case, intimately familiar with the underlying law.[176] That law may have to be carefully spelled out for the court.

Moreover, it will not do to make disingenuous arguments, toying with these underlying legal principles. Usually, this will not succeed, with the court spotting the ploy, observing something along this line: the reasoning is "more creative than persuasive."[177] Occasionally, however, as this opinion attests, the court just might adopt one or more of these types of arguments, to the chagrin of many.

# Other Difficult Court Opinions

What follows is an inventory of court opinions comprising part of the law of tax-exempt organizations that, while it cannot be said were wrongly decided, are difficult to apply, in whole or in part, in a real-world context. These opinions are in alphabetical order.

## AIRLIE FOUNDATION v. UNITED STATES[178]

CASE STUDY

### INTRODUCTION TO THE CASE

In a dramatic application (resurrection?) of the commerciality doctrine, a court ruled that an organization operating a conference center cannot be tax-exempt as a charitable or educational organization because of a distinctively commercial hue associated with its operations.

### SUMMARY OF THE FACTS

The organization is a nonprofit corporation formed in 1960 and recognized by the IRS as a tax-exempt charitable and educational organization in 1963. Its multiple purposes include the operation of a conference center for educational organizations, and the sponsoring and assisting of other organizations in holding meetings, seminars, and conferences.

The organization fulfills its mission principally by organizing, hosting, conducting, and sponsoring educational conferences at its facilities. It has played a role in the development of programs in fields such as civil and human rights, international relations, public policy, the environment, medical education, mental health, and disability. The organization sponsors events such as lectures, concerts, and art shows without charge, and provides meeting space for nonprofit organizations, overnight accommodations for participants in its cultural programs, and public use of its grounds for large-scale charitable events.

On average, the organization annually hosts about 600 groups. It derives approximately 85 percent of its operating revenue from fees (paid by what the court characterized as "clients") and about 8 percent of its revenue from its endowment. An average of 20 percent of the organization's conference events are for governmental agencies, 50 percent from "nonprofit and/or educational" organizations, and 30 to 40 percent from others. At most, 10 percent of the organization's "clients" use its facility for private events, and another 10 percent at most represent private commercial clients "pursuing their private interests."

Industry data indicates that the organization's average daily rate was almost 20 percent lower than the average rates for nearby conference centers. The expected operating pretax profit margin for a commercial conference center should be about 20 percent of gross revenues; the organization's actual operations during the years reviewed reflected a pretax profit margin of 4 percent, after the exclusion of grants, investment income, and unusual items.

In 1999, there were 651 "events." The organization fully subsidized 4.75 percent of these events and partially subsidized another 12.5 percent. Subsidies varied depending on the "patrons" but included "discounts" of 10, nearly 50, and 80 percent.

In 1988, the IRS revoked the tax-exempt status of this organization, retroactive to 1976. The agency's assertions were that private inurement was taking place, to the benefit of the organization's founder and his family, and that the conference center was being operated in a commercial manner. This court in 1993 upheld the revocation of exemption, basing it solely on the private inurement argument (see the July 1993 issue).

The organization reapplied to the IRS in 1999 for recognition as a tax-exempt charitable and educational organization. The agency denied this recognition in 2003, having concluded, once again, that the conference center was being operated for a commercial purpose.

The organization asserted that its present conference activities are undertaken principally in advancement of its charitable and educational purposes. Contending that its conference activities differ substantially from those of commercial conference centers, the organization offered:

- Its conference fees are comparable to, and in some instances lower than, those of other nonprofit conference centers and are substantially lower than those of commercial conference centers.

- It engages in "very little" advertising, and its "limited promotional activities" using the Internet are "less commercial" than those of other tax-exempt conference centers.

- It has not unreasonably accumulated reserves.

The IRS nonetheless asserted that this operation of a conference center reflects a "commercial hue."

## SUMMARY OF THE LAW

The court observed that, in applying the operational test, "courts have relied on what has come to be termed the 'commerciality' doctrine." In "many instances," it wrote, courts have found that, due to the commercial nature in which an organization conducts its activities, the entity is operated for "nonexempt commercial purposes" rather than for exempt purposes.

The court stated that among the "major factors" courts have considered in "assessing commerciality" are competition with for-profit entities, extent and degree of low-cost services provided, pricing policies, and reasonableness of financial reserves. Additional factors were said to include whether the organization uses "commercial promotional methods (e.g., advertising)" and the extent to which the organization receives charitable contributions.

## SUMMARY OF THE OPINION

The court observed that the organization in this case "engages in conduct of both a commercial and exempt nature." It thus concluded that the organization's entitlement to tax-exempt status "turns largely" on the *primary purpose test*. Using that test, the court found undue commerciality.

The organization was cast as an "intermediary" and was said to "not directly benefit the public." Its conference patrons were not limited to tax-exempt organizations. The conference center was found to be in competition with commercial organizations because of income derived from weddings and "special events." The organization was portrayed as maintaining a "commercial website" and paying "significant advertising and promotional expenses."

Although the organization was found to be operating "in important respects" in an "exempt fashion," the court nonetheless detected a "distinctive 'commercial hue' to the way [the organization] carries out its business."

## COMMENTARY

It is difficult to believe that a court opinion of this nature can appear in modern times. A development such as this was hard enough to grasp more than 10 years ago,[179] but to have this happen in the early going of the twenty-first century is stunning. How many tax exemptions would fall if the law is as it is articulated in this opinion?

Much lies in perceptions here: the organization had to know it lost when the court referred to those using the conference center as "clients" and "patrons" and to the organization's program activities as "events." The organization was chastised for maintaining a "commercial website," whatever that is, without any discussion of what may be a "tax-exempt website." It was penalized for paying advertising and promotional expenses, a common practice of thousands of exempt organizations (colleges, universities, healthcare providers, to name just a few).

There is no discussion in the opinion of relevant statutory law, which clearly contemplates wholly fee-based charitable and educational organizations.[180] Once again (this is so tiring), the absence of charitable contributions was noted (they are not required for exemption). The court largely ignored the arguments advanced by the organization.

The court could have concluded that activities such as weddings and like events were unrelated businesses and allowed overall tax exemption. (The court did not even acknowledge this possibility.) This matter of *competition* with for-profit entities is getting out of hand; there are thousands of exempt organizations that engage in such competitive activities.

Reading this opinion, one is led to believe that a tax-exempt charitable and educational organization cannot compete with for-profit organizations, cannot advertise (except perhaps incidentally), cannot maintain reserves, cannot earn an excess of revenue over expenses, and cannot maintain a web site. This is not the law.[181]

## GUIDE FOR PLANNERS

This opinion illustrates that the commerciality doctrine remains a potent force in the law of tax-exempt organizations and that the elements of the doctrine articulated in the principal court opinion on the subject[182] continue to be the factors utilized in subsequent court opinions in applying the doctrine. This doctrine is guaranteed to provide ample opportunity for headaches for planners in the years to come

## ANCLOTE PSYCHIATRIC CENTER, INC. V. COMM'R[183]

CASE STUDY

## INTRODUCTION TO THE CASE

A court concluded that the sale of the assets of a tax-exempt hospital to an entity controlled by insiders of the hospital resulted in private inurement because the assets were sold in a transaction that was not at arm's-length, thus causing the assets to be sold for less than their fair market value.

## SUMMARY OF THE FACTS

This nonprofit psychiatric hospital was recognized as a tax-exempt organization in 1958. By 1980, the board of directors of the hospital was looking for ways to generate funds to expand the institution and to otherwise support its educational and research goals.

In 1981, the hospital hired a tax lawyer to advise it as to conversion to a for-profit entity. The lawyer realized that the board did not want to relinquish control of the hospital and that the organization needed access to the hospital to conduct research. These factors precluded sale of the institution to outsiders. Therefore, a plan was devised to sell the hospital to a for-profit corporation controlled by the board members of the exempt organization.

An appraiser determined, using the asset-based approach, that the fair market value of the hospital in 1981 was between $3.5 and $4.3 million. The IRS issued a private letter ruling in 1982, holding that the sale would be on an arm's-length basis and thus would not jeopardize the organization's tax-exempt status. The sale closed, effective May 1983, with a purchase price of $6.3 million, consisting of $4.3 million in cash and notes, and $1.8 million in assumed liabilities. The lawyer who designed the transaction represented the for-profit corporation in the deal, and another lawyer represented the nonprofit organization; the deal was a negotiated one. Because of confusion over the funding of pension plans, the purchase price was in fact $6.6 million.

The hospital expanded over the ensuing months and obtained a certificate of need for additional beds. The operating assets were sold in 1985 to a large health-care provider, for $29.6 million. In 1990, the hospital was sold for $4.3 million.

## SUMMARY OF THE LAW

A tax-exempt charitable organization may not allow its net earnings to inure to the benefit of persons having a personal and private interest in the activities of the organization. These persons are known as *insiders,* and the doctrine is that of proscribing *private inurement.* Private inurement can arise where the organization's assets are sold to insiders at a price representing less than fair market value.

## SUMMARY OF THE OPINION

This opinion opened with the court stating that the issue of revocation "turns on the question [of] whether petitioner's sale of its hospital in May 1983 was for less than fair market value."[184] Later, the court wrote that "fair market value plays an important role but is not determinative herein."[185]

The court found that the lawyers who negotiated this sale, "as far as the legal as distinguished from the financial aspects of the sale were concerned, acted independently and in good faith and sought to protect the interests" of their clients.[186] The court continued, however, to observe that "there are serious questions as to the extent to which the negotiations adequately took into account certain financial aspects of the transaction which may cause the negotiations and the resulting sale price to be categorized as not being at arm's length and therefore giving rise to inurement."[187]

The court noted an array of elements that were either not taken into account or inadequately taken into account in arriving at the price, including various changes in the values of assets between 1981 and 1983, valuations of adjacent properties that were transferred as part of the deal, the value of the certificate of need, the impact of changes in Medicare reimbursement policy, and the sales of the hospital in 1985 and 1990. Factoring in these elements, the court concluded that the fair market value of the assets transferred was $7.8 million.

The court was not unmindful of the subsequent sales, particularly the one in 1985. Summarizing the law on this point, the court wrote that "evidence as to [a] latter category of events may be admitted because of its potential relevance even though it may ultimately be determined that such evidence does not have an impact on the determination of fair market value."[188] As to this case, the court cryptically wrote that "other evidence could provide a basis for concluding that the elements which impacted the 1985 sale may have been sufficiently known or anticipated at the time of the 1983 sale."[189]

The difference of about $1.2 million in the value of the sales price was found to be "substantial."[190] The value of $7.8 million was found to "fall outside the upper limit of any reasonable range of fair market values."[191]

The negotiations between the lawyers were found to be "fatally flawed because of their apparent failure to take into account the obvious and substantial" increases in asset values in 1981 through 1983.[192]

The court rejected reliance on the independent appraisal in that, by the time of closing, it was more than 18 months old.

## COMMENTARY

This is an important court opinion in the law of tax-exempt organizations. It presaged the first of the intermediate sanctions cases;[193] other cases of this genre may be expected to emerge.

What this and like cases entail is the sale of assets by exempt organizations to directors or other insiders. There is nothing inherently wrong with this practice; such transactions are to be tested against the standard of reasonableness.

Generally, nothing unusual develops from a law standpoint as the result of this type of transaction. By contrast, on occasion, something happens to cause an adverse outcome from the exempt organization's standpoint. Sometimes a court is simply overwhelmed by the complexity of the facts of the case and proceeds to an erroneous decision.[194] Usually, in these few exceptional cases, however, the trouble starts because of a straightforward and unavoidable reason: the facts are reviewed on the basis of hindsight.

## GUIDE FOR PLANNERS

There are lessons to be learned from this opinion. One is obvious: parties to these types of transactions should not rely on stale appraisals. Another lesson is that a favorable ruling from the IRS is not necessarily protection; these cases are, as noted, viewed in hindsight, perhaps many years later.

A third lesson (if the court was correct) is that lawyers or others negotiating this type of a transaction may not blindly rely on a current appraisal but must (somehow) independently assure themselves that all relevant items are properly valued. It is odd that the court did not chide the appraiser in the slightest for failing to take certain elements into account in determining value—instead, the court faulted the lawyers. Indeed, the court scolded the hospital's officers and directors for not considering the value of an asset that was excluded from consideration by the appraiser.[195]

A fourth lesson—perhaps the most terrifying one—is that the IRS and the courts can take into account events and actions that occur subsequent to the transaction. The parties, too, are supposed to peer into the future and take into account, in determining value, events that have yet to occur. If the court is correct (and, as a practical matter, it cannot be), it is not enough to value items that are *known*—consideration must also be accorded matters that may be *anticipated*.

## BRANCH MINISTRIES V. ROSSOTTI[196]                    CASE STUDY

### INTRODUCTION TO THE CASE

A federal court of appeals upheld the revocation by the IRS of the tax-exempt status of a church that participated and intervened in a political campaign in opposition to a candidate for public office.

### SUMMARY OF THE FACTS

Four days before the 1992 presidential election, Branch Ministries, a tax-exempt church, placed full-page advertisements in two nationally circulated newspapers in which it urged Christians not to vote for the then presidential candidate William J. Clinton because of his position on certain social and moral issues.

The advertisements proclaimed: "Christians Beware. Do not put the economy ahead of the Ten Commandments." They contained the assertions that Clinton supported abortion on demand, homosexuality, and the distribution of condoms to teenagers in public schools. The text also stated: "Bill Clinton is promoting policies that are in rebellion to God's laws." And: "How then can we vote for Bill Clinton?" The advertisements stated that they were sponsored by the Church and others, and solicited charitable contributions.

Soon after the election, the IRS engaged in a church tax inquiry. The notice stated that the "general subject matter of the inquiry concerns political expenditures which you may have paid or incurred." One month later, the Church responded, taking the position that the advertisements were not participation in a political campaign but instead constituted a "warning to members of the Body of Christ." The IRS eventually revoked the exemption of the Church because of its involvement in politics.

Although it was not required to do so, the Church had applied to the IRS for and received recognition of tax-exempt status.

### SUMMARY OF THE LAW

A church and any other type of a tax-exempt charitable organization is precluded from participating or intervening (including publishing or distributing of statements) in any political campaign on behalf of or in opposition to any candidate for public office.

The IRS has the authority to revoke the tax exemption of a church.[197]

There is a strong presumption that the IRS is properly discharging its official duties when it makes prosecutorial decisions. To prevail on a selective prosecution claim, the party must clearly establish that the prosecutorial decision had a discriminatory effect and that it was motivated by a discriminatory purpose or intent. A showing of *discriminatory effect* in this context requires the party to demonstrate that similarly situated persons of other religions or political beliefs have not been prosecuted. *Discriminatory purpose* may be established either with direct evidence of intent or with evidence concerning the unequal application of the law, statistical disparities, and other indirect evidence of intent.

## ANALYSIS

In defending against this revocation, the Church mustered three arguments that were considered—and rejected—by the appellate court.

### IRS Authority

The Church asserted that the IRS lacks the statutory authority to revoke the tax-exempt status of a bona fide church. The reasoning underlying this position was:

- The Internal Revenue Code exemption provision refers to tax-exempt status for *religious* organizations; it does not mention *churches*.

- The law that exempts certain organizations from the requirement of having to apply for recognition of tax-exempt status[198] specifically exempts *churches*.

- Therefore, the tax-exempt status of the Church is not derived from the exemption provision but is implied from the lack of any section in the Code for the taxation of churches.

- Consequently, the IRS is powerless to apply any of the rules in the exemption provision to the Church (including the prohibition on political campaign activities) and to revoke the Church's tax-exempt status.

This line of reasoning met with the response of the appellate court that it is "more creative than persuasive."[199] The court observed that, obviously, every church is a religious organization—it is an IRC § 501(c)(3) entity. The authority of the IRS to revoke the exemption of a church is reflected in the church tax examination rules. Thus, the court was amply satisfied that the IRS had the statutory authority to revoke the tax exemption of the Church.

As to the Church's exempt status, the court also noted that the Church sought and received a determination letter from the IRS that it is an IRC § 501(c)(3) entity. Thus, the court held that the IRS had the authority to revoke the ruling that it issued.

### Freedom of Religious Rights

The Church claimed that the revocation of its tax exemption violated its right to freely exercise its religion under the First Amendment to the U.S. Constitution and the Religious Freedom Restoration Act. For that contention to be sustained, the Church initially had to establish that its free exercise right was substantially burdened. The court held that the Church failed to satisfy this test.

The Church asserted that a revocation of exemption would threaten its existence. It maintained that a loss of its tax-exempt status would make its members reluctant to make charitable gifts to it, which contributions were necessary to its survival, and would obligate it to pay taxes. Yet the case law shows that these financial burdens do not meet the substantiality test.

Also, the appellate court observed that the impact of the Church's revocation of exempt status is "likely to be more symbolic than substantial."[200] Inasmuch as churches do not have to apply for recognition of exemption, the Church may hold itself out as an exempt organization—as long as it does not intervene in political campaigns. Contributions would not be taxable in any event, since gifts are not income. Moreover, the Church can reapply for a determination as to its tax-exempt status.

The Church argued that it is substantially burdened because it has no alternative means by which to communicate its sentiments about candidates for public office. The court, however, stated that the Church has the option of creating a related advocacy organization[201] that in turn can establish a political action committee.[202] It observed that the advocacy entity should be incorporated and should maintain records demonstrating that contributions to the Church are not being used to support political campaign activities.

The Church also failed in its claim that the IRS had violated the Church's free speech rights by engaging in viewpoint discrimination. The appellate court wrote that the restrictions imposed by IRC § 501(c)(3) are "viewpoint neutral": "they prohibit intervention in favor of [or in opposition to] all candidates for public office by all [charitable] tax-exempt organizations, regardless of candidate, party, or viewpoint."[203]

### Selective Prosecution

The Church asserted that the IRS engaged in selective prosecution and, in so doing, violated the Church's equal protection rights. In support of this claim, the Church submitted hundreds of pages of copies of newspaper articles reporting political campaign activities in, or by the pastors of, other churches that have not had their exemption revoked. Examples included reports of explicit endorsements of Democratic candidates by members of the clergy and many instances in which favored candidates were invited to address congregations from the pulpit. The Church complained that despite this widespread and widely reported involvement by other churches in political campaigns, it has been the only one to have had its tax-exempt status revoked for engaging in political campaign activity. The Church attributed this alleged discrimination to the political bias of the IRS.

The appellate court stated that to establish selective prosecution, the Church had to prove that it was singled out for prosecution from among others similarly situated and that the prosecution was improperly motivated, being based on some arbitrary classification. This burden is "demanding," the court wrote, because the law presumes that government prosecutors have properly discharged their official duties.[204]

During oral argument, the lawyers for the IRS conceded that if some of the church-sponsored political activities cited by the Church were accurately reported, the churches involved could have lost their tax exemption. The appellate court, however, ruled that the Church failed to establish selective prosecution because it failed to demonstrate that it was "similarly situated" to any of these other churches.[205] Wrote the court: "None of the reported activities involved the placement of advertisements in newspapers with nationwide circulations opposing a candidate and soliciting tax deductible contributions to defray their cost."[206]

Because the Church failed to establish that it was singled out for prosecution from among others who were similarly situated, the court did not examine whether the IRS was improperly motivated in undertaking the prosecution.

## COMMENTARY

The trial and appellate court opinions are unsettling. There can be no doubt that these courts were correct in their application of the law. The Church, as a public charity, engaged in prohibited political campaign activity, and the IRS clearly had the authority to revoke the Church's tax exemption. To be sure, one can argue that the Church was involved in religious ministry or outreach, but it still participated and intervened in a presidential campaign, and that it cannot do and maintain its exempt status.

Yet, it is puzzling that the IRS did not first issue a warning to the Church. The newspaper advertisements were a first-time offense. There have been many instances where representatives of the IRS have visited with clergy and explained that tax-exempt churches are not allowed to engage in political campaign activity, without taking punitive action.

Even more perplexing is why the IRS did not simply impose the tax on political campaign expenditures[207] rather than revoke the exemption. The agency has the discretion to levy the tax and not revoke the exemption. (It also, as this case illustrates, has the authority to revoke exemption and not levy the tax. The agency further has the authority to do both.) Thus, these questions remain unanswered: why did the IRS apply the punitive approach of revocation of exemption, and was this heavy-handedness, designed to send a message? The agency, of course, is under no compunction to explain its decision making in this regard; neither court addressed the point.

The trial and appellate courts nimbly sidestepped the selective prosecution contention, albeit on questionable grounds. The Church had made a colorable showing as to selective prosecution, presenting the court with instances in which political campaign activity took place in churches, such as candidates campaigning from the pulpit during worship services and endorsements by clergy, with the IRS doing nothing about the violations (many of which have taken place in the shadow of the IRS's national office).

The courts did not find any evidence of selective prosecution because no instance was brought to it of a church engaged in precisely the type of political campaign activity as was involved in the case—namely, media endorsements. The fact that churches participated in other types of political campaign activities was considered irrelevant. If a political candidate gives a campaign address during a church service or a member of the clergy officially endorses a political candidate (both of which have occurred many times), those are certainly instances in which a "political act" can be "easily attributed" to an otherwise exempt church. Indeed, in the minds of some at least, that type of campaigning and/or endorsing is a more egregious transgression of the law than advertisements in the public media.

With regard to the selective prosecution claim, it should not make much difference which type of political campaign activity was involved, inasmuch as all types of activity of this nature are equally barred. This aspect of the court's opinion—a critical one—rested on a proverbial distinction without a difference.

### Guide for Planners

The planner can extract several lessons from these two opinions, most of them quite clearcut. One of these lessons is that the IRS sweepingly interprets and applies the proscription on political campaign activities applicable to public charities. Another lesson is that the IRS has complete discretion—at least until a court says otherwise—whether to, in these cases, do nothing, publicly or privately chide the charitable organization, impose the tax on impermissible legislative expenditures, and/or revoke tax-exempt status. (It would be helpful, nonetheless, for the agency to offer some guidance on its criteria for assessing the tax and/or abrogating exempt status.)

The contours of the selective prosecution argument are, in general, outside the scope of this analysis and, more specifically, subtle and elusive. The courts' eliding away from a finding of selective prosecution because evidence of previous examples of the *precise* form of political campaign activity involved in the case was not presented to the trial court—even though many other instances of political campaign activities by churches was evidenced—is troubling. Indeed, in the fall of 2003, former President Clinton appeared in the midst of a church service, Bible in hand and speaking with the accompaniment of the church choir, to appeal to voters to reject the then pending recall proposal concerning California Governor Gray Davis or, if necessary, vote in favor of Mr. Davis; it is unlikely that the tax-exempt status of this church will be disturbed. It was, after all, the Clinton Administration that prosecuted this case.

The planner should be particularly interested in the courts' rejection of the free speech arguments on the ground that a church can legitimately and blithely indirectly engage in political campaign activity by setting up a related exempt social welfare organization that in turn establishes a political action committee. It is, in practice, not easy to create and sustain this type of trifurcated structure.

## Caracci v. Comm'r[208]

CASE STUDY

### Introduction to the Case

The U.S. Tax Court, in the first of the intermediate sanctions decisions, upheld imposition of the tax penalties on disqualified persons but refused to allow the IRS to revoke the tax-exempt status of the three healthcare organizations that participated in the excess benefit transactions.

### Summary of the Facts

Related individuals founded, and served as directors, officers, or employees of, three tax-exempt home healthcare agencies. Years later, these entities "converted" to for-profit ones, by transferring all of their assets to newly created S corporations, all controlled by these family members. This was done because of changes in Medicare compensation practices, enabling the shareholders of the new corporations to deduct anticipated future losses. The transfer date was October 1, 1995.

An appraisal stated that the value of the assets of the tax-exempt entities was less than their liabilities. The government's witness took the position that the fair market value of the transferred assets exceeded assumed liabilities by about $20 million.

The court concluded that the fair market value of the transferred assets was $18.7 million, that the assumed liabilities totaled $13.5 million, and thus that the net value of these assets was $5.2 million. The value of the exempt organizations' transferred assets, in the words of the court, "far exceeded" the consideration paid by the for-profit entities.[209]

## Law and Analysis

The intermediate sanctions rules[210] are effective for transactions occurring after September 13, 1995. (Had the parties acted two weeks earlier, the sanctions would have been avoided.) The assets transfers were found by the court to be *excess benefit transactions*. The S corporations and their shareholders were found to be *disqualified persons*.

Each of the disqualified persons was held to be jointly and severally liable for the initial and additional intermediate sanctions penalties. These transactions have not been *corrected*. The court thus did not decide the matter of *abatement*.

The court elected to not revoke the tax-exempt status of the "dormant" nonprofit entities. The court observed that the correction process may require a transfer of the assets back to the exempt organizations. It was noted that if the exempt status of these entities were to be removed at this stage, the entities would not be able to receive the assets.

## Commentary

Like so many of the intermediate sanctions cases to come, the heart of this one was the valuation issue. Here, the issue was the fair market value of property; in other cases, the issue will be the fair value of compensation. Indeed, most of this opinion is devoted to the analysis as to the proper determination of that value.

The difficult aspect of this case was the court's judgment that the tax-exempt statuses of the nonprofit entities should not be revoked. The legislative history of the intermediate sanctions rules states that these penalties are to be the "sole sanction" imposed in cases where the "excess benefit does not rise to a level where it calls into question whether, on the whole, the organization functions as a charitable or other tax-exempt organization."[211] In other words, revocation of exemption *and* imposition of the penalty taxes are to occur only where the excess benefit is egregious.

This case was found to not warrant revocation of exemption; it was held not to be an "unusual case."[212] The court wrote: "The dormant state of the . . . tax-exempt entities precludes calling into question whether, on the whole, they are functioning tax-exempt entities."[213] But that statement makes no sense. Why does the "dormant state" of these organizations "preclude" that analysis? The court observed that these exempt entities "have not since the transfers been operated contrary to their tax-exempt purpose."[214] That is true—but they have not been operated at all! The disqualified persons stripped the charitable entities of all of their assets, rendering them unavoidably dormant.

Because all of the assets (and liabilities) of these tax-exempt organizations were transferred in excess benefit transactions, it would seem that the cases are sufficiently egregious to merit revocation of the exemptions. It is true that that approach would preclude correction by transferring the assets back to the charitable entities. But that is likely to be the case in any of the intermediate sanctions fact patterns.

## GUIDE FOR PLANNERS

With this opinion, the Tax Court—although it is by no means clear why—raised the standard for revocation of tax-exempt status in an intermediate sanctions case. With this holding as authority, the planner is in a stronger position, than would otherwise be the case, to fend off IRS attempts to levy the intermediate sanctions penalties *and* revoke exemption.

Still, the Tax Court's position in this case is probably incorrect. The court did not adhere to the standard in the legislative history of the intermediate sanctions rules as to the propriety of revocation of tax-exempt status. Thus, more litigation on this point will have to ensue before the planner can become comfortable with this higher standard.

## EXACTO SPRING CORP. V. COMM'R[215]                    CASE STUDY

### INTRODUCTION TO THE CASE

A U.S. Court of Appeals for the Seventh Circuit issued an opinion that dramatically changed the approach to determining the reasonableness of compensation paid to executives of closely held corporations—with interesting implications for the determination of the compensation of executives of charitable and other nonprofit organizations.

### SUMMARY OF THE FACTS

The fact pattern of these cases is, by now, a familiar one: a closely held corporation is compensating a talented, energetic, hard-working individual. This individual is the company's founder, principal owner, and chief executive officer. The company is paying the individual a salary, which the IRS finds excessive.

The IRS sets a lower amount of salary as a reasonable amount. The agency finds the balance of the amount paid to be a nondeductible dividend; it assesses the company for additional taxes. Both parties obtain expert witnesses; the matter is litigated, with the trial court (usually the Tax Court) finding reasonable compensation to be approximately midway between the IRS's figure and the amount of compensation actually paid. In some instances, the court's decision is appealed.

The court of appeals in this case wrote, however, that the "judges of the Tax Court are not equipped by training or experience to determine the salaries of corporate officers; no judges are."[216]

In this case, the individual was paid $1.3 million in year one and $1 million in year two. The IRS thought the amounts should be $381,000 and $400,000. The Tax Court decided the appropriate amounts were $900,000 and $700,000. (A study of these numbers reveals that the Tax Court seems to have added the IRS's determination of the maximum amount this individual should have been paid in each of the years at issue to the amount he was in fact paid, then decided the reasonable amount of compensation was that number divided by two.)

## SUMMARY OF THE LAW

The Tax Court evaluated this individual's compensation against a backdrop of seven factors. This is termed the *multifactor test*. The factors looked at were the type and extent of the services rendered, the scarcity of qualified employees, the qualifications and prior earning capacity of the employee, the contributions of the employee to the business venture, the net earnings of the employer, the prevailing compensation paid to employees with comparable jobs, and the peculiar characteristics of the employer's business.

## SUMMARY OF THE OPINION

The court of appeals pronounced this multifactor test to be "redundant, incomplete, and unclear."[217] Its several criticisms of this approach are discussed below. Essentially, this appellate court believed that the multifactor test "does not provide adequate guidance to a rational decision."[218] It preferred a "much simpler and more purposive test."[219] The test the court devised is the *independent investor test*.

According to this appellate court, the multifactor test is in the process of being replaced by the independent investor test. This replacement test is based on the return on investment expected by the company's investors (real or hypothetical)— a percentage determined by an expert witness. (In this case, the expert witness that met with approval by the court of appeals—it happened to be the IRS's— determined that investors in a firm like the one in the case would expect a 13 percent return on investment.)

The appellate court went on to say that when the investors in a company are obtaining a "far higher return than they had any reason to expect," the executive's salary is "presumptively reasonable."[220] This is the case, even though the executive's salary is "'exorbitant' . . . (as it might appear to a judge or other modestly paid official)."[221]

Under this approach, the presumption can be rebutted by a showing by the government that although the executive's salary was reasonable, the company "did not in fact intend to pay him that amount as salary, that his salary really did include a concealed dividend though it need not have."[222] This is material because, to be deductible, an expenditure must be a "bona fide expense" as well as reasonable in amount.

There seems to be another rebuttable presumption as a component of the independent investor test. This is: if the executive's salary was approved by the other owners of the corporation, who are independent of the executive—that is, who had no incentive to disguise a dividend as salary—that approval "goes far" to rebut any evidence of "bad faith."[223]

## COMMENTARY

It is premature to conclude that the independent investor test has prevailed—nationally—over the multifactor test. In addition to the Seventh Circuit, the Second Circuit has embraced the independent investor test.[224] The Seventh Circuit wrote that another federal court of appeals, the Ninth Circuit, has adopted this test,[225] although that seems to be a strained reading of the opinion. The Ninth Circuit has applied the multifactor test but then used the independent investor test to interpret one of the factors.[226] By contrast, the First Circuit has elected to stick with the multifactor test.[227]

Whatever the substance and progress of the independent investor test in the context of closely held corporations may be, it does not have much if anything to do with nonprofit organizations, which do not have investors (at least not in the conventional sense of that word). An analogy can be made to a *constituency* or to *beneficiaries,* but they generally are more difficult to identify and usually are constantly changing, and there is no parallel to a return on investment.

Thus, the law in this regard as established by the courts may be evolving to the point at which the tests for determining the reasonableness of compensation are different for nonprofit organizations and for-profit organizations. If this becomes the case, the former will continue to use the multifactor test and the latter, the independent investor test.

Should this occur, the trend unfolding until recently would end; no longer would current developments concerning the determination of reasonable compensation in the for-profit context inform the law concerning the determination of reasonable compensation in the nonprofit context. If this is in fact the trend, it will take several years to be complete.

The difficulty is that the Seventh Circuit in this decision has harshly exposed the inherent flaw in the multifactor test—a flaw that remains when the test is applied in the nonprofit setting. The flaw is that, as this appellate court so nicely stated the matter, judges "are not equipped by training or experience to determine the salaries of corporate officers." If the multifactor test is to continue to be applied with respect to the compensation of executives of charitable and other nonprofit organizations, that fact must be faced and some alternative resolution (such as referral of that question of fact to a panel of experts) achieved.

Otherwise, the Seventh Circuit was too rough in its characterization of the multifactor test. The court wrote that the test is "nondirective."[228] This means that the test does not contain rules as to how much weight to give each factor. That fact, however, is inherent in any facts-and-circumstances test. A court should have the freedom to weigh factors in the context of a particular case.

Another criticism was that many of the factors are "vague."[229] Examples provided were the type of services rendered and the characteristics of the employer's business. Yet these factors are not "vague"; they are quite clear and easily adopted in the setting of the facts in a particular case.

A third criticism of the multifactor test in this case is that it would allow this type of an executive to receive a "huge" salary while not providing any services.[230] That, however, was because the Tax Court in the case used seven factors but not an obvious one, which is the number of hours worked. Whether the employee is full-time or part-time should always be one of the factors deployed in application of a multifactor test.

A fourth criticism is that the multifactor test "invites the Tax Court [or any other trial court] to set itself up as a superpersonnel department of closely held corporations, a role unsuitable for courts."[231] This was noted above; it is also true with respect to nonprofit organizations. The test enables judges to decide what positions are comparable, what types of businesses should pay what salaries, and the like. Courts are not inherently competent to do that, to be sure, but the problem lies not in the concept of comparability but who is doing the comparing.

Another criticism relates to the way the Tax Court has been handling these cases. The court has offered up, in the words of the Seventh Circuit, "arbitrary deci-sions based on uncanalized discretion or unprincipled rules of thumb."[232] In this case, the Tax Court apparently, as to year two, for example, added $1 million and $400,000, a total of $1.4 million, then divided that number by two to arrive at a reasonable compensation amount of $700,000. The appellate court excoriated the Tax Court because of this exercise: "One would have to be awfully naïve to believe that the [multi]factor test generated this pleasing symmetry."[233]

Also, in this case, all of the factors either favored the executive or were neutral, yet the Tax Court ruled that his compensation was excessive. (The court of appeals wrote that he passed the multifactor test "with flying colors" and that the conclusion of the lower court thus was "stunning."[234]) The appellate court noted that the "government's lawyer was forced to concede at the argument of the appeal that she could not deny the possibility that the Tax Court had pulled its figures for [the executive's] allowable compensation out of a hat."[235] Consequently, the criticism of the multifactor test goes more to the arbitrary manner in which the courts have applied it and far less to any inherent deficiencies.

## Guide for Planners

Thus, in the meantime, nonprofit organizations, and their planners, should continue to assess the reasonableness of compensation by means of a multifactor test.[236]

At the same time, this opinion unequivocally addresses the fundamental fact that judges and other lawyers generally are not trained to resolve the fact issue as to valuation—although as the Tax Court has demonstrated, judges can more than adequately rise to this occasion.[237]

## Fund for the Study of Economic Growth & Tax Reform v. Internal Revenue Service[238]

CASE STUDY

## Introduction to the Case

A fund affiliated with a nonprofit tax law revision study commission was held precluded from tax-exempt status as a charitable organization on the ground that it functioned in a partisan manner as part of its efforts to further the study of tax reform.

## Summary of the Facts

In the late 1990s, the leadership of the House of Representatives and the Senate established a commission to study alternatives to the federal income tax. The commission was headed by former Representative Jack Kemp; it became known as the Kemp Commission. The fund was established to raise money to support the Commission's work, which did not receive any federal funding.

The report of the Kemp Commission, submitted to Congress, focused only on development of a flat tax system and not on other alternatives for tax reform, including retention of today's federal income tax.

## Summary of the Law

An organization that wants to be tax-exempt as a charitable one may not engage in attempts to influence legislation to an extent that is more than insubstantial. An organization that violates this rule is an *action organization*.

This type of organization can engage in activities that are *educational*. It cannot, however, engage in activities (other than incidentally) that amount to *propaganda*.

## Summary of the Opinion

The courts in this case blurred the distinction between the activities of the Commission and those of the Fund. They observed that the organizations focused only on a flat tax system and not other alternatives for tax system restructuring, including retention of the present system. A U.S. flat tax can be created only by legislation.

Also, the organizations were seen as engaging in propagandizing rather than engaging in educational undertakings. If the Commission's report had consisted solely of the pros and cons of the various alternatives to restructuring of the federal system for calculating and collecting taxes, the report would have been a product of an educational effort. Instead, by concentrating only on one option—a flat tax—and advocating that choice, the organizations engaged in activities consisting of propaganda.

The court of appeals in this case found it reasonable to "conclude that the Commission had not set out to study tax reform generally and only later concluded that a flat tax was preferable to the present system of taxation. Rather, the indications are that the Commission assumed a conclusion—the preferability of a flat tax—and then tried to sell this conclusion both to Congress and the President, and to the public more broadly."[239]

The appellate court also offered up these thoughts: "We are not holding that any organization which studies an issue touching on legislation, reaches a conclusion with respect to that issue, and then argues the merits of that conclusion must necessarily be characterized as an 'action' organization." This court added: "We are simply holding that an organization which assumes a conclusion with respect to a highly public and controversial legislative issue and then goes into the business of selling that conclusion may properly be designated an 'action' organization."[240]

The courts concluded that the Commission and the Fund were free to lobby. They cannot do so, however, with the benefit of the subsidy of tax exemption.

## COMMENTARY

These distinctions made by the appellate court in this case do not accurately reflect the state of the law. A tax-exempt charitable organization may not engage in lobbying efforts to more than an insubstantial extent, nor may it (other than to an insubstantial extent) engage in propagandizing. The court's observation was nonsensical phraseology. There is nothing in the law that causes pre-lobbying "study" to immunize the subsequent lobbying from being characterized as attempts to influence legislation. It does not make any difference whether lobbying activity was intended at the outset or subsequently decided upon. There is no difference, from a law standpoint, between arguing the merits of a conclusion in a legislative setting and attempting to "sell" a conclusion.

Advocacy is advocacy, whether it is characterized as "arguing the merits" of a conclusion or being "in the business of selling" that conclusion. Also, it makes no difference whether the conclusion being advocated by a charitable organization was preceded by "study" or based on an "assumption."

Further, it is irrelevant whether the legislative issue involved is "highly public and controversial." The rules as to lobbying by charities do not differentiate between legislation that is eristic or mundane.

## GUIDE FOR PLANNERS

Lesson: It is not necessary, for these rules to be triggered, for a specific item of legislation to be moving through a legislature. If the organization's primary objective can be attained only by legislative action, it is an action organization.[241]

## GRAHAM V. COMM'R[242]

CASE STUDY

### INTRODUCTION TO THE CASE

The U.S. Tax Court concluded that the self-dealing rules did not apply to certain transactions involving a private foundation because the ostensible disqualified person was not such a person in that he was not (albeit barely) a substantial contributor to the foundation.

### SUMMARY OF THE FACTS

The petitioner in this case, Mr. Graham, was indicted for federal income tax evasion. He needed, but lacked, about $200,000 to pay his lawyer. He turned to a colleague, Mr. Hofheinz, for assistance. Mr. Hofheinz had previously made unsecured loans to Mr. Graham totaling more than $1 million. Mr. Hofheinz, a lawyer and a businessman who had participated in several of Mr. Graham's business deals, was unwilling to loan more money to Mr. Graham.

Mr. Hofheinz, however, had a third role: the trustee of a private foundation. At his direction, the foundation purchased Mr. Graham's personal residence, which had a fair market value of $535,000. (The residence was purchased for $630,000, which was its tax assessment value.) The agreement between the private foundation and Mr. and Mrs. Graham provided that: (1) Mr. Graham would receive $250,000 (so he could pay his lawyer); (2) he could later ask for and receive $135,000; and (3) Mr. and Mrs. Graham could continue to live in the residence rent-free for three years. They were responsible for payment of taxes and insurance on the residence.

Mr. Hofheinz believed that the purchase of this residence was a "good deal" for the foundation, in that the purchase price was far enough below the property's value so as to allow the foundation a substantial profit on a subsequent sale.

Mr. Graham entered into a plea bargain in connection with the indictment. This required him to pay fines and back taxes of (coincidentally) $135,000. This sum he obtained from Mr. Hofheinz, pursuant to the agreement.

About three years later, the Graham-Hofheinz relationship deteriorated. The latter began proceedings to evict Mr. and Mrs. Graham from the residence. Mrs. Graham filed for bankruptcy. In that proceeding, Mrs. Graham showed that the residence was owned by a corporation, that she was its sole shareholder, and thus that the sale of the residence was invalid because Mr. Graham did not have any interest in it, so he lacked the ability to sell it.

A backdated document between Messrs. Graham and Hofheinz (these guys were quite a pair) stated that the $135,000 was for the Graham's furniture. Yet, the furniture remained in their possession. The foundation did not file a claim to the furniture in Mrs. Graham's bankruptcy proceeding. There, Mr. Graham testified that the $135,000 was consideration provided in exchange for the residence. The bankruptcy court concluded that the transaction was a sale of the residence, although it did not determine what constituted the consideration exchanged for the residence. (It is not known from the Tax Court opinion why Mrs. Graham's argument as to why Mr. Graham lacked any ownership in the house was rejected.) That decision was affirmed on appeal.

The IRS asserted that Mr. Graham made a bargain sale of the residence to the private foundation, so that he became a substantial contributor with respect to the foundation. The IRS then contended that acts of self-dealing took place over a seven-year period, and assessed taxes and penalties totaling $2,722,390.

At trial, the *government's* witness testified that the agreement to pay the $135,000 was at the time worth $131,905 and that the value of three years of rent was $111,371 (taking into account the tenants' payment of taxes and insurance).

The total contributions received by this private foundation by the close of the year in which the ostensible sale of the residence occurred was $2,371,589.

## Summary of the Law

A private foundation and disqualified persons with respect to it generally cannot engage in transactions together, inasmuch as they are prohibited acts of self-dealing.[243] Self-dealing transactions include sales and leases of property, loans, and other transfers of a foundation's assets.

One way for a person to become a disqualified one is to be a substantial contributor with respect to a private foundation.[244] A *substantial contributor* is a person who, in the aggregate, contributed more than $5,000 to the private foundation, where that amount is more than 2 percent of the total contributions received by the foundation before the close of the tax year of the foundation in which the contribution is received by the foundation from that person.[245] Contributions are valued at their fair market value as of the time they are received by the foundation.[246]

The private benefit doctrine is applicable with respect to private foundations.

The Tax Court agreed with the bankruptcy court, as well as with the IRS, that the sale occurred when the residence was transferred to the foundation. It also agreed with Mr. Graham that the consideration paid by the foundation for the residence consisted of three elements: the initial payment ($250,000), the promise to pay $135,000 ($131,905), and the rent-free use of the residence ($111,371). The consideration thus totaled $493,276.

Two percent of the total contributions received by the foundation, as of the close of the transaction year, was $47,432. The difference between the fair market value of the residence ($535,000) and the consideration paid ($493,276) is $41,724. Inasmuch as $41,724 is $5,708 shy of the requisite 2 percent amount ($47,432), Mr. Graham was not a substantial contributor to the foundation. He thus was not a disqualified person, and thus acts of self-dealing did not occur. The Tax Court so found, and Mr. Graham was not liable for the $2.7 million in taxes and penalties.

## COMMENTARY

There are lessons to be learned from this case (aside from evidencing how wonderful the law of tax-exempt organizations is). One is the power of valuation. If the residence had been valued much higher than $535,000 (remember, its purchase price for the Grahams and its tax assessment value was $630,000), Mr. Graham would have been a substantial contributor. He barely escaped as it was. Moreover, he was able to avoid the self-dealing rules thanks to the uncontradicted testimony of the IRS's expert! The opinion does not explain why the value of the property declined by $95,000 (over less than four years) or why Mr. Graham didn't have his own expert witness. (As it turned out, the IRS's witness did the job for him.)

Suppose that the 2 percent figure had been exceeded. Would Mr. Graham in fact have been a substantial contributor? Before one can be a *substantial contributor,* one has to be a *contributor*. The Tax Court did not make a determination on that point. Mr. Graham contended he never had *donative intent*, so he was not a substantial contributor. Given the facts of this case, that is probably true.

Now comes the mystery. Why was this private foundation's tax-exempt status not revoked? The private benefit doctrine applies in the foundation setting. That doctrine does not require the involvement of an insider (disqualified person). Clearly, the foundation, which had Mr. Hofheinz as its sole trustee, provided private benefit to Mr. Graham and that benefit was hardly insubstantial. Mr. Hofheinz used foundation resources to provide assistance to a fellow businessman, under circumstances and pursuant to terms that were, to say the least, unconventional. Mr. Graham could not have gotten the assistance that he received from Mr. Hofheinz (the foundation) from any other source. It is true that the foundation received (ultimately) the residence, but it is unlikely that it would have made that investment absent the Graham-Hofheinz relationship. Mr. Hofheinz's testimony that purchase of the residence seemed like a good deal for the foundation is not enough to dispel private benefit. Indeed, the proposal to cause the foundation to purchase the residence evolved as an alternative to another loan by Mr. Hofheinz to Mr. Graham. It is surprising that the IRS did not raise this issue.

## GUIDE FOR PLANNERS

This is one of the few cases where the instruction for the planner is found in what did *not* happen. The lesson is that even if the self-dealing rules (or the private inurement or the excess benefit transaction rules) do not apply, for the reason that the self-dealer (or other recipient of an unwarranted benefit) is not a disqualified person (or not an insider), the analysis should not be terminated—rather, the planner should press on, to determine the outcome of application of the private benefit doctrine.

## LIVING FAITH, INC. V. COMM'R[247]

CASE STUDY

## INTRODUCTION TO THE CASE

A federal court of appeals concluded that a nonprofit organization operated for a substantial commercial purpose and thus did not qualify for tax-exempt status.

## SUMMARY OF THE FACTS

This organization was established for the purpose of keeping with the doctrines of the Seventh-day Adventist Church, although it is independent from and does not receive any funding from the Church. Adherents of this religion believe that the concept of health is permeated with religious meaning. Good health, according to their view, promotes virtuous conduct and is furthered by a vegetarian diet and abstention from tobacco, alcohol, and caffeine. Ill health is seen as promoting sin.

The organization operated two vegetarian restaurants and health food stores, in a manner consistent with these religious beliefs. These facilities are open to the public and operate under the name of "Country Life." Country Life is a worldwide chain of independently operated restaurants and food stores. The organization is licensed to use the name. The guidelines of the license require the facilities to employ Church management and maintain a good working relationship with the Church. They also require that management have business ability, undergo six months of training in operating a Country Life restaurant, and maintain good business relations with suppliers and the community.

The hours of operation of these facilities are less than those of commercial facilities; they are closed on Saturdays. Meal and food prices are set at market rates. Buffet prices at its restaurants are about three times the wholesale cost of the food, a formula common in the food business. Retail prices at the health food stores are maintained at levels recommended by its wholesalers. The organization's prices are similar to, and in some instances higher than, those of other vegetarian restaurants and health food stores. Products sold at the health food stores include grocery items (such as packaged and bulk foods), vitamins, spices, and toiletries.

The organization disseminates various informational materials that promote both religious teachings and the Country Life restaurants. Literature is placed by the counter, the door, the end of the buffet line, and on each table. The organization offers books on religious subjects at no charge to its patrons. These practices it labeled "literature evangelism," which has caused a few individuals to join the Church.

Before the facilities open, the organization conducts a devotional talk by a staff member, hymn singing, and a Bible reading for workers. One Saturday a month, the organization provides the public an opportunity to sample vegetarian cooking by offering free meals. Those who attend may also peruse the Church literature and other information about the Church. The organization offers to the public a five-week cooking school that promotes vegetarian cooking. Classes meet on a weekly basis, during hours when the restaurants and food stores are closed, for a modest price. It offers weekly Bible study class, free of charge, during hours when the facilities are closed. It occasionally provides meals to the needy in exchange for chores, and has collected and donated to charity organizations about 100 bags of used clothing.

The organization generated net income in the two years at issue. Stipends are paid to its five-member staff. Several members of the staff also serve as officers and directors of the organization. Three of these are ordained deacons of the Church.

The organization stated that profits realized from its operations will be used to expand its health ministry in accordance with Church tenets. Its future plans include establishment of an "outpost evangelism program" where people may live in harmony with the principles of the Bible and the writings of the Church's founder.

The organization contended that it operated its restaurants and health food stores with the tax-exempt purpose of furthering the religious work of the Church, as a health ministry.

The sole issue was whether this organization was "operated exclusively" for exempt purposes.

## Summary of the Law

The focus in a case such as this is on an organization's purposes rather than its activities. Nonexempt purposes are permitted if they are insubstantial. A substantial nonexempt purpose defeats tax-exempt charitable status.

A single activity may be carried on for more than one purpose. Whether an activity has a substantial nonexempt purpose is a question of fact to be determined under the facts and circumstances of each case. When undertaking this inquiry, the courts look to various objective criteria. Relevant evidence includes the particular manner in which an organization's activities are conducted, the commercial hue of those activities, competition with commercial entities, and the existence and amount of annual or accumulated profits.

An organization's purpose may be inferred from its manner of operations. An organization's activities, and not solely its members' devotion to their work, determine entitlement to tax exemption. In short, an entity's activities provide a useful indicia of its purpose or purposes.

## Summary of the Opinion

The organization asserted that good health is an especially important component of the Church and that the County Life operations further this religious purpose.

The appellate court agreed that an organization's good faith assertion of an exempt purpose is relevant to the analysis of its exempt status; nonetheless, the court could not "accept the view that such an assertion be dispositive."[248] It added: "Put simply, saying one's purpose is exclusively religious doesn't necessarily make it so."[249]

The appellate court observed that although an organization is not disqualified from tax-exempt status solely because its primary activity constitutes a business, when it conducts a business with an "apparently commercial character" as its primary activity, that fact weighs heavily against exemption.[250] The organization, the primary activity of which consists of operating restaurants and food stores, "engages in precisely such conduct."[251] Its operations were seen as "presumptively commercial."[252]

The court found it "significant" that the organization is in "direct competition with other restaurants."[253] Competition with commercial firms was seen as "strong evidence" of the predominance of nonexempt commercial endeavors. The organization—which operates in a shopping center—failed to demonstrate that its business does not compete with other restaurants and food stores. Its prices, for example, are set competitively with area businesses, using pricing formulas common in the retail food business. This "lack of below-cost pricing militates against granting an exemption," the court wrote.[254] Indeed, the court added, the "profit-making price structure looms large" in its analysis of the organization's purposes.[255]

That the organization competes with other commercial enterprises was also indicated by its informational activities, which were also "promotional."[256] The use of promotional materials and "commercial catch phrases" to enhance sales are relevant factors in determining whether an organization operates in the same manner as that of any profitable commercial enterprise. A tract was said to contain religious references and "significant commercial overtones."[257] Another tract promoted the Bible study classes and vegetarian cooking classes, also stating: "We want to serve you better with expanded hours and services."[258] These materials were said to contain a "strong commercial hue" and to provide an "indicia of a forbidden commercial purpose."[259]

The organization's outlays for advertising ($15,000 over two years) was seen as another relevant factor in determining that the organization was engaging in activities for a nonexempt purpose. So, too, was its "lack of plans to solicit contributions."[260] The organization's failure to show a profit, while relevant in determining the presence or absence of commercial purposes, was "only one factor among several," and it did not per se entitle the organization to tax exemption.[261] This was especially so in this case, where the lack of profits occur during the organization's initial years of existence. "Consistent and substantial operating losses" were heralded as a factor supporting exemption.[262]

Still other factors revealed evidence of a commercial purpose. One was the organization's hours of operation. The Bible study classes and free meals occurred after hours and did not interfere with "routine business operations."[263] The organization utilized promotional materials and "commercial catch phrases" to enhance sales.[264] The organization advertised its services and food. The organization paid salaries. Management was required to have "business ability."[265] They were provided six months' training in a Country Life store. The organization did not receive charitable contributions.

The court wrote that "it is difficult to see how the experience of dining or shopping" at the organization's restaurant and health food stores "differs, if it does, from the same experience one might have while dining or shopping at other vegetarian restaurants and health food stores."[266] Granting tax exemption to this organization "would necessarily disadvantage its for-profit competitors."[267]

The appellate court also rejected the organization's assertions that the Tax Court's positions were contrary to the free exercise clause of the First Amendment.

## COMMENTARY

This is one of the most significant court opinions in the law of tax-exempt organizations. It is the clearest explication of the commerciality doctrine by a federal court of appeals. This opinion is somewhat in conflict with an opinion issued by the U.S. Court of Appeals for the Third Circuit, issued in 1984 (and ignored in the opinion by the Seventh Circuit), where that court of appeals held that a comparable analysis by the Tax Court was too stringent, making the court "uncomfortable" with this approach.

If this opinion reflects the law on the point, tremulous times lie ahead for many of the nation's tax-exempt charitable, educational, scientific, and religious organizations, and those who would join their ranks. Thousands of the exempt organizations in the United States would have their exemptions revoked if the above criteria were applied to them.

## GUIDE FOR PLANNERS

Of all of the elements comprising the law of tax-exempt organizations, the commerciality doctrine may be the one that bedevils the planner the most.[268]

The doctrine is unevenly applied; it is not clearly articulated. Many charitable organizations are operating today in blatant violation—knowingly or unknowingly—of the doctrine's precepts. These may be the least of the planner's worries in this regard, however.

What is fundamentally troubling about the commerciality doctrine lies in its details: the components of the doctrine. If the underlying assumption of the doctrine is accepted—that is, that a charitable organization can lose or be denied tax-exempt status because it is operated in a commercial manner—the legitimacy of these components remains.

It may be that the matter of competition is a valid component—although healthcare facilities, schools, publishing organizations, consulting entities, and more compete all the time with for-profit corporations. The matter of pricing may be appropriate—although the inadequate generation of funds that leaves an organization annually operating at a loss is not likely to enable the entity to survive for many years. The desire of the court in *Living Faith* to see "below-cost pricing" is just not credible or practical in the modern world.

The matter of "promotional" activities is also problematic; many public charities (such as hospitals and colleges) advertise their services. Some have "catch phrases" that they use in this process. It is hard to conceive, today, of an organization losing its tax-exempt status because of promotional endeavors.

Beyond these factors, the *Living Faith* opinion devolved into elements that the planner can safely ignore. That facts that an organization uses the services of employees, does not rely heavily on volunteers, has hours of operation that comport with those of for-profit organizations, and expects those who work for it to have "business ability" are, in the modern world, hardly the stuff of nonexempt functions.

The planner will continue to discover that there are those (it is hard to believe but true) who assert that an organization that does not receive an appreciable amount of charitable contributions cannot qualify as a tax-exempt charitable organization. This is a stunning assertion, one that makes no sense in today's world. For that matter, it has not been a plausible argument for more than three decades—since Congress enacted the rules concerning service provider publicly supported organizations, which are entities that can be charitable organizations even though their funding is confined to exempt function revenue (income from the sale of goods and/or services).[269]

## NOTE

The IRS, which endorses the commerciality doctrine, is beginning to use it in applying the unrelated business income rules.[270]

## VIGILANT HOSE CO. OF EMMITSBURG v. UNITED STATES[271]

CASE STUDY

### INTRODUCTION TO THE CASE

A federal district court held that the proceeds derived by a tax-exempt organization from gambling operations were not taxable as unrelated business income, in that the economic activity did not rise to the level of a business, and held that the exempt organization was not involved in a joint venture with for-profit companies.

### SUMMARY OF THE FACTS

The organization operated a volunteer fire department. It was classified as a tax-exempt social welfare organization.[272] It raised funds to support its fire-fighting activities by receiving the proceeds from the operation of "tip jars" placed in three taverns.

A "tip jar" is a gambling device in which patrons purchase sealed pieces of paper containing numbers, series of numbers, or symbols that may entitle the patron to cash or other prizes. In this case, the tip jar operations were allowed pursuant to state statute and a county ordinance, which permit this type of gambling for the benefit of nonprofit organizations. The pieces of paper are purchased by the nonprofit organization from the county.

Pursuant to the ordinance, the "operator" of the tip jars and the nonprofit organization involved must jointly apply for and obtain a permit from the county. To obtain the permit, the applicants must establish the bona fide nonprofit status of the sponsoring organization. At least 70 percent of the tip jar proceeds must be paid over to the nonprofit organization. These laws were complied with in this case.

The IRS asserted that the net tip jar proceeds received by this volunteer fire department constituted unrelated business income. The taxes for the two years under audit were about $28,000.

## SUMMARY OF THE OPINION

For a nonprofit, tax-exempt organization to become subject to the unrelated business income tax, the activity generating the net income must be a *business*. Generally, a business is "any activity which is carried on for the sale of goods or the performance of services."[273] Courts have held that, for these tax rules to apply, the exempt organization must have engaged in extensive business activities over a substantial period of time.[274]

The court in this case concluded that the organization's tip jar activities were not extensive. The organization's role was limited to jointly applying for the gaming permit and purchasing the tip jar tickets. The significant and substantial portion of the gambling activity was the sale of the tip jar tickets at the participating taverns.

Having failed to prevail on the argument that the economic activity was a business, the IRS contended that the relationship between the tax-exempt organization and the three taverns was a *joint venture*. Under this argument, the activities of the employees of the taverns were imputed to the exempt organization.

This argument also failed. The court observed that other than sporadically supplying new tip jar tickets and renewing permits, the fire department did not have any "ongoing connection" with the operation of the tip jars.[275] Any outside control over the operations was exercised by the county's permit office. The organization did not seek out or solicit the three taverns; they chose the volunteer fire department as the nonprofit organization that would be benefited.

## COMMENTARY

There is much to this case. First, it is difficult to convince a court that an economic activity benefiting a tax-exempt organization is not a *business* for unrelated business income tax purposes. This is one of the rare occasions that a tax-exempt organization has prevailed on this point.

Second, the court rejected the argument as to the presence of a joint venture. The IRS has become quite fond of asserting the presence of a joint venture in an effort to either preclude or deny tax-exempt status or find a business for the purpose of taxation. A joint venture can be imposed on parties as a matter of law. The IRS's win in the first of the whole hospital joint venture cases[276] has emboldened it in this regard. This is evident in light of the breathtaking assertion in this case that there was a joint venture between the volunteer fire department and the three taverns assisting it. Those who minimize the potential of the IRS's joint venture argument should be sobered by this decision.

## GUIDE FOR PLANNERS

This opinion is of significance for planners for two reasons. One is that it illustrates the point that a court can find an activity to not be a business without using the statutory definition of that term.

The other reason—and this is the difficult part—is that it shows how the IRS can impose the concept of a joint venture on a set of facts where the parties did not intend to have a venture and the planner missed the point. From the agency's standpoint, a joint venture can lurk in many cases, such as a fundraising arrangement, a management contract, or a lease. This court rejected the IRS's attempt to force a joint venture structure onto the facts, but the planner cannot be assured that will always happen.

## Notes

1. E.g., Better Bus. Bureau of Wash., D.C. v. United States, 326 U.S. 279 (1945). See *Tax-Exempt Organizations,* § 4.4.
2. E.g., Trinidad v. Sagrada Orden de Predicadores de la Provincia del Santisimo Rosario de Filipinas, 263 U.S. 578 (1924). See *Tax-Exempt Organizations,* § 25.1(d).
3. E.g., est of Haw. v. Comm'r, 71 T.C. 1067 (1979), *aff'd,* 647 F.2d 170 (9th Cir. 1981). See *Tax-Exempt Organizations,* § 19.10. See pages 280–282 below.
4. E.g., Eastern Ky. Welfare Rights Org. v. Simon, 506 F.2d 1278 (D.C. Cir. 1974). See *Tax-Exempt Organizations,* § 6.3.
5. A court, in summarizing the community benefit standard applicable to healthcare entities (see Chapter 1, text accompanied by note 35) wrote that the purpose of a community board is "more complex than giving wealthy self-styled philanthropists something to do on the rare occasion that they are not playing golf." St. David's Health Care Sys., Inc. v. United States, 2002-1 U.S.T.C. ¶ 50,452 (W.D. Tex. 2002), *vacated and remanded,* 349 F.3d 232 (5th Cir. 2003). This court also expressed its exasperation with the language of a federal tax regulation, observing that "[s]adly, the last sentence of the section is a horrible amalgamation of negatives arranged like an inside joke prompting laughter only from seasoned and sadistic bureaucrats." (Following a trial ordered on the remand, a jury, on March 4, 2004, found that the healthcare system should retain its tax-exempt status.)
6. E.g., Stanbury Law Firm, P.A. v. Internal Revenue Serv., 221 F.3d 1059 (8th Cir. 2000). See *Private Foundations,* § 15.1. See pages 292–294 below.
7. E.g., United Cancer Council, Inc. v. Comm'r, 165 F.3d 1173 (7th Cir. 1999), *rev'g and remanding* 109 T.C. 326 (1997). See *Tax-Exempt Organizations,* § 19.3. See pages 266–270 below.
8. 743 F.2d 148 (3d Cir. 1984).
9. Id. at 151.
10. Id.
11. Id.
12. Id.
13. Id.
14. Id.
15. Id.
16. Id. at 152.
17. Id.
18. Id.
19. Id.
20. Id. at 153.
21. Id. at 154.
22. Id.
23. Id. at 155.
24. Id. at 156.

25. Id.
26. Id. at 157.
27. Id. at 158.
28. Id. at 159.
29. Id.
30. Id.
31. Id.
32. Id.
33. *Tax-Exempt Organizations,* chap. 5.
34. Living Faith, Inc. v. Comm'r, 950 F.2d 365 (7th Cir. 1991). See pages 314–318 below.
35. 743 F.2d at 152. note 8 above.
36. Note 7 above, *rev'g and remanding* 109 T.C. 326 (1997).
37. 109 T.C. at 387, note 7 above.
38. Id.
39. Id. at 388.
40. Id.
41. Id. at 396.
42. 165 F.3d at 1176, note 7 above.
43. Id. at 1175.
44. Id. at 1176.
45. Id.
46. Id. at 1178.
47. Id.
48. Id. at 1176.
49. Id. at 1179.
50. Id. at 1178.
51. Id.
52. Id.
53. 109 T.C. at 387, note 7 above.
54. 165 F.3d at 1179, note 7 above.
55. Id. at 1180.
56. Granzow v. Comm'r, 739 F.2d 265, 268 (7th Cir. 1984).
57. Nationalist Movement v. Comm'r, 37 F.3d 216, 219 (5th Cir. 1994).
58. Orange County Agric. Soc'y, Inc. v. Comm'r, 893 F.2d 529, 532 (2d Cir. 1990).
59. Church By Mail, Inc. v. Comm'r, 765 F.2d 1387, 1390 (9th Cir. 1985).
60. Fund for the Study of Econ. Growth & Tax Reform v. IRS, 161 F.3d 755, 759 (D.C. Cir. 1998).
61. The opinion reads as though the preparation of it was entrusted to a tyro law clerk, who deferred the writing of it until the close of a long weekend that was preceded with great festivity, including the consumption of a variety of substances, some of which may have been legal.
62. 165 F.3d at 1179, note 7 above.
63. Id. at 1176.
64. 109 T.C. at 396, note 7 above.
65. 165 F.2d at 1176, note 7 above.
66. Id. at 1177.
67. Id. at 1178.
68. IRC § 4958(f)(1)(A).
69. See text accompanied by notes 39–40 above.

70. 165 F.3d at 1179, note 7 above.
71. IRC § 4941.
72. IRC § 4941(d)(1).
73. American Campaign Acad. v. Comm'r, 92 T.C. 1053 (1989).
74. Id.
75. See pages 276–280 below.
76. 67 Fed. Reg. 3080 (Jan. 23, 2002).
77. See, however, the text of note 176 below.
78. 118 T.C. 528 (2002).
79. IRC § 170(f)(10).
80. IRC § 170(f)(8).
81. Reg. § 1.170A-13(f)(6).
82. Hernandez v. Comm'r, 490 U.S. 680, 690 (1989).
83. United States v. American Bar Endowment, 477 U.S. 105, 116, 118 (1985).
84. 118 T.C. at 535, note 78 above.
85. Id.
86. Id. at 536.
87. IRC § 170(f)(10).
88. 118 T.C. at 536, note 78 above.
89. Id.
90. 826 F. Supp. 537 (D.D.C. 1993), *aff'd,* 95-1 U.S.T.C. ¶ 50,279 (D.C. Cir. 1995).
91. 826 F. Supp. at 539.
92. Id. at 550.
93. Id. at 552.
94. Id. at 551.
95. Id. at 553.
96. Id.
97. Note 73 above.
98. 82 T.C. at 1069, note 73 above.
99. Id. at 1070.
100. Id. at 1072.
101. Id. at 1073.
102. Id. at 1074.
103. Id. at 1075.
104. Id. at 1074.
105. Id. at 1075.
106. Rev. Rul. 68-504, 1968-2 C.B. 211.
107. Rev. Rul. 75-196, 1975-1 C.B. 155.
108. 71 T.C. 1067 (1979).
109. Id. at 1080.
110. Id.
111. Id.
112. Id.
113. Id.
114. Id. at 1081.
115. Id.
116. Id.

117. Id.
118. Id.
119. Id. at 1082.
120. Id.
121. Id.
122. Id.
123. E.g., Andrew Megosh, Lary Scollick, Mary Jo Salins, and Cheryl Chasin, "Private Benefit Under IRC 501(c)(3)," Part I, Topic H, IRS Exempt Organizations Continuing Professional Education Technical Instruction Program for Fiscal Year 2001.
124. 49 F.3d 1395 (9th Cir. 1995), aff'g 65 T.C.M. 2191 (1993).
125. IRC § 42.
126. 49 F.3d at 1396, note 124 above.
127. 65 T.C.M. at 2195, note 124 above.
128. 49 F.3d at 1397, note 124 above.
129. IRC § 42(h)(5).
130. Pursuant to IRC § 501(c)(3).
131. 49 F.3d at 1398, note 124 above.
132. IRC § 42(h)(5)(B).
133. IRC § 469(h).
134. 49 F.3d at 1398, note 124 above. See IRC § 42(h)(5)(C).
135. 49 F.3d at 1398, note 124 above.
136. Id.
137. Id. at 1396.
138. Id.
139. 58 F.3d at 404.
140. IRC § 501(c)(3).
141. Plumstead Theatre Soc'y, Inc. v. Comm'r, 74 T.C. 1324 (1980), aff'd, 675 F.2d 244 (9th Cir. 1982).
142. 58 F.3d at 404, note 139 above.
143. IRC §§ 168(h)(6)(A)(i), 512(c).
144. Rev. Rul. 98-15, 1998-1 C.B. 718.
145. 114 T.C. 498 (2000).
146. Id. at 501.
147. Id. at 508.
148. Id. at 509.
149. Id. at 510.
150. Id.
151. Id.
152. Id. at 510–11.
153. Id. at 511.
154. See Bruce R. Hopkins, "The Meaning of Tax-Exempt Status in the Work of Certification Organizations," in *The Licensure and Certification Mission: Legal, Social, and Political Foundations,* eds. Craig G. Schoon and I. Leon Smith, ch. 1 (New York: Professional Examination Service, 2000).
155. Addis v. Comm'r, note 78 above.
156. See text accompanied by note 18 above.
157. See Chapter 4, pages 95–96.
158. E.g., Sadie Copeland, Steve Grodnitsky, and Debra Cowen, "Beauty Pageants: Private Benefit Worth Watching," Topic B, IRS Exempt Organizations Continuing Professional Education Technical Instruction Program for Fiscal Year 2002.

159. The import of this opinion in relation to the matter of selection of an organization's name is the subject of Chapter 1, pages 8–9.
160. 84 T.C.M. 506 (2002).
161. Id. at 508.
162. Id.
163. E.g., Priv. Ltr. Rul. 200343027, where a for-profit farm established and operated by the founder of a private foundation subsequently, after his death, became a functionally related business and a program-related investment for the foundation as a demonstration project. Perhaps it is necessary for the founder to be deceased before the activity can qualify for charitable status.
164. 221 F.3d 1059 (8th Cir. 2000).
165. IRC § 6103(a).
166. IRC § 6104(b).
167. Stanbury Law Firm, P.A. v. Internal Revenue Serv., note 164 above, 221 F.3d at 1062.
168. Id.
169. IRC § 509(a)(1).
170. IRC § 508(b).
171. Stanbury Law Firm v. Internal Revenue Serv., note 164 above, at 221 F.3d at 1062.
172. Id.
173. For this proposition, the court cited IRC § 7428(b)(1), although the more appropriate citation is IRC § 7428(a)(1)(A).
174. Stanbury Law Firm v. Internal Revenue Serv., note 164 above, at 221 F.3d at 1062.
175. IRC § 7428(a)(1)(B).
176. Thus, for example, the U.S. Court of Appeals for the Seventh Circuit wrote that a fundraising company was not in control of a charitable organization, with the Tax Court accused of using a definition of the word *control* that "is not used elsewhere, so far as we can determine, in the law, including the federal tax law" (note 52 above), when an almost identical definition of the term was in the intermediate sanctions rules (see Chapter 4, page 62). What was the extent of the appellate court's "determination"?
177. See text accompanied by notes 232, 239, and 240 below.
178. 2003-2 U.S.T.C. ¶ 50,719 (D.D.C. 2003). This is the same organization that is the subject of the opinion referenced at pages 274–276 above.
179. Living Faith, Inc. v. Comm'r, note 34 above, *aff'g* 60 T.C.M. 710 (1990).
180. IRC § 509(a)(2).
181. E.g., Presbyterian & Reformed Publ'g Co. v. Comm'r, note 8 above.
182. Living Faith, Inc. v. United States, note 34 above.
183. 76 T.C.M. 175 (1998).
184. Id. at 176.
185. Id. at 182.
186. Id.
187. Id. at 183.
188. Id.
189. Id.
190. Id. at 186.
191. Id.
192. Id. at 187.
193. Caracci v. Comm'r, 118 T.C. 379 (2002).
194. See the discussion of Airlie Found., Inc. v. United States, pages 295–297 above.

195. 76 T.C.M. at 187, note 183 above.
196. 40 F. Supp. 2d 15 (D.D.C. 1999), *aff'd,* 211 F.3d 137 (D.C. Cir. 2000).
197. IRC § 7611(d)(1)(A)(i), (ii).
198. IRC § 508.
199. 211 F.3d at 141, 196 above.
200. Id. at 142.
201. That is, a related IRC § 501(c)(4) entity.
202. That is, an IRC § 527 entity.
203. 211 F.3d at 144, note 196 above.
204. Id.
205. Id.
206. Id.
207. IRC § 4955.
208. 118 T.C. 379 (2002).
209. Id. at 415.
210. See Chapter 4, pages 71–78.
211. H. Rep. 104-506, 104th Cong., 2d sess., at 59, n. 15.
212. 118 T.C. at 417, note 208 above.
213. Id.
214. Id. at 418.
215. 196 F.3d 833 (7th Cir. 1999).
216. Id. at 835.
217. Id.
218. Id.
219. Id.
220. Id.
221. Id. at 836.
222. Id. at 839.
223. Id.
224. Dexsil Corp. v. Comm'r, 147 F.3d 96 (2d Cir. 1998).
225. Rapco, Inc. v. Comm'r, 85 F.3d 950 (2d Cir. 1996).
226. Labelgraphics, Inc. v. Comm'r, 221 F.3d 1091 (9th Cir. 2000).
227. Haffner's Serv. Stations, Inc. v. Comm'r, 326 F.3d 1 (1st Cir. 2003).
228. 196 F.3d at 835, note 215 above.
229. Id.
230. Id. at 837.
231. Id.
232. Id.
233. Id.
234. Id. at 837.
235. Id. at 838.
236. The U.S. Tax Court, on August 3, 2000, received the first of the intermediate sanctions cases concerning the issue of excessive compensation (Peters v. Comm'r, Tax Court Docket No. 8446-00). The IRS, in the notice of deficiency issued in the case, stated that seven factors were taken into consideration in determining that compensation paid to a trustee of a charitable organization was unreasonable. The last of these factors was the independent investor test, with the IRS writing: "It is not probable [that] an outside investor would approve of such a compensation plan as reasonable." See *Intermediate Sanctions* § 4.6(b)(v).

237. See, for example, the discussion of valuation in the Caracci v. Comm'r, pages 304–306 above.

238. 997 F. Supp. 15 (D.D.C. 1998), *aff'd*, 161 F.3d 755 (D.C. Cir. 1999).

239. 161 F.3d at 760.

240. Id. at 760 n. 9.

241. See Chapter 5, pages 108–109.

242. 83 T.C.M. 1137 (2002).

243. IRC § 4941.

244. IRC § 4946(a)(1)(A), (2).

245. IRC § 507(d)(2)(A).

246. IRC § 507(d)(2)(B)(i); Reg. § 1.507-6(c)(2).

247. Note 34 above.

248. 950 F.2d at 372, note 34 above.

249. Id.

250. Id. at 373.

251. Id.

252. Id.

253. Id.

254. Id.

255. Id.

256. Id.

257. Id.

258. Id.

259. Id.

260. Id. at 374.

261. Id.

262. Id.

263. Id.

264. Id. at 373.

265. Id. at 375.

266. Id.

267. Id.

268. *Tax-Exempt Organizations,* chap. 25. Also see the discussion of the case of Presbyterian Publ'g Co. v. United States, pages 263–265 above.

269. See Chapter 5, pages 88–89. These rules were not referenced in the *Living Faith* opinion.

270. E.g., Tech. Adv. Mem. 200021056.

271. 2001-2 U.S.T.C. ¶ 50,458 (D. Md.).

272. That is, an IRC § 501(c)(4) entity.

273. IRC § 513(c).

274. E.g., American Acad. of Family Physicians v. United States, 91 F.3d 1155 (8th Cir. 1996).

275. Vigilant Hose Co. of Emmitsburg v. United States, note 271 above, 2001-2 U.S.T.C. ¶ 50,458, at 89,022.

276. Redlands Surgical Services v. Comm'r, 113 T.C. 47, *aff'd,* 242 F.3d 904 (9th Cir. 2001).

# CHAPTER 12

# The Legal Audit

On occasion, the planner for one or more tax-exempt organizations is called on to conduct an audit of an organization's operations, to determine if—or the extent to which—the organization is in compliance with federal and state law, and emerging corporate governance concepts. If the planner is a lawyer, this undertaking is referred to as the *legal audit*. Other subjects that may be reviewed, albeit often outside the context of a legal audit, include accounting principles, ethics enforcement programs, and compliance with watchdog agency standards.

In this chapter, the planner is provided with checklists, based in part on—and generally following the order of—the previous chapters of this book. Thus, the emphasis here is on aspects of the legal audit, although obviously much of what is offered is usable by planners other than lawyers (such as accountants, fundraisers, management consultants) and organizations' management.

## INVENTORY OF BASICS [See Chapter 1.]

- What is the nonprofit organization's formal name?
- Does the organization operate under a different name? If so, what is it?
- Are the organization and the planner satisfied that this name is (or these names are) the most appropriate name(s) for the organization?
- What is the organization's mailing address?
- What is the organization's e-mail address?
- Does the organization have a web site? If so, what is the address?
- When the organization was established, was consideration given to forming it as a for-profit organization? If so, what were the reasons for creating the entity as a nonprofit organization?
- What are the organization's purposes?
- Does the organization's articles of organization appropriately reflect these purposes?

- When was the organization's statement of purposes in the articles most recently written or amended?
- Does the organization have a procedure for periodic review of its statement of purposes?
- What are the organization's activities?
- How does this list of activities correlate with Form 990, Part III?
- Have any material activities been added or terminated in the previous three years?
- If so, how are these developments reflected in relation to Form 990, Part VI, question 76?
- What is the organization's principal state of operation? Why was that state selected?
- What is the organization's legal form?
- What is the date of formation of the organization?
- What is the type of the organization's articles of organization? Provide a copy of the document.
- Have the articles of organization been reviewed to be certain that all of the requisite provisions are in the document?
- Why was this legal form selected?
- If the organization is not incorporated, why?
- Does the organization have members? If so, describe.
- Does the organization have committees? If so, describe.
- Does the organization have bylaws? If so, provide a copy of the document.
- If so, have the bylaws been reviewed to be certain that all of the requisite provisions are in the document?
- Is the organization in compliance with state and local filing requirements, such as annual corporate and fundraising reports?
- How is the organization funded?
- Does the organization indemnify any person? If so, describe.
- Does the organization provide any form of guarantee? If so, describe.
- Does the organization have any insurance coverage? If so, describe.
- If the organization is incorporated, who is the registered agent?
- Does the organization do business in one or more states other than the state in which it is located? If so, what are those other states?
- If so, is the organization in compliance with the initial and ongoing filing requirements of the other state(s)? [The planner should review these documents.]
- If so, and if the organization is incorporated, who is the registered agent in the other state(s)?
- Is the organization under the scrutiny of a watchdog agency? If so, describe.
- Has the organization ever undergone an IRS audit? If so, what was (were) the outcome(s)?

- Has the organization ever received a private ruling from the IRS? If so, describe the circumstances and provide a copy of the ruling.
- Has the organization previously undergone a legal audit? If so, what was (were) the outcome(s)?

## CORPORATE GOVERNANCE [See Chapter 1.]

- What is the name of the organization's governing board (generically referred to as the board of directors)?
- Identify the individuals who comprise the organization's board of directors.
- How are these individuals selected?
- Identify the organization's officers.
- How are these individuals selected?
- Identify the organization's key employees.
- On what basis were these individuals determined to be key?
- Are the proceedings of the meetings of the board of directors reflected in minutes? [These should be reviewed by the planner.]
- Are the proceedings of other meetings reflected in minutes? [If so, these should be reviewed by the planner.]
- Are minutes reviewed by a lawyer before circulation to the board of directors (and/or other body)?
- Does the full board of directors vote on the compensation of the organization's chief executive officer and/or other personnel?
- Does the organization have a mission statement? If so, provide a copy.
- Does the organization have a business plan? If so, provide a copy.
- Does the organization have a case statement? If so, provide a copy.
- Does the organization have an employees' handbook? [If so, the planner should review it.]
- Does the organization have a code of ethics? If so, provide a copy.
- Does the organization have a conflict-of-interest policy? If so, provide a copy.
- If so, do the appropriate individuals annually sign affirmation statements? [If so, the planner should review these.]
- Does the organization currently have a business relationship with one or more directors? If so, discuss.
- Does the organization currently have a business relationship with one or more officers? If so, discuss.
- Has the board of directors reviewed the operations of the organization in light of corporate governance principles? If so, what was the outcome?
- Does each member of the board of directors have a board book? [If so, the planner should review it.]

- Does the board of directors have an e-mail communications system? If so, is there a policy as to when this system should not be used?
- Is there a policy as to board members' attendance at meetings?
- Do board members read material about nonprofit boards?
- Do board members attend seminars about nonprofit organization management and law?
- Does the board of directors periodically have retreats?

## EXTERNAL RELATIONSHIPS [See Chapter 1.]

- Does the organization use the services of one or more lawyers? If so, describe.
- Does the organization use the services of one or more accountants? If so, describe.
- Does the organization use the services of a fundraising consultant (individual) or company? If so, describe.
- Does the organization use the services of a professional solicitor? If so, describe.
- Does the organization use the services of a management company? If so, describe.
- Does the organization use the services of any other independent contractor? If so, describe. [Examples are investment advisers, lobbyists, public relations consultants, and political campaign consultants.]
- Is the organization a party to a lease(s)? If so, provide a copy(ies).
- Is the organization a party to any other contract(s)? If so, provide a copy(ies).
- Does the organization have a formal relationship with another tax-exempt organization(s)? If so, describe?
- Does the organization have a for-profit subsidiary? If so, discuss. [See below.]
- Is the organization a partner in a partnership? If so, discuss. [See below.]
- Is the organization a member of a limited liability company? If so, discuss. [See below.]
- Is the organization a member of another type of joint venture? If so, discuss. [See below.]
- Is the organization the sole member of a limited liability company? If so, discuss. [See below.]
- Is the organization the beneficiary of a trust(s)? If so, discuss. [See below.]
- Is the organization the beneficiary of an insurance policy(ies)? If so, discuss.
- Is the organization referenced in one or more wills or estate plans? If so, discuss.

## TAX-EXEMPT STATUS [See Chapter 2.]

- Is the organization tax-exempt under federal income tax law? If so, pursuant to which section of the Internal Revenue Code?

- Is the organization exempt from the payment of state and/or local tax? If so, describe. [This includes sales, use, tangible personal property, intangible personal property, and real property taxation.]

- Has the organization's federal income tax exemption been recognized by the IRS? If so, provide a copy of the determination letter or ruling.

- Does the organization have a copy of its application for recognition of exemption? If so, provide a copy.

- If the organization's tax exemption has not been recognized by the IRS, should consideration be given to acquisition of that recognition?

- Is the organization subject to the federal unrelated business income tax? If not, explain. [See below.]

- Is the organization's net investment income subject to federal taxation? If yes, explain.

- If the organization is exempt from federal income taxation by reason of IRC § 501(c)(3), what is the primary reason for that exemption (charitable, educational, religious, scientific, or other)?

- If the organization provides benefits, services, and/or products for a fee, how is that fee determined?

- Is there any content on the organization's web site that may pertain to the organization's tax-exempt status?

- If an application for recognition of exempt status is in preparation, is it being reviewed by a lawyer?

- Subsequent to the issuance of a determination letter or ruling as to exempt status by the IRS, have there been any material changes in the activities of the organization? If so, describe.

- Subsequent to the issuance of such a document, have there been any amendments to the organization's governing instruments? If so, describe.

- Subsequent to the issuance of such a document, has there been any change in the organization's form? If so, describe.

- Is the organization a central organization in connection with the group exemption rules? If so, describe.

- Is the organization a subordinate organization in connection with the group exemption rules? If so, describe.

## Private Inurement Doctrine [See Chapter 3.]

- Is the organization subject to the private inurement doctrine?
- The insiders with respect to the organization are the following persons: [Insert list.]
- Is the organization's board an independent board or a captive board?
- Does the organization pay compensation to an insider?

- If so, is the organization assured that the amount and terms of the compensation are reasonable?
- What is the basis for that assurance?
- Is the compensation based, in whole or in part, on the revenue flow of the organization?
- Is the organization borrowing money from an insider?
- If so, is the organization assured that the terms of the arrangement are reasonable?
- If so, what is the basis for that assurance?
- Is the organization lending money to an insider?
- If so, is the organization assured that the terms of the arrangement are reasonable?
- If so, what is the basis for that assurance?
- Is the organization renting property to an insider?
- If so, is the organization assured that the terms of the arrangement are reasonable?
- If so, what is the basis for that assurance?
- Is the organization renting property from an insider?
- If so, is the organization assured that the terms of the arrangement are reasonable?
- If so, what is the basis for that assurance?
- Is the organization making facilities or services available to an insider?
- If so, is the organization assured that the terms of the arrangement are reasonable?
- If so, what is the basis for that assurance?
- Is the organization selling property to an insider?
- If so, is the organization assured that the terms of the transaction are reasonable?
- If so, what is the basis for that assurance?
- Is the organization purchasing property from an insider?
- If so, is the organization assured that the terms of the transaction are reasonable?
- If so, what is the basis for that assurance?
- Is the organization a partner in a partnership involving an insider?
- If so, is the organization assured that the terms of the arrangement are reasonable?
- If so, what is the basis for that assurance?
- Is the organization a member of another type of joint venture involving an insider?
- If so, is the organization assured that the terms of the arrangement are reasonable?
- If so, what is the basis for that assurance?
- Is the organization taking the position that a benefit to an insider is incidental? If so, describe.

## PRIVATE BENEFIT DOCTRINE [See Chapter 3.]

- Is the organization subject to the private benefit doctrine?
- Does the organization pay compensation?

- If so, is the organization assured that the amount and terms of the compensation are reasonable?
- Is the compensation based, in whole or in part, on the revenue flow of the organization?
- What is the basis for that assurance?
- Is the organization borrowing money?
- If so, is the organization assured that the terms of the arrangement are reasonable?
- If so, what is the basis for that assurance?
- Is the organization lending money?
- If so, is the organization assured that the terms of the arrangement are reasonable?
- If so, what is the basis for that assurance?
- Is the organization renting property?
- If so, is the organization assured that the terms of the arrangement are reasonable?
- If so, what is the basis for that assurance?
- Is the organization renting property?
- If so, is the organization assured that the terms of the arrangement are reasonable?
- If so, what is the basis for that assurance?
- Is the organization making facilities or services available?
- If so, is the organization assured that the terms of the arrangement are reasonable?
- If so, what is the basis for that assurance?
- Is the organization selling property?
- If so, is the organization assured that the terms of the transaction are reasonable?
- If so, what is the basis for that assurance?
- Is the organization purchasing property?
- If so, is the organization assured that the terms of the transaction are reasonable?
- If so, what is the basis for that assurance?
- Is the organization a partner in a partnership?
- If so, is the organization assured that the terms of the arrangement are reasonable?
- If so, what is the basis for that assurance?
- Is the organization a member of another type of joint venture?
- If so, is the organization assured that the terms of the arrangement are reasonable?
- If so, what is the basis for that assurance?
- Is the organization taking the position that a benefit being provided is incidental? If so, describe.

## EXCESS BENEFIT TRANSACTIONS [See Chapter 3.]

- Is the organization subject to the intermediate sanctions rules?
- The disqualified persons with respect to the organization are the following persons: [Insert list.]

- Does this list include members of the family of disqualified persons? [If not, add to list.]
- Does the list of disqualified persons include entities controlled by disqualified persons? [If not, add to list.]
- Does the organization pay compensation to a disqualified person?
- If so, is the organization assured that the amount and terms of the compensation are reasonable?
- Is the compensation based, in whole or in part, on the revenue flow of the organization?
- What is the basis for that assurance?
- Is the organization borrowing money from a disqualified person?
- If so, is the organization assured that the terms of the arrangement are reasonable?
- If so, what is the basis for that assurance?
- Is the organization lending money to a disqualified person?
- If so, is the organization assured that the terms of the arrangement are reasonable?
- If so, what is the basis for that assurance?
- Is the organization renting property to a disqualified person?
- If so, is the organization assured that the terms of the arrangement are reasonable?
- If so, what is the basis for that assurance?
- Is the organization renting property from a disqualified person?
- If so, is the organization assured that the terms of the arrangement are reasonable?
- If so, what is the basis for that assurance?
- Is the organization making facilities or services available to a disqualified person?
- If so, is the organization assured that the terms of the arrangement are reasonable?
- If so, what is the basis for that assurance?
- Is the organization selling property to a disqualified person?
- If so, is the organization assured that the terms of the transaction are reasonable?
- If so, what is the basis for that assurance?
- Is the organization purchasing property from a disqualified person?
- If so, is the organization assured that the terms of the transaction are reasonable?
- If so, what is the basis for that assurance?
- Is the organization a partner in a partnership involving a disqualified person?
- If so, is the organization assured that the terms of the arrangement are reasonable?
- If so, what is the basis for that assurance?
- Is the organization a member of another type of joint venture involving a disqualified person?
- If so, is the organization assured that the terms of the arrangement are reasonable?

- If so, what is the basis for that assurance?
- Is the organization properly treating an economic benefit as consideration for the performance of services? Describe.
- Has the organization indirectly provided an excess benefit? If so, describe.
- Has the organization provided an excess benefit for the use of a disqualified person? If so, describe.
- Has the organization reported an excess benefit transaction on an annual information return? If so, describe.
- Is the organization properly utilizing the initial contract exception? If so, describe.
- Is the organization properly utilizing the rebuttable presumption of reasonableness? If so, describe.
- Did an organization manager knowingly participate in an excess benefit transaction?
- Are any penalty excise taxes properly calculated?
- Has an excess benefit transaction been corrected? If so, describe.
- Does the organization have a policy for indemnifying disqualified persons subject to a penalty tax? If so, describe.
- Does the organization maintain insurance coverage for payment or reimbursement of penalty excise taxes? If so, describe.
- Is the organization taking the position that a benefit to a disqualified person is incidental? If so, describe.

## SELF-DEALING RULES [See Chapters 3, 4.]

- Is the organization a private foundation?
- The disqualified persons with respect to the organization are the following persons: [Insert list.]
- Is the organization engaging in an act of self-dealing directly with a disqualified person?
- Is the organization engaging in an act of self-dealing indirectly with a disqualified person?
- Is the organization providing an improper benefit for the use of a disqualified person?
- Is the organization relying on the personal services exception?
- Did a foundation manager knowingly participate in a self-dealing transaction?
- Are any penalty excise taxes properly calculated?
- Has a self-dealing transaction been corrected? If so, describe.
- Is the organization taking the position that a benefit to a disqualified person is incidental? If so, describe.

## ACTIONS BY ORGANIZATION [See Chapter 3.]

- What persons are authorized to act on behalf of the organization?
- Does the board of directors act by majority vote or unanimous consent?
- When is action taken by an officer considered an act of the organization?
- When is action taken by an employee considered an act of the organization?
- Does the organization have one or more persons designated as agents?
- If so, under what circumstances is the act of an agent considered an act of the organization?

## PUBLIC CHARITY CLASSIFICATION [See Chapter 4.]

- Is the organization a public charity because it is an institution?
- Is the organization a public charity because it is a donative publicly supported charity? [If the answer is no, the following 12 questions are inapplicable.]
- Has the organization's total amount of support, for these purposes, been properly determined?
- What is the organization's current public support ratio?
- Is this ratio above or below one-third of total support?
- Is the reviewer satisfied that the numbers involved, including the 2 percent threshold, are accurate?
- Has there been a correct determination as to which payments are gifts and which are some other form of revenue?
- Has there been a correct determination as to which payments are grants and which are forms of exempt function revenue?
- Are grants from other donative publicly supported charities properly included in full as public support?
- Are grants from other charitable organizations, which are described in the donative publicly supported charities rules, properly included in full as public support?
- Are grants from governmental units properly included in full as public support?
- Is support from various persons properly aggregated or not aggregated?
- Have all gifts and grants been examined in relation to the unusual grant rule? If so, what was the outcome?
- Has application of the facts-and-circumstances test been analyzed? If so, why? What was the outcome?
- Is the organization a public charity because it is a service provider publicly supported charity? [If the answer is no, the following 14 questions are inapplicable.]
- Has the organization's total amount of support, for these purposes, been properly determined?
- Has the organization properly identified all of the disqualified persons with respect to it?

- Are any calculations as to substantial contributor classification correct?
- Have all foundation managers been correctly identified?
- What is the organization's current public support ratio?
- Is this ratio above or below one-third of total support?
- Is the reviewer satisfied that the numbers involved are accurate?
- Has there been a correct determination as to which payments are gifts and which are some other form of revenue?
- Has there been a correct determination as to which payments are grants and which are forms of exempt function revenue?
- Are grants from governmental units properly included in full as public support?
- Is support from various persons properly aggregated or not aggregated?
- Have all gifts and grants been examined in relation to the unusual grant rule? If so, what was the outcome?
- Has the organization's investment income been correctly calculated?
- Is the investment income amount above or below one-third of total support?
- Is the organization a supporting organization? [If the answer is no, the following 22 questions are inapplicable.]
- Is the organization in compliance with the supporting organization organizational test?
- Identify the organization's supported entity or entities.
- Explain whether each of the supported organizations is an institution, a donative publicly supported charity, or a service provider publicly supported charity.
- If the relationship between a supported organization and a supporting organization is that of parent and subsidiary, explain how that relationship is manifested.
- If the relationship is that of common control, explain how that relationship is manifested.
- If the relationship is that of "operated in connection with," explain how that relationship is manifested.
- Is the supported organization(s) formally identified in the supporting organization's articles of organization?
- How does the supporting organization support or benefit the supported organization(s)?
- If the organization is a fundraising organization, is it in compliance with federal disclosure requirements? [See Chapter 10.]
- If the organization is a fundraising organization, is it in compliance with applicable state fundraising regulation law?
- If the organization is a fundraising organization, is it in compliance with applicable local fundraising regulation law?
- Does the supporting organization conduct program activities or is it engaged in fundraising in support of a supported organization's programs?

- Does the supporting organization function as a holding company?
- Is the supporting organization a member of a joint venture? [See Chapter 7.]
- Does the supporting organization have a taxable subsidiary? [See Chapter 6.]
- Has a title-holding company been reviewed as an alternative to the supporting organization?
- Has a single-member limited liability company been reviewed as an alternative to the supporting organization? [See Chapter 7.]
- Was the supporting organization created by one or more donors (as opposed to one or more supported organizations)?
- Are one or more supported organizations noncharitable entities?
- If so, does each noncharitable entity qualify as the type of tax-exempt organization that can utilize a supporting organization?
- If so, does each noncharitable entity satisfy the service provider publicly supported charity rules?
- Is the supporting organization controlled by disqualified persons? If not, where is the control manifested?
- Has the organization's public charity status been reviewed by the IRS? If so, what was the outcome?
- Has the organization's public charity status been changed by IRS ruling? If so, provide a copy of that document.
- Is the organization currently within an advance ruling period?
- If so, what is the organization's current public support ratio?
- Does the organization expect to receive the requisite amount of public support by the close of the advance ruling period?
- Does the organization have a plan for receiving that amount of public support? If so, what is it?
- Does the organization have a contingency plan for avoiding private foundation status if the requisite amount of public support is not received during the advance ruling period? If so, what is it?
- Does this contingency plan (if any) entail use of a supporting organization? [If so, see above.]
- Have any of the private foundation termination rules been utilized? If so, explain.
- If the organization is a private foundation, is the organization in compliance with the private foundation organizational test? [If the organization is not a private foundation, this question and the following 10 questions are inapplicable.]
- If the organization is a private foundation, is it in compliance with the self-dealing rules?
- If the organization is a private foundation, is it in compliance with the minimum distribution requirements?

- If the organization is a private foundation, is it in compliance with the excess business holdings rules?
- If the organization is a private foundation, is it in compliance with the jeopardizing investments rules?
- If the organization is a private foundation, is it in compliance with the taxable expenditures rules as to lobbying activities?
- If the organization is a private foundation, is it in compliance with the taxable expenditures rules as to political campaign activities?
- If the organization is a private foundation, is it in compliance with the taxable expenditures rules concerning grants to noncharitable organizations?
- If the organization is a private foundation, is it in compliance with the taxable expenditures rules concerning grants to individuals?
- If the organization is a private foundation, is it in compliance with the taxable expenditures rules concerning noncharitable expenditures?
- If the organization is a private foundation, is it properly calculating, reporting, and paying the tax on net investment income?
- If the planner is advising a donor, is the charitable deduction for each contribution to a charitable organization properly calculated?
- If the planner is advising a donor, is a donor-advised fund being contemplated as an alternative to a private foundation, a supporting organization, or another type of public charity?

## LEGISLATIVE ACTIVITIES [See Chapter 5.]

- Does the organization attempt to influence legislation?
- If so, what is the extent of these lobbying activities?
- How is this "extent" measured?
- If the organization is a public charity, is this "extent" of lobbying consistent with its tax-exempt status? If so, why?
- If the organization is a public charity, can its primary objective be attained only by legislative action?
- Does the organization engage in direct lobbying?
- Does the organization engage in grassroots lobbying?
- If the organization is a public charity, is it under the substantial part test? Does it comply with that test?
- Is this organization properly reporting its lobbying activities on its annual information return?
- If the organization is a public charity, is it under the expenditure test? Does it comply with that test?
- Is this organization properly reporting its lobbying activities on its annual information return?

- If the organization has elected the expenditure test, is it relying on one or more exceptions provided by these rules?
- If the organization has not elected the expenditure test, why not?
- If the organization elected the expenditure test, when did it do so? Provide a copy of Form 5768.
- If the organization has elected the expenditure test, does it have mixed-purpose expenditures?
- If the organization has elected the expenditure test, does the organization pay for mass media advertisements?
- If the organization has elected the expenditure test, does it have one or more affiliated organizations?
- If the organization has elected the expenditure test, is it properly taking into account the lobbying expenditures of affiliated organizations?
- If the organization has elected the expenditure test, does the organization have a separate fundraising unit? If so, are total exempt purpose expenditures properly calculated?
- If the organization is a public charity under the substantial part test, has it paid any tax on excessive lobbying expenditures?
- If the organization is a public charity under the expenditure test, has it paid any tax on excessive lobbying expenditures?
- If the organization is a tax-exempt charitable entity, has it ever had its exemption revoked because of its lobbying activities?
- If the organization is a private foundation, what are its lobbying activities? Is it relying on one or more exceptions?
- If the organization is a public charity, does it use a related tax-exempt social welfare organization to conduct lobbying activities?
- If the answer to the preceding question is yes, is the planner satisfied that the principles as to bifurcation are being followed?
- If the organization is a public charity and the answer to the question before the preceding one is no, has consideration been given to such use of a social welfare organization?
- If the organization is a tax-exempt social welfare organization, what are its lobbying activities, if any?
- If the organization is a tax-exempt business league, what are its lobbying activities, if any?
- If the organization is a business league, is it in conformity with the rules concerning the deductibility of dues as a business expense?
- If the organization is any other type of tax-exempt organization, what are its lobbying activities, if any?

- Does the organization engage in research? If so, how are the research activities treated in relation to the lobbying rules?
- Does the organization engage in attempts to influence legislation by means of the Internet?
- Does the organization provide a web site link to one or more other organizations?
- If the organization attempts to influence legislation by means of the Internet, is it in compliance with the foregoing rules?

## POLITICAL CAMPAIGN ACTIVITIES

- Does the organization engage in political campaign activities?
- If so, what is the extent of these political campaign activities?
- Is the organization a public charity? If so, how is it in compliance with the proscription on political campaign activities?
- If the organization is a public charity, is it, in complying with the proscription, relying on the proposition that a candidate is not involved?
- If the organization is a public charity, is it, in complying with the proscription, relying on the proposition that a campaign is not involved?
- If the organization is a public charity, is it, in complying with the proscription, relying on the proposition that a public office is not involved?
- If the organization is a public charity, is it, in complying with the proscription, asserting that an activity is not a participation or intervention in a political campaign?
- Is the organization a social welfare organization? If so, how is it in compliance with the rules?
- If the organization is a social welfare organization, does it have a related political organization?
- If the organization is a social welfare organization, has it ever paid (or been requested to pay) the political organizations tax?
- Is the organization a business league? If so, how is it in compliance with the rules?
- If the organization is a business league, does it have a related political organization?
- If the organization is a business league, has it ever paid (or been requested to pay) the political organizations tax?
- Is the organization any other type of tax-exempt organization? If so, how is it in compliance with the rules?
- If the organization is another type of tax-exempt organization, does it have a related political organization?
- If the organization is another type of tax-exempt organization, has it ever paid (or been requested to pay) the political organizations tax?

- If the organization is a public charity, does it have a related political organization that does not engage in political campaign activities?

- If the organization is a public charity, has it ever paid (or been requested to pay) the political organizations tax?

- If the organization is a public charity, has there ever been an assertion that any of its legislative activities constitute political campaign activities?

- Is the organization itself a political organization?

- Is the organization a private foundation? Is it in compliance with the proscription on political campaign activity?

- If the organization is a public charity, and is affiliated with one or more other tax-exempt noncharitable organizations that engage in political campaign activity, is the planner satisfied that this activity is not tainting the tax-exempt status of the charitable organization?

- Is the organization taking the position that political campaign activities are being undertaken by an individual in his or her personal capacity and not as a representative of the organization?

- If the organization is a public charity, is it taking the position that it is engaging in permissible voter education activities?

- Does the organization engage in political campaign activities by means of the Internet?

- Does the organization provide a web site link to one or more other organizations?

- If the organization engages in political campaign activities by means of the Internet, is it in compliance with the foregoing rules?

## OTHER FORMS OF ADVOCACY [See Chapter 5.]

- Does the tax-exempt organization engage in activities such as litigation, demonstrations, picketing, and boycotts?

- If so, does the organization regard these as exempt functions?

- If so, and the organization is a charitable organization, ascertain why these activities are charitable and/or educational in nature.

- If the organization is a charitable organization, is it taking the position that such activities are a means to achievement of exempt ends?

- If the organization is a charitable organization, is it in compliance with the law that it may not engage in activities that are contrary to public policy?

- Has the tax-exempt organization been charged with a violation of civil law?

- Has the tax-exempt organization been charged with a violation of criminal law?

- Is there a basis for either type of charge, if it has not occurred?

## Subsidiaries in General [See Chapter 6.]

- Does the tax-exempt organization have one or more subsidiaries?
- If so, identify them.
- If the exempt organization does not presently have a subsidiary, is it contemplating one (or more)?
- Should the exempt organization have one or more subsidiaries?
- Is protection against legal liability a factor?
- Is preservation of tax-exempt status a factor?
- Identify the legal form of each of these subsidiaries (if any).
- Identify the control mechanism utilized for each of these subsidiaries (if any).

## Bifurcation Basics [See Chapter 6.]

- Does each of the entities have one or more real and substantial business functions?
- What is the nature of the overlap of the boards of directors?
- What is the nature of the overlap of officers?
- What is the nature of the overlap of employees?
- Are the organizations in the same location?
- Is there a sharing of office space, furniture, and/or equipment?
- Is the parent (exempt) organization involved in the day-to-day management of the subsidiary? If not, why not?
- Can a case be made that the subsidiary is merely an extension of the parent?
- Can a case be made that the parent-subsidiary relationship is a sham?
- If the two organizations were treated as one for tax purposes, what would be the impact on the tax-exempt status of the parent?
- Is there a contract between the organizations concerning fees, reimbursements of costs, employee-sharing, and the like?

## Tax-Exempt Subsidiaries [See Chapter 6.]

- What is the form of the tax-exempt subsidiary?
- What is the purpose of the exempt subsidiary? Responses include lobbying ___, political campaign activity ___, fundraising ___, certification ___, conduct of exempt functions ___ (program), and/or maintenance of an endowment ___.
- If the activity of the subsidiary is fundraising, does the organization have fundraising as its sole function?
- If the activity of the subsidiary is maintenance of an endowment, does the size of the endowment adversely affect the organization's fundraising ability?

- Is the subsidiary a supporting organization? If so, what type of supporting organization?
- If the subsidiary is a charitable organization and is not a supporting organization, what is the public charity status of the subsidiary?
- If the subsidiary is a charitable organization and is not a supporting organization, why is it not a supporting organization?
- What is the tax-exempt status of the parent? IRC § _____.
- What is the tax-exempt status of the subsidiary? IRC § _____.

## TAXABLE SUBSIDIARIES [See Chapter 6.]

- What is the form of the subsidiary?
- What is the purpose of the subsidiary?
- If the purpose of the subsidiary is unrelated business, what is the size of the subsidiary in relation to the tax-exempt parent?
- How was the subsidiary capitalized? If money was involved, what was the amount?
- Is a liquidation of the subsidiary being contemplated? If so, what would be the tax consequences?
- Is the subsidiary a partner in or member of a joint venture?
- Is the parent exempt organization a partner in or member of a joint venture? Should that role be performed by the/a subsidiary?
- Is the parent exempt organization contemplating becoming a partner in or member of a joint venture? Should that role be performed by the/a subsidiary?
- Is the organization engaged in social enterprise? If so, describe the interrelationship with use of a taxable subsidiary (if any).

## REVENUE FROM SUBSIDIARY [See Chapter 6.]

- Does the subsidiary pay revenue to the tax-exempt parent?
- If so, what is the nature of this revenue? Categories include dividend ___, interest ___, rent ___, royalty ___, annuity ___, capital gain ___, or grant ___ .
- Does the parent pay tax on some or all of the revenue received from the subsidiary?
- If no, should tax be paid?
- If the parent is a charitable organization, what is the impact (if any) of revenue from the subsidiary on the parent's public charity status?

## JOINT VENTURES BASICS [See Chapter 7.]

- Is the tax-exempt organization a partner in a partnership or a member of any other form of joint venture?

- If so, what is the legal form of this joint venture?
- What is the documentation associated with the formation of the venture and the exempt organization's participation in it?
- Why did the tax-exempt organization become involved in the venture?
- If it is a partnership, is the exempt organization a general partner or a limited partner?
- In relation to the exempt organization's purposes, is the business being conducted by the joint venture related or unrelated?
- Are there facts that suggest that the exempt organization may be deemed to be involved in a joint venture?
- Is the aggregate approach rule being followed?
- Has the tax-exempt organization given consideration to use of a subsidiary as a participant in the venture?

## JOINT VENTURES—OTHER ELEMENTS [See Chapter 7.]

- How does the organization's involvement in the venture further its exempt purposes?
- If the exempt organization is (or will be) a general partner in the venture, what are the ways by which the organization is (or will be) insulated from the day-to-day responsibilities of general partner (see above list of factors)?
- Is the rate of return on the capital investment of the limited partners reasonable?
- Does the documentation make it clear that the fulfillment of charitable purposes by the venture takes precedence over the maximization of profit?
- Has the venture itself entered into a contract, particularly a management contract? If so, with whom?
- What is the extent of the charitable organization's resources that are (or will be) transferred to the venture? All, a primary portion, or an insubstantial portion?
- Is there an argument that the charitable organization has lost control of itself to one or more for-profit co-venturers?
- Have management contracts, leases, royalty agreements, and the like been reviewed to see if a joint venture lurks in the facts?
- Is there potential for application of the doctrines of private benefit, private inurement, and/or intermediate sanctions?
- Is the business in the venture related or unrelated to the purposes of the exempt organization?
- Do any of the unrelated business income modification rules apply?

## UNRELATED BUSINESS ANALYSIS [See Chapter 8.]

- Is the tax-exempt organization involved subject to the unrelated business rules?

- What are the businesses (programs and other endeavors) that are conducted by the organization?
- What definition of the term *business* is being used in this analysis?
- Identify undertakings of the organization that do not qualify as businesses (if any).
- Is the fragmentation rule being properly applied by the organization?
- Identify each business that is regularly carried on.
- Is a business of the organization conducted only on a seasonal basis?
- Has the organization outsourced any of its activities?
- If so, does the contract involved provide that the other party to the contract is an agent of the tax-exempt organization?
- Does the organization expend any preparatory time? How extensive is this amount of time?
- Ascertain each business that is related to the organization's exempt purposes. What is the rationale for the relatedness?
- Ascertain each business that is substantially related to the organization's exempt purposes. What is the rationale for the substantiality?
- Ascertain each business that is unrelated to the organization's exempt purposes.
- Is any of the income from one or more unrelated businesses sheltered from unrelated business income taxation by statute? If so, identify the law(s).
- Are one or more unrelated business activities sheltered from unrelated business income by statute? If so, identify the law(s).
- Does the organization engage in fundraising?
- If so, are any of the fundraising activities unrelated businesses?
- Does the organization have unrelated debt-financed income?
- Does the organization receive income from a controlled entity?
- Is the organization correctly ascertaining the expenses that can be deducted in computing unrelated business taxable income?
- Is the organization conducting an unrelated business at a loss, where the loss can be offset against gain from one or more other unrelated businesses?
- How much unrelated business activity can the exempt organization engage in without endangering its tax-exempt status?
- Should one or more unrelated businesses be transferred to another organization?
- If so, what should the form of that organization be?
- Is the organization contemplating an unrelated business that should be initiated in another organization?
- If so, what should the form of that organization be?

## COMMERCIALITY DOCTRINE [See Chapter 8.]

- Does the organization engage in activities that compete with for-profit organizations?

- What factors does the organization take into account in determining the amount of its fees?
- Does the organization advertise one or more of its activities?
- Does the organization have a catchphrase, jingle, or the like?
- Does the organization have employees?
- If so, are they provided any special training?
- Does the organization utilize the services of volunteers?
- Does the organization receive any charitable contributions?
- What is the outcome when the commerciality doctrine is applied to the organization?

## ANNUAL INFORMATION RETURNS [See Chapter 9.]

- Is the organization required to file annual information returns?
- If so, which return is the appropriate one? Form 990 ___. Form 990-EZ ___. Form 990-PF ___. Other ___.
- If not, what is the basis for the nonfiling exception? Church ___. Other religious organization ___. Small organization ___. Affiliate of a governmental unit ___.
- Is the planner satisfied that these returns are accurate?
- Does the planner, on an ongoing basis, evaluate the content of the organization's web site?
- For example, in the case of reporting by charitable organizations, are the appropriate distinctions being made between contributions, grants, and exempt function income?
- Likewise, are the appropriate distinctions being made between direct public support and indirect public support?
- Likewise, is revenue from one or more special events being properly reported?
- Likewise, is the organization accurately reporting its expenses on a functional basis?
- Likewise, has the organization adequately stated its primary purpose?
- Likewise, is the organization accurately (and fully) reporting its program service accomplishments?
- Likewise, has the organization properly identified all of its key employees?
- Likewise, is the organization properly answering the question as to the conduct of any activities not previously reported to the IRS?
- Likewise, is the organization properly answering the question as to any changes in the organization's organizing or governing documents?
- Likewise, has the organization properly answered the question as to the making of any political expenditures?
- Likewise, has the organization properly answered the question as to compliance with the public disclosure (inspection) requirements?

- Likewise, has the organization properly answered the question concerning the quid pro quo disclosure requirements?
- Likewise, has the organization properly answered the question as to the receipt of nondeductible gifts?
- Likewise, has the organization properly answered the question as to the payment of tax because of legislative or political campaign activities?
- Likewise, has the organization properly answered the question as to its involvement in any excess benefit transactions?
- Likewise, is the organization properly reporting its related income, unrelated income, and income shielded from taxation by statute?
- Likewise, does the organization control one or more organizations?
- Likewise, is the organization the owner of one or more disregarded entities?
- Likewise, has the organization received any funds to pay premiums on a personal benefit contract?
- Likewise, is the organization properly reporting compensation arrangements?
- Likewise, is the organization properly reporting any transactions with insiders?
- Likewise, is the organization engaging in any transactions with noncharitable organizations?
- Likewise, is the organization properly calculating its public support ratio (if applicable)?
- Likewise, is the organization properly reporting information about contributions to it?
- Likewise, is the organization filing a copy of the annual information return with one or more states?

## DISCLOSURE REQUIREMENTS [See Chapter 10.]

- Has the organization (if required to do so) made a copy of its application for recognition of exemption available to those who request it?
- Is this practice ongoing?
- Is the organization's application posted on the Internet?
- Does the organization have copies of the application available to timely respond to requests for it?
- Is there any basis for application of the harassment campaign exception?
- How is the organization responding to the question on Form 990, Part VI, question 83a, with respect to its application for recognition of exemption?
- Has the organization made one or more copies of its annual information return available to those who request it or them?
- Is this practice ongoing?

- Are one or more of the organization's annual information returns posted on the Internet?
- How is the organization responding to the question on Form 990, Part VI, line 83a, with respect to its annual information return?
- Does the organization receive charitable contributions?
- Is the organization in compliance with the charitable gift substantiation requirements?
- Is the organization taking the position that it is providing goods or services in consideration for contributions?
- If so, is it providing a good faith estimate of those goods or services? How is that estimate amount determined?
- By what means is the organization providing written acknowledgments of gifts?
- In this context, how is the organization treating donors' understandings and expectations?
- Does the organization receive quid pro quo charitable contributions?
- Is the organization in compliance with the quid pro quo contributions disclosure requirements?
- How is the good faith estimate amount determined?
- How is donative intent being determined?
- How is the organization responding to the question on Form 990, Part VI, line 83b?
- If the organization is not a charitable entity, is it in compliance with the rules concerning disclosure of nondeductibility of contributions?
- Is the organization in compliance with the IRS's safe-harbor rules?
- If not, how is the organization complying with these rules?
- How is the organization responding to the questions on Form 990, Part VI, lines 84a and b?
- Is the organization working with its donors to be certain that they are in compliance with the rules requiring disclosure to the IRS of certain gifts of property?
- Is the organization properly completing Form 8283, Section B, Part IV?
- Is the organization timely receiving copies of Form 8283, Section B?
- Is the organization timely disclosing dispositions of contributed property to the IRS by means of Form 8282?
- Has or is the organization consuming or distributing contributed property in furtherance of its exempt purposes?
- Has or is the organization transferring contributed property to another charitable organization?
- Is the organization working with its donors to be certain that they are in compliance with the rules requiring appraisals of certain gifts of property?

- Does the organization offer to the public information or services that is available to the public without charge from the federal government?

- If so, is the organization in compliance with the rules requiring disclosure of that availability?

- Has the organization received or is it now receiving any funds to pay premiums on one or more personal benefit contracts?

- Has the organization paid or is it paying premiums on one or more personal benefit contracts?

- How is the organization responding to the questions on Form 990, Part X?

- Is the organization involved in one or more tax shelters?

- Is the organization involved in a listed transaction?

- Is the organization involved in a reportable transaction?

## COURT OPINIONS [See Chapter 11.]

- How are you [the planner] advising your clients as to applicability of the commerciality doctrine?

- How are you determining which persons are insiders and/or disqualified persons with respect to tax-exempt organizations?

- In application of the contributions substantiation requirements, how are you advising clients to treat expectations and understandings?

- How are you, in your practice, applying the private benefit doctrine?

- In establishing a tax-exempt organization, how are you treating exempt functions performed by one or more founders personally?

- When clients obtain appraisals of property, are you evaluating the accuracy of the appraisals?

- Do these appraisals take into account future events that may impact the valuation?

- If the intermediate sanctions penalties are being applied, is revocation of tax exemption also being attempted? If so, how are you evaluating the standard for the revocation?

- When clients obtain opinions as to the reasonableness of compensation, are you evaluating the reports to determine if all of the relevant factors have been taken into consideration?

- In advising charitable organizations as to the federal tax rules concerning lobbying, are you making distinctions between organizations that are advocating the merits of a studied issue and those that are selling an assumed conclusion?

- Also, as to the lobbying rules, are you differentiating between legislative issues that are highly public and controversial and those that are not?

- When applying the private inurement, intermediate sanctions, and/or self-dealing rules, are you also applying the private benefit doctrine?

# Form 1023

| Form **1023**<br>(Rev. September 1998)<br>Department of the Treasury<br>Internal Revenue Service | **Application for Recognition of Exemption**<br>**Under Section 501(c)(3) of the Internal Revenue Code** | OMB No. 1545-0056<br>**Note:** *If exempt status is approved, this application will be open for public inspection.* |
|---|---|---|

Read the instructions for each Part carefully.
**A User Fee must be attached to this application.**
If the required information and appropriate documents are not submitted along with Form 8718 (with payment of the appropriate user fee), the application may be returned to you.
**Complete the Procedural Checklist on page 8 of the instructions.**

**Part I    Identification of Applicant**

| **1a** Full name of organization (as shown in organizing document) | | **2** Employer identification number (EIN)<br>(If none, see page 3 of the **Specific Instructions**.) |
|---|---|---|
| **1b** c/o Name (if applicable) | | **3** Name and telephone number of person to be contacted if additional information is needed |
| **1c** Address (number and street) | Room/Suite | |
| | | (    ) |
| **1d** City, town, or post office, state, and ZIP + 4. If you have a foreign address, see **Specific Instructions** for Part I, page 3. | | **4** Month the annual accounting period ends |
| | | **5** Date incorporated or formed |
| **1e** Web site address | | **6** Check here if applying under section:<br>**a** ☐ 501(e) **b** ☐ 501(f) **c** ☐ 501(k) **d** ☐ 501(n) |

**7** Did the organization previously apply for recognition of exemption under this Code section or under any other section of the Code? . . . . . . . . . . . . . . . . . . . . . . . . . . .    ☐ **Yes** ☐ **No**
If "Yes," attach an explanation.

**8** Is the organization required to file Form 990 (or Form 990-EZ)? . . . . . . . . . . . .    ☐ **N/A** ☐ **Yes** ☐ **No**
If "No," attach an explanation (see page 3 of the **Specific Instructions**).

**9** Has the organization filed Federal income tax returns or exempt organization information returns? . . .    ☐ **Yes** ☐ **No**
If "Yes," state the form numbers, years filed, and Internal Revenue office where filed.

**10** Check the box for the type of organization. ATTACH A CONFORMED COPY OF THE CORRESPONDING ORGANIZING DOCUMENTS TO THE APPLICATION BEFORE MAILING. (See **Specific Instructions** for Part I, Line 10, on page 3.) See also Pub. 557 for examples of organizational documents.

**a** ☐ Corporation—Attach a copy of the Articles of Incorporation (including amendments and restatements) showing approval by the appropriate state official; also include a copy of the bylaws.

**b** ☐ Trust—    Attach a copy of the Trust Indenture or Agreement, including all appropriate signatures and dates.

**c** ☐ Association— Attach a copy of the Articles of Association, Constitution, or other creating document, with a declaration (see instructions) or other evidence the organization was formed by adoption of the document by more than one person; also include a copy of the bylaws.

If the organization is a corporation or an unincorporated association that has not yet adopted bylaws, check here ▶    ☐

I declare under the penalties of perjury that I am authorized to sign this application on behalf of the above organization and that I have examined this application, including the accompanying schedules and attachments, and to the best of my knowledge it is true, correct, and complete.

**Please**
**Sign**    ▶
**Here**    ----------------------------    ----------------------------    ----------------------------
                    (Signature)                    (Type or print name and title or authority of signer)                    (Date)

**For Paperwork Reduction Act Notice, see page 7 of the instructions.**                    Cat. No. 17133K

| Part II | Activities and Operational Information |
| --- | --- |

1   Provide a detailed narrative description of all the activities of the organization—past, present, and planned. **Do not merely refer to or repeat the language in the organizational document.** List each activity separately in the order of importance based on the relative time and other resources devoted to the activity. Indicate the percentage of time for each activity. Each description should include, as a minimum, the following: **(a)** a detailed description of the activity including its purpose and how each acitivity furthers your exempt purpose; **(b)** when the activity was or will be initiated; and **(c)** where and by whom the activity will be conducted.

2   What are or will be the organization's sources of financial support? List in order of size.

3   Describe the organization's fundraising program, both actual and planned, and explain to what extent it has been put into effect. Include details of fundraising activities such as selective mailings, formation of fundraising committees, use of volunteers or professional fundraisers, etc. Attach representative copies of solicitations for financial support.

**Part II**  Activities and Operational Information *(Continued)*

4  Give the following information about the organization's governing body:

| **a** Names, addresses, and titles of officers, directors, trustees, etc. | **b** Annual compensation |
|---|---|
| | |

**c** Do any of the above persons serve as members of the governing body by reason of being public officials or being appointed by public officials? . . . . . . . . . . . . . . . . . . . . . . . . . . .  ☐ **Yes** ☐ **No**
If "Yes," name those persons and explain the basis of their selection or appointment.

**d** Are any members of the organization's governing body "disqualified persons" with respect to the organization (other than by reason of being a member of the governing body) or do any of the members have either a business or family relationship with "disqualified persons"? (See **Specific Instructions** for Part II, Line 4d, on page 3.) . . . . . . . . . . . . . . . . . . . . . . . . . . . .  ☐ **Yes** ☐ **No**
If "Yes," explain.

5  Does the organization control or is it controlled by any other organization? . . . . . . . . . . .  ☐ **Yes** ☐ **No**
Is the organization the outgrowth of (or successor to) another organization, or does it have a special relationship with another organization by reason of interlocking directorates or other factors? . . . . .  ☐ **Yes** ☐ **No**
If either of these questions is answered "Yes," explain.

6  Does or will the organization directly or indirectly engage in any of the following transactions with any political organization or other exempt organization (other than a 501(c)(3) organization): **(a)** grants; **(b)** purchases or sales of assets; **(c)** rental of facilities or equipment; **(d)** loans or loan guarantees; **(e)** reimbursement arrangements; **(f)** performance of services, membership, or fundraising solicitations; or **(g)** sharing of facilities, equipment, mailing lists or other assets, or paid employees? . . . . . . .  ☐ **Yes** ☐ **No**
If "Yes," explain fully and identify the other organizations involved.

7  Is the organization financially accountable to any other organization? . . . . . . . . . . . . .  ☐ **Yes** ☐ **No**
If "Yes," explain and identify the other organization. Include details concerning accountability or attach copies of reports if any have been submitted.

**Part II**    Activities and Operational Information *(Continued)*

**8**   What assets does the organization have that are used in the performance of its exempt function? (Do not include property producing investment income.) If any assets are not fully operational, explain their status, what additional steps remain to be completed, and when such final steps will be taken. If none, indicate "N/A."

**9**   Will the organization be the beneficiary of tax-exempt bond financing within the next 2 years?. . . .    ☐ **Yes** ☐ **No**

**10a** Will any of the organization's facilities or operations be managed by another organization or individual under a contractual agreement?. . . . . . . . . . . . . . . . . . . . . . . . . . .    ☐ **Yes** ☐ **No**
**b**   Is the organization a party to any leases?   . . . . . . . . . . . . . . . . . . . . . .    ☐ **Yes** ☐ **No**
         If either of these questions is answered "Yes," attach a copy of the contracts and explain the relationship between the applicant and the other parties.

**11**  Is the organization a membership organization?   . . . . . . . . . . . . . . . . . . . . .    ☐ **Yes** ☐ **No**
         If "Yes," complete the following:
**a**   Describe the organization's membership requirements and attach a schedule of membership fees and dues.

**b**   Describe the organization's present and proposed efforts to attract members and attach a copy of any descriptive literature or promotional material used for this purpose.

**c**   What benefits do (or will) the members receive in exchange for their payment of dues?

**12a** If the organization provides benefits, services, or products, are the recipients required, or will they be required, to pay for them?. . . . . . . . . . . . . . . . . . . . . . . . .    ☐ **N/A** ☐ **Yes** ☐ **No**
         If "Yes," explain how the charges are determined and attach a copy of the current fee schedule.

**b**   Does or will the organization limit its benefits, services, or products to specific individuals or classes of individuals?. . . . . . . . . . . . . . . . . . . . . . . . . . . . . . .    ☐ **N/A** ☐ **Yes** ☐ **No**
         If "Yes," explain how the recipients or beneficiaries are or will be selected.

**13**  Does or will the organization attempt to influence legislation? . . . . . . . . . . . . . . .    ☐ **Yes** ☐ **No**
         If "Yes," explain. Also, give an estimate of the percentage of the organization's time and funds that it devotes or plans to devote to this activity.

**14**  Does or will the organization intervene in any way in political campaigns, including the publication or distribution of statements?   . . . . . . . . . . . . . . . . . . . . . . . . . . . .    ☐ **Yes** ☐ **No**
         If "Yes," explain fully.

| Part III | Technical Requirements |
|---|---|

**1**  Are you filing Form 1023 within 15 months from the end of the month in which your organization was
created or formed?  . . . . . . . . . . . . . . . . . . . . . . . . . . . . . . . . .  ☐ **Yes** ☐ **No**
If you answer "Yes," do not answer questions on lines 2 through 6 below.

**2**  If one of the exceptions to the 15-month filing requirement shown below applies, check the appropriate box and proceed
to question 7.

**Exceptions**—You are not required to file an exemption application within 15 months if the organization:

☐ **a**  Is a church, interchurch organization of local units of a church, a convention or association of churches, or an
integrated auxiliary of a church. See **Specific Instructions,** Line 2a, on page 4;

☐ **b**  Is not a private foundation and normally has gross receipts of not more than $5,000 in each tax year; or

☐ **c**  Is a subordinate organization covered by a group exemption letter, but only if the parent or supervisory organization
timely submitted a notice covering the subordinate.

**3**  If the organization does not meet any of the exceptions on line 2 above, are you filing Form 1023 within
27 months from the end of the month in which the organization was created or formed?.  . . . . . .  ☐ **Yes** ☐ **No**

If "Yes," your organization qualifies under Regulation section 301.9100-2, for an automatic 12-month
extension of the 15-month filing requirement. Do not answer questions 4 through 6.

If "No," answer question 4.

**4**  If you answer "No" to question 3, does the organization wish to request an extension of time to apply
under the "reasonable action and good faith" and the "no prejudice to the interest of the government"
requirements of Regulations section 301.9100-3? . . . . . . . . . . . . . . . . . . . . . .  ☐ **Yes** ☐ **No**

If "Yes," give the reasons for not filing this application within the 27-month period described in question 3.
See **Specific Instructions,** Part III, Line 4, before completing this item. Do not answer questions 5 and 6.

If "No," answer questions 5 and 6.

**5**  If you answer "No" to question 4, your organization's qualification as a section 501(c)(3) organization can
be recognized only from the date this application is filed. Therefore, do you want us to consider the
application as a request for recognition of exemption as a section 501(c)(3) organization from the date
the application is received and not retroactively to the date the organization was created or formed?  .  ☐ **Yes** ☐ **No**

**6**  If you answer "Yes" to question 5 above and wish to request recognition of section 501(c)(4) status for the period beginning
with the date the organization was formed and ending with the date the Form 1023 application was received (the effective
date of the organization's section 501(c)(3) status), check here ▶ ☐   and attach a completed page 1 of Form 1024 to this
application.

**Part III**    **Technical Requirements** *(Continued)*

7   Is the organization a private foundation?
   ☐ **Yes**   (Answer question 8.)
   ☐ **No**    (Answer question 9 and proceed as instructed.)

8   If you answer "Yes" to question 7, does the organization claim to be a private operating foundation?
   ☐ **Yes**   (Complete Schedule E.)
   ☐ **No**

After answering question 8 on this line, go to line 14 on page 7.

9   If you answer "No" to question 7, indicate the public charity classification the organization is requesting by checking the box below that most appropriately applies:

**THE ORGANIZATION IS NOT A PRIVATE FOUNDATION BECAUSE IT QUALIFIES:**

| | | |
|---|---|---|
| **a** ☐ | As a church or a convention or association of churches (CHURCHES MUST COMPLETE SCHEDULE A.) | Sections 509(a)(1) and 170(b)(1)(A)(i) |
| **b** ☐ | As a school (MUST COMPLETE SCHEDULE B.) | Sections 509(a)(1) and 170(b)(1)(A)(ii) |
| **c** ☐ | As a hospital or a cooperative hospital service organization, or a medical research organization operated in conjunction with a hospital (These organizations, except for hospital service organizations, MUST COMPLETE SCHEDULE C.) | Sections 509(a)(1) and 170(b)(1)(A)(iii) |
| **d** ☐ | As a governmental unit described in section 170(c)(1). | Sections 509(a)(1) and 170(b)(1)(A)(v) |
| **e** ☐ | As being operated solely for the benefit of, or in connection with, one or more of the organizations described in **a** through **d**, **g**, **h**, or **i** (MUST COMPLETE SCHEDULE D.) | Section 509(a)(3) |
| **f** ☐ | As being organized and operated exclusively for testing for public safety. | Section 509(a)(4) |
| **g** ☐ | As being operated for the benefit of a college or university that is owned or operated by a governmental unit. | Sections 509(a)(1) and 170(b)(1)(A)(iv) |
| **h** ☐ | As receiving a substantial part of its support in the form of contributions from publicly supported organizations, from a governmental unit, or from the general public. | Sections 509(a)(1) and 170(b)(1)(A)(vi) |
| **i** ☐ | As normally receiving not more than one-third of its support from gross investment income and more than one-third of its support from contributions, membership fees, and gross receipts from activities related to its exempt functions (subject to certain exceptions). | Section 509(a)(2) |
| **j** ☐ | The organization is a publicly supported organization but is not sure whether it meets the public support test of **h** or **i**. The organization would like the IRS to decide the proper classification. | Sections 509(a)(1) and 170(b)(1)(A)(vi) or Section 509(a)(2) |

**If you checked one of the boxes a through f in question 9, go to question
14. If you checked box g in question 9, go to questions 11 and 12.
If you checked box h, i, or j, in question 9, go to question 10.**

**Part III**    **Technical Requirements** *(Continued)*

**10**    If you checked box **h, i,** or **j** in question 9, has the organization completed a tax year of at least 8 months?

  ☐ **Yes**—Indicate whether you are requesting:

   ☐ A definitive ruling. (Answer questions 11 through 14.)

   ☐ An advance ruling. (Answer questions 11 and 14 and attach two Forms 872-C completed and signed.)

  ☐ **No—You must request an advance ruling by completing and signing two Forms 872-C and attaching them to the Form 1023.**

**11**    If the organization received any unusual grants during any of the tax years shown in Part IV-A, **Statement of Revenue and Expenses,** attach a list for each year showing the name of the contributor; the date and the amount of the grant; and a brief description of the nature of the grant.

**12**    If you are requesting a definitive ruling under section 170(b)(1)(A)(iv) or (vi), check here ▶ ☐  and:

**a** Enter 2% of line 8, column (e), Total, of Part IV-A . . . . . . . . . . . . . . ─────────

**b** Attach a list showing the name and amount contributed by each person (other than a governmental unit or "publicly supported" organization) whose total gifts, grants, contributions, etc., were more than the amount entered on line **12a** above.

**13**    If you are requesting a definitive ruling under section 509(a)(2), check here ▶ ☐  and:

**a** For each of the years included on lines 1, 2, and 9 of Part IV-A, attach a list showing the name of and amount received from each "disqualified person." (For a definition of "disqualified person," see **Specific Instructions,** Part II, Line 4d, on page 3.)

**b** For each of the years included on line 9 of Part IV-A, attach a list showing the name of and amount received from each payer (other than a "disqualified person") whose payments to the organization were more than $5,000. For this purpose, "payer" includes, but is not limited to, any organization described in sections 170(b)(1)(A)(i) through (vi) and any governmental agency or bureau.

| **14**    Indicate if your organization is one of the following. If so, complete the required schedule. (Submit only those schedules that apply to your organization. **Do not submit blank schedules.**) | Yes | No | If "Yes," complete Schedule: |
|---|---|---|---|
| Is the organization a church? . . . . . . . . . . . . . . . . | | | A |
| Is the organization, or any part of it, a school? . . . . . . . . . . . . . . . | | | B |
| Is the organization, or any part of it, a hospital or medical research organization? . . . . . . | | | C |
| Is the organization a section 509(a)(3) supporting organization? . . . . . . . . . . . | | | D |
| Is the organization a private operating foundation? . . . . . . . . . . . . . . . | | | E |
| Is the organization, or any part of it, a home for the aged or handicapped? . . . . . . . | | | F |
| Is the organization, or any part of it, a child care organization? . . . . . . . . . . . | | | G |
| Does the organization provide or administer any scholarship benefits, student aid, etc.? . . . . | | | H |
| Has the organization taken over, or will it take over, the facilities of a "for profit" institution? . . . | | | I |

Form 1023 (Rev. 9-98)

**Part IV**   **Financial Data**

*Complete the financial statements for the current year and for each of the 3 years immediately before it. If in existence less than 4 years, complete the statements for each year in existence. If in existence less than 1 year, also provide proposed budgets for the 2 years following the current year.*

### A. Statement of Revenue and Expenses

| | | Current tax year | 3 prior tax years or proposed budget for 2 years | | | |
|---|---|---|---|---|---|---|
| | | **(a)** From ....... to | **(b)** ........... | **(c)** ........... | **(d)** ........... | **(e) TOTAL** |
| **Revenue** | 1 Gifts, grants, and contributions received (not including unusual grants—see page 6 of the instructions). . . . . . | | | | | |
| | 2 Membership fees received . . | | | | | |
| | 3 Gross investment income (see instructions for definition) . . | | | | | |
| | 4 Net income from organization's unrelated business activities not included on line 3 . . . . . | | | | | |
| | 5 Tax revenues levied for and either paid to or spent on behalf of the organization . . . . | | | | | |
| | 6 Value of services or facilities furnished by a governmental unit to the organization without charge (not including the value of services or facilities generally furnished the public without charge) . . . . | | | | | |
| | 7 Other income (not including gain or loss from sale of capital assets) (attach schedule) . . | | | | | |
| | 8 **Total** (add lines 1 through 7) | | | | | |
| | 9 Gross receipts from admissions, sales of merchandise or services, or furnishing of facilities in any activity that is not an unrelated business within the meaning of section 513. Include related cost of sales on line 22 . . . . . . | | | | | |
| | 10 **Total** (add lines 8 and 9) . . | | | | | |
| | 11 Gain or loss from sale of capital assets (attach schedule). . . | | | | | |
| | 12 Unusual grants. . . . . . | | | | | |
| | 13 **Total** revenue (add lines 10 through 12) . . . . . . . | | | | | |
| **Expenses** | 14 Fundraising expenses . . . | | | | | |
| | 15 Contributions, gifts, grants, and similar amounts paid (attach schedule) . . . . . . . | | | | | |
| | 16 Disbursements to or for benefit of members (attach schedule) . | | | | | |
| | 17 Compensation of officers, directors, and trustees (attach schedule) . . . . . . | | | | | |
| | 18 Other salaries and wages . . | | | | | |
| | 19 Interest . . . . . . . . | | | | | |
| | 20 Occupancy (rent, utilities, etc.) . | | | | | |
| | 21 Depreciation and depletion . . | | | | | |
| | 22 Other (attach schedule) . . . | | | | | |
| | 23 **Total** expenses (add lines 14 through 22) . . . . . . . | | | | | |
| | 24 Excess of revenue over expenses (line 13 minus line 23) | | | | | |

| Part **IV** | **Financial Data** *(Continued)* |
|---|---|

| **B. Balance Sheet** (at the end of the period shown) | Current tax year |
|---|---|
| | Date ................ |

### Assets

| | | | |
|---|---|---|---|
| 1 | Cash . . . . . . . . . . . . . . . . . . . . . . . . . | **1** | |
| 2 | Accounts receivable, net . . . . . . . . . . . . . . . . . | **2** | |
| 3 | Inventories . . . . . . . . . . . . . . . . . . . . . . | **3** | |
| 4 | Bonds and notes receivable (attach schedule) . . . . . . . . . . | **4** | |
| 5 | Corporate stocks (attach schedule) . . . . . . . . . . . . . . | **5** | |
| 6 | Mortgage loans (attach schedule) . . . . . . . . . . . . . | **6** | |
| 7 | Other investments (attach schedule) . . . . . . . . . . . . . | **7** | |
| 8 | Depreciable and depletable assets (attach schedule) . . . . . . . . | **8** | |
| 9 | Land . . . . . . . . . . . . . . . . . . . . . . . . | **9** | |
| 10 | Other assets (attach schedule) . . . . . . . . . . . . . . . | **10** | |
| 11 | **Total assets** (add lines 1 through 10) . . . . . . . . . . . . . | **11** | |

### Liabilities

| | | | |
|---|---|---|---|
| 12 | Accounts payable . . . . . . . . . . . . . . . . . . . | **12** | |
| 13 | Contributions, gifts, grants, etc., payable . . . . . . . . . . . . | **13** | |
| 14 | Mortgages and notes payable (attach schedule) . . . . . . . . . . | **14** | |
| 15 | Other liabilities (attach schedule) . . . . . . . . . . . . . . | **15** | |
| 16 | **Total liabilities** (add lines 12 through 15) . . . . . . . . . . . | **16** | |

### Fund Balances or Net Assets

| | | | |
|---|---|---|---|
| 17 | Total fund balances or net assets . . . . . . . . . . . . . . | **17** | |
| 18 | **Total liabilities and fund balances or net assets** (add line 16 and line 17) . . . . | **18** | |

If there has been any substantial change in any aspect of the organization's financial activities since the end of the period shown above, check the box and attach a detailed explanation . . . . . . . . . . . . . . . . . . . . . . . . . ▶ ☐

## Schedule A. Churches

**1**  Provide a brief history of the development of the organization, including the reasons for its formation.

**2**  Does the organization have a written creed or statement of faith?. . . .  ☐ **Yes**  ☐ **No**

If "Yes," attach a copy.

**3**  Does the organization require prospective members to renounce other religious beliefs or their membership in other churches or religious orders to become members? . . . . . . . . . . . . . . . . . . . . . . .  ☐ **Yes**  ☐ **No**

**4**  Does the organization have a formal code of doctrine and discipline for its members? . . . . . . . . . . . . . . . . . . . . . .  ☐ **Yes**  ☐ **No**

If "Yes," describe.

**5**  Describe the form of worship and attach a schedule of worship services.

**6**  Are the services open to the public?. . . . . . . . . . . . . . . .  ☐ **Yes**  ☐ **No**

If "Yes," describe how the organization publicizes its services and explain the criteria for admittance.

**7**  Explain how the organization attracts new members.

**8**  **(a)** How many active members are currently enrolled in the church?

**(b)** What is the average attendance at the worship services?

**9**  In addition to worship services, what other religious services (such as baptisms, weddings, funerals, etc.) does the organization conduct?

## Schedule A. Churches *(Continued)*

**10** Does the organization have a school for the religious instruction of the young? . . . . . . . . . . . . . . . . . . . . . . . . . . . . . . . . . . . . □ **Yes**    □ **No**

**11** Were the current deacons, minister, and/or pastor formally ordained after a prescribed course of study? . . . . . . . . . . . . . . . . . . . . . . . . . □ **Yes**    □ **No**

**12** Describe the organization's religious hierarchy or ecclesiastical government.

**13** Does the organization have an established place of worship? . . . . . . . □ **Yes**    □ **No**

If "Yes," provide the name and address of the owner or lessor of the property and the address and a description of the facility.

If the organization has no regular place of worship, state where the services are held and how the site is selected.

**14** Does (or will) the organization license or otherwise ordain ministers (or their equivalent) or issue church charters? . . . . . . . . . . . . . . . . . . . . □ **Yes**    □ **No**

If "Yes," describe in detail the requirements and qualifications needed to be so licensed, ordained, or chartered.

**15** Did the organization pay a fee for a church charter? . . . . . . . . . . . □ **Yes**    □ **No**

If "Yes," state the name and address of the organization to which the fee was paid, attach a copy of the charter, and describe the circumstances surrounding the chartering.

**16** Show how many hours a week the minister/pastor and officers each devote to church work and the amount of compensation paid to each of them. If the minister or pastor is otherwise employed, indicate by whom employed, the nature of the employment, and the hours devoted to that employment.

## Schedule A. Churches *(Continued)*

**17** Will any funds or property of the organization be used by any officer, director, employee, minister, or pastor for his or her personal needs or convenience?    ☐ **Yes**    ☐ **No**

If "Yes," describe the nature and circumstances of such use.

**18** List any officers, directors, or trustees related by blood or marriage.

**19** Give the name of anyone who has assigned income to the organization or made substantial contributions of money or other property. Specify the amounts involved.

## Instructions

Although a church, its integrated auxiliaries, or a convention or association of churches is not required to file Form 1023 to be exempt from Federal income tax or to receive tax-deductible contributions, such an organization may find it advantageous to obtain recognition of exemption. In this event, you should submit information showing that your organization is a church, synagogue, association or convention of churches, religious order or religious organization that is an integral part of a church, and that it is carrying out the functions of a church.

In determining whether an admittedly religious organization is also a church, the IRS does not accept any and every assertion that such an organization is a church. Because beliefs and practices vary so widely, there is no single definition of the word "church" for tax purposes. The IRS considers the facts and circumstances of each organization applying for church status.

The IRS maintains two basic guidelines in determining that an organization meets the religious purposes test:

**1.** That the particular religious beliefs of the organization are truly and sincerely held, and

**2.** That the practices and rituals associated with the organization's religious beliefs or creed are not illegal or contrary to clearly defined public policy.

In order for the IRS to properly evaluate your organization's activities and religious purposes, it is important that all questions in Schedule A be answered.

The information submitted with Schedule A will be a determining factor in granting the "church" status requested by your organization. In completing the schedule, consider the following points:

**1.** The organization's activities in furtherance of its beliefs must be exclusively religious, and

**2.** An organization will not qualify for exemption if it has a substantial nonexempt purpose of serving the private interests of its founder or the founder's family.

# Schedule B. Schools, Colleges, and Universities

**1** Does, or will, the organization normally have: **(a)** a regularly scheduled curriculum, **(b)** a regular faculty of qualified teachers, **(c)** a regularly enrolled student body, and **(d)** facilities where its educational activities are regularly carried on? . . . . . . . . . . . . . . . . . . . . . . . . . . . . . ☐ **Yes** ☐ **No**
If "No," do not complete the rest of Schedule B.

**2** Is the organization an instrumentality of a state or political subdivision of a state? . . . . . . . . ☐ **Yes** ☐ **No**
If "Yes," document this in Part II and do not complete items 3 through 10 of Schedule B. (See instructions on the back of Schedule B.)

**3** Does or will the organization (or any department or division within it) discriminate in any way on the basis of race with respect to:

**a** Admissions? . . . . . . . . . . . . . . . . . . . . . . . . . . . . . . . . . . . . ☐ **Yes** ☐ **No**
**b** Use of facilities or exercise of student privileges? . . . . . . . . . . . . . . . . . . . . . ☐ **Yes** ☐ **No**
**c** Faculty or administrative staff? . . . . . . . . . . . . . . . . . . . . . . . . . . . . . ☐ **Yes** ☐ **No**
**d** Scholarship or loan programs? . . . . . . . . . . . . . . . . . . . . . . . . . . . . . ☐ **Yes** ☐ **No**
If "Yes" for any of the above, explain.

**4** Does the organization include a statement in its charter, bylaws, or other governing instrument, or in a resolution of its governing body, that it has a racially nondiscriminatory policy as to students? . . . . ☐ **Yes** ☐ **No**

Attach whatever corporate resolutions or other official statements the organization has made on this subject.

**5a** Has the organization made its racially nondiscriminatory policies known in a manner that brings the policies to the attention of all segments of the general community that it serves? . . . . . . . . ☐ **Yes** ☐ **No**

If "Yes," describe how these policies have been publicized and how often relevant notices or announcements have been made. If no newspaper or broadcast media notices have been used, explain.

**b** If applicable, attach clippings of any relevant newspaper notices or advertising, or copies of tapes or scripts used for media broadcasts. Also attach copies of brochures and catalogs dealing with student admissions, programs, and scholarships, as well as representative copies of all written advertising used as a means of informing prospective students of the organization's programs.

**6** Attach a numerical schedule showing the racial composition, as of the current academic year, and projected to the extent feasible for the next academic year, of: **(a)** the student body, and **(b)** the faculty and administrative staff.

**7** Attach a list showing the amount of any scholarship and loan funds awarded to students enrolled and the racial composition of the students who have received the awards.

**8a** Attach a list of the organization's incorporators, founders, board members, and donors of land or buildings, whether individuals or organizations.

**b** State whether any of the organizations listed in **8a** have as an objective the maintenance of segregated public or private school education, and, if so, whether any of the individuals listed in **8a** are officers or active members of such organizations.

**9a** Enter the public school district and county in which the organization is located.

**b** Was the organization formed or substantially expanded at the time of public school desegregation in the above district or county? . . . . . . . . . . . . . . . . . . . . . . . . . . . . . . . ☐ **Yes** ☐ **No**

**10** Has the organization ever been determined by a state or Federal administrative agency or judicial body to be racially discriminatory? . . . . . . . . . . . . . . . . . . . . . . . . . . . . . . ☐ **Yes** ☐ **No**

If "Yes," attach a detailed explanation identifying the parties to the suit, the forum in which the case was heard, the cause of action, the holding in the case, and the citations (if any) for the case. Also describe in detail what changes in the organization's operation, if any, have occurred since then.

**For more information, see back of Schedule B.**

# Instructions

A "school" is an organization that has the primary function of presenting formal instruction, normally maintains a regular faculty and curriculum, normally has a regularly enrolled student body, and has a place where its educational activities are carried on.

The term generally corresponds to the definition of an "educational organization" in section 170(b)(1)(A)(ii). Thus, the term includes primary, secondary, preparatory and high schools, and colleges and universities. The term does not include organizations engaged in both educational and noneducational activities unless the latter are merely incidental to the educational activities. A school for handicapped children is included within the term, but an organization merely providing handicapped children with custodial care is not.

For purposes of Schedule B, "Sunday schools" that are conducted by a church are not included in the term "schools," but separately organized schools (such as parochial schools, universities, and similar institutions) are included in the term.

A private school that otherwise meets the requirements of section 501(c)(3) as an educational institution will not qualify for exemption under section 501(a) unless it has a racially nondiscriminatory policy as to students.

This policy means that the school admits students of any race to all the rights, privileges, programs, and activities generally accorded or made available to students at that school and that the school does not discriminate on the basis of race in the administration of its educational policies, admissions policies, scholarship and loan programs, and athletic or other school-administered programs.

The IRS considers discrimination on the basis of race to include discrimination on the basis of color and national or ethnic origin. A policy of a school that favors racial minority groups in admissions, facilities, programs, and financial assistance will not constitute discrimination on the basis of race when the purpose and effect is to promote the establishment and maintenance of that school's racially nondiscriminatory policy as to students.

See Rev. Proc. 75-50, 1975-2 C.B. 587, for guidelines and recordkeeping requirements for determining whether private schools that are applying for recognition of exemption have racially nondiscriminatory policies as to students.

## Line 2

An instrumentality of a state or political subdivision of a state may qualify under section 501(c)(3) if it is organized as a separate entity from the governmental unit that created it and if it otherwise meets the organizational and operational tests of section 501(c)(3). See Rev. Rul. 60-384, 1960-2 C.B. 172. Any such organization that is a school is not a private school and, therefore, is not subject to the provisions of Rev. Proc. 75-50.

Schools that incorrectly answer "Yes" to line 2 will be contacted to furnish the information called for by lines 3 through 10 in order to establish that they meet the requirements for exemption. To prevent delay in the processing of your application, be sure to answer line 2 correctly and complete lines 3 through 10, if applicable.

# Schedule C. Hospitals and Medical Research Organizations

☐ Check here if claiming to be a hospital; complete the questions in Section I of this schedule; and write "N/A" in Section II.
☐ Check here if claiming to be a medical research organization operated in conjunction with a hospital; complete the questions in Section II of this schedule; and write "N/A" in Section I.

| Section I | Hospitals |
|---|---|

**1a** How many doctors are on the hospital's courtesy staff?. . . . . . . . . . . . . . . _____

**b** Are all the doctors in the community eligible for staff privileges? . . . . . . . . . . . . ☐ **Yes** ☐ **No**
If "No," give the reasons why and explain how the courtesy staff is selected.

**2a** Does the hospital maintain a full-time emergency room?. . . . . . . . . . . . . . . ☐ **Yes** ☐ **No**
**b** What is the hospital's policy on administering emergency services to persons without apparent means to pay?

**c** Does the hospital have any arrangements with police, fire, and voluntary ambulance services for the delivery or admission of emergency cases? . . . . . . . . . . . . . . . . . . . ☐ **Yes** ☐ **No**
Explain.

**3a** Does or will the hospital require a deposit from persons covered by Medicare or Medicaid in its admission practices? . . . . . . . . . . . . . . . . . . . . . . . . . . . . ☐ **Yes** ☐ **No**
If "Yes," explain.

**b** Does the same deposit requirement, if any, apply to all other patients?. . . . . . . . . . . ☐ **Yes** ☐ **No**
If "No," explain.

**4** Does or will the hospital provide for a portion of its services and facilities to be used for charity patients? ☐ **Yes** ☐ **No**
Explain the policy regarding charity cases. Include data on the hospital's past experience in admitting charity patients and arrangements it may have with municipal or government agencies for absorbing the cost of such care.

**5** Does or will the hospital carry on a formal program of medical training and research?. . . . . . . ☐ **Yes** ☐ **No**
If "Yes," describe.

**6** Does the hospital provide office space to physicians carrying on a medical practice? . . . . . . . ☐ **Yes** ☐ **No**
If "Yes," attach a list setting forth the name of each physician, the amount of space provided, the annual rent, the expiration date of the current lease and whether the terms of the lease represent fair market value.

| Section II | Medical Research Organizations |
|---|---|

**1** Name the hospitals with which the organization has a relationship and describe the relationship.

**2** Attach a schedule describing the organization's present and proposed (indicate which) medical research activities; show the nature of the activities, and the amount of money that has been or will be spent in carrying them out. (Making grants to other organizations is not direct conduct of medical research.)

**3** Attach a statement of assets showing their fair market value and the portion of the assets directly devoted to medical research.

**For more information, see back of Schedule C.**

# Additional Information

## Hospitals

To be entitled to status as a "hospital," an organization must have, as its principal purpose or function, the providing of medical or hospital care or medical education or research. "Medical care" includes the treatment of any physical or mental disability or condition, the cost of which may be taken as a deduction under section 213, whether the treatment is performed on an inpatient or outpatient basis. Thus, a rehabilitation institution, outpatient clinic, or community mental health or drug treatment center may be a hospital if its principal function is providing the above-described services.

On the other hand, a convalescent home or a home for children or the aged is not a hospital. Similarly, an institution whose principal purpose or function is to train handicapped individuals to pursue some vocation is not a hospital. Moreover, a medical education or medical research institution is not a hospital, unless it is also actively engaged in providing medical or hospital care to patients on its premises or in its facilities on an inpatient or outpatient basis.

## Cooperative Hospital Service Organizations

Cooperative hospital service organizations (section 501(e)) should not complete Schedule C.

## Medical Research Organizations

To qualify as a medical research organization, the principal function of the organization must be the direct, continuous, and active conduct of medical research in conjunction with a hospital that is described in section 501(c)(3), a Federal hospital, or an instrumentality of a governmental unit referred to in section 170(c)(1).

For purposes of section 170(b)(1)(A)(iii) only, the organization must be set up to use the funds it receives in the active conduct of medical research by January 1 of the fifth calendar year after receipt. The arrangement it has with donors to assure use of the funds within the 5-year period must be legally enforceable.

As used here, "medical research" means investigations, experiments, and studies to discover, develop, or verify knowledge relating to the causes, diagnosis, treatment, prevention, or control of human physical or mental diseases and impairments.

For further information, see Regulations section 1.170A-9(c)(2).

# Schedule D. Section 509(a)(3) Supporting Organizations

| **1a** Organizations supported by the applicant organization:<br>Name and address of supported organization | **b** Has the supported organization received a ruling or determination letter that it is not a private foundation by reason of section 509(a)(1) or (2)? | |
|---|---|---|
| .................................................................... | ☐ **Yes** | ☐ **No** |
| .................................................................... | ☐ **Yes** | ☐ **No** |
| .................................................................... | ☐ **Yes** | ☐ **No** |
| .................................................................... | ☐ **Yes** | ☐ **No** |
| .................................................................... | ☐ **Yes** | ☐ **No** |

**c** If "No" for any of the organizations listed in **1a,** explain.

**2** Does the supported organization have tax-exempt status under section 501(c)(4), 501(c)(5), or 501(c)(6)?  ☐ **Yes** ☐ **No**
If "Yes," attach: **(a)** a copy of its ruling or determination letter, and **(b)** an analysis of its revenue for the current year and the preceding 3 years. (Provide the financial data using the formats in Part IV-A (lines 1–13) and Part III (lines 11, 12, and 13).)

**3** Does your organization's governing document indicate that the majority of its governing board is elected or appointed by the supported organizations? . . . . . . . . . . . . . . . . . . . .  ☐ **Yes** ☐ **No**
If "Yes," skip to line 9.
If "No," you must answer the questions on lines 4 through 9.

**4** Does your organization's governing document indicate the common supervision or control that it and the supported organizations share? . . . . . . . . . . . . . . . . . . . . . . . .  ☐ **Yes** ☐ **No**
If "Yes," give the article and paragraph numbers. If "No," explain.

**5** To what extent do the supported organizations have a significant voice in your organization's investment policies, in the making and timing of grants, and in otherwise directing the use of your organization's income or assets?

**6** Does the mentioning of the supported organizations in your organization's governing instrument make it a trust that the supported organizations can enforce under state law and compel to make an accounting?  ☐ **Yes** ☐ **No**
If "Yes," explain.

**7a** What percentage of your organization's income does it pay to each supported organization?

**b** What is the total annual income of each supported organization?

**c** How much does your organization contribute annually to each supported organization?

**For more information, see back of Schedule D.**

## Schedule D. Section 509(a)(3) Supporting Organizations *(Continued)*

8   To what extent does your organization conduct activities that would otherwise be carried on by the supported organizations? Explain why these activities would otherwise be carried on by the supported organizations.

9   Is the applicant organization controlled directly or indirectly by one or more "disqualified persons" (other than one who is a disqualified person solely because he or she is a manager) or by an organization that is not described in section 509(a)(1) or (2)?  . . . . . . . . . . . . . . . . . . . . . . . . .  ☐ **Yes** ☐ **No**
If "Yes," explain.

## Instructions

For an explanation of the types of organizations defined in section 509(a)(3) as being excluded from the definition of a private foundation, see Pub. 557, Chapter 3.

### Line 1

List each organization that is supported by your organization and indicate in item **1b** if the supported organization has received a letter recognizing exempt status as a section 501(c)(3) public charity as defined in section 509(a)(1) or 509(a)(2). If you answer "No" in **1b** to any of the listed organizations, please explain in **1c.**

### Line 3

Your organization's governing document may be articles of incorporation, articles of association, constitution, trust indenture, or trust agreement.

### Line 9

For a definition of a "disqualified person," see **Specific Instructions,** Part II, Line 4d, on page 3 of the application's instructions.

# Schedule E. Private Operating Foundations

| Income Test | | Most recent tax year |
|---|---|---|
| **1a** Adjusted net income, as defined in Regulations section 53.4942(a)-2(d) . . . . . . . . . | 1a | |
| **b** Minimum investment return, as defined in Regulations section 53.4942(a)-2(c) . . . . . . . | 1b | |
| **2** Qualifying distributions: | | |
| **a** Amounts (including administrative expenses) paid directly for the active conduct of the activities for which organized and operated under section 501(c)(3) (attach schedule) . . . . . . . . . | 2a | |
| **b** Amounts paid to acquire assets to be used (or held for use) directly in carrying out purposes described in section 170(c)(1) or 170(c)(2)(B) (attach schedule) . . . . . . . . . . . . . . . | 2b | |
| **c** Amounts set aside for specific projects that are for purposes described in section 170(c)(1) or 170(c)(2)(B) (attach schedule). . . . . . . . . . . . . . | 2c | |
| **d Total** qualifying distributions (add lines 2a, b, and c) . . . . . . . . . . . . . . . | 2d | |
| **3** Percentages: | | |
| **a** Percentage of qualifying distributions to adjusted net income (divide line 2d by line 1a) . . . . . | 3a | % |
| **b** Percentage of qualifying distributions to minimum investment return (divide line 2d by line 1b). . . (Percentage must be at least 85% for 3a or 3b) | 3b | % |
| **Assets Test** | | |
| **4** Value of organization's assets used in activities that directly carry out the exempt purposes. Do not include assets held merely for investment or production of income (attach schedule) . . . . . . | 4 | |
| **5** Value of any stock of a corporation that is controlled by applicant organization and carries out its exempt purposes (attach statement describing corporation) . . . . . . . . . . . . . . | 5 | |
| **6** Value of all qualifying assets (add lines 4 and 5) . . . . . . . . . . . . . . . . | 6 | |
| **7** Value of applicant organization's total assets . . . . . . . . . . . . . . . . . | 7 | |
| **8** Percentage of qualifying assets to total assets (divide line 6 by line 7—percentage must exceed 65%) | 8 | % |
| **Endowment Test** | | |
| **9** Value of assets not used (or held for use) directly in carrying out exempt purposes: | | |
| **a** Monthly average of investment securities at fair market value. . . . . . . . . . . . . | 9a | |
| **b** Monthly average of cash balances. . . . . . . . . . . . . . . . . . . . | 9b | |
| **c** Fair market value of all other investment property (attach schedule). . . . . . . . . . . | 9c | |
| **d Total** (add lines 9a, b, and c). . . . . . . . . . . . . . . . . . . . . . | 9d | |
| **10** Acquisition indebtedness related to line 9 items (attach schedule) . . . . . . . . . . . | 10 | |
| **11** Balance (subtract line 10 from line 9d) . . . . . . . . . . . . . . . . . . . | 11 | |
| **12** Multiply line 11 by 3⅓% (⅔ of the percentage for the minimum investment return computation under section 4942(e)). Line 2d above must equal or exceed the result of this computation . . . . . . . | 12 | |
| **Support Test** | | |
| **13** Applicant organization's support as defined in section 509(d) . . . . . . . . . . . . . | 13 | |
| **14** Gross investment income as defined in section 509(e) . . . . . . . . . . . . . . . | 14 | |
| **15** Support for purposes of section 4942(j)(3)(B)(iii) (subtract line 14 from line 13) . . . . . . . . | 15 | |
| **16** Support received from the general public, five or more exempt organizations, or a combination of these sources (attach schedule). . . . . . . . . . . . . . . . . . . . . . | 16 | |
| **17** For persons (other than exempt organizations) contributing more than 1% of line 15, enter the total amounts that are more than 1% of line 15 . . . . . . . . . . . . . . . . . . | 17 | |
| **18** Subtract line 17 from line 16 . . . . . . . . . . . . . . . . . . . . . . | 18 | |
| **19** Percentage of total support (divide line 18 by line 15—must be at least 85%) . . . . . . . . | 19 | % |
| **20** Does line 16 include support from an exempt organization that is more than 25% of the amount of line 15? . . . . . . . . . . . . . . . . . . . . . . . . . . . . . . | ☐ Yes ☐ No | |

**21** Newly created organizations with less than 1 year's experience: Attach a statement explaining how the organization is planning to satisfy the requirements of section 4942(j)(3) for the income test and one of the supplemental tests during its first year's operation. Include a description of plans and arrangements, press clippings, public announcements, solicitations for funds, etc.

**22** Does the amount entered on line 2a above include any grants that the applicant organization made?   ☐ Yes ☐ No
If "Yes," attach a statement explaining how those grants satisfy the criteria for "significant involvement" grants described in section 53.4942(b)-1(b)(2) of the regulations.

**For more information, see back of Schedule E.**

# Instructions

If the organization claims to be an operating foundation described in section 4942(j)(3) and—

**a.** Bases its claim to private operating foundation status on normal and regular operations over a period of years; or

**b.** Is newly created, set up as a private operating foundation, and has at least 1 year's experience;

provide the information under the **income test and under one of the three supplemental tests** (assets, endowment, or support). If the organization does not have at least 1 year's experience, provide the information called for on line 21. If the organization's private operating foundation status depends on its normal and regular operations as described in **a** above, attach a schedule similar to Schedule E showing the data in tabular form for the 3 years preceding the most recent tax year. (See Regulations section 53.4942(b)-1 for additional information before completing the "Income Test" section of this schedule.) Organizations claiming section 4942(j)(5) status must satisfy the income test and the endowment test.

A "private operating foundation" described in section 4942(j)(3) is a private foundation that spends substantially all of the smaller of its adjusted net income (as defined below) or its minimum investment return directly for the active conduct of the activities constituting the purpose or function for which it is organized and operated. The foundation must satisfy the income test under section 4942(j)(3)(A), as modified by Regulations section 53.4942(b)-1, and one of the following three supplemental tests: **(1)** the assets test under section 4942(j)(3)(B)(i); **(2)** the endowment test under section 4942(j)(3)(B)(ii); or **(3)** the support test under section 4942(j)(3)(B)(iii).

Certain long-term care facilities described in section 4942(j)(5) are treated as private operating foundations for purposes of section 4942 only.

"Adjusted net income" is the excess of gross income determined with the income modifications described below for the tax year over the sum of deductions determined with the deduction modifications described below. Items of gross income from any unrelated trade or business and the deductions directly connected with the unrelated trade or business are taken into account in computing the organization's adjusted net income.

## Income Modifications

The following are income modifications (adjustments to gross income):

**1.** Section 103 (relating to interest on certain governmental obligations) does not apply. Thus, interest that otherwise would have been excluded should be included in gross income.

**2.** Except as provided in **3** below, capital gains and losses are taken into account only to the extent of the net short-term gain. Long-term gains and losses are disregarded.

**3.** The gross amount received from the sale or disposition of certain property should be included in gross income to the extent that the acquisition of the property constituted a qualifying distribution under section 4942(g)(1)(B).

**4.** Repayments of prior qualifying distributions (as defined in section 4942(g)(1)(A)) constitute items of gross income.

**5.** Any amount set aside under section 4942(g)(2) that is "not necessary for the purposes for which it was set aside" constitutes an item of gross income.

## Deduction Modifications

The following are deduction modifications (adjustments to deductions):

**1.** Expenses for the general operation of the organization according to its charitable purposes (as contrasted with expenses for the production or collection of income and management, conservation, or maintenance of income-producing property) should not be taken as deductions. If only a portion of the property is used for production of income subject to section 4942 and the remainder is used for general charitable purposes, the expenses connected with that property should be divided according to those purposes. Only expenses related to the income-producing portion should be taken as deductions.

**2.** Charitable contributions, deductible under section 170 or 642(c), should not be taken into account as deductions for adjusted net income.

**3.** The net operating loss deduction prescribed under section 172 should not be taken into account as a deduction for adjusted net income.

**4.** The special deductions for corporations (such as the dividends-received deduction) allowed under sections 241 through 249 should not be taken into account as deductions for adjusted net income.

**5.** Depreciation and depletion should be determined in the same manner as under section 4940(c)(3)(B).

Section 265 (relating to the expenses and interest connected with tax-exempt income) should not be taken into account.

You may find it easier to figure adjusted net income by completing column (c), Part 1, Form 990-PF, according to the instructions for that form.

An organization that has been held to be a private operating foundation will continue to be such an organization only if it meets the income test and either the assets, endowment, or support test in later years. See Regulations section 53.4942(b) for additional information. No additional request for ruling will be necessary or appropriate for an organization to maintain its status as a private operating foundation. However, data related to the above tests must be submitted with the organization's annual information return, Form 990-PF.

# Schedule F. Homes for the Aged or Handicapped

**1**   What are the requirements for admission to residency? Explain fully and attach promotional literature and application forms.

**2**   Does or will the home charge an entrance or founder's fee? . . . . . . . . . . . . . . . . . ☐ **Yes** ☐ **No**
If "Yes," explain and specify the amount charged.

**3**   What periodic fees or maintenance charges are or will be required of its residents?

**4a**  What established policy does the home have concerning residents who become unable to pay their regular charges?

**b**   What arrangements does the home have or will it make with local and Federal welfare units, sponsoring organizations, or others to absorb all or part of the cost of maintaining those residents?

**5**   What arrangements does or will the home have to provide for the health needs of its residents?

**6**   In what way are the home's residential facilities designed to meet some combination of the physical, emotional, recreational, social, religious, and similar needs of the aged or handicapped?

**7**   Provide a description of the home's facilities and specify both the residential capacity of the home and the current number of residents.

**8**   Attach a sample copy of the contract or agreement the organization makes with or requires of its residents.

**For more information, see back of Schedule F.**

# Instructions

### Line 1

Provide the criteria for admission to the home and submit brochures, pamphlets, or other printed material used to inform the public about the home's admissions policy.

### Line 2

Indicate whether the fee charged is an entrance fee or a monthly charge, etc. Also, if the fee is an entrance fee, is it payable in a lump sum or on an installment basis?

### Line 4

Indicate the organization's policy regarding residents who are unable to pay. Also, indicate whether the organization is subsidized for all or part of the cost of maintaining those residents who are unable to pay.

### Line 5

Indicate whether the organization provides health care to the residents, either directly or indirectly, through some continuing arrangement with other organizations, facilities, or health personnel. If no health care is provided, indicate "N/A."

## Schedule G. Child Care Organizations

**1** Is the organization's primary activity the providing of care for children away from their homes?. . . . . . . . . . . . . . . . . . . . . . . . . . . . . . ☐ **Yes**    ☐ **No**

**2** How many children is the organization authorized to care for by the state (or local governmental unit), and what was the average attendance during the past 6 months, or the number of months the organization has been in existence if less than 6 months?

**3** How many children are currently cared for by the organization?

**4** Is substantially all (at least 85%) of the care provided for the purpose of enabling parents to be gainfully employed or to seek employment? . . . ☐ **Yes**    ☐ **No**

**5** Are the services provided available to the general public?. . . . . . . . . ☐ **Yes**    ☐ **No**
   If "No," explain.

**6** Indicate the category, or categories, of parents whose children are eligible for the child care services (check as many as apply):

☐  low-income parents

☐  any working parents (or parents looking for work)

☐  anyone with the ability to pay

☐  other (explain)

## Instructions

**Line 5**

If your organization's services are not available to the general public, indicate the particular group or groups that may utilize the services.

REMINDER—If this organization claims to operate a school, then it must also fill out Schedule B.

## Schedule H. Organizations Providing Scholarship Benefits, Student Aid, etc., to Individuals

**1a** Describe the nature and the amount of the scholarship benefit, student aid, etc., including the terms and conditions governing its use, whether a gift or a loan, and how the availability of the scholarship is publicized. If the organization has established or will establish several categories of scholarship benefits, identify each kind of benefit and explain how the organization determines the recipients for each category. Attach a sample copy of any application the organization requires individuals to complete to be considered for scholarship grants, loans, or similar benefits. (Private foundations that make grants for travel, study, or other similar purposes are required to obtain advance approval of scholarship procedures. See Regulations sections 53.4945-4(c) and (d).)

**b** If you want this application considered as a request for approval of grant procedures in the event we determine that the organization is a private foundation, check here . . . . . . . . . . . . . . . . . . . . . . . . . . . . ▶ ☐

**c** If you checked the box in **1b** above, check the box(es) for which you wish the organization to be considered.

☐ 4945(g)(1)          ☐ 4945(g)(2)          ☐ 4945(g)(3)

**2** What limitations or restrictions are there on the class of individuals who are eligible recipients? Specifically explain whether there are, or will be, any restrictions or limitations in the selection procedures based upon race or the employment status of the prospective recipient or any relative of the prospective recipient. Also indicate the approximate number of eligible individuals.

**3** Indicate the number of grants the organization anticipates making annually . . . . . . . . . ▶

**4** If the organization bases its selections in any way on the employment status of the applicant or any relative of the applicant, indicate whether there is or has been any direct or indirect relationship between the members of the selection committee and the employer. Also indicate whether relatives of the members of the selection committee are possible recipients or have been recipients.

**5** Describe any procedures the organization has for supervising grants (such as obtaining reports or transcripts) that it awards and any procedures it has for taking action if the terms of the grant are violated.

**For more information, see back of Schedule H.**

## Additional Information

Private foundations that make grants to individuals for travel, study, or other similar purposes are required to obtain advance approval of their grant procedures from the IRS. Such grants that are awarded under selection procedures that have not been approved by the IRS are subject to a 10% excise tax under section 4945. (See Regulations sections 53.4945-4(c) and (d).)

If you are requesting advance approval of the organization's grant procedures, the following sections apply to line **1c:**

4945(g)(1)—The grant constitutes a scholarship or fellowship grant that meets the provisions of section 117(a) prior to its amendment by the Tax Reform Act of 1986 and is to be used for study at an educational organization (school) described in section 170(b)(1)(A)(ii).

4945(g)(2)—The grant constitutes a prize or award that is subject to the provisions of section 74(b), if the recipient of such a prize or award is selected from the general public.

4945(g)(3)—The purpose of the grant is to achieve a specific objective, produce a report or other similar product, or improve or enhance a literary, artistic, musical, scientific, teaching, or other similar capacity, skill, or talent of the grantee.

# Schedule I. Successors to "For Profit" Institutions

1   What was the name of the predecessor organization and the nature of its activities?

2   Who were the owners or principal stockholders of the predecessor organization? (If more space is needed, attach schedule.)

| Name and address | Share or interest |
| --- | --- |
| | |
| | |
| | |
| | |

3   Describe the business or family relationship between the owners or principal stockholders and principal employees of the predecessor organization and the officers, directors, and principal employees of the applicant organization.

4a   Attach a copy of the agreement of sale or other contract that sets forth the terms and conditions of sale of the predecessor organization or of its assets to the applicant organization.

b   Attach an appraisal by an independent qualified expert showing the fair market value at the time of sale of the facilities or property interest sold.

5   Has any property or equipment formerly used by the predecessor organization been rented to the applicant organization or will any such property be rented? . . . . . . . . . . . . . . . . . . . . . . . . .   ☐ **Yes** ☐ **No**
   If "Yes," explain and attach copies of all leases and contracts.

6   Is the organization leasing or will it lease or otherwise make available any space or equipment to the owners, principal stockholders, or principal employees of the predecessor organization? . . . . . .   ☐ **Yes** ☐ **No**
   If "Yes," explain and attach a list of these tenants and a copy of the lease for each such tenant.

7   Were any new operating policies initiated as a result of the transfer of assets from a profit-making organization to a nonprofit organization? . . . . . . . . . . . . . . . . . . . . . . . . . . .   ☐ **Yes** ☐ **No**
   If "Yes," explain.

## Additional Information

A "for profit" institution for purposes of Schedule I includes any organization in which a person may have a proprietary or partnership interest, hold corporate stock, or otherwise exercise an ownership interest. The institution need not have operated for the purpose of making a profit.

⊕

# Form 1024

| Form **1024**<br>(Rev. September 1998)<br>Department of the Treasury<br>Internal Revenue Service | **Application for Recognition of Exemption**<br>**Under Section 501(a)** | OMB No. 1545-0057<br><br>If exempt status is approved,<br>this application will be open<br>for public inspection. |

Read the instructions for each Part carefully. **A User Fee must be attached to this application.**
If the required information and appropriate documents are not submitted along with Form 8718 (with payment of the appropriate user fee), the application may be returned to the organization.
**Complete the Procedural Checklist on page 6 of the instructions.**

**Part I. Identification of Applicant** (Must be completed by all applicants; also complete appropriate schedule.) Submit only the schedule that applies to your organization. Do not submit blank schedules.

Check the appropriate box below to indicate the section under which the organization is applying:

a ☐ Section 501(c)(2)—Title holding corporations (Schedule A, page 7)

b ☐ Section 501(c)(4)—Civic leagues, social welfare organizations (including certain war veterans' organizations), or local associations of employees (Schedule B, page 8)

c ☐ Section 501(c)(5)—Labor, agricultural, or horticultural organizations (Schedule C, page 9)

d ☐ Section 501(c)(6)—Business leagues, chambers of commerce, etc. (Schedule C, page 9)

e ☐ Section 501(c)(7)—Social clubs (Schedule D, page 11)

f ☐ Section 501(c)(8)—Fraternal beneficiary societies, etc., providing life, sick, accident, or other benefits to members (Schedule E, page 13)

g ☐ Section 501(c)(9)—Voluntary employees' beneficiary associations (Parts I through IV and Schedule F, page 14)

h ☐ Section 501(c)(10)—Domestic fraternal societies, orders, etc., not providing life, sick, accident, or other benefits (Schedule E, page 13)

i ☐ Section 501(c)(12)—Benevolent life insurance associations, mutual ditch or irrigation companies, mutual or cooperative telephone companies, or like organizations (Schedule G, page 15)

j ☐ Section 501(c)(13)—Cemeteries, crematoria, and like corporations (Schedule H, page 16)

k ☐ Section 501(c)(15)—Mutual insurance companies or associations, other than life or marine (Schedule I, page 17)

l ☐ Section 501(c)(17)—Trusts providing for the payment of supplemental unemployment compensation benefits (Parts I through IV and Schedule J, page 18)

m ☐ Section 501(c)(19)—A post, organization, auxiliary unit, etc., of past or present members of the Armed Forces of the United States (Schedule K, page 19)

n ☐ Section 501(c)(25)—Title holding corporations or trusts (Schedule A, page 7)

| 1a Full name of organization (as shown in organizing document) | 2 Employer Identification number (EIN) (if none, see **Specific Instructions** on page 2) |
| --- | --- |
| 1b c/o Name (if applicable) | 3 Name and telephone number of person to be contacted if additional information is needed |
| 1c Address (number and street) / Room/Suite | |
| 1d City, town or post office, state, and ZIP + 4  If you have a foreign address, see **Specific Instructions** for Part I, page 2. | (     ) |

| 1e Web site address | 4 Month the annual accounting period ends | 5 Date incorporated or formed |
| --- | --- | --- |

6 Did the organization previously apply for recognition of exemption under this Code section or under any other section of the Code?   ☐ Yes   ☐ No
If "Yes," attach an explanation.

7 Has the organization filed Federal income tax returns or exempt organization information returns?   . . . . . . .   ☐ Yes   ☐ No
If "Yes," state the form numbers, years filed, and Internal Revenue office where filed.

8 Check the box for the type of organization. ATTACH A CONFORMED COPY OF THE CORRESPONDING ORGANIZING DOCUMENTS TO THE APPLICATION BEFORE MAILING.

a ☐ Corporation— Attach a copy of the Articles of Incorporation (including amendments and restatements) showing approval by the appropriate state official; also attach a copy of the bylaws.

b ☐ Trust— Attach a copy of the Trust Indenture or Agreement, including all appropriate signatures and dates.

c ☐ Association— Attach a copy of the Articles of Association, Constitution, or other creating document, with a declaration (see instructions) or other evidence that the organization was formed by adoption of the document by more than one person. Also include a copy of the bylaws.

If this is a corporation or an unincorporated association that has not yet adopted bylaws, check here   . . . . . ▶ ☐

PLEASE
SIGN
HERE ▶

I declare under the penalties of perjury that I am authorized to sign this application on behalf of the above organization, and that I have examined this application, including the accompanying schedules and attachments, and to the best of my knowledge it is true, correct, and complete.

. . . . . . . . . . . . . . . . . . . . . . . . . . . . . . . . . . . . . . . . . . . . . . . . . . . . . . . . . . . . . . . . . . . . . . . . . . . . . . . . . .
(Signature)                    (Type or print name and title or authority of signer)                    (Date)

**For Paperwork Reduction Act Notice, see page 5 of the instructions.**

**Part II. Activities and Operational Information** (Must be completed by all applicants)

1    Provide a detailed narrative description of all the activities of the organization—past, present, and planned. Do not merely refer to or
     repeat the language in the organizational document. List each activity separately in the order of importance based on the relative time and
     other resources devoted to the activity. Indicate the percentage of time for each activity. Each description should include, as a minimum,
     the following: **(a)** a detailed description of the activity including its purpose and how each activity furthers your exempt purpose; **(b)** when
     the activity was or will be initiated; and **(c)** where and by whom the activity will be conducted.

2    List the organization's present and future sources of financial support, beginning with the largest source first.

## Part II. Activities and Operational Information (continued)

3   Give the following information about the organization's governing body:

| **a**   Names, addresses, and titles of officers, directors, trustees, etc. | **b**  Annual compensation |
|---|---|
|  |  |

4   If the organization is the outgrowth or continuation of any form of predecessor, state the name of each predecessor, the period during which it was in existence, and the reasons for its termination. Submit copies of all papers by which any transfer of assets was effected.

5   If the applicant organization is now, or plans to be, connected in any way with any other organization, describe the other organization and explain the relationship (e.g., financial support on a continuing basis; shared facilities or employees; same officers, directors, or trustees).

6   If the organization has capital stock issued and outstanding, state: **(1)** class or classes of the stock; **(2)** number and par value of the shares; **(3)** consideration for which they were issued; and **(4)** if any dividends have been paid or whether your organization's creating instrument authorizes dividend payments on any class of capital stock.

7   State the qualifications necessary for membership in the organization; the classes of membership (with the number of members in each class); and the voting rights and privileges received. If any group or class of persons is required to join, describe the requirement and explain the relationship between those members and members who join voluntarily. Submit copies of any membership solicitation material. Attach sample copies of all types of membership certificates issued.

8   Explain how your organization's assets will be distributed on dissolution.

## Part II. Activities and Operational Information (continued)

9   Has the organization made or does it plan to make any distribution of its property or surplus funds to shareholders or
members? . . . . . . . . . . . . . . . . . . . . . . . . . . . . . . . . . . . . . .   ☐ Yes ☐ No
If "Yes," state the full details, including: **(1)** amounts or value; **(2)** source of funds or property distributed or to be
distributed; and **(3)** basis of, and authority for, distribution or planned distribution.

10   Does, or will, any part of your organization's receipts represent payments for services performed or to be performed? .   ☐ Yes ☐ No
If "Yes," state in detail the amount received and the character of the services performed or to be performed.

11   Has the organization made, or does it plan to make, any payments to members or shareholders for services performed
or to be performed? . . . . . . . . . . . . . . . . . . . . . . . . . . . . . . . . .   ☐ Yes ☐ No
If "Yes," state in detail the amount paid, the character of the services, and to whom the payments have been, or will
be, made.

12   Does the organization have any arrangement to provide insurance for members, their dependents, or others (including
provisions for the payment of sick or death benefits, pensions, or annuities)? . . . . . . . . . . . . .   ☐ Yes ☐ No
If "Yes," describe and explain the arrangement's eligibility rules and attach a sample copy of each plan document and
each type of policy issued.

13   Is the organization under the supervisory jurisdiction of any public regulatory body, such as a social welfare agency,
etc.? . . . . . . . . . . . . . . . . . . . . . . . . . . . . . . . . . . . . . . .   ☐ Yes ☐ No
If "Yes," submit copies of all administrative opinions or court decisions regarding this supervision, as well as copies of
applications or requests for the opinions or decisions.

14   Does the organization now lease or does it plan to lease any property? . . . . . . . . . . . . . .   ☐ Yes ☐ No
If "Yes," explain in detail. Include the amount of rent, a description of the property, and any relationship between the
applicant organization and the other party. Also, attach a copy of any rental or lease agreement. (If the organization is
a party, as a lessor, to multiple leases of rental real property under similar lease agreements, please attach a single
representative copy of the leases.)

15   Has the organization spent or does it plan to spend any money attempting to influence the selection, nomination, election,
or appointment of any person to any Federal, state, or local public office or to an office in a political organization? . .   ☐ Yes ☐ No
If "Yes," explain in detail and list the amounts spent or to be spent in each case.

16   Does the organization publish pamphlets, brochures, newsletters, journals, or similar printed material?   . . . . .   ☐ Yes ☐ No
If "Yes," attach a recent copy of each.

**Part III. Financial Data** (Must be completed by all applicants)

Complete the financial statements for the current year and for each of the 3 years immediately before it. *If in existence less than 4 years, complete the statements for each year in existence. **If in existence less than 1 year, also provide proposed budgets for the 2 years following the current year.***

### A. Statement of Revenue and Expenses

| Revenue | (a) Current Tax Year From ___ To | 3 Prior Tax Years or Proposed Budget for Next 2 Years (b) ___ | (c) ___ | (d) ___ | (e) Total |
|---|---|---|---|---|---|
| 1 Gross dues and assessments of members | | | | | |
| 2 Gross contributions, gifts, etc. | | | | | |
| 3 Gross amounts derived from activities related to the organization's exempt purpose (attach schedule) (Include related cost of sales on line 9.) | | | | | |
| 4 Gross amounts from unrelated business activities (attach schedule) | | | | | |
| 5 Gain from sale of assets, excluding inventory items (attach schedule) | | | | | |
| 6 Investment income (see page 3 of the instructions) | | | | | |
| 7 Other revenue (attach schedule). | | | | | |
| 8 Total revenue (add lines 1 through 7) | | | | | |
| **Expenses** | | | | | |
| 9 Expenses attributable to activities related to the organization's exempt purposes. | | | | | |
| 10 Expenses attributable to unrelated business activities | | | | | |
| 11 Contributions, gifts, grants, and similar amounts paid (attach schedule). | | | | | |
| 12 Disbursements to or for the benefit of members (attach schedule) | | | | | |
| 13 Compensation of officers, directors, and trustees (attach schedule) | | | | | |
| 14 Other salaries and wages. | | | | | |
| 15 Interest. | | | | | |
| 16 Occupancy. | | | | | |
| 17 Depreciation and depletion | | | | | |
| 18 Other expenses (attach schedule) | | | | | |
| 19 Total expenses (add lines 9 through 18) | | | | | |
| 20 Excess of revenue over expenses (line 8 minus line 19) | | | | | |

### B. Balance Sheet (at the end of the period shown)

Current Tax Year as of _____

**Assets**

| | | |
|---|---|---|
| 1 | Cash. | 1 |
| 2 | Accounts receivable, net. | 2 |
| 3 | Inventories. | 3 |
| 4 | Bonds and notes receivable (attach schedule) | 4 |
| 5 | Corporate stocks (attach schedule). | 5 |
| 6 | Mortgage loans (attach schedule) | 6 |
| 7 | Other investments (attach schedule) | 7 |
| 8 | Depreciable and depletable assets (attach schedule) | 8 |
| 9 | Land. | 9 |
| 10 | Other assets (attach schedule) | 10 |
| 11 | **Total assets** | 11 |

**Liabilities**

| | | |
|---|---|---|
| 12 | Accounts payable. | 12 |
| 13 | Contributions, gifts, grants, etc., payable. | 13 |
| 14 | Mortgages and notes payable (attach schedule). | 14 |
| 15 | Other liabilities (attach schedule) | 15 |
| 16 | **Total liabilities.** | 16 |

**Fund Balances or Net Assets**

| | | |
|---|---|---|
| 17 | Total fund balances or net assets | 17 |
| 18 | **Total liabilities and fund balances or net assets** (add line 16 and line 17) | 18 |

If there has been any substantial change in any aspect of the organization's financial activities since the end of the period shown above, check the box and attach a detailed explanation. ▶ ☐

## Part IV. Notice Requirements (Sections 501(c)(9) and 501(c)(17) Organizations Only)

**1**   Section 501(c)(9) and 501(c)(17) organizations:

Are you filing Form 1024 within 15 months from the end of the month in which the organization was created or formed as required by section 505(c)? . . . . . . . . . . . . . . . . . . . . . . . . . . . . . . .   ☐ **Yes** ☐ **No**

If "Yes," skip the rest of this Part.

If "No," answer question 2.

**2**   If you answer "No" to question 1, are you filing Form 1024 within 27 months from the end of the month in which the organization was created or formed? . . . . . . . . . . . . . . . . . . . . . . . . . . . .   ☐ **Yes** ☐ **No**

If "Yes," your organization qualifies under Regulation section 301.9100-2 for an automatic 12-month extension of the 15-month filing requirement. Do not answer questions 3 and 4.

If "No," answer question 3.

**3**   If you answer "No" to question 2, does the organization wish to request an extension of time to apply under the "reasonable action and good faith" and the "no prejudice to the interest of the government" requirements of Regulations section 301.9100-3? . . . . . . . . . . . . . . . . . . . . . . . . . . . . . .   ☐ **Yes** ☐ **No**

If "Yes," give the reasons for not filing this application within the 27-month period described in question 2. See Specific Instructions, Part IV, Line 3, page 4, before completing this item. Do not answer question 4.

If "No," answer question 4.

**4**   If you answer "No" to question 3, your organization's qualification as a section 501(c)(9) or 501(c)(17) organization can be recognized only from the date this application is filed. Therefore, does the organization want us to consider its application as a request for recognition of exemption as a section 501(c)(9) or 501(c)(17) organization from the date the application is received and not retroactively to the date the organization was created or formed? . . . . . . . .   ☐ **Yes** ☐ **No**

## Schedule A    Organizations described in section 501(c)(2) or 501(c)(25) (Title holding corporations or trusts)

1    State the complete name, address, and EIN of each organization for which title to property is held and the number and type of the applicant organization's stock held by each organization.

2    If the annual excess of revenue over expenses has not been or will not be turned over to the organization for which title to property is held, state the purpose for which the excess is or will be retained by the title holding organization.

3    In the case of a corporation described in section 501(c)(2), state the purpose of the organization for which title to property is held (as shown in its governing instrument) and the Code sections under which it is classified as exempt from tax. If the organization has received a determination or ruling letter recognizing it as exempt from taxation, please attach a copy of the letter.

4    In the case of a corporation or trust described in section 501(c)(25), state the basis whereby each shareholder is described in section 501(c)(25)(C). For each organization described that has received a determination or ruling letter recognizing that organization as exempt from taxation, please attach a copy of the letter.

5    With respect to the activities of the organization.

a    Is any rent received attributable to personal property leased with real property? . . . . . . . . . . . . . ☐ Yes ☐ No

If "Yes," what percentage of the total rent, as reported on the financial statements in Part III, is attributable to personal property?

b    Will the organization receive income which is incidentally derived from the holding of real property, such as income from operation of a parking lot or from vending machines? . . . . . . . . . . . . . . . . . . ☐ Yes ☐ No

If "Yes," what percentage of the organization's gross income, as reported on the financial statements in Part III, is incidentally derived from the holding of real property?

c    Will the organization receive income other than rent from real property or personal property leased with real property or income which is incidentally derived from the holding of real property? . . . . . . . . . . . ☐ Yes ☐ No

If "Yes," describe the source of the income.

# Instructions

Line 1.—Provide the requested information on each organization for which the applicant organization holds title to property. Also indicate the number and types of shares of the applicant organization's stock that are held by each.

Line 2.—For purposes of this question, "excess of revenue over expenses" is all of the organization's income for a particular tax year less operating expenses.

Line 3.—Give the exempt purpose of each organization that is the basis for its exempt status and the Internal Revenue Code section

that describes the organization (as shown in its IRS determination letter).

Line 4.—Indicate if the shareholder is one of the following:

1. A qualified pension, profit-sharing, or stock bonus plan that meets the requirements of the Code;

2. A government plan;

3. An organization described in section 501(c)(3); or

4. An organization described in section 501(c)(25).

Form 1024 (Rev. 9-98)                                                                                          Page **8**

| **Schedule B** | Organizations Described in Section 501(c)(4) (Civic leagues, social welfare organizations (including posts, councils, etc., of veterans' organizations not qualifying or applying for exemption under section 501(c)(19)) or local associations of employees.) |

1  Has the Internal Revenue Service previously issued a ruling or determination letter recognizing the applicant organization (or any predecessor organization listed in question 4, Part II of the application) to be exempt under section 501(c)(3) and later revoked that recognition of exemption on the basis that the applicant organization (or its predecessor) was carrying on propaganda or otherwise attempting to influence legislation or on the basis that it engaged in political activity? . .  ☐ **Yes** ☐ **No**

If "Yes," indicate the earliest tax year for which recognition of exemption under section 501(c)(3) was revoked and the IRS district office that issued the revocation.

2  Does the organization perform or plan to perform (for members, shareholders, or others) services, such as maintaining the common areas of a condominium; buying food or other items on a cooperative basis; or providing recreational facilities or transportation services, job placement, or other similar undertakings?. . . . . . . . . . . . . . .  ☐ **Yes** ☐ **No**

If "Yes," explain the activities in detail, including income realized and expenses incurred. Also, explain in detail the nature of the benefits to the general public from these activities. (If the answer to this question is explained in Part II of the application (pages 2, 3, and 4), enter the page and item number here.)

3  If the organization is claiming exemption as a homeowners' association, is access to any property or facilities it owns or maintains restricted in any way? . . . . . . . . . . . . . . . . . . . . . . . . . . .  ☐ **Yes** ☐ **No**

If "Yes," explain.

4  If the organization is claiming exemption as a local association of employees, state the name and address of each employer whose employees are eligible for membership in the association. If employees of more than one plant or office of the same employer are eligible for membership, give the address of each plant or office.

| Schedule C | Organizations described in section 501(c)(5) (Labor, agricultural, including fishermen's organizations, or horticultural organizations) or section 501(c)(6) (business leagues, chambers of commerce, etc.) |
|---|---|

1  Describe any services the organization performs for members or others. (If the description of the services is contained in Part II of the application, enter the page and item number here.)

2  Fishermen's organizations only.—What kinds of aquatic resources (not including mineral) are cultivated or harvested by those eligible for membership in the organization?

3  Labor organizations only.—Is the organization organized under the terms of a collective bargaining agreement? . . ☐ **Yes**  ☐ **No**

If "Yes," attach a copy of the latest agreement.

Form 1024 (Rev. 9-98)                                                                                                    Page **11**

| **Schedule D** | **Organizations described in section 501(c)(7) (Social clubs)** |

**1**  Has the organization entered or does it plan to enter into any contract or agreement for the management or operation of its property and/or activities, such as restaurants, pro shops, lodges, etc.? . . . . . . . . . . . . . . .   ☐ **Yes** ☐ **No**

If "Yes," attach a copy of the contract or agreement. If one has not yet been drawn up, please explain the organization's plans.

**2**  Does the organization seek or plan to seek public patronage of its facilities or activities by advertisement or otherwise?   ☐ **Yes** ☐ **No**
If "Yes," attach sample copies of the advertisements or other requests.
If the organization plans to seek public patronage, please explain the plans.

**3a**  Are nonmembers, other than guests of members, permitted or will they be permitted to use the club facilities or participate in or attend any functions or activities conducted by the organization? . . . . . . . . . . . . . . . . .   ☐ **Yes** ☐ **No**
If "Yes," describe the functions or activities in which there has been or will be nonmember participation or admittance. (Submit a copy of the house rules, if any.)

**b**  State the amount of nonmember income included in Part III of the application, lines 3 and 4, column (a) . . . . . .
**c**  Enter the percent of gross receipts from nonmembers for the use of club facilities . . . . . . . . . . .   %
**d**  Enter the percent of gross receipts received from investment income and nonmember use of the club's facilities  . .   %

**4a**  Does the organization's charter, bylaws, other governing instrument, or any written policy statement of the organization contain any provision that provides for discrimination against any person on the basis of race, color, or religion? . .   ☐ **Yes** ☐ **No**

**b**  If "Yes," state whether or not its provision will be kept.

**c**  If the organization has such a provision that will be repealed, deleted, or otherwise stricken from its requirements, state when this will be done. . . . . . . . . . . . . . . . . . . . . . . . . . . . . . . . . . .  _____
**d**  If the organization formerly had such a requirement and it no longer applies, give the date it ceased to apply  . . .  _____
**e**  If the organization restricts its membership to members of a particular religion, check here and attach the explanation specified in the instructions . . . . . . . . . . . . . . . . . . . . . . . . . . . . . . . . . .  ☐

**See reverse side for instructions**

# Instructions

**Line 1.**—Answer "Yes," if any of the organization's property or activities will be managed by another organization or company.

**Lines 3b, c, and d.**—Enter the figures for the current year. On an attached schedule, furnish the same information for each of the prior tax years for which you completed Part III of the application.

**Line 4e.**—If the organization restricts its membership to members of a particular religion, the organization must be:

1. An auxiliary of a fraternal beneficiary society that:

**a.** Is described in section 501(c)(8) and exempt from tax under section 501(a), and

**b.** Limits its membership to members of a particular religion; or

**2.** A club that, in good faith, limits its membership to the members of a particular religion in order to further the teachings or principles of that religion and not to exclude individuals of a particular race or color.

If you checked **4e,** your explanation must show how the organization meets one of these two requirements.

| **Schedule E** | **Organizations described in section 501(c)(8) or 501(c)(10) (Fraternal societies, orders, or associations)** |

**1**  Is the organization a college fraternity or sorority, or chapter of a college fraternity or sorority? . . . . . . .  ☐ Yes  ☐ No
If "Yes," read the instructions for Line 1, below, before completing this schedule.

**2**  Does or will your organization operate under the lodge system? . . . . . . . . . . . . . .  ☐ Yes  ☐ No
If "No," does or will it operate for the exclusive benefit of the members of an organization operating under the lodge system? . . . . . . . . . . . . . . . . . . . . . . . . . . . . . . . . . . . .  ☐ Yes  ☐ No

**3**  Is the organization a subordinate or local lodge, etc.? . . . . . . . . . . . . . . . . . .  ☐ Yes  ☐ No
If "Yes," attach a certificate signed by the secretary of the parent organization, under the seal of the organization, certifying that the subordinate lodge is a duly constituted body operating under the jurisdiction of the parent body.

**4**  Is the organization a parent or grand lodge? . . . . . . . . . . . . . . . . . . . . . .  ☐ Yes  ☐ No
If "Yes," attach a schedule for each subordinate lodge in active operation showing: (a) its name and address; (b) the number of members in it; and (c) how often it holds periodic meetings.

# Instructions

**Line 1.**—To the extent that they qualify for exemption from Federal income tax, college fraternities and sororities generally qualify as organizations described in section 501(c)(7). Therefore, if the organization is a college fraternity or sorority, refer to the discussion of section 501(c)(7) organizations in Pub. 557. If section 501(c)(7) appears to apply to your organization, complete Schedule D instead of this schedule.

**Line 2.**—Operating under the lodge system means carrying on activities under a form of organization that is composed of local branches, chartered by a parent organization, largely self-governing, and called lodges, chapters, or the like.

| Schedule F | Organizations described in section 501(c)(9) (Voluntary employees' beneficiary associations) |
|---|---|

1   Describe the benefits available to members. Include copies of any plan documents that describe such benefits and the terms and conditions of eligibility for each benefit.

2   Are any employees or classes of employees entitled to benefits to which other employees or classes of employees are not entitled?   . . . . . . . . . . . . . . . . . . . . . . . . . . . . . . . . . . . . . . . . . . . □ **Yes** □ **No**
If "Yes," explain.

3   Give the following information for each plan as of the last day of the most recent plan year and enter that date here. If there is more than one plan, attach a separate schedule   . . . . . . . . . . . . . . . . . . . . . . .   ___/___/___
(mo.)  (day)  (yr.)

a   Total number of persons covered by the plan who are highly compensated individuals (See instructions below.)  . . .   _____
b   Number of other employees covered by the plan. . . . . . . . . . . . . . . . . . . . . . . . . . . .   _____
c   Number of employees not covered by the plan . . . . . . . . . . . . . . . . . . . . . . . . . . . .   _____
d   Total number employed* . . . . . . . . . . . . . . . . . . . . . . . . . . . . . . . . . . . . .   _____

* Should equal the total of **a**, **b**, and **c**—if not, explain any difference. Describe the eligibility requirements that prevent those employees not covered by the plan from participating.

4   State the number of persons, if any, other than employees and their dependents (e.g., the proprietor of a business whose employees are members of the association) who are entitled to receive benefits  . . . . . . . . . . . . ▶

# Instructions

**Line 3a.**—A "highly compensated individual" is one who:

**(a)** Owned 5% or more of the employer at any time during the current year or the preceding year.

**(b)** Received more than $80,000 (adjusted for inflation) in compensation from the employer for the preceding year, and

**(c)** Was among the top 20% of employees by compensation for the preceding year. However, the employer can choose not to have **(c)** apply.

**Schedule G** **Organizations described in section 501(c)(12) (Benevolent life insurance associations, mutual ditch or irrigation companies, mutual or cooperative telephone companies, or like organizations)**

**1** Attach a schedule in columnar form for each tax year for which the organization is claiming exempt status. On each schedule:

**a** Show the total gross income received from members or shareholders.

**b** List, by source, the total amounts of gross income received from other sources.

**2** If the organization is claiming exemption as a local benevolent insurance association, state:

**a** The counties from which members are accepted or will be accepted.

**b** Whether stipulated premiums are or will be charged in advance, or whether losses are or will be paid solely through assessments.

**3** If the organization is claiming exemption as a "like organization," explain how it is similar to a mutual ditch or irrigation company, or a mutual or cooperative telephone company.

**4** Are the rights and interests of members in the organization's annual savings determined in proportion to their business with it? . . . . . . . . . . . . . . . . . . . . . . . . . . . . . . . . . . . . .  ☐ **Yes** ☐ **No**

If "Yes," does the organization keep the records necessary to determine at any time each member's rights and interests in such savings, including assets acquired with the savings? . . . . . . . . . . . . . . . . . . . .  ☐ **Yes** ☐ **No**

**5** If the organization is a mutual or cooperative telephone company and has contracts with other systems for long-distance telephone services, attach copies of the contracts.

# Instructions

Mutual or cooperative electric or telephone companies should show income received from qualified pole rentals separately. Mutual or cooperative telephone companies should also show separately the gross amount of income received from nonmember telephone companies for performing services that involve their members and the gross amount of income received from the sale of display advertising in a directory furnished to their members.

Do not net amounts due or paid to other sources against amounts due or received from those sources.

| Schedule H | Organizations described in section 501(c)(13) (Cemeteries, crematoria, and like corporations) |
|---|---|

**1** Attach the following documents:

**a** Complete copy of sales contracts or other documents, including any "debt" certificates, involved in acquiring cemetery or crematorium property.

**b** Complete copy of any contract your organization has that designates an agent to sell its cemetery lots.

**c** A copy of the appraisal (obtained from a disinterested and qualified party) of the cemetery property as of the date acquired.

**2** Does your organization have, or does it plan to have, a perpetual care fund? . . . . . . . . . . . . . . . . .  ☐ **Yes** ☐ **No**

If "Yes," attach a copy of the fund agreement and explain the nature of the fund (cash, securities, unsold land, etc.)

**3** If your organization is claiming exemption as a perpetual care fund for an organization described in section 501(c)(13), has the cemetery organization, for which funds are held, established exemption under that section? . . . . . . .  ☐ **Yes** ☐ **No**

If "No," explain.

Form 1024 (Rev. 9-98) Page **17**

| Schedule I | Organizations described in section 501(c)(15) (Small insurance companies or associations) |

1   Is the organization a member of a controlled group of corporations as defined in section 831(b)(2)(B)(ii)? (Disregard section 1563(b)(2)(B) in determining whether the organization is a member of a controlled group.) . . . . . . . . . . . ☐ **Yes** ☐ **No**

If "Yes," include on lines 2 through 5 the total amount received by the organization and all other members of the controlled group.

If "No," include on lines 2 through 5 only the amounts that relate to the applicant organization.

| | | (a) Current Year | 3 Prior Tax Years | | |
| | | From _____ To | (b) ·········· | (c) ·········· | (d) ·········· |
|---|---|---|---|---|---|
| 2 | Direct written premiums . . . . . . . . . . . . . . | | | | |
| 3 | Reinsurance assumed . . . . . . . . . . . . . . | | | | |
| 4 | Reinsurance ceded . . . . . . . . . . . . . . . | | | | |
| 5 | Net written premiums ((line 2 plus line 3) minus line 4) . . . . | | | | |
| 6 | If you entered an amount on line 3 or line 4, attach a copy of the reinsurance agreements the organization has entered into. | | | | |

## Instructions

**Line 1.**—Answer "Yes," if the organization would be considered a member of a controlled group of corporations if it were not exempt from tax under section 501(a). In applying section 1563(a), use a "more than 50%" stock ownership test to determine whether the applicant or any other corporation is a member of a controlled group.

**Line 2.**— In addition to other direct written premiums, include on line 2 the full amount of any prepaid or advance premium in the year the prepayment is received. For example, if a $5,000 premium for a 3-year policy was received in the current year, include the full $5,000 amount in the Current Year column.

| Schedule J | Organizations described in section 501(c)(17) (Trusts providing for the payment of supplemental unemployment compensation benefits) |
|---|---|

**1** If benefits are provided for individual proprietors, partners, or self-employed persons under the plan, explain in detail.

**2** If the plan provides other benefits in addition to the supplemental unemployment compensation benefits, explain in detail and state whether the other benefits are subordinate to the unemployment benefits.

**3** Give the following information as of the last day of the most recent plan year and enter that date here . . . . . . . ─────────

**a** Total number of employees covered by the plan who are shareholders, officers, self-employed persons, or highly compensated (See Schedule F instructions for line 3a on page 14.) . . . . . . . . . . . . . . . . ─────────

**b** Number of other employees covered by the plan . . . . . . . . . . . . . . . . . . . . ─────────

**c** Number of employees not covered by the plan . . . . . . . . . . . . . . . . . . . . . ─────────

**d** Total number employed*. . . . . . . . . . . . . . . . . . . . . . . . . . . . . ─────────

* Should equal the total of **a, b,** and **c**—if not, explain the difference. Describe the eligibility requirements that prevent those employees not covered by the plan from participating.

**4** At any time after December 31, 1959, did any of the following persons engage in any of the transactions listed below with the trust: the creator of the trust or a contributor to the trust; a brother or sister (whole or half blood), a spouse, an ancestor, or a lineal descendant of such a creator or contributor; or a corporation controlled directly or indirectly by such a creator or contributor?

**Note:** *If you know that the organization will be, or is considering being, a party to any of the transactions (or activities) listed below, check the "Planned" box. Give a detailed explanation of any "Yes" or "Planned" answer in the space below.*

**a** Borrow any part of the trust's income or corpus? . . . . . . . . . . . . . . . . . . ☐ **Yes** ☐ **No** ☐ **Planned**

**b** Receive any compensation for personal services? . . . . . . . . . . . . . . . . . . ☐ **Yes** ☐ **No** ☐ **Planned**

**c** Obtain any part of the trust's services? . . . . . . . . . . . . . . . . . . . . . ☐ **Yes** ☐ **No** ☐ **Planned**

**d** Purchase any securities or other properties from the trust? . . . . . . . . . . . . . . ☐ **Yes** ☐ **No** ☐ **Planned**

**e** Sell any securities or other property to the trust? . . . . . . . . . . . . . . . . . . ☐ **Yes** ☐ **No** ☐ **Planned**

**f** Receive any of the trust's income or corpus in any other transaction? . . . . . . . . . . ☐ **Yes** ☐ **No** ☐ **Planned**

**5** Attach a copy of the Supplemental Unemployment Benefit Plan and related agreements.

Form 1024 (Rev. 9-98)                                                                                          Page **19**

| Schedule K | Organizations described in section 501(c)(19)—A post or organization of past or present members of the Armed Forces of the United States, auxiliary units or societies for such a post or organization, and trusts or foundations formed for the benefit of such posts or organizations. |
|---|---|

**1**   *To be completed by a post or organization of past or present members of the Armed Forces of the United States.*

**a**   Total membership of the post or organization.

**b**   Number of members who are present or former members of the U.S. Armed Forces

**c**   Number of members who are cadets (include students in college or university ROTC programs or at armed services academies only), or spouses, widows, or widowers of cadets or past or present members of the U.S. Armed Forces

**d**   Does the organization have a membership category other than the ones set out above? . . . . . . . . . . ☐ **Yes** ☐ **No**

   If "Yes," please explain in full. Enter number of members in this category . . . . . . . . . . . . .

**e**   If you wish to apply for a determination that contributions to your organization are deductible by donors, enter the number of members from line 1b who are war veterans, as defined below. . . . . . . . . . . . . . .

   A war veteran is a person who served in the Armed Forces of the United States during the following periods of war: April 21, 1898, through July 4, 1902; April 6, 1917, through November 11, 1918; December 7, 1941, through December 31, 1946; June 27, 1950, through January 31, 1955; and August 5, 1964, through May 7, 1975.

**2**   *To be completed by an auxiliary unit or society of a post or organization of past or present members of the Armed Forces of the United States.*

**a**   Is the organization affiliated with and organized according to the bylaws and regulations formulated by such an exempt post or organization? . . . . . . . . . . . . . . . . . . . . . . . . . . . . . ☐ **Yes** ☐ **No**
   If "Yes," submit a copy of such bylaws or regulations.

**b**   How many members does your organization have? . . . . . . . . . . . . . . . . . . . . .

**c**   How many are themselves past or present members of the Armed Forces of the United States, or are their spouses, or persons related to them within two degrees of blood relationship? (Grandparents, brothers, sisters, and grandchildren are the most distant relationships allowable.) . . . . . . . . . . . . . . . . . . . . . .

**d**   Are all of the members themselves members of a post or organization, past or present members of the Armed Forces of the United States, spouses of members of such a post or organization, or related to members of such a post or organization within two degrees of blood relationship? . . . . . . . . . . . . . . . . . . . ☐ **Yes** ☐ **No**

**3**   *To be completed by a trust or foundation organized for the benefit of an exempt post or organization of past or present members of the Armed Forces of the United States.*

**a**   Will the corpus or income be used solely for the funding of such an exempt organization (including necessary related expenses)? . . . . . . . . . . . . . . . . . . . . . . . . . . . . . . . . . ☐ **Yes** ☐ **No**
   If "No," please explain.

**b**   If the trust or foundation is formed for charitable purposes, does the organizational document contain a proper dissolution provision as described in section 1.501(c)(3)-1(b)(4) of the Income Tax Regulations? . . . . . . . . . . . ☐ **Yes** ☐ **No**

# Form 990

| Form **990** | **Return of Organization Exempt From Income Tax** | OMB No. 1545-0047 |
|---|---|---|
| | Under section 501(c), 527, or 4947(a)(1) of the Internal Revenue Code (except black lung benefit trust or private foundation) | 20**03** |
| Department of the Treasury<br>Internal Revenue Service | ▶ The organization may have to use a copy of this return to satisfy state reporting requirements. | Open to Public Inspection |

**A** For the 2003 calendar year, or tax year beginning _____, 2003, and ending _____, 20 ____

| B Check if applicable: | Please use IRS label or print or type. See Specific Instructions. | C Name of organization | | D Employer identification number |
|---|---|---|---|---|
| ☐ Address change | | | | |
| ☐ Name change | | Number and street (or P.O. box if mail is not delivered to street address) | Room/suite | E Telephone number |
| ☐ Initial return | | | | ( ) |
| ☐ Final return | | City or town, state or country, and ZIP + 4 | | F Accounting method: ☐ Cash ☐ Accrual |
| ☐ Amended return | | | | ☐ Other (specify) ▶ |
| ☐ Application pending | | | | |

● **Section 501(c)(3) organizations and 4947(a)(1) nonexempt charitable trusts must attach a completed Schedule A (Form 990 or 990-EZ).**

**H and I are not applicable to section 527 organizations.**
H(a) Is this a group return for affiliates? ☐ Yes ☐ No
**G** Website: ▶
H(b) If "Yes," enter number of affiliates ▶ ..............
**J** **Organization type** (check only one) ▶ ☐ 501(c) ( ) ◀ (insert no.) ☐ 4947(a)(1) or ☐ 527
H(c) Are all affiliates included? ☐ Yes ☐ No
(If "No," attach a list. See instructions.)
**K** Check here ▶ ☐ if the organization's gross receipts are normally not more than $25,000. The organization need not file a return with the IRS; but if the organization received a Form 990 Package in the mail, it should file a return without financial data. **Some states require a complete return.**
H(d) Is this a separate return filed by an organization covered by a group ruling? ☐ Yes ☐ No
**I** Group Exemption Number ▶
**M** Check ▶ ☐ if the organization is **not** required to attach Sch. B (Form 990, 990-EZ, or 990-PF).
**L** Gross receipts: Add lines 6b, 8b, 9b, and 10b to line 12 ▶

## Part I Revenue, Expenses, and Changes in Net Assets or Fund Balances (See page 18 of the instructions.)

| | | | | |
|---|---|---|---|---|
| **1** | Contributions, gifts, grants, and similar amounts received: | | | |
| **a** | Direct public support | 1a | | |
| **b** | Indirect public support | 1b | | |
| **c** | Government contributions (grants) | 1c | | |
| **d** | **Total** (add lines 1a through 1c) (cash $ _____ noncash $ _____ ) | | 1d | |
| **2** | Program service revenue including government fees and contracts (from Part VII, line 93) | | 2 | |
| **3** | Membership dues and assessments | | 3 | |
| **4** | Interest on savings and temporary cash investments | | 4 | |
| **5** | Dividends and interest from securities | | 5 | |
| **6a** | Gross rents | 6a | | |
| **b** | Less: rental expenses | 6b | | |
| **c** | Net rental income or (loss) (subtract line 6b from line 6a) | | 6c | |
| **7** | Other investment income (describe ▶ ) | | 7 | |
| **8a** | Gross amount from sales of assets other than inventory | (A) Securities 8a | (B) Other | |
| **b** | Less: cost or other basis and sales expenses. | 8b | | |
| **c** | Gain or (loss) (attach schedule) | 8c | | |
| **d** | Net gain or (loss) (combine line 8c, columns (A) and (B)) | | 8d | |
| **9** | Special events and activities (attach schedule). If any amount is from **gaming**, check here ▶ ☐ | | | |
| **a** | Gross revenue (not including $ _____ of contributions reported on line 1a) | 9a | | |
| **b** | Less: direct expenses other than fundraising expenses | 9b | | |
| **c** | Net income or (loss) from special events (subtract line 9b from line 9a) | | 9c | |
| **10a** | Gross sales of inventory, less returns and allowances | 10a | | |
| **b** | Less: cost of goods sold | 10b | | |
| **c** | Gross profit or (loss) from sales of inventory (attach schedule) (subtract line 10b from line 10a) | | 10c | |
| **11** | Other revenue (from Part VII, line 103) | | 11 | |
| **12** | **Total revenue** (add lines 1d, 2, 3, 4, 5, 6c, 7, 8d, 9c, 10c, and 11) | | 12 | |
| **13** | Program services (from line 44, column (B)) | | 13 | |
| **14** | Management and general (from line 44, column (C)) | | 14 | |
| **15** | Fundraising (from line 44, column (D)) | | 15 | |
| **16** | Payments to affiliates (attach schedule) | | 16 | |
| **17** | **Total expenses** (add lines 16 and 44, column (A)) | | 17 | |
| **18** | Excess or (deficit) for the year (subtract line 17 from line 12) | | 18 | |
| **19** | Net assets or fund balances at beginning of year (from line 73, column (A)) | | 19 | |
| **20** | Other changes in net assets or fund balances (attach explanation) | | 20 | |
| **21** | Net assets or fund balances at end of year (combine lines 18, 19, and 20) | | 21 | |

*(Left margin labels: Revenue, Expenses, Net Assets)*

For Paperwork Reduction Act Notice, see the separate instructions. Cat. No. 11282Y Form **990** (2003)

Form 990 (2003)                                                                                                          Page **2**

| **Part II** | **Statement of Functional Expenses** | All organizations must complete column (A). Columns (B), (C), and (D) are required for section 501(c)(3) and (4) organizations and section 4947(a)(1) nonexempt charitable trusts but optional for others. (See page 22 of the instructions.) |

| Do not include amounts reported on line 6b, 8b, 9b, 10b, or 16 of Part I. | | **(A)** Total | **(B)** Program services | **(C)** Management and general | **(D)** Fundraising |
|---|---|---|---|---|---|
| 22 | Grants and allocations (attach schedule) . . (cash $ _____ noncash $ _____ ) | 22 | | | |
| 23 | Specific assistance to individuals (attach schedule) | 23 | | | |
| 24 | Benefits paid to or for members (attach schedule). | 24 | | | |
| 25 | Compensation of officers, directors, etc. . . . | 25 | | | |
| 26 | Other salaries and wages . . . . . . . | 26 | | | |
| 27 | Pension plan contributions . . . . . . | 27 | | | |
| 28 | Other employee benefits . . . . . . | 28 | | | |
| 29 | Payroll taxes . . . . . . . . . | 29 | | | |
| 30 | Professional fundraising fees . . . . . . | 30 | | | |
| 31 | Accounting fees . . . . . . . . . | 31 | | | |
| 32 | Legal fees . . . . . . . . . | 32 | | | |
| 33 | Supplies . . . . . . . . . . | 33 | | | |
| 34 | Telephone . . . . . . . . . | 34 | | | |
| 35 | Postage and shipping . . . . . . | 35 | | | |
| 36 | Occupancy . . . . . . . . . | 36 | | | |
| 37 | Equipment rental and maintenance . . . . | 37 | | | |
| 38 | Printing and publications . . . . . | 38 | | | |
| 39 | Travel . . . . . . . . . . | 39 | | | |
| 40 | Conferences, conventions, and meetings . . | 40 | | | |
| 41 | Interest . . . . . . . . . . | 41 | | | |
| 42 | Depreciation, depletion, etc. (attach schedule) | 42 | | | |
| 43 | Other expenses not covered above (itemize): **a** ......... | 43a | | | |
| **b** | ........................................... | 43b | | | |
| **c** | ........................................... | 43c | | | |
| **d** | ........................................... | 43d | | | |
| **e** | ........................................... | 43e | | | |
| 44 | Total functional expenses (add lines 22 through 43). *Organizations completing columns (B)–(D), carry these totals to lines 13—15* . | 44 | | | |

**Joint Costs.** Check ▶ ☐ if you are following SOP 98-2.
Are any joint costs from a combined educational campaign and fundraising solicitation reported in **(B)** Program services? . ▶ ☐ **Yes** ☐ **No**
If "Yes," enter **(i)** the aggregate amount of these joint costs $_____ ; **(ii)** the amount allocated to Program services $_____ ;
**(iii)** the amount allocated to Management and general $_____ ; and **(iv)** the amount allocated to Fundraising $_____

| **Part III** | **Statement of Program Service Accomplishments** (See page 25 of the instructions.) |

What is the organization's primary exempt purpose? ▶...................................................................

All organizations must describe their exempt purpose achievements in a clear and concise manner. State the number of clients served, publications issued, etc. Discuss achievements that are not measurable. (Section 501(c)(3) and (4) organizations and 4947(a)(1) nonexempt charitable trusts must also enter the amount of grants and allocations to others.)

**Program Service Expenses**
(Required for 501(c)(3) and (4) orgs., and 4947(a)(1) trusts; but optional for others.)

**a** ...........................................................................................................................
...........................................................................................................................
...........................................................................................................................
(Grants and allocations   $                                    )

**b** ...........................................................................................................................
...........................................................................................................................
...........................................................................................................................
(Grants and allocations   $                                    )

**c** ...........................................................................................................................
...........................................................................................................................
...........................................................................................................................
(Grants and allocations   $                                    )

**d** ...........................................................................................................................
...........................................................................................................................
...........................................................................................................................
(Grants and allocations   $                                    )

**e** Other program services (attach schedule)    (Grants and allocations   $                    )

**f Total of Program Service Expenses** (should equal line 44, column (B), Program services) . . . . . ▶

Form **990** (2003)

**Part IV**   **Balance Sheets** (See page 25 of the instructions.)

| Note: | | *Where required, attached schedules and amounts within the description column should be for end-of-year amounts only.* | **(A)** Beginning of year | | **(B)** End of year |
|---|---|---|---|---|---|
| | 45 | Cash—non-interest-bearing . . . . . . . . . . . . . | | 45 | |
| | 46 | Savings and temporary cash investments . . . . . . . . . | | 46 | |
| | 47a | Accounts receivable . . . . . . .   **47a** | | | |
| | b | Less: allowance for doubtful accounts . .   **47b** | | 47c | |
| | 48a | Pledges receivable . . . . . . .   **48a** | | | |
| | b | Less: allowance for doubtful accounts . .   **48b** | | 48c | |
| | 49 | Grants receivable . . . . . . . . . . . . . . . | | 49 | |
| | 50 | Receivables from officers, directors, trustees, and key employees (attach schedule) . . . . . . . . . . . . . . . . . | | 50 | |
| | 51a | Other notes and loans receivable (attach schedule). . . . . . . . . .   **51a** | | | |
| | b | Less: allowance for doubtful accounts . .   **51b** | | 51c | |
| | 52 | Inventories for sale or use . . . . . . . . . . . . . | | 52 | |
| | 53 | Prepaid expenses and deferred charges . . . . . . . . . | | 53 | |
| | 54 | Investments—securities (attach schedule). . . ▶ ☐ Cost ☐ FMV | | 54 | |
| | 55a | Investments—land, buildings, and equipment: basis . . . . . . . .   **55a** | | | |
| | b | Less: accumulated depreciation (attach schedule). . . . . . . . . . .   **55b** | | 55c | |
| | 56 | Investments—other (attach schedule) . . . . . . . . . . | | 56 | |
| | 57a | Land, buildings, and equipment: basis . .   **57a** | | | |
| | b | Less: accumulated depreciation (attach schedule). . . . . . . . . . .   **57b** | | 57c | |
| | 58 | Other assets (describe ▶ _____ ) | | 58 | |
| | 59 | **Total assets** (add lines 45 through 58) (must equal line 74) . . . . | | 59 | |
| | 60 | Accounts payable and accrued expenses . . . . . . . . . . | | 60 | |
| | 61 | Grants payable . . . . . . . . . . . . . . . . . | | 61 | |
| | 62 | Deferred revenue . . . . . . . . . . . . . . . . | | 62 | |
| | 63 | Loans from officers, directors, trustees, and key employees (attach schedule). . . . . . . . . . . . . . . . . . . | | 63 | |
| | 64a | Tax-exempt bond liabilities (attach schedule) . . . . . . . . | | 64a | |
| | b | Mortgages and other notes payable (attach schedule) . . . . . | | 64b | |
| | 65 | Other liabilities (describe ▶ _____ ) | | 65 | |
| | 66 | **Total liabilities** (add lines 60 through 65) . . . . . . . . . . | | 66 | |
| | | **Organizations that follow SFAS 117, check here** ▶ ☐ **and complete lines 67 through 69 and lines 73 and 74.** | | | |
| | 67 | Unrestricted. . . . . . . . . . . . . . . . . . | | 67 | |
| | 68 | Temporarily restricted . . . . . . . . . . . . . . | | 68 | |
| | 69 | Permanently restricted . . . . . . . . . . . . . . | | 69 | |
| | | **Organizations that do not follow SFAS 117, check here** ▶ ☐ **and complete lines 70 through 74.** | | | |
| | 70 | Capital stock, trust principal, or current funds . . . . . . . | | 70 | |
| | 71 | Paid-in or capital surplus, or land, building, and equipment fund . . | | 71 | |
| | 72 | Retained earnings, endowment, accumulated income, or other funds | | 72 | |
| | 73 | **Total net assets or fund balances** (add lines 67 through 69 **or** lines 70 through 72; column (A) **must** equal line 19; column (B) **must** equal line 21). . . | | 73 | |
| | 74 | **Total liabilities and net assets / fund balances** (add lines 66 and 73) | | 74 | |

Row labels for left margin: **Assets** (lines 45–59), **Liabilities** (lines 60–66), **Net Assets or Fund Balances** (lines 67–74).

Form 990 is available for public inspection and, for some people, serves as the primary or sole source of information about a particular organization. How the public perceives an organization in such cases may be determined by the information presented on its return. Therefore, please make sure the return is complete and accurate and fully describes, in Part III, the organization's programs and accomplishments.

Form 990 (2003)                                                                                      Page **4**

| **Part IV-A** | **Reconciliation of Revenue per Audited Financial Statements with Revenue per Return** (See page 27 of the instructions.) |

| **Part IV-B** | **Reconciliation of Expenses per Audited Financial Statements with Expenses per Return** |

**Part IV-A**

a  Total revenue, gains, and other support per audited financial statements . . ▶  **a**

b  Amounts included on line **a** but not on line 12, Form 990:

(1) Net unrealized gains on investments . . $

(2) Donated services and use of facilities $

(3) Recoveries of prior year grants . . . $

(4) Other (specify):

.........................  $

Add amounts on lines (1) through (4) ▶  **b**

c  Line **a** minus line **b**. . . . . ▶  **c**

d  Amounts included on line 12, Form 990 but not on line **a:**

(1) Investment expenses not included on line 6b, Form 990 . . . $

(2) Other (specify):

.........................  $

Add amounts on lines (1) and (2)  ▶  **d**

e  Total revenue per line 12, Form 990 (line **c** plus line **d**) . . . . . . ▶  **e**

**Part IV-B**

a  Total expenses and losses per audited financial statements . . ▶  **a**

b  Amounts included on line **a** but not on line 17, Form 990:

(1) Donated services and use of facilities $

(2) Prior year adjustments reported on line 20, Form 990 . . . . $

(3) Losses reported on line 20, Form 990 . $

(4) Other (specify):

.........................  $

Add amounts on lines (1) through (4)▶  **b**

c  Line **a** minus line **b** . . . . . ▶  **c**

d  Amounts included on line 17, Form 990 but not on line **a:**

(1) Investment expenses not included on line 6b, Form 990. . . $

(2) Other (specify):

.........................  $

Add amounts on lines (1) and (2)  ▶  **d**

e  Total expenses per line 17, Form 990 (line **c** plus line **d**) . . . . . ▶  **e**

| **Part V** | **List of Officers, Directors, Trustees, and Key Employees** (List each one even if not compensated; see page 27 of the instructions.) |

| **(A)** Name and address | **(B)** Title and average hours per week devoted to position | **(C)** Compensation (If not paid, enter -0-.) | **(D)** Contributions to employee benefit plans & deferred compensation | **(E)** Expense account and other allowances |
|---|---|---|---|---|
| ........................................... | | | | |
| ........................................... | | | | |
| ........................................... | | | | |
| ........................................... | | | | |
| ........................................... | | | | |
| ........................................... | | | | |
| ........................................... | | | | |
| ........................................... | | | | |
| ........................................... | | | | |
| ........................................... | | | | |
| ........................................... | | | | |
| ........................................... | | | | |
| ........................................... | | | | |

75  Did any officer, director, trustee, or key employee receive aggregate compensation of more than $100,000 from your organization and all related organizations, of which more than $10,000 was provided by the related organizations?  ▶  ☐ **Yes**  ☐ **No**
   If "Yes," attach schedule—see page 28 of the instructions.

Form **990** (2003)

Form 990 (2003)                                                                                              Page **5**

| **Part VI** | **Other Information** (See page 28 of the instructions.) | | Yes | No |
|---|---|---|---|---|

**76** Did the organization engage in any activity not previously reported to the IRS? If "Yes," attach a detailed description of each activity . | **76** | | |

**77** Were any changes made in the organizing or governing documents but not reported to the IRS? . . . | **77** | | |
If "Yes," attach a conformed copy of the changes.

**78a** Did the organization have unrelated business gross income of $1,000 or more during the year covered by this return?. | **78a** | | |
  **b** If "Yes," has it filed a tax return on **Form 990-T** for this year? . . . . . . . . . . . | **78b** | | |

**79** Was there a liquidation, dissolution, termination, or substantial contraction during the year? If "Yes," attach a statement | **79** | | |

**80a** Is the organization related (other than by association with a statewide or nationwide organization) through common membership, governing bodies, trustees, officers, etc., to any other exempt or nonexempt organization? . . . | **80a** | | |
  **b** If "Yes," enter the name of the organization ▶ ........................................................
................................................ and check whether it is ☐ exempt **or** ☐ nonexempt.

**81a** Enter direct and indirect political expenditures. See line 81 instructions . . . | **81a** |
  **b** Did the organization file **Form 1120-POL** for this year?. . . . . . . . . | **81b** | | |

**82a** Did the organization receive donated services or the use of materials, equipment, or facilities at no charge or at substantially less than fair rental value? . . . . . . . . . . . . . . . | **82a** | | |
  **b** If "Yes," you may indicate the value of these items here. Do not include this amount as revenue in Part I or as an expense in Part II. (See instructions in Part III.) . . | **82b** |

**83a** Did the organization comply with the public inspection requirements for returns and exemption applications? | **83a** | | |
  **b** Did the organization comply with the disclosure requirements relating to quid pro quo contributions? . . | **83b** | | |

**84a** Did the organization solicit any contributions or gifts that were not tax deductible? . . . . . . . | **84a** | | |
  **b** If "Yes," did the organization include with every solicitation an express statement that such contributions or gifts were not tax deductible? . . . . . . . . . . . . . . . . . . . | **84b** | | |

**85** *501(c)(4), (5), or (6) organizations.* **a** Were substantially all dues nondeductible by members? . . . . . . | **85a** | | |
  **b** Did the organization make only in-house lobbying expenditures of $2,000 or less? . . . . | **85b** | | |
If "Yes" was answered to either 85a or 85b, **do not** complete 85c through 85h below unless the organization received a waiver for proxy tax owed for the prior year.
  **c** Dues, assessments, and similar amounts from members . . . . . . | **85c** |
  **d** Section 162(e) lobbying and political expenditures . . . . . . . | **85d** |
  **e** Aggregate nondeductible amount of section 6033(e)(1)(A) dues notices . . | **85e** |
  **f** Taxable amount of lobbying and political expenditures (line 85d less 85e) . . | **85f** |
  **g** Does the organization elect to pay the section 6033(e) tax on the amount on line 85f? . . . . . . . | **85g** | | |
  **h** If section 6033(e)(1)(A) dues notices were sent, does the organization agree to add the amount on line 85f to its reasonable estimate of dues allocable to nondeductible lobbying and political expenditures for the following tax year?. . . . . . . . . . . . . . . . . . . . . | **85h** | | |

**86** *501(c)(7) orgs.* Enter: **a** Initiation fees and capital contributions included on line 12 . | **86a** |
  **b** Gross receipts, included on line 12, for public use of club facilities. . . . . | **86b** |

**87** *501(c)(12) orgs.* Enter: **a** Gross income from members or shareholders. . . . | **87a** |
  **b** Gross income from other sources. (Do not net amounts due or paid to other sources against amounts due or received from them.) . . . . . . . | **87b** |

**88** At any time during the year, did the organization own a 50% or greater interest in a taxable corporation or partnership, or an entity disregarded as separate from the organization under Regulations sections 301.7701-2 and 301.7701-3? If "Yes," complete Part IX . . . . . . . . | **88** | | |

**89a** *501(c)(3) organizations.* Enter: Amount of tax imposed on the organization during the year under:
section 4911 ▶ _____ ; section 4912 ▶ _____ ; section 4955 ▶ _____
  **b** *501(c)(3) and 501(c)(4) orgs.* Did the organization engage in any section 4958 excess benefit transaction during the year or did it become aware of an excess benefit transaction from a prior year? If "Yes," attach a statement explaining each transaction. . . . . . . . . . . . . . . | **89b** | | |
  **c** Enter: Amount of tax imposed on the organization managers or disqualified persons during the year under sections 4912, 4955, and 4958. . . . . . . . . . . . . . . . . ▶ _____
  **d** Enter: Amount of tax on line 89c, above, reimbursed by the organization. . . . . . . . . ▶ _____

**90a** List the states with which a copy of this return is filed ▶ ........................................................
  **b** Number of employees employed in the pay period that includes March 12, 2003 (See instructions.) | **90b** |

**91** The books are in care of ▶ ............................................ Telephone no. ▶ ( ........ )
Located at ▶ ........................................................ ZIP + 4 ▶ ........................

**92** *Section 4947(a)(1) nonexempt charitable trusts filing Form 990 in lieu of* **Form 1041**—Check here . . . . . . . ▶ ☐
and enter the amount of tax-exempt interest received or accrued during the tax year . . ▶ | **92** |

Form **990** (2003)

Form 990 (2003)                                                                Page **6**

## Part VII    Analysis of Income-Producing Activities (See page 33 of the instructions.)

**Note:** Enter gross amounts unless otherwise indicated.

| | Unrelated business income | | Excluded by section 512, 513, or 514 | | (E) Related or exempt function income |
|---|---|---|---|---|---|
| | (A) Business code | (B) Amount | (C) Exclusion code | (D) Amount | |
| **93** Program service revenue: | | | | | |
| a _____ | | | | | |
| b _____ | | | | | |
| c _____ | | | | | |
| d _____ | | | | | |
| e _____ | | | | | |
| f Medicare/Medicaid payments . . . . . | | | | | |
| g Fees and contracts from government agencies | | | | | |
| **94** Membership dues and assessments . . . | | | | | |
| **95** Interest on savings and temporary cash investments | | | | | |
| **96** Dividends and interest from securities . . . | | | | | |
| **97** Net rental income or (loss) from real estate: | | | | | |
| a debt-financed property . . . . . . . | | | | | |
| b not debt-financed property . . . . . . | | | | | |
| **98** Net rental income or (loss) from personal property | | | | | |
| **99** Other investment income . . . . . . . | | | | | |
| **100** Gain or (loss) from sales of assets other than inventory | | | | | |
| **101** Net income or (loss) from special events . . | | | | | |
| **102** Gross profit or (loss) from sales of inventory . | | | | | |
| **103** Other revenue: a _____ | | | | | |
| b _____ | | | | | |
| c _____ | | | | | |
| d _____ | | | | | |
| e _____ | | | | | |
| **104** Subtotal (add columns (B), (D), and (E)) . . | | | | | |

**105** Total (add line 104, columns (B), (D), and (E)). . . . . . . . . . . . . ▶ _____

**Note:** Line 105 plus line 1d, Part I, should equal the amount on line 12, Part I.

## Part VIII    Relationship of Activities to the Accomplishment of Exempt Purposes (See page 34 of the instructions.)

| Line No. ▼ | Explain how each activity for which income is reported in column (E) of Part VII contributed importantly to the accomplishment of the organization's exempt purposes (other than by providing funds for such purposes). |
|---|---|
| | |
| | |
| | |
| | |

## Part IX    Information Regarding Taxable Subsidiaries and Disregarded Entities (See page 34 of the instructions.)

| (A) Name, address, and EIN of corporation, partnership, or disregarded entity | (B) Percentage of ownership interest | (C) Nature of activities | (D) Total income | (E) End-of-year assets |
|---|---|---|---|---|
| | % | | | |
| | % | | | |
| | % | | | |
| | % | | | |

## Part X    Information Regarding Transfers Associated with Personal Benefit Contracts (See page 34 of the instructions.)

(a) Did the organization, during the year, receive any funds, directly or indirectly, to pay premiums on a personal benefit contract? . . ☐ Yes ☐ No

(b) Did the organization, during the year, pay premiums, directly or indirectly, on a personal benefit contract? ☐ Yes ☐ No

**Note:** If "Yes" to **(b),** file **Form 8870 and Form 4720** (see instructions).

**Please Sign Here**

Under penalties of perjury, I declare that I have examined this return, including accompanying schedules and statements, and to the best of my knowledge and belief, it is true, correct, and complete. Declaration of preparer (other than officer) is based on all information of which preparer has any knowledge.

▶ _____     _____
Signature of officer                                    Date

▶ _____
Type or print name and title.

**Paid Preparer's Use Only**

| Preparer's signature ▶ | | Date | Check if self-employed ▶ ☐ | Preparer's SSN or PTIN (See Gen. Inst. W) |
|---|---|---|---|---|
| Firm's name (or yours if self-employed), address, and ZIP + 4 ▶ | | | EIN ▶ | |
| | | | Phone no. ▶ ( ) | |

Form **990** (2003)

| SCHEDULE A<br>(Form 990 or 990-EZ)<br><br>Department of the Treasury<br>Internal Revenue Service | **Organization Exempt Under Section 501(c)(3)**<br>(Except Private Foundation) and Section 501(e), 501(f), 501(k),<br>501(n), or Section 4947(a)(1) Nonexempt Charitable Trust<br>**Supplementary Information—(See separate instructions.)**<br>▶ **MUST be completed by the above organizations and attached to their Form 990 or 990-EZ** | OMB No. 1545-0047<br><br>20**03** |
|---|---|---|

| Name of the organization | Employer identification number |
|---|---|
| | |

**Part I**  Compensation of the Five Highest Paid Employees Other Than Officers, Directors, and Trustees
(See page 1 of the instructions. List each one. If there are none, enter "None.")

| (a) Name and address of each employee paid more than $50,000 | (b) Title and average hours per week devoted to position | (c) Compensation | (d) Contributions to employee benefit plans & deferred compensation | (e) Expense account and other allowances |
|---|---|---|---|---|
| | | | | |
| | | | | |
| | | | | |
| | | | | |
| | | | | |

| Total number of other employees paid over $50,000 .  .  .  .  .  .  .  .  .  .  ▶ | | | | |
|---|---|---|---|---|

**Part II**  Compensation of the Five Highest Paid Independent Contractors for Professional Services
(See page 2 of the instructions. List each one (whether individuals or firms). If there are none, enter "None.")

| (a) Name and address of each independent contractor paid more than $50,000 | (b) Type of service | (c) Compensation |
|---|---|---|
| | | |
| | | |
| | | |
| | | |
| | | |

| Total number of others receiving over $50,000 for professional services .  .  .  .  .  .  .  ▶ | | |
|---|---|---|

For Paperwork Reduction Act Notice, see the Instructions for Form 990 and Form 990-EZ.        Cat. No. 11285F        Schedule A (Form 990 or 990-EZ) 2003

**Part III    Statements About Activities** (See page 2 of the instructions.)

| | Yes | No |
|---|---|---|

**1** During the year, has the organization attempted to influence national, state, or local legislation, including any attempt to influence public opinion on a legislative matter or referendum? If "Yes," enter the total expenses paid or incurred in connection with the lobbying activities ▶ $ _____ (Must equal amounts on line 38, Part VI-A, or line I of Part VI-B.)    **1**

Organizations that made an election under section 501(h) by filing Form 5768 must complete Part VI-A. Other organizations checking "Yes" must complete Part VI-B AND attach a statement giving a detailed description of the lobbying activities.

**2** During the year, has the organization, either directly or indirectly, engaged in any of the following acts with any substantial contributors, trustees, directors, officers, creators, key employees, or members of their families, or with any taxable organization with which any such person is affiliated as an officer, director, trustee, majority owner, or principal beneficiary? *(If the answer to any question is "Yes," attach a detailed statement explaining the transactions.)*

**a** Sale, exchange, or leasing of property?    **2a**

**b** Lending of money or other extension of credit?    **2b**

**c** Furnishing of goods, services, or facilities?    **2c**

**d** Payment of compensation (or payment or reimbursement of expenses if more than $1,000)?    **2d**

**e** Transfer of any part of its income or assets?    **2e**

**3a** Do you make grants for scholarships, fellowships, student loans, etc.? (If "Yes," attach an explanation of how you determine that recipients qualify to receive payments.)    **3a**

**b** Do you have a section 403(b) annuity plan for your employees?    **3b**

**4** Did you maintain any separate account for participating donors where donors have the right to provide advice on the use or distribution of funds?    **4**

**Part IV    Reason for Non-Private Foundation Status** (See pages 3 through 6 of the instructions.)

The organization is not a private foundation because it is: (Please check only **ONE** applicable box.)

**5** ☐ A church, convention of churches, or association of churches. Section 170(b)(1)(A)(i).

**6** ☐ A school. Section 170(b)(1)(A)(ii). (Also complete Part V.)

**7** ☐ A hospital or a cooperative hospital service organization. Section 170(b)(1)(A)(iii).

**8** ☐ A Federal, state, or local government or governmental unit. Section 170(b)(1)(A)(v).

**9** ☐ A medical research organization operated in conjunction with a hospital. Section 170(b)(1)(A)(iii). **Enter the hospital's name, city, and state ▶** ......................................................................................

**10** ☐ An organization operated for the benefit of a college or university owned or operated by a governmental unit. Section 170(b)(1)(A)(iv). (Also complete the **Support Schedule** in Part IV-A.)

**11a** ☐ An organization that normally receives a substantial part of its support from a governmental unit or from the general public. Section 170(b)(1)(A)(vi). (Also complete the **Support Schedule** in Part IV-A.)

**11b** ☐ A community trust. Section 170(b)(1)(A)(vi). (Also complete the **Support Schedule** in Part IV-A.)

**12** ☐ An organization that normally receives: **(1) more than 33⅓%** of its support from contributions, membership fees, and gross receipts from activities related to its charitable, etc., functions—subject to certain exceptions, and **(2) no more than 33⅓%** of its support from gross investment income and unrelated business taxable income (less section 511 tax) from businesses acquired by the organization after June 30, 1975. See section 509(a)(2). (Also complete the **Support Schedule** in Part IV-A.)

**13** ☐ An organization that is not controlled by any disqualified persons (other than foundation managers) and supports organizations described in: **(1)** lines 5 through 12 above; or **(2)** section 501(c)(4), (5), or (6), if they meet the test of section 509(a)(2). (See section 509(a)(3).)

Provide the following information about the supported organizations. (See page 5 of the instructions.)

| **(a)** Name(s) of supported organization(s) | **(b)** Line number from above |
|---|---|
| | |
| | |
| | |

**14** ☐ An organization organized and operated to test for public safety. Section 509(a)(4). (See page 6 of the instructions.)

Schedule A (Form 990 or 990-EZ) 2003

Schedule A (Form 990 or 990-EZ) 2003    Page **3**

**Part IV-A** **Support Schedule** (Complete only if you checked a box on line 10, 11, or 12.) *Use cash method of accounting.*

Note: *You may use the worksheet in the instructions for converting from the accrual to the cash method of accounting.*

| Calendar year (or fiscal year beginning in) ▶ | (a) 2002 | (b) 2001 | (c) 2000 | (d) 1999 | (e) Total |
|---|---|---|---|---|---|
| **15** Gifts, grants, and contributions received. (Do not include unusual grants. See line 28.). . | | | | | |
| **16** Membership fees received . . . . . . | | | | | |
| **17** Gross receipts from admissions, merchandise sold or services performed, or furnishing of facilities in any activity that is related to the organization's charitable, etc., purpose . . . | | | | | |
| **18** Gross income from interest, dividends, amounts received from payments on securities loans (section 512(a)(5)), rents, royalties, and unrelated business taxable income (less section 511 taxes) from businesses acquired by the organization after June 30, 1975 . . | | | | | |
| **19** Net income from unrelated business activities not included in line 18 . . . . | | | | | |
| **20** Tax revenues levied for the organization's benefit and either paid to it or expended on its behalf. . . . . . . . . . . . | | | | | |
| **21** The value of services or facilities furnished to the organization by a governmental unit without charge. Do not include the value of services or facilities generally furnished to the public without charge. . . . . . . | | | | | |
| **22** Other income. Attach a schedule. Do not include gain or (loss) from sale of capital assets | | | | | |
| **23** Total of lines 15 through 22. . . . . . | | | | | |
| **24** Line 23 minus line 17. . . . . . . . | | | | | |
| **25** Enter 1% of line 23 . . . . . . . . | | | | | ///// |

**26** **Organizations described on lines 10 or 11:**    **a** Enter 2% of amount in column (e), line 24. . . . ▶    **26a**

**b** Prepare a list for your records to show the name of and amount contributed by each person (other than a governmental unit or publicly supported organization) whose total gifts for 1999 through 2002 exceeded the amount shown in line 26a. **Do not file this list with your return.** Enter the total of all these excess amounts ▶ **26b**

**c** Total support for section 509(a)(1) test: Enter line 24, column (e) . . . . . . . . . . . ▶ **26c**

**d** Add: Amounts from column (e) for lines:  18 _____  19 _____
22 _____  26b _____  . . . . ▶ **26d**

**e** Public support (line 26c minus line 26d total)  . . . . . . . . . . . . . . . . ▶ **26e**

**f** **Public support percentage (line 26e (numerator) divided by line 26c (denominator))** . . . . . ▶ **26f**    %

**27** **Organizations described on line 12:**    **a** For amounts included in lines 15, 16, and 17 that were received from a "disqualified person," prepare a list to show the name of, and total amounts received in each year from, each "disqualified person." **Do not file this list with your return.** Enter the sum of such amounts for each year:

(2002) ......................... (2001) ......................... (2000) ......................... (1999) ...........................

**b** For any amount included in line 17 that was received from each person (other than "disqualified persons"), prepare a list for your records to show the name of, and amount received for each year, that was more than the **larger** of **(1)** the amount on line 25 for the year or **(2)** $5,000. (Include in the list organizations described in lines 5 through 11, as well as individuals.) **Do not file this list with your return.** After computing the difference between the amount received and the larger amount described in **(1)** or **(2),** enter the sum of these differences (the excess amounts) for each year:

(2002) ......................... (2001) ......................... (2000) ......................... (1999) ...........................

**c** Add: Amounts from column (e) for lines:  15 _____  16 _____
17 _____  20 _____  21 _____  . . . . . ▶ **27c**

**d** Add: Line 27a total  . _____  and line 27b total . . _____  . . . . . ▶ **27d**

**e** Public support (line 27c total minus line 27d total). . . . . . . . . . . ▶ **27e**

**f** Total support for section 509(a)(2) test: Enter amount from line 23, column (e). . ▶ **27f**

**g** **Public support percentage (line 27e (numerator) divided by line 27f (denominator)).** . . . . . ▶ **27g**    %

**h** **Investment income percentage (line 18, column (e) (numerator) divided by line 27f (denominator)). ▶** **27h**    %

**28** **Unusual Grants:** For an organization described in line 10, 11, or 12 that received any unusual grants during 1999 through 2002, prepare a list for your records to show, for each year, the name of the contributor, the date and amount of the grant, and a brief description of the nature of the grant. **Do not file this list with your return.** Do not include these grants in line 15.

Schedule A (Form 990 or 990-EZ) 2003

Schedule A (Form 990 or 990-EZ) 2003                                                                                                Page **4**

### Part V  Private School Questionnaire (See page 7 of the instructions.)
**(To be completed ONLY by schools that checked the box on line 6 in Part IV)**

| | | Yes | No |
|---|---|---|---|
| **29** | Does the organization have a racially nondiscriminatory policy toward students by statement in its charter, bylaws, other governing instrument, or in a resolution of its governing body? | **29** | |
| **30** | Does the organization include a statement of its racially nondiscriminatory policy toward students in all its brochures, catalogues, and other written communications with the public dealing with student admissions, programs, and scholarships? | **30** | |
| **31** | Has the organization publicized its racially nondiscriminatory policy through newspaper or broadcast media during the period of solicitation for students, or during the registration period if it has no solicitation program, in a way that makes the policy known to all parts of the general community it serves? | **31** | |

If "Yes," please describe; if "No," please explain. (If you need more space, attach a separate statement.)

------------------------------------------------------------------------------------------
------------------------------------------------------------------------------------------
------------------------------------------------------------------------------------------
------------------------------------------------------------------------------------------

| | | Yes | No |
|---|---|---|---|
| **32** | Does the organization maintain the following: | | |
| **a** | Records indicating the racial composition of the student body, faculty, and administrative staff? | **32a** | |
| **b** | Records documenting that scholarships and other financial assistance are awarded on a racially nondiscriminatory basis? | **32b** | |
| **c** | Copies of all catalogues, brochures, announcements, and other written communications to the public dealing with student admissions, programs, and scholarships? | **32c** | |
| **d** | Copies of all material used by the organization or on its behalf to solicit contributions? | **32d** | |

If you answered "No" to any of the above, please explain. (If you need more space, attach a separate statement.)

------------------------------------------------------------------------------------------
------------------------------------------------------------------------------------------

| | | Yes | No |
|---|---|---|---|
| **33** | Does the organization discriminate by race in any way with respect to: | | |
| **a** | Students' rights or privileges? | **33a** | |
| **b** | Admissions policies? | **33b** | |
| **c** | Employment of faculty or administrative staff? | **33c** | |
| **d** | Scholarships or other financial assistance? | **33d** | |
| **e** | Educational policies? | **33e** | |
| **f** | Use of facilities? | **33f** | |
| **g** | Athletic programs? | **33g** | |
| **h** | Other extracurricular activities? | **33h** | |

If you answered "Yes" to any of the above, please explain. (If you need more space, attach a separate statement.)

------------------------------------------------------------------------------------------
------------------------------------------------------------------------------------------
------------------------------------------------------------------------------------------

| | | Yes | No |
|---|---|---|---|
| **34a** | Does the organization receive any financial aid or assistance from a governmental agency? | **34a** | |
| **b** | Has the organization's right to such aid ever been revoked or suspended? | **34b** | |
| | If you answered "Yes" to either 34a or b, please explain using an attached statement. | | |
| **35** | Does the organization certify that it has complied with the applicable requirements of sections 4.01 through 4.05 of Rev. Proc. 75-50, 1975-2 C.B. 587, covering racial nondiscrimination? If "No," attach an explanation | **35** | |

Schedule A (Form 990 or 990-EZ) 2003

**Part VI-A**    **Lobbying Expenditures by Electing Public Charities** (See page 9 of the instructions.)
(To be completed **ONLY** by an eligible organization that filed Form 5768)

Check ▶ **a** ☐ if the organization belongs to an affiliated group.    Check ▶ **b** ☐ if you checked "a" and "limited control" provisions apply.

| | **Limits on Lobbying Expenditures**<br>(The term "expenditures" means amounts paid or incurred.) | | **(a)**<br>Affiliated group<br>totals | **(b)**<br>To be completed<br>for ALL electing<br>organizations |
|---|---|---|---|---|
| 36 | Total lobbying expenditures to influence public opinion (grassroots lobbying) . . . . | **36** | | |
| 37 | Total lobbying expenditures to influence a legislative body (direct lobbying) . . . . . | **37** | | |
| 38 | Total lobbying expenditures (add lines 36 and 37) . . . . . . . . . . . . | **38** | | |
| 39 | Other exempt purpose expenditures . . . . . . . . . . . . . . . | **39** | | |
| 40 | Total exempt purpose expenditures (add lines 38 and 39). . . . . . . . . . | **40** | | |
| 41 | Lobbying nontaxable amount. Enter the amount from the following table— | | | |
| | **If the amount on line 40 is—**     **The lobbying nontaxable amount is—** | | | |
| | Not over $500,000 . . . . . . 20% of the amount on line 40 . . . . . ⎫ | | | |
| | Over $500,000 but not over $1,000,000 . . $100,000 plus 15% of the excess over $500,000 ⎬ | | | |
| | Over $1,000,000 but not over $1,500,000 . $175,000 plus 10% of the excess over $1,000,000 ⎬ **41** | | | |
| | Over $1,500,000 but not over $17,000,000 . $225,000 plus 5% of the excess over $1,500,000 ⎬ | | | |
| | Over $17,000,000 . . . . . . . $1,000,000 . . . . . . . . ⎭ | | | |
| 42 | Grassroots nontaxable amount (enter 25% of line 41) . . . . . . . . . . | **42** | | |
| 43 | Subtract line 42 from line 36. Enter -0- if line 42 is more than line 36 . . . . . . | **43** | | |
| 44 | Subtract line 41 from line 38. Enter -0- if line 41 is more than line 38 . . . . . . | **44** | | |

**Caution:** *If there is an amount on either line 43 or line 44, you must file Form 4720.*

### 4-Year Averaging Period Under Section 501(h)

(Some organizations that made a section 501(h) election do not have to complete all of the five columns below.
See the instructions for lines 45 through 50 on page 11 of the instructions.)

| | Calendar year (or<br>fiscal year beginning in) ▶ | **Lobbying Expenditures During 4-Year Averaging Period** | | | | |
|---|---|---|---|---|---|---|
| | | **(a)**<br>2003 | **(b)**<br>2002 | **(c)**<br>2001 | **(d)**<br>2000 | **(e)**<br>Total |
| 45 | Lobbying nontaxable amount . . . . . . | | | | | |
| 46 | Lobbying ceiling amount (150% of line 45(e)) . | | | | | |
| 47 | Total lobbying expenditures . . . . . . | | | | | |
| 48 | Grassroots nontaxable amount . . . . . | | | | | |
| 49 | Grassroots ceiling amount (150% of line 48(e)) | | | | | |
| 50 | Grassroots lobbying expenditures . . . . | | | | | |

**Part VI-B**    **Lobbying Activity by Nonelecting Public Charities**
(For reporting only by organizations that did not complete Part VI-A) (See page 12 of the instructions.)

During the year, did the organization attempt to influence national, state or local legislation, including any attempt to influence public opinion on a legislative matter or referendum, through the use of:

| | | **Yes** | **No** | **Amount** |
|---|---|---|---|---|
| **a** | Volunteers. . . . . . . . . . . . . . . . . . . . . . . . . . . | | | |
| **b** | Paid staff or management (Include compensation in expenses reported on lines **c** through **h.**) . . . | | | |
| **c** | Media advertisements . . . . . . . . . . . . . . . . . . . . . | | | |
| **d** | Mailings to members, legislators, or the public . . . . . . . . . . . . . . | | | |
| **e** | Publications, or published or broadcast statements . . . . . . . . . . . . . | | | |
| **f** | Grants to other organizations for lobbying purposes . . . . . . . . . . . . . | | | |
| **g** | Direct contact with legislators, their staffs, government officials, or a legislative body . . . . . | | | |
| **h** | Rallies, demonstrations, seminars, conventions, speeches, lectures, or any other means . . . . . | | | |
| **i** | Total lobbying expenditures (Add lines **c** through **h.**) . . . . . . . . . . . . . . . | | | |

If "Yes" to any of the above, also attach a statement giving a detailed description of the lobbying activities.

**Part VII**    **Information Regarding Transfers To and Transactions and Relationships With Noncharitable Exempt Organizations** (See page 12 of the instructions.)

**51**    Did the reporting organization directly or indirectly engage in any of the following with any other organization described in section 501(c) of the Code (other than section 501(c)(3) organizations) or in section 527, relating to political organizations?

| | | Yes | No |
|---|---|---|---|
| **a** Transfers from the reporting organization to a noncharitable exempt organization of: | | | |
| (i) Cash | **51a(i)** | | |
| (ii) Other assets | **a(ii)** | | |
| **b** Other transactions: | | | |
| (i) Sales or exchanges of assets with a noncharitable exempt organization | **b(i)** | | |
| (ii) Purchases of assets from a noncharitable exempt organization | **b(ii)** | | |
| (iii) Rental of facilities, equipment, or other assets | **b(iii)** | | |
| (iv) Reimbursement arrangements | **b(iv)** | | |
| (v) Loans or loan guarantees | **b(v)** | | |
| (vi) Performance of services or membership or fundraising solicitations | **b(vi)** | | |
| **c** Sharing of facilities, equipment, mailing lists, other assets, or paid employees | **c** | | |

**d** If the answer to any of the above is "Yes," complete the following schedule. Column (b) should always show the fair market value of the goods, other assets, or services given by the reporting organization. If the organization received less than fair market value in any transaction or sharing arrangement, show in column (d) the value of the goods, other assets, or services received:

| (a)<br>Line no. | (b)<br>Amount involved | (c)<br>Name of noncharitable exempt organization | (d)<br>Description of transfers, transactions, and sharing arrangements |
|---|---|---|---|
| | | | |
| | | | |
| | | | |
| | | | |
| | | | |
| | | | |
| | | | |
| | | | |
| | | | |
| | | | |
| | | | |
| | | | |
| | | | |
| | | | |

**52a** Is the organization directly or indirectly affiliated with, or related to, one or more tax-exempt organizations described in section 501(c) of the Code (other than section 501(c)(3)) or in section 527?  ▶  ☐ **Yes**  ☐ **No**

**b** If "Yes," complete the following schedule:

| (a)<br>Name of organization | (b)<br>Type of organization | (c)<br>Description of relationship |
|---|---|---|
| | | |
| | | |
| | | |
| | | |
| | | |
| | | |
| | | |
| | | |
| | | |
| | | |
| | | |
| | | |
| | | |
| | | |

| Schedule B | Schedule of Contributors | OMB No. 1545-0047 |
|---|---|---|
| (Form 990, 990-EZ, or 990-PF) | | |
| Department of the Treasury Internal Revenue Service | Supplementary Information for line 1 of Form 990, 990-EZ, and 990-PF (see Instructions) | 2003 |

| Name of organization | Employer identification number |
|---|---|
| | |

**Organization type** (check one):

**Filers of:**                    **Section:**

Form 990 or 990-EZ          ☐ 501(c)(    ) (enter number) organization

                             ☐ 4947(a)(1) nonexempt charitable trust **not** treated as a private foundation

                             ☐ 527 political organization

Form 990-PF                  ☐ 501(c)(3) exempt private foundation

                             ☐ 4947(a)(1) nonexempt charitable trust treated as a private foundation

                             ☐ 501(c)(3) taxable private foundation

---

Check if your organization is covered by the **General Rule** or a **Special Rule. (Note:** *Only a section 501(c)(7), (8), or (10) organization can check box(es) for both the General Rule and a Special Rule—see instructions.)*

**General Rule—**

☐ For organizations filing Form 990, 990-EZ, or 990-PF that received, during the year, $5,000 or more (in money or property) from any one contributor. (Complete Parts I and II.)

**Special Rules—**

☐ For a section 501(c)(3) organization filing Form 990, or Form 990-EZ, that met the 33⅓% support test of the regulations under sections 509(a)(1)/170(b)(1)(A)(vi) and received from any one contributor, during the year, a contribution of the greater of $5,000 or 2% of the amount on line 1 of these forms. (Complete Parts I and II.)

☐ For a section 501(c)(7), (8), or (10) organization filing Form 990, or Form 990-EZ, that received from any one contributor, during the year, aggregate contributions or bequests of more than $1,000 for use *exclusively* for religious, charitable, scientific, literary, or educational purposes, or the prevention of cruelty to children or animals. (Complete Parts I, II, and III.)

☐ For a section 501(c)(7), (8), or (10) organization filing Form 990, or Form 990-EZ, that received from any one contributor, during the year, some contributions for use *exclusively* for religious, charitable, etc., purposes, but these contributions did not aggregate to more than $1,000. (If this box is checked, enter here the total contributions that were received during the year for an *exclusively* religious, charitable, etc., purpose. Do not complete any of the Parts unless the **General Rule** applies to this organization because it received nonexclusively religious, charitable, etc., contributions of $5,000 or more during the year.)  . . . . . . . . . . . . . . . . . . . . . . . . . . . . . ▶ $ _____

**Caution:** *Organizations that are not covered by the General Rule and/or the Special Rules do not file Schedule B (Form 990, 990-EZ, or 990-PF), but they **must** check the box in the heading of their Form 990, Form 990-EZ, or on line 1 of their Form 990-PF, to certify that they do not meet the filing requirements of Schedule B (Form 990, 990-EZ, or 990-PF).*

---

**For Paperwork Reduction Act Notice, see the Instructions for Form 990 and Form 990-EZ.**          Cat. No. 30613X          Schedule B (Form 990, 990-EZ, or 990-PF) (2003)

| Name of organization | Employer identification number |
|---|---|
| | |

**Part I**    **Contributors** (See Specific Instructions.)

| (a) No. | (b) Name, address, and ZIP + 4 | (c) Aggregate contributions | (d) Type of contribution |
|---|---|---|---|
| ____ | ................................................<br>................................................<br>................................................ | $ .......................... | Person ☐<br>Payroll ☐<br>Noncash ☐<br>(Complete Part II if there is a noncash contribution.) |

| (a) No. | (b) Name, address, and ZIP + 4 | (c) Aggregate contributions | (d) Type of contribution |
|---|---|---|---|
| ____ | ................................................<br>................................................<br>................................................ | $ .......................... | Person ☐<br>Payroll ☐<br>Noncash ☐<br>(Complete Part II if there is a noncash contribution.) |

| (a) No. | (b) Name, address, and ZIP + 4 | (c) Aggregate contributions | (d) Type of contribution |
|---|---|---|---|
| ____ | ................................................<br>................................................<br>................................................ | $ .......................... | Person ☐<br>Payroll ☐<br>Noncash ☐<br>(Complete Part II if there is a noncash contribution.) |

| (a) No. | (b) Name, address, and ZIP + 4 | (c) Aggregate contributions | (d) Type of contribution |
|---|---|---|---|
| ____ | ................................................<br>................................................<br>................................................ | $ .......................... | Person ☐<br>Payroll ☐<br>Noncash ☐<br>(Complete Part II if there is a noncash contribution.) |

| (a) No. | (b) Name, address, and ZIP + 4 | (c) Aggregate contributions | (d) Type of contribution |
|---|---|---|---|
| ____ | ................................................<br>................................................<br>................................................ | $ .......................... | Person ☐<br>Payroll ☐<br>Noncash ☐<br>(Complete Part II if there is a noncash contribution.) |

| (a) No. | (b) Name, address, and ZIP + 4 | (c) Aggregate contributions | (d) Type of contribution |
|---|---|---|---|
| ____ | ................................................<br>................................................<br>................................................ | $ .......................... | Person ☐<br>Payroll ☐<br>Noncash ☐<br>(Complete Part II if there is a noncash contribution.) |

| Name of organization | Employer identification number |
|---|---|
|  |  |

**Part I**   Contributors (See Specific Instructions.)

| (a)<br>No. | (b)<br>Name, address, and ZIP + 4 | (c)<br>Aggregate contributions | (d)<br>Type of contribution |
|---|---|---|---|
| —— | ................................................. <br> ................................................. <br> ................................................. | $............................ | Person ☐ <br> Payroll ☐ <br> Noncash ☐ <br> (Complete Part II if there is a noncash contribution.) |
| —— | ................................................. <br> ................................................. <br> ................................................. | $............................ | Person ☐ <br> Payroll ☐ <br> Noncash ☐ <br> (Complete Part II if there is a noncash contribution.) |
| —— | ................................................. <br> ................................................. <br> ................................................. | $............................ | Person ☐ <br> Payroll ☐ <br> Noncash ☐ <br> (Complete Part II if there is a noncash contribution.) |
| —— | ................................................. <br> ................................................. <br> ................................................. | $............................ | Person ☐ <br> Payroll ☐ <br> Noncash ☐ <br> (Complete Part II if there is a noncash contribution.) |
| —— | ................................................. <br> ................................................. <br> ................................................. | $............................ | Person ☐ <br> Payroll ☐ <br> Noncash ☐ <br> (Complete Part II if there is a noncash contribution.) |
| —— | ................................................. <br> ................................................. <br> ................................................. | $............................ | Person ☐ <br> Payroll ☐ <br> Noncash ☐ <br> (Complete Part II if there is a noncash contribution.) |

Schedule B (Form 990, 990-EZ, or 990-PF) (2003)

| Name of organization | Employer identification number |
|---|---|
| | |

**Part I**   Contributors (See Specific Instructions.)

| (a) No. | (b) Name, address, and ZIP + 4 | (c) Aggregate contributions | (d) Type of contribution |
|---|---|---|---|
| _____ | ................................................. ................................................. ................................................. ................................................. | $............................. | Person ☐ <br> Payroll ☐ <br> Noncash ☐ <br> (Complete Part II if there is a noncash contribution.) |
| _____ | ................................................. ................................................. ................................................. ................................................. | $............................. | Person ☐ <br> Payroll ☐ <br> Noncash ☐ <br> (Complete Part II if there is a noncash contribution.) |
| _____ | ................................................. ................................................. ................................................. ................................................. | $............................. | Person ☐ <br> Payroll ☐ <br> Noncash ☐ <br> (Complete Part II if there is a noncash contribution.) |
| _____ | ................................................. ................................................. ................................................. ................................................. | $............................. | Person ☐ <br> Payroll ☐ <br> Noncash ☐ <br> (Complete Part II if there is a noncash contribution.) |
| _____ | ................................................. ................................................. ................................................. ................................................. | $............................. | Person ☐ <br> Payroll ☐ <br> Noncash ☐ <br> (Complete Part II if there is a noncash contribution.) |
| _____ | ................................................. ................................................. ................................................. ................................................. | $............................. | Person ☐ <br> Payroll ☐ <br> Noncash ☐ <br> (Complete Part II if there is a noncash contribution.) |

Schedule B (Form 990, 990-EZ, or 990-PF) (2003)

| Name of organization | Employer identification number |
|---|---|
| | |

**Part II**    Noncash Property (See Specific Instructions.)

| (a) No. from Part I | (b) Description of noncash property given | (c) FMV (or estimate) (see instructions) | (d) Date received |
|---|---|---|---|
| ―― | | $ ......................... | ........../...../.......... |
| ―― | | $ ......................... | ........../...../.......... |
| ―― | | $ ......................... | ........../...../.......... |
| ―― | | $ ......................... | ........../...../.......... |
| ―― | | $ ......................... | ........../...../.......... |
| ―― | | $ ......................... | ........../...../.......... |

| Name of organization | Employer identification number |
|---|---|

**Part II**    Noncash Property (See Specific Instructions.)

| (a) No. from Part I | (b) Description of noncash property given | (c) FMV (or estimate) (see instructions) | (d) Date received |
|---|---|---|---|
| —— | ........................................ | $ ......................... | ........../...../.......... |
| —— | ........................................ | $ ......................... | ........../...../.......... |
| —— | ........................................ | $ ......................... | ........../...../.......... |
| —— | ........................................ | $ ......................... | ........../...../.......... |
| —— | ........................................ | $ ......................... | ........../...../.......... |
| —— | ........................................ | $ ......................... | ........../...../.......... |

Schedule B (Form 990, 990-EZ, or 990-PF) (2003)

Page _____ to _____ of **Part III**

**Name of organization**

**Employer identification number**

| **Part III** | *Exclusively* religious, charitable, etc., individual contributions to section 501(c)(7), (8), or (10) organizations aggregating more than $1,000 for the year. (Complete columns (a) through (e) and the following line entry.) |
|---|---|

For organizations completing Part III, enter the total of *exclusively* religious, charitable, etc., contributions of **$1,000 or less** for the year. (Enter this information once—see instructions.) ▶ $

| (a) No. from Part I | (b) Purpose of gift | (c) Use of gift | (d) Description of how gift is held |
|---|---|---|---|
| ——— | | | |

| (e) Transfer of gift | |
|---|---|
| Transferee's name, address, and ZIP + 4 | Relationship of transferor to transferee |
| | |

| (a) No. from Part I | (b) Purpose of gift | (c) Use of gift | (d) Description of how gift is held |
|---|---|---|---|
| ——— | | | |

| (e) Transfer of gift | |
|---|---|
| Transferee's name, address, and ZIP + 4 | Relationship of transferor to transferee |
| | |

| (a) No. from Part I | (b) Purpose of gift | (c) Use of gift | (d) Description of how gift is held |
|---|---|---|---|
| ——— | | | |

| (e) Transfer of gift | |
|---|---|
| Transferee's name, address, and ZIP + 4 | Relationship of transferor to transferee |
| | |

| (a) No. from Part I | (b) Purpose of gift | (c) Use of gift | (d) Description of how gift is held |
|---|---|---|---|
| ——— | | | |

| (e) Transfer of gift | |
|---|---|
| Transferee's name, address, and ZIP + 4 | Relationship of transferor to transferee |
| | |

Schedule B (Form 990, 990-EZ, or 990-PF) (2003)

Schedule B (Form 990, 990-EZ, or 990-PF) (2003)

| Name of organization | Employer identification number |
|---|---|
| | |

**Part III**  *Exclusively* religious, charitable, etc., individual contributions to section 501(c)(7), (8), or (10) organizations aggregating more than $1,000 for the year. (Complete columns **(a)** through **(e)** and the following line entry.)

For organizations completing Part III, enter the total of *exclusively* religious, charitable, etc., contributions of **$1,000 or less** for the year. (Enter this information once—see instructions.)  ▶ $

| (a) No. from Part I | (b) Purpose of gift | (c) Use of gift | (d) Description of how gift is held |
|---|---|---|---|
| ____ | | | |

| (e) Transfer of gift | |
|---|---|
| Transferee's name, address, and ZIP + 4 | Relationship of transferor to transferee |
| | |

| (a) No. from Part I | (b) Purpose of gift | (c) Use of gift | (d) Description of how gift is held |
|---|---|---|---|
| ____ | | | |

| (e) Transfer of gift | |
|---|---|
| Transferee's name, address, and ZIP + 4 | Relationship of transferor to transferee |
| | |

| (a) No. from Part I | (b) Purpose of gift | (c) Use of gift | (d) Description of how gift is held |
|---|---|---|---|
| ____ | | | |

| (e) Transfer of gift | |
|---|---|
| Transferee's name, address, and ZIP + 4 | Relationship of transferor to transferee |
| | |

| (a) No. from Part I | (b) Purpose of gift | (c) Use of gift | (d) Description of how gift is held |
|---|---|---|---|
| ____ | | | |

| (e) Transfer of gift | |
|---|---|
| Transferee's name, address, and ZIP + 4 | Relationship of transferor to transferee |
| | |

Schedule B (Form 990, 990-EZ, or 990-PF) (2003)

# Form 990-T

| Form **990-T** | **Exempt Organization Business Income Tax Return** (and proxy tax under section 6033(e)) | OMB No. 1545-0687 |
|---|---|---|
| Department of the Treasury Internal Revenue Service | For calendar year 2003 or other tax year beginning ........... , 2003, and ending ........... , 20 ..... ▶ **See separate instructions.** | 2003 |

| A ☐ Check box if address changed | Name of organization ( ☐ check box if name changed and see instructions) | **D Employer identification number** (Employees' trust, see instructions for Block D on page 7.) |
|---|---|---|
| **B Exempt under section** ☐ 501( )( ) ☐ 408(e)  ☐ 220(e) ☐ 408A  ☐ 530(a) ☐ 529(a) | **Please Print or Type** | Number, street, and room or suite no. (If a P.O. box, see page 7 of instructions.) |
|  |  | City or town, state, and ZIP code |

**E New unrelated bus. activity codes** (See instructions for Block E on page 7.)

| C Book value of all assets at end of year | F Group exemption number (see instructions for Block F on page 7) ▶ |
|---|---|

G Check organization type ▶ ☐ 501(c) corporation ☐ 501(c) trust ☐ 401(a) trust ☐ Other trust

H Describe the organization's primary unrelated business activity. ▶

I During the tax year, was the corporation a subsidiary in an affiliated group or a parent-subsidiary controlled group? . . ▶ ☐ Yes ☐ No
If "Yes," enter the name and identifying number of the parent corporation. ▶

J The books are in care of ▶ _____ Telephone number ▶ ( )

### Part I    Unrelated Trade or Business Income

| | | (A) Income | (B) Expenses | (C) Net |
|---|---|---|---|---|
| 1a | Gross receipts or sales | | | |
| b | Less returns and allowances _____ c Balance ▶ **1c** | | | |
| 2 | Cost of goods sold (Schedule A, line 7) . . . . **2** | | | |
| 3 | Gross profit (subtract line 2 from line 1c) . . . . . **3** | | | |
| 4a | Capital gain net income (attach Schedule D) . . . . . **4a** | | | |
| b | Net gain (loss) (Form 4797, Part II, line 18) (attach Form 4797) **4b** | | | |
| c | Capital loss deduction for trusts . . . . . . . **4c** | | | |
| 5 | Income (loss) from partnerships and S corporations (attach statement) **5** | | | |
| 6 | Rent income (Schedule C) . . . . . . . . **6** | | | |
| 7 | Unrelated debt-financed income (Schedule E) . . . . **7** | | | |
| 8 | Interest, annuities, royalties, and rents from controlled organizations (Schedule F) . . . . . . . **8** | | | |
| 9 | Investment income of a section 501(c)(7), (9), or (17) organization (Schedule G) . . . . . . **9** | | | |
| 10 | Exploited exempt activity income (Schedule I) . . . . **10** | | | |
| 11 | Advertising income (Schedule J) . . . . . . . **11** | | | |
| 12 | Other income (see page 9 of the instructions—attach schedule) **12** | | | |
| 13 | **Total** (combine lines 3 through 12) . . . . . . . **13** | | | |

### Part II    Deductions Not Taken Elsewhere (See page 9 of the instructions for limitations on deductions.)
(Except for contributions, deductions must be directly connected with the unrelated business income.)

| 14 | Compensation of officers, directors, and trustees (Schedule K) . . . . . . . . . . | **14** | |
|---|---|---|---|
| 15 | Salaries and wages . . . . . . . . . . . . . . . . . . . . . | **15** | |
| 16 | Repairs and maintenance . . . . . . . . . . . . . . . . . . . | **16** | |
| 17 | Bad debts . . . . . . . . . . . . . . . . . . . . . . . | **17** | |
| 18 | Interest (attach schedule) . . . . . . . . . . . . . . . . . . | **18** | |
| 19 | Taxes and licenses . . . . . . . . . . . . . . . . . . . . | **19** | |
| 20 | Charitable contributions (see page 11 of the instructions for limitation rules) . . . . . | **20** | |
| 21 | Depreciation (attach Form 4562) . . . . . . . . . . **21** | | |
| 22 | Less depreciation claimed on Schedule A and elsewhere on return . **22a** | **22b** | |
| 23 | Depletion . . . . . . . . . . . . . . . . . . . . . . . | **23** | |
| 24 | Contributions to deferred compensation plans . . . . . . . . . . . . . | **24** | |
| 25 | Employee benefit programs . . . . . . . . . . . . . . . . . . | **25** | |
| 26 | Excess exempt expenses (Schedule I) . . . . . . . . . . . . . . . | **26** | |
| 27 | Excess readership costs (Schedule J) . . . . . . . . . . . . . . . | **27** | |
| 28 | Other deductions (attach schedule) . . . . . . . . . . . . . . . . | **28** | |
| 29 | **Total deductions** (add lines 14 through 28) . . . . . . . . . . . . . . | **29** | |
| 30 | Unrelated business taxable income before net operating loss deduction (subtract line 29 from line 13). | **30** | |
| 31 | Net operating loss deduction . . . . . . . . . . . . . . . . . . | **31** | |
| 32 | Unrelated business taxable income before specific deduction (subtract line 31 from line 30) . . | **32** | |
| 33 | Specific deduction (Generally $1,000, but see line 33 instructions for exceptions) . . . . . | **33** | |
| 34 | **Unrelated business taxable income** (subtract line 33 from line 32). If line 33 is greater than line 32, enter the smaller of zero or line 32 . . . . . . . . . . . . . . . . | **34** | |

For Paperwork Reduction Act Notice, see instructions.          Cat. No. 11291J          Form **990-T** (2003)

## Part III    Tax Computation

**35**   **Organizations Taxable as Corporations** (see instructions for tax computation on page 12). Controlled group members (sections 1561 and 1563)—check here ☐ . **See instructions** and:

a   Enter your share of the $50,000, $25,000, and $9,925,000 taxable income brackets (in that order):

(1) |$ _____|_|   (2) |$ _____|_|   (3) |$ _____|_|

b   Enter organization's share of: **(1)** additional 5% tax (not more than $11,750)   |$ _____|

(2) additional 3% tax (not more than $100,000) . . . . . . . . . |$ _____|

c   Income tax on the amount on line 34 . . . . . . . . . . . . . . . . ▶ | **35c** | |

**36**   **Trusts Taxable at Trust Rates** (see instructions for tax computation on page 13) Income tax on the amount on line 34 from: ☐ Tax rate schedule or ☐ Schedule D (Form 1041) . . . . ▶ | **36** | |

**37**   **Proxy tax** (see page 13 of the instructions) . . . . . . . . . . . . . . ▶ | **37** | |

**38**   Alternative minimum tax . . . . . . . . . . . . . . . . . . . . . | **38** | |

**39**   **Total** (add lines 37 and 38 to line 35c or 36, whichever applies) . . . . . . . . . | **39** | |

## Part IV    Tax and Payments

**40a** Foreign tax credit (corporations attach Form 1118; trusts attach Form 1116) | **40a** | |

b   Other credits (see page 13 of the instructions) . . . . . . | **40b** | |

c   General business credit—Check here and indicate which forms are attached: ☐ Form 3800   ☐ Form(s)(specify) ▶ .................... | **40c** | |

d   Credit for prior year minimum tax (attach Form 8801 or 8827) . . . | **40d** | |

e   **Total credits** (add lines 40a through 40d) . . . . . . . . . . . . . | **40e** | |

**41**   Subtract line 40e from line 39 . . . . . . . . . . . . . . . . . . | **41** | |

**42**   Other taxes. Check if from: ☐ Form 4255 ☐ Form 8611 ☐ Form 8697 ☐ Form 8866 ☐ Other (attach schedule) . | **42** | |

**43**   **Total tax** (add lines 41 and 42) . . . . . . . . . . . . . | **43** | |

**44a** Payments: A 2002 overpayment credited to 2003 . . . . . | **44a** | |

b   2003 estimated tax payments . . . . . . . . . . . . . | **44b** | |

c   Tax deposited with Form 8868 . . . . . . . . . | **44c** | |

d   Foreign organizations—Tax paid or withheld at source (see instructions) | **44d** | |

e   Backup withholding (see instructions) . . . . . . . . . | **44e** | |

f   Other credits and payments (see instructions) . . . . . | **44f** | |

**45**   **Total payments** (add lines 44a through 44f) . . . . . . . . . . . . . | **45** | |

**46**   Estimated tax penalty (see page 4 of the instructions). Check ▶ ☐ if Form 2220 is attached . | **46** | |

**47**   **Tax due**—If line 45 is less than the total of lines 43 and 46, enter amount owed . . . . . ▶ | **47** | |

**48**   **Overpayment**—If line 45 is larger than the total of lines 43 and 46, enter amount overpaid . ▶ | **48** | |

**49**   Enter the amount of line 48 you want: **Credited to 2004 estimated tax** ▶     **Refunded** ▶ | **49** | |

## Part V    Statements Regarding Certain Activities and Other Information (See instructions on page 15.)

| | | Yes | No |
|---|---|---|---|
| **1** | At any time during the 2003 calendar year, did the organization have an interest in or a signature or other authority over a financial account in a foreign country (such as a bank account, securities account, or other financial account)? If "Yes," the organization may have to file Form TD F 90-22.1. If "Yes," enter the name of the foreign country here ▶ .................................................................. | | |
| **2** | During the tax year, did the organization receive a distribution from, or was it the grantor of, or transferor to, a foreign trust? If "Yes," see page 15 of the instructions for other forms the organization may have to file. | | |
| **3** | Enter the amount of tax-exempt interest received or accrued during the tax year ▶ $ | | |

### Schedule A—Cost of Goods Sold — Enter method of inventory valuation ▶

| | | | | | | | |
|---|---|---|---|---|---|---|---|
| **1** | Inventory at beginning of year | **1** | | **6** | Inventory at end of year . . . | **6** | |
| **2** | Purchases . . . . . . . | **2** | | **7** | **Cost of goods sold.** Subtract line 6 from line 5. (Enter here and on line 2, Part I.) . . . . . . . | **7** | |
| **3** | Cost of labor . . . . . . . | **3** | | | | | |
| **4a** | Additional section 263A costs (attach schedule) . . . . . | **4a** | | **8** | Do the rules of section 263A (with respect to property produced or acquired for resale) apply to the organization? . . . . . . . . . . | Yes | No |
| **b** | Other costs (attach schedule) | **4b** | | | | | |
| **5** | **Total**—Add lines 1 through 4b | **5** | | | | | |

**Sign Here** ▶

Under penalties of perjury, I declare that I have examined this return, including accompanying schedules and statements, and to the best of my knowledge and belief, it is true, correct, and complete. Declaration of preparer (other than taxpayer) is based on all information of which preparer has any knowledge.

| | | | | May the IRS discuss this return with the preparer shown below (see instructions)? ☐ Yes ☐ No |
|---|---|---|---|---|
| ▶ Signature of officer | Date | ▶ Title | | |

**Paid Preparer's Use Only**

| Preparer's signature ▶ | | Date | Check if self-employed ☐ | Preparer's SSN or PTIN |
|---|---|---|---|---|
| Firm's name (or yours if self-employed), address, and ZIP code ▶ | | | EIN | |
| | | | Phone no. ( ) | |

Form **990-T** (2003)

## Schedule C—Rent Income (From Real Property and Personal Property Leased With Real Property)
(See instructions on page 16.)

**1** Description of property

(1) _____

(2) _____

(3) _____

(4) _____

| | 2 Rent received or accrued | | 3 Deductions directly connected with the income in columns 2(a) and 2(b) (attach schedule) |
|---|---|---|---|
| | **(a)** From personal property (if the percentage of rent for personal property is more than 10% but not more than 50%) | **(b)** From real and personal property (if the percentage of rent for personal property exceeds 50% or if the rent is based on profit or income) | |
| (1) | | | |
| (2) | | | |
| (3) | | | |
| (4) | | | |
| Total | | Total | |

**Total income** (Add totals of columns 2(a) and 2(b). Enter here and on line 6, column (A), Part I, page 1.) . . ▶

**Total deductions.** Enter here and on line 6, column (B), Part I, page 1 . . ▶

## Schedule E—Unrelated Debt-Financed Income (See instructions on page 16.)

| 1 Description of debt-financed property | 2 Gross income from or allocable to debt-financed property | 3 Deductions directly connected with or allocable to debt-financed property | |
|---|---|---|---|
| | | **(a)** Straight line depreciation (attach schedule) | **(b)** Other deductions (attach schedule) |
| (1) | | | |
| (2) | | | |
| (3) | | | |
| (4) | | | |

| 4 Amount of average acquisition debt on or allocable to debt-financed property (attach schedule) | 5 Average adjusted basis of or allocable to debt-financed property (attach schedule) | 6 Column 4 divided by column 5 | 7 Gross income reportable (column 2 × column 6) | 8 Allocable deductions (column 6 × total of columns 3(a) and 3(b)) |
|---|---|---|---|---|
| (1) | | % | | |
| (2) | | % | | |
| (3) | | % | | |
| (4) | | % | | |
| | | | Enter here and on line 7, column (A), Part I, page 1. | Enter here and on line 7, column (B), Part I, page 1. |

**Totals** . . . . . . . . . . . . . . . . . . . . . . . . . . . . . ▶

**Total dividends-received deductions** included in column 8 . . . . . . . . . . . . . . . . . ▶

## Schedule F—Interest, Annuities, Royalties, and Rents From Controlled Organizations (See instructions on page 17.)

| | | Exempt Controlled Organizations | | | |
|---|---|---|---|---|---|
| 1 Name of Controlled Organization | 2 Employer Identification Number | 3 Net unrelated income (loss) (see instructions) | 4 Total of specified payments made | 5 Part of column (4) that is included in the controlling organization's gross income | 6 Deductions directly connected with income in column (5) |
| (1) | | | | | |
| (2) | | | | | |
| (3) | | | | | |
| (4) | | | | | |

Nonexempt Controlled Organizations

| 7 Taxable Income | 8 Net unrelated income (loss) (see instructions) | 9 Total of specified payments made | 10 Part of column (9) that is included in the controlling organization's gross income | 11 Deductions directly connected with income in column (10) |
|---|---|---|---|---|
| (1) | | | | |
| (2) | | | | |
| (3) | | | | |
| (4) | | | | |
| | | | Add columns 5 and 10. Enter here and on line 8, Column (A), Part I, page 1. | Add columns 6 and 11. Enter here and on line 8, Column (B), Part I, page 1. |

**Totals** . . . . . . . . . . . . . . . . . . . . . . . . ▶

## Schedule G—Investment Income of a Section 501(c)(7), (9), or (17) Organization
(See instructions on page 18.)

| 1 Description of income | 2 Amount of income | 3 Deductions directly connected (attach schedule) | 4 Set-asides (attach schedule) | 5 Total deductions and set-asides (col. 3 plus col. 4) |
|---|---|---|---|---|
| (1) | | | | |
| (2) | | | | |
| (3) | | | | |
| (4) | | | | |
| Totals . . . . . . . ▶ | Enter here and on line 9, column (A), Part I, page 1. | | | Enter here and on line 9, column (B), Part I, page 1. |

## Schedule I—Exploited Exempt Activity Income, Other Than Advertising Income
(See instructions on page 18.)

| 1 Description of exploited activity | 2 Gross unrelated business income from trade or business | 3 Expenses directly connected with production of unrelated business income | 4 Net income (loss) from unrelated trade or business (column 2 minus column 3). If a gain, compute cols. 5 through 7. | 5 Gross income from activity that is not unrelated business income | 6 Expenses attributable to column 5 | 7 Excess exempt expenses (column 6 minus column 5, but not more than column 4). |
|---|---|---|---|---|---|---|
| (1) | | | | | | |
| (2) | | | | | | |
| (3) | | | | | | |
| (4) | | | | | | |
| Totals . . . . . . . ▶ | Enter here and on line 10, col. (A), Part I, page 1. | Enter here and on line 10, col. (B), Part I, page 1. | | | | Enter here and on line 26, Part II, page 1. |

## Schedule J—Advertising Income (See instructions on page 19.)

### Part I    Income From Periodicals Reported on a Consolidated Basis

| 1 Name of periodical | 2 Gross advertising income | 3 Direct advertising costs | 4 Advertising gain or (loss) (col. 2 minus col. 3). If a gain, compute cols. 5 through 7. | 5 Circulation income | 6 Readership costs | 7 Excess readership costs (column 6 minus column 5, but not more than column 4). |
|---|---|---|---|---|---|---|
| (1) | | | | | | |
| (2) | | | | | | |
| (3) | | | | | | |
| (4) | | | | | | |
| Totals (carry to Part II, line (5)) . . . . . . . ▶ | | | | | | |

### Part II    Income From Periodicals Reported on a Separate Basis (For each periodical listed in Part II, fill in columns 2 through 7 on a line-by-line basis.)

| | | | | | | |
|---|---|---|---|---|---|---|
| (1) | | | | | | |
| (2) | | | | | | |
| (3) | | | | | | |
| (4) | | | | | | |
| (5) Totals from Part I | | | | | | |
| Totals, Part II (lines 1-5) . . . ▶ | Enter here and on line 11, col. (A), Part I, page 1. | Enter here and on line 11, col. (B), Part I, page 1. | | | | Enter here and on line 27, Part II, page 1. |

## Schedule K—Compensation of Officers, Directors, and Trustees (See instructions on page 19.)

| 1 Name | 2 Title | 3 Percent of time devoted to business | 4 Compensation attributable to unrelated business |
|---|---|---|---|
| | | % | |
| | | % | |
| | | % | |
| | | % | |
| Total—Enter here and on line 14, Part II, page 1 . . . . . . . . . . . . . . . . . . . . ▶ | | | |

# Inventory of IRS Forms

The planner, in the tax-exempt organizations setting, should have a working familiarity with, at a minimum, the following IRS forms:

- 872-C (request for extension of statute of limitations for newly formed publicly supported organizations)
- 990 (annual information return filed by most exempt organizations)
- 990-EZ (annual information return filed by small exempt organizations)
- 990-PF (annual information return filed by private foundations)
- 990-T (unrelated business income tax return)
- 1023 (application for recognition of exemption filed by charitable organizations)
- 1024 (application for recognition of exemption filed by most other exempt organizations)
- 1120-POL (return filed by some political organizations)
- 2848 (power of attorney)
- 4720 (reporting of various taxes)
- 8282 (reporting of dispositions of contributed property)
- 8283 (reporting of certain noncash charitable contributions)
- 8718 (user fee payments)
- 8734 (reporting of public support following close of advance ruling period)
- 8868 (request for extension of time to file annual information return)
- 8871 (notice filed by new political organizations)
- 8872 (political organizations report of contributions and expenditures)
- SS-4 (application for employer identification number)

# Inventory of Tax Penalties

The planner, in the tax-exempt organizations setting, should be aware of (and strive to avoid imposition of) the following penalties:

- IRC § 170(f)(10)(F) (excise tax on charitable organizations involvement with personal benefit contracts)
- IRC § 527(f) (income tax on exempt organizations political expenditures)
- IRC § 4911 (excise tax on excess expenditures to influence legislation)
- IRC § 4912 (excise tax on certain disqualifying lobbying expenditures)
- IRC § 4941 (excise tax on private foundation self-dealing)
- IRC § 4942 (excise tax on private foundation inadequate income distribution)
- IRC § 4943 (excise tax on private foundation excess business holdings)
- IRC § 4944 (excise tax on private foundations jeopardizing investments)
- IRC § 4945 (excise tax on private foundations taxable expenditures)
- IRC § 4953 (excise tax on excess contributions to black lung benefit trusts)
- IRC § 4955 (excise tax on charitable organizations political campaign activity expenditures)
- IRC § 4958 (excise tax on disqualified persons with respect to public charities)
- IRC § 6652(c)(1)(A) (penalty for late or incomplete annual information return)
- IRC § 6652(c)(1)(B)(ii) (annual information return responsible person penalty)
- IRC § 6652(c)(1)(C) (penalty for failure to comply with annual information return inspection requirements)
- IRC § 6652(c)(1)(D) (penalty for failure to comply with application for recognition of exemption or notice inspection requirements)
- IRC § 6662 (accuracy-related penalty)
- IRC § 6663 (fraud penalty)

- IRC § 6684 (penalty for willful violation of private foundation rules)
- IRC § 6685 (penalty for willful failure to comply with exempt organizations public inspection requirements)
- IRC § 6694 (penalty for understatement of taxpayer's liability by an income tax return preparer)
- IRC § 6695 (penalty with respect to preparation of income tax returns for others)
- IRC § 6700 (penalty for promotion of abusive tax shelter)
- IRC § 6701 (penalty for aiding and abetting understatement of tax liability)
- IRC § 6707 (penalty for failure to register tax shelters)
- IRC § 6708 (penalty for failure to maintain lists of investors in potentially abusive tax shelters)
- IRC § 6710 (penalty for failure to disclose that certain contributions are nondeductible)
- IRC § 6711 (penalty for failure to disclose that certain information or service is available from the federal government)
- IRC § 6714 (penalty for failure to comply with quid pro quo contribution disclosure requirements)
- IRC § 6721 (penalty for failure to file correct information returns)
- IRC § 7602 (penalty for filing frivolous income tax return)
- IRC § 7203 (penalty for willful failure to keep tax records and file returns)
- IRC § 7206 (penalty for making fraudulent and otherwise false statements)
- IRC § 7207 (penalty for filing of fraudulent returns or statements)

# Other Bodies of Law

The planner, in the tax-exempt organizations setting, will be largely concerned with the federal tax, and state corporate and fundraising regulation, laws. There will be occasion, however, for the applicability of other laws, namely:

- Antitrust (federal and state)
- Banking
- Bond financing
- Campaign finance
- Consumer protection
- Constitutional
- Education
- Employment
- Environmental
- Estate administration
- Federal (other)
- Health
- Insurance
- International
- Investment
- Labor
- Local laws (e.g., county ordinances)
- Postal
- Probate
- Securities (federal and state)

- State (other)
- Tax law (state and local)
- Trust

# Table of Cases

# Table of IRS Revenue Rulings

# Table of IRS Private Determinations

# Index